Dodge Challenger & Plymouth Sapporo Automotive Repair Manual

Larry Holt
and John H Haynes Member of the Guild of Motoring Writers

Models covered:
Dodge Challenger and Plymouth Sapporo. All models 1978 thru 1983.
1600cc (1.6 liter), 2000cc (2 liter) and 2600cc (2.6 liter) engines,
manual 5-speed and automatic transmissions

ISBN 0 85696 699 1

Printed in the USA *(7W3 – 699)*

ABCDE
FGHI

Haynes Publishing Group
Sparkford Nr Yeovil
Somerset BA22 7JJ England

Haynes North America, Inc
861 Lawrence Drive
Newbury Park
California 91320 USA

Acknowledgements

Thanks are due to Chrysler Motors Corporation, USA, who gave us permission to reproduce certain illustrations and provided technical information. The Champion Sparking Plug Company, UK, provided the illustrations of spark plug conditions.

About this manual

Its purpose

The purpose of this manual is to help you get the best value from your vehicle. It can do so in several ways. It can help you decide what work must be done even if you choose to get it done by a dealer service department or a repair shop; it provides information and procedures for routine maintenance and servicing; and it offers diagnostic and repair procedures to follow when trouble occurs.

It is hoped that you will use the manual to tackle the work yourself. For many simpler jobs, doing it yourself may be quicker than arranging an appointment to get the vehicle into a shop and making the trips to leave it and pick it up. More importantly, a lot of money can be saved by avoiding the expense the shop must pass on to you to cover its labor and overhead costs. An added benefit is the sense of satisfaction and accomplishment that you feel after having done the job yourself.

Using the manual

The manual is divided into Chapters. Each Chapter is divided into numbered Sections, which are headed in bold type between horizontal lines. Each Section consists of consecutively numbered paragraphs.

The two types of illustrations used (figures and photographs), are referenced by a number preceding their captions. Figure reference numbers denote Chapter and numerical sequence in the Chapter; i.e. Fig. 12.4 means Chapter 12, figure number 4. Figure captions are followed by a Section number which ties the figure to a specific portion of the text. All photographs apply to the Chapter in which they appear, and the reference number pinpoints the pertinent Section and paragraph; i.e. 3.2 means Section 3, paragraph 2.

Procedures, once described in the text, are not normally repeated. When it is necessary to refer to another Chapter, the reference will be given as Chapter and Section number; i.e. Chapter 1/16. Cross references given without use of the word 'Chapter' apply to Sections and/or paragraphs in the same Chapter. For example, 'see Section 8' means in the same Chapter.

Reference to the left or right side of the vehicle is based on the assumption that one is sitting in the driver's seat facing forward.

Even though extreme care has been taken during the preparation of this manual, neither the publisher nor the author can accept responsibility for any errors in, or omissions from, the information given.

Introduction to the Dodge Challenger and Plymouth Sapporo

This manual covers the service and repair operations for the Challenger and Sapporo models. Introduced in 1978, they span the years through 1983. They were imported by the Chrysler Corporation and built by the Mitsubushi Motors Corporation in Japan.

For 1978-79, there were three engine sizes available: 1600 cc, 2000 cc and 2600 cc, with a choice of either a 5-speed manual or automatic transmission. All models have 4-cylinder engines featuring overhead cam and Silent Shafts for smoother and quieter performance. In addition, the models built for the USA are equipped with the MCA Jet Valves, a pollution control system designed to help meet exhaust emissions standards.

From 1980 through 1983, the 2600 cc engine was the only one offered, with the 1983 models incorporating an electronic digital instrument panel. The electronic voice alert 'Talking Car' is also an option.

On all models, the design is conventional, having an in-line engine and transmission with a driveshaft transferring the drive to the rear axle.

The front suspension is independent with coil springs and MacPherson struts. The rear suspension uses coil springs with a four-link axle location and double-action telescopic shock absorbers.

The front brakes are disc, while the rear are drums (with disc optional) and assisted with a power booster.

Contents

Dodge Challenger

Plymouth Sapporo

General dimensions

Length (A)	179.2 in (4570 mm)
Width (B)	65.9 in (1675 mm)
Height (C)	53.5 in (1355 mm)
Wheelbase (D)	99.6 in (2530 mm)
Tracking (E)	54.1 in (1375 mm)
Tracking (F)	53.3 in (1355 mm)
Ground clearance	6.3 in (160 mm)
Curb weight	2767 lb (1255 kg)

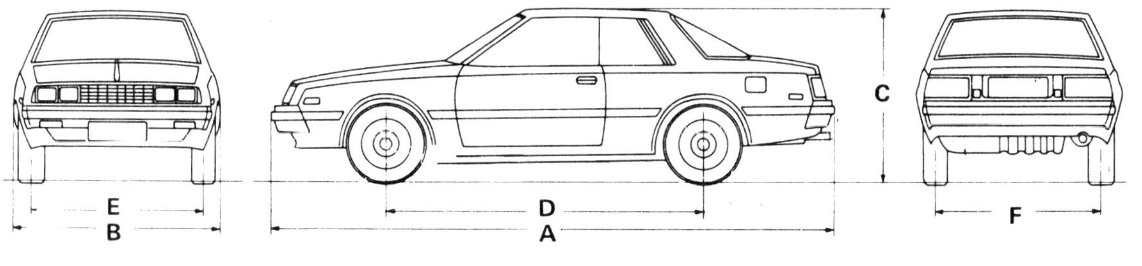

Vehicle general dimensions

(Refer to Specifications)

Buying parts

Buying spare parts

Replacement parts are available from many sources, which generally fall into one of two categories - authorized dealer parts departments and independent retail auto parts stores. Our advice concerning these parts is as follows:

Retail auto parts stores: Good auto parts stores will stock frequently needed components which wear out relatively fast, such as clutch components, exhaust systems, brake parts, tune-up parts, etc. These stores often supply new or reconditioned parts on an exchange basis, which can save a considerable amount of money. Discount auto parts stores are often very good places to buy materials and parts needed for general vehicle maintenance such as oil, grease, filters, spark plugs, belts, touch-up paint, bulbs, etc. They also usually sell tools and general accessories, have convenient hours, charge lower prices and can often be found not far from home.

Authorized dealer parts department: This is the best source for parts which are unique to the vehicle and not generally available elsewhere (such as major engine parts, transmission parts, trim pieces, etc.).

Warranty information: If the vehicle is still covered under warranty, be sure that any replacement parts purchased - regardless of the source - do not invalidate the warranty!

To be sure of obtaining the correct parts, have engine and chassis numbers available and, if possible, take the old parts along for positive identification.

Vehicle identification numbers

The Vehicle Identification Number (VIN) is located on a plate attached to the top left side of the instrument panel and is visible through the windshield.

The chassis number stamping location is on the top center of the firewall in the engine compartment.

The vehicle safety certification label is attached to the face of the door pillar. This label shows the month and year manufactured, Gross Vehicle Weight Rating (GVWR) and again, the Vehicle Identification Number (VIN).

The vehicle model and engine model nameplate is riveted on the firewall in the engine compartment.

The engine model and serial number is stamped on the right front top edge of the cylinder block.

The manual transmission serial number is stamped on the clutch housing of the transmission case. The automatic transmission serial number is stamped on the transmission case.

The body color plate is located on the headlight support panel (illustration).

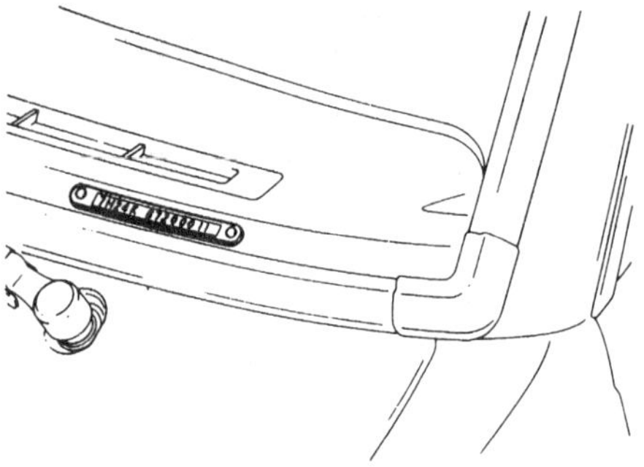

Vehicle identification number location

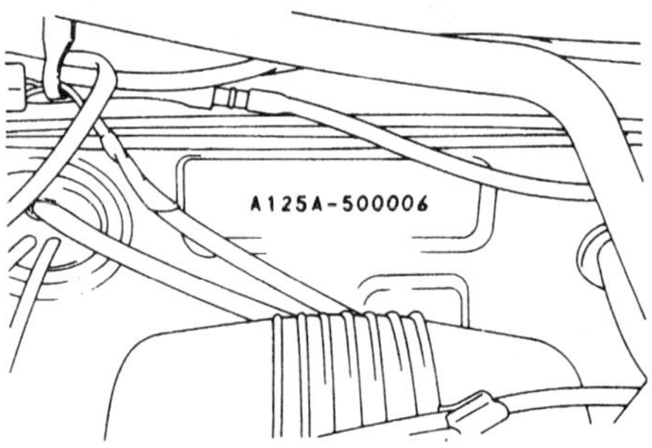

Vehicle chassis number firewall location

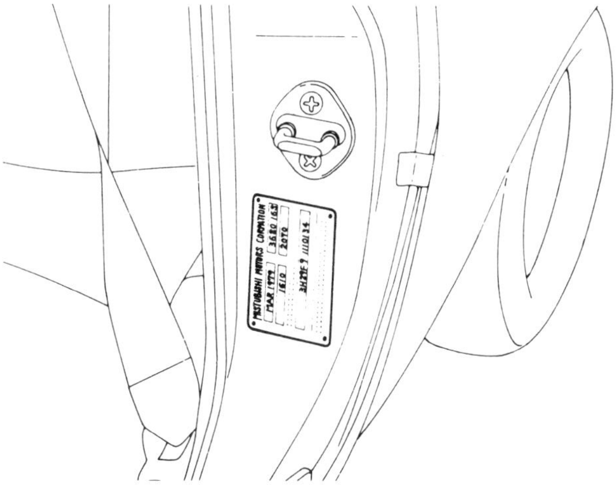

Vehicle safety label location

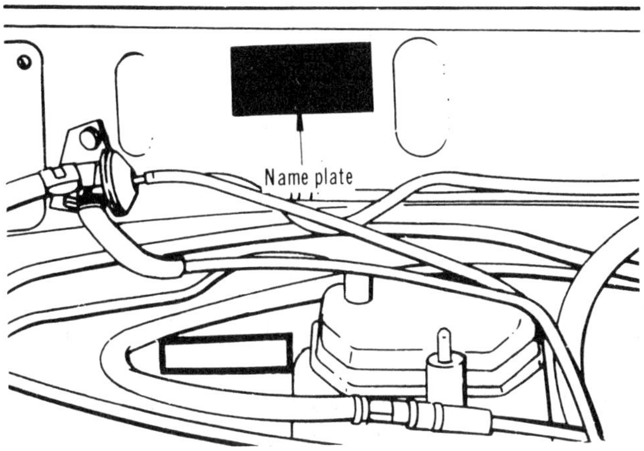

Vehicle nameplate firewall location

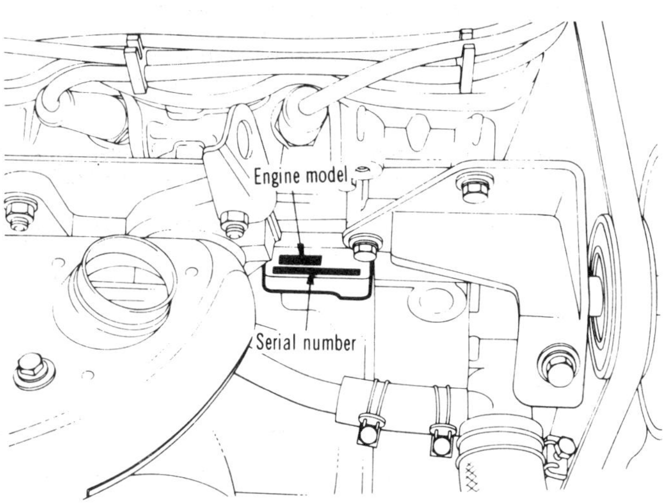

Engine model and serial number location

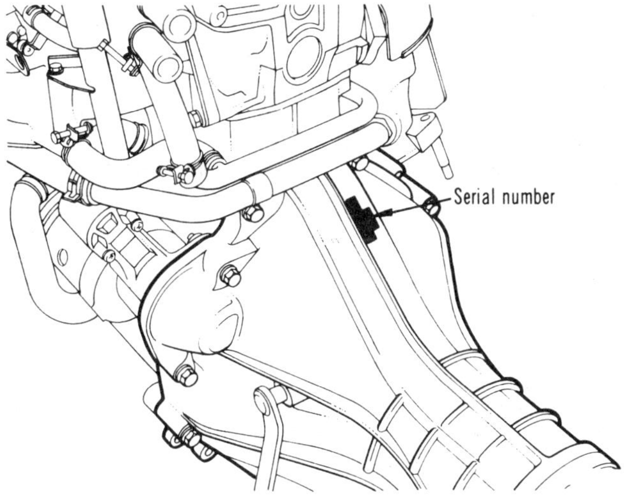

Manual transmission number location

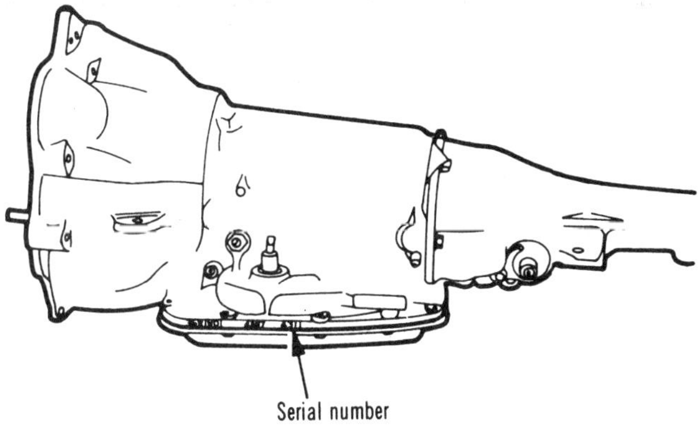

Automatic transmission number location

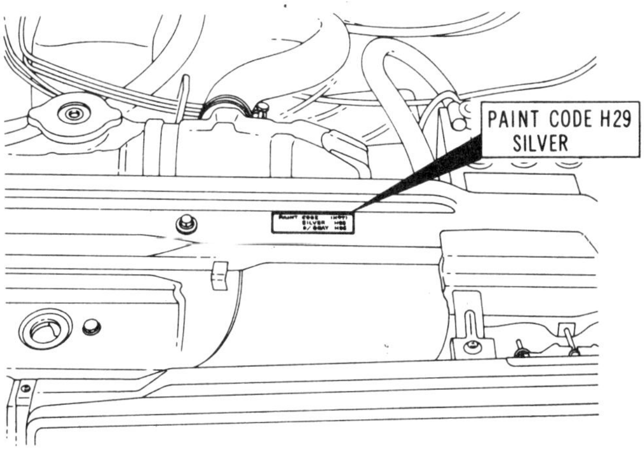

Vehicle body color plate location

Maintenance techniques, tools and working facilities

Maintenance techniques

There are a number of techniques involved in maintenance and repair that will be referred to throughout this manual. Application of these techniques will enable the home mechanic to be more efficient, better organized and capable of performing the various tasks properly, which will ensure that the repair job is thorough and complete.

Fasteners

Fasteners are nuts, bolts, studs and screws used to hold two or more parts together. There are a few things to keep in mind when working with fasteners. Almost all of them use a locking device of some type; either a lock washer, locknut, locking tab or thread adhesive. All threaded fasteners should be clean and straight, with undamaged threads and undamaged corners on the hex head where the wrench fits. Develop the habit of replacing damaged nuts and bolts with new ones. Special locknuts with nylon or fiber inserts can only be used once. If they are removed, they lose their locking ability and must be replaced with new ones.

Rusted nuts and bolts should be treated with a penetrating fluid to ease removal and prevent breakage. Some mechanics use turpentine in a spout-type oil can, which works quite well. After applying the rust penetrant, let it "work" for a few minutes before trying to loosen the nut or bolt. Badly rusted fasteners may have to be chiseled or sawed off or removed with a special nut breaker, available at tool stores.

If a bolt or stud breaks off in an assembly, it can be drilled and removed with a special tool commonly available for this purpose. Most automotive machine shops can perform this task, as well as other repair procedures (such as repair of threaded holes that have been stripped out).

Flat washers and lock washers, when removed from an assembly should always be replaced exactly as removed. Replace damaged washers with new ones. Always use a flat washer between a lock washer and any soft metal surface (such as aluminum), thin sheet metal or plastic.

Fastener sizes

For a number of reasons, automobile manufacturers are making wider and wider use of metric fasteners. Therefore, it is important to be able to tell the difference between standard (sometimes called U.S., English or SAE) and metric hardware, since they cannot be interchanged.

All bolts, whether standard or metric, are sized according to diameter, thread pitch and length. For example, a standard $\frac{1}{2}$ – 13 x 1 bolt is $\frac{1}{2}$ inch in diameter, has 13 threads per inch and is 1 inch long. An M12 – 1.75 x 25 metric bolt is 12 mm in diameter, has a thread pitch of 1.75 mm (the distance between threads) and is 25 mm long. The 2 bolts are nearly identical, and easily confused, but they are not interchangeable.

In addition to the differences in diameter, thread pitch and length, metric and standard bolts can also be distinguished by examining the bolt heads. To begin with, the distance across the flats on a standard bolt head is measured in inches, while the same dimension on a metric bolt is measured in millimeters (the same is true for nuts). As a result, a standard wrench should not be used on a metric bolt and a metric wrench should not be used on a standard bolt. Also, standard bolts have slashes radiating out from the center of the head to denote the grade or strength of the bolt (which is an indication of the amount of

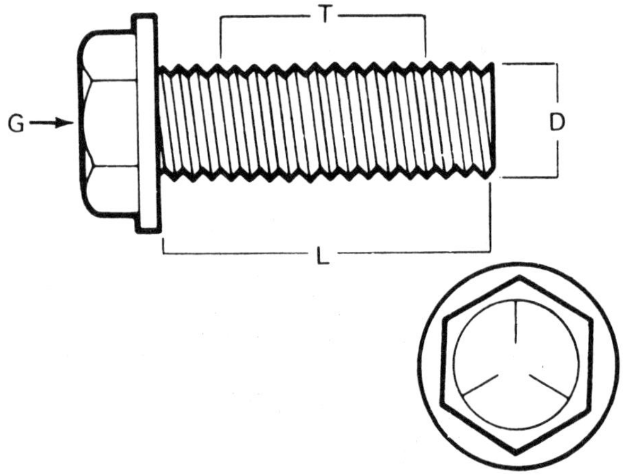

Standard (SAE) bolt dimensions and grade marks

G – Grade marks (bolt strength)
L – Length (in inches)
T – Thread pitch (number of threads per inch)
D – Nominal diameter (in inches)

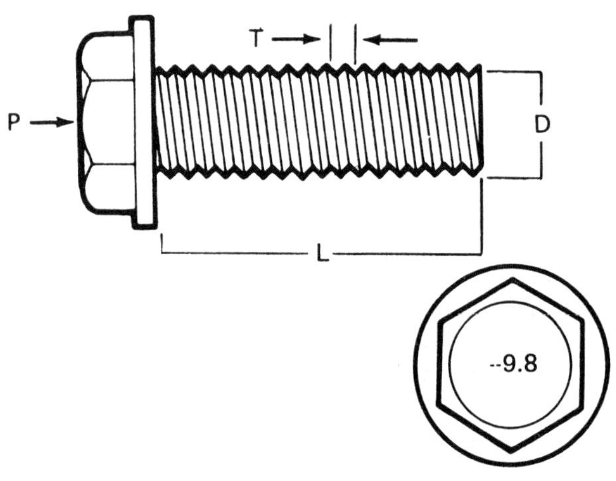

Metric bolt dimensions/grade marks

P – Property class (bolt strength)
L – Length (in millimeters)
T – Thread pitch (distance between threads; in millimeters)
D – Nominal diameter (in millimeters)

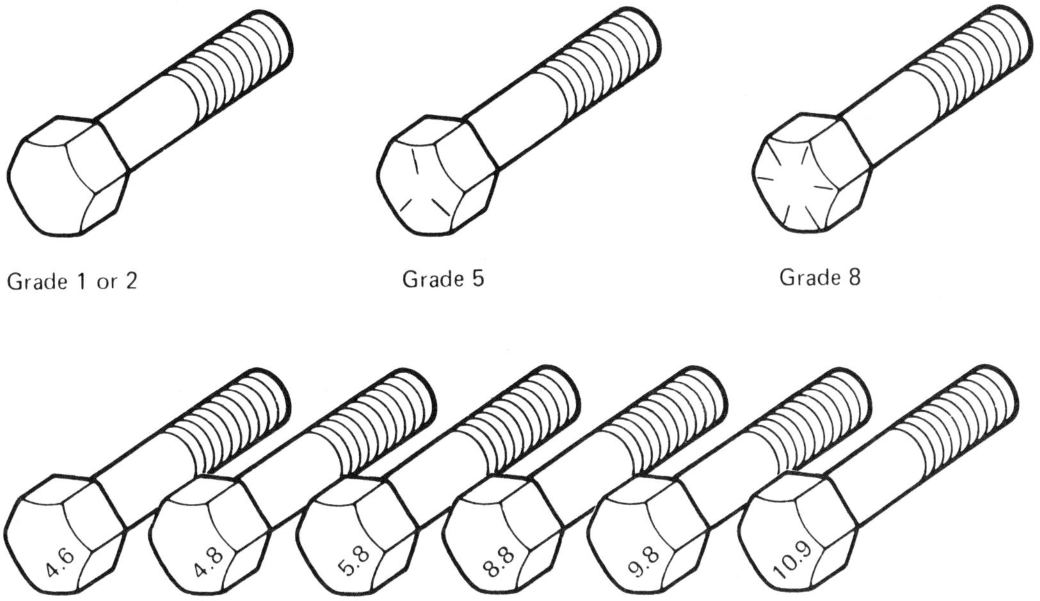

Bolt strength markings (top – standard SAE; bottom – metric)

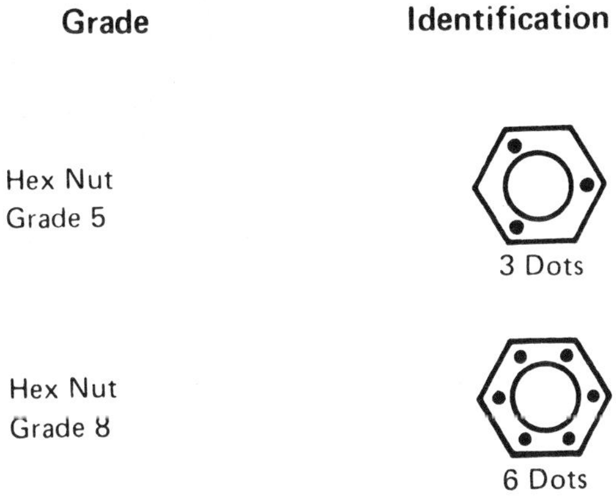

Standard hex nut strength markings

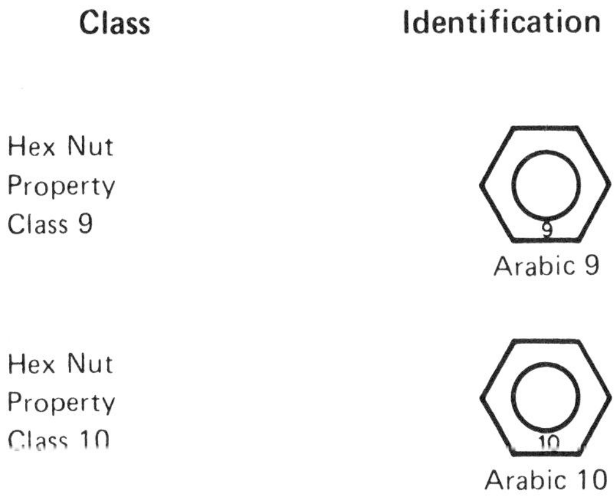

Metric hex nut strength markings

torque that can be supplied to it). The greater the number of slashes, the greater the strength of the bolt (grades 0 through 5 are commonly used on automobiles). Metric bolts have a property class (grade) number, rather than a slash, molded into their heads to indicate bolt strength. In this case, the higher the number the stronger the bolt (property class numbers 8.8, 9.8 and 10.9 are commonly used on automobiles).

Strength markings can also be used to distinguish standard hex nuts from metric hex nuts. Standard nuts have dots stamped into one side, while metric nuts are marked with a number. The greater the number of dots, or the higher the number, the greater the strength of the nut.

Metric studs are also marked on their ends according to property class (grade). Larger studs are numbered (the same as metric bolts), while smaller studs carry a geometric code to denote grade.

It should be noted that many fasteners, especially Grades 0 through 2, have no distinguishing marks on them. When such is the

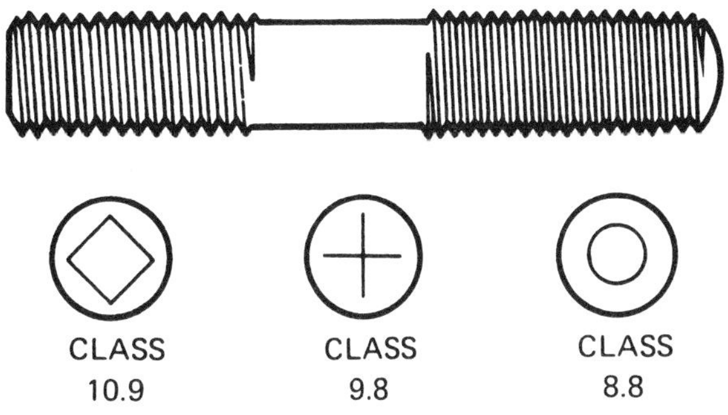

Metric stud strength markings

case, the only way to determine whether it is standard or metric is to measure the thread pitch or compare it to a known fastener of the same size.

Since fasteners of the same size (both standard and metric) may have different strength ratings, be sure to reinstall any bolts, studs or nuts removed from your vehicle in their original locations. Also, when replacing a fastener with a new one, make sure that the new one has a strength rating equal to or greater than the original.

Tightening sequences and procedures

Most threaded fasteners should be tightened to a specific torque value (torque is basically a twisting force). Over-tightening the fastener can weaken it and lead to eventual breakage, while under-tightening can cause it to eventually come loose. Bolts, screws and studs, depending on the materials they are made of and their thread diameters, have specific torque values (many of which are noted in the Specifications at the beginning of each Chapter). Be sure to follow the torque recommendations closely. For fasteners not assigned a specific torque, a general torque value chart is presented here as a guide. As was previously mentioned, the sizes and grade of a fastener determine the amount of torque that can safely be applied to it. The figures listed here are approximate for Grade 2 and Grade 3 fasteners (higher grades can tolerate higher torque values).

	ft-lb	Nm
Metric thread sizes		
M-6	6 to 9	9 to 12
M-8	14 to 21	19 to 28
M-10	28 to 40	38 to 54
M-12	50 to 71	68 to 96
M-14	80 to 140	109 to 154
Pipe thread sizes		
$\frac{1}{8}$	5 to 8	7 to 10
$\frac{1}{4}$	12 to 18	17 to 24
$\frac{3}{8}$	22 to 33	30 to 44
$\frac{1}{2}$	25 to 35	34 to 47
U.S. thread sizes		
$\frac{1}{4}$ - 20	6 to 9	9 to 12
$\frac{5}{16}$ - 18	12 to 18	17 to 24
$\frac{5}{16}$ - 24	14 to 20	19 to 27
$\frac{3}{8}$ - 16	22 to 32	30 to 43
$\frac{3}{8}$ - 24	27 to 38	37 to 51
$\frac{7}{16}$ - 14	40 to 55	55 to 74
$\frac{7}{16}$ - 20	40 to 60	55 to 81
$\frac{1}{2}$ - 13	55 to 80	75 to 108

Fasteners laid out in a pattern (i.e. cylinder head bolts, oil pan bolts, differential cover bolts, etc.) must be loosened and tightened in a definite sequence to avoid warping the component. This sequence will normally be shown in the appropriate Chapter. If a specific pattern is not given, the following procedures can be used to prevent warping. Initially, the bolts or nuts should be assembled finger-tight only. Next, they should be tightened one full turn each, in a criss-cross or diagonal pattern. After each one has been tightened one full turn, return to the first one and tighten them all one half turn, following the same pattern. Finally, tighten each of them one-quarter turn at a time until they all have been tightened to the proper torque value. To loosen and remove them the procedure would be reversed.

Component disassembly

Component disassembly should be done with care and purpose to help ensure that the parts go back together properly. Always keep track of the sequence in which parts are removed. Make note of special characteristics or marks on parts that can be installed more than one way (such as a grooved thrust washer on a shaft). It is a good idea to lay the disassembled parts out on a clean surface in the order that they were removed. It may also be helpful to make simple sketches or take instant photos of components before removal.

When removing fasteners from an assembly, keep track of their locations. Sometimes threading a bolt back in a part or putting the washers and nut back on a stud can prevent mixups later. If nuts and bolts cannot be returned to their original locations, they should be kept in a compartmented box or a series of small boxes. A cupcake or muffin tin is ideal for this purpose, since each cavity can hold the bolts and nuts from a particular area (i.e. oil pan bolts, valve cover bolts, engine mount bolts, etc.). A pan of this type is especially helpful when working on assemblies with very small parts such as the carburetor, alternator, valve train or interior dash and trim pieces. The cavities can be marked with paint or tape to identify the contents.

Whenever wiring looms, harnesses or connectors are separated, it's a good idea to identify them with numbered pieces of masking tape so that they can be easily reconnected.

Gasket sealing surfaces

Throughout any vehicle, gaskets are used to seal the mating surfaces between two parts and keep lubricants, fluids, vacuum or pressure contained in an assembly.

Many times these gaskets are coated with a liquid or paste-type gasket sealing compound before assembly. Age, heat and pressure can sometimes cause the two parts to stick together so tightly that they are very difficult to separate. Often, the assembly can be loosened by striking it with a soft-faced hammer near the mating surfaces. A regular hammer can be used if a block of wood is placed between the hammer and the part. Do not hammer on cast parts or parts that could be easily damaged. With any particularly stubborn part, always recheck to see that every fastener has been removed.

Avoid using a screwdriver or bar to pry apart an assembly, as they can easily mar the gasket sealing surfaces of the parts (which must remain smooth). If prying is absolutely necessary, use an old broom handle, but keep in mind that extra clean-up will be necessary if the wood splinters.

After the parts are separated, the old gasket must be carefully scraped off and the gasket surfaces cleaned. Stubborn gasket material can be soaked with rust penetrant or treated with a special chemical to soften it so that it can be easily scraped off. A scraper can be fashioned from a piece of copper tubing by flattening and sharpening one end. Copper is recommended because it is usually softer than the surfaces to be scraped, which reduces the chance of gouging the part. Some gaskets can be removed with a wire brush, but regardless of the method used, the mating surfaces must be left clean and smooth. If, for some reason the gasket surface is gouged, then a gasket sealer thick enough to fill scratches will have to be used upon reassembly of the components. For most applications, a non-drying (or semi-drying) gasket sealer should be used.

Hose removal tips

Caution: *If the vehicle is equipped with air conditioning, do not disconnect any of the a/c hoses without first having the system de-*

pressurized by a dealer service department or air conditioning specialist.

Hose removal precautions closely parallel gasket removal precautions. Avoid scratching or gouging the surface that the hose mates against or the connection may leak. This is especially true for radiator hoses. Because of various chemical reactions, the rubber in hoses can bond itself to the metal spigot that the hose fits over. To remove a hose, first loosen the hose clamps that secure it to the spigot. Then, with slip-joint pliers, grab the hose at the clamp and rotate it around the spigot. Work it back-and-forth until it is completely free, then pull it off. Silicone or other lubricants will ease removal if they can be applied between the hose and the spigot. Apply the same lubricant to the inside of the hose and the outside of the spigot to simplify installation.

As a last resort (and if the hose is to be replaced with a new one anyway), the rubber can be slit with a knife and the hose peeled from its spigot. If this must be done, be careful that the metal connection is not damaged.

If a hose clamp is broken or damaged, do not re-use it. Wire-type clamps usually weaken with age, so it is a good idea to replace them with screw-type clamps whenever a hose is removed.

Tools

A selection of good tools is a basic requirement for anyone who plans to maintain and repair his or her own vehicle. For the owner who has few tools, if any, the initial investment might seem high, but when compared to the spiraling costs of professional auto maintenance and repair, it is a wise one.

To help the owner decide which tools are needed to perform the tasks detailed in this manual, the following tool lists are offered: *Maintenance and minor repair, Repair and overhaul* and *Special.* The newcomer to practical mechanics should start off with the *Maintenance and minor repair* tool kit, which is adequate for the simpler jobs performed on a vehicle. Then, as his confidence and experience grow, he can tackle more difficult tasks, buying additional tools as they are needed. Eventually the basic kit will be expanded into the *Repair and overhaul* tool set. Over a period of time, the experienced do-it-yourselfer will assemble a tool set complete enough for most repair and overhaul procedures and will add tools from the *Special* category when he feels the expense is justified by the frequency of use.

Maintenance and minor repair tool kit

The tools in this list should be considered the minimum for performance of routine maintenance, servicing and minor repair work. We recommend the purchase of combination wrenches (box end and open end combined in one wrench); while more expensive than open-ended ones, they offer the advantages of both types of wrench.

Combination wrench set ($\frac{1}{4}$ in to 1 in or 6 mm to 19 mm)
Adjustable wrench – 8 in
Spark plug wrench (with rubber insert)
Spark plug gap adjusting tool
Feeler gauge set
Brake bleeder wrench
Standard screwdriver ($\frac{5}{16}$ in x 6 in)
Phillips screwdriver (No.2 x 6 in)
Combination pliers – 6 in
Hacksaw and assortment of blades
Tire pressure gauge
Grease gun
Oil can
Fine emery cloth
Wire brush
Battery post and cable cleaning tool
Oil filter wrench
Funnel (medium size)
Safety goggles
Jack stands (2)
Drain pan

Note: *If basic tune-ups are going to be a part of routine maintenance, it will be necessary to purchase a good quality stroboscopic timing light and a combination tachometer/dwell meter. Although they are included in the list of Special tools, they are mentioned here because they are absolutely necessary for tuning most vehicles properly.*

Repair and overhaul tool set

These tools are essential for anyone who plans to perform major repairs and are in addition to those in the *Maintenance and minor repair tool kit.* Included is a comprehensive set of sockets which, though expensive, are invaluable because of their versatility (especially when various extensions and drives are available). We recommend the $\frac{1}{2}$ in drive over the $\frac{3}{8}$ in drive. Although the larger drive is bulky and more expensive, it has the capability of accepting a very wide range of large sockets (ideally, the mechanic would have a $\frac{3}{8}$ in drive set and a $\frac{1}{2}$ in drive set).

Socket set(s)
Reversible ratchet
Extension – 10 in
Universal joint
Torque wrench (same size drive as sockets)
Ballpein hammer – 8 oz
Soft-faced hammer (plastic/rubber)
Standard screwdriver ($\frac{1}{4}$ in x 6 in)
Standard screwdriver (stubby – $\frac{5}{16}$ in)
Phillips screwdriver (No.3 x 8 in)
Phillips screwdriver (stubby – No.2)
Pliers – vise grip
Pliers – lineman's
Pliers – needle nose
Pliers – snap-ring (internal and external)
Cold chisel – $\frac{1}{2}$ in
Scriber
Scraper (made from flattened copper tubing)
Center punch
Pin punches ($\frac{1}{16}$, $\frac{1}{8}$, $\frac{3}{16}$ in)
Steel rule/straightedge – 12 in
Allen wrench set ($\frac{1}{8}$ to $\frac{3}{8}$ in or 4 mm to 10 mm)
A selection of files
Wire brush (large)
Jack stands (second set)
Jack (scissor or hydraulic type)

Note: *Another tool which is often useful is an electric drill motor with a chuck capacity of $\frac{3}{8}$ in (and a set of good quality drill bits).*

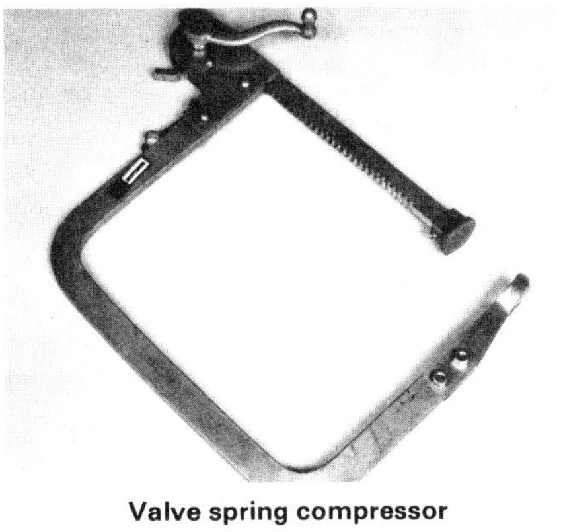

Valve spring compressor

Piston ring groove cleaning tool

Piston ring compressor

Piston ring removal and installation tool

Cylinder ridge reamer

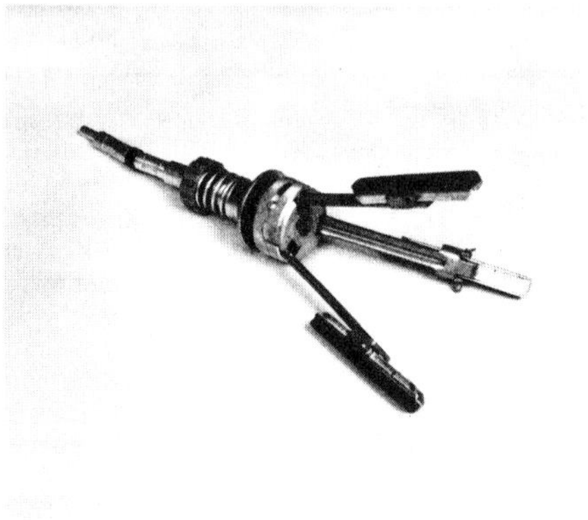

Cylinder surfacing hone

Cylinder bore gauge

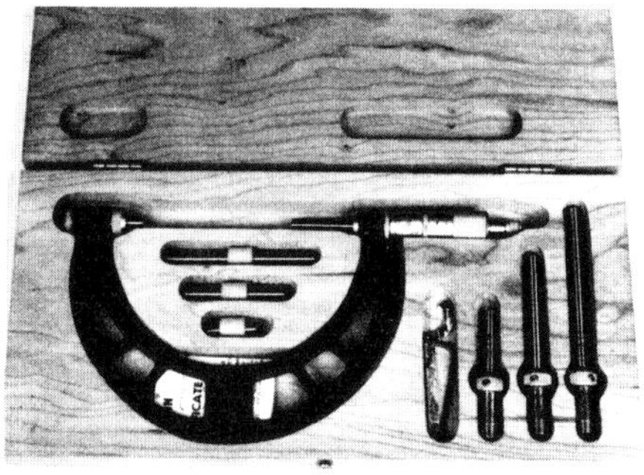

Micrometer set

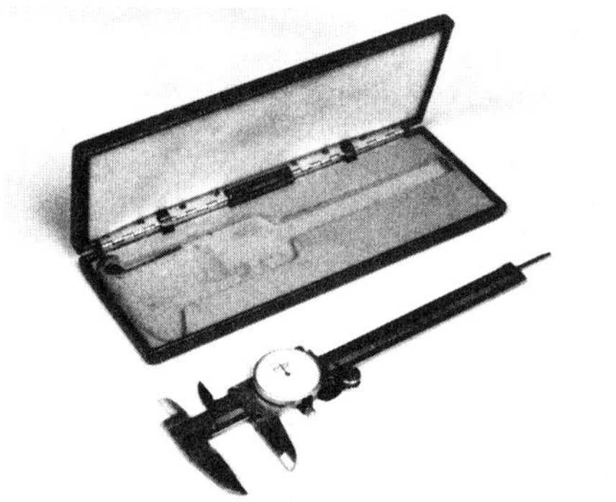

Dial caliper

Hydraulic lifter removal tool

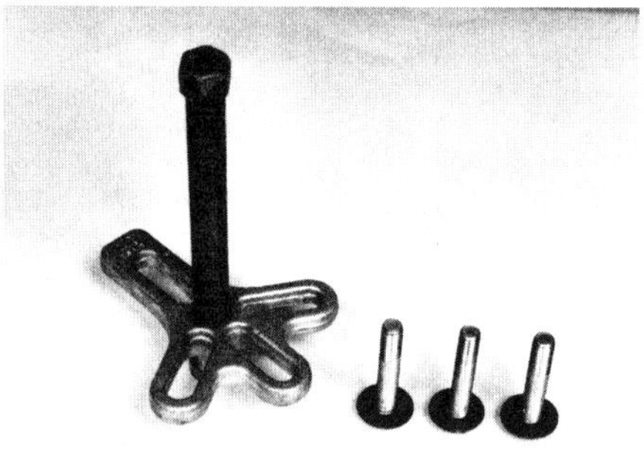

Universal type puller

Dial indicator set

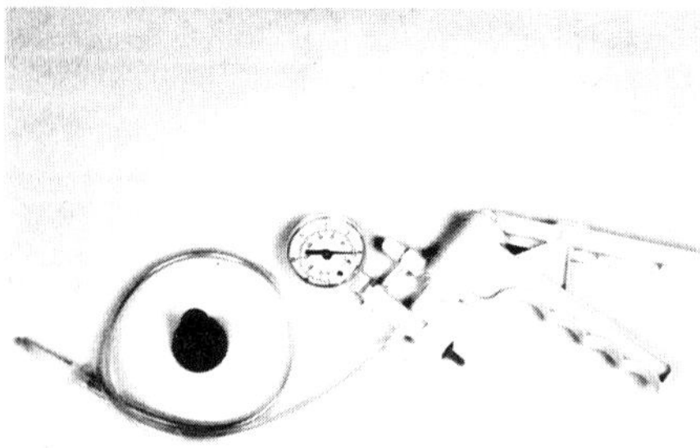

Hand-operated vacuum pump

Brake shoe spring tool

Special tools

The tools in this list include those which are not used regularly, are expensive to buy, or which need to be used in accordance with their manufacturer's instructions. Unless these tools will be used frequently, it is not very economical to purchase many of them. A consideration would be to split the cost and use between yourself and a friend or friends. In addition, most of these tools can be obtained from a tool rental shop on a temporary basis.

This list contains only those tools and instruments widely available to the public, and not those special tools produced by vehicle manufacturers for distribution to dealer service departments. Occasionally, references to the manufacturer's special tools are included in the text of this manual. Generally, an alternate method of doing the job without the special tool is offered. However, sometimes there is no alternative to their use. Where this is the case, and the tool cannot be purchased or borrowed, the work should be turned over to the dealer, a repair shop or an automotive machine shop.

Valve spring compressor
Piston ring groove cleaning tool
Piston ring compressor
Piston ring installation tool
Cylinder compression gauge
Cylinder ridge reamer
Cylinder surfacing hone
Cylinder bore gauge
Micrometer(s) and/or dial calipers
Hydraulic lifter removal tool
Balljoint separator
Universal-type puller
Impact screwdriver
Dial indicator set
Stroboscopic timing light (inductive pickup)
Hand-operated vacuum/pressure pump
Tachometer/dwell meter
Universal electrical multimeter
Cable hoist
Brake spring removal and installation tools
Floor jack

Buying tools

For the do-it-yourselfer who is just starting to get involved in vehicle maintenance and repair, there are a couple of options available when purchasing tools. If maintenance and minor repair is the extent of the work to be done, the purchase of individual tools is satisfactory. If, on the other hand, extensive work is planned, it would be a good idea to purchase a modest tool set from one of the large retail chain stores. A set can usually be bought at substantial savings over the individual tool prices (and they often come with a tool box). As additional tools are needed, add-on sets, individual tools and a larger tool box can be purchased to expand the tool selection. Building a tool set gradually allows the cost of the tools to be spread over a longer period of time and gives the mechanic the freedom to choose only those tools that will actually be used.

Tool stores will often be the only source of some of the special tools that are needed, but regardless of where tools are bought, try to avoid cheap ones (especially when buying screwdrivers and sockets) because they won't last very long. The expense involved in replacing cheap tools will eventually be greater than the initial cost of quality tools.

Care and maintenance of tools

Good tools are expensive, so it makes sense to treat them with respect. Keep them in a clean and usable condition and store them properly when not in use. Always wipe off any dirt, grease or metal chips before putting them away. Never leave tools lying around in the work area. Upon completion of a job, always check closely under the hood for tools that may have been left there (so they don't get lost during a test drive).

Some tools, such as screwdrivers, pliers, wrenches and sockets, can be hung on a panel mounted on the garage or workshop wall, while others should be kept in a tool box or tray. Measuring instruments, gauges, meters, etc. must be carefully stored where they cannot be damaged by weather or impact from other tools.

When tools are used with care and stored properly, they will last a very long time. Even with the best of care, tools will wear out if used frequently. When a tool is damaged or worn out, replace it; subsequent jobs will be safer and more enjoyable if you do.

Working facilities

Not to be overlooked when discussing tools is the workshop. If anything more than routine maintenance is to be carried out, some sort of suitable work area is essential.

It is understood, and appreciated, that many home mechanics do not have a good workshop or garage available and end up removing an engine or doing major repairs outside. It is recommended, however, that the overhaul or repair be completed under the cover of a roof.

A clean, flat workbench or table of comfortable working height is an absolute necessity. The workbench should be equipped with a vise that has a jaw opening of at least 4 inches.

As mentioned previously, some clean, dry storage space is also required for tools, as well as the lubricants, fluids, cleaning solvents, etc. which soon become necessary.

Sometimes waste oil and fluids, drained from the engine or transmission during normal maintenance or repairs, present a disposal problem. To avoid pouring oil on the ground or into the sewage system, simply pour the used fluids into large containers, seal them with caps and deliver them to a local recycling center or disposal facility. Plastic jugs (such as old antifreeze containers) are ideal for this purpose.

Always keep a supply of old newspapers and clean rags available. Old towels are excellent for mopping up spills. Many mechanics use rolls of paper towels for most work because they are readily available and disposable. To keep the area under the vehicle clean, a large cardboard box can be cut open and flattened to protect the garage or shop floor.

Whenever working over a painted surface (such as when leaning over a fender to service something under the hood), always cover it with an old blanket or bedspread to protect the finish. Vinyl covered pads, made especially for this purpose, are available at auto parts stores.

Automotive chemicals and lubricants

A number of automotive chemicals and lubricants are available for use in vehicle maintenance and repair. They include a wide variety of products ranging from cleaning solvents and degreasers to lubricants and protective sprays for rubber, plastic and vinyl.

Contact point/spark plug cleaner is a solvent used to clean oily film and dirt from points, grime from electrical connectors and oil deposits from spark plugs. It is oil free and leaves no residue. It can also be used to remove gum and varnish from carburetor jets and other orifices.

Carburetor cleaner is similar to contact point/spark plug cleaner but it is a stronger solvent and may leave a slight oily residue. It is not recommended for cleaning electrical components or connections.

Brake system cleaner is used to remove grease or brake fluid from brake system components where clean surfaces are absolutely necessary and petroleum-based solvents cannot be used. It also leaves no residue.

Silicone-based lubricants are used to protect rubber parts such as hoses, weatherstripping and grommets and are used as lubricants for hinges and locks.

Multi-purpose grease is an all-purpose lubricant used whenever grease is more practical than a liquid lubricant such as oil. Some multi-purpose grease is white and specially formulated to be more resistant to water than ordinary grease.

Bearing grease/wheel bearing grease is a heavy grease used where increased loads and friction are encountered (i.e. wheel bearings, universal joints, etc.).

High temperature wheel bearing grease is designed to withstand the extreme temperatures encountered by wheel bearings in disc brake equipped vehicles. It usually contains molybdenum disulfide, which is a 'dry' type lubricant.

Gear oil (sometimes called gear lube) is a specially designed oil used in differentials, manual transmissions and transfer cases, as well as other areas where high friction, high temperature lubrication is required. It is available in a number of viscosities (weights) for various applications.

Motor oil, of course, is the lubricant specially formulated for use in the engine. It normally contains a wide variety of additives to prevent corrosion and reduce foaming and wear. Motor oil comes in various weights (viscosity ratings) of from 5 to 80. The recommended weight of the oil depends on the seasonal temperature and the demands on the engine. Light oil is used in cold climates and under light load conditions; heavy oil is used in hot climates and where high loads are encountered. Multi-viscosity oils are designed to have characteristics of both light and heavy oils and are available in a number of weights from 5W-20 to 20W-50.

Oil additives range from viscosity index improvers to slick chemical treatments that purportedly reduce friction. It should be noted that most oil manufacturers caution against using additives with their oils.

Gas additives perform several functions, depending on their chemical makeup. They usually contain solvents that help dissolve gum and varnish that build up on carburetor and intake parts. They also serve to break down carbon deposits that form on the inside surfaces of the combustion chambers. Some additives contain upper cylinder lubricants for valves and piston rings.

Brake fluid is a specially formulated hydraulic fluid that can withstand the heat and pressure encountered in brake systems. Care must be taken that this fluid does not come in contact with painted surfaces or plastics. An opened container should always be resealed to prevent contamination by water or dirt.

Undercoating is a petroleum-based, tar-like substance that is designed to protect metal surfaces on the underside of a vehicle from corrosion. It also acts as a sound deadening agent by insulating the bottom of the vehicle.

Weatherstrip cement is used to bond weatherstripping around doors, windows and trunk lids. It is sometimes used to attach trim pieces as well.

Degreasers are heavy-duty solvents used to remove grease and grime that accumulate on engine and chassis components. They can be sprayed or brushed on and, depending on the type, are rinsed with either water or solvent.

Solvents are used alone or in combination with degreasers to clean parts and assemblies during repair and overhaul. The home mechanic should use only solvents that are non-flammable and that do not produce irritating fumes.

Gasket sealing compounds may be used in conjunction with gaskets, to improve their sealing capabilities, or alone, to seal metal-to-metal joints. Many gaskets can withstand extreme heat, some are impervious to gasoline and lubricants, while others are capable of filling and sealing large cavities. Depending on the intended use, gasket sealers either dry hard or stay relatively soft and pliable. They are usually applied by hand, with a brush, or are sprayed on the gasket sealing surfaces.

Thread cement is an adhesive locking compound that prevents threaded fasteners from loosening because of vibration. It is available in a variety of types for different applications.

Moisture dispersants are usually sprays that can be used to dry out electrical components such as the distributor, fuse block and wiring connectors. Some types can also be used as a treatment for rubber and as a lubricant for hinges, cables and locks.

Waxes and polishes are used to help protect painted and plated surfaces from the weather. Different types of paint may require the use of different types of wax or polish. Some polishes utilize a chemical or abrasive cleaner to help remove the top layer of oxidized (dull) paint in older vehicles. In recent years, many non-wax polishes that contain a wide variety of chemicals such as polymers and silicones have been introduced. These non-wax polishes are usually easier to apply and last longer than conventional waxes and polishes.

Jacking and towing

Jacking

The jack supplied with the vehicle should be used for raising the vehicle during a tire change or when placing jackstands under the frame. **Under no circumstances should work be performed beneath the vehicle or the engine started while this jack is being used as the only means of support.**

All vehicles are supplied with a scissors-type jack which fits into a notch in the vertical rocker panel flange nearest to the wheel being changed.

The vehicle should be on level ground with the wheels blocked and the transmission in Park (automatic) or Reverse (manual). Pry off the hub cap (if equipped) using the tapered end of the lug wrench. Loosen the wheel nuts one half turn and leave them in place until the wheel is raised off the ground.

Place the jack under the side of the vehicle in the jacking notch. Use the supplied wrench to turn the jackscrew clockwise until the wheel is raised off the ground. Remove the wheel nuts, pull off the wheel and replace it with the spare.

With the beveled side in, replace the wheel nuts and tighten them until snug. Lower the vehicle by turning the jackscrew counterclockwise. Remove the jack and tighten the nuts in a diagonal fashion. Replace the hubcap by placing it into position and using the heel of your hand or a rubber mallet to seat it.

Towing

The vehicle can be towed with all four wheels on the ground provided speeds do not exceed 35 mph and the distance is not over 50 miles, otherwise transmission damage can result.

Towing equipment specifically designed for that purpose should

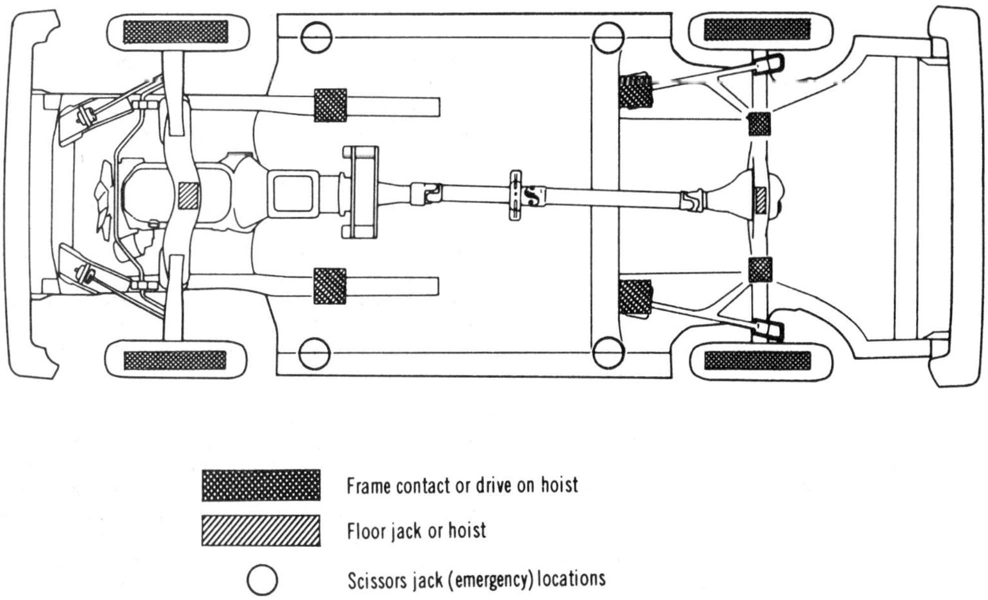

Vehicle frame and body lifting points

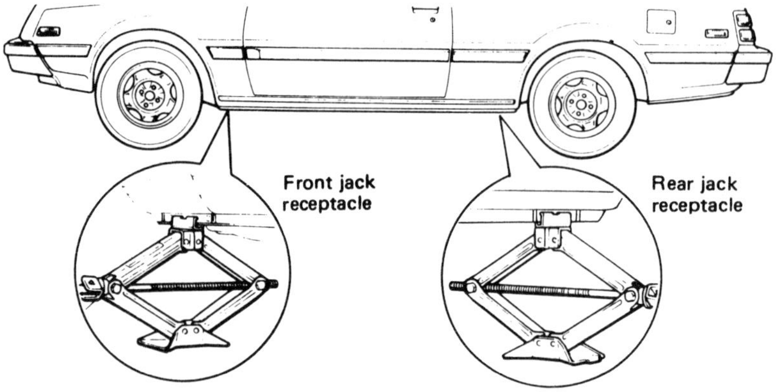

Jack lifting and support points

be used and should be attached to the main structural members of the vehicle and not the bumper or brackets.

Safety is a major consideration when towing a vehicle and all applicable state and local laws must be obeyed. A safety chain system must be used for all towing.

While towing, the parking brake should be fully released and the transmission should be in Neutral. The steering must be unlocked (ignition switch in the Off position). Remember that power steering and power brakes will not work with the engine off.

Vehicles with manual transmissions can be towed considerably farther and faster than vehicles with automatic transmissions. Make sure the fluid levels are full on both the transmission and the differential before attempting a long distance tow. The shift lever must be in Neutral.

Booster battery (jump) starting

If the vehicle will not start because the starter does not operate or barely turns over, suspect a dead battery. Remove and clean the battery cables (see Battery maintenance, Chapter 1), reconnect them and try to start the engine again. If the headlights do not work, or dim when the starter is operated, or the radio does not work, it is probable that the problem is a dead battery. If the lights shine brightly when the starter is operated, the problem is with the starter motor or its wiring.

A vehicle with a dead battery can be started using a set of jumper cables and a second vehicle that is operating. Make sure both vehicles have 12-volt batteries (which have six filler holes; 6-volt batteries have three filler holes). Your eyes should be shielded; safety goggles are a good idea. Before connecting the batteries, make sure that the ignition switch is in the Off position.

1 If possible, bring both cars nose-to-nose and open the hoods. Some imported vehicles have their batteries in the trunk or under the rear seat. Position these vehicles so that the batteries are as close to one another as possible. **Do not allow the cars to touch.**

2 Set both parking brakes. Put manual transmissions in Neutral and automatics in Park.

3 Remove the vent caps from both batteries and allow any built-up gases to excape. Cover the vent holes with clean rags.

4 Determine which of the battery posts in each vehicle is the positive terminal. The positive post is generally larger than the negative post; it may be marked with a plus sign (+) or Pos.

5 Attach the *red* booster cable to the positive terminals of both batteries.

6 The other battery post in each vehicle is the negative one. If the posts have different diameters, the negative one will be smaller. It may be marked with a minus sign (–) or Neg.

7 Attach one end of the *black* cable to the negative terminal of the *good* battery. Attach the other end to a good ground on the *dead* vehicle, such as an unpainted bolt or flange on the engine or chassis.

8 Make sure all hands and cables are clear of the fans and other moving parts on both vehicles. Then, start the engine of the vehicle with the good battery and have an assistant accelerate it moderately.

9 Attempt to start the second engine. If it still will not start, check for additional problems in the ignition and fuel systems.

10 If the 'dead' engine now starts, keep it running and carefully remove the cables in the opposite order from which they were attached (*black* cable from the dead vehicle, then from the good one; *red* cable from the dead vehicle, then from the good one).

11 Replace the vent caps and discard the rags.

12 Drive the formerly stalled car for at least 30 minutes to recharge its battery. If this problem recurs, refer to Battery maintenance in Chapter 1 or replace your battery with a new one.

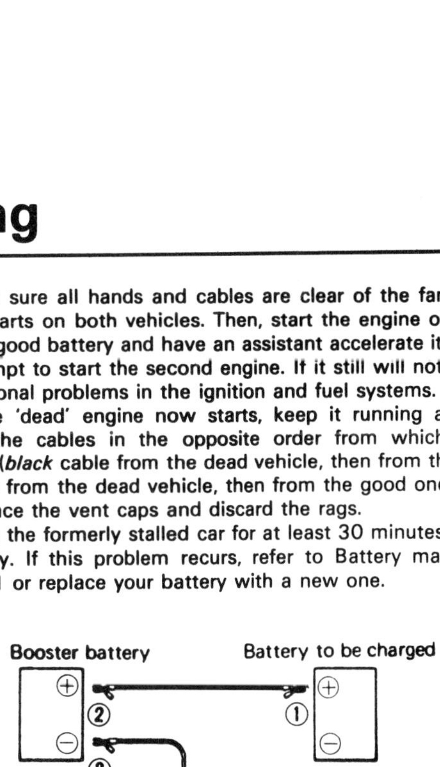

Battery booster cable hook-up sequence

Safety first!

Regardless of how enthusiastic you may be about getting on with the job at hand, take the time to ensure that your safety is not jeopardized. A moment's lack of attention can result in an accident, as can failure to observe certain simple safety precautions. The possibility of an accident will always exist, and the following points should not be considered a comprehensive list of all dangers. Rather, they are intended to make you aware of the risks and to encourage a safety conscious approach to all work you carry out on your vehicle.

Essential DOs and DON'Ts

DON'T rely on a jack when working under the vehicle. Always use approved jackstands to support the weight of the vehicle and place them under the recommended lift or support points.
DON'T attempt to loosen extremely tight fasteners (i.e. wheel lug nuts) while the vehicle is on a jack — it may fall.
DON'T start the engine without first making sure that the transmission is in Neutral (or Park where applicable) and the parking brake is set.
DON'T remove the radiator cap from a hot cooling system — let it cool or cover it with a cloth and release the pressure gradually.
DON'T attempt to drain the engine oil until you are sure it has cooled to the point that it will not burn you.
DON'T touch any part of the engine or exhaust system until it has cooled sufficiently to avoid burns.
DON'T siphon toxic liquids such as gasoline, antifreeze and brake fluid by mouth, or allow them to remain on your skin.
DON'T inhale brake lining dust — it is potentially hazardous (see *Asbestos* below)
DON'T allow spilled oil or grease to remain on the floor — wipe it up before someone slips on it.
DON'T use loose fitting wrenches or other tools which may slip and cause injury.
DON'T push on wrenches when loosening or tightening nuts or bolts. Always try to pull the wrench toward you. If the situation calls for pushing the wrench away, push with an open hand to avoid scraped knuckles if the wrench should slip.
DON'T attempt to lift a heavy component alone — get someone to help you.
DON'T rush or take unsafe shortcuts to finish a job.
DON'T allow children or animals in or around the vehicle while you are working on it.
DO wear eye protection when using power tools such as a drill, sander, bench grinder, etc. and when working under a vehicle.
DO keep loose clothing and long hair well out of the way of moving parts.
DO make sure that any hoist used has a safe working load rating adequate for the job.
DO get someone to check on you periodically when working alone on a vehicle.
DO carry out work in a logical sequence and make sure that everything is correctly assembled and tightened.
DO keep chemicals and fluids tightly capped and out of the reach of children and pets.
DO remember that your vehicle's safety affects that of yourself and others. If in doubt on any point, get professional advice.

Asbestos

Certain friction, insulating, sealing, and other products — such as brake linings, brake bands, clutch linings, torque converters, gaskets, etc. — contain asbestos. *Extreme care must be taken to avoid inhalation of dust from such products since it is hazardous to health.* If in doubt, assume that they *do* contain asbestos.

Fire

Remember at all times that gasoline is highly flammable. Never smoke or have any kind of open flame around when working on a vehicle. But the risk does not end there. A spark caused by an electrical short circuit, by two metal surfaces contacting each other, or even by static electricity built up in your body under certain conditions, can ignite gasoline vapors, which in a confined space are highly explosive. Do not, under any circumstances, use gasoline for cleaning parts. Use an approved safety solvent.

Always disconnect the battery ground (–) cable *at the battery* before working on any part of the fuel system or electrical system. Never risk spilling fuel on a hot engine or exhaust component.

It is strongly recommended that a fire extinguisher suitable for use on fuel and electrical fires be kept handy in the garage or workshop at all times. Never try to extinguish a fuel or electrical fire with water.

Fumes

Certain fumes are highly toxic and can quickly cause unconsciousness and even death if inhaled to any extent. Gasoline vapor falls into this category, as do the vapors from some cleaning solvents. Any draining or pouring of such volatile fluids should be done in a well ventilated area.

When using cleaning fluids and solvents, read the instructions on the container carefully. Never use materials from unmarked containers.

Never run the engine in an enclosed space, such as a garage. Exhaust fumes contain carbon monoxide, which is extremely poisonous. If you need to run the engine, always do so in the open air, or at least have the rear of the vehicle outside the work area.

If you are fortunate enough to have the use of an inspection pit, never drain or pour gasoline and never run the engine while the vehicle is over the pit. The fumes, being heavier than air, will concentrate in the pit with possibly lethal results.

The battery

Never create a spark or allow a bare light bulb near the battery. The battery normally gives off a certain amount of hydrogen gas, which is highly explosive.

Always disconnect the battery ground (–) cable *at the battery* before working on the fuel or electrical systems.

If possible, loosen the filler caps or cover when charging the battery from an external source. Do not charge at an excessive rate or the battery may burst.

Take care when adding water and when carrying a battery. The electrolyte, even when diluted, is very corrosive and should not be allowed to contact clothing or skin.

Always wear eye protection when cleaning the battery to prevent the caustic deposits from entering your eyes.

Household current

When using an electric power tool, inspection light, etc., which operates on household current, always make sure that the tool is correctly connected to its plug and that, where necessary, it is properly grounded. Do not use such items in damp conditions and, again, do not create a spark or apply excessive heat in the vicinity of fuel or fuel vapor.

Secondary ignition system voltage

A severe electric shock can result from touching certain parts of the ignition system (such as the spark plug wires) when the engine is running or being cranked, particularly if components are damp or the insulation is defective. In the case of an electronic ignition system, the secondary system voltage is much higher and could prove fatal.

Troubleshooting

Contents

This section provides an easy-reference guide to the more common faults which may occur during the operation of your vehicle. These faults and their probable causes are grouped under their respective systems i.e. Engine, Cooling system, etc., and also refer to the Chapter and/or Section which deals with the problem.

Remember that successful troubleshooting is not a mysterious 'black art' practiced only by professional mechanics, it's simply the result of a bit of knowledge combined with an intelligent, systematic approach to the problem. Always work by a process of elimination, starting with the simplest solution and working through to the most complex – and never overlook the obvious. Anyone can forget to fill the gas tank or leave the lights on overnight, so don't assume that you are above such oversights.

Finally, always get clear in your mind why a problem has occurred and take steps to ensure that it doesn't happen again. if the electrical system fails because of a poor connection, check all other connections in the system to make sure that they don't fail as well; if a particular fuse continues to blow, find out why – don't just go on replacing fuses. Remember, failure or incorrect functioning of a small component can often be indicative of potential failure or incorrect functioning of a more important component or system.

1 Engine will not rotate when attempting to start

1 Battery terminal connection loose or corroded. Check the cable terminals at the battery; tighten or clean off corrosion as necessary.
2 Battery discharged or faulty. If the cable connectors are clean and tight on the battery posts, turn the key to the On position and switch on the headlights and/or windshield wipers. If these fail to function, the battery is discharged.
3 Automatic transmission not fully engaged in Park or clutch not fully depressed.
4 Broken, loose or disconnected wiring in the starting circuit. Inspect all wiring and connectors at the battery, starter solenoid and ignition switch.
5 Starter motor pinion jammed on flywheel ring gear. If manual transmission, place transmission in gear and rock the vehicle to manually turn the engine. Remove starter and inspect pinion (Chapter 2) and flywheel (Chapter 2) at earliest convenience.
6 Starter solenoid faulty (Chapter 5).
7 Starter motor faulty (Chapter 5).
8 Ignition switch faulty (Chapter 5 or 11).

2 Engine rotates but will not start

1 Fuel tank empty.
2 Battery discharged (engine rotates slowly). Check the operation of electrical components as described in previous Section (Chapter 1).
3 Battery terminal connections loose or corroded. See previous Section.
4 Carburetor flooded and/or fuel level in carburetor incorrect. This will usually be accompanied by a strong fuel odor from under the hood. Wait a few minutes, depress the accelerator pedal all the way to the floor and attempt to start the engine.
5 Choke control inoperative (Chapters 1 and 4).
6 Fuel not reaching carburetor. With ignition switch in Off position, open hood, remove the top plate of air cleaner assembly and observe the top of the carburetor (manually move choke plate back if necessary). Have an assistant depress the accelerator pedal fully and make sure that fuel spurts into carburetor. If not, check fuel filter (Chapters 1 and 4), fuel lines and fuel pump (Chapter 4).
7 Excessive moisture on, or damage to, ignition components (Chapter 5).
8 Worn, faulty or incorrectly adjusted spark plugs (Chapter 1).
9 Broken, loose or disconnected wiring in the starting circuit (see previous Section).
10 Distributor loose, causing ignition timing to change. Turn the distributor as necessary to start the engine, then set ignition timing as soon as possible (Chapter 1).
11 Ignition condenser faulty (Chapter 1).
12 Broken, loose or disconnected wires at the ignition coil, or faulty coil (Chapter 5).

3 Starter motor operates without rotating engine

1 Starter pinion sticking. Remove the starter (Chapter 5) and inspect.
2 Starter pinion or engine flywheel teeth worn or broken. Remove the inspection cover at the rear of the engine and inspect.

4 Engine hard to start when cold

1 Battery discharged or low. Check as described in Section 1.
2 Choke control inoperative or out of adjustment (Chapter 4).
3 Carburetor flooded (see Section 2).
4 Fuel supply not reaching the carburetor (see Section 4).
5 Carburetor worn and in need of overhauling (Chapter 4).

5 Engine hard to start when hot

1 Choke sticking in the closed position (Chapter 4).
2 Carburetor flooded (see Section 2).
3 Air filter in need of replacement (Chapter 1).
4 Fuel not reaching the carburetor (see Section 4).

6 Starter motor noisy or excessively rough in engagement

1 Pinion or flywheel gear teeth worn or broken. Remove the inspection cover at the rear of the engine and inspect.
2 Starter motor retaining bolts loose or missing.

7 Engine starts but stops immediately

1 Loose or faulty electrical connections at distributor, coil or alternator.
2 Insufficient fuel reaching the carburetor. Disconnect the fuel line at the carburetor and remove the filter (Chapter 1 or 4). Place a container under the disconnected fuel line. Observe the flow of fuel from the line. If little or none at all, check for blockage in the lines and/or replace the fuel pump (Chapter 4).
3 Vacuum leak at the gasket surfaces of the intake manifold and/or carburetor. Make sure that all mounting bolts (nuts) are tightened to specifications and that all vacuum hoses connected to the carburetor and manifold are positioned properly and in good condition.

8 Engine 'lopes' while idling or idles erratically

1 Vacuum leakage. Check mounting bolts (nuts) at the carburetor and intake manifold for tightness. Check that all vacuum hoses are connected and in good condition. Use a mechanic's stethoscope or a length of fuel line hose held against your ear to listen for vacuum leaks while the engine is running. A hissing sound will be heard. A soapy water solution will also detect leaks. Check the carburetor and intake manifold gasket surfaces.
2 Leaking EGR valve or plugged PCV valve (Chapter 6).
3 Air filter clogged and in need of replacement (Chapter 1 or 4).
4 Fuel pump not delivering sufficient fuel to the carburetor (see Section 7).
5 Carburetor out of adjustment (Chapter 4).
6 Leaking head gasket. If this is suspected, take the vehicle to a repair shop or dealer where this can be pressure checked without the need to remove the heads.
7 Timing chain/belt and/or timing gears worn and in need of replacement (Chapter 1).
8 Camshaft lobes worn, necessitating the removal of the camshaft for inspection (Chapter 2).

9 Engine misses at idle speed

1 Spark plugs faulty or not gapped properly (Chapter 1 or 5).
2 Faulty spark plug wires (Chapter 1 or 5).

3 Carburetor choke not operating properly (Chapter 4).
4 Sticking or faulty emissions systems (see checking procedures in Chapter 6).
5 Clogged fuel filter and/or foreign matter in fuel. Remove the fuel filter (Chapter 1 or 4) and inspect.
6 Vacuum leaks at carburetor, intake manifold or hose connections. Check as described in Section 8.
7 Incorrect idle speed (Chapter 1 or 4) or idle mixture (Chapter 4).
8 Incorrect ignition timing (Chapter 1 or 5).
9 Uneven or low cylinder compression. Remove plugs and use compression tester as per manufacturer's instructions.

10 Engine misses throughout driving speed range

1 Carburetor fuel filter clogged and/or impurities in the fuel system (Chapter 1 or 4). Also check fuel flow at the carburetor (see Section 7).
2 Faulty or incorrectly gapped spark plugs (Chapter 1 or 5).
3 Incorrectly set ignition timing (Chapter 1 or 5).
4 Check for a cracked distributor cap, disconnected distributor wires or damage to the distributor components (Chapter 1 or 5).
5 Leaking spark plug wires (Chapter 1 or 5).
6 Emission system components faulty (Chapter 6).
7 Low or uneven cylinder compression pressures. Remove spark plugs and test compression with gauge.
8 Weak or faulty ignition system (see Chapter 5).
9 Vacuum leaks at carburetor, intake manifold or vacuum hoses (see Section 8).

11 Engine stalls

1 Carburetor idle speed incorrectly set (Chapter 1 or 4).
2 Carburetor fuel filter clogged and/or water and impurities in the fuel system (Chapter 1 or 4).
3 Choke improperly adjusted or sticking (Chapter 4).
4 Distributor components damp, points out of adjustment or damage to distributor cap, rotor, etc. (Chapter 1 or 5).
5 Emission system components faulty (see checking procedures in Chapter 6).
6 Faulty or incorrectly gapped spark plugs (Chapter 1 or 5). Also check spark plug wires (Chapter 1 or 5).
7 Vacuum leak at the carburetor, intake manifold or vacuum hoses. Check as described in Section 8.
8 Valve clearances incorrectly set (Chapter 1 or 2).

12 Engine lacks power

1 Incorrect ignition timing (Chapter 1 or 5).
2 Excessive play in distributor shaft. At the same time check for worn rotor, faulty distributor cap, wires, etc. (Chapter 1 or 5).
3 Faulty or incorrectly gapped spark plugs (Chapter 1 or 5).
4 Carburetor not adjusted or excessively worn (Chapter 4).
5 Weak coil or condenser (Chapter 5).
6 Faulty ignition coil (Chapter 5).
7 Brakes binding (Chapter 1 or 9).
8 Automatic transmission fluid level incorrect, causing slippage (Chapter 1 or 7).
9 Manual transmission clutch slipping (Chapter 8).
10 Fuel filter clogged and/or impurities in the fuel system (Chapter 1 or 4).
11 Emission control system not functioning properly (Chapter 6).
12 Use of sub-standard fuel. Fill tank with proper octane fuel.
13 Low or uneven cylinder compression pressures. Test with compression tester, which will detect leaking valves and/or blown head gasket.

13 Engine backfires

1 Emission system not functioning properly (Chapter 6).
2 Ignition timing incorrect (Section 3).
3 Carburetor in need of adjustment or worn excessively (Chapter 4).
4 Vacuum leak at carburetor, intake manifold or vacuum hoses. Check as described in Section 8.
5 Valve clearances incorrectly set, and/or valves sticking (Chapter 1 or 2).

14 Pinging or knocking engine sounds during hard acceleration or uphill

1 Incorrect grade of fuel. Fill tank with fuel of the proper octane rating.
2 Ignition timing incorrect (Chapter 1 or 5).
3 Carburetor in need of adjustment (Chapter 4).
4 Improper spark plugs. Check plug type with that specified on tune-up decal located inside engine compartment. Also check plugs and wires for damage (Chapter 1 or 4).
5 Worn or damaged distributor components (Chapter 5).
6 Faulty emission system (Chapter 6).
7 Vacuum leak (Check as described in Section 8).

15 Engine 'diesels' (continues to run) after switching off

1 Idle speed too fast (Chapter 1 or 5).
2 Electrical solenoid at side of carburetor not functioning properly (not all models, see Chapter 4).
3 Ignition timing incorrectly adjusted (Chapter 1 or 5).
4 Air cleaner valve not operating properly (Chapter 4).
5 Excessive engine operating temperatures. Probable causes of this are: malfunctioning thermostat, clogged radiator, faulty water pump (see Chapter 3).

Engine electrical

16 Battery will not hold a charge

1 Alternator drivebelt defective or not adjusted properly (Chapter 1 or 5).
2 Electrolyte level too low or too weak (Chapter 1 or 5).
3 Battery terminals loose or corroded (Chapter 1 or 5).
4 Alternator not charging properly (Chapter 5).
5 Loose, broken or faulty wiring in the charging circuit (Chapter 5).
6 Short in vehicle circuitry causing a continual drain on battery.
7 Battery internal defect.

17 Ignition light fails to go out

1 Fault in alternator or charging circuit (Chapter 5).
2 Alternator drivebelt defective or not properly adjusted (Chapter 5).

18 Ignition light fails to come on when key is turned on

1 Ignition light bulb faulty (Chapter 10).
2 Alternator faulty (Chapter 5).
3 Fault in the printed circuit, dash wiring or bulb holder (Chapter 10).

Engine fuel system

19 Excessive fuel consumption

1 Dirty or choked air filter element (Chapter 1 or 4).
2 Incorrectly set ignition timing (Chapter 1 or 5).
3 Choke sticking or improperly adjusted (Chapter 4).
4 Emission system not functioning properly (not all vehicles, see Chapter 6).
5 Carburetor idle speed and/or mixture not adjusted properly (Chapter 1 or 4).
6 Carburetor internal parts worn or damaged (Chapter 4).
7 Low tire pressure or incorrect tire size (Chapter 1 or 11).

20 Fuel leakage and/or fuel odor

1 Leak in a fuel feed or vent line (Chapter 4).
2 Tank overfilled. Fill only to automatic shut-off.
3 Emission system filter in need of replacement (Chapter 1).
4 Vapor leaks from system lines (Chapter 4).
5 Carburetor internal parts excessively worn or out of adjustment (Chapter 4).

Engine cooling system

21 Overheating

1 Insufficient coolant in system (Chapter 1 or 3).
2 Fan belt defective or not adjusted properly (Chapter 1 or 3).
3 Radiator core blocked or radiator grille dirty and restricted (Chapter 3).
4 Thermostat faulty (Chapter 3).
5 Fan blades broken or cracked (Chapter 3).
6 Radiator cap not maintaining proper pressure. Have cap pressure tested by gas station or repair shop.
7 Ignition timing incorrect (Chapter 1 or 5).

22 Overcooling

1 Thermostat faulty (Chapter 3).
2 Inaccurate temperature gauge (Chapter 10).

23 External coolant leakage

1 Deteriorated or damaged hoses. Loose clamps at hose connections (Chapter 3).
2 Water pump seals defective. If this is the case, water will drip from the 'weep' hole in the water pump body (Chapter 3).
3 Leakage from radiator core or header tank. This will require the radiator to be professionally repaired (see Chapter 3 for removal procedures).
4 Engine drain plugs or water jacket freeze plugs leaking (Chapter 2 or 3).

24 Internal coolant leakage

Note: *Internal coolant leaks can usually be detected by examining the oil. Check the dipstick and inside of valve cover for water deposits and an oil consistency like that of a milkshake.*
1 Faulty cylinder head gasket. Have the system pressure-tested professionally or remove the cylinder heads (Chapter 2) and inspect.
2 Cracked cylinder bore or cylinder head. Dismantle engine and inspect (Chapter 2).

25 Coolant loss

1 Overfilling system (Chapter 1).
2 Coolant boiling away due to overheating (see causes in Section 15).
3 Internal or external leakage (see Sections 23 and 24).
4 Faulty radiator cap. Have the cap pressure tested.

26 Poor coolant circulation

1 Inoperative water pump. A quick test is to pinch the top radiator hose closed with your hand while the engine is idling, then let it loose. You should feel a surge of coolant if the pump is working properly (Chapter 3).
2 Restriction in cooling system. Drain, flush and refill the system (Chapter 1). If it appears necessary, remove the radiator (Chapter 3) and have it reverse-flushed or professionally cleaned.
3 Fan drivebelt defective or not adjusted properly (Chapter 1).
4 Thermostat sticking (Chapter 3).

Clutch

27 Fails to release (pedal depressed to the floor) – shift lever does not move freely in and out of Reverse

1 Improper linkage adjustment (Chapter 8).
2 Clutch fork off ball stud. Look under the vehicle, on the left side of the transmission.
3 Clutch disc warped, bent or damaged (Chapter 8).

28 Clutch slips (engine speed increases with no increases in vehicle speed)

1 Linkage in need of adjustment (Chapter 8).
2 Clutch disc oil soaked or lining worn. Remove disc (Chapter 8) and inspect.
3 Clutch disc not seated in. It may take 30 or 40 normal starts for a new disc to seat.

29 Grabbing (chattering) on take-up

1 Oil on clutch disc lining. Remove disc (Chapter 8) and inspect. Correct any leakage source.
2 Worn or loose engine or transmission mounts. These units move slightly when clutch is released. Inspect mounts and bolts.
3 Worn splines on clutch disc hub. Remove clutch components (Chapter 8) and inspect.
4 Warped pressure plate or flywheel. Remove clutch components and inspect.

30 Squeal or rumble with clutch fully engaged (pedal released)

1 Improper adjustment; no freeplay (Chapter 8).
2 Release bearing binding on transmission bearing retainer. Remove clutch components (Chapter 8) and check bearing. Remove any burrs or nicks, clean and relubricate before reinstallation.
3 Weak linkage return spring. Replace the spring.

31 Squeal or rumble with clutch fully disengaged (pedal depressed)

1 Worn, faulty or broken release bearing (Chapter 8).
2 Worn or broken pressure plate springs (or diaphragm fingers) (Chapter 8).

32 Clutch pedal stays on floor when disengaged

1 Binding linkage or release bearing. Inspect linkage or remove clutch components as necessary.
2 Linkage springs being over-extended. Adjust linkage for proper freeplay. Make sure proper pedal stop (bumper) is installed.

Manual transmission

Note: *All the following Sections are contained within Chapter 7A unless noted.*

33 Noisy in Neutral with engine running

1 Input shaft bearing worn.
2 Damaged main drive gear bearing.
3 Worn countergear bearings.
4 Worn or damaged countergear shims.

34 Noisy in all gears

Any of the above causes, and/or insufficient lubricant (see checking procedures in Chapter 1 or 7).

35 Noisy in one particular gear

1 Worn, damaged or chipped gear teeth for that particular gear.
2 Worn or damaged synchronizer for that particular gear.

36 Slips out of high gear

1 Transmission loose on clutch housing.
2 Shift rods interfering with engine mounts or clutch lever.
3 Shift rods not working freely.
4 Damaged mainshaft pilot bearing.
5 Dirt between transmission case and clutch housing or misalignment of transmission (Chapter 7).
6 Worn or improperly adjusted linkage (Chapter 7).

37 Difficulty in engaging gears

1 Clutch not releasing completely (see clutch adjustment, Chapter 8).
2 Loose, damaged or out of adjustment shift linkage. Make a thorough inspection, replacing parts as necessary. Adjust as described in Chapter 8.

38 Oil leakage

1 Excessive amount of lubricant in transmission (see Chapter 1 or 7 for correct checking procedures). Drain lubricant as required.
2 Side cover loose or gasket damaged.
3 Rear oil seal or speedometer oil seal in need of replacement (Section 6).

Automatic transmission

Note: *Due to the complexity of the automatic transmission, it is difficult for the home mechanic to properly diagnose and service this component. For problems other than the following, the vehicle should be taken to a reputable mechanic.*

39 Fluid leakage

1 Automatic transmission fluid is a deep red color. Fluid leaks should not be confused with engine oil which can easily be blown by air flow to the transmission.
2 To pinpoint a leak, first remove all built-up dirt and grime from around the transmission. Degreasing agents and/or steam cleaning will achieve this. With the underside clean, drive the vehicle at low speeds so that air flow will not blow the leak far from its source. Raise the vehicle and determine where the leak is coming from. Common areas of leakage are:

a) *Fluid pan:* tighten mounting bolts and/or replace pan gasket as necessary (see Chapter 7B)
b) *Rear extension:* tighten bolts and/or replace oil seal as necessary (Chapter 7B)
c) *Filler pipe:* replace the rubber seal where pipe enters transmission case
d) *Transmission oil lines:* tighten connectors where lines enter transmission case and/or replace lines
e) *Vent pipe:* transmission over-filled and/or water in fluid (see checking procedures, Chapter 1 or 7B)
f) *Speedometer connector:* replace the O-ring where speedometer cable enters transmission case

40 General shift mechanism problems

1 Chapter 7B deals with checking and adjusting the shift linkage on automatic transmissions. Common problems which may be attributed to poorly adjusted linkage are:

a) Engine starting in gears other than Park or Neutral
b) Indicator on quadrant pointing to a gear other than the one actually being used
c) Vehicle will not hold firm when in Park position

2 Refer to Chapter 7B to adjust the manual linkage.

41 Transmission will not downshift with the accelerator pedal pressed to the floor

Chapter 7B deals with adjusting the downshift cable or downshift switch to enable the transmission to downshift properly.

42 Engine will start in gears other than P (Park) or N (Neutral)

Chapter 7B deals with adjusting the Neutral start switches used with automatic transmissions.

43 Transmission slips, shifts rough, is noisy or has no drive in forward or reverse gears

1 There are many probable causes for the above problems, but the home mechanic should concern himself with only one possibility: fluid level.
2 Before taking the vehicle to a specialist, check the level of the fluid and condition of the fluid as described in Chapter 1 or 7B. Correct fluid level as necessary or change the fluid and filter if needed. If the problem persists, have a professional diagnose the probable cause.

Driveshaft

44 Leakage of fluid at front of driveshaft

Defective transmission rear oil seal. See Chapter 7B for replacement procedures. While this is done, check the splined yoke for burrs or a rough condition which may be damaging the seal. If found, these can be dressed with crocus cloth or a fine stone.

45 Knock or clunk when the transmission is under initial load (just after transmission is put into gear)

1 Loose or disconnected rear suspension components. Check all mounting bolts and bushings (Chapter 11).
2 Loose driveshaft bolts. Inspect all bolts and nuts and tighten to specified torque (Chapter 8).
3 Worn or damaged universal joint bearings. Test for wear (Chapter 8).

46 Metallic grating sound consistent with vehicle speed

Pronounced wear in the universal joint bearings. Check for wear (Chapter 8).

47 Vibration

Note: *Before it can be assumed that the driveshaft is at fault, make sure the tires are perfectly balanced and perform the following test.*
1 Install a tachometer inside the vehicle to monitor engine speed as the vehicle is driven. Drive the vehicle and note the engine speed at which the vibration (roughness) is most pronounced. Now, shift the transmission to a different gear and bring the engine speed to the same point.

2 If the vibration occurs at the same engine speed (rpm) regardless of which gear the transmission is in, the driveshaft is NOT at fault since the driveshaft speed varies.
3 If the vibration decreases or is eliminated when the transmission is in a different gear at the same engine speed, refer to the following probable causes.
4 Bent or dented driveshaft. Inspect and replace as necessary (Chapter 8).
5 Undercoating or built-up dirt, etc. on the driveshaft. Clean the shaft thoroughly and retest.
6 Worn universal joint bearings. Remove and inspect (Chapter 8).
7 Driveshaft and/or companion flange out of balance. Check for missing weights on the shaft. Remove driveshaft (Chapter 8) and reinstall 180° from original position. Retest. Have driveshaft professionally balanced if problem persists.

Rear axle

48 Noise – same when in Drive as when vehicle is coasting

1 Road noise. No corrective procedures available.
2 Tire noise. Inspect tires and tire pressures (Chapter 1).
3 Front wheel bearings loose, worn or damaged (Chapter 1).

49 Vibration

See probable causes under *Driveshaft*. Proceed under the guidelines listed for the driveshaft. If the problem persists, check the rear wheel bearings by raising the rear of the vehicle and spinning the wheels by hand. Listen for evidence of rough (noisy) bearings. Remove and inspect (Chapter 8).

50 Oil leakage

1 Pinion oil seal damaged (Chapter 8).
2 Axle shaft oil seals damaged (Chapter 8).
3 Differential inspection cover leaking. Tighten mounting bolts or replace the gasket as required (Chapter 8).

Brakes

Note: *Before assuming a brake problem exists, make sure that the tires are in good condition and properly inflated (see Chapter 1), the front end alignment is correct and that the vehicle is not unequally loaded.*

51 Vehicle pulls to one side during braking

1 Defective, damaged or oil contaminated brake pad on one side. Inspect as described in Chapter 1 or 9.
2 Excessive wear of brake pad material or disc on one side. Inspect and correct as necessary.
3 Loose or disconnected front suspension components. Inspect and tighten all bolts to specifications (Chapter 11).
4 Defective caliper assembly. Remove caliper and inspect for stuck piston or damage (Chapter 9).

52 Noise (high-pitched squeal without the brakes applied)

Front brake pads worn out. This noise comes from the wear sensor rubbing against the disc. Replace pads with new ones immediately (Chapter 9).

53 Excessive brake pedal travel

1 Partial brake system failure. Inspect entire system (Chapter 9) and correct as required.
2 Insufficient fluid in master cylinder. Check (Chapter 1) and add fluid and bleed system if necessary.
3 Rear brakes not adjusting properly. Make a series of starts and stops while the vehicle is in Reverse. If this does not correct the situation, remove drums and inspect self-adjusters (Chapter 9).

54 Brake pedal feels spongy when depressed

1 Air in hydraulic lines. Bleed the brake system (Chapter 9).
2 Faulty flexible hoses. Inspect all system hoses and lines. Replace parts as necessary.
3 Master cylinder mounting nuts/bolts loose. Inspect and tighten to specified torque.
4 Master cylinder faulty (Chapter 9).

55 Excessive effort required to stop vehicle

1 Power brake booster not operating properly (Chapter 9).
2 Excessively worn linings or pads. Inspect and replace if necessary (Chapter 9).
3 One or more caliper pistons (front wheels) or wheel cylinders (rear wheels) seized or sticking. Inspect and rebuild as required (Chapter 9).
4 Brake linings or pads contaminated with oil or grease. Inspect and replace as required (Chapter 9).
5 New pads or linings installed and not yet 'bedded in'. It will take awhile for the new material to seat against the drum (or rotor).

56 Pedal travels to the floor with little resistance

Little or no fluid in the master cylinder reservoir caused by leaking wheel cylinder(s), leaking caliper piston(s), loose, damaged or disconnected brake lines. Inspect entire system and correct as necessary.

57 Brake pedal pulsates during brake application

1 Wheel bearings not adjusted properly or in need of replacement (Chapter 11).
2 Caliper not sliding properly due to improper installation or obstructions. Remove and inspect (Chapter 9).
3 Rotor not within specifications. Remove the rotor (Chapter 9) and check for excessive lateral runout and parallelism. Have the rotor professionally machined or replace it with a new one.

Suspension and steering

58 Vehicle pulls to one side

1 Tire pressures uneven (Chapter 1).
2 Defective tire (Chapter 1).
3 Excessive wear in suspension or steering components (Chapter 11).
4 Front end in need of alignment. Take vehicle to a qualified specialist.
5 Front brakes dragging. Inspect braking system as described in Chapter 9.

59 Shimmy, shake or vibration

1 Tire or wheel out of balance or out of round. Have professionally balanced.
2 Loose, worn or out of adjustment wheel bearings (Chapter 11).
3 Shock absorbers and/or suspension components worn or damaged (Chapter 11).

60 Excessive pitching and/or rolling around corners or during braking

1 Defective shock absorbers. Replace as a set (Chapter 11).
2 Broken or weak springs and/or suspension components. Inspect as described in Chapter 11.

61 Excessively stiff steering

1 Lack of lubricant in steering gearbox (manual) or power steering fluid reservoir (Chapter 11).
2 Incorrect tire pressures (Chapter 1).
3 Lack of lubrication at steering joints (Chapter 1).
4 Front end out of alignment.
5 See also section titled *Lack of power assistance.*

62 Excessive play in steering

1 Loose wheel bearings (Chapter 11).
2 Excessive wear in suspension or steering components (Chapter 11).
3 Steering gearbox out of adjustment (Chapter 11).

63 Lack of power assistance

1 Steering pump drivebelt faulty or not adjusted properly (Chapter 1).
2 Fluid level low (Chapter 1).
3 Hoses or pipes restricting the flow. Inspect and replace parts as necessary.
4 Air in power steering system. Bleed system (Chapter 11).

64 Excessive tire wear (not specific to one area)

1 Incorrect tire pressures (Chapter 1).
2 Tires out of balance. Have professionally balanced.
3 Wheels damaged. Inspect and replace as necessary.
4 Suspension or steering components excessively worn (Chapter 11).

65 Excessive tire wear on outside edge

1 Inflation pressures not correct (Chapter 1).
2 Excessive speed on turns.
3 Front end alignment incorrect (excessive toe-in). Have professionally aligned.
4 Suspension arm bent or twisted.

66 Excessive tire wear on inside edge

1 Inflation pressures incorrect (Chapter 1).
2 Front end alignment incorrect (toe-out). Have professionally aligned.
3 Loose or damaged steering components (Chapter 11).

67 Tire tread worn in one place

1 Tires out of balance. Balance tires professionally.
2 Damaged or buckled wheel. Inspect and replace if necessary.
3 Defective tire.

Chapter 1 Tune-up and routine maintenance

Contents

Specifications

Note: *Additional specifications and torque figures can be found in each individual Chapter.*

Capacities

Engine oil capacity (with a new filter)	
1600 cc engine	4.2 US qt (4.0 liters)
2000 cc engine	4.5 US qt (4.3 liters)
2600 cc engine	5.2 US qt (5.0 liters)
Coolant system capacity (includes heater and reserve)	
1600 cc engine	7.7 US qt (7.3 liters)
2000 cc engine	9.5 US qt (9.0 liters)
2600 cc engine	9.7 US qt (9.2 liters)
Manual transmission	
1600 cc engine	2.1 US qt (2 liters)
2000 cc engine	2.4 US qt (2.3 liters)
2600 cc engine	2.4 US qt (2.3 liters)
Automatic transmission	6.8 US qt (6.4 liters)
Rear axle	2.7 US pt (1.3 liters)
Power steering	2.2 US pt (1.06 liters)
Brakes	1.5 US pt (0.8 liter)
Fuel tank	15.8 US gal (60 liters)

Lubricants

Engine oil	SAE 10W 30, 40 or 50; API classification, SE or SF
Cooling system	High-quality Ethylene Glycol
Manual transmission	SAE 80W; API classification, GL-4
Automatic transmission	Dexron II type
Rear axle	SAE 90W; API classification, GL-4, GL-5
Power steering	ATF Dexron II
Brake system	Conform to DOT 3
Front wheel bearings	MPG NLGI grade 2 EP

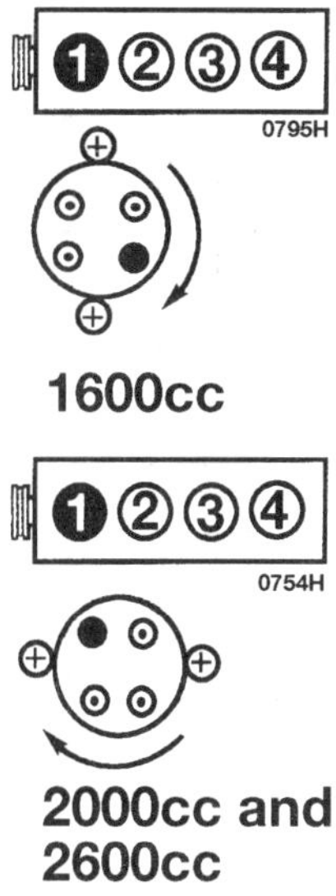

Cylinder location and distributor rotation

Tires

Tire inflation pressure	24 psi (165 kPa)
Tire size	70R14 (P195)

Front balljoint deflection

Front balljoint deflection	0.06 in (1.5 mm)

Braking system

Disc pad thickness limit	0.04 in (1.0 mm)
Drum lining thickness limit	0.04 in (1.0 mm)
Pedal height	7.1 in (180 mm)
Pedal free play	0.4 to 0.6 in (10 to 15 mm)
Parking brake stroke	4 to 6 notches
Pedal-to-wall clearance	1.6 in (40 mm)
Parking brake lever movement	0.24 in (6 mm)
Pedal movement	0.12 in (3 mm)
Disc thickness – front limit	0.43 in (11 mm)
Disc runout limit	0.006 in (0.15 mm)
Drum inside dia. limit	9.08 in (230.6 mm)
Disc thickness – rear limit	0.33 in (8.4 mm)

Cooling system

Thermostat	
Valve open temperature	190°F (88°C)
Full open temperature	212°F (100°C)
Radiator checking pressure	22.7 psi (157 kPa)
Radiator cap opening pressure	
High pressure side	10.7 to 14.9 psi (73.5 to 103.0 kPa)
Vacuum side	– 0.7 psi – 43.9 kPa)

Fuel cap relief valve opening pressure

Fuel cap relief valve opening pressure	– 0.46 to – 0.82 psi (–3.1 to –5.7 kPa)

Engine and ignition

Firing order	1 – 3 – 4 – 2
Spark plug gap	
USA	0.039 to 0.043 in (1.0 to 1.1 mm)
Canada	0.028 to 0.031 in (0.7 to 0.8 mm)
Spark plug type	See tune-up decal under the hood
Ignition timing	See tune-up decal under the hood
Valve clearance (engine hot)	
Intake and Jet valve	0.006 in (0.15 mm)
Exhaust valve	0.010 in (0.25 mm)
Contact breaker point gap	0.018 to 0.021 in (0.45 to 0.55 mm)
Distributor dwell angle	52° ± 3°
Engine compression pressure	149 psi (1.03 mPa) @ 250 rpm

Clutch

Pedal height	7.5 in (190 mm)
Pedal stroke	6 in (150 mm)
Pedal free play	0.6 to 0.8 in (15 to 20 mm)

Alternator

Alternator and power steering belt tension (deflection with 22 lbs pressure)	$\frac{1}{4}$ to $\frac{3}{8}$ in (7 to 10 mm)
Alternator brush length limit	0.315 in (8 mm)

Starter brush length limit

Starter brush length limit	0.453 in (11.5 mm)

Torque specifications

	ft-lb	Nm
Engine oil pan drain plug	44 to 57	59 to 78
Engine oil filter	Hand-tighten	
Oil pump brace bolt	20 to 30	26 to 40
Front axle hub	14.5 to 0 to 3.6	19.6 to 0 to 4.9
Rear axle drain plug	36 to 51	49 to 69
Rear axle filler plug	29 to 43	39 to 59
Brake tube flare nut	9 to 12	13 to 17
Lug nuts		
Steel wheel	51 to 58	69 to 78
Aluminum wheel	58 to 72	78 to 98
Starter mount bolt	16 to 23	22 to 31
Spark plug		
1978 U and F engines only	18 to 21.5	25 to 29
All others	15 to 21	20 to 29
Windshield wiper pivot shaft	7 to 12	10 to 16
Transmission drain plug	43	59
Transmission filler plug	22 to 25	29 to 34
Valve cover bolts	4 to 5	5 to 6
Alternator support bolt	14 to 18	20 to 25
Alternator brace bolt	8.5 to 11	12 to 15

1 Introduction

This Chapter was designed to help the home mechanic maintain his (or her) car for peak performance, economy, safety and long life.

On the following pages you will find a maintenance schedule along with Sections which deal specifically with each item on the schedule. Included are visual checks, adjustments and item replacements.

Servicing your car using the time/mileage maintenance schedule and the sequenced Sections will give you a planned program of maintenance. Keep in mind that it is a full plan, and maintaining only a few items at the specified intervals will not give you the same results.

You will find as you service your car that many of the procedures can, and should, be grouped together, due to the nature of the job at hand. Examples of this are as follows:

If the car is fully raised for a chassis inspection, this is the ideal time for the following checks: manual transaxle fluid, exhaust system, suspension, steering and the fuel system.

If the tires and wheels are removed, as during a routine tire rotation, go ahead and check the brakes and wheel bearings at the same time.

If you must borrow or rent a torque wrench, you will do best to service the spark plugs and/or repack (or replace) the wheel bearings all in the same day to save time and money.

The first step of this or any maintenance plan is to prepare yourself before the actual work begins. Read through the appropriate Sections for all work that is to be performed before you begin. Gather together all necessary parts and tools. If it appears you could have a problem during a particular job, don't hesitate to ask advice from your local parts man or dealer service department.

Fig. 1.1 Engine compartment components

1 *Fuel check valve*
2 *Purge control valve*
3 *Engine oil fill*
4 *Air cleaner filter*
5 *Windshield wiper motor*
6 *Brake fluid reservoir*
7 *Ignition coil*
8 *Battery*
9 *Distributor*
10 *Radiator*
11 *Radiator cap*
12 *Engine drivebelt*
13 *ECS canister*
14 *Windshield washer fluid*
15 *Radiator overfill reservoir*
16 *Air conditioner receiver/dryer*
17 *Engine oil check dipstick*
18 *Two-way valve*

Fig. 1.2 Engine underside components

1 *Engine oil filter*
2 *Radiator drain plug*
3 *Balljoint grease fittings*
4 *Transmission control*
5 *Transmission drain plug*
6 *Engine drain plug*

2 Tune-up sequence

The term 'tune-up' is loosely used for any general operation that puts the engine back in its proper running condition. A tune-up is not a specific operation, but rather a combination of individual operations, such as replacing the spark plugs, adjusting the idle speed, setting the ignition timing, etc.

If, from the time the car is new, the routine maintenance schedule (Section 3) is followed closely and frequent checks are made of fluid levels and high wear items, as suggested throughout this Manual, the engine will be kept in relatively good running condition and the need for additional tune-ups will be minimized.

More likely than not, however, there will be times when the engine is running poorly due to lack of regular maintenance. This is even more likely if a used car is bought which has not received regular and frequent maintenance checks. In such cases an engine tune-up will be needed outside of the regular routine maintenance intervals.

The following series of operations are those most often needed to bring a generally poor running engine back into a proper state of tune.

Minor tune-up

Clean, inspect and test battery (Sec 35)
Check all engine-related fluids (Sec 4)
Test engine compression (Sec 36)
Check and adjust drivebelts (Sec 21)
Replace spark plugs (Sec 31)
Inspect distributor cap and rotor (Sec 32)
Check breaker points and dwell angle (Sec 33)
Inspect spark plug and coil wires (Sec 32)
Replace oil filter (Sec 6)
Check and adjust idle speed (Sec 27)
Check and adjust timing (Sec 14)
Check and adjust fuel/air mixture (Sec 27)
Replace fuel filter (Sec 24)
Replace PCV valve (Sec 23)
Adjust valve clearances (Sec 28)
Check cooling system (Sec 10)

Major tune-up

(the above operations and those listed below)
Check vacuum advance system (Chapter 6)
Check EGR system (Chapter 6)
Test alternator and regulator (Chapter 5)
Test ignition system (Chapter 5)
Test charging system (Chapter 5)
Check fuel system (Chapter 4)

3 Routine maintenance intervals

Note: *The following maintenance intervals are recommended by the manufacturer. In the interest of vehicle longevity, we recommend shorter intervals on certain operations such as fluid and filter replacements.*

7500 miles (12 000 km)

Change engine oil (Sec 6)

15 000 miles (24 000 km)

Check and adjust valve clearances (Sec 28)
Change engine oil (Sec 6)
Replace engine oil filter (Sec 6)
Check and adjust drivebelts (Sec 21)
Check cooling system (Sec 10)
Inspect disc brake pads (Sec 8)
Check brake hoses (Sec 8)
Inspect tires (Sec 5)

22 500 miles (36 000 km)

Change engine oil (Sec 6)

30 000 miles (48 000 km)

Check and adjust valve clearances (Sec 28)
Clean carburetor choke and linkage (Sec 26)
Replace air cleaner filter (Sec 22)
Replace spark plugs (Sec 31)
Change engine oil (Sec 6)
Replace engine oil filter (Sec 6)
Replace drivebelts (Sec 21)
Drain, flush and refill cooling system (Sec 34)
Inspect brake lines and fluid level (Sec 8)
Inspect disc brake pads (Sec 8)
Inspect drum brake shoes and cylinders (Sec 8)
Check brake hoses (Sec 8)
Inspect balljoint and steering seals (Sec 12)
Inspect for leaks in front wheel bearings (Sec 12)
Check manual transmission fluid level (Sec 7)
Check rear axle fluid level (Sec 7)
Inspect tires for wear (Sec 5)

37 500 miles (60 000 km)

Change engine oil (Sec 6)

45 000 miles (72 000 km)

Check and adjust valve clearance (Sec 28)
Change engine oil (Sec 6)
Replace engine oil filter (Sec 6)
Check and adjust drivebelts (Sec 21)
Inspect disc brake pads (Sec 8)
Check brake hoses (Sec 8)
Inspect tires for wear (Sec 5)

50 000 miles (80 000 km)

Check and adjust ignition timing (Sec 14)
Replace fuel filter (Sec 24)
Check fuel system for leaks (Sec 9)
Check ignition cables (Sec 32)
Check all rubber hoses (Sec 38)
Check crankcase emission control system (Sec 23)
Check evaporative emission control system (Sec 25)
Replace ECS canister (Sec 25)
Replace brake fluid (Sec 39)

Severe operating conditions

Severe operating conditions are defined as:

Frequent short trips or long periods of idling
Driving at sustained high speeds during hot weather (over 90°F, +32°C)
Towing a trailer for long distances
Driving in temperatures below 10°F (-12°C) for 60 or more days
Driving 2000 miles (3200 km) or more per month

If the vehicle has been operated under severe conditions, follow these maintenance intervals:

Change engine oil and filter every 2000 miles (3200 km) or two months
Clean and regap the spark plugs every 6000 miles (9600 km)
Drain and refill the automatic transaxle every 22 500 miles (36 000 km) if the vehicle is driven 2000 or more miles per month
Change the air and fuel filters more frequently

4 Fluid levels check (weekly)

1 There are a number of components on a vehicle which rely on the use of fluids to perform their job. Through the normal operation of the vehicle, these fluids are used up and must be replenished before damage occurs. See the lubricant specification Section for the specific fluid to be used when adding is required. When checking fluid levels, it is important that the vehicle is on a level surface.

Engine oil

2 The engine oil level is checked with a dipstick, which is located at the side of the engine block. This dipstick travels through a tube and into the oil pan at the bottom of the engine.

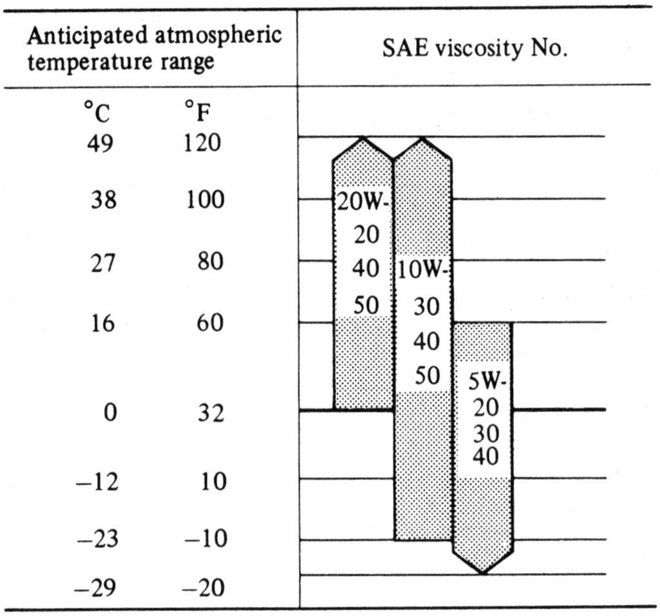

Fig. 1.3 Engine oil temperature/viscosity table (Sec 4)

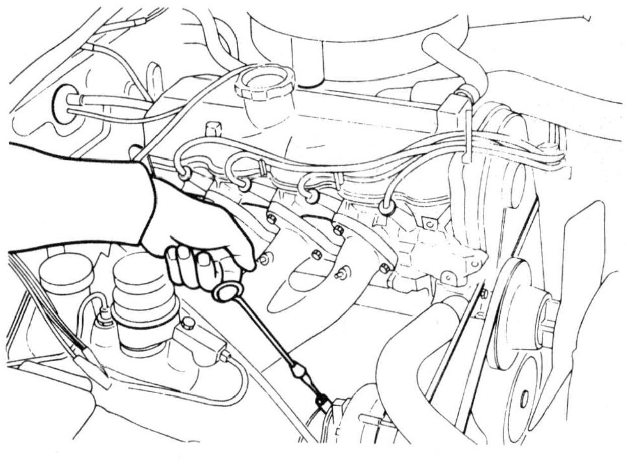

Fig. 1.4 Engine oil level check (Sec 4)

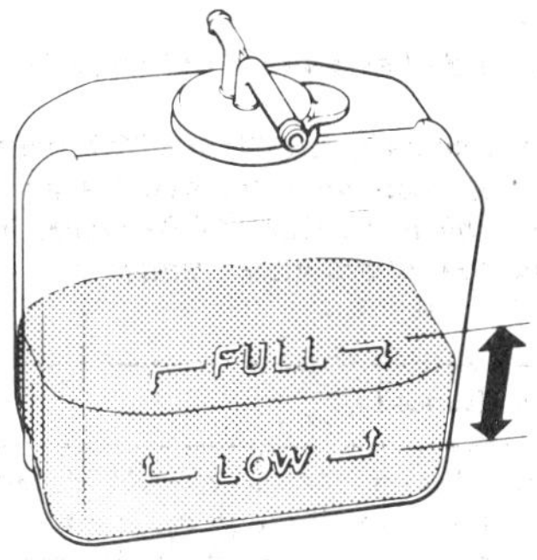

Fig. 1.5 Radiator reserve tank level check (Sec 4)

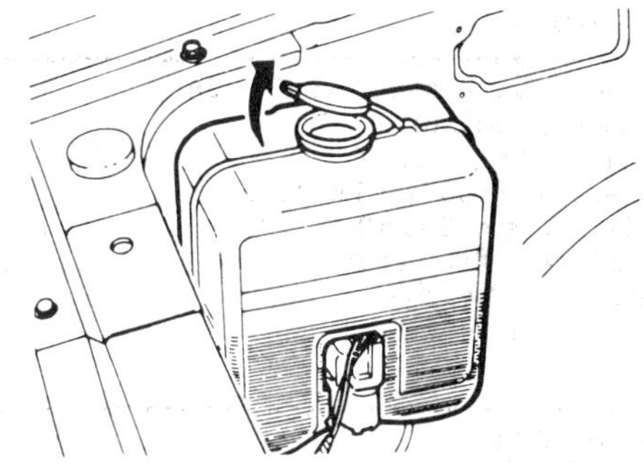

Fig. 1.6 Windshield washer fluid level check (Sec 4)

3 The oil level should be checked preferably before the vehicle has been driven, or about 15 minutes after the engine has been shut off. If the oil is checked immediately after driving the vehicle, some of the oil will remain in the upper engine components, thus giving an inaccurate reading on the dipstick.
4 Pull the dipstick from its tube and wipe all the oil from the end with a clean rag. Insert the clean dipstick all the way back into the oil pan and pull it out again. Observe the oil at the end of the dipstick. At its highest point, the level should be between the Add and Full marks.
5 It takes approximately 1 quart of oil to raise the level from the Add mark to the Full mark on the dipstick. Do not allow the level to drop below the Add mark, as this may cause engine damage due to oil starvation. On the other hand, do not overfill the engine by adding oil above the Full mark, as this may result in oil-fouled spark plugs, oil leaks or oil seal failures.
6 Oil is added to the engine after removing a twist-off cap located on the rocker arm cover. An oil can spout or funnel will reduce spills as the oil is poured in.
7 Checking the oil level can also be an important preventative maintenance step. If you find the oil level dropping abnormally, it is an indication of oil leakage or internal engine wear which should be corrected. If there are water droplets in the oil, or if it is milky looking, this also indicates component failure and the engine should be checked immediately. The condition of the oil can also be checked along with the level. With the dipstick removed from the engine, take your thumb and index finger and wipe the oil up the dipstick, looking for small dirt particles or engine filings which will cling to the dipstick. This is an indication that the oil should be drained and fresh oil added (Section 6).

Coolant

8 Most vehicles are equipped with a pressurized coolant recovery system which makes coolant level checks very easy. A clear or white coolant reservoir, attached to the inner fender panel, is connected by a hose to the radiator cap. As the engine heats up during operation, coolant is forced from the radiator, through the connecting tube and into the reservoir. As the engine cools, this coolant is automatically drawn back into the radiator to keep the level correct.
9 The coolant level should be checked when the engine is cold. Merely observe the level of fluid in the reservoir, which should be between the Low and the Full marks on the side of the reservoir. If the system is completely cooled, also check the level in the radiator by removing the cap.
10 If your particular vehicle is not equipped with a coolant recovery system, the level should be checked by removing the radiator cap. However, the cap should not under any circumstances be removed while the system is hot, as escaping steam could cause serious injury. Wait until the engine has completely cooled, then wrap a thick cloth around the cap and turn it to its first stop. If any steam escapes from the cap, allow the engine to cool further. Then remove the cap and check the level in the radiator. It should be about 1 in below the bottom of the filler neck.
11 If only a small amount of coolant is required to bring the system up to the proper level, regular water can be used. However, to maintain the proper antifreeze/water mixture in the system, both should be mixed together to replenish a low level. High-quality

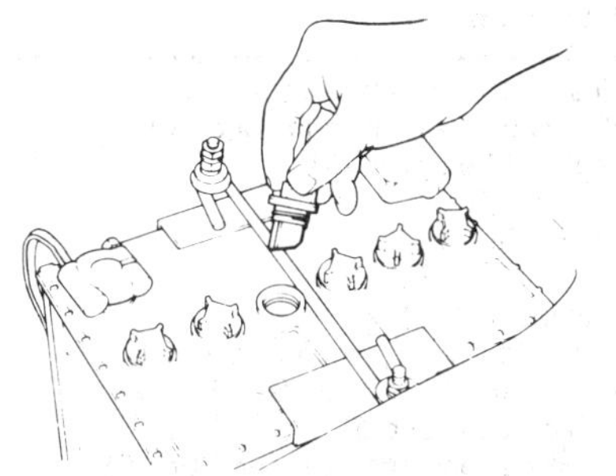

Fig. 1.7 Maintain battery electrolyte level (Sec 4)

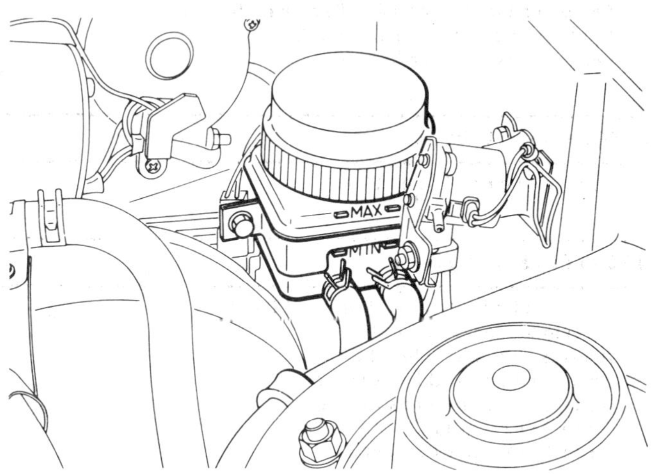

Fig. 1.8 Brake reservoir fluid level check (Sec 4)

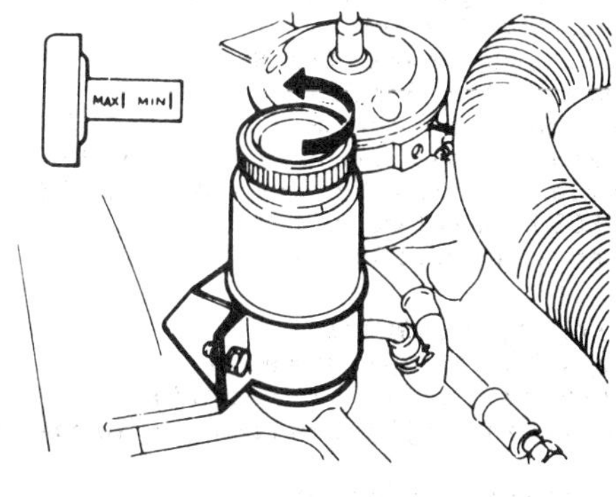

Fig. 1.9 Power steering fluid level check (Sec 4)

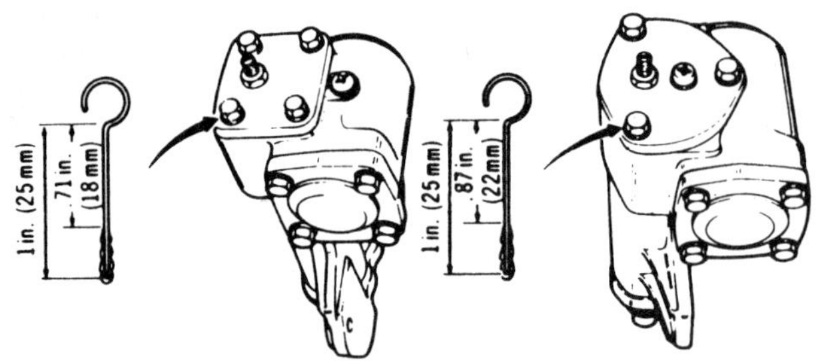

Small size gear box
97.5 CID (1600 c.c.) engine

Large size gear box
121.7 CID (2000 c.c.) engine

Fig. 1.10 Manual steering fluid level check (Sec 4)

antifreeze offering protection to -20°F should be mixed with water in the proportion specified on the container. Do not allow antifreeze to come in contact with your skin or painted surfaces of the car. Flush contacted areas immediately with plenty of water. **Caution:** *Antifreeze can be fatal to children and pets. They like it because it is sweet. Just a few licks can cause death. Wipe up garage floor and drip pan coolant drippings immediately. Keep antifreeze containers covered. Repair leaks in your cooling system immediately.*

12 On systems with a recovery tank, coolant should be added to the reservoir after removing the cap at the top of the reservoir. Coolant should be added directly into the radiator on systems without a coolant recovery tank.

13 As the coolant level is checked, observe the condition of the coolant. It should be relatively clear. If the fluid is brown or a rust color, this is an indication that the system should be drained, flushed and refilled (Sec 34).

14 If the cooling system requires repeated additions to keep the proper level, have the radiator pressure cap checked for proper sealing ability. Also check for leaks in the system (cracked hoses, loose hose connections, leaking gaskets, etc). (Section 10).

Windshield washer

15 The fluid for the windshield washer system is located in a plastic reservoir. The level inside the reservoir should be maintained at the Full mark.

16 A good quality washer solvent should be added through the plastic cap whenever replenishing is required. Do not use plain water alone in this system, especially in cold climates where the water could freeze.

Battery electrolyte

17 There are certain precautions to be taken when working on or near the battery: a) Never expose a battery to open flame or sparks which could ignite the hydrogen gas given off by the battery; b) Wear protective clothing and eye protection to reduce the possibility of the corrosive sulfuric acid solution inside the battery harming you; if the fluid is splashed or spilled, flush the contacted area immediately with plenty of water; c) Remove all metal jewelry which could contact the positive terminal and another grounded metal source, thus causing a short circuit; d) Always keep batteries and battery acid out of the reach of children.

18 The caps on the top of the battery should be removed periodically to check for a low water level. This check will be more critical during the warm summer months.

19 Remove each of the caps and add distilled water to bring the level of each cell to the split ring in the filler opening.

20 At the same time the battery water level is checked, the overall condition of the battery and its related components should be inspected. If corrosion is found on the cable ends or battery terminals, remove the cables and clean away all corrosion using a baking soda/water solution or a wire brush cleaning tool designed for this purpose. See Section 35 for complete battery care and servicing.

Brake fluid reservoir

21 The brake fluid reservoir is located on the left side of the engine compartment, just above the fender well.

22 Check that the brake fluid level is between the upper and lower level markings on the reservoir. If it is low, you will have to add brake fluid to bring it up to the proper level.

23 Before removing the cap on the reservoir, use a rag to clean all dirt and grease from around the cap area. If any foreign matter enters the reservoir with the cap removed, blockage in the brake system lines can occur. Also, make sure all painted surfaces around the reservoir are covered, as brake fluid will ruin paint.

24 Carefully lift the cap off the cylinder and set it aside, taking care not to set it on a painted surface.

25 Carefully pour the specified brake fluid into the reservoir to bring it up to the proper level. Be careful not to spill the fluid on painted surfaces. Be sure the specified fluid is used, as mixing different types of brake fluid can cause damage to the system (see lubricant specification or your owner's manual). **Note:** *Change the brake fluid every 4 years (50 000 miles) as described in Section 39.*

26 At this time, the fluid and reservoir can be inspected for contamination. Normally, the braking system will not need periodic draining and refilling, but if rust deposits, dirt particles or water droplets are seen in the fluid, the system should be dismantled, drained and refilled with fresh fluid.

27 Reinstall the reservoir cap. Make sure the lid is properly seated to prevent fluid leakage and/or system pressure loss.

28 The brake fluid in the reservoir will drop slightly as the brake shoes or pads at each wheel wear down during normal operation. If it requires repeated replenishing to keep it at the proper level, this is an indication of leakage in the brake system which should be corrected immediately (Section 8).

29 If upon checking the reservoir fluid level you discover that one or both reservoirs is empty or nearly empty, the braking system should be bled (Chapter 9). When the fluid level gets low, air can enter the system and should be removed by bleeding the brakes.

Power steering

30 Unlike manual steering, the power steering system relies on fluid which may, over a period of time, require replenishing.

31 The reservoir for the power steering pump is located near the front of the engine, on the right side.

32 The power steering fluid level should be checked only after the vehicle has been driven, with the fluid at operating temperature. The front wheels should be pointed straight ahead.

33 With the engine shut off, use a rag to clean the reservoir cap and the areas around the cap. This will help to prevent foreign material from falling into the reservoir when the cap is removed.

34 Twist off the reservoir cap which has a built-in dipstick attached to it. Pull off the cap and clean off the fluid at the bottom of the dipstick with a clean rag. Now reinstall the dipstick/cap assembly to get a fluid level reading. Remove the dipstick/cap and observe the fluid level. It should be at the Full hot mark on the dipstick.

35 If additional fluid is required, pour the specified lubricant directly into the reservoir using a funnel to prevent spills.

36 If the reservoir requires frequent fluid additions, all power steering hoses, hose connections, the power steering pump and the steering box should be carefully checked for leaks.

Manual steering

37 It is unlikely that the manual steering gearbox oil would ever need replenishing, but it should be checked occasionally.

38 With the vehicle on a level surface, remove the bolt from the lower right corner of the gearbox upper cover.

39 Insert a thin screwdriver into the hole. The oil level should be 0.8 in (20 mm) below the hole.

40 Add oil of the recommended type and grade if necessary, but do not overfill. Replace the bolt and tighten it securely.

41 If the gearbox requires oil, check for leaks and have them repaired if any are found.

5 Tire wear and tire pressure check

1 Periodically inspecting the tires can not only prevent you from being stranded with a flat tire, but can also give you clues as to possible problems with the steering and suspension systems before major damage occurs.

2 Proper tire inflation adds miles to the life of the tires, allows the

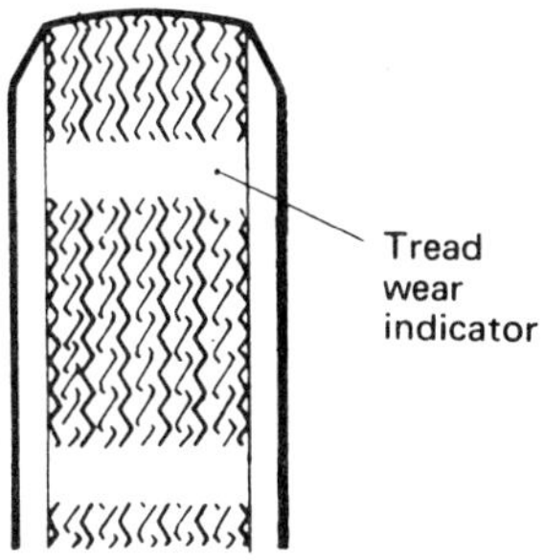

Fig. 1.11 Tire wear visual check (Sec 5)

vehicle to achieve maximum gas mileage and contributes to overall riding comfort.

3 When inspecting the tire, first check the wear on the tread. Irregularities in the tread pattern (cupping, flat spots, more wear on one side than the other) are indications of front end alignment and/or balance problems (see chart in Chapter 11). If any of these conditions are found you should take the vehicle to a wheel alignment shop to correct the problem.

4 Also check the tread area for cuts or punctures. Many times a nail or tack will imbed itself into the tire tread and yet the tire will holds its air pressure for a short time. In most cases, a repair shop or gas station can repair the punctured tire.

5 It is also important to check the sidewalls of the tire, both inside and outside. Check for the rubber being deteriorated, cut or punctured. Also inspect the inboard side of the tire for signs of brake fluid leakage, indicating a thorough brake inspection is needed immediately (Section 8).

6 Incorrect tire pressure cannot be determined merely by looking at the tire. This is especially true for radial tires. A tire pressure gauge must be used. If you do not already have a reliable gauge, it is a good idea to purchase one and keep it in the glove box. Built-in pressure gauges at gas stations are often unreliable. If you are in doubt as to the accuracy of your gauge, many repair shops have master pressure gauges which you can use for comparison purposes.

7 Always check tire inflation when the tires are cold. Cold, in this case, means that the vehicle has not been driven more than one mile after sitting for three hours or more. It is normal for the pressure to increase 4 to 8 pounds or more when the tires are hot.

8 Unscrew the valve cap protruding from the wheel and firmly press the gauge onto the valve stem. Observe the reading on the gauge and check this figure against the recommended tire pressure for your vehicle.

9 Check all tires and add air as necessary to bring all tires up to the recommended pressure levels. Do not forget the spare tire. Be sure to reinstall the valve caps, which will keep dirt and moisture out of the valve stem mechanism.

6 Engine oil and oil filter change

1 Frequent oil changes may be the best form of preventative maintenance available for the home mechanic. When engine oil is old, it gets diluted and contaminated, which ultimately leads to premature engine wear.

2 Although some sources recommend oil filter changes every other oil change, we feel that the minimal cost of an oil filter and the relative ease with which it is installed dictate that a new filter be used whenever the oil is changed.

3 The tools necessary for a normal oil and filter change are: a wrench to fit the drain plug at the bottom of the oil pan; an oil filter wrench to remove the old filter; a container with at least six-quart capacity to drain the old oil into; and a funnel or oil can spout to help pour fresh oil into the engine.

4 In addition, you should have plenty of clean rags and newspaper handy to mop up any spills. Access to the underside of the car is greatly improved if it can be lifted on a hoist, driven onto ramps or supported by jackstands. Do not work under a vehicle which is supported only by a bumper, hydraulic or scissors-type jack.

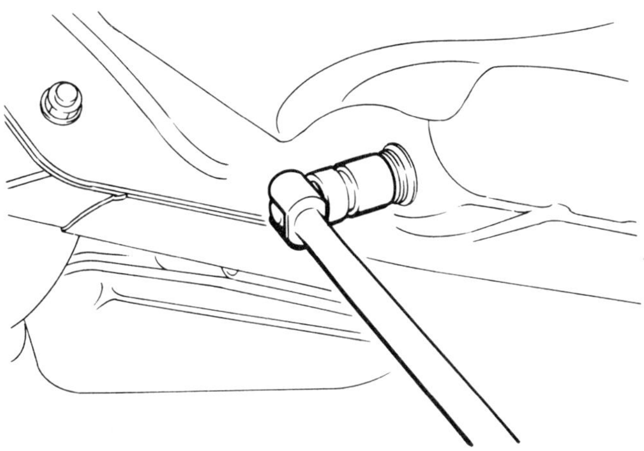

Fig. 1.12 Engine oil drain plug (Sec 6)

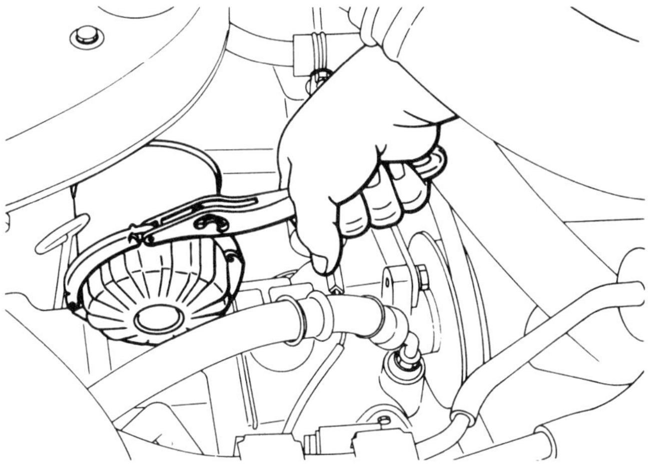

Fig. 1.13 Engine oil filter replacement (Sec 6)

5 If this is your first change on the vehicle, it is a good idea to crawl underneath and familiarize yourself with the locations of the oil drain plug and the oil filter. Since the engine and exhaust components will be warm during the actual work, it is best to figure out any potential problems before the vehicle and its accessories are hot.

6 Allow the engine to warm up to normal operating temperature. If the new oil or any tools are needed, use this warm-up time to gather everything necessary for the job. The correct type of oil to buy for your application can be found in *Lubricant Specifications* in the front of this Chapter.

7 With the engine oil warm (warm engine oil will drain better and more built-up sludge will be removed with the oil), raise the vehicle for access beneath. Make sure it is firmly supported. If jackstands are used, they should be placed towards the front of the frame rails which run the length of the vehicle.

8 Move all necessary tools, rags and newspapers under the vehicle. Position the drain pan under the drain plug. Keep in mind that the oil will initially flow from the pan with some force, so place the pan accordingly.

9 Being careful not to touch any of the hot exhaust pipe components, use the wrench to remove the drain plug near the bottom of the oil pan. Depending on how hot the oil has become, you may want to wear gloves while unscrewing the plug the final few turns.

10 Allow the old oil to drain into the pan. It may be necessary to move the pan farther under the engine as the oil flow reduces to a trickle.

11 After all the oil has drained, clean the drain plug thoroughly with a clean rag. Small metal filings may cling to this plug, which would immediately contaminate your new oil.
12 Clean the area around the drain plug opening and reinstall the drain plug. Tighten the plug securely with your wrench according to the specified torque.
13 Move the drain pan into position under the oil filter.
14 Now use the filter wrench to loosen the oil filter. Chain or metal band-type filter wrenches may distort the filter canister, but don't worry too much about this as the filter will be discarded anyway.
15 Sometimes the oil filter is on so tight it cannot be loosened, or is inaccessible with a filter wrench. As a last resort, you can punch a metal bar or long screwdriver directly through the bottom of the canister and use this as a T-bar to turn the filter. If this must be done, be prepared for oil to spurt out of the canister as it is punctured.
16 Completely unscrew the old filter. Be careful, it is full of oil. Empty the old oil inside the filter into the drain pan.
17 Compare the old filter with the new one to make sure they are of the same type.
18 Use a clean rag to remove all oil, dirt and sludge from the area where the oil filter mounts to the engine. Check the old filter to make sure the rubber gasket is not stuck to the engine mounting surface. If this gasket is stuck to the engine (use a flashlight if necessary) remove it.
19 Smear a light coat of fresh oil onto the rubber seal of the new oil filter.
20 Screw the new filter to the engine following the tightening directions printed on the filter canister or packing box. Most filter manufacturers recommend against using a filter wrench due to possible overtightening and damage to the canister or the rubber seal.
21 Remove all tools, rags, etc., from under the vehicle, being careful not to spill the oil in the drain pan. Lower the vehicle off its support stands.
22 Move to the engine compartment and locate the oil filler cap on the valve cover, near the front of the engine.
23 If an oil can spout is used, push the spout into the top of the oil can and pour the fresh oil through the filler opening. A funnel placed into the opening may also be used.
24 Pour about three qts. of fresh oil into the engine. Wait a few minutes to allow the oil to drain to the pan, then check the level on the oil dipstick (see Section 4 if necessary). If the oil level is at or near the lower Add mark, start the engine and allow the new oil to circulate.
25 Run the engine for only about a minute and then shut it off. Immediately look under the vehicle and check for leaks at the oil pan drain plug and around the oil filter. If either is leaking, retighten and recheck them.
26 With the new oil circulated and the filter now completely full, recheck the level on the dipstick and add enough oil to bring the level to the Full mark on the dipstick.
27 During the first few trips after an oil change, make it a point to check for leaks and proper oil level.
28 The old oil drained from the engine cannot be reused in its present state and should be disposed of. Oil reclamation centers, auto repair shops and gas stations will normally accept the oil which can be refined and used again. After the oil has cooled, it can be drained into a suitable container (capped plastic jugs, topped bottles, milk cartons, etc.) for transport to one of these disposal sites.

7 Fluid levels check – 6 month

Automatic transmission

1 The fluid inside the transmission must be at normal operating temperature to get an accurate reading on the dipstick. This is done by driving the vehicle for several miles, making frequent starts and stops to allow the transmission to shift through all gears.
2 Park the vehicle on a level surface. With the parking brake engaged and the engine idling, select each gear momentarily, ending with the selector lever in the N (Neutral) position.
3 Remove the transmission dipstick (located on the right side, near the rear of the engine) and wipe all the fluid from the end of the dipstick with a clean rag.
4 Push the dipstick back into the transmission until the cap seats firmly on the dipstick tube. Now remove the dipstick again and observe the fluid on the end. The highest point of fluid should be between the Full mark and $\frac{1}{4}$ inch below the Full mark.
5 If the fluid is at or below the Add mark, add sufficient fluid to raise the level to the Full mark. One pint of fluid will raise the level from Add to Full. Fluid should be added directly into the dipstick guide tube, using a funnel to prevent spills.
6 It is important that the transmission must not be overfilled. Under no circumstances should the fluid level be above the Full mark on the dipstick, as this could cause internal damage to the transmission. The

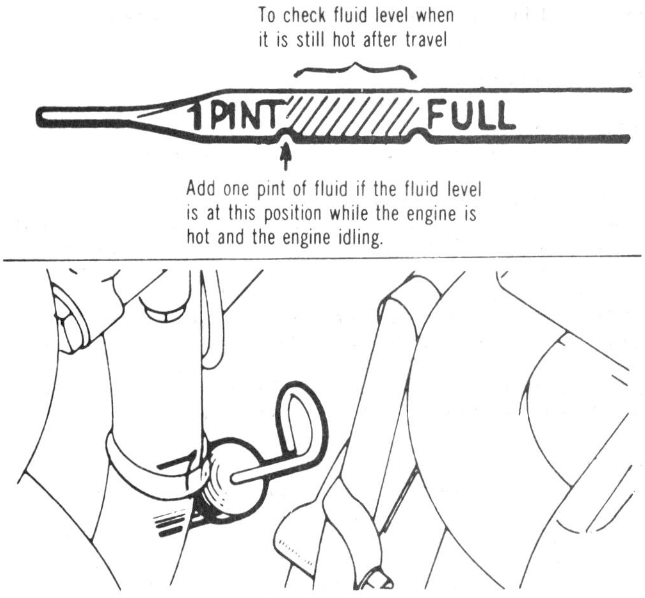

Fig. 1.14 Automatic transmission check (Sec 7)

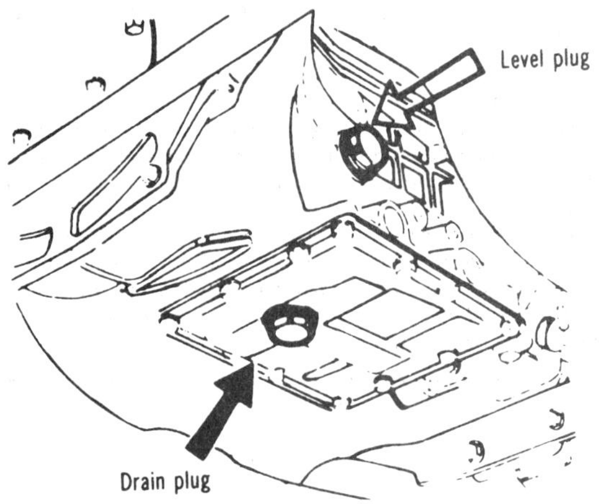

Fig. 1.15 Manual transmission check (Sec 7)

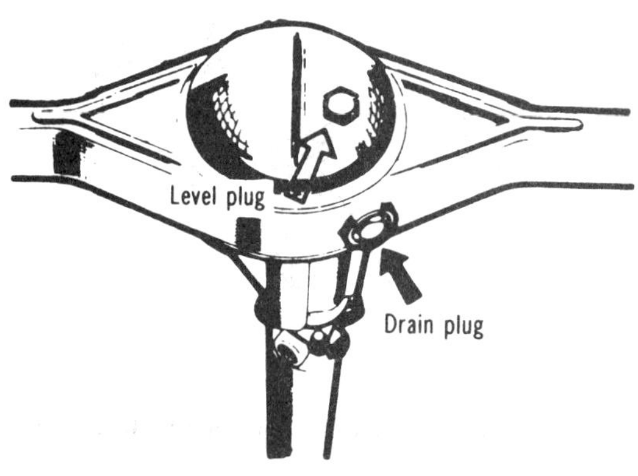

Fig. 1.16 Rear axle level check (Sec 7)

best way to prevent overfilling is to add fluid a little at a time, driving the vehicle and checking the level between additions.
7 Use only transmission fluid specified by the manufacturer. This information can be found in the *Lubricant Specification* Section.
8 The condition of the fluid should also be checked along with the level. If the fluid at the end of the dipstick is a dark reddish-brown color, or if the fluid has a 'burnt' smell, the transmission fluid should be replaced. If you are in doubt about the condition of the fluid, purchase some new fluid and compare the two for color and smell.

Manual transmission

9 Manual transmissions do not have a dipstick. The fluid level is checked by removing a plug in the left side of the transmission case. Locate this plug and use a rag to clean the plug and the area around it.
10 With the vehicle components cold, remove the plug. If fluid immediately starts leaking out, thread the plug back into the transmission because the fluid level is all right. If there is no fluid leakage, completely remove the plug and place your little finger inside the hole. The fluid level should be just at the bottom of the plug hole.
11 If the transmission needs more fluid, use a syringe to squeeze the appropriate lubricant into the plug hole to bring the fluid up to the proper level.
12 Thread the plug back into the transmission and tighten it securely. Drive the vehicle and check for leaks around the plug.

Rear axle

13 Like the manual transmission, the rear axle has an inspection and fill plug which must be removed to check the fluid level.
14 Remove the plug which is located at the rear of the differential. Use your little finger to reach inside the differential housing to feel the level of the fluid. It should be at the bottom of the plug hole.
15 If this is not the case, add the proper lubricant through the plug hole. A syringe or a small funnel can be used for this.
16 Make certain the correct lubricant is used.
17 Tighten the plug securely and check for leaks after the first few miles of driving.

Air conditioning

18 It is important to have the correct amount of oil in the refrigerant system. Too little oil gives inadequate lubrication and can cause the compressor to fail. Too much oil will increase the discharge air temperature.
19 Before the compressor oil level can be checked, the system must be discharged. **Caution**: *Do not attempt to do this yourself; the refrigerant can cause serious injuries and respiratory irritation. Take your vehicle to a qualified service center or dealer service department to have the oil level checked.*

8 Brake system check

1 The brakes should be inspected every time the wheels are removed or a whenever fault is suspected. Indications of a potential braking system fault are: the car pulls to one side when the brake pedal is depressed; noises coming from the brakes when they are applied; excessive brake pedal travel; pulsating pedal; and leakage of fluid, usually seen on the inside of the tire or wheel.

Hoses and brake lines

2 Visually check all flexible hoses and rigid tubing in the brake system.
3 In doing this, look for cracked rubber, bent or pinched tubes and leaks from the brake system onto components near brake connections.
4 If any item needs to be replaced, refer to Chapter 9 for removal and installation.

Brake pedal

5 Physically check for smooth pedal movement and a firm feel.
6 Apply normal pressure to the brake pedal and if it feels spongy or gradually moves closer to the floorboard, refer to the bleeding procedure or the height and freeplay adjustments in Chapter 9.

Disc brakes (front or rear)

7 Disc brakes can be visually checked without the need to remove any parts except the wheels.
8 Raise the vehicle and place it securely on jackstands. Remove the front wheels *(see Jacking and towing* at the front of this Manual if necessary).
9 Now visible is the disc brake caliper which contains the pads. There is an outer brake pad and an inner pad. Both should be inspected.
10 Most later model vehicles come equipped with a 'wear sensor' attached to the inner pad. This is a small, bent piece of metal which is visible from the inboard side of the brake caliper. When the pads wear to a danger limit, the metal sensor rubs against the disc and makes a screeching sound.
11 Inspect the pad thickness by looking through the cut-out inspection hole in the caliper body. If the pad lining material is below specifications, the pads should be replaced. Keep in mind that the lining material is riveted or bonded to a metal backing shoe and the metal portion is not included in this measurement.
12 Since it will be difficult to measure the exact thickness of the remaining lining material, if you are in doubt as to the pad quality, remove the pads for further inspection or replacement. See Chapter 9 for disc brake pad replacement.
13 Before installing the wheels, check for any leakage around the brake hose connections.

1

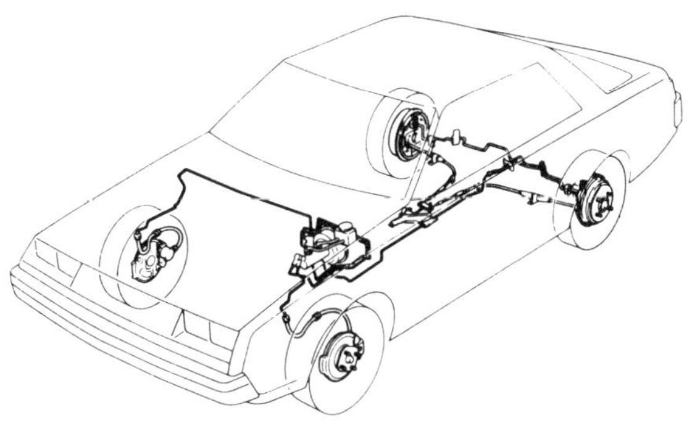

Fig. 1.17 Brake lines with rear drum brakes (Sec 8)

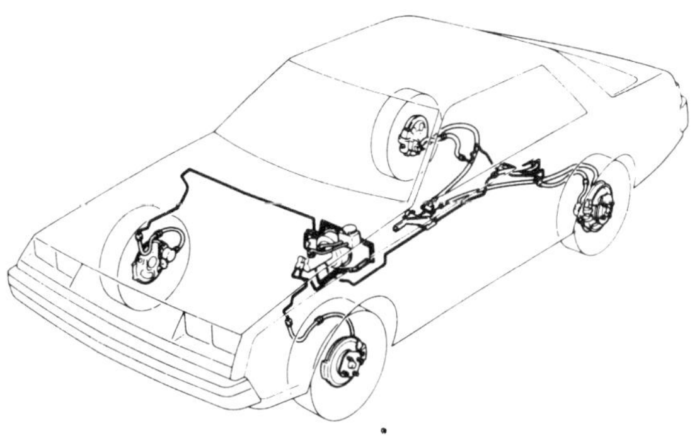

Fig. 1.18 Brake lines with rear disc brakes (Sec 8)

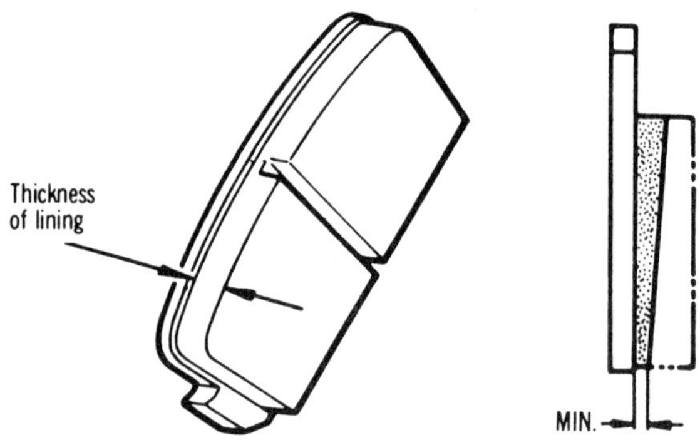

Fig. 1.19 Disc brake pad check (Sec 8)

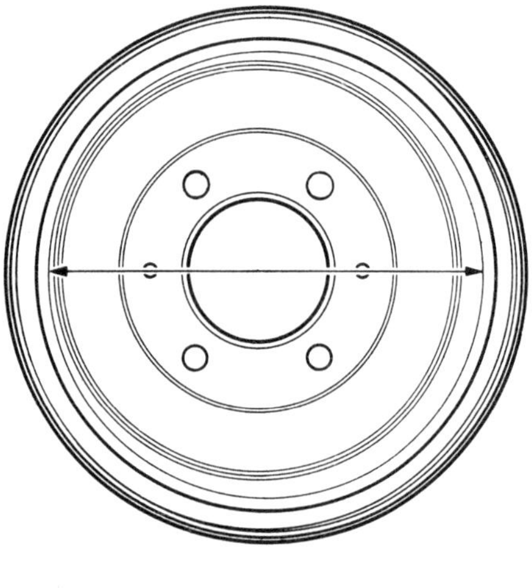

Fig. 1.20 Rear brake check (Sec 8)

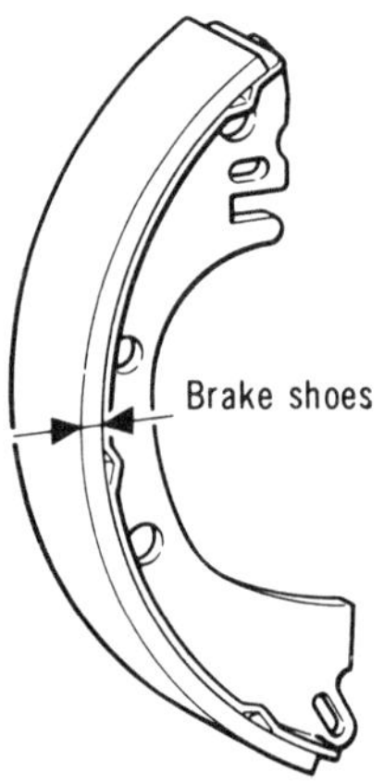

Fig. 1.21 Rear brake shoe pad check (Sec 8)

14 Also check the condition of the disc for scoring, gouging or burnt spots. If these conditions exist, the hub/rotor assembly should be removed for servicing (see Section 38). If the disc is worn or damaged, it can be resurfaced by an automotive machine shop.

Drum brakes (rear)

15 Raise the vehicle and support it firmly on jackstands. Block the front tires to prevent the car from rolling, however, do not apply the parking brake as this will lock the drums into place.
16 Remove the wheels, referring to *Jacking and towing* at the front of this Manual if necessary.
17 Mark the hub so it can be reinstalled in the same place. Use a scribe, chalk, etc., on the drum and center hub and backing plate.
18 Pull the brake drum off the axle and brake assembly. If this proves difficult, make sure the parking brake is released, then squirt some penetrating oil around the center hub area. Allow the oil to soak in and try again to pull the drum off. Then, if the drum cannot be pulled off, the brake shoes will have to be adjusted inward. This is done by first removing the lanced cutout in the drum or backing plate with a hammer and chisel. With this lanced area punched in, rotate the drum until the opening lines up with the adjuster wheel. Pull the lever off the sprocket and then use a small screwdriver to turn the sprocket wheel which will move the linings away from the drums.
19 With the drum removed, carefully brush away any accumulations of dirt and dust. Do not blow this out with compressed air or in any similar fashion. Make an effort not to inhale this dust as it contains asbestos and is harmful to your health.
20 Observe the thickness of the lining material on both the front and rear brake shoes. If the material has worn away to within the specified limits of the recessed rivets or metal backing, the shoes should be replaced. If the linings look worn, but you are unable to determine their exact thickness, compare them with a new set at the auto parts store. The shoes should also be replaced if they are cracked, glazed (shiny surface), or wet with brake fluid.
21 Check that all the brake assembly springs are connected and in good condition.
22 Check the brake components for any signs of fluid leakage. With your finger, carefully pry back the rubber cups on the wheel cylinder located at the top of the brake shoes. Any leakage is an indication that the wheel cylinders should be overhauled immediately (Chapter 9). Also check the hoses and connections for signs of leakage.
23 Wipe the inside of the drum with a clean rag and denatured alcohol. Again, be careful not to breathe the dangerous asbestos dust.
24 Check the inside of the drum for cracks, scores, deep scratches or hard spots which will appear as small discolorations. If these imperfections cannot be removed with fine emery cloth, the drum must be taken to a machine shop equipped to turn the drums. Refer to Chapter 9 for a more detailed brake drum inspection procedure.
25 If after the inspection process all parts are in good working condition, reinstall the brake drum. Install the wheel and lower the car to the ground.

Parking brake

26 The easiest way to check the operation of the parking brake is to park the car on a steep hill, with the parking brake set and the transmission in Neutral. If the parking brake cannot prevent the car from rolling, it is in need of adjustment (see Chapter 9).
27 Visually check the cable for any crimped areas or bends along its length and frayed edges. If these conditions exist, see Chapter 9 for replacement.

9 Fuel system check

1 There are certain precautions to be taken when inspecting or servicing the fuel system components. Work in a well ventilated area and do not allow open flames (cigarettes, appliance pilot lights, etc.) to get near the work area. Mop up spills immediately and do not store fuel-soaked rags where they could ignite.
2 The fuel system is under some amount of pressure, so if any fuel lines are disconnected for servicing, be prepared to catch the fuel as it spurts out. Plug all disconnected fuel lines immediately after disconnection to prevent the tank from emptying itself.
3 The fuel system is most easily checked with the vehicle raised on a hoist where the components under the vehicle are readily visible and accessible.
4 If the smell of gasoline is noted while driving, or after the vehicle has sat in the sun, the system should be thoroughly inspected immediately.
5 Remove the gas filler cap and check for damage, corrosion and a proper sealing imprint on the gasket. The filler cap is also equipped with a vacuum-type relief valve. Check the relief valve opening pressure and compare with the specifications. Relief valve failure may be caused by deteriorated packing or it could be clogged or damaged. Replace the cap with a new one if necessary.
6 With the vehicle raised, inspect the gas tank and filler neck for

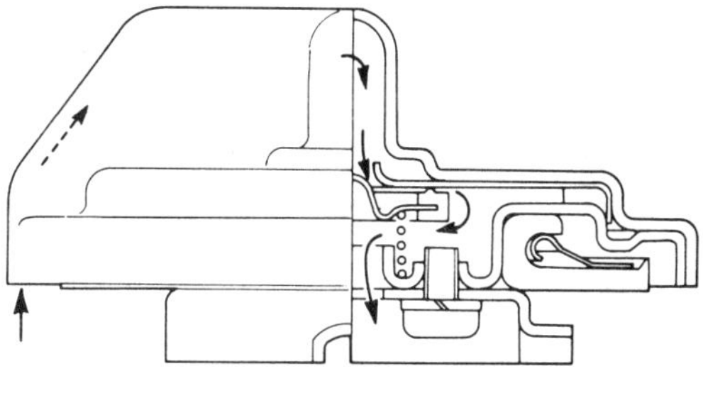

Fig. 1.22 Check fuel filler cap relief valve (Sec 9)

punctures, cracks or any damage. The connection between the filler neck and the tank is especially critical. Sometimes a rubber filler neck will leak due to loose clamps or deteriorated rubber; problems a home mechanic can usually rectify.

7 Do not under any circumstances try to repair a fuel tank yourself (except rubber components) unless you have considerable experience. A welding torch or any open flames can easily cause the fuel vapors to explode if the proper precautions are not taken.

8 Carefully check all rubber hoses and metal lines leading away from the fuel tank. Check for loose connections, deteriorated hose, crimped lines or damage of any kind. Follow these lines up to the front of the vehicle, carefully inspecting them all the way. Repair or replace damaged sections as necessary.

9 The fuel filter is the cartridge type, which can be replaced easily and normally requires no cleaning. If the amount of water inside is slight and no clogging is noticed, you can clean it. Remove the filter from the left side of the engine compartment (refer to Section 24) and, with the outlet pointing downward, spray compressed air into the inlet.

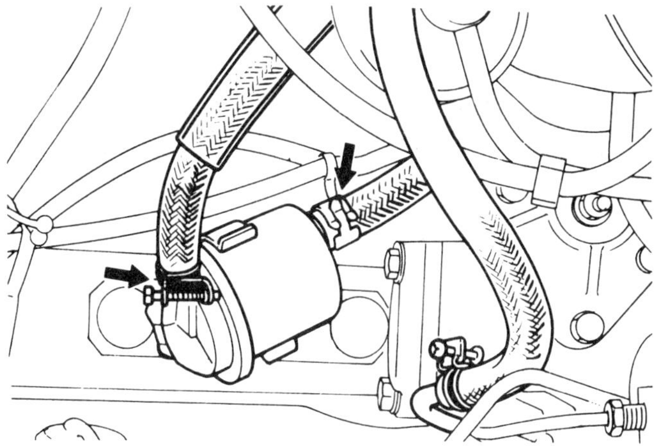

Fig. 1.23 Remove fuel filter to check (Sec 9)

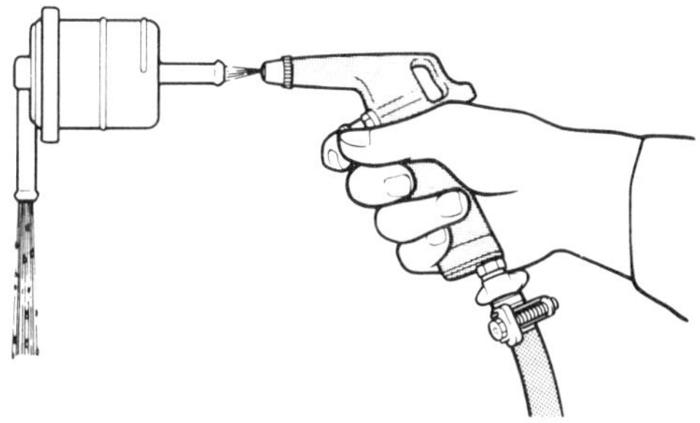

Fig. 1.24 Cleaning fuel filter with compressed air (Sec 9)

10 Cooling system check

1 Many major failures can be attributed to a faulty cooling system. If equipped with an automatic transmission, the cooling system also plays an important role in transmission life.

2 The cooling system should be checked with the engine cold. Do this before the vehicle is driven for the day or after it has been shut off for one or two hours.

3 Remove the radiator cap and thoroughly clean the cap (inside and out) with clean water. Also clean the filler neck on the radiator. All traces of corrosion should be removed.

4 Carefully check the upper and lower radiator hoses along with the smaller diameter heater hoses. Inspect their entire length, replacing any hose which is cracked, swollen or shows signs of deterioration. Cracks may become more apparent if the hose is squeezed.

5 Also check that all hose connections are tight. A leak in the cooling system will usually show up as white or rust colored deposits on the areas adjoining the leak.

6 Use compressed air or a soft brush to remove bugs, leaves, etc., from the front of the radiator or air conditioning condenser. Be careful not to damage the delicate cooling fins, or cut yourself on the sharp fins.

7 Inspect the cap valve and spring for deterioration or broken packing. Also check the valve opening pressure and compare with Specifications. If necessary, replace the cap with a new one.

8 Have the cooling system pressure checked and compare with the Specifications at the front of this Chapter.

9 To remove and check the thermostat, see Chapter 3.

10 Check the specific gravity (cooling capabilities) of the cooling system.

11 The cooling system reserve tank level should be kept between the Full and Low marks on the tank.

12 To check the reserve system, make sure all coolant levels are full. Open the radiator drain plug and see if coolant is drawn from the reserve tank to the radiator. If not, check for leaks at the filler neck, cap or reserve tank tube. It may be necessary to test the cap or pressure test the cooling system to locate a leak.

13 To replace any hoses, refer to Chapter 3.

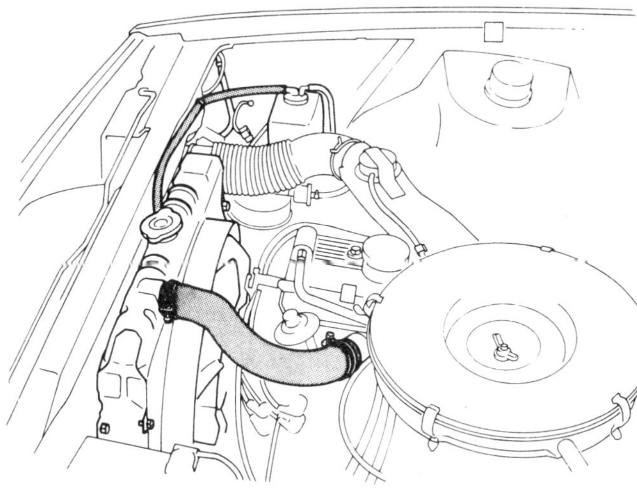

Fig. 1.25 Upper radiator hose check (Sec 10)

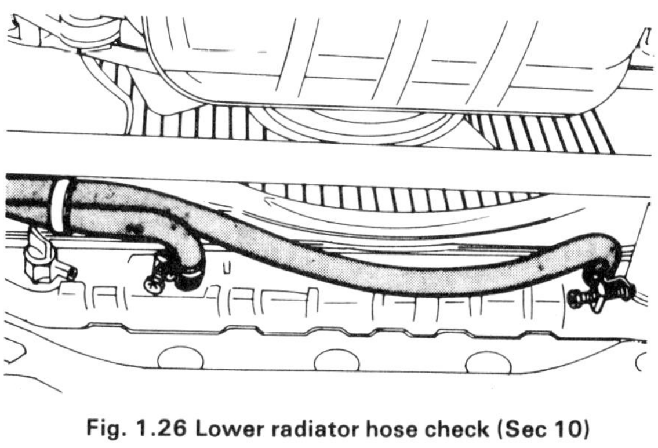

Fig. 1.26 Lower radiator hose check (Sec 10)

1

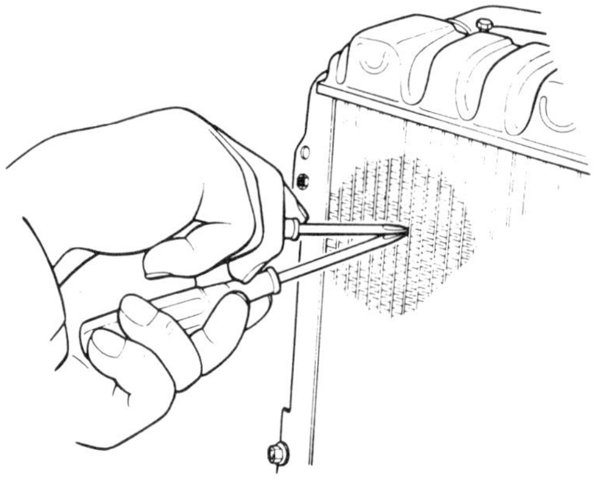

Fig. 1.27 Straightening radiator cooling fins (Sec 10)

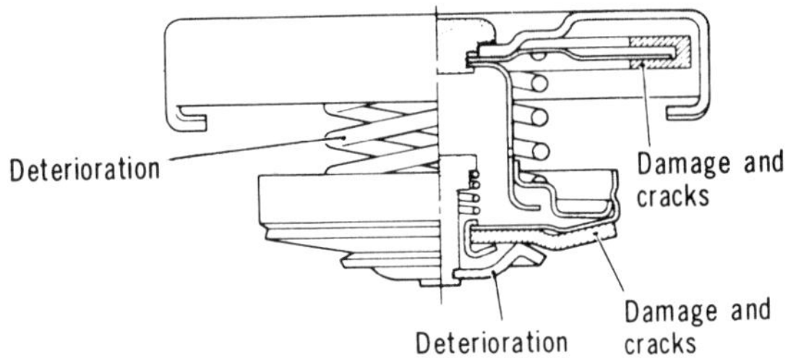

Fig. 1.28 Radiator cap inspection (Sec 10)

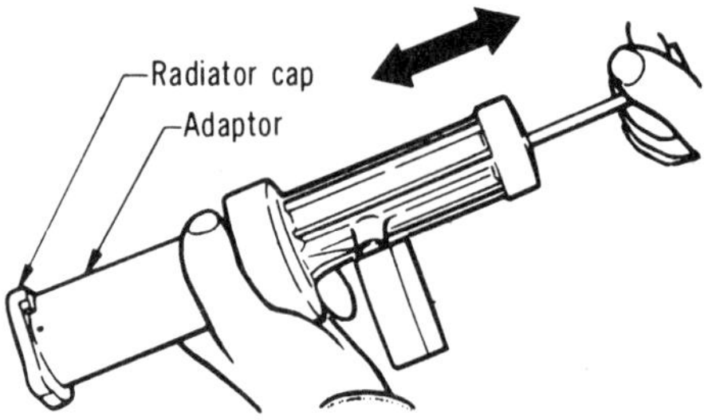

Fig. 1.29 Pressure test radiator cap (Sec 10)

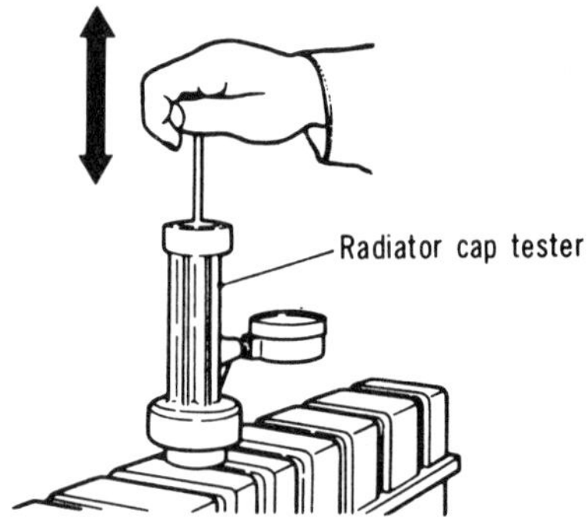

Fig. 1.30 Pressure test the cooling system (Sec 10)

11 Air conditioning system check

1 The following maintenance steps should be performed on a regular basis to ensure that the air conditioner continues to operate at peak efficiency.

a) Check the tension of the a/c compressor drivebelt and adjust if necessary. Refer to Chapter 1, Section 19.
b) Visually inspect the condition of the hoses, checking for any cracking, hardening or other deterioration. **Note:** *Do not replace without first having the system discharged.*
c) Check that the fins of the condenser are not covered with foreign material, such as leaves or bugs. A soft brush and compressed air can be used to remove them.

2 The a/c compressor should be run for about 10 minutes at least once every month. This is especially important to remember during the winter months because long-term non-use can cause hardening of the internal seals.
3 Due to the complexity of the air conditioning system and the special equipment required to effectively work on it, accurate trouble-shooting and repair of the system cannot be expected of the home mechanic and should be left to a professional. In any case, due to the toxic nature of the refrigerant, prior to disconnecting any part of the system, the car should be taken to a dealer or other qualified shop to have the system discharged. If the system should lose its cooling action, some causes can be diagnosed by the home mechanic. Look for other symptoms of trouble such as those in the following list. In all cases, it 's a good idea to have the system serviced by a professional.

a) If bubbles appear in the sight glass (located at the top of the receiver drier), this is an indication of either a small refrigerant leak or air in the refrigerant. If air is in the refrigerant, the receiver drier is suspect and should be replaced.
b) If the view glass takes on a mist-like appearance or shows many bubbles, this indicates a large refrigerant leak. In such a case, do not operate the compressor at all until the fault has been corrected.
c) Sweating or frosting of the expansion valve inlet indicates that the expansion valve is clogged or defective. It should be cleaned or replaced as necessary.
d) Sweating or frosting of the suction line (which runs between the suction throttle valve and the compressor) indicates that the expansion valve is stuck open or defective. It should be corrected or replaced as necessary.
e) Frosting on the evaporator indicates a defective suction throttle valve, requiring replacement of the valve.
f) Frosting of the high pressure liquid line (which runs between the condenser, receiver drier and expansion valve) indicates that either the drier or the high pressure line is restricted. The line will have to be cleared or the receiver drier replaced.
g) The combination of bubbles in the sight glass, a very hot suction line and, possibly, overheating of the engine is an indication that either the condenser is not operating properly or the refrigerant is overcharged. Check the tensions of the fan belt and adjust if necessary (Chapter 1). Check for foreign matter covering the fins of the condenser and clean if necessary. Also check for proper operation of the cooling system. If no fault can be found in these checks, the condenser may need to be replaced.

4 To replace the drivebelt or any hoses, refer to Chapter 3.

12 Suspension and steering check

1 Whenever the front of the vehicle is raised for service, it is a good idea to visually check the suspension and steering components for wear.
2 Indications of a fault in these systems are: excessive play in the steering wheel before the front wheels react; excessive sway around corners or body movement over rough roads; binding at some point as the steering wheel is turned.
3 Before the vehicle is raised for inspection, test the shock absorbers by pushing downward to rock the vehicle at each corner. If you push the vehicle down and it does not come back to a level position without

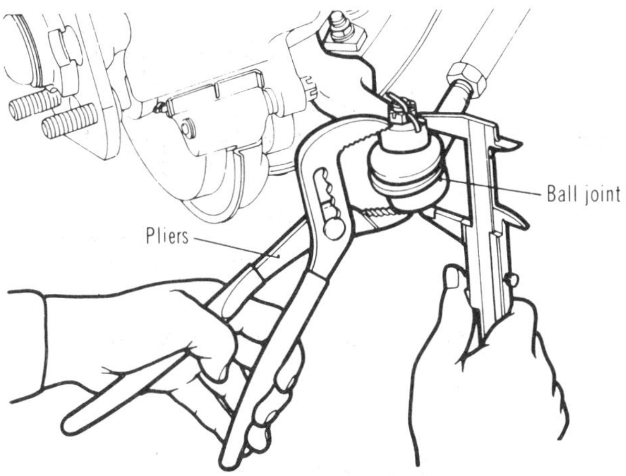

Fig. 1.31 Front balljoint deflection check (Sec 12)

one or two bounces, the shocks are worn and need to be replaced. As this is done, check for squeaks and strange noises from the suspension components. Information on shock absorber and suspension components can be found in Chapter 11.

4 Now, raise the front end of the vehicle and support it firmly on jack stands placed under the frame rails. Because of the work to be done, make sure the vehicle cannot fall from the stands.

5 Grab the top and bottom of the front tire with your hands and rock the tire/wheel on its spindle. If there is movement of more than .059 in, the wheel bearings should be serviced (see Section 38).

6 Crawl under the vehicle and check for loose bolts, broken or disconnected parts and deteriorated rubber bushings on all suspension and steering components. Look for grease or fluid leaking from around the steering box. Check the power steering hoses and their connections for leaks. Check the balljoints for wear.

7 Have an assistant turn the steering wheel from side-to-side and check the steering components for free movement, chafing or binding. If the steering does not react with the movement of the steering wheel, try to determine where the slack is located.

8 Check for balljoint deflection by squeezing the balljoint with channel-lock pliers and a suitable caliper measuring instrument.

13 Exhaust system check

1 With the exhaust system cold (at least three hours after being driven), check the complete exhaust system from its starting point at the engine to the end of the tailpipe. This is best done on a hoist where full access is available.

2 Check the pipes and their connections for signs of leakage and/or corrosion indicating a potential failure. Check that all brackets and hangers are in good condition and are tight.

3 At the same time, inspect the underside of the body for holes, corrosion, open seams, etc., which may allow exhaust gases to enter the passenger compartment. Seal all body openings with silicone or body putty.

4 Rattles and other driving noises can often be traced to the exhaust system, especially the mounts and hangers. Try to move the pipes and muffler. If the components can come into contact with the body or driveline parts, secure the exhaust system with new mountings.

5 This is also an ideal time to check the running condition of the engine by inspecting the very end of the tailpipe. The exhaust deposits here are an indication of engine tune. If the pipe is black and sooty, or bright white deposits are found here, the engine is in need of a tune-up including a thorough carburetor inspection and adjustment.

14 Ignition timing check and adjustment

1 All vehicles are equipped with a tune-up decal on the underside of the hood. This decal lists important ignition timing settings and procedures to be followed which are specific to that vehicle. Information on the tune-up decal supersedes the information given in this Section. The decal should be followed if information on it is different from that given here.

2 At the specified intervals, when the distributor has been removed or a change made in the fuel type, the ignition timing must be checked and adjusted if necessary.

3 Before attempting to check the timing, make sure that the transmission is in Neutral (or Park) with the parking brake set. Turn off the air conditioner and lights. Make sure the idle speed is as specified.

4 Connect a timing light in accordance with the manufacturer's instructions. Generally, the light will be connected to power and ground terminals and to the number one spark plug in some fashion. The number one spark plug is the one closest to the front of the engine.

5 Locate the numbered timing tag on the front of the engine. It is

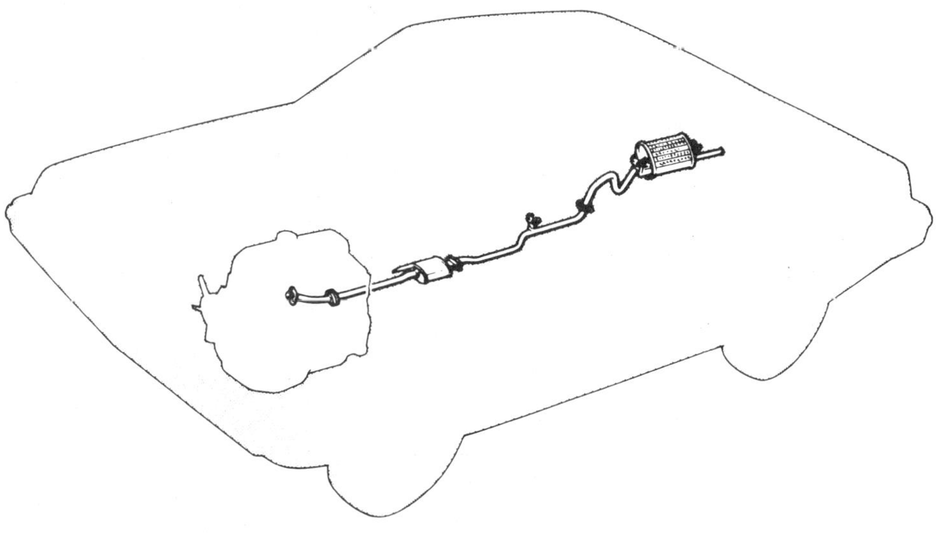

Fig. 1.32 Exhaust system checks (Sec 13)

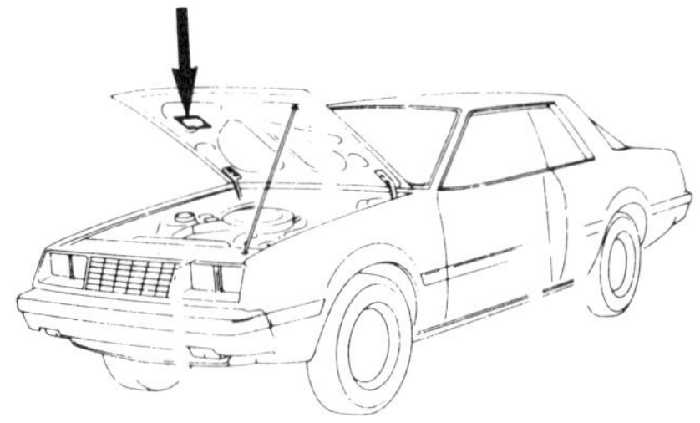

Fig. 1.33 Under-hood tune-up decal (arrow) (Sec 14)

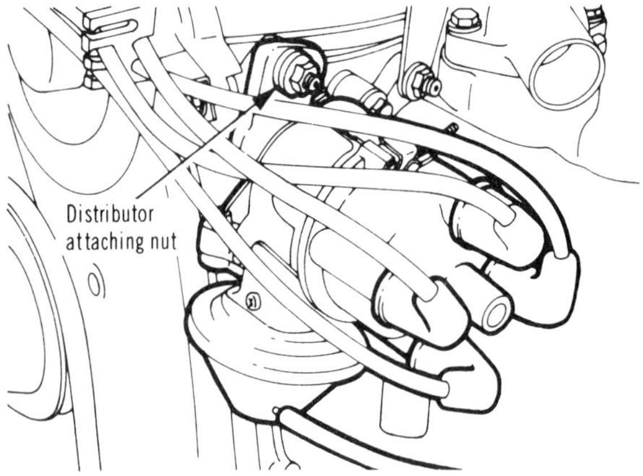

Fig. 1.34 Point-type distributor (Sec 14)

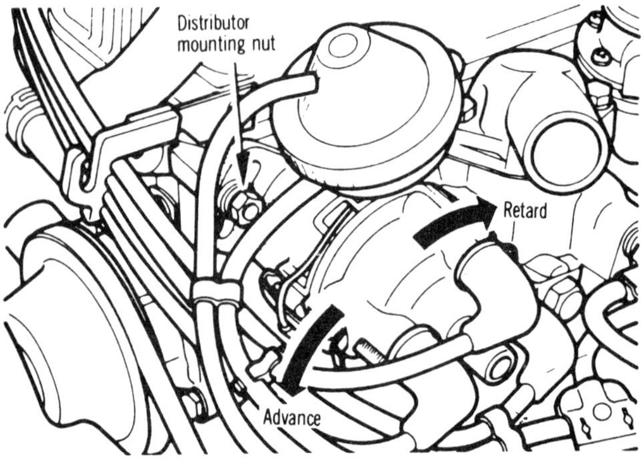

Fig. 1.35 Pointless-type distributor (electronic) (Sec 14)

just behind and above the pulley on the crankshaft. If necessary, clean it off with solvent so that the printing and small raised lines are clearly visible.

6 Locate the notch on the rear flange of the crankshaft pulley. It may be necessary to have an assistant turn the starter on and off (in short bursts), without starting the engine, to bring this notch into a position where it can be easily cleaned and marked. Stay clear of all moving engine parts if the engine is turned over in this manner.

7 Use white soapstone, chalk or paint to mark the notch in the crankshaft pulley. Also, mark the timing tab line which represents the number of degrees of ignition advance required in the Specifications (Chapter 5) or the tune-up decal on the underside of the hood. Each line on the timing tab represents 5°. The letters BTDC stand for Before Top Dead Center (advance) and the letter T indicates Top Dead Center (TDC). Thus if your vehicle specifications call for 5° BTDC, you will mark the timing tab line just before the T.

8 Check that the wiring for the timing light is clear of all moving engine parts, then start the engine.

9 Point the flashing timing light at the timing marks. Again, be careful not to come in contact with moving parts of the engine. The marks you made should appear stationary and be lined up opposite each other. If the marks are in alignment, the timing is correct. If the marks are not aligned, turn off the engine.

10 Loosen the locknut at the base of the distributor just enough to enable you to turn the distributor (see Chapter 5 for further details if necessary).

11 Restart the engine and slowly turn the distributor until the timing marks are aligned.

12 Shut off the engine and tighten the locknut. Be careful not to disturb the distributor.

13 Start the engine and recheck the timing to make sure the marks did not shift when you tightened the distributor locknut.

14 Disconnect the timing light and remove any tools from under the hood. Drive the vehicle and listen for pinging noises. These will be most noticeable when the engine is hot and under load (climbing a hill, accelerating from stop). If the engine is pinging, the ignition timing is too far advanced (before top dead center). Reconnect the timing light and turn the distributor to move the mark on the pulley one or two degrees closer to the T on the timing tab. Road test the vehicle again.

15 To keep pinging at a minimum and allow vehicle operation at the specified timing setting, it is a good idea to use gasoline of the same octane rating at all times. Switching fuel brands and octane levels can decrease performance and economy and possibly damage the engine.

15 Fastener check

1 Since nuts, bolts, screws, etc., may eventually work loose as a result of vibration and shock, it is a good idea to periodically check and tighten them to avoid damage to and possible loss of components.

2 Chassis parts that should be carefully checked include front and rear suspension components and steering and brake system parts.

3 Body parts that may loosen in time include seats and seat belt systems, doors and hood components.

4 As a final precaution, check the operation of all hinges and locks.

16 Chassis lubrication

1 A grease gun and a cartridge filled with grease are usually the only equipment necessary to lubricate the chassis components. Occasionally on later model vehicles, plugs will be installed rather than grease fittings, in which case grease fittings will have to be purchased and installed.

2 Look under the vehicle to see if grease fittings or solid plugs are installed. If there are plugs, remove them with the correct wrench and buy grease fittings which will thread into the component. A dealer or auto parts store will be able to find replacement fittings. Straight, as well as angled, fittings are available for easy greasing.

3 For easier access under the vehicle, raise the vehicle with a jack and place jackstands under the frame. Make sure it is firmly supported by the stands.

4 Before you do any greasing, force a little of the grease out the nozzle to remove any dirt from the end of the gun. Wipe the nozzle clean with a rag.

5 With the grease gun, plenty of clean rags and the location diagram, go under the vehicle to begin lubricating the components.

6 Wipe the grease fitting nipple clean and push the nozzle firmly over the fitting nipples. Squeeze the trigger on the grease gun to force grease into the component. The balljoints (one upper and one lower for each wheel) should be lubricated until the rubber reservoir is firm to the touch. Do not pump too much grease into these fittings as this could rupture the reservoir. For all other suspension and steering fittings, continue pumping grease into the nipple until grease seeps out of the joint between the two components. If the grease seeps out around the grease gun nozzle, the nipple is clogged or the nozzle is not fully seated around the fitting nipple. Re-secure the gun nozzle to the fitting and try again. If necessary, replace the fitting.

7 Wipe the excess grease from the components and the grease fitting. Follow these procedures for the remaining fittings.

8 Check the universal joints on the driveshaft; some have fittings, some are factory sealed. About two pumps is all that is required for grease type universal joints. While you are under the vehicle, clean and lubricate the parking brake cable along with its cable guides and levers. This can be done by smearing some of the chassis grease onto the cable and its related parts with your fingers.
9 Lower the vehicle to the ground for the remaining body lubrication process.
10 Open the hood and smear a little chassis grease on the hood latch mechanism. If the hood has an inside release, have an assistant pull the release knob from inside the car as you lubricate the cable at the latch.
11 Lubricate all the hinges (door, hood, etc.) with a few drops of light engine oil to keep them in proper working order.
12 Finally, the key lock cylinders can be lubricated with spray-on graphite which is available at auto parts stores.

17 Universal joints check

1 Wear in the needle roller bearings is characterized by vibration in the transmission, 'clunks' on taking up the drive, and in extreme cases of lack of lubrication, metallic squeaking and ultimately grating and shrieking sounds as the bearings break up.
2 It is easy to check if the needle roller bearings are worn with the shaft in position, by trying to turn it with one hand, the other hand holding the rear axle flange when the rear universal joint is being checked, and the front half coupling when the front universal joint is being checked. Any movement between the shaft and the couplings is indicative of considerable wear.
3 A further test for wear is to attempt to lift the shaft and note any movement between the yokes of the joints.
4 If wear is evident, either fit a new driveshaft assembly complete or replace the universal joints, as described later in Chapter 8.

18 Clutch pedal check and adjustment

1 If equipped with a manual transmission, it is important to have the clutch pedal height and free play correctly adjusted.
2 The height of the pedal is the distance it sits away from the floor. Measure this distance and if it is not within the range specified, make adjustments by referring to Chapter 8.
3 Clutch pedal free play is the distance the clutch pedal moves before the mechanical linkage actually begins to disengage the clutch disc from the flywheel and pressure plate.
4 To check the free play, slowly depress the clutch pedal until the resistance offered by the clutch release mechanism is felt. The pedal will suddenly become much more difficult to move.
5 Measure the distance the clutch pedal has travelled and compare it to the Specifications. If adjustment is required, refer to Chapter 8 for the step-by-step procedure to follow.

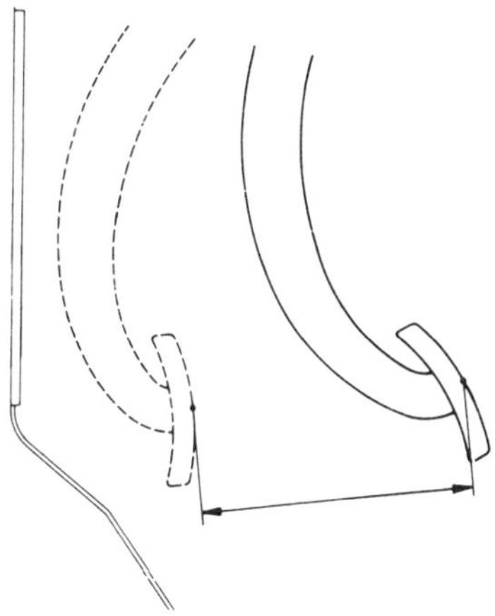

Fig. 1.36 Measure of clutch pedal height/travel (Sec 18)

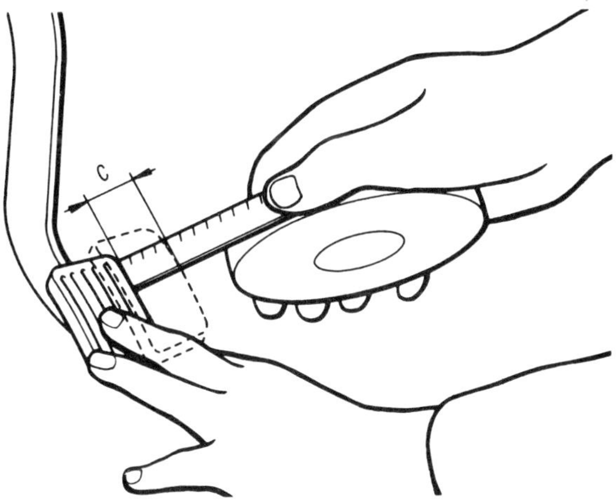

Fig. 1.37 Clutch pedal freeplay check (Sec 18)

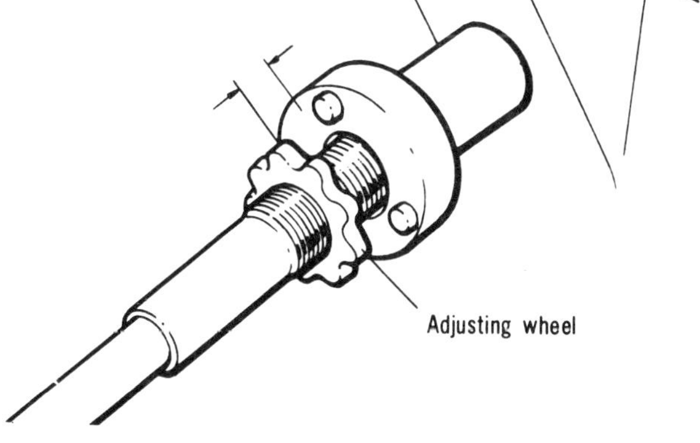

Fig. 1.38 Clutch cable adjustment wheel (Sec 18)

19 Clutch cable check and replacement

1 On vehicles with manual transmissions, clutch cables take a lot of abuse and need to be periodically inspected.
2 Check the cable for ease of movement, frayed edges along its length and any crimped or bent sections.
3 Replace the cable, if necessary, by referring to Chapter 8. If the cable does not need to be replaced, wipe some grease on the exposed metal to keep it from deteriorating.

20 Tire rotation

1 The tires should be rotated at the specified intervals and whenever uneven wear is noticed. Since the vehicle will be raised and the tires removed anyway, this is a good time to check the brakes (Section 8) and/or repack the wheel bearings (Section 37). Read over these sections if this is to be done at the same time.
2 The location for each tire in the rotation sequence depends on the type of tire used on your vehicle. Tire type can be determined by reading the raised printing on the sidewall of the tire.
3 See the information in *Jacking and Towing* at the front of this manual for the proper procedures to follow in raising the vehicle and changing a tire; however, if the brakes are to be checked do not apply the parking brake as stated. Make sure the tires are blocked to prevent the vehicle from rolling.

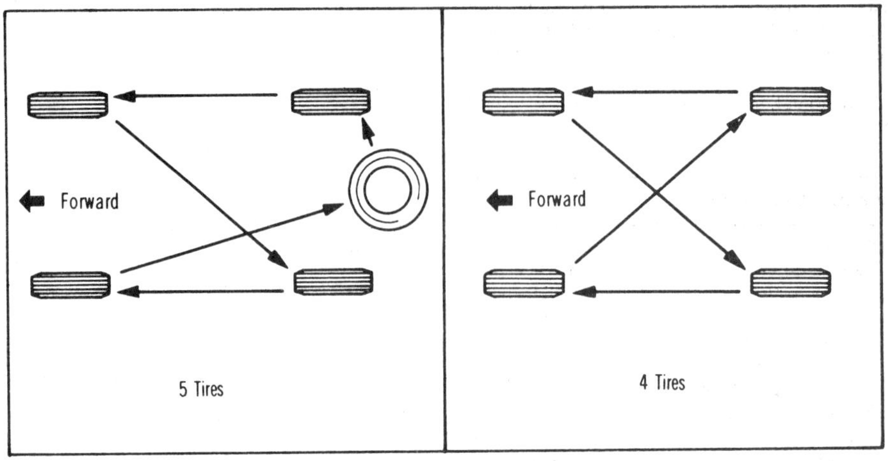

Fig. 1.39 Bias tire rotation sequence (Sec 20)

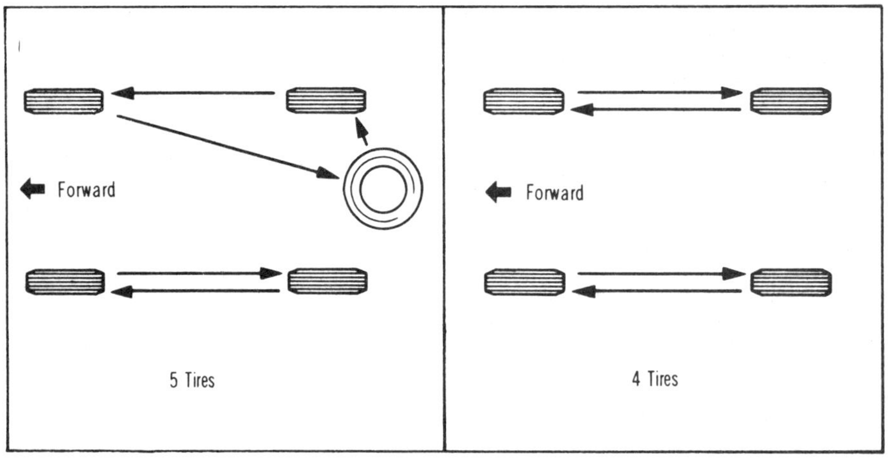

Fig. 1.40 Radial tire rotation sequence (Sec 20)

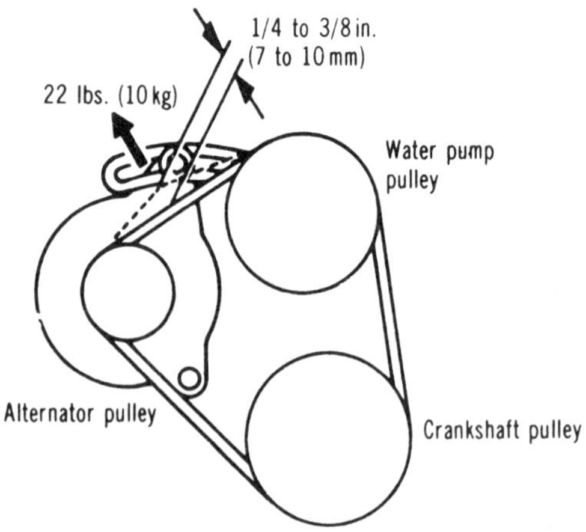

Fig. 1.41 1600 cc engine belt adjustment (Sec 21)

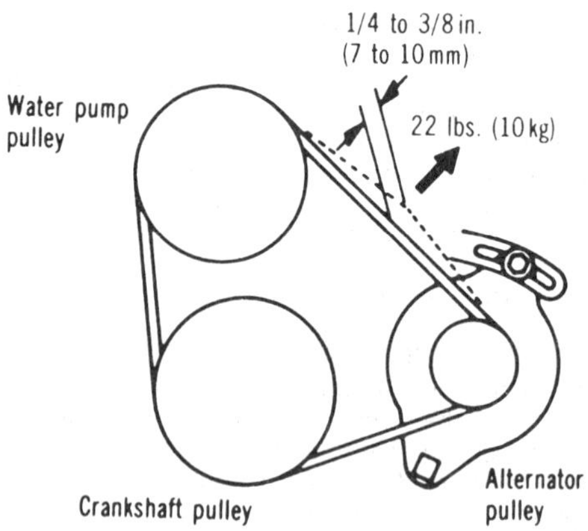

Fig. 1.42 2000 cc and 2600 cc engine belt adjustment (Sec 21)

4 Preferably, the entire vehicle should be raised at the same time. This can be done on a hoist or by jacking up each corner of the vehicle and then lowering it onto jackstands placed under the frame rails. Always use four jackstands and make sure the vehicle is firmly supported all around.
5 After rotation, check and adjust the tire pressures as necessary and be sure to check wheel nut tightness.

21 Drivebelt check, adjustment and replacement

1 The drivebelts, or V-belts as they are sometime called at the front of the engine play an important role in the overall operation of the vehicle and its components. Due to their function and material make-up, the belts are prone to failure after a period of time and should be inspected and adjusted periodically to prevent major engine or component damage.
2 The number of belts used on a particular vehicle depends on the accessories installed. Drivebelts are used to turn: the alternator; power steering pump; water pump; fan; and air conditioning compressor. Depending on the pulley arrangement, a single belt may be used for more than one of these components.
3 With the engine off, open the hood and locate the various belts at the front of the engine. Using your fingers (and a flashlight if necessary). move along the belts checking for cracks or separation. Also check for fraying and glazing which gives the belt a shiny appearance. Both sides of the belts should be inspected, which means you will have to twist the belt to check the underside.
4 The tension of each belt is checked by pushing on the belt at a distance halfway between the pulleys. Push firmly with your thumb and see how much the belt moves downward (deflects). Compare your measurements to the ones specified.
5 If it is found necessary to adjust the belt tension, either to make the belt tighter or looser, this is done by moving the belt-driven accessory on its bracket.
6 For each component there will be an adjustment or strap bolt and a pivot bolt. Both bolts must be loosened slightly to enable you to move the component.
7 After the bolts have been loosened, move the component away from the engine (to tighten the belt) or toward the engine (to loosen) the belt). Hold the accessory in this position and check the belt tension. If it is correct, tighten the bolts until snug, then recheck the tension. If it is all right, fully tighten the bolts.
8 It will often be necessary to use some sort of pry bar to move the accessory while the belt is adjusted. If this must be done to gain the proper leverage, be very careful not to damage the component being moved, or the part being pried against.
9 For drivebelt replacement refer to Chapter 3.

22 Air cleaner filter check and replacement

1 At the specified intervals, the air filter should be replaced with a new one. A thorough program of preventative maintenance would call for the filter to be inspected periodically between changes.
2 The air filter is located inside the air cleaner housing on the top of the engine. To remove the filter, unscrew the wing nut at the top of the air cleaner, unsnap the four spring-type clamps, and lift off the top plate.
3 While the top plate is off, be careful not to drop anything down into the carburetor.
4 Lift the air filter out of the housing.
5 To check the filter, hold it up to strong sunlight, or place a flashlight or droplight on the inside of the ring-shaped filter. If you can see light coming through the paper element, the filter is all right. Check all the way around the filter. A filter not completely clogged with dirt and dust can also be cleaned with compressed air. Before doing this, gently tap the filter against the palm of your hand to remove the bulk of the larger particles.
6 Wipe the inside of the air cleaner clean with a rag.
7 Place the old filter (if in good condition) or the new filter (if specified interval has elapsed) back into the air cleaner housing. Make sure it seats properly in the bottom of the housing.
8 Reinstall the top plate with the four clamps and wing nut. Be sure to align the arrow stamped on the plate with the arrow stamped on the snorkel tube.

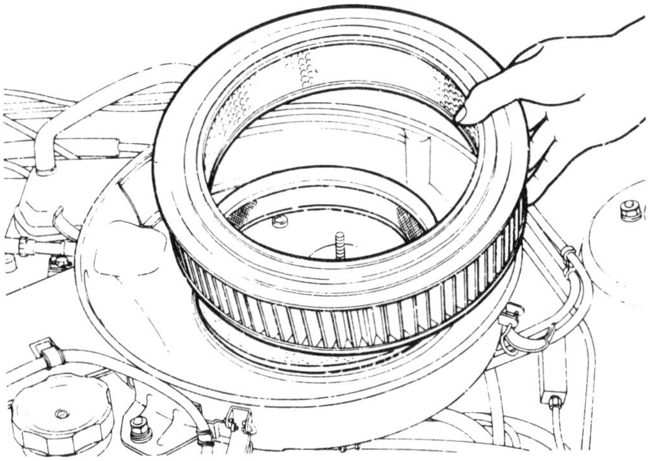

Fig. 1.43 Remove air filter to check (Sec 22)

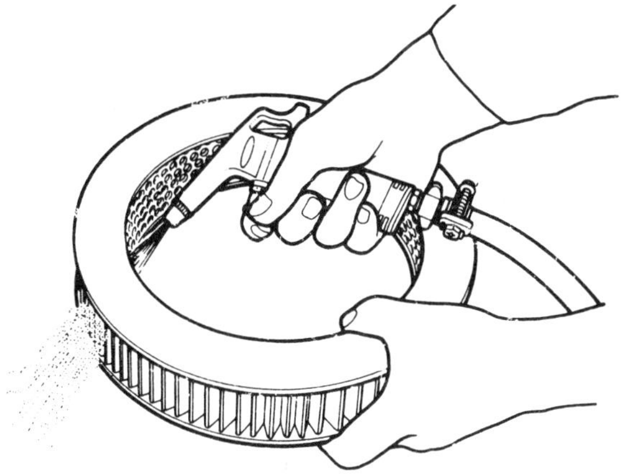

Fig. 1.44 Cleaning filter with compressed air (Sec 22)

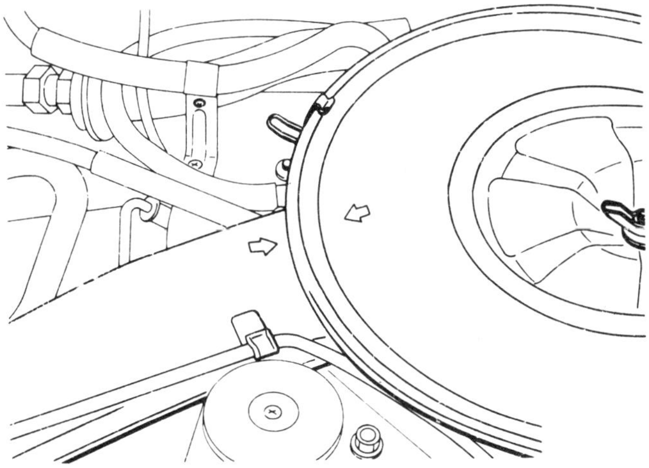

Fig. 1.45 Align marks when installing air cleaner cover (Sec 22)

1

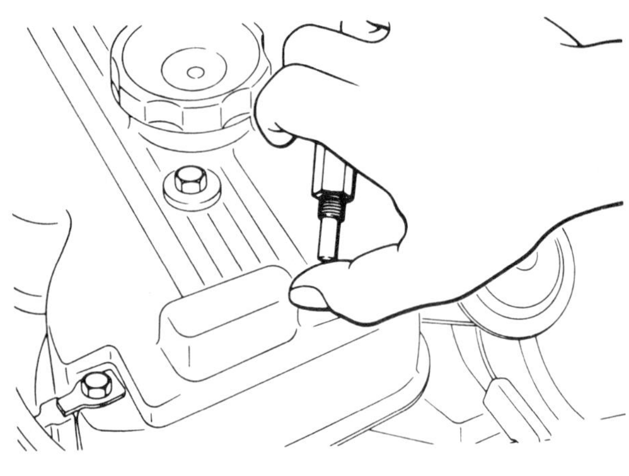

Fig. 1.46 PCV valve check with engine running (Sec 23)

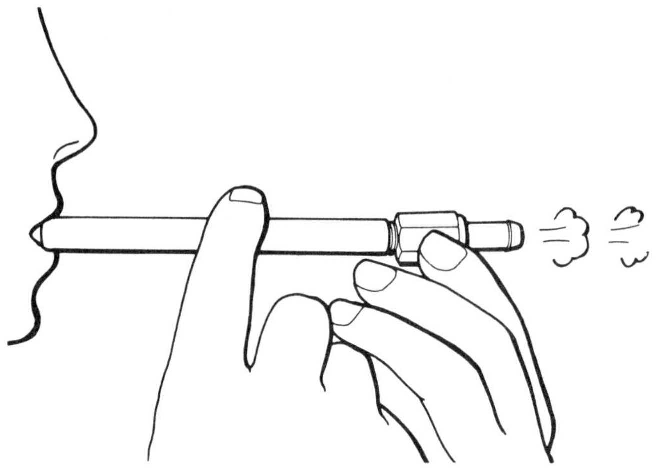

Fig. 1.47 PCV valve check by removing valve from engine (Sec 23)

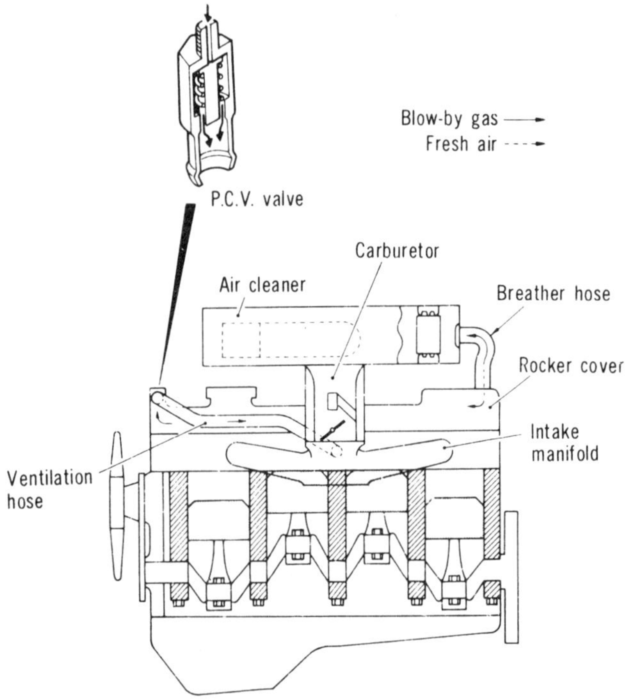

Fig. 1.48 PCV valve location (Sec 23)

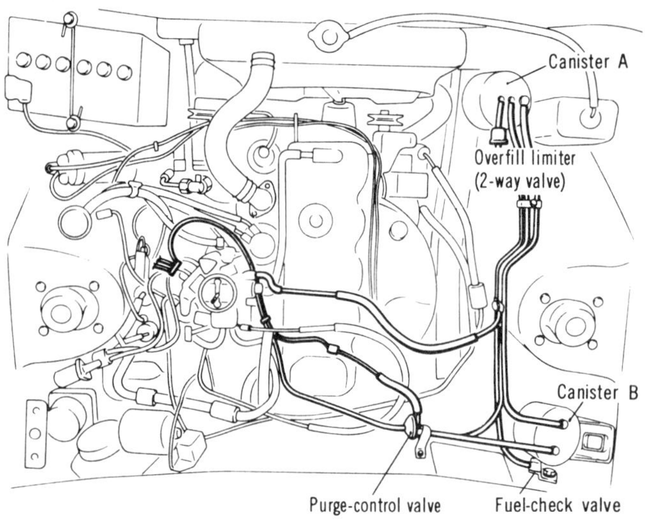

Fig. 1.49 ECS system and canister locations (Sec 25)

23 PCV valve check and replacement

1 The PCV valve is located on the front of the valve cover. It is connected to a short rubber hose, which is in turn connected to the metal PCV tube.
2 To check the valve with the engine running, remove it from the valve cover (still attached to the hose). If it is not clogged, a hissing noise will be heard as air passes through it. A strong vacuum should also be felt when your finger is placed over the inlet.
3 You can also check the valve with the engine off by completely removing it from the engine. Blow into the threaded opening and if the pressure cannot pass through, replace it with a new one.
4 When purchasing a replacement PCV valve, make sure it is the proper type.
5 Loosen the clamp that secures the hose to the PCV valve and disconnect the hose from the valve.
6 Unscrew the valve from the valve cover. Compare the old valve with the new one to make sure they are the same.
7 Screw the new valve into the manifold and connect the hose to it. More information on the PCV system can be found in Chapter 6.

24 Fuel filter replacement

1 Check the filter by referring to Section 9.
2 Replace the filter when recommended by removing it from the retaining cup and disconnecting both hoses. Be prepared to catch some gasoline in a rag when the hoses are disconnected and take care not to get any gasoline in your eyes. Pull the hose clamps off the hoses and discard them.
3 Slide new hose clamps onto both hoses. Connect the hoses to the new filter, taking care that the fuel inlet and outlet spigots are in the proper position. Install the hose clamps on both hoses approximately $\frac{1}{4}$ in back from the hose ends.
4 Push the fuel filter back into the mounting bracket. Check to make sure that it is held securely and that the hoses are not kinked.
5 Start the vehicle and check for leaks.

25 ECS and canister check and replacement

1 The function of the ECS emissions system is to draw fuel vapors from the tank and carburetor, store them in a charcoal-filled canister, and then burn them during normal engine operation.
2 The charcoal canister should be replaced at the specified intervals. If, however, a fuel odor is detected, the canister and system hoses should be inspected immediately.

3 The canister is located at the front right side of the engine compartment. It has three hoses attached to the top side. In order to facilitate removal of the canister, release the flexible rubber snorkel tube from the air cleaner housing and the front grille support.
4 Loosen and slide back the hose clamps on the three hoses and pull the hoses off the canister. Loosen the spring type clamp at the rear of the canister and lift the canister out of its holder.
5 Place a new canister into position in the holder, tighten the spring-type clamp and replace the hoses and hose clamps. Install the flexible rubber snorkel tube between the air cleaner housing and the front grille support.
6 The ECS system is explained in more detail in Chapter 6.

26 Carburetor choke check and adjustment

1 The choke only operates when the engine is cold, so this check can be performed before the vehicle has been started for the day.
2 Open the hood and remove the top plate of the air cleaner assembly. Place the top plate and wing nut aside, out of the way of moving engine components.
3 Look at the top of the carburetor at the center of the air cleaner housing. You will notice a flat plate at the carburetor opening.
4 Have an assistant press the accelerator pedal to the floor. The plate should close fully. Start the engine while you observe the plate at the carburetor. Do not position your face directly over the carburetor, as the engine could backfire, causing serious burns. When the engine starts, the choke plate should open slightly.
5 Allow the engine to continue running at an idle speed. As the engine warms up to operating temperature, the plate should slowly open, allowing more air to enter through the top of the carburetor.
6 After a few minutes, the choke plate should be fully open to the vertical position.
7 You will notice that the engine speed corresponds with the plate opening. With the plate fully closed, the engine should run at a fast idle speed. As the plate opens, the engine speed will decrease.
8 If during the above checks a fault is detected, refer to Chapter 4 for specific information on adjusting and servicing the choke components.

27 Idle speed and fuel/air mixture check and adjustment

1 Engine idle speed is the speed at which the engine operates when no accelerator pedal pressure is applied. This speed is critical to the performance of the engine itself, as well as many engine sub-systems.
2 A hand-held tachometer must be used when adjusting idle speed to get an accurate reading. The exact hook-up for these meters varies with the manufacturer, so follow the particular directions included.
3 Before any attempt is made to adjust the idle speed make sure that the air cleaner is in place with all vacuum lines connected and the choke valve fully open. The engine must be at normal operating temperature with the transmission in Neutral and all electrical accessories Off. Apply the parking brake and block the wheels to prevent accidental movement of the vehicle.
4 Check the ignition timing (Section 14) and the carburetor float level (Chapter 4) before proceeding.
5 Locate the idle speed adjusting screw (SAS) on the carburetor.
6 Using the tachometer and a screwdriver, adjust the curb idle speed if found to be different from the Specifications. Turn the SAS screw in or out accordingly to make the adjustment.
7 If you have air conditioning, a further adjustment must be made. After setting the curb idle speed to Specifications, switch the air conditioner on.
8 The throttle opener is now activated, which raises the engine rpm to compensate for the drain on the engine from the air conditioner.
9 Turn the throttle opener screw in or out, as necessary, to again achieve the correct curb idle speed specified.
10 When the air conditioner switch is turned off, the engine should return to the specified curb idle speed.
11 The fuel/air mixture is pre-set at the factory and made tamperproof by means of a plug. This adjustment should never need changing unless the carburetor is overhauled and is fully explained in Chapter 4.

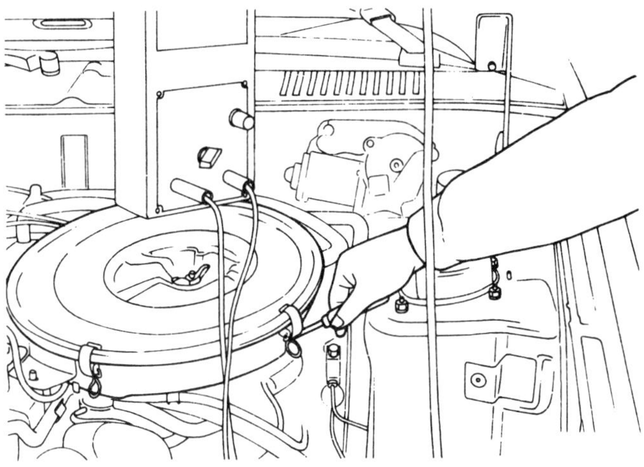

Fig. 1.50 Reading engine curb idle speed (Sec 27)

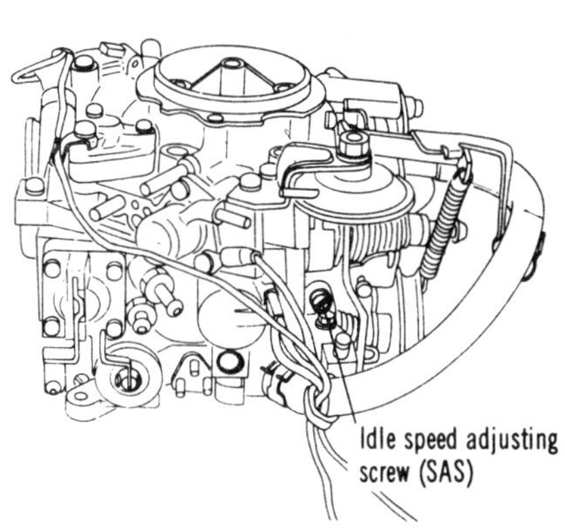

Fig. 1.51 Curb idle speed adjustment screw (Sec 27)

1

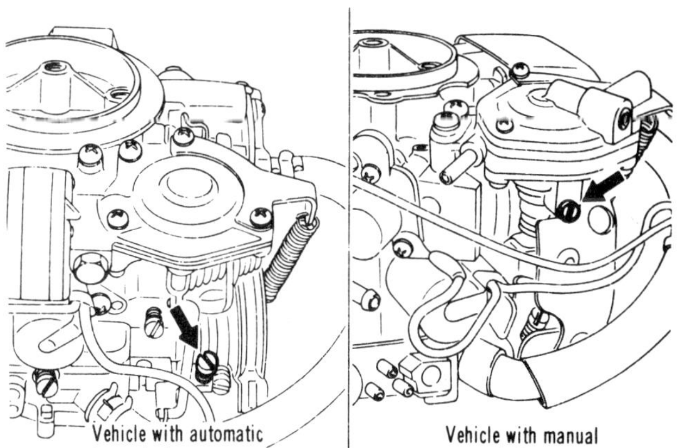

Fig. 1.52 Throttle opener adjustment screw (Sec 27)

28 Valve clearance check and adjustment

1 The intake, exhaust and Jet Valve clearances must be periodically checked and adjusted to ensure efficient and trouble-free engine operation. Always adjust the Jet Valve clearance before adjusting the intake valve clearance. Also, whenever the cylinder head is removed, or the bolts re-torqued, the valve clearances must be readjusted.
2 The engine must be at normal operating temperature when the valve clearances are adjusted.

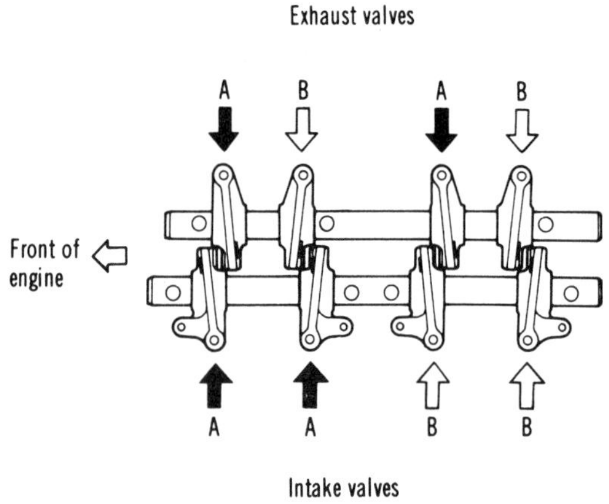

Fig. 1.53 Valve location and orientation (Sec 28)

Fig. 1.54 Valve clearance and adjustment (Sec 28)

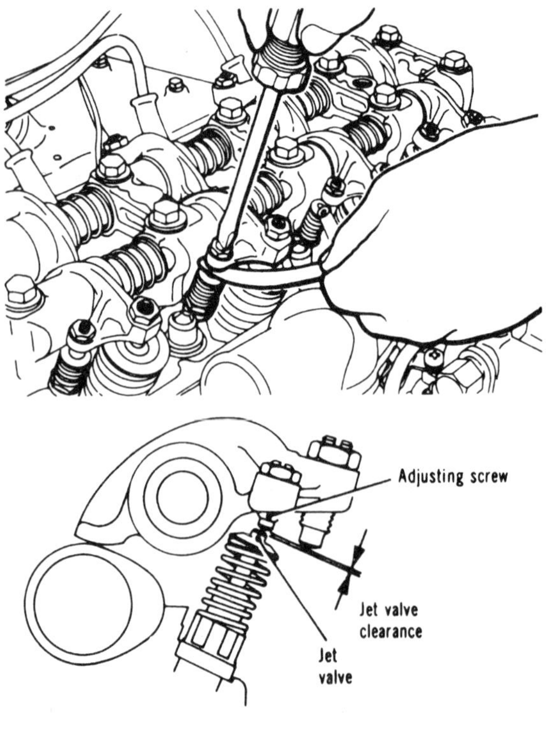

Fig. 1.55 Jet valve clearance and adjustment (Sec 28)

3 With the engine stopped, remove the air cleaner assembly. Detach the throttle cable, the carburetor vent tube, and the CECS hoses from the top of the valve cover. Remove the spark plug leads from the spark plugs. Pull the wire lead out of the center terminal of the distributor cap and ground it to the engine block. Also, remove the spark plugs so that each piston can easily be positioned at Top Dead Center (TDC) on the compression stroke.

4 Unfasten the distributor cap, remove the bolts attaching the valve cover and lift off the valve cover with the distributor cap and spark plug wire harness attached to it.

5 While watching the rocker arms for the number one cylinder, rotate the engine in a clockwise direction (with a wrench on the large bolt at the front of the crankshaft) until the exhaust valve is closing and the intake valve has just started to open. The intake valve is on the carburetor side of the engine, the exhaust valve is on the exhaust manifold side of the engine. Line up the notch in the pulley (on the front of the crankshaft) with the T on the timing marks tab (on the timing chain case). At this point, the number 4 piston will be at TDC on the compression stroke and the number 4 cylinder valve clearances can be adjusted. Remember, the Jet Valve clearance is always adjusted before the intake and exhaust valve clearance.

6 The intake valve and Jet Valve adjusting screws are located on a common rocker arm. Loosen the locknut on the intake valve adjusting screw and back off the adusting screw at least two full turns.

7 Loosen the locknut on the Jet Valve adjusting screw. Turn the Jet Valve adjusting screw counterclockwise and insert a .006 in (0.15 mm) feeler gauge between the Jet Valve stem and the adjusting screw.

8 Carefully tighten the adjusting screw until you can feel a slight drag on the feeler gauge as it is withdrawn from between the stem and adjusting screw. **Note:** *Since the Jet Valve spring is relatively weak, use special care not to force the Jet Valve open. Be particularly careful if the adjusting screw is hard to turn.*

9 Hold the adjusting screw with a screwdriver to keep it from turning and tighten the locknut. Recheck the clearance to make sure it hasn't changed.

10 Next, adjust the intake valve clearance. Insert a .006 in (0.15 mm) feeler gauge between the intake valve stem and the adjusting screw.

11 Carefully tighten the adjusting screw until you can feel a slight drag on the feeler gauge as it is withdrawn from between the stem and adjusting screw.

12 Hold the adjusting screw with a screwdriver, to keep it from turning, and tighten the locknut. Recheck the clearance to make sure it hasn't changed.

13 Loosen the locknut on the exhaust valve adjusting screw. Turn the adjusting screw counterclockwise and insert a .010 in (0.25 mm) feeler gauge between the valve stem and the adjusting screw.

14 Carefully tighten the adjusting screw until you can feel a slight drag on the feeler gauge as it is withdrawn from between the stem and adjusting screw.

15 Hold the adjusting screw with a screwdriver to keep it from turning and tighten the locknut. Recheck the clearance to make sure it hasn't changed.

16 Repeat the procedure to adjust the valve clearances for cylinders 1, 2 and 3. Use the following table for determining when the pistons are at TDC.

Exhaust valve closing, intake valve opening	Adjust valve clearances at
No. 1 cylinder	No. 4 cylinder
No. 2 cylinder	No. 3 cylinder
No. 3 cylinder	No. 2 cylinder
No. 4 cylinder	No. 1 cylinder

17 Install the valve cover (using a new gasket), distributor cap, spark plugs, throttle cable, carburetor vent tubes, CECS hoses and air cleaner assembly. Push the lead wire into the center terminal of the distributor cap and attach the spark plug wires to the spark plugs.

18 Start and run the engine. Check for oil leakage between the valve cover and the cylinder head.

29 Hot air intake system check

1 All models are equipped with a thermostatically controlled air cleaner which directs air to the carburetor from different locations depending upon engine temperature.

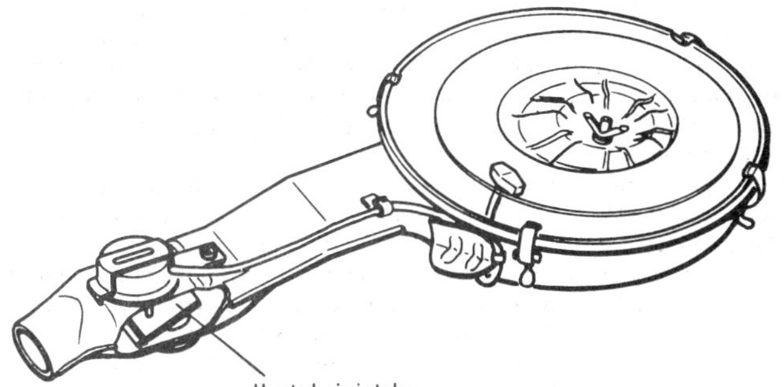

Fig. 1.56 Hot air intake check (Sec 29)

2 This is a simple visual check; however, if access is tight, a small mirror may have to be used.
3 Open the hood and locate the baffle inside the air cleaner assembly. It will be located inside the long snorkel of the air cleaner. Check that the flexible air hose(s) are securely attached and not damaged.
4 If there is a flexible air duct attached to the end of the snorkel, leading to an area behind the grille, disconnect it at the snorkel. This will enable you to look through the end of the snorkel and see the baffle inside.
5 The testing must be done when the engine and outside air are cold (below 72°F). Start the engine and look through the snorkel at the baffle, which should move to a closed position. With the baffle closed, air cannot enter through the end of the snorkel, but instead enters the air cleaner through the duct attached to the exhaust manifold.
6 As the engine warms up to operating temperature, the baffle should open to allow air through the snorkel end. Depending on ambient temperature, this may take 10 to 15 minutes. To speed up this check you can reconnect the snorkel air duct, drive the car and then check to see if the baffle is fully open.
7 If the hot intake system is not operating properly, see Chapter 6 for more information.

30 Vacuum hose and connection check

1 Check for damage or air leakage in the rubber hoses and connections.
2 Inspect the surface of the hoses for heat and mechanical damage. Hard and brittle rubber, cracking, tears, cuts, abrasions and excessive swelling indicate deterioration of the rubber.
3 If any of these symptoms are present, replace the hoses or connections with new ones.

31 Spark plug check and replacement

1 The spark plugs are located on the right side of the engine and are easily accessible for servicing.
2 In most cases, the tools necessary for a spark plug replacement job are: a plug wrench or spark plug socket which fits onto a ratchet wrench (this special socket will be insulated inside to protect the porcelain insulator) and a feeler gauge to check and adjust the spark plug gap.
3 The best policy to follow when replacing the spark plugs is to purchase the new spark plugs beforehand, adjust them to the proper gap and then replace each plug one at a time. When buying the new spark plugs it is important that the correct plug is purchased for your specific engine. This information can be found on the tune-up decal located under the hood of your vehicle or in the factory owner's manual. If differences exist between these sources, purchase the spark plug type specified on the tune-up decal as this information was printed for your specific engine.
4 With the new spark plugs at hand, allow the engine to thoroughly cool before attempting the removal. During this cooling time, each of the new spark plugs can be inspected for defects and the gap can be checked.
5 The gap is checked by inserting the proper thickness gauge between the electrodes at the tip of the plug. The gap between these electrodes should be the same as that given in the Specifications or on the tune-up decal. The wire should just touch each of the electrodes. If the gap is incorrect, use the notched adjuster on the feeler gauge body to bend the curved side electrode slightly until the proper gap is achieved. Also, at this time check for cracks in the spark plug body, indicating the spark plug should be replaced with a new one. If the side electrode is not exactly over the center one, use the notched adjuster to align the two.
6 Cover the fenders of the vehicle to prevent damage to exterior paint.
7 With the engine cool, remove the spark plug wire from one spark plug. Do this by grabbing the boot at the end of the wire, not the wire itself. Sometimes it is necessary to use a twisting motion while the boot and plug wire is pulled free. Using a plug removal tool is the easiest and safest method.
8 If compressed air is available, use this to blow any dirt or foreign material away from the spark plug area. A common bicycle pump will also work. The idea here is to eliminate the possibility of material falling into the engine cylinder as the spark plug is removed.
9 Now place the spark plug wrench or socket over the plug and remove it from the engine by turning in a counterclockwise motion.
10 Compare the spark plug with those shown in this Chapter to get an indication of the overall running condition of the engine.
11 Carefully insert one of the new plugs into the spark plug hole and tighten it by hand. Since the cylinder head on your engine is aluminum, you must be especially careful not to cross-thread the spark plug in the hole. If resistance is felt as you thread the spark plug in by hand, back it out and start again. *Do not, under any circumstances, force the spark plug into the hole with a wrench or socket.*
12 Finally tighten the spark plug with the wrench or socket. It is best to use a torque wrench for this to ensure the plug is seated correctly. The correct torque figure is given in Specifications.
13 Before pushing the spark plug wire onto the end of the plug, inspect it following the procedures outlined in Section 32.
14 Install the plug wire to the new spark plug, again using a twisting motion on the boot until it is firmly seated on the spark plug. Make sure the wire is routed away from the hot exhaust manifold.
15 Follow the above procedures for the remaining spark plugs, replacing each one at a time to prevent mixing up the spark plug wires.

32 Spark plug wires and distributor cap check and replacement

1 The spark plug wires should be checked at the recommended intervals or whenever new spark plugs are installed.
2 The wires should be inspected one at a time to prevent mixing up the order which is essential for proper engine operation.
3 Disconnect the plug wire from the spark plug. A removal tool can be used for this, or you can grab the rubber boot, twist slightly and then pull the wire free. Do not pull on the wire itself, only on the rubber boot.
4 Inspect inside the boot for corrosion, which will look like a white, crusty powder. Some vehicles use a conductive white grease which should not be mistaken for corrosion.
5 Now push the wire and boot back onto the end of the spark plug. It should be a tight fit on the plug end. If not, remove the wires and use a pair of pliers to carefully crimp the metal connector inside the wire boot until the fit is secure.
6 Now using a clean rag, clean the wire its entire length. Remove all built-up dirt and grease. As this is done, inspect for burns, cracks or any other form of damage.
7 Disconnect the wire at the distributor (again, pulling and twisting only on the rubber boot). Check for corrosion and a tight fit in the same manner as the spark plug end. A small amount of white grease can be applied to the inside of the plug wire boot to aid in the removal/installation of the boot onto the spark plug and help provide conductivity between plug and wire.
8 Check the remaining spark plug wires in the same way, making sure they are securely fastened at the distributor and spark plug.
9 A visual check of the spark plug wires can also be made. In a

darkened garage (make sure there is ventilation), start the engine and observe each plug wire. Be careful not to come into contact with any moving engine parts. If there is a break or fault in the wire, you will be able to see arcing or a small spark at the damaged area.
10 If it is decided the spark plug wires are in need of replacement, purchase a new set for your specific engine model. Wire sets can be purchased which are pre-cut to the proper size and with the rubber boots already installed. Remove and replace each wire individually to prevent mix-ups in the firing sequence.
11 Remove the distributor cap and inspect it for cracks or damage. Closely examine the contacts on the inside of the cap for excessive corrosion or damage. Slight scoring is normal. Again, if in doubt as to the quality of the cap, replace it with a new on as described in Chapter 5.
12 It is important that the distributor is lubricated every six months or 6000 miles whichever comes sooner.
13 Remove the distributor cap and rotor arm. Apply a single drop of engine or machine oil to the contact breaker pivot and the vacuum rod eye.
14 Smear oil onto the surface of the cam and apply as many drops of oil as it will absorb to the cam felt.
15 Apply two drops of oil to the recess in the top of the cam spindle and reinstall the rotor and distributor cap.

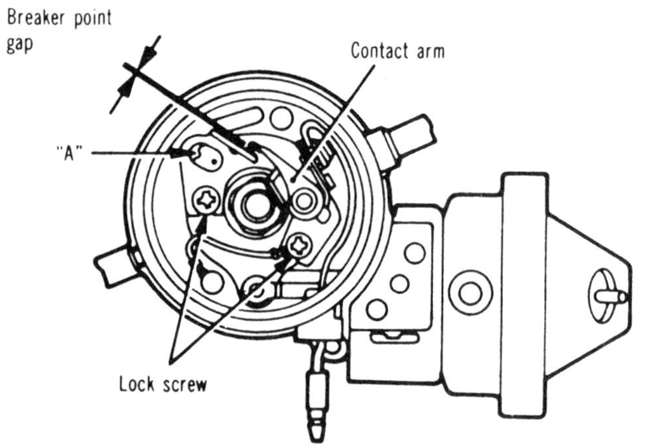

Fig. 1.57 Contact breaker point gap adjustment (Sec 33)

33 Contact point replacement and dwell angle adjustment

Note: *This procedure is for point-type distributors only and not pointless-type (electronic).*
1 Although the contact points can be cleaned and dressed with a fine-cut contact file, it may be false economy for the home mechanic to attempt this. Due to the inaccessibility of the distributor components, it is more practical to merely replace the contact points during tune-ups.
2 The contact point set and condenser are replaced as one complete assembly. Point alignment and spring tension are factory set and require no further adjustment.
3 Whenever distributor servicing is required, as in contact point replacement, it is a good idea to use magnetized tools to prevent screws or nuts from falling down into the distributor body, requiring distributor disassembly to retrieve.

Contact point replacement

4 Remove the distributor cap by placing a screwdriver on the slotted head of the latch. Press down on the latch and give a $\frac{1}{4}$ turn to release the curved section at the bottom of the latch.
5 With both latches disengaged from the distributor body, place the cap (with the spark plug wires still attached) out of the way. Use a length of wire or tape if necessary.
6 Remove the rotor, which is now visible at the top of the distributor shaft. In most cases the rotor is held in place with two screws. On some models, the rotor is merely pushed onto the shaft and can simply be lifted away. Place the rotor in a safe place where it cannot be damaged.
7 Loosen the two screws which secure the contact point set assembly to the breaker plate. Do not completely remove these screws, as most point sets have slots at these locations. Slide the point set off the breaker plate.
8 Disconnect the primary and condenser wire leads at the point set. These wires may be attached with a small nut (which should be loosened, but not removed) a small standard screw, or by a quick-disconnect terminal which requires the tangs to be pressed together to unlock.
9 The contact breaker point assembly can now be removed from the distributor.
10 The condenser can now be removed from the breaker plate. Loosen the mounting strap screw and slide the condenser out of the bracket, or completely remove the condenser and strap depending on the exact attachment.
11 Before installing the new points and condenser, clean all lubricant, dirt, etc., from the breaker plate and the rotating cam surface of the distributor shaft.
12 Place the new condenser into position and tighten its retaining screw.
13 Slide the new contact point set onto the breaker plate and tighten the two attaching screws.
14 Connect the primary and condenser electrical leads to the new point assembly. Make sure the leads are positioned the same as they were on removal.
15 Although the final gap between the contact points will be adjusted later (dwell angle), it is best to get an initial gap to start the engine. With the points in position and tightened to the breaker plate, see that the points rubbing block is resting on one of the high points of the center cam. To move the center cam, have an assistant just click the ignition key in short bursts. If equipped with a manual transmission, place the shifter in gear and rock the car back and forth.
16 With the rubbing block on a cam high point (points fully open), place a blade-type feeler gauge between the contacts. Make sure the point gap meets the specifications. If not correct, use a screwdriver in slot A to turn the points which will open and close the gap.
17 Before installing the rotor, inspect it for cracks or damage. Carefully check the condition of the metal contact at the top of the rotor for excessive burning or pitting. If in doubt as to its quality, replace it with a new one.
18 Install the rotor. Both types are keyed to go onto the shaft only one way. Rotors having attached screws will have raised pegs on the bottom. Make sure the rotor is firmly seated.
19 Install the distributor cap, locking the two latches under the distributor body.
20 Start the engine and check the dwell angle and the ignition timing (Section 14).

Point dwell angle adjustment

21 On modern engines, setting the contact breaker gap using feeler gauges must be regarded as a basic adjustment only. For optimum engine performance, the dwell angle must be checked. The dwell angle is the number of degrees through which the distributor cam turns during the period between the instants of closure and opening of the contact breaker points. Checking the dwell angle not only gives a more accurate setting of the contact breaker gap but this method also evens out any variations in the gap which could be caused by wear in the distributor shaft or its bushings or a difference in height of any of the cam peaks.
22 The angle should be checked with a dwell meter connected in accordance with the makers' instructions. Refer to Specifications for the correct dwell angle. If the dwell angle is found to be too large, increase the points gap, if too small, reduce the gap. Always adjust the dwell angle before checking the ignition timing.

For a COLOR version of this spark plug diagnosis page, please see the inside rear cover of this manual

CARBON DEPOSITS

Symptoms: Dry sooty deposits indicate a rich mixture or weak ignition. Causes misfiring, hard starting and hesitation.

Recommendation: Check for a clogged air cleaner, high float level, sticky choke and worn ignition points. Use a spark plug with a longer core nose for greater anti-fouling protection.

OIL DEPOSITS

Symptoms: Oily coating caused by poor oil control. Oil is leaking past worn valve guides or piston rings into the combustion chamber. Causes hard starting, misfiring and hesition.

Recommendation: Correct the mechanical condition with necessary repairs and install new plugs.

TOO HOT

Symptoms: Blistered, white insulator, eroded electrode and absence of deposits. Results in shortened plug life.

Recommendation: Check for the correct plug heat range, over-advanced ignition timing, lean fuel mixture, intake manifold vacuum leaks and sticking valves. Check the coolant level and make sure the radiator is not clogged.

PREIGNITION

Symptoms: Melted electrodes. Insulators are white, but may be dirty due to misfiring or flying debris in the combustion chamber. Can lead to engine damage.

Recommendation: Check for the correct plug heat range, over-advanced ignition timing, lean tuel mixture, clogged cooling system and lack of lubrication.

HIGH SPEED GLAZING

Symptoms: Insulator has yellowish, glazed appearance. Indicates that combustion chamber temperatures have risen suddenly during hard acceleration. Normal deposits melt to form a conductive coating. Causes misfiring at high speeds.

Recommendation: Install new plugs. Consider using a colder plug if driving habits warrant.

GAP BRIDGING

Symptoms: Combustion deposits lodge between the electrodes. Heavy deposits accumulate and bridge the electrode gap. The plug ceases to fire, resulting in a dead cylinder.

Recommendation: Locate the faulty plug and remove the deposits from between the electrodes.

NORMAL

Symptoms: Brown to grayish-tan color and slight electrode wear. Correct heat range for engine and operating conditions.

Recommendation: When new spark plugs are installed, replace with plugs of the same heat range.

ASH DEPOSITS

Symptoms: Light brown deposits encrusted on the side or center electrodes or both. Derived from oil and/or fuel additives. Excessive amounts may mask the spark, causing misfiring and hesitation during acceleration.

Recommendation: If excessive deposits accumulate over a short time or low mileage, install new valve guide seals to prevent seepage of oil into the combustion chambers. Also try changing gasoline brands.

WORN

Symptoms: Rounded electrodes with a small amount of deposits on the firing end. Normal color. Causes hard starting in damp or cold weather and poor fuel economy.

Recommendation: Replace with new plugs of the same heat range.

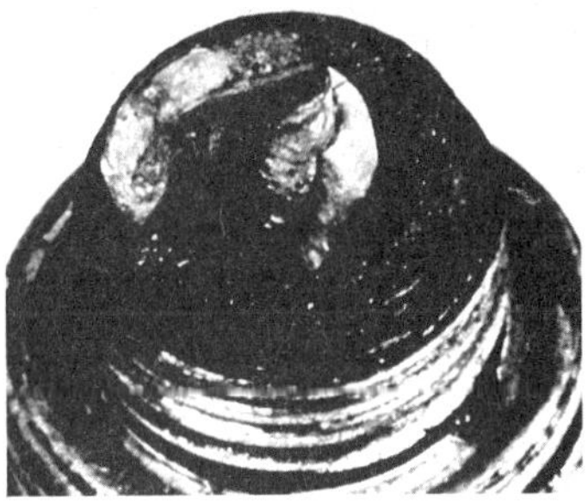

DETONATION

Symptoms: Insulators may be cracked or chipped. Improper gap setting techniques can also result in a fractured insulator tip. Can lead to piston damage.

Recommendation: Make sure the fuel anti-knock values meet engine requirements. Use care when setting the gaps on new plugs. Avoid lugging the engine.

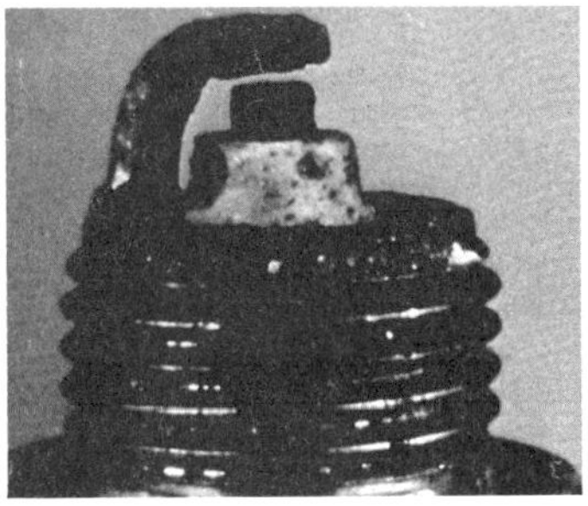

SPLASHED DEPOSITS

Symptoms: After long periods of misfiring, deposits can loosen when normal combustion temperature is restored by an overdue tune-up. At high speeds, deposits flake off the piston and are thrown against the hot insulator, causing misfiring.

Recommendation: Replace the plugs with new ones or clean and reinstall the originals.

MECHANICAL DAMAGE

Symptoms: May be caused by a foreign object in the combustion chamber or the piston striking an incorrect reach (too long) plug. Causes a dead cylinder and could result in piston damage.

Recommendation: Remove the foreign object from the engine and/or install the correct reach plug.

34 Fluid changes – 24 month

Radiator

1 Periodically, the cooling system should be drained, flushed and refilled to replenish the antifreeze mixture and prevent the formation of rust and corrosion which can impair the performance of the cooling system and ultimately cause engine damage.
2 At the same time the cooling system is serviced, all hoses and the radiator pressure cap should be inspected and replaced if faulty (see Section 10).
3 As antifreeze is a poisonous solution, take care not to spill any of the cooling mixture on the vehicle's paint or your own skin. If this happens, rinse immediately with plenty of clear water. Also, it is advisable to consult your local authorities about the dumping of antifreeze before draining the cooling system. In many areas reclamation centers have been set up to collect automobile oil and drained antifreeze/water mixtures rather than allowing these liquids to be added to the sewage and water facilities.
4 With the engine cold, remove the radiator pressure cap.
5 Move a large container under the radiator to catch the water/antifreeze mixture as it is drained.
6 Drain the radiator by opening the drain petcock at the bottom of the radiator.
7 Remove the engine coolant drain plug from the right side of the engine. This will allow the coolant to drain from the engine itself.
8 Disconnect the overflow tube and remove the coolant reserve system reservoir. Flush it out with clean water.
9 Place a cold water hose (a common garden hose is fine) in the radiator filler neck at the top of the radiator and flush the system until the water runs clear at all drain points.
10 In severe cases of contamination or clogging of the radiator, remove it (see Chapter 3) and reverse flush it. This involves simply inserting a cold pressure hose in the bottom radiator outlet to allow the clear water to run against the normal flow, draining through the top. A radiator repair shop should be consulted if further cleaning or repair is necessary.
11 Where the coolant is regularly drained and the system refilled with the correct antifreeze/inhibitor mixture there should be no need to employ chemical cleaners or descalers.
12 To refill the system, install the drain plug securely in the engine. Special thread sealing tape (available at auto parts stores) should be used on the drain plug in the engine block. Install the reserve system reservoir and the overflow hose.
13 Fill the radiator to the base of the filler neck and then add more coolant to the coolant reserve system reservoir until it reaches the Full mark.
14 Run the engine until normal operating temperature is reached and with the engine idling, add coolant up to the correct level (see Section 4). Install the reservoir cap.
15 Always refill the system with a mixture of high quality ethylene glycol-based antifreeze and water in the proportion called for on the antifreeze container or in your owner's manual. Chapter 3 also contains information on antifreeze mixtures.
16 Keep a close watch on the coolant level and the various cooling hoses during the first few miles of driving. Tighten the hose clamps and/or add more coolant mixture as necessary.

Rear axle

17 The vehicle should be driven for a few minutes before draining the rear axle fluid. This practice will tend to warm up the fluid and ensure complete drainage.
18 Move a drain pan, rags, newspapers, and tools under the rear of the vehicle. With the drain pan under the differential, remove the drain plug from the bottom of the housing. While the fluid is draining, remove the inspection plug.
19 After the fluid has completely drained, wipe the area around the drain hole with a clean rag and install the drain plug.
20 Fill the housing (through the inspection hole) with the recommended lubricant until the level is even with the bottom of the inspection hole. Install the inspection plug.
21 After driving the vehicle, check for leaks at the drain and inspection plugs.
22 When the job is complete, check for metal filings or chips in the drained fluid, which indicates that the differential should be thoroughly inspected and repaired (see Chapter 8 for more information).

Manual transmission

23 Move a drain pan (at least 5 pint capacity), rags, newspapers and a $\frac{1}{2}$ in drive ratchet with extension under the center of the car.
24 With the drain pan under the transmission, use the wrench and extension to loosen the drain plug.
25 Once loosened, carefully unscrew it with your fingers until you can remove it from the transmission case.
26 Allow all of the oil to drain into the pan. Then, replace the drain plug and tighten it to the specified torque.
27 Now remove the transmission inspection plug on the side of the transmission housing. Using a hand pump, syringe or funnel fill the transmission with the correct amount and grade of fluid (see Specifications), until the level is just at the bottom of the inspection plug hole.
28 Now reinstall the inspection plug, torqueing it to Specifications.

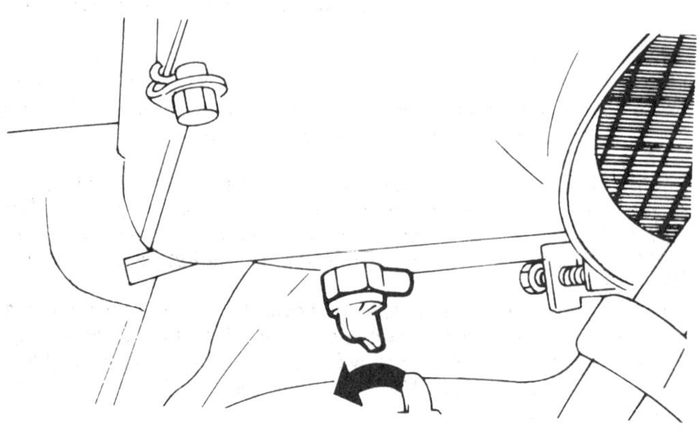

Fig. 1.58 Radiator drain plug (Sec 34)

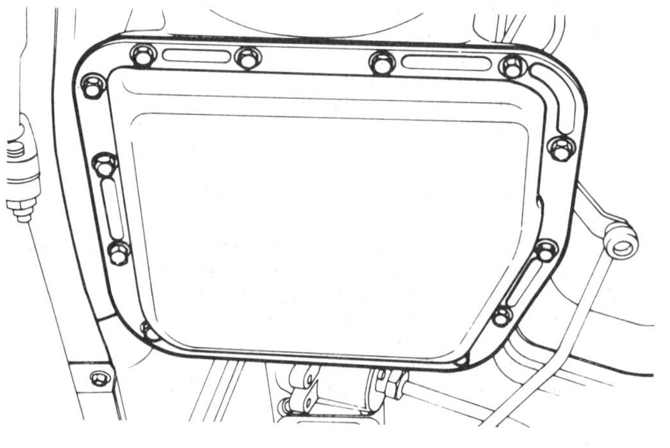

Fig. 1.59 Automatic transmission oil pan fluid draining (Sec 34)

Automatic transmission

29 At the specified time intervals, the transmission fluid should be changed and the filter replaced with a new one. Since there is no drain plug, the transmission oil pan must be removed from the bottom of the transmission to drain the fluid.
30 Before any draining, purchase the specified transmission fluid (see *Lubricant Specifications)* and a new filter. The necessary gaskets should be included with the filter; if not, purchase an oil pan gasket and a strainer-to-valve body gasket.
31 Other tools necessary for this job include: jackstands to support the vehicle in a raised position; wrench to remove the oil pan bolts; standard screwdriver; drain pan capable of holding at least 8 pints; newspapers and clean rags.
32 The fluid should be drained immediately after the vehicle has been driven. This will remove any built-up sediment better than if the fluid were cold. Because of this, it may be wise to wear protective gloves (fluid temperature can exceed 350° in a hot transmission).
33 After the vehicle has been driven to warm up the fluid, raise it and place it on jackstands for access underneath. Make sure it is firmly supported by the four stands placed under the frame rails.
34 Move the necessary equipment under the vehicle, being careful not to touch any of the hot exhaust components.
35 Place the drain pan under the transmission oil pan and remove the oil pan bolts along the rear and sides of the pan. Loosen, but do not remove, the bolts at the front of the pan.
36 Carefully pry the pan downward at the rear, allowing the hot fluid to drain into the drain pan. If necessary, use a screwdriver to break the gasket seal at the rear of the pan; however, do not damage the pan or transmission in the process.
37 Support the pan and remove the remaining bolts at the front of the pan. Lower the pan and drain the remaining fluid into the drain receptacle. As this is done, check the fluid for metal particles which may be an indication of internal failure.

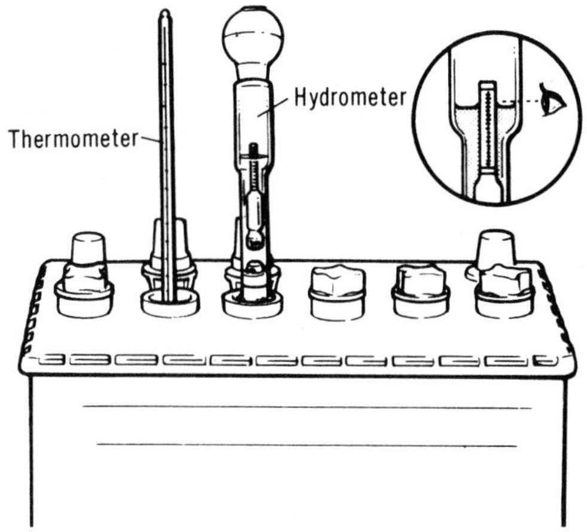

Fig. 1.60 Check battery specific gravity with a hydrometer (Sec 35)

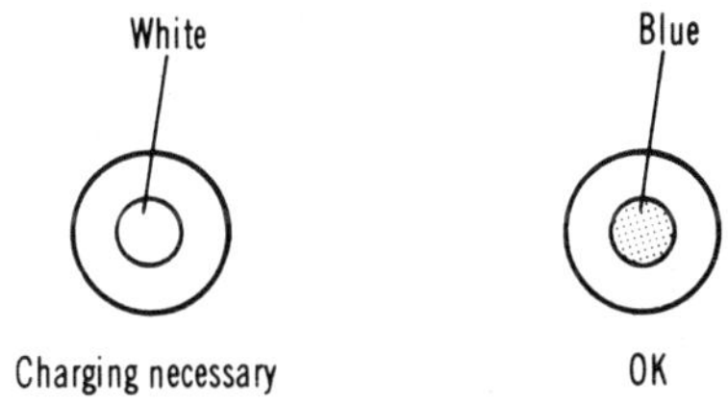

Fig. 1.61 Maintenance free battery test indicator (Sec 35)

35 Battery maintenance

Checking

Caution: *Hydrogen gas, which is highly flammable, is always present in the battery cells so keep lighted tobacco or any other open flames away from the battery. The electrolyte inside the battery is actually dilute sulfuric acid, which can be hazardous to your skin and cause damage if splashed in the eyes. It will also ruin clothes and painted surfaces.*
1 Check the battery case for cracks and evidence of leakage.
2 To check the electrolyte level in the battery, remove all vent caps. If the battery water level is low, add distilled water until the level is above the cell plates. There is an indicator on the side of the battery casing to help you judge when enough water has been added. Do not overfill.
3 Periodically check the specific gravity of the electrolyte with a hydrometer. This is especially important during cold weather. If the reading is below the specification, the battery should be recharged.
4 Check the tightness of the battery terminals to ensure good electrical connections. The terminals can be cleaned with a stiff wire brush. Corrosion can be kept to a minimum by applying a layer of petroleum jelly or grease to the terminal and cable connectors after they are assembled.
5 Inspect the entire length of the battery cables for corrosion, cracks and frayed conductors.
6 Check that the rubber protector over the positive terminal is not torn or missing. It should completely cover the terminal.
7 Make sure that the battery is securely mounted.
8 The battery case and caps should be kept clean and dry. If corrosion is evident, clean the battery.
9 If the vehicle is not being used for an extended period, disconnect the battery cables and have it charged approximately every six weeks.

Cleaning

10 Corrosion on the battery hold-down components and inner fender panels can be removed by washing with a solution of water and baking soda. Once the area has been thoroughly cleaned, rinse it with clear water.
11 Corrosion on the battery case and terminals can also be removed with a solution of water and baking soda and a stiff brush. Be careful that none of the solution is splashed into your eyes or onto your skin (wear protective gloves). Do not allow any of the baking soda and water solution to get into the battery cells. Rinse the battery thoroughly once it is clean.
12 Metal parts of the vehicle which have been damaged by spilled battery acid should be painted with a zinc-based primer and paint. Do this only after the area has been thoroughly cleaned and dried.

Charging

13 As was mentioned before, if the battery's specific gravity is below the specified amount, the battery must be recharged.
14 If the battery is to remain in the vehicle during charging, disconnect the cables from the battery to prevent damage to the electrical system.
15 When batteries are being charged, hydrogen gas, which is very explosive and flammable is produced. Do not smoke or allow an open flame near a charging or a recently charged battery. Also, do not plug in the battery charger until the connections have been made at the battery posts.
16 The average time necessary to charge a battery at the normal rate is from 12 to 16 hours (sometimes longer). Always charge the battery slowly. A quick charge or boost charge is hard on a battery and will shorten its life. Use a battery charger that is rated at no more than 3½ amperes.
17 Remove all of the vent caps and cover the velt holes with a clean cloth to prevent the spattering of electrolyte. Hook the battery charger leads to the battery posts (positive to positive, negative to negative), then plug in the charger. Make sure it is set at 12 volts if it has a selector switch.
18 Watch the battery closely during charging to make sure that it does not overheat.
19 The battery can be considered fully charged when it is gassing freely and there is no increase in specific gravity during three successive readings taken at hourly intervals. Overheating of the battery during charging at normal charging rates, excessive gassing and continual low specific gravity readings are an indication that the battery should be replaced with a new one.

Maintenance-free battery

20 Some models are equipped with maintenance-free batteries which do not require the addition of water or electrolyte.
21 The top of the battery should be kept clean and free from dirt and moisture so that the battery does not become partially discharged by leakage through dampness and dirt. Clean the top of the battery with a baking soda and water solution, making sure that it does not enter the battery.
22 Once every three months, remove the battery and inspect the securing bolts, battery clamp bolts and leads for corrosion (white fluffy deposits which are brittle to the touch).
23 Clean the battery posts with a battery cleaning tool or wire brush.
24 Clean the battery cable terminals with a wire brush until the corrosion is removed and the metal in the terminal contact area is bright.
25 Apply grease or petroleum jelly around the base of the battery posts and install the battery cables (positive cables first) and tighten the terminal cable nuts securely.
26 If any doubt exists about the state of charge of the battery, it should be tested by a dealer or properly equipped shop.
27 The maintenance-free battery has a built-in test indicator (hydrometer). It should not be used to determine if the battery is charged or discharged.
28 If the battery needs charging, stop the charging when the blue dot appears or when the maximum charge is reached.
29 If the blue dot does not appear after the maximum length of time, do not over-charge. Replace it with a new one.

36 Engine compression check

1 A compression check will tell you what mechanical condition the engine is in. Specifically, it can tell you if the compression is down due to leakage caused by worn piston rings, defective valves and seats or a blown head gasket.
2 Begin by cleaning the area around the spark plugs before you remove them. This will keep dirt from falling into the cylinders while you are performing the compression test.
3 Remove the coil high-tension lead from the distributor and ground it on the engine block. Block the throttle and choke valves wide open.
4 With the compression gauge in the number one cylinder's spark plug hole, crank the engine over at least four compression strokes and observe the gauge. The compression should build up quickly in a healthy engine. Low compression on the first stroke, followed by gradually increasing pressure on successive strokes, indicates worn piston rings. A low compression reading on the first stroke, which does not build up during successive strokes, indicates leaking valves or a defective head gasket. Record the highest gauge reading obtained.
5 Repeat the procedure for the remaining cylinders and compare the results to the Specifications. Compression readings 10% above or below the specified amount can be considered normal.
6 Pour a couple of teaspoons of engine oil (a squirt can works great for this) into each cylinder, through the spark plug hole, and repeat the test.
7 If the compression increases after the oil is added, the piston rings are definitely worn. If the compression does not increase significantly, the leakage is occurring at the valves or head gasket.
8 If two adjacent cylinders have equally low compression, there is a strong possibility that the head gasket between them is blown. The appearance of coolant in the combustion chambers or the crankcase would verify this condition.
9 If the compression is higher than normal, the combustion chambers are probably coated with carbon deposits. If that is the case, the cylinder head should be removed and decarbonized.
10 If compression is way down, or varies greatly between cylinders, it would be a good idea to have a leak-down test performed by a reputable automotive repair shop. This test will pinpoint exactly where the leakage is occurring and how severe it is.

37 Front wheel bearing check and repacking

1 In most cases, the front wheel bearings will not need servicing until the brake pads are changed. However, these bearings should be checked whenever the front wheels are raised for any reason.
2 With the vehicle securely supported on jackstands, spin the wheel and check for noise, rolling resistance or free play. Now grab the top of the wheel with one hand and the bottom of the wheel with the other. Move the tire in and out on the spindle. If there is noticeable movement, the bearings should be checked, then repacked with grease or replaced, if necessary.
3 Remove the wheel/tire from the hub.
4 Refer to Chapter 9 and remove the brake caliper assembly and bracket.
5 Remove the dust cap from the hub with a screwdriver (photo) or pry bar. Remove the cotter pin, the nut and the special washer from the end of the spindle (photo). Pull the hub assembly out slightly, then push it back to its original position. This should slide the outer bearing off the spindle enough so that it can be removed by hand. As you slide it off, note how the bearing is installed. Next, pull off the hub, which will contain the inner bearing and the seal (photo).
6 Use a screwdriver or pry bar to pry out the seal on the rear of the hub. Note how it is installed. The inner bearing can now be removed from the hub. Again, note how it is installed.
7 Use clean parts solvent to remove all traces of the old grease from

37.5a Remove the dust cap from the end of the hub

37.5b Pull out the cotter key

37.5c Remove the nut and washer and the outer bearing is exposed

37.5d Pull out the hub to dislodge the bearing

the bearings and spindle. Do not wash the hub in solvent unless the brake disc is separated from the hub first. A small brush may prove useful; however, make sure no bristles from the brush are left inside the bearing cage. Allow the parts to air dry.

8 Carefully inspect the bearings for cracks, heat discoloration, bent rollers, etc. Check the bearing races inside the hub for cracks, scoring or uneven surfaces. If the bearing races are in need of replacement, the job is best left to a repair shop which can press the new races into position.

9 Use an approved high temperature wheel bearing grease to pack the bearings. Work the grease fully into the bearings, forcing the grease between the rollers, cone and cage.

10 Apply a thin coat of grease to the spindle at the outer bearing seat, inner bearing seat, shoulder and seal seat.

11 Put a small quantity of grease inboard at each bearing race inside the hub. Using your fingers, form a dam at these points to provide extra grease availability and to keep thinned grease from flowing out of the bearing.

12 Place the grease-packed inner bearing into the rear of the hub and put a little more grease outboard of the bearing. Do not get any grease on the brake disc.

13 Place a new seal over the inner bearing and tap the seal into place with a flat piece of wood and hammer until it is flush with the hub.

14 Carefully place the hub assembly onto the spindle and push the grease-packed outer bearing into position.

15 Install the washer and spindle nut. While rotating the hub in a forward direction, tighten the nut to 21.7 ft-lbs (using a torque wrench) to seat the bearings. Completely loosen the nut and then retighten it to 5.8 ft-lbs. Install the cotter pin. If the slot on the nut does not line up with the cotter pin hole, loosen the nut (30° maximum) to align them.

16 Bend the ends of the new cotter pin until they are flat against the nut. Cut off any extra length which could interfere with the dust cap.

17 Install the dust cap, tapping it into place with a rubber mallet.

18 Install the brake caliper support bracket and caliper assembly.

19 Slip the tire/wheel into place and tighten the mounting nuts.

20 Grab the top and bottom of the tire and check the bearings in the same manner as described at the beginning of this Section.

21 Lower the vehicle to the ground and fully tighten the wheel nuts.

38 Underhood hoses check and replacement

Caution: *Replacement of air conditioner hoses should be left to a dealer or a/c specialist who can depressurize the system and perform the work safely.*

1 The high temperature present under the hood can cause deterioration of the numerous rubber and plastic hoses.

2 Periodic inspection should be made for cracking, loose clamps and leaking because some of the hoses are part of the emissions system and can affect the engine's running and idling.

3 Remove the air cleaner if necessary and trace the entire length of each hose. Squeeze the hose to check for cracks and look for swelling, discoloration and leaks.

4 If the vehicle has considerable mileage or one or more of the hoses is suspect, it is a good idea to replace all of the hoses at one time.

5 Measure the length and inside diameter of each hose and obtain and cut the replacement to size. As original equipment hose clamps are often good for only one or two uses, it is a good idea to replace them with screw-type clamps.

6 Replace each hose one at a time to eliminate the possibility of confusion. Hoses attached to the heater system, choke or ported vacuum switches contain radiator coolant so newspapers or rags should be kept handy to catch the spillage when they are disconnected.

7 After installation, run the engine until up to operating temperature, shut it off and check for leaks. After the engine has cooled, retighten all of the screw-type clamps.

39 Fluid changes – 48 month

Power steering

1 Before beginning this maintenance operation, make sure that you have purchased enough new power steering fluid of the recommended type *(see Lubricant Specification and capacities)* to refill the system. You will also need two jackstands, a drain pan, some newspapers and clean rags and common hand tools.

2 Raise the front of the vehicle and support it securely on jackstands. The front wheels must be free to turn from side-to-side, so locate the jackstands accordingly.

3 Working from the top of the engine compartment, position a container of at least one quart capacity under the return and oil cooler tube to reservoir connections.

4 Loosen the hose clamp, pull the tubes apart and allow the fluid to drain into the container. Let the hose hang down under the vehicle so that it will drain into the pan.

5 Start the engine and allow it to idle, then slowly turn the steering wheel from lock-to-lock several times. This will ensure complete draining of the system. Shut off the engine.

6 Once the system has drained completely, reconnect the hoses and tighten the hose clamps.

7 Fill the reservoir to within $\frac{1}{2}$ inch of the top with new power steering fluid of the recommended type.

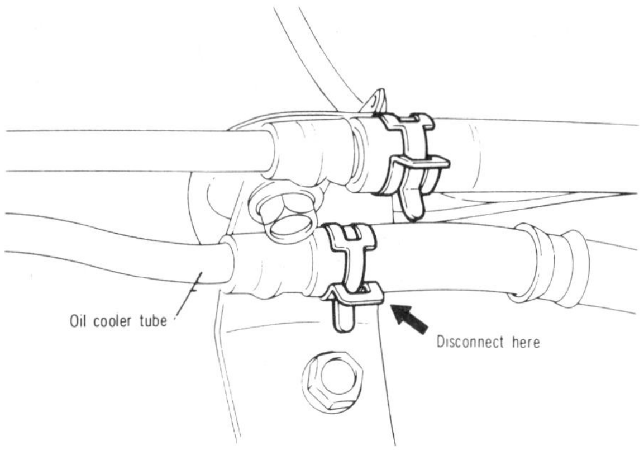

Fig. 1.62 Disconnect return and oil cooler tubes for power steering draining (Sec 39)

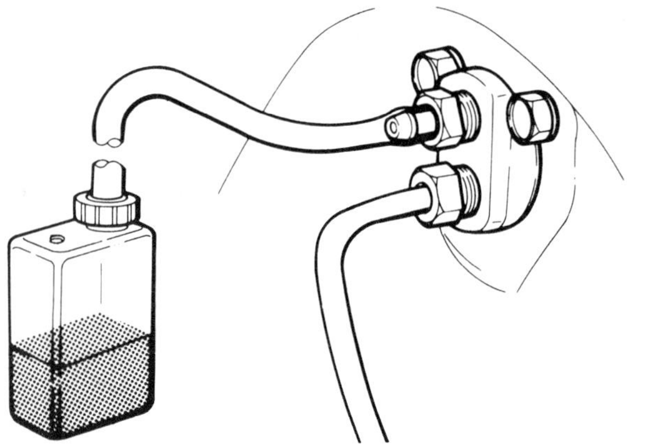

Fig. 1.63 Use vinyl tube and container to drain brakes (Sec 39)

8 Start the engine, allow it to idle and turn the steering wheel from lock-to-lock several times. Check the fluid level and add more as necessary.
9 Repeat the procedures until the level in the reservoir stabilizes.
10 Lower the vehicle and test drive it, then check for leaks at the reservoir hose connections.

Brakes

Caution: *Brake fluid is corrosive to paint. If it is spilled, wipe it up immediately and flush with water.*
11 Since brake fluid absorbs moisture and becomes contaminated in other ways while in use, it should be drained, flushed and filled with new fluid.
12 Before draining the old fluid, make sure you purchase at least twice as much fluid as the holding capacity of the reservoir and that it is the recommended type (see *Capacities and Lubricant Specification)*. Also, obtain enough clear vinyl hose (size to fit bleeder nipple) to cut into four separate two-foot lengths. You will also need four containers of one quart capacity.
13 Remove the reservoir cap and siphon or dip out as much old fluid as you can. Place the nylon tubes on each of the four wheel bleeder screws and place the tubes into the containers.
14 An assistant would be helpful at this point. Refill the brake reservoir with new brake fluid and open all of the bleeder valves. Now, have your assistant pump the brakes while you add new brake fluid to the reservoir.
15 Keep the reservoir level up to the lower level mark. This will keep air entering the system to a minimum which will aid the bleeding procedure later on.
16 Periodically check your farthest drain container during this period to see when all of the old fluid is out of the system. You can usually tell the old fluid from the new. **Note**: *Have your assistant stop pumping the brake pedal as you do this check.*
17 When you feel that the system is completely flushed, retighten the bleeder screws, fill the reservoir and put the reservoir cap back on.
18 Finally, bleed the system according to the procedure in Chapter 9.

Manual steering

19 The manual steering gearbox is normally filled with lubricant for life. Unless a severe leak occurs, necessitating a complete overhaul, changing the lubricant will not be required.
20 The steering gearbox can be drained, but only by completely removing it from the vehicle and draining it through the filler hole. This is not recommended unless the gearbox is being removed for another problem.

Air conditioning

21 The air conditioning system refrigerant can be drained and refilled. **Caution**: *Do not attempt to do this yourself; the refrigerant used is pressurized and can cause serious injuries and respiratory irritation.*
22 Leave any draining/refilling of the air conditioning system to a professional who knows the dangers and how to handle them with the right equipment.

40 Headlight check and adjustment

1 The best and most accurate way to have your headlights checked

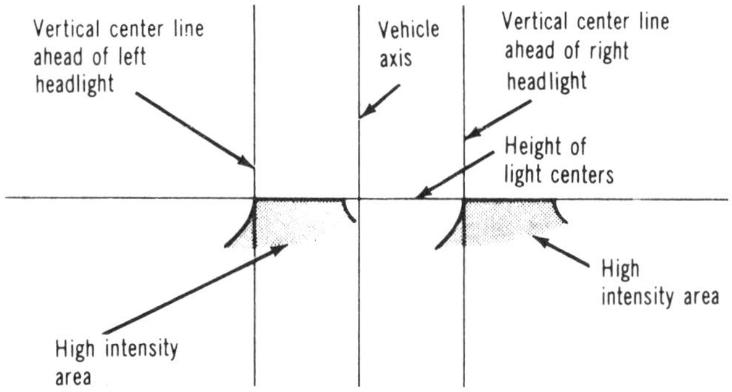

Fig. 1.64 Headlight low-beam adjustment pattern (Sec 40)

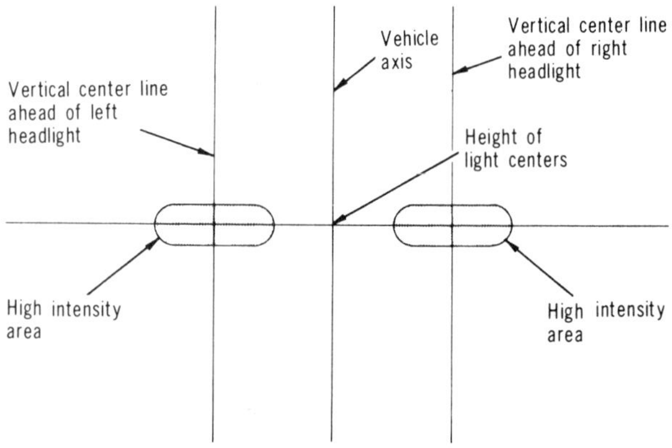

Fig. 1.65 Headlight high-beam adjustment pattern (Sec 40)

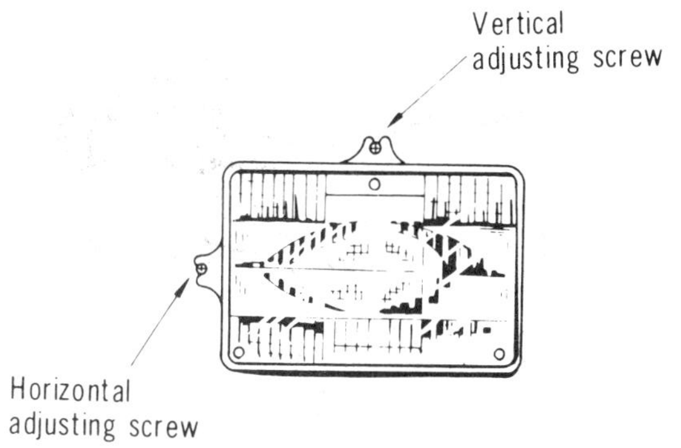

Fig. 1.66 Headlight direction adjustment screws (Sec 40)

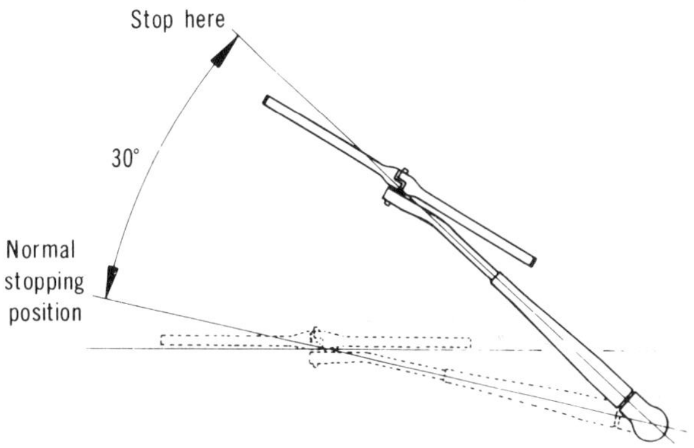

Fig. 1.67 Correct wiper position to check arm alignment (Sec 41)

and adjusted, is to have it done by someone who has the right headlight calibration equipment.

2 The diagrams shown can be used as a quick fix until your headlights can be accurately calibrated. The vehicle must be 25 ft from the wall used for the check and on a level surface.

3 Place a vertical tape on the wall in line with the vehicle centerline. Also, a vertical tape for each headlight.

4 Place a horizontal tape corresponding with the centerline of the headlights. Make adjustment by turning the appropriate adjusting screws.

41 Windshield wiper system check, adjustment and replacement

Wiper blades

1 If the wiping action is jerky and unsatisfactory, check the blade contact against the windshield glass. If it is excessively strong, loosen the arm set nut, remove it and then retighten it.

2 Check the blades and if permanent distortion has occurred, you should replace the blades with new ones.

3 Wet the windshield and see if the water is wiped away completely. If there is water remaining, there is wax or dirt on the glass or the rubber blades. Saturate a sponge in washer fluid and thoroughly clean the glass and blades.

Wiper arms

4 If the jerky movement still persists, you can check the wiper arm alignment. Operate the wipers and then stop them (by using the ignition key) when they are in a position approximately 30° above their normal stopping position.

5 With the wipers in this position, remove the blades, and check the parallel condition of the top end of the arm and the surface of the glass.

6 If your wiper arm seems to be out of alignment, grip the end of the arm with a pair of pliers and carefully twist it until you obtain the desired effect.

7 When installing new wiper blades, be careful not to install them in the reverse direction; this will cause the blades to squeak and prematurely deteriorate.

Washer jets

8 If the position of the washer jet spray is incorrect, adjust by changing the mounting position of the washer nozzle holder.

9 If the amount of fluid coming out of the jet is insufficient or none at all, check the tubes for kinks, the clips for excessive tightness or the fluid to be frozen.

10 The correct mixing ratio for windshield washing fluid for all seasons is four parts washer liquid to one part water. Washer liquid bought in a store has its own antifreeze ingredients to guard against freezing. **Caution**: *Do not add radiator antifreeze. It will damage your vehicle's exterior paint.*

11 Finally, adjust the stopping position of the windshield wipers. Contact of the wipers anywhere other than the windshield for any length of time will cause the rubber of the blades to form to that shape and not wipe the windshield clean.

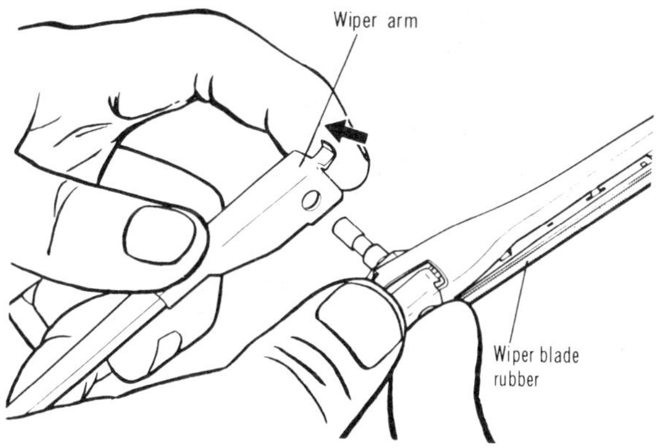

Fig. 1.68 Correct wiper blade installation (Sec 41)

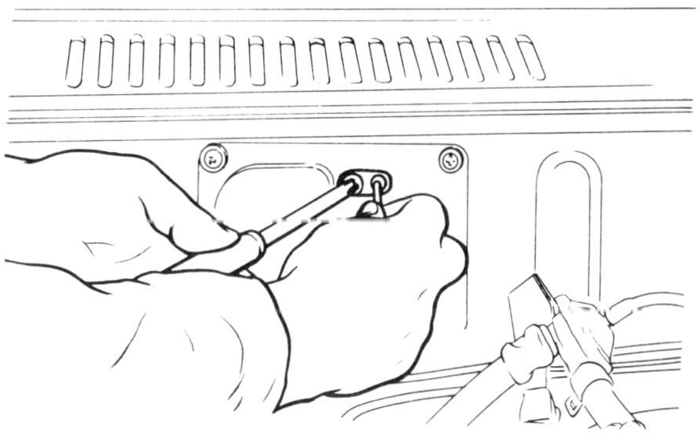

Fig. 1.69 Washer jet position adjustment (Sec 41)

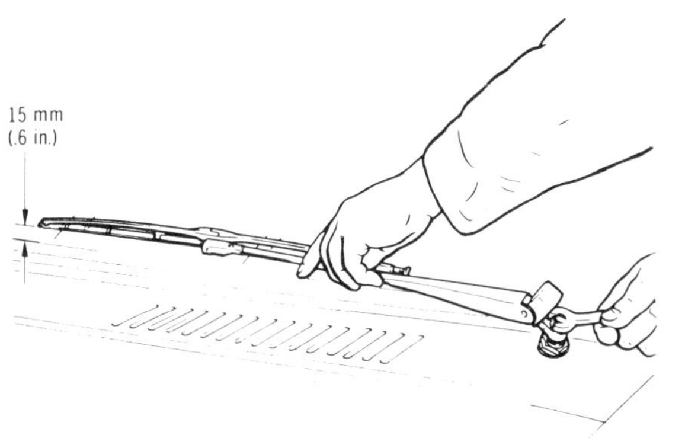

Fig. 1.70 Wiper arm stopping position adjustment (Sec 41)

Chapter 2 Engine

Contents

Specifications

Engine – 4G3 series (1600 cc K-engine)

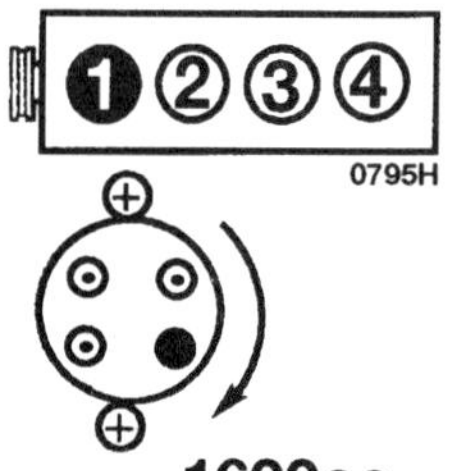

1600cc

Firing order 1-3-4-2

Cylinder location and distributor rotation

General

Bore and stroke	3.03 x 3.39 in (77.0 x 86.1 mm)
Actual displacement	97.5 cu in (1597 cc)
Compression ratio	8.5:1
Compression pressure	149 psi
Maximum Cyl-to-Cyl variation	15 psi
Valve clearances (cold)	
Intake and Jet valves	0.003 in (0.07 mm)
Exhaust valves	0.007 in (0.17 mm)

Cylinder

Standard bore size	3.028 to 3.029 in (76.90 to 76.93 mm)
Out-of-roundness/taper	0.0008 in (0.02 mm) max

Pistons and rings

Standard piston diameter	3.028 in (76.9 mm)
Oversizes available (pistons/rings)	0.010, 0.020, 0.030, 0.039 in (0.25, 0.50, 0.75, 1.00 mm)
Piston-to-cylinder clearance	0.0008 to 0.0016 in (0.02 to 0.04 mm)

Connecting rod

Bend or distortion	0.001 in (0.03 mm) max

Crankshaft

Connecting rod journal diameter	1.772 in (45.0 mm)
Connecting rod bearing oil clearance	0.0004 to 0.0028 in (0.01 to 0.06 mm)
Out-of-roundness/taper	0.0004 in (0.01 mm) max
Bearing undersizes	0.010, 0.020, 0.030 in (0.25, 0.50, 0.75 mm)

Undersize rework dimension of pin	
0.010 in (0.25 mm)	1.7612 to 1.7618 in (44.735 to 44.75 mm)
0.020 in (0.50 mm)	1.7514 to 1.7520 in (44.485 to 44.50 mm)
0.030 in (0.75 mm)	1.7415 to 1.7421 in (44.235 to 44.25 mm)
Undersize rework dimension of main bearing journal	
0.010 in (0.25 mm)	2.2337 to 2.2342 in (56.735 to 56.75 mm)
0.020 in (0.50 mm)	2.2238 to 2.2244 in (56.485 to 56.50 mm)
0.030 in (0.75 mm)	2.2140 to 2.2146 in (56.235 to 56.25 mm)
Runout	0.001 in (0.03 mm) max
Endplay	0.002 to 0.007 in (0.05 to 0.18 mm)

Cylinder head

Warpage	0.004 in (0.1 mm) max
Camshaft bearing oil clearance	0.002 to 0.004 in (0.05 to 0.09 mm)
Camshaft lobe height	
Intake	1.4116 to 1.4316 in (35.86 to 36.36 mm)
Exhaust	1.4197 to 1.4397 in (35.91 to 36.41 mm)
Camshaft endplay	0.002 to 0.006 in (0.05 to 0.15 mm)
Valve margin width	0.039 in (1.0 mm) min
Valve spring free length	1.823 in (46.3 mm)
Preload/length	1.469 in (37.3 mm) at 61.7 lbs

Jet Valve

Stem diameter	0.1693 in (4.3 mm)
Spring free length	1.1654 in (29.6 mm)
Preload/length	0.846 in (21.5 mm) at 55 lbs

Balancer shaft

Front journal diameter	
Right shaft	1.535 in (39.0 mm)
Left shaft	0.728 in (18.5 mm)
Rear journal diameter	1.417 in (36.0 mm)
Bearing oil clearances	
Right shaft front bearing	0.0008 to 0.0024 in (0.02 to 0.06 mm)
All others	0.0016 to 0.031 in (0.04 to 0.08 mm)

Flywheel

Out-of-round	0.005 in (0.13 mm) max

Oil pump (Silent Shaft engine) – refer to illustration

Gear endplay B	0.0024 to 0.0047 in (0.06 to 0.12 mm)
Shaft-to-cover clearance	0.0008 to 0.0019 in (0.02 to 0.05 mm)
Tip clearance A	
Driven gear	0.0039 to 0.0078 in (0.1 to 0.2 mm)
Drive gear	0.0059 to 0.0098 in (0.15 to 0.25 mm)
Maximum tip clearance (both gears)	0.0158 to 0.0275 in (0.4 to 0.7 mm)
Gear-to-bearing side clearance C	0.0008 to 0.0020 in (0.02 to 0.05 mm)
Drive gear-to-rear bearing clearance D	0.0016 to 0.0028 in (0.04 to 0.07 mm)

Oil pump (non-Silent Shaft engine)

Side clearance	0.0024 to 0.0047 in (0.06 to 0.12 mm)
Tip clearance	0.0016 to 0.0047 in (0.04 to 0.12 mm)
Body clearance	0.0039 to 0.0063 in (0.10 to 0.16 mm)
Shaft-to-cover clearance	0.0008 to 0.0020 in (0.02 to 0.05 mm)

Engine – 4G5 series (2000 cc U and 2600 cc F-engines)

General

	U-engine	F-engine
Bore and stroke	3.31 x 3.54 in (84.0 x 90.0 m)	3.59 x 3.86 in (91.1 x 98.0 mm)
Actual displacement	121.7 cid (1995 cc)	155.9 cid (2555 cc)
Compression ratio	8.5:1	8.2:1
Compression pressure	149 psi	149 psi
Maximum cyl-to-cyl variation	15 psi	15 psi
Valve clearance		
Intake (cold) and Jet valves	0.003 in (0.07 mm)	0.003 in (0.07 mm)
Exhaust valves	0.007 in (0.17 mm)	0.007 in (0.17 mm)

Cylinder

Standard bore	3.301 in (84.0 mm)	3.587 in (91.1 mm)
Out-of-roundness/taper	0.0008 in (0.02 mm) max	0.0008 in (0.02 mm) max

Pistons and rings

Standard piston diameter	3.3071 in (84.0 mm)	3.587 in (91.1 mm)
Oversizes available (both engines)	0.010, 0.020, 0.030 0.039 in (0.25, 0.50, 0.75, 1.00 mm)	

Crankshaft	U and F engines
Bend or distortion	0.001 in (0.03 mm) max
Out-of-roundness/taper of pin	0.0004 in (0.01 mm)
Out-of-roundness/taper of main bearing journal	0.0004 in (0.01 mm)
Undersize rework dimension of pin	
0.010 in (0.25 mm)	2.0762 to 2.0768 in (52.735 to 52.75 mm)
0.020 in (0.50 mm)	2.0663 to 2.0669 in (52.485 to 52.50 mm)
0.030 in (0.75 mm)	2.0565 to 2.0571 in (52.235 to 52.25 mm)
Undersize rework dimension of main bearing journal	
0.010 in (0.25 mm)	2.5880 to 2.5886 in (65.735 to 65.75 mm)
0.020 in (0.50 mm)	2.5781 to 2.5787 in (52.485 to 52.50 mm)
0.030 in (0.75 mm)	2.5683 to 2.5689 in (52.235 to 52.25 mm)
End play	0.002 to 0.007 in (0.05 to 0.175 mm)

Cylinder head	
Warpage	0.002 in (0.05 mm) max
Camshaft bearing oil clearance	0.002 to 0.004 in (0.05 to 0.10 mm)
Camshaft lobe height	
Intake	1.660 in (42.18 mm)
Exhaust	1.663 in (42.24 mm)
Endplay of camshaft	0.004 to 0.008 in (0.1 to 0.2 mm)
Thickness of valve head (standard)	
Intake	0.047 in (1.2 mm)
Exhaust	0.079 in (2.0 mm)
Thickness of valve head (minimum)	
Intake	0.028 in (0.7 mm)
Exhaust	0.039 in (1.0 mm)
Valve spring free length	1.869 in (47.5 mm)
Preload/length	1.59 in (40.4 mm) at 61 lbs

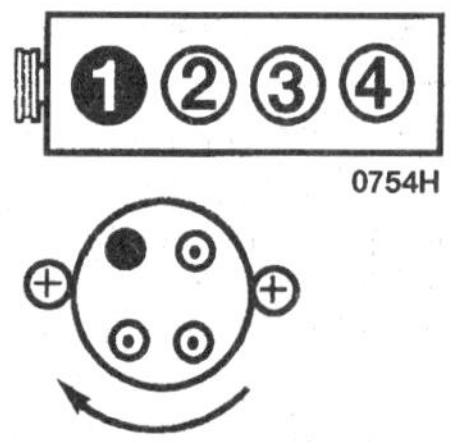

2000cc and 2600cc

Cylinder location and distributor rotation

Jet Valve	
Stem diameter	0.1693 in (4.3 mm)
Spring free length	1.1654 in (29.6 mm)
Preload/length	0.846 in (21.5 mm) at 5.5 lbs

Balancer shaft	
Front journal diameter	0.9055 in (23.0 mm)
Rear journal diameter	1.6929 in (43.0 mm)
Oil clearance	
Front	0.0008 to 0.0024 in (0.02 to 0.06 mm)
Rear	0.0020 to 0.0035 in (0.05 to 0.09 mm)

Flywheel	
Out-of-roundness	0.005 in (0.13 mm) max

Oil pump	
Body-to-gear clearance	0.0041 to 0.0059 in (0.105 to 0.15 mm)
Bearing-to-gear clearance (drive gear rear end)	0.0017 to 0.0026 in (0.044 to 0.066 mm)
Gear endplay	0.0024 to 0.0047 in (0.06 to 0.12 mm)
Bearing-to-gear clearance	0.0008 to 0.0018 in (0.02 to 0.046 mm)

Torque specifications	ft-lb	Nm
Front insulator-to-crossmember bolts	22 to 29	29 to 39
Front insulator-to-engine mount nuts	10 to 14	13 to 19
Rear insulator-to-engine support bracket bolts (U and F engines)	10 to 14	13 to 19
Rear insulator-to-engine support bracket bolts (K engine)	4 to 7	5 to 10
Rear insulator-to-transmission nuts		
1979 models	14 to 17	20 to 23.5
1980 models	11 to 14	15 to 20
Engine support bracket-to-vehicle body bolts	7	9.5
Engine mount-to-engine block bolts (U and F engines)	29 to 36	39 to 49
Engine mount-to-engine block bolts (K engine)	44 to 50	59 to 68
Cylinder head-to-timing chaincase bolt	11 to 15	15 to 21
Cylinder head bolt (U and F engine)	65 to 72	89 to 98
Cylinder head bolt (K engine)	51 to 54	69 to 73
Camshaft bearing cap bolt	14 to 15	17 to 20
Camshaft sprocket bolt (U and F engine)	37 to 43	49 to 58
Camshaft sprocket bolt (K engine)	44 to 57	59 to 78
Valve cover bolts	4 to 5	5 to 6
Heater joint	15 to 28	20 to 39
Main bearing cap bolts (U and F engines)	55 to 61	74 to 83
Main bearing cap bolts (K engine)	37 to 39	49 to 53
Connecting rod cap bolts (U and F engines)	33 to 34	45 to 47
Connecting rod cap bolts (K engine)	24 to 25	32 to 34
Flywheel bolts (M/T only)	94 to 101	128 to 137
Driveplate bolts (A/T only)	83 to 90	112.7 to 121.5

Crankshaft pulley bolt (U and F engines)	80 to 94	108 to 127
Crankshaft pulley bolt (K engine)	7.5 to 8.5	10 to 11
Crankshaft sprocket bolt (K engine)	44 to 50	59 to 68
Oil pump sprocket bolt	22 to 28	29 to 39
Oil pan bolts	4.5 to 5.5	6 to 7
Oil pan drain plug	44 to 57	59 to 78
Oil pump bolts (U and F engines)	6 to 7	8 to 9
Oil pump cover (K engine)	11 to 13	15 to 17
Intake/exhaust manifold nuts	11 to 14	15 to 19
Exhaust pipe-to-manifold nuts	11 to 18	15 to 24
Silent shaft chamber cover bolts (U and F engines)	3 to 4	4 to 5
Silent Shaft sprocket bolts (U and F engines)	22 to 28	29 to 39
Silent Shaft-to-oil pump gear bolt	22 to 28	29 to 39
Oil pressure sending unit	11 to 15	15 to 21
Jet Valve	13 to 15	18 to 21
Timing belt tensioner nut (K engine)	16 to 21	22 to 29

1 General information

The 1600 cc engine (coded K) was available for the years 1978 thru 1980. It has a belt-driven camshaft and is manufactured in two versions; those with the Silent Shaft balancer system and those without it. Lubrication is handled by a trochoid-type oil pump mounted on the front of the engine under the timing belt cover. This oil pump is driven by a cogged-type timing belt.

The 2000 cc engine (coded U) was only available in 1978 and has all the characteristics of the 2600 cc engine. The only difference being displacement, which results from different bore/stroke combinations.

The 2600 cc engine (coded F) was carried from the start in 1978 through to 1983. Both the 2000 cc and 2600 engines have chain-driven camshafts and Silent Shaft balancer systems. Their lubrication is handled by a gear-type pump mounted on the front of the engine under the timing chain cover. This oil pump is driven by the Silent Shaft chain.

The Silent Shaft counterbalancing system cancels the engine's power pulses and produces relatively vibration-free operation.

All engines are in-line vertical four cylinders. Their crankshafts ride in five renewable insert-type main bearings, with the center bearing assigned the additional task of controlling crankshaft end thrust.

Their pistons have two compression rings and one oil control ring. The piston pins are the semi-floating type, being a press fit in the small end of the connecting rod. The connecting rod big ends are also fitted with renewable insert-type plain bearings.

These engines are liquid-cooled, utilizing a centrifugal impeller-type pump driven by a belt from the crankshaft to circulate coolant around the cylinders and combustion chambers and through the intake manifold. The oil is filtered continuously by a cartridge-type filter mounted on the side of the engine.

Only vehicles sold in the US are equipped with a Jet Valve assembly, which reduces certain exhaust emissions.

2 Engine oil and oil filter - check and replacement

See Chapter 1 for the engine oil and oil filter check and replacement.

3 Drivebelt - check, adjustment and replacement

See Chapter 1 for all engines drivebelt checks, adjustments and replacement procedures.

4 Engine compression - check

See Chapter 1 to check the engine compression.

5 Repairs possible with the engine in the vehicle

1 Many major repair operations can be accomplished without removing the engine from the vehicle.

2 It is a very good idea to clean the engine compartment and the exterior of the engine with some type of pressure washer before any work is begun. A clean engine will make the job easier and will prevent the possibility of getting dirt into internal areas of the engine.

3 Remove the hood and cover the fenders to provide as much working room as possible and to prevent damage to the painted surfaces.

4 If oil or coolant leaks develop, indicating a need for gasket or seal replacement, the repairs can generally be made with the engine in the vehicle. The oil pan gasket, the cylinder head gasket, intake and exhaust manifold gaskets, timing chain case gaskets and the front and rear crankshaft oil seals are accessible with the engine in place. In the case of the rear crankshaft oil seal, the transmission, the clutch components and the flywheel must be removed first.

5 Exterior engine components such as the starter motor, the alternator, the distributor, the fuel pump and the carburetor, as well as the intake and exhaust manifolds, are quite easily removed for repair with the engine in place.

6 Since the cylinder head can be removed without pulling the engine, valve servicing can also be accomplished with the engine in the vehicle.

7 Repairs to or inspection of the camshaft, the timing chain/belt assembly, the Silent Shafts and chain/belt assembly and the oil pump are all possible with the engine in place

8 In extreme cases caused by a lack of necessary equipment, repair or replacement of piston rings, pistons, connecting rods and rod bearings and reconditioning of the cylinder bores is possible with the engine in the vehicle. This practice is not recommended because of the cleaning and preparation work that must be done to the components involved.

6 Engine overhaul - general note

1 It is not always easy to determine when, or if, an engine should be completely overhauled, as a number of factors must be considered.

2 High mileage is not necessarily an indication that an overhaul is needed while low mileage, on the other hand, does not preclude the need for an overhaul. Frequency of servicing is probably the single most important consideration. An engine that has regular (and frequent) oil and filter changes, as well as other required maintenance, will most likely give many thousands of miles of reliable service. Conversely, a neglected engine may require an overhaul very early in its life.

3 Excessive oil consumption is an indication that piston rings and/or valve guides are in need of attention. Make sure that oil leaks are not responsible before deciding that the rings and guides are bad. Have a cylinder compression or leak-down test performed by an experienced tune-up mechanic to determine for certain the extent of the work required.

4 If the engine is making obvious knocking or rumbling noises, the connecting rod and/or main bearings are probably at fault. Check the oil pressure with a gauge (installed in place of the oil pressure sending unit. If it is extremely low, the bearings and/or oil pump are probably worn out.

5 Loss of power, rough running, excessive valve train noise and high fuel consumption rates may also point to the need for an overhaul

(especially if they are all present at the same time). If a complete tune-up does not remedy the situation, major mechanical work is the only solution.

6 An engine overhaul generally involves restoring the internal parts to the specifications of a new engine. During an overhaul, the piston rings are replaced and the cylinder walls are reconditioned (rebored and/or honed). If a rebore is done, then new pistons are also required. The main and connecting rod bearings are replaced with new ones and, if necessary, the crankshaft may be reground to restore the journals. Generally, the valves are serviced as well, since they are usually in less-than-perfect condition at this point. While the engine is being overhauled, other components such as the carburetor, the distributor, the starter and the alternator can be rebuilt also. The end result should be a like-new engine that will give as many trouble-free miles as the original.

7 Before beginning the engine overhaul, read through the entire procedure to familiarize yourself with the scope and requirements of the job. Overhauling an engine is not that difficult, but it is time-consuming. Plan on the vehicle being tied up for a minimum of two weeks, especially if parts must be taken to an automotive machine shop for repair or reconditioning. Check on availability of parts and make sure that any necessary special tools and equipment are obtained in advance. Most work can be done with typical shop hand tools, although a number of precision measuring tools are required for inspecting parts to determine if they must be replaced. Often a reputable automotive machine shop will handle the inspection of parts and offer advice concerning reconditioning and replacement. As a general rule, time is the primary cost of an overhaul, so it doesn't pay to install worn or sub-standard parts.

8 As a final note, to ensure maximum life and minimum trouble from a rebuilt engine, everything must be assembled with care in a spotlessly clean environment.

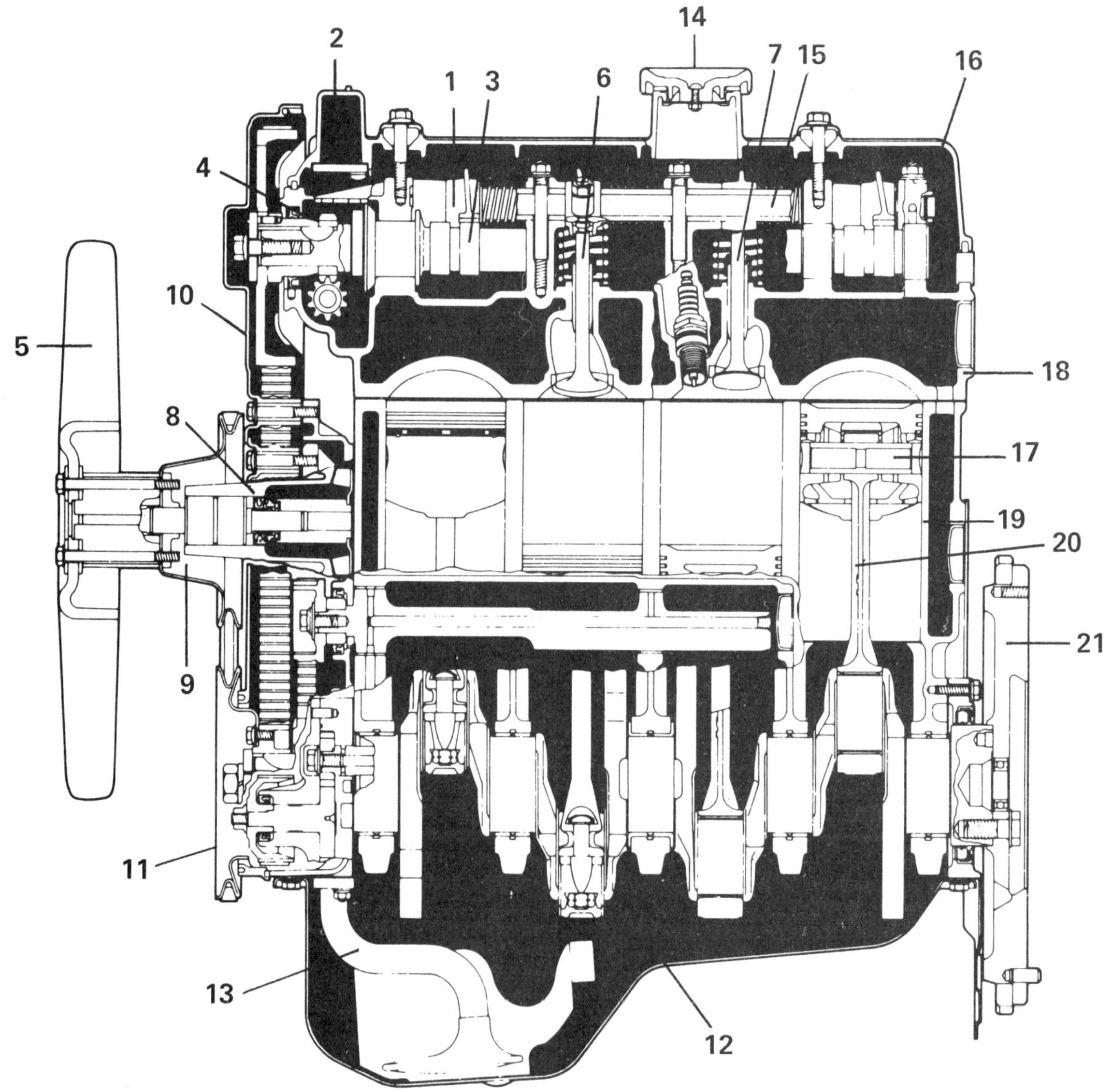

Fig. 2.1 1600 cc engine sectional view

1 Rocker arm	*7 Exhaust valve*	*12 Oil pan*	*17 Piston*
2 Breather	*8 Water pump*	*13 Oil screen*	*18 Cylinder head*
3 Camshaft	*9 Water pump pulley*	*14 Oil filler cap*	*19 Cylinder block*
4 Camshaft sprocket	*10 Belt case*	*15 Rocker arm shaft*	*20 Connecting rod*
5 Cooling fan	*11 Crankshaft pulley*	*16 Rocker cover*	*21 Flywheel*
6 Intake valve			

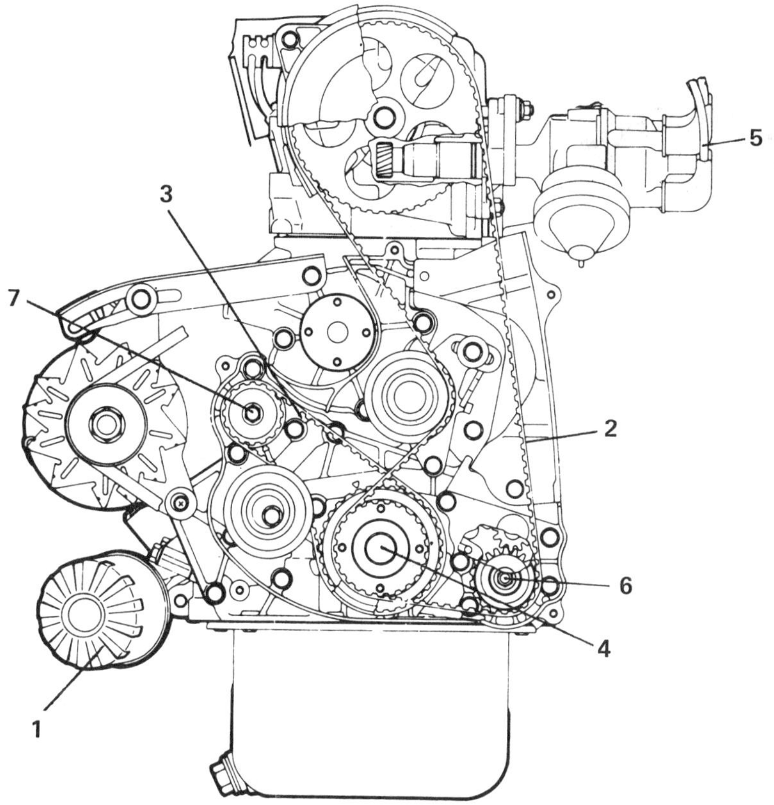

Fig. 2.2 1600 cc engine timing belt train

1 Oil filter
2 Timing belt
3 Silent Shaft belt
4 Crankshaft
5 Distributor
6 Left Silent Shaft
7 Right Silent Shaft

Fig. 2.3 2000 cc and 2600 cc engine sectional view

1 Rocker arm
2 Breather
3 Camshaft
4 Camshaft sprocket
5 Cooling fan
6 Intake valve
7 Exhaust valve
8 Water pump
9 Water pump pulley
10 Chain case
11 Crankshaft pulley
12 Oil pan
13 Oil screen
14 Oil filler cap
15 Rocker arm shaft
16 Rocker cover
17 Piston
18 Cylinder head
19 Cylinder block
20 Connecting rod
21 Flywheel

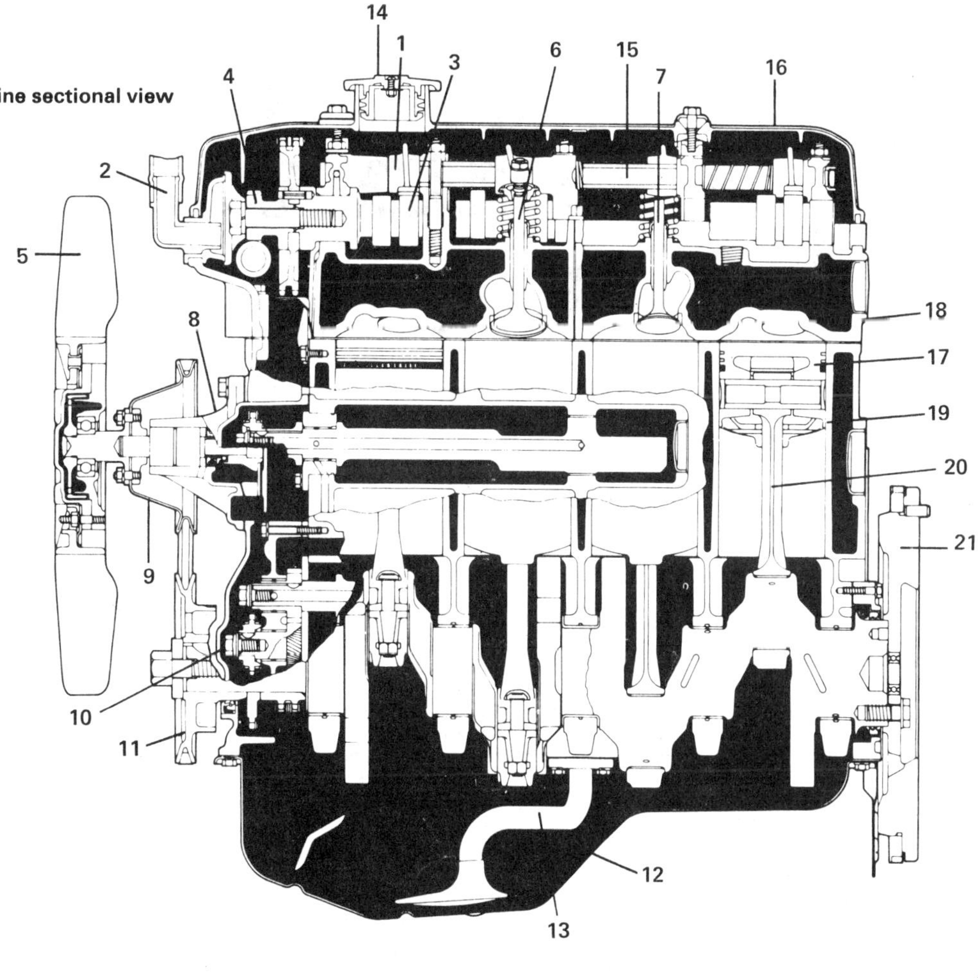

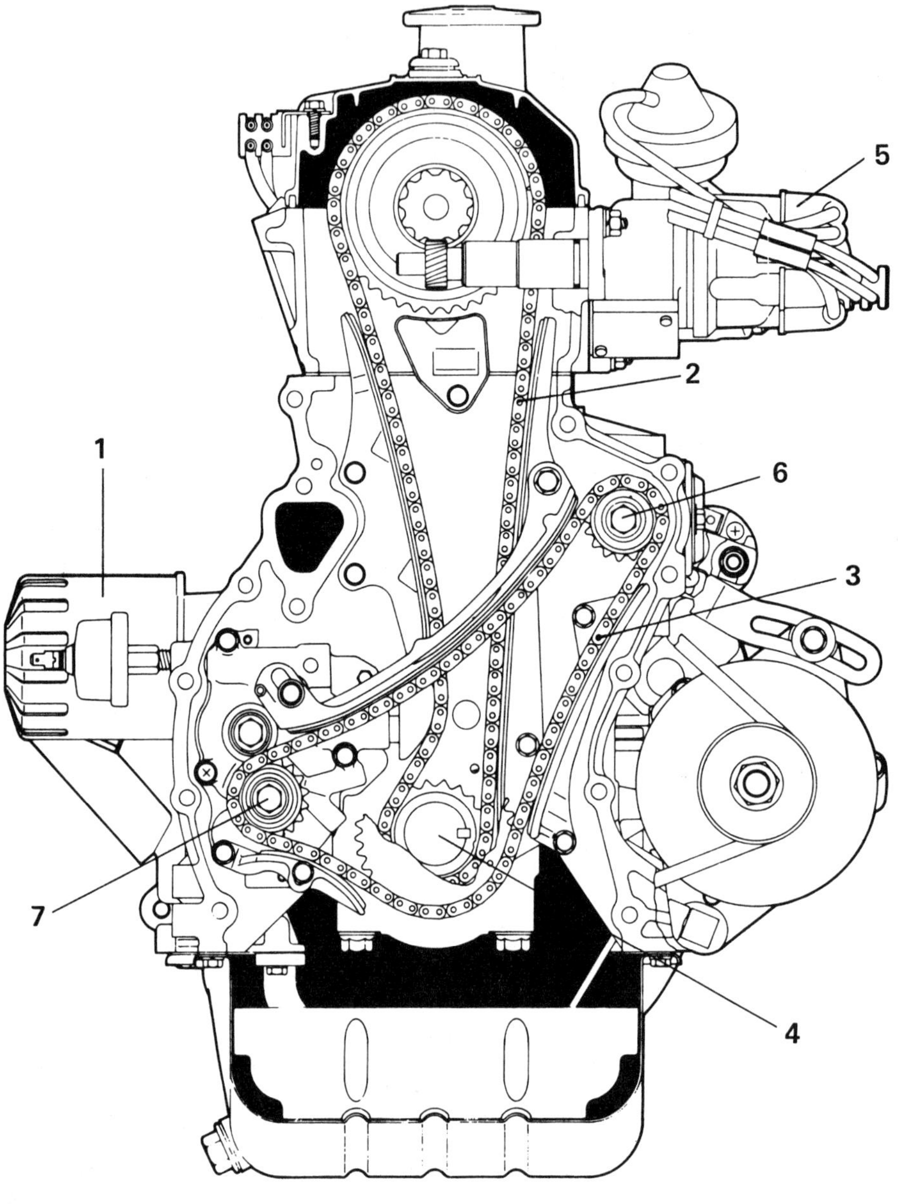

Fig. 2.4 2000 cc and 2600 cc engine timing chain train

1 *Oil filter*
2 *Timing chain*
3 *Silent Shaft chain*
4 *Crankshaft*
5 *Distributor*
6 *Left Silent Shaft*
7 *Right Silent Shaft*

7 Engine – removal

1 The engine can be removed from the vehicle in either of two ways. One would be with the engine and transmission intact, as a unit. The other would be with the engine separated from the transmission before being removed from the vehicle. The procedure outlined here is for removing the engine and transmission as a unit. If you choose to remove only the engine, leaving the transmission in place in the vehicle, refer to Chapter 7 for the procedure to follow for separating the transmission from the engine.

2 Whichever engine removal method is used, a suitable means of lifting the engine must be available. Ideally, a small crane mounted on wheels should be rented or borrowed. These are readily available, and easy to use. An alternative would be to suspend a chain fall or cable hoist from the garage ceiling beams, or a framework fabricated from large timbers. Regardless of which type of hoist support is utilized, it must be strong enough to support the full weight of the engine and transmission. Do not take chances or cut corners here, as serious injury and damage to the engine and vehicle could result.

3 The following sequence of operations does not necessarily need to be performed in the order given. It is, rather, a checklist of everything that must be disconnected or removed before the engine and transmission can be lifted out of the vehicle. If your vehicle is equipped with an automatic transmission the engine removal procedure will be slightly different. It is very important that all linkages, electrical wiring, hoses and cables are removed or disconnected before attempting to lift the engine clear of the vehicle, so double-check everything thoroughly.

4 Scribe or mark with paint the location of the hood hinge brackets on the hood (to ensure proper alignment of the hood upon reinstallation). Loosen and remove the bolts attaching the hood to the brackets and lift the hood carefully away from the vehicle (with the help of an assistant).

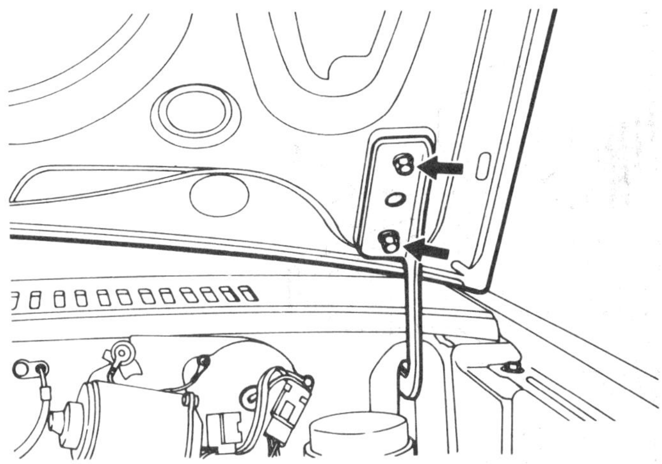

Fig. 2.5 Mark and remove hood from hinges (Sec 7)

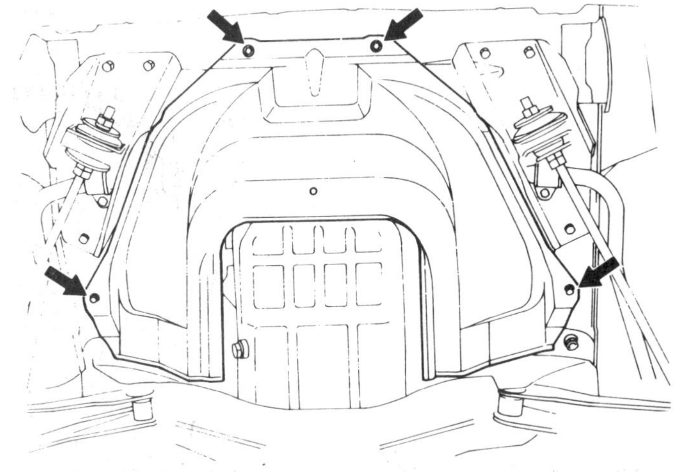

Fig. 2.6 Engine mud cover removal (Sec 7)

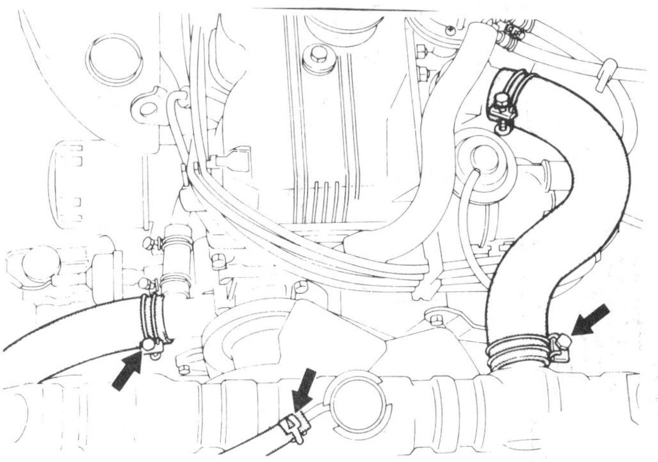

Fig. 2.7 Radiator hoses removal (Sec 7)

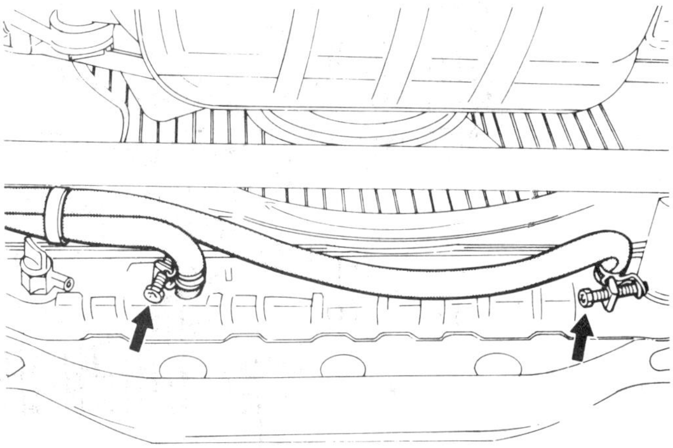

Fig 2.8 Automatic transmission oil cooler lines removal (Sec 7)

5 Raise the vehicle and set it on jackstands. (Refer to *Jacking and Towing).*

6 Disconnect both battery cables from the battery (negative first, then positive), remove the battery hold-down and lift the battery out of the vehicle.

7 Remove the mud cover under the engine.

8 Drain the engine oil and the transmission lubricant (refer to Chapter 1).

9 Remove the radiator pressure cap, then drain the coolant from the radiator and the engine block. The radiator drain petcock is located on the lower left side of the radiator. The engine block drain is located on the lower right side of the engine, underneath the exhaust manifold. Once the coolant has been drained, removed the radiator hoses by loosening and sliding back the hose clamps and pulling the hoses off the radiator and engine. If your vehicle is equipped with an automatic transmission, disconnect and plug the transmission fluid cooling lines at the bottom of the radiator. Do not allow any dirt to enter the lines or fittings.

10 If your vehicle is equipped with a fan shroud, remove both the upper and lower sections. Each section is held in place by bolts and a sheetmetal screw.

11 Remove the bolts attaching the fan clutch to the water pump flange and lift the fan and clutch assembly away from the engine.

12 Remove the bolts attaching the radiator to the vehicle (photo), and

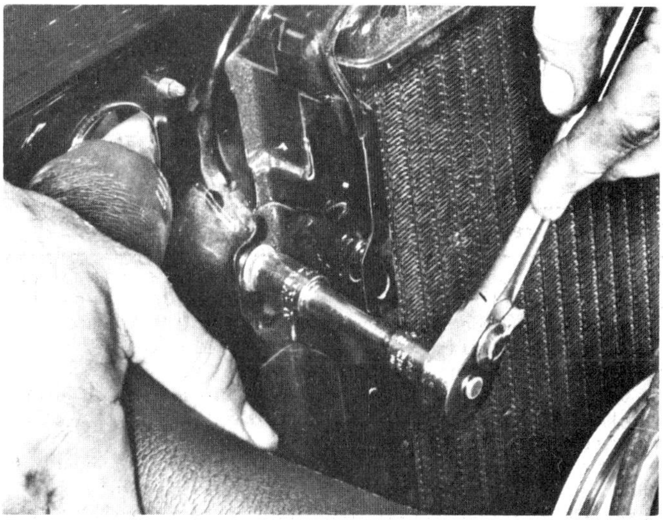

7.12 Remove the radiator mounting bolts

2

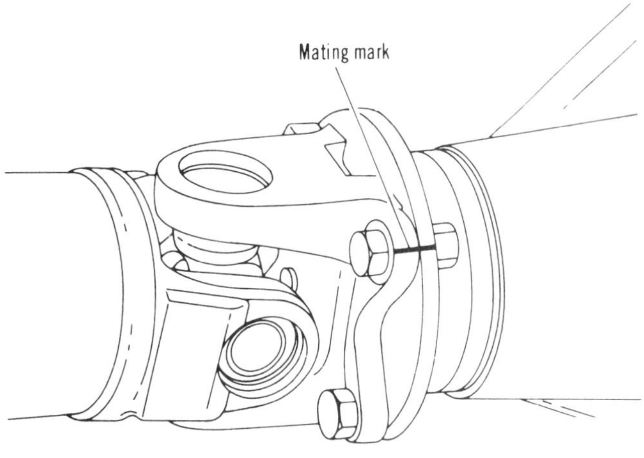

Fig. 2.9 Match mark the driveshaft universal (Sec 7)

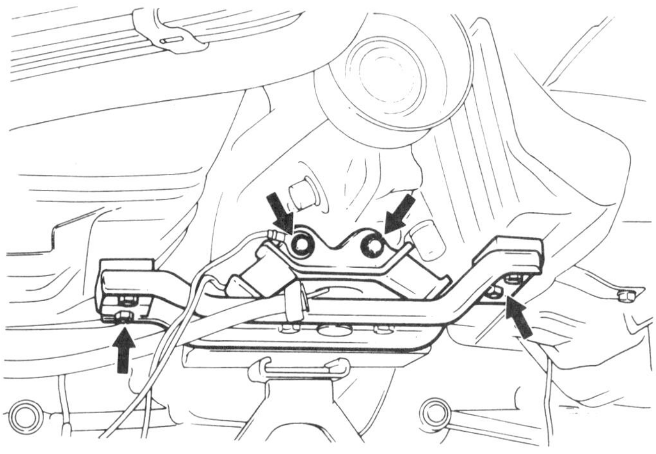

Fig. 2.10 Rear engine supports removal (Sec 7)

remove the overflow tube where it attaches at the radiator filler neck. Lift the radiator out of the vehicle and store it where it will not be damaged.

13 Remove the rubber snorkel connecting the air cleaner housing to the headlight support channel.

14 Disconnect the wire from the oil pressure sending unit on the right side of the engine (photo).

15 If the vehicle is equipped with power steering, remove the nut and the washer attaching the pulley to the power steering pump shaft (photo). Loosen the power steering pump pivot bolts and the adjusting bolt. Remove the drive belt from the pulley and slide the pulley off the front of the power steering pump shaft. Remove the pivot bolts and the adjustment bolt and pull the power steering pump, with the hoses still attached, out of the mounting bracket. Tie the pump out of the way, making sure that the hoses are not kinked or twisted.

16 On vehicles sold in the US only, remove the nut attaching the heat shield to the right front engine mount (photo) and lift the heat shield away from the engine.

17 Remove the electrical ground strap connecting the firewall heat shield to the exhaust manifold.

18 Remove the top cover from the air cleaner. It is held in place by spring clips and a wing nut. Lift out the filter element. Disconnect the various hoses leading to the air cleaner housing and remove the air cleaner housing from the engine.

19 Pull the vacuum hose off of the purge control valve (photo), then remove the carburetor float bowl vent hose (at the valve cover) (photo) and the bracket that supports the purge hose (photo).

20 Remove the throttle cable housing brackets at the carburetor and the valve cover (photo), and disconnect the throttle cable from the carburetor.

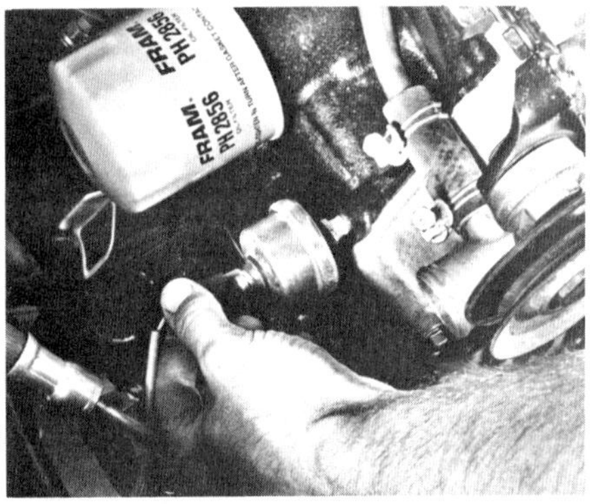

7.14 Disconnect wire from the oil pressure sending unit

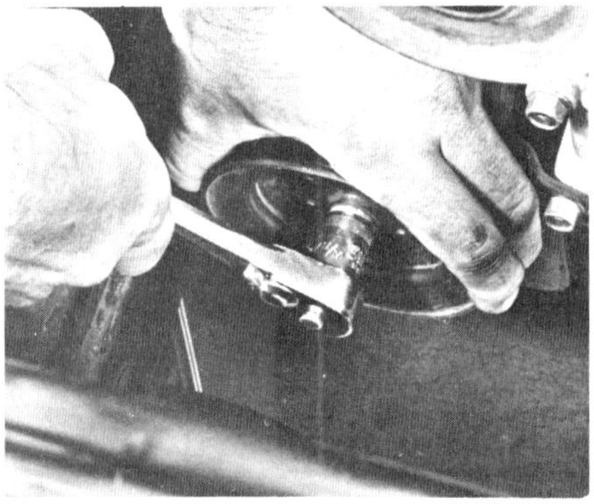

7.15 Remove the power steering pump drive pulley

7.16 Remove the heat shield from the right motor mount

7.19a Remove the vacuum hose from the purge control valve

7.19b Remove the carburetor float bowl vent hose

7.19c Remove the purge hose bracket

7.20 Remove the throttle cable bracket from the valve cover

7.21 Remove the heater hose from the intake manifold

7.22a Remove the power brake vacuum hose from the intake manifold

7.22b Remove the vacuum hoses from the throttle positioner and the air switching valve

7.25 Disconnect the fuel hoses from the carburetor

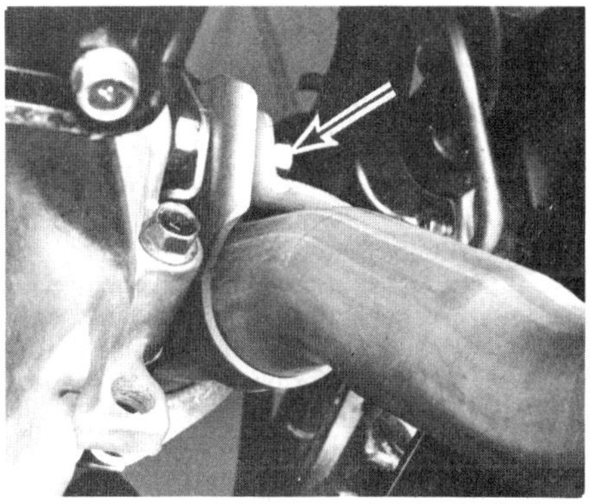
7.26 Remove the exhaust pipe bracket bolt (arrow)

21 Disconnect the heater hoses from the intake manifold fitting (photo) and the water pump transfer tube fitting at the rear of the engine.
22 Disconnect the power brake vacuum hose from the intake manifold fitting (photo). Disconnect the vacuum hose from the diaphragm at the left rear corner of the carburetor (a/c only). Disconnect the vacuum hose (color-coded yellow) from the air switching valve on the front left corner of the carburetor (photo).
23 Disconnect the electrical connector just below and to the left of the carburetor. Remove the wire from the coolant temperature sending unit just behind the distributor. Remove the coil wire from the center tower of the distributor and unplug the primary circuit connector on the distributor body.
24 If your vehicle is equipped with air conditioning, disconnect the air conditioning compressor electrical lead. Remove the compressor and tie it out of the way.
25 Disconnect and plug the fuel hoses at the fuel pump, and the fuel hoses at the carburetor (photo). Disconnect the plastic tie-wraps, as necessary, to separate the fuel hoses, vacuum lines and electrical wiring. Slip all the belts off their pulleys and lift off the water pump pulley.
26 Remove the exhaust pipe by referring to Section 12 (photo).
27 Match mark the universal joint flange yoke and the transmission flange yoke. Remove the bolts retaining the universal to the transmission and carefully lay the front of the driveshaft on the ground.
28 Disconnect the speedometer cable where it enters the transmission (photo). Bend back the retaining strap that holds the speedometer cable housing to the frame crossmember and pull the speedometer cable away from the engine and transmission. Lay it on top of the left frame rail to keep it out of the way. Push forward on the parking brake lever and disengage the cable from the lever. Loosen the parking brake cable housing clamp in front of the frame crossmember and slide the cable housing forward to free the cable from the support bracket on the crossmember. Lay the cable on top of the left frame rail to keep it out of the way. Remove the pin attaching the rear parking brake cable balancer to the parking brake lever.
29 Disconnect the wiring harness from the back-up light switch, just behind the steering box. Disconnect the clutch cable from the clutch control lever at the transmission bellhousing. Back off the clutch cable adjuster and put as much free play as possible in the cable. Pull the rubber dust cover from the end of the clutch cable and slip the clutch cable through the mounting boss on the transmission bellhousing. Lay the clutch cable on top of the left frame rail to keep it out of the way.
30 Disconnect the bayonet-type connector from the starter solenoid on the lower left side of the engine. Disconnect the battery lead from the solenoid.

2

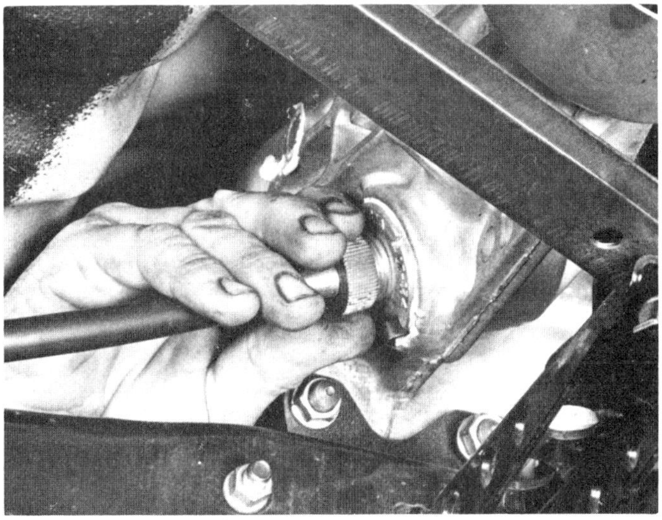
7.28 Disconnect the speedometer cable from the transmission

7.33 Loosen the transmission support crossmember bolts

7.36 Remove the gearshift control lever assembly

31 Disconnect the bayonet-type connector and the battery lead from the alternator. Tie the electrical harness out of the way, so that it will not interfere with the engine removal. Separate the battery ground cable from the engine block immediately behind the alternator. Remove the alternator pivot and adjusting bolts and lift the alternator away from the engine.
32 Remove the fuel line retaining strap from the left motor mount. At this point, double-check all around the engine to make sure that all electrical harnesses, vacuum lines, fuel lines, hoses, cables, and so forth, have been disconnected or removed.
33 Loosen the bolts holding each of the motor mounts to the frame and loosen, but do not remove, the bolts on each side of the crossmember that supports the rear of the transmission where it connects to the frame rails (photo). Also, remove the nuts on the transmission mount at the top of the crossmember.
34 If your vehicle is equipped with a center console, remove the screws that attach it to the vehicle. Loosen the jam nuts on the shift lever and unscrew the shift knob. Lift the console away from the shift lever and unplug the electrical connector behind the console.
35 Remove the screws that attach the shifter boot retainer plate to the tunnel. Lift off the retainer plate and pull back the rubber boot. It has a lip that fits over the sheet metal of the tunnel. Take care not to tear it as you pull the boot back.
36 Remove the bolts attaching the control lever assembly to the transmission (photo) and slip the control lever assembly off. If your vehicle is equipped with a 5-speed transmission, place the shift lever in First gear before removing the control lever assembly.
37 Support the transmission with a jack or some other suitable support and remove the bolts and nuts on the transmission support crossmember.
38 Secure a short length of heavy chain between the hoisting brackets on the engine. Attach the engine hoist lifting hook to the chain and raise the hoist slightly to take the weight off the front motor mounts. Remove the bolts from each of the motor mounts and carefully hoist the engine while the jack supporting the transmission is removed. Gradually move the engine up and forward by moving the hoist and lower the transmission. Continue hoisting the engine until it clears the front of the vehicle, then pull forward on the hoist. Do not allow the engine to swing freely. Lower the engine to the floor.

8 Engine mounts – inspection and replacement

1 Now, with the engine removed, is a good time to inspect the metal and especially the rubber mounts on which the engine rests.
2 Check the support insulators and rubber pads for cracks and splitting.
3 Make sure that the mounting brackets are not bent or cracked near the weld seams. Replace any parts, if necessary, with new ones.

9 Separating the engine and transmission

1 Remove the splash shield from the bottom of the transmission bellhousing and block the engine and transmission securely in an upright position.
2 Remove the starter motor from the left side of the bellhousing. It is held in place by bolts.
3 Remove the bolts attaching the transmission to the engine block.
4 Support the transmission near the front and pull straight back until it is completely free from the engine. If it is allowed to fall, damage to the input shaft could result.

10 Engine disassembly/reassembly – general note

1 To completely disassemble the engine, remove the following items in the order given:

Engine external components	*(Section 11)*
Oil pan and screen	*(Section 13)*
Camshaft and rocker arms	*(Section 15)*
Cylinder head	*(Section 17)*
Valves and Jet Valves	*(Section 19)*
Timing belt/chain and sprockets	*(Section 21 or 22)*
Silent Shaft belt/chain and sprockets	*(Section 25 or 26)*
Left Silent Shaft	*(Section 28)*
Oil pump and right Silent Shaft	*(Section 30 or 32)*
Pistons and connecting rods	*(Section 34)*
Crankshaft	*(Section 35)*

2 Engine reassembly is basically the reverse of disassembly. Install the following items in the order given:

Crankshaft	*(Section 35)*
Pistons and connecting rods	*(Section 34)*
Oil pump and right Silent Shaft	*(Section 30 or 32)*
Left Silent Shaft	*(Section 28)*
Silent Shaft belt/chain and sprockets	*(Section 25 or 26)*
Timing belt/chain and sprockets	*(Section 21 or 22)*
Valves and Jet Valves	*(Section 19)*
Cylinder head	*(Section 17)*
Camshaft and rocker arms	*(Section 15)*
Oil pan and screen	*(Section 13)*
Engine external components	*(Section 11)*

11 External engine components – removal and installation

Removal

Note: *When removing the external components from the engine, pay close attention to details that may be helpful or important during*

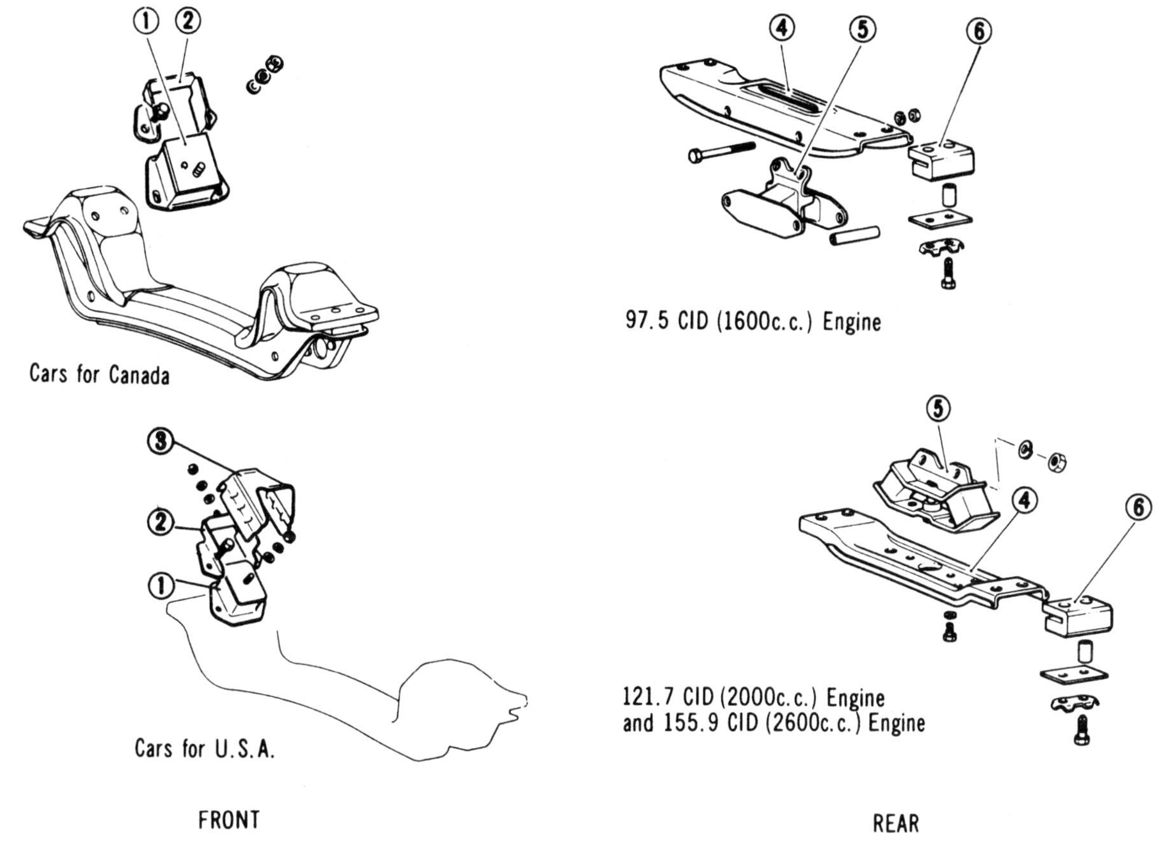

Fig. 2.11 Engine mountings – exploded view (Sec 8)

1 Front insulator
2 Roll restrictor
3 Heat deflection plate
4 Engine support bracket (rear)
5 Rear insulator
6 Pad

2

installation. Look for the correct positioning of gaskets, seals, spacers, pins, washers, bolts and other small items. If necessary, refer to the illustrations and use them as a guide during disassembly.

1 It is much easier to dismantle and repair the engine if it is mounted on a portable-type engine stand. These stands can often be rented, for a reasonable fee, from an equipment rental yard.
2 If a stand is not available, it is possible to dismantle the engine with it blocked up on a sturdy workbench or on the floor. Be extra careful not to tip or drop the engine when working without a stand.
3 Before the engine can be mounted on a stand, the flywheel, the dust shield and the rear seal housing must be removed. Remove the flywheel and dust shield by referring to Chapter 7A, then loosen and remove the bolts attaching the seal housing to the rear of the engine block and the oil pan. Carefully remove the housing. Try not to let the oil separator inside the seal housing fall out of place. To prevent confusion during reassembly note how the oil separator is installed. You may have to tap the seal housing lightly with a soft-faced hammer to break it loose. Do not pry between the seal housing and engine block, as damage to the gasket sealing surfaces may result. At this point, the engine is ready to mount on the stand.
4 Remove the left engine mount insulator and metal roll restrictor. They are attached by a nut. Remove the bolts attaching the left engine mounting bracket to the engine block and remove the engine mount bracket. Next, remove the insulator, the roll restrictor and the motor mount bracket from the right side of the engine. Store the right and left motor mount bracket components separately to avoid confusion during reassembly. Be sure to inspect the metal parts for cracks and the rubber parts for deterioration and delamination from the metal. If any defects are found, replace the parts with new ones.
5 If your vehicle is equipped with air conditioning, remove the upper and lower compressor brackets from the engine block. Remove the air conditioning idler pulley bracket from the upper right side of the engine.
6 Remove the bolts and lift the power steering pump bracket away from the lower right side of the engine.
7 Pull the crankcase emissions control system hose off the fitting at the rear of the valve cover and release it from the clamp on the valve cover. Remove the bowl vent tube from the metal pipe attached to the valve cover. Remove the rubber hose connecting the fitting at the rear of the intake manifold to the coolant transfer tube.
8 Remove the nuts and bolt attaching the intake manifold to the engine cylinder head and lift the manifold and the carburetor, as an assembly, from the head. Note the position of the engine hoisting bracket attached to the rear intake manifold studs.
9 Remove the nuts attaching the fuel pump to the cylinder head, and slip off the fuel pump and the insulator.
10 Remove the distributor cap by depressing and turning the spring loaded screws on the cap. Remove the distributor mounting nut and slip the distributor out of the engine by pulling straight out on it.
11 Loosen and slide back the hose clamp on the rubber hose connecting the water pump to the coolant transfer tube. Remove the bolts attaching the water pump to the front of the engine and pull the water pump off. You may have to tap lightly on the pump body with a soft-faced hammer to break the gasket seal.
12 Remove the coolant transfer tube. It is held in place by a bracket on the right side of the engine and a bracket at the rear of the engine.
13 Unscrew and remove the oil pressure sending unit at the right front side of the engine.
14 Remove the bolts attaching the spark plug lead brackets to the valve cover and lift the distributor cap and spark plug leads away from the engine as an assembly.
15 Unscrew and remove the oil filter and take out the oil dipstick. Remove the exhaust manifold by referring to Section 12.

Installation

16 Once the engine has been assembled to the point where all internal parts, the timing chain cover, the oil pan and the cylinder head are in place, the exterior components can be installed. At this point, if the engine is mounted on a stand, it should be removed from the stand so that the rear oil seal housing can be installed.
17 Lubricate the seal contact surface of the flange at the rear of the crankshaft with multi-purpose grease.
18 After noting which side is facing out, use a hammer and punch to drive the oil seal out of the housing. Lay a new seal in place (with the correct side out) and seat it in the housing with a hammer and a block of wood. Tap the seal around its entire circumference to seat it squarely in the housing.
19 Place the oil separator into the housing with the oil hole facing down (toward the bottom of the case) and the tabs pointing out. One or two strategically-placed dabs of heavy grease will help keep the separator positioned properly.
20 Apply a thin, even coat of silicone-type gasket sealer to both sides of the new gasket and to the exposed portion of the oil pan gasket, then install the oil seal housing. Make sure the oil separator does not fall out of place. Tap the seal housing very gently with a soft-faced hammer (photo) to seat it properly. Install the attaching bolts and tighten them securely.
21 Install the dust shield and the flywheel by referring to Chapter 7A and slip the oil dipstick into its tube.
22 After coating its threads with a thread sealant or sealing tape, screw the oil pressure sending unit into the block and tighten it securely (photo).
23 Lubricate the rubber gasket on the new oil filter and install it on the engine.
24 Install the motor mount brackets, the insulator and the roll restrictors into place on the block. The insulators have alignment pins which must fit into the holes in the brackets. Tighten the bolts/nuts to the specified torque (photo).
25 Attach the air conditioner compressor brackets to the block and tighten the bolts securely (if so equipped).
26 Install the water pump and tighten the mounting bolts securely. Be sure to coat both sides of the gasket with silicone-type gasket sealer. Install the rubber hose and the coolant transfer tube.
27 Install the hose clamps and tighten the transfer tube mounting bolts.
28 Install the air conditioner idler pulley and the power steering pump bracket (if so equipped).
29 Next, install the fuel pump. Use a new gasket and coat both sides with silicone-type gasket sealer. Tighten the mounting nuts securely.
30 Coat both sides of the areas immediately around the coolant passages in the intake manifold gasket with a silicone-type gasket sealer, then install the intake manifold/carburetor assembly in place on the engine. Do not allow any gasket sealer to get in the jet air passages in the manifold and head.
31 Slip the engine hoisting bracket into place on the rear studs (photo) then install the nuts (and the bolt) and tighten them to the specified torque. When tightening, start at the center of the manifold and work out toward the ends. Tighten each fastener in sequence, a little at a time, until they are all at the specified torque.
32 Slip the rubber coolant hose onto the intake manifold spigot (photo) and tighten the hose clamps securely.
33 Using a new gasket, install the exhaust manifold and tighten the nuts to the specified torque. Be sure to install the engine hoist bracket to the front (photo) and the SAS pipe bracket and electrical ground strap to the rear of the manifold (photo) before tightening the nuts. When tightening, start at the center of the manifold and work out toward the ends. Tighten each nut in sequence, a little at a time, until they are all at the specified torque.
34 Attach the heat shields to the exhaust manifold (photo). The bolts that hold the upper shield in place must have the large washers on them.
35 Coat the Secondary Air Supply System air pipe fitting threads with an anti-seize compound, then thread the fitting into the top of the exhaust manifold and tighten it finger tight. Install the air pipe bracket bolt, then tighten the fitting and the bolt securely.
36 Make sure the number 1 piston is at top dead center on the

11.20 Tap the rear oil seal housing with a soft-faced hammer

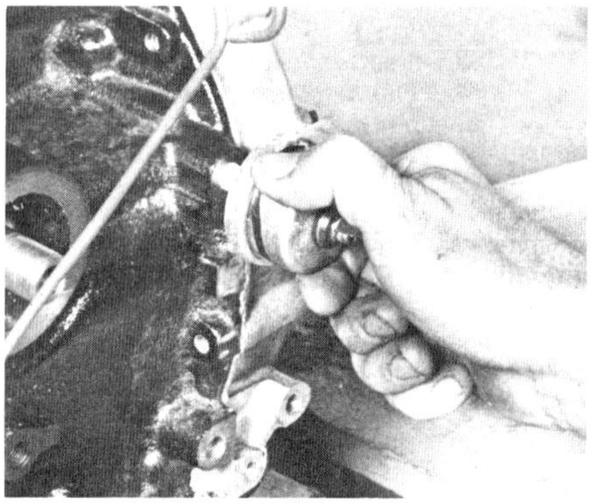

11.22 Install the oil pressure sending unit

11.24 Install the insulator (note the alignment pin)

11.31 Install the engine hoisting bracket before tightening the intake manifold nuts

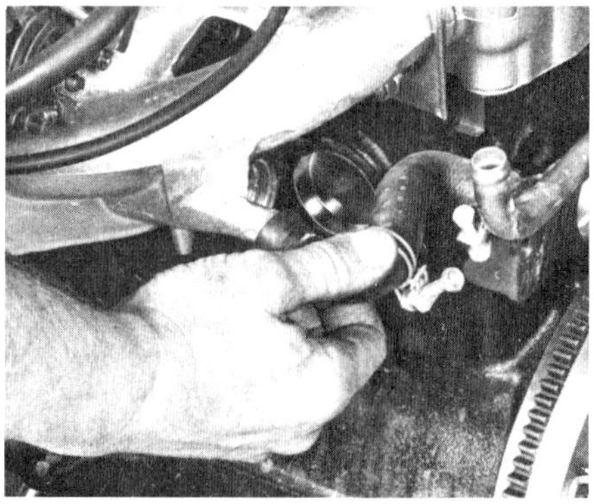

11.32 Install the coolant hose onto the intake manifold

11.33a Install the engine hoisting bracket onto the front exhaust manifold mounting studs

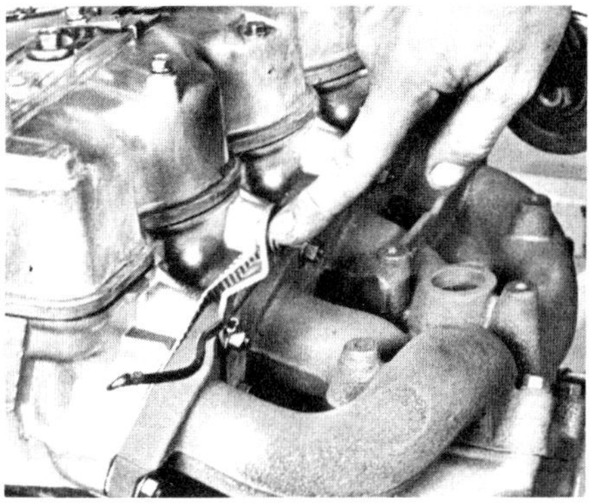

11.33b Attach the SAS pipe bracket and the grounding strap to the rear exhaust manifold studs

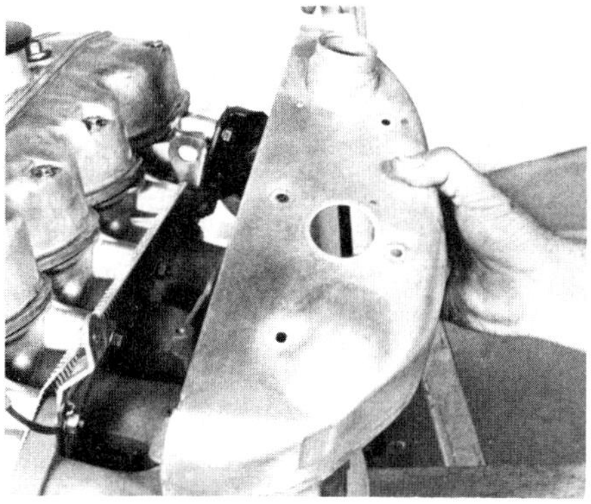

11.34 Install the upper heat shield to the exhaust manifold

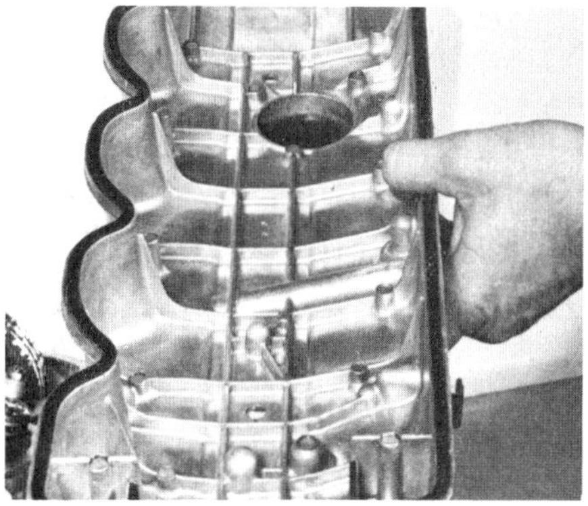

11.39 Install the new valve cover seal

compression stroke, then install the distributor. Line up the mating marks on the distributor housing (a line) and the driven gear (a punch mark). Slide the distributor into place in the cylinder head while lining up the mark on the distributor hold-down flange with the center of the stud. Make sure the distributor is completely seated, then install the mounting nut and tighten it securely.
37 Remove the valve cover. Coat the sealing surfaces of the cylinder head with silicone-type gasket sealer, then install the breather at the front and the semi-circular seal at the rear of the head.
38 Add the specified amount of the recommended type of oil to the engine. Pour it directly over the camshaft so that the lobes are thoroughly lubricated.
39 Coat the valve cover gasket sealing surface of the breather at the front of the head with silicone-type gasket sealer. Lay a new rubber seal in place in the valve cover and install the cover in place on the engine. Install the attaching bolts, using new rubber seals and tighten them securely (photo).
40 Slip the rubber carburetor bowl vent tube onto the metal tube mounted on the valve cover, then slide the hose clamp into place. Attach the crankcase breather hose to the spigot at the rear of the valve cover.
41 Attach the clutch, the starter motor and the transmission to the engine.

12 Exhaust pipe/manifold – removal and installation

1 Remove the nuts and washers holding the exhaust pipe to the exhaust manifold and remove the bolt attaching the exhaust pipe bracket to the transmission bellhousing (photo).
2 Remove the bolts at the exhaust pipe-to-muffler flange and the bolt at the rear exhaust pipe mounting bracket, immediately in front of the muffler.
3 Lift the exhaust pipe out from under the vehicle and set it aside.
4 Remove the exhaust pipe bracket from the right side of the transmission bellhousing.
5 Take off the Secondary Air Supply System air pipe by removing the bracket bolts and the fitting on top of the exhaust manifold. Separate the heat shields attached to the exhaust manifold.
6 Remove the nuts attaching the manifold to the head and lift the exhaust manifold away from the engine.
7 Installation is the reverse of removal.

13 Oil pan and screen – removal and installation

Note: *The following procedure is best done with the engine turned upside-down.*

Removal

1 Remove the bolts securing the oil pan to the engine block.
2 Tap on the pan with a soft-faced hammer, to break the gasket seal, and lift the oil pan off the engine.
3 Using a gasket scraper, scrape off all traces of the old gasket from the engine block, the timing chain cover and the oil pan. Be especially careful not to nick or gouge the gasket sealing surface of the timing chain cover as it is made of aluminum and is quite soft.
4 Remove the bolts holding the oil screen in place. Remove the screen.
5 Clean and inspect the pan and screen by referring to Section 14.

Installation

6 Turn the engine upside-down.
7 Before installing the oil pan, apply a thin coat of silicone-type gasket sealer to the engine block sealing surfaces. Lay a new oil pan gasket in place and carefully apply a coat of gasket sealer to the exposed side of the gasket.
8 Gently lay the oil pan in place. Be careful not to disturb the gasket. Install the bolts. Start with the bolts closest to the center of the pan and tighten them to the specified torque using a criss-cross pattern. Do not overtighten them or leakage may occur.

14 Oil pan and screen – inspection

1 Thoroughly clean the oil pan and screen in solvent and wipe dry. 2
2 Inspect the exterior of the pan for signs of damage or excessive rust. Check the gasket sealing surface for distortion. If any of these things are evident, a new pan must be obtained.
3 Check the oil screen for failure, damage or cracking. If it is defective, replace it with a new one.

15 Camshaft and rocker arms – removal and installation

Removal

1 Remove the bolts, washers and rubber seals attaching the valve cover to the cylinder head and lift off the cover. Remove the breather grommet from the front of the cylinder head and the circular seal from the rear of the cylinder head.

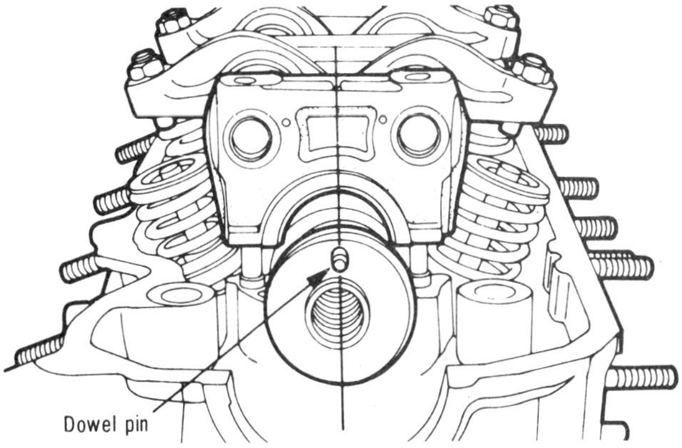

Fig. 2.12 Correct camshaft installation (Sec 15)

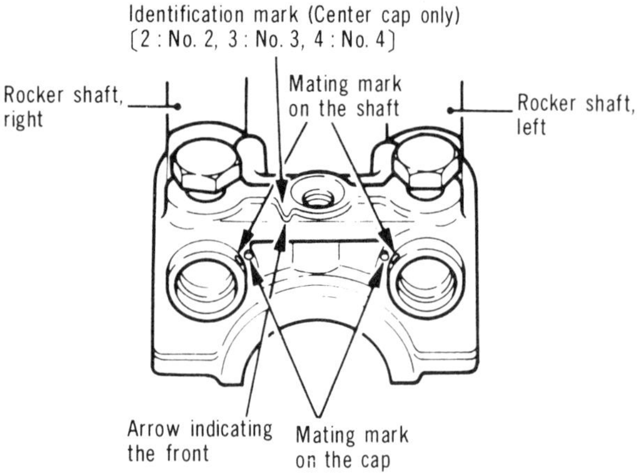

Fig. 2.13 Correct rocker arm shaft assembly (Sec 15)

15.2 Align the mark on the pulley with the T on the timing tab

2 Rotate the engine with a wrench on the large bolt at the front of the crankshaft until the number 1 piston is at top dead center on the compression stroke. To do this, watch the rocker arms for the number 1 cylinder valves while slowly rotating the crankshaft in a clockwise direction (viewed from the front). When the intake valve closes, continue rotating the crankshaft until the mark on the pulley is aligned with the T on the timing tab (photo).

3 Locate the timing mark on the camshaft sprocket and make sure the plated link of the cam chain is opposite the mark.

4 Remove the camshaft sprocket bolt and oil shield from the front of the camshaft (photo). Hold the large bolt on the end of the crankshaft (to keep the engine from turning) while loosening the bolt. Remove the distributor drivegear from the front of the camshaft by tapping it with a soft-faced hammer. Pull the camshaft sprocket (with the chain in place) off the camshaft, and allow it to rest on the sprocket holder.

5 Loosen the camshaft bearing cap bolts, $\frac{1}{2}$-turn each, in sequence, until all pressure from the valve springs has been released. Then remove the inner bolts and lift the rocker arm shaft assembly away from the cylinder head with the end bolts in place. Do not disassemble the components any further, unless new parts are required. Carefully lift the camshaft out of the cylinder head and store it where it will not be damaged.

Installation

6 Make sure the bearing journals on the camshaft are clean, then carefully lay it in place in the head. Do not lubricate the camshaft lobes at this time. Rotate the camshaft until the dowel pin on the front is positioned at the top.

7 Loosen the jam nuts on the valve clearance adjusting bolts and back the adjusting bolts out a minimum of two full turns.

8 Wipe the camshaft bearing cap bearing surfaces clean and apply a coat of clean multi-purpose grease (or engine assembly lube) to each of them. Also, apply a very small amount of grease to the end of each valve stem. Lay the rocker arm shaft assembly in place with the number 1 bearing cap at the front of the engine. Install the camshaft bearing cap bolts and tighten them to 7 ft-lb in the following order: center, number 2, number 4, front, rear. Repeat the procedure, tightening them to the final specified torque.

9 Next, lift up on the camshaft sprocket (with the chain attached) and slip it into place on the end of the camshaft. The dowel pin on the cam should slip into the hole in the sprocket.

10 Install the distributor drivegear (again, line up the dowel pin and hole), the oil shield and the bolt. Tighten the bolt to the specified torque (photo). To keep the camshaft and crankshaft from turning, install 2 of the flywheel mounting bolts in the rear flange of the crankshaft (180° apart), then wedge a large screwdriver between the bolts. Also, tighten the large bolt on the front of the crankshaft to the specified torque at this time.

11 The camshaft end play can be checked with a dial indicator set or a feeler gauge.

12 If a feeler gauge is used, gently pry the camshaft all the way

15.4 Remove the bolt and oil shield from the camshaft

15.10 Tighten the camshaft sprocket mounting bolt

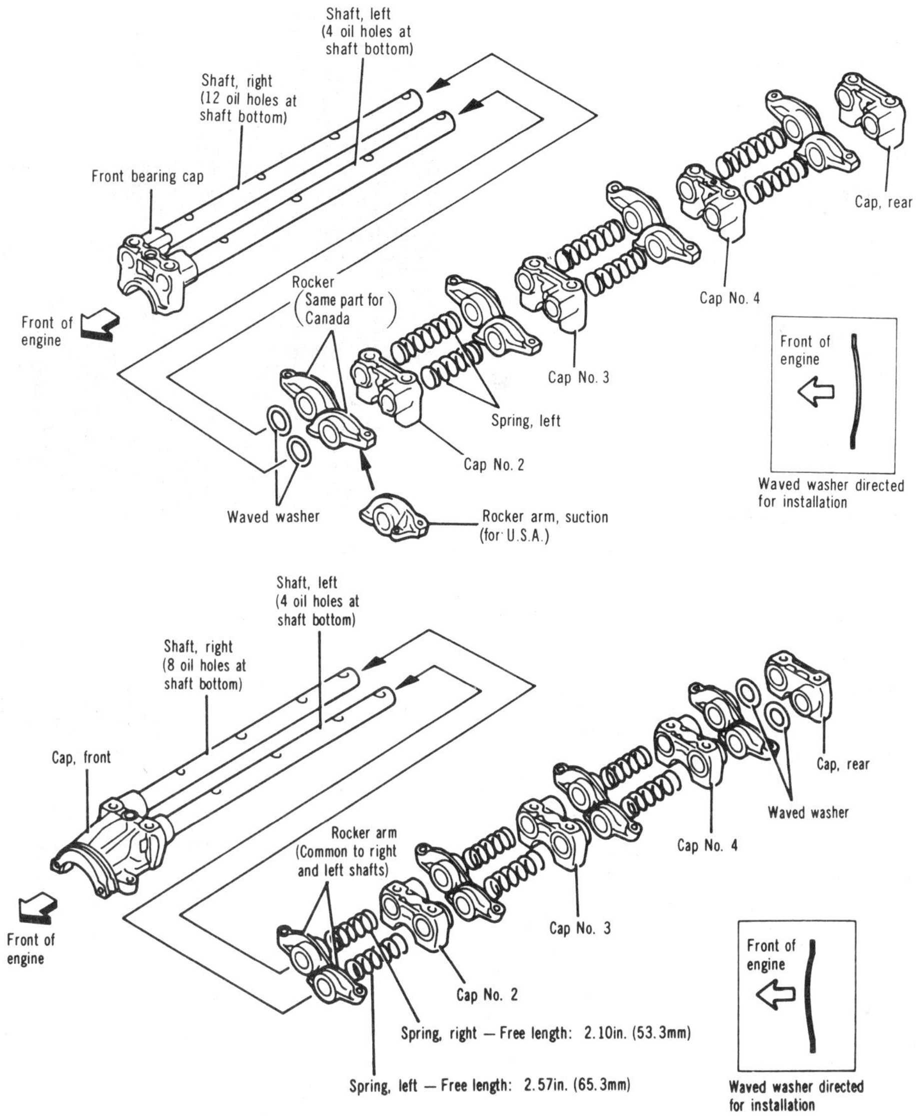

Fig. 2.14 Rocker arm shaft and components – exploded view (2000 cc and 2600 cc top, 1600 cc bottom) (Sec 15)

toward the front of the engine. Slip a feeler gauge between the flange at the front of the camshaft and the number 1 (front) cam bearing cap. Compare the measured endplay to the Specifications.

13 If a dial indicator is used, mount it at the front of the engine with the indicator stem touching the head of the bolt that attaches the sprocket to the camshaft. Carefully pry the camshaft all the way toward the front of the engine, then zero the dial indicator. Gently pry the camshaft as far as possible in the opposite direction and observe the needle movement on the dial indicator, which will indicate the amount of endplay. Compare it to the Specifications.

14 Next, adjust the valve clearances using the 'cold engine' specifications.

16 Camshaft and rocker arms – inspection

Camshaft

1 Inspect the camshaft bearing journals for excessive wear and evidence of seizure (photo). If the journals are damaged, the bearing surfaces in the head and bearing caps are probably damaged as well. Both the camshaft and cylinder head will have to be replaced with new ones.

2 Check the cam lobes for pitting, grooves, scoring or flaking.

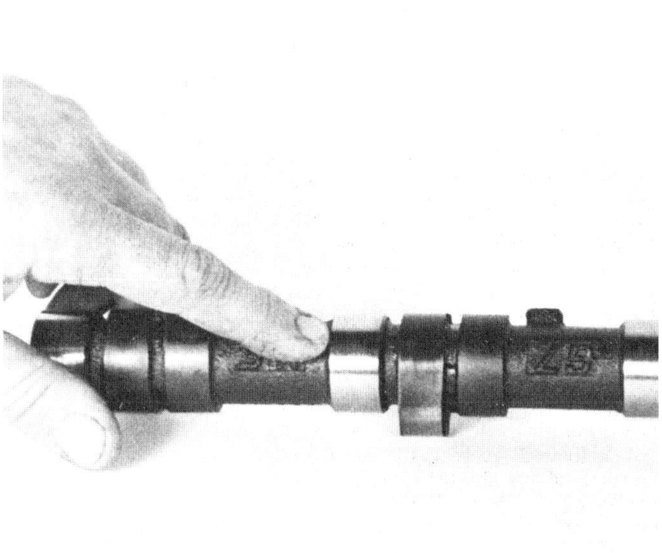

16.1 Inspect the bearing journals for excessive wear or seizure

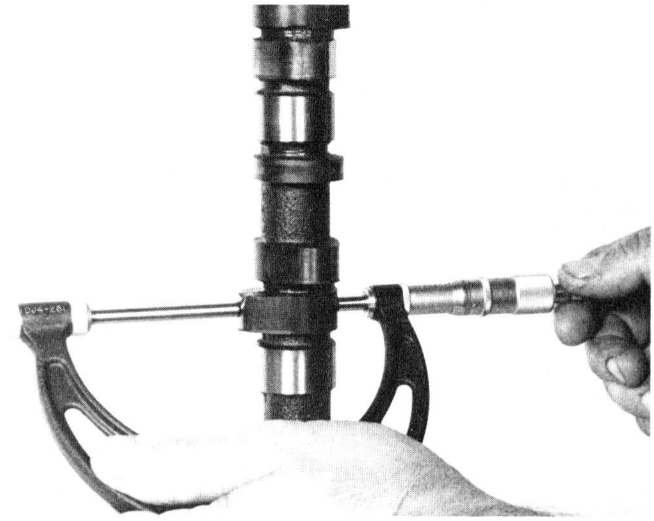

16.2 Measure the cam lobe height

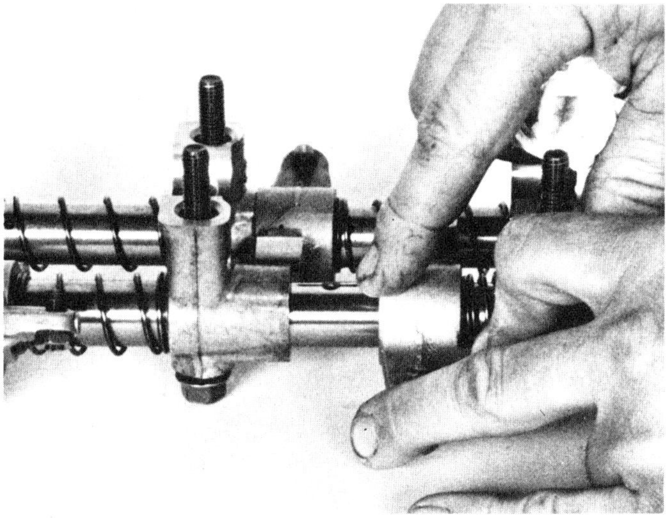

16.5 Check the rocker arm shafts for wear

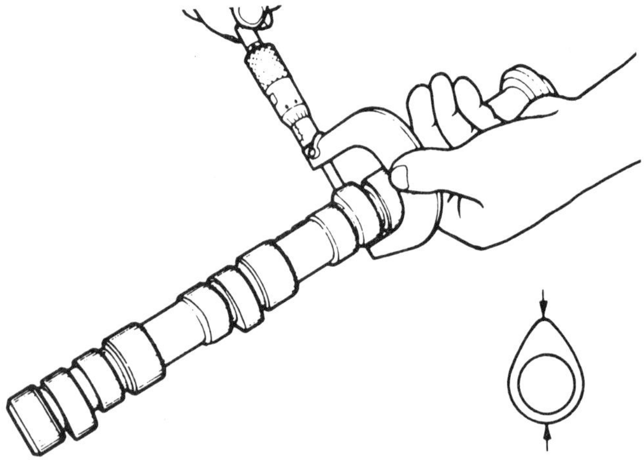

Fig. 2.15 Cam height check (Sec 16)

Measure the cam lobe height and compare it to the Specifications (photo). If the lobe height is less than the minimum specified and/or the lobes are damaged, a new camshaft must be obtained.

Rocker arm assembly

3 Check the rocker arm faces (that contact the camshaft lobes) and the ends of the adjusting screws (that contact the valve stems) for pitting, excessive wear and roughness.

4 Check the adjusting screw threads for damage. Make sure they can be threaded in and out of the rocker arms.

5 Slide each rocker arm along its shaft, against the locating spring pressure, and check the rocker arm shafts for excessive wear and evidence of scoring in the areas that normally contact the rocker arms (photo).

6 Any damaged or excessively worn parts must be replaced with new ones. Refer to the exploded view of the rocker arm assembly components, which will enable you to correctly disassemble and reassemble them.

17 Cylinder head – removal and installation

Removal

1 Remove the bolts attaching the cylinder head to the timing chain cover (at the very front of the cylinder head). Remove the bolts

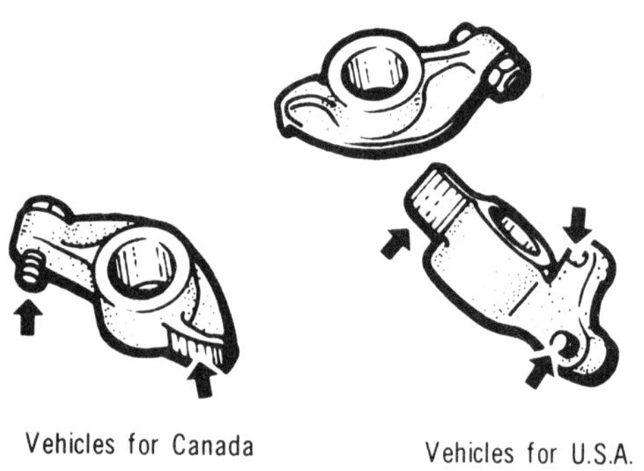

Fig. 2.16 Rocker arm check (Sec 16)

attaching the cylinder head to the engine block. Turn them $\frac{1}{4}$ of a turn each, in the sequence shown, until they are all loose enough to remove by hand.

2 Remove the cylinder head by lifting it straight up and off the engine block. Do not pry between the cylinder head and the engine block, as damage to the gasket sealing surfaces may result. Instead use a soft-faced hammer to tap the cylinder head and break the gasket seal.

3 Lift off the old head gasket. Clean the gasket surface.

Installation

4 Before installing the cylinder head, the timing chain and sprockets, the Silent Shaft chain and sprockets and the timing chain case must be in place on the engine.

5 Make sure the gasket sealing surfaces of the engine block and cylinder head are clean and oil-free, then lay the new head gasket in place on the block (no sealant) with the manufacturer's stamped mark facing up (photo). Use the dowel pins in the top of the block to properly locate the gasket.

6 Carefully set the cylinder head in place on the block. Use the dowel pins to properly align it.

7 Install the head bolts and tighten them, in the sequence shown, to $\frac{1}{3}$ of the specified torque. Repeat the procedure, using the same sequence, tightening them to $\frac{2}{3}$ of the specified torque. Repeat the procedure one last time, tightening them to the final specified torque.

8 Install the small head bolts (with washers) in the very front of the head and tighten them to the specified torque.

9 Wipe the camshaft bearing surfaces in the cylinder head clean and apply a coat of clean multi-purpose grease (or engine assembly lube) to each of them.

17.5 Install the new head gasket

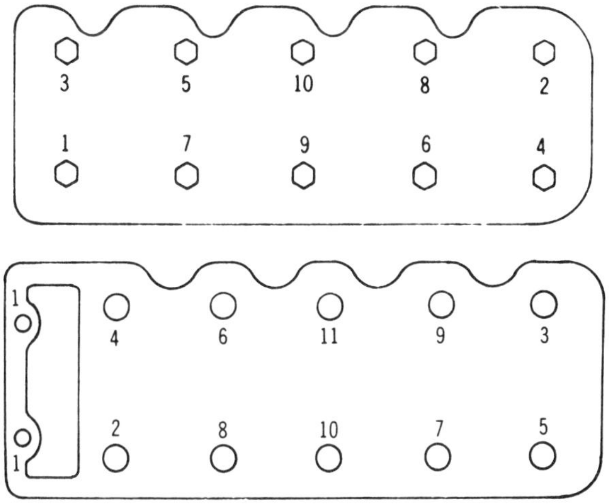

Fig. 2.17 Head bolt removal sequence (1600 cc top, 2000 cc and 2600 cc bottom) (Sec 17)

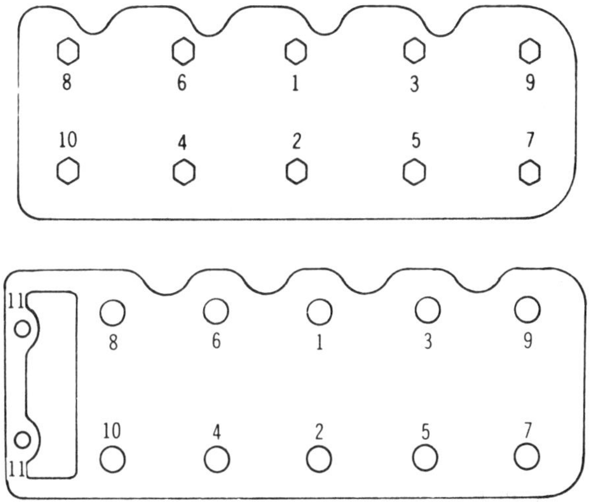

Fig. 2.18 Head bolt tightening sequence (1600 cc top, 2000 cc and 2600 cc bottom) (Sec 17)

18 Valves and cylinder head – servicing

1 Because of the complex nature of the job and the special tools and equipment required, servicing of the valves, the valve seats and the valve guides (commonly known as a 'valve job') is best left to a professional.

2 The home mechanic can remove and disassemble the head, do the initial cleaning and inspection, then reassemble and deliver the head to a dealer service department or a reputable automotive machine shop for the actual valve servicing.

3 The dealer service department, or automotive machine shop, will remove the valves and springs, recondition or replace the valves and valve seats, recondition or replace the valve guides, check and replace the valve springs, spring retainers and keepers (as necessary), replace the valve seals with new ones, reassemble the valve components and make sure the installed spring height is correct. The cylinder head gasket surface will also be resurfaced if it is warped.

4 After the valve job has been performed by a professional, the head will be in like-new condition. When the head is returned, be sure to clean it again, very thoroughly (before installation on the engine), to remove any metal particles and abrasive grit that may still be present from the valve service or head resurfacing operations. Use compressed air, if available, to blow out all the oil holes and passages.

19 Valves – removal, inspection and installation

Removal

1 Cylinder head disassembly involves removal and disassembly of the Jet Valves and removal of the intake and exhaust valves and their related components.

2 Using a 6-point deep socket and a breaker bar, carefully remove the Jet Valve assemblies from the cylinder head. Do not tilt the socket, as the Jet Valve stems can be bent very easily by the force exerted on the valve spring retainer (which will cause defective Jet Valve operation). Label each Jet Valve assembly so it can be reinstalled in the same hole it was removed from.

3 Disassemble each Jet Valve by carefully compressing the spring and removing the keepers, the valve spring retainer and the valve spring. Slide the valve out of the body and pull off the seal with pliers (discard the oil seals, as they should not be reused). Keep the parts for each Jet Valve assembly separate (photo) so that they are not accidentally interchanged with parts from other Jet Valve assemblies.

4 Before the valves are removed, arrange to label and store them, along with their related components, so that they can be kept separate and reinstalled in the same valve guides they were removed from. Also, measure the valve spring installed height (for each valve) and

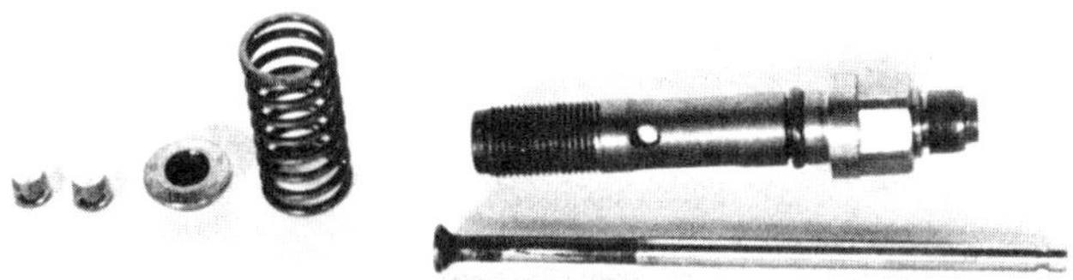

19.3 Jet Valve components

19.4 Measure the installed height of the valve springs

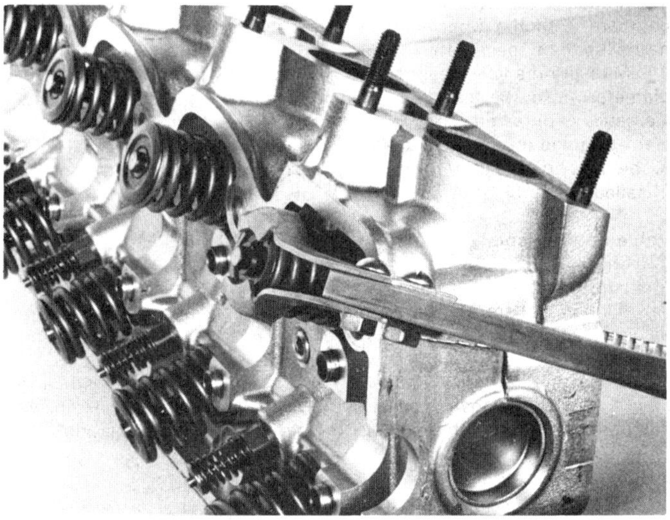

19.5 Compress the valve spring with a valve spring compressor

19.6 Intake/exhaust valve components

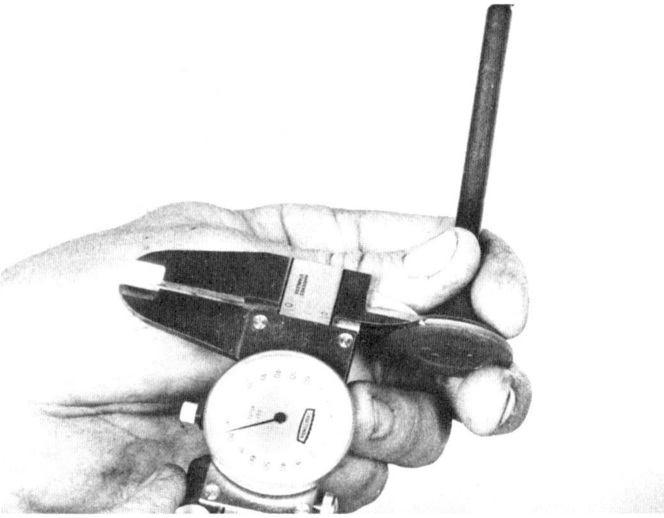

19.10 Measure the valve margin width

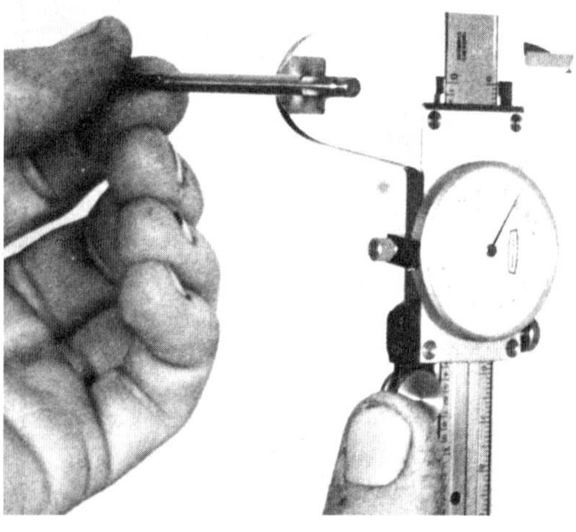

19.11 Measure the valve stem diameter

compare it to the Specifications (photo). If it is greater than specified, the valve seats and valve faces need attention.

5 Compress the valve spring on the first valve with a spring compressor (photo) then remove the keepers and the retainer from the valve assembly. Carefully release the valve spring compressor and remove the spring, the spring seat and the valve from the head. If the valve binds in the guide (won't pull through), push it back into the head and deburr the area around the keeper groove with a fine file.

6 Repeat the procedure for the remaining valves. Remember to keep all the parts for each valve in order so that they can be reinstalled in the same position (photo).

7 Once the valves have been removed and safely stored, pull off the valve stem seals with pliers and discard them; the old seals should never be reused.

8 Refer to Section 20 for cylinder head cleaning and inspection procedures.

Inspection

Valves

9 Carefully inspect each valve face for cracks, pitting and burned spots. Check the valve stem and neck for cracks. Rotate the valve and check for any obvious indication that it is bent. Check the end of the stem for pitting and excessive wear. The presence of any of the above conditions indicates a need for valve service by a professional.

10 Measure the width of the valve margin (on each valve) and compare it to the Specifications (photo). Any valve with a margin narrower than specified will have to be replaced with a new one.

11 Measure the valve stem diameter (photo). By subtracting the stem diameter from the valve guide diameter, the valve stem-to-guide clearance is obtained. Compare the results to the Specifications. If the stem-to-guide clearance is greater than specified, the guides will have to be reconditioned or replaced and new valves may have to be installed, depending on the condition of the old ones.

Valve components

12 Check each valve spring for wear (on the ends) and pitting. Measure the free length (photo) and compare it to the Specifications. Any springs that are shorter than specified have sagged and should not be reused. Stand the spring on a flat surface and check it for squareness.

13 Check the spring retainers and keepers for obvious wear and cracks. Any questionable parts should not be reused, as extensive damage will occur in the event of failure during engine operation.

Jet Valve assemblies

14 Make sure the Jet Valve slides freely in the Jet Valve body. It should have no detectable side play. Check the valve head and seat for cracks and pitting. Check the spring for wear (on the ends) and cracks.

19.12 Measure the free length of the valve spring

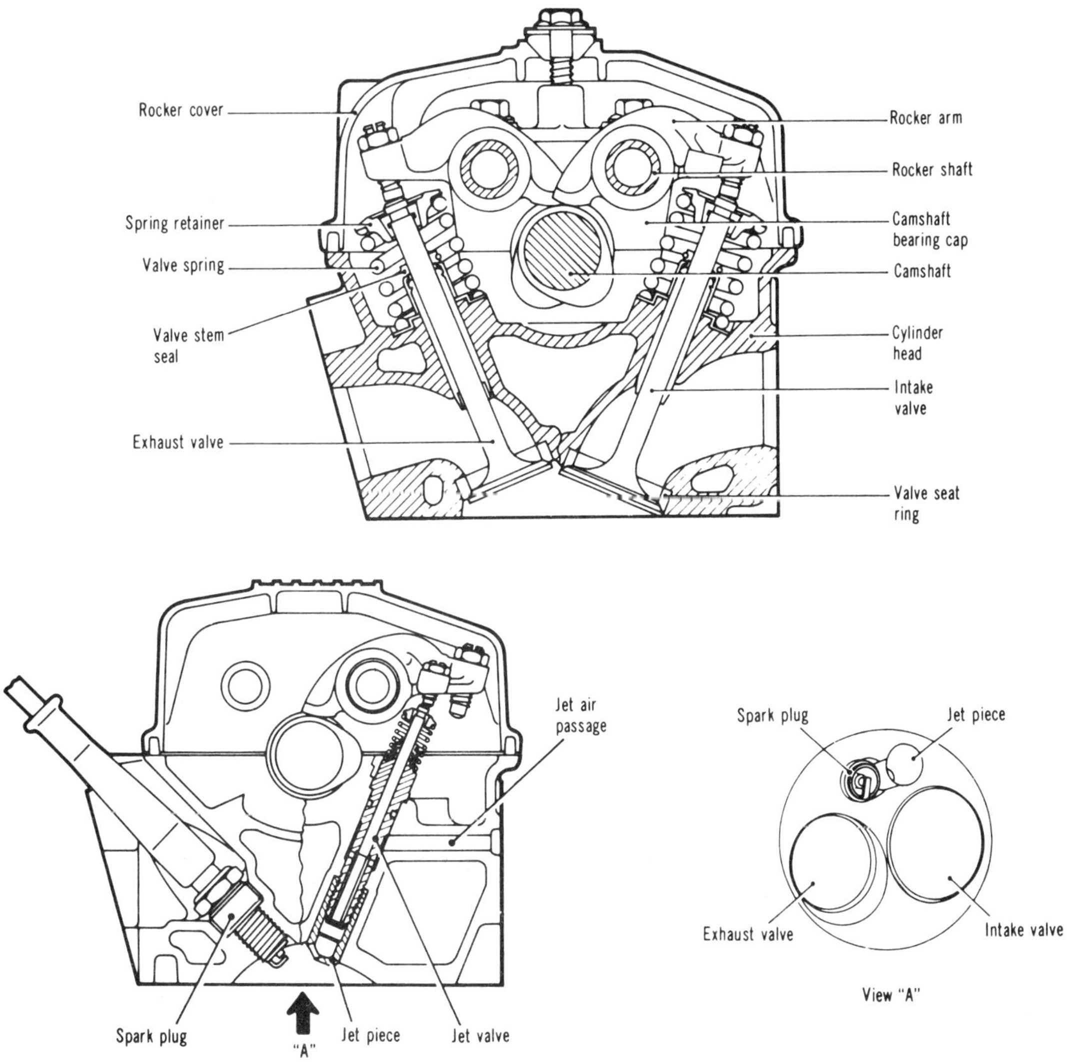

Fig. 2.19 Cylinder head/valves – sectional view (Sec 19)

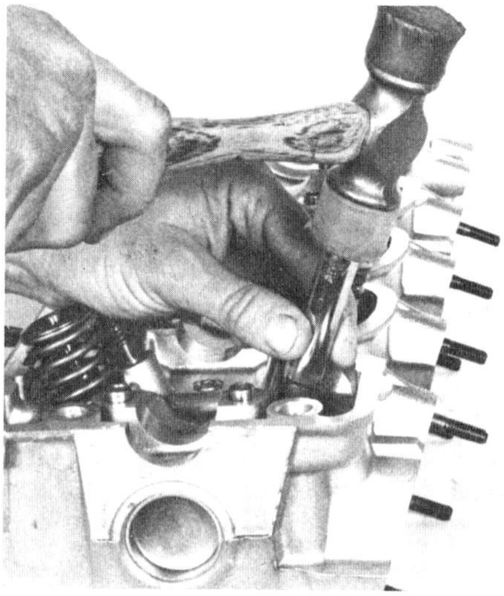

19.21 Install new valve guide seals with a hammer and a deep-well socket

Measure the valve spring free length and diameter of the valve stem. Compare the results to the Specifications.
15 If defects are found in any of the Jet Valve components, the entire valve assembly should be replaced with a new one.
16 Be sure to check the remaining Jet Valve assemblies.
17 If the inspection process indicates that the valve components are in generally poor condition and worn beyond the limits specified, which is usually the case in an engine that is being overhauled, reassemble the valves in the cylinder head and refer to Section 18 for valve servicing recommendations.
18 If the inspection process turns up no excessively worn parts, and if the valve faces and seats are in good condition, the valve train components can be reinstalled in the cylinder head without major servicing.

Installation

19 Regardless of whether or not the head was sent to an automotive machine shop for valve servicing, make sure it is clean before beginning reassembly.
20 If the head was sent out for valve servicing, the valves and related components will already be in place. Begin the reassembly procedure with step 24.
21 Lay all the spring seats in position, then install new seals on each of the valve guides. Using a hammer and an appropriate size deep socket, gently tap each seal into place until it is properly seated on its guide (photo). Do not twist or cock the seals during installation, as they will not seal properly on the valve stems.
22 Next, install the valves (taking care not to damage the new seals), the springs, the retainers and the keepers. Coat the valve stems with clean multi-purpose grease (or engine assembly lube) before slipping them into the guides, and install the springs with the painted side next to the retainer. When compressing the springs with the valve spring compressor, do not let the retainers contact the valve guide seals. Make certain that the keepers are securely locked in their retaining grooves.
23 Double-check the installed valve spring height. If it was correct before disassembly, it should still be within the specified limits.
24 Install new seals on each of the Jet Valve bodies. Gently tap them into place with a hammer and the appropriate size deep socket. Lubricate and install the valves and make sure the stems slide smoothly in the valve bodies. Install the springs, the retainers and the keepers. When compressing the springs, be careful not to damage the valve stems or the new seals.
25 Install a new O-ring on each Jet Valve body and apply a thin coat of clean engine oil or multi-purpose grease to each O-ring, the Jet Valve threads and the Jet Valve seating surfaces.
26 Carefully thread the Jet Valve assemblies into the cylinder head and tighten them to the specified torque. Be careful not to tilt the socket, as the valve stems can be bent very easily.

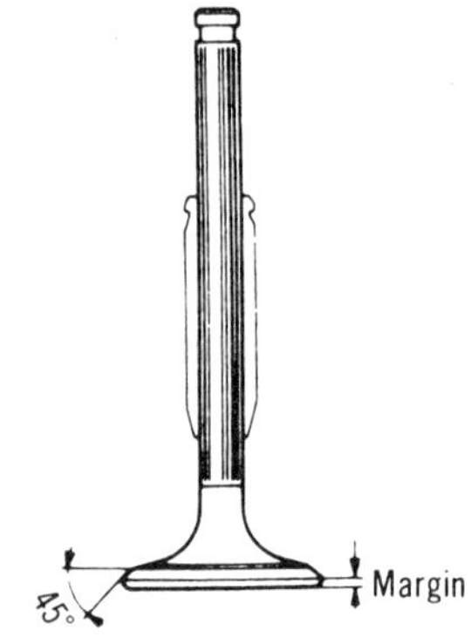

Fig. 2.20 Valve check points (Sec 19)

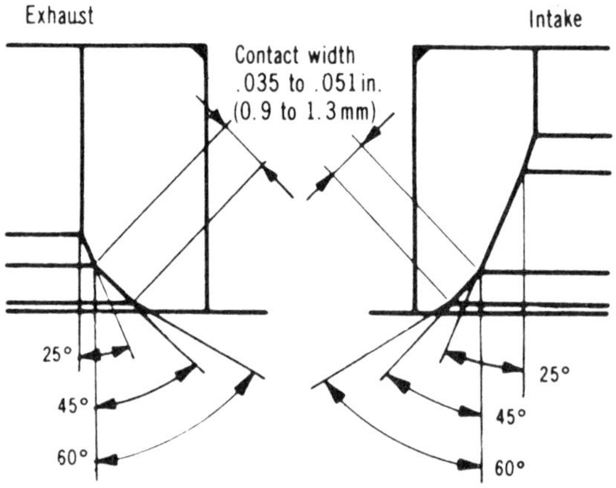

Fig. 2.21 Valve seat re-conditioning dimensions (Sec 19)

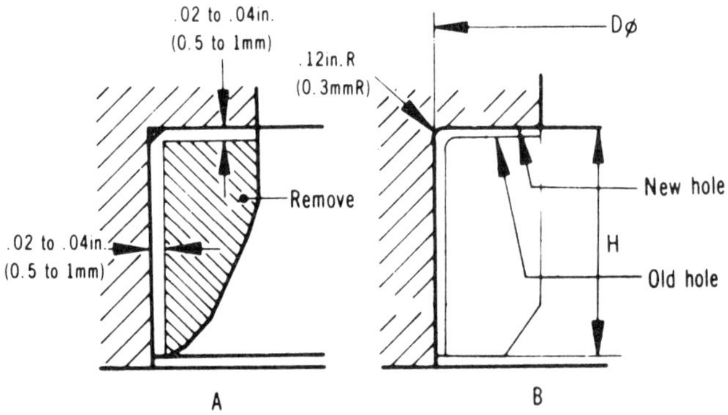

Fig. 2.22 Valve seat insert replacement (Sec 19)

20 Cylinder head – cleaning and inspection

1 Thorough cleaning of the cylinder head and related valve train components, followed by a detailed inspection, will enable you to decide how much valve service work must be done during the engine overhaul.

Cleaning

2 Scrape away any traces of old gasket material and sealing compound from the head gasket, the intake manifold and the exhaust manifold sealing surfaces. Work slowly and do not nick or gouge the soft aluminum of the head.
3 Carefully scrape all carbon deposits out of the combustion

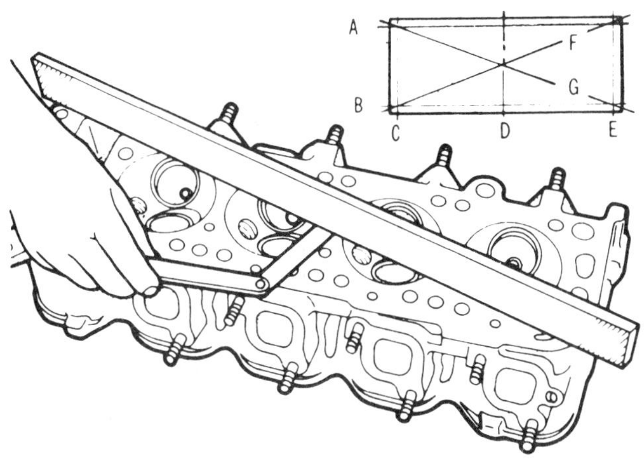

Fig. 2.23 Cylinder head distortion check points (Sec 20)

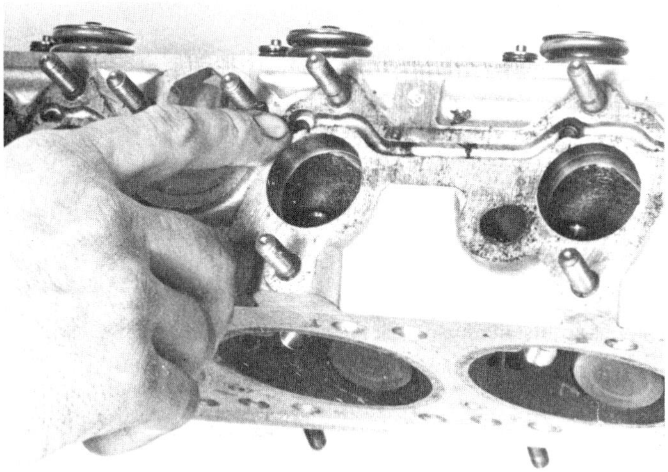

20.5 Make sure the Jet air passages, the EGR gas ports and the oil supply holes are clean

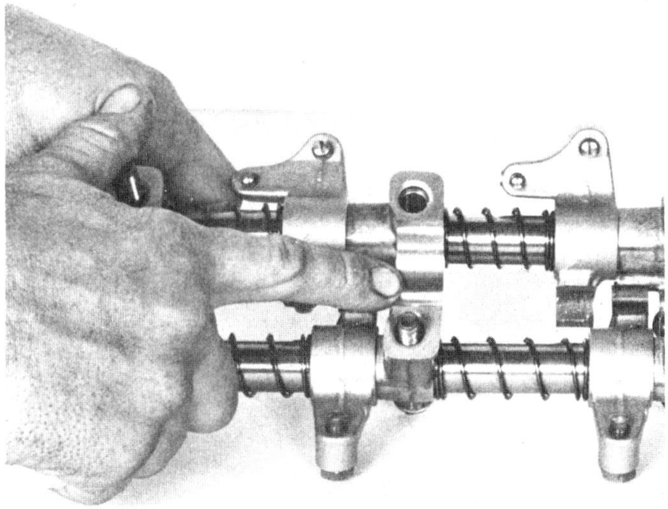

20.14 Inspect the camshaft bearing cap bearing surfaces

chamber areas. A hand-held wire brush or a piece of fine emery cloth can be used once the majority of deposits have been scraped away. Do not use a wire brush mounted in a drill motor, as the head material is soft and can be eroded away by the wire brush.

4 Remove any scale that may be built up around the coolant passages.

5 Run a stiff wire brush through the oil holes, the EGR gas ports and the jet air passages to remove any deposits that may have formed in those areas (photo).

6 It is a good idea to run an appropriate size tap into each of the threaded holes to remove any corrosion or thread sealant that may be present. Be very careful when cleaning aluminum threads; they can be damaged easily with a tap. If compressed air is available, use it to clear the holes of debris produced by this operation. Clean the exhaust and intake manifold stud threads in a similar manner with an appropriate size die. Clean the camshaft bearing cap bolt threads with a wire brush.

7 Next, clean the cylinder head with solvent and dry it thoroughly. Compressed air will speed the drying process and ensure that all holes and recessed areas are clean. **Note**: *Decarbonizing chemicals are available and may prove useful when cleaning cylinder heads and valve train components. They are very caustic and should be used with caution. Be sure to follow the directions on the container.*

8 Clean the camshaft with solvent and dry it thoroughly.

9 Without dismantling the rocker arm assembly, clean it with solvent (make sure all oil holes are clear) and dry it thoroughly. Compressed air, if it is available, will speed up the drying process and make it much easier.

10 Clean all the valve springs, keepers, retainers and spring seats with solvent and dry them thoroughly. Do the parts from one valve at a time, so that no mixing of parts between valves occurs.

11 Scrape off any heavy deposits that may have formed on the valves, then use a motorized wire brush to remove deposits from the valve heads and stems. Again, make sure the valves do not get mixed up.

12 Clean the Jet Valve components with solvent. Do one Jet Valve at a time so parts are not accidentally interchanged. Carefully remove any deposits from the Jet Valve stem and head with a fine wire brush. Do not bend the valve stem in the process.

Inspection

13 Inspect the head very carefully for cracks, evidence of coolant leakage and other damage. If cracks are found, a new head is in order. 2

14 Check the camshaft bearing surfaces in the head and the bearing caps (photo). If there is evidence of excessive wear, scoring or seizure, the cylinder head will have to be replaced with a new one to restore the camshaft bearing surfaces and proper oil clearance.

15 Using a straightedge and feeler gauge, check the head gasket mating surfaces for warpage at the points shown. If the head is warped beyond the limits given in the Specifications, it can be resurfaced at an automotive machine shop.

16 Examine the valve seats in each of the combustion chambers. If they are pitted, cracked or burned, the head will require valve service that is beyond the scope of the home mechanic.

17 Measure the inside diameters of the valve guides (at both ends and the center of the guide) with a small hole gauge and a 0-to-1 in micrometer. Record the measurements for future reference. These measurements, along with the valve stem diameter measurements, will enable you to compute the valve stem-to-guide clearance. This clearance, when compared to the Specifications, will be one factor that will determine the extent of the valve service work required. The guides are measured at the ends and at the center to determine if they are worn in a bell-mouth pattern (more wear at the ends). If they are, guide reconditioning or replacement is an absolute must.

21 Timing belt/sprockets (1600 only) – removal and installation

Removal

1 Remove the upper and lower front timing belt covers, then remove the crankshaft sprocket mounting bolt. To keep the crankshaft from turning, install two flywheel mounting bolts in the rear crankshaft flange (180° apart) and wedge a large screwdriver between the bolts.

2 Loosen the belt tensioner nut and bolt, push the tensioner to the left and tighten the nut so that the tensioner does not spring back.

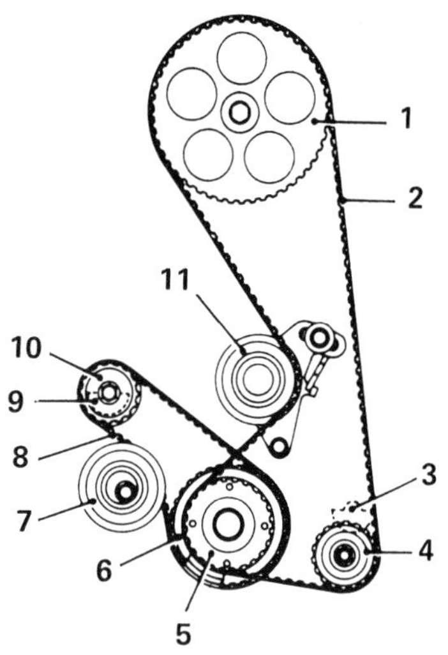

Fig. 2.24 Timing/Silent Shaft belt system (Sec 21)

1 *Camshaft sprocket*
2 *Timing belt*
3 *Left Silent Shaft*
4 *Oil pump sprocket*
5 *Crankshaft sprocket (small)*
6 *Crankshaft sprocket (large)*
7 *Silent Shaft belt tensioner*
8 *Silent Shaft belt*
9 *Right Silent Shaft*
10 *Silent Shaft sprocket*
11 *Timing belt tensioner*

3 After the tensioner has been released, slip the belt off the sprockets.
4 Remove the tensioner, the camshaft sprocket, the small crankshaft sprocket, the flange and spacer.
5 On the engines without Silent Shafts, also remove the upper and lower rear timing belt covers.
6 **Note**: *Engines without Silent Shaft are finished at this point. Proceed to Section 25.*

Installation

7 Installation is the reverse of removal. On engines without Silent Shafts, install the upper and lower rear timing belt covers.
8 Slip the spacer, the flange and the small sprocket onto the crankshaft, then install the sprocket mounting bolt and tighten it to the specified torque. Turn the crankshaft until the roll pin on the sprocket is aligned with the pointer on the lower case cover.
9 Apply a thin coat of engine oil to the outside of the camshaft. Next, install the camshaft sprocket, tighten the bolt to the specified torque and align the match marks on the sprocket and cover.
10 Install the tensioner spring, then install the tensioner and temporarily tighten the nut. The front end of the spring (bent at right angles) fits over the projection on the tensioner and the other end (straight) rests against the water pump body. Next, push the lower flange to the left, align the holes and install the bolt.
11 Push the tensioner to the left as far as possible and temporarily tighten the nut, then slip the timing belt onto the sprockets. The belt should be installed first on the crankshaft sprocket, then on the oil pump and camshaft sprockets. Check to make sure that the timing marks on the individual sprockets are properly aligned.
12 Temporarily install the crankshaft pulley to prevent misalignment of the belt as the crankshaft is turned, then loosen the tensioner mounting bolt and nut. The tensioner will be moved by the spring and will apply tension to the belt. Make sure the belt is completely meshed with each of the sprockets.
13 Tighten the tensioner mounting nut and bolt. Be sure to tighten the nut before tightening the bolt, or the tensioner may be turned and the belt given more tension than required.
14 Once again, check to ensure that the timing marks on all of the sprockets are properly aligned, then turn the crankshaft clockwise through a complete rotation. This will apply the proper tension to the

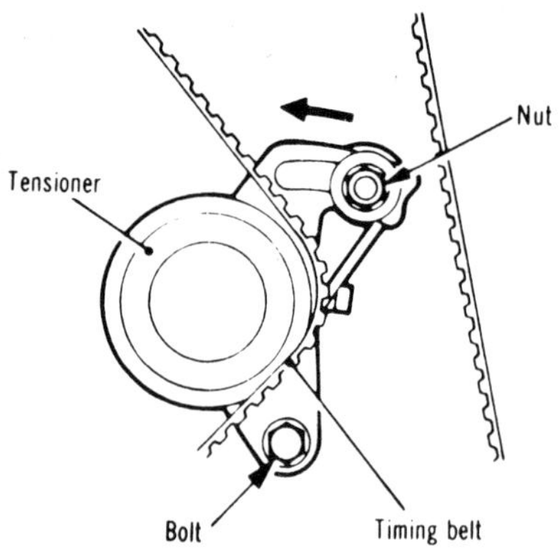

Fig. 2.25 Loosen/adjust timing belt with tensioner (Sec 21)

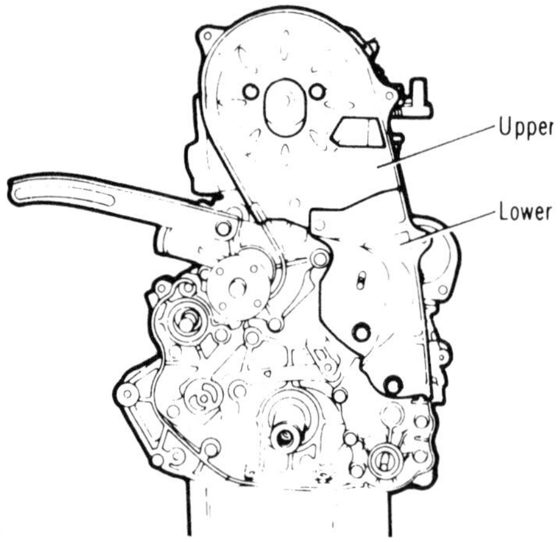

Fig. 2.26 Installation of rear upper and under covers (Sec 21)

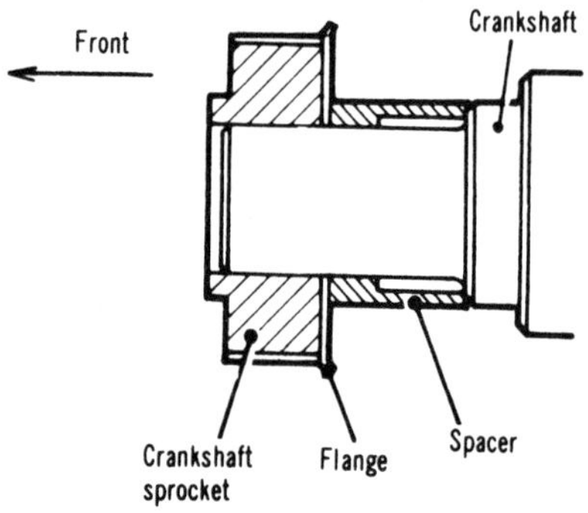

Fig. 2.27 Installing spacer, flange and sprocket (Sec 21)

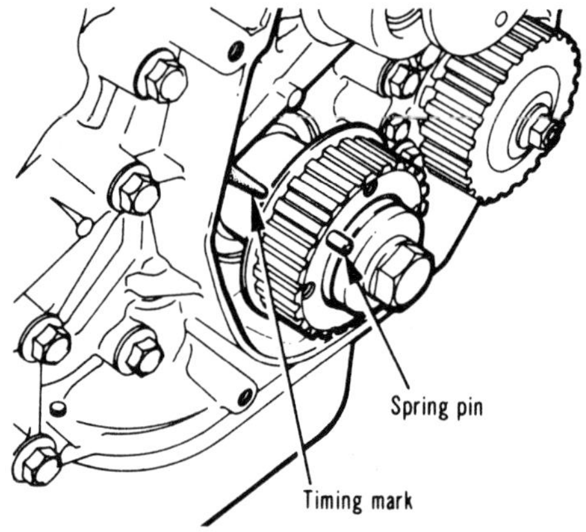

Fig. 2.28 Timing mark alignment (Sec 21)

timing belt. Make sure that the crankshaft is turned smoothly in a clockwise direction and do not push or shake the belt.
15 Loosen the tensioner mounting bolt and nut. The trailing side of the belt will tighten automatically. Now retighten them; first the nut and then the bolt.
16 Check to ensure that when the center of the tension side of the belt and the under cover are held between the thumb and the forefinger the clearance between the belt and the cover is 0.47 in (12 mm).
17 Remove the crankshaft pulley and install the upper and lower front timing belt covers.
18 Refer to Section 26 for the final timing belt adjustment.

22 Silent Shafts belt/sprockets (1600 only) – removal and installation

1 To remove the Silent Shafts, first remove the oil pump sprocket. To do this, remove the pump sprocket nut. Then remove the plug at the bottom of the left side of the cylinder block.
2 Insert an appropriate screwdriver into this plug hole to keep the left Silent Shaft in position. Remove the pump sprocket.
3 Loosen the right Silent Shaft sprocket bolt until it can be loosened by hand and leave it there.
4 Now, remove the Silent Shaft tensioner and the Silent Shaft belt.
5 Remove the large crankshaft sprocket and the right Silent Shaft sprocket.
6 Now you can remove the bolts holding the rear upper and lower timing belt covers. Remove both covers.
7 Remove the bolts holding the water pump in place and remove the pump.
8 To remove the oil pump, see Section 28.

Installation

9 Install the water pump and tighten the bolts according to the Specifications.
10 Install the rear upper and lower covers and torque them to Specifications. Because the lower of the bolts also retains the oil pump, it should be tightened to the same torque as the oil pump cover mounting bolts.
11 Install the spacer to the end of the right Silent Shaft. Apply a thin coat of engine oil to the outer surface before installing it. Install the chamfered end first. Make sure that the oil seal lip has not been rolled back by the spacer.
12 Install the right Silent Shaft sprocket with its bolt finger tight. Install the large crankshaft sprocket and align the timing marks on both sprockets with their timing marks on the front case.
13 Install the Silent Shaft belt making sure that there is no slack on its tension side, then the tensioner. Make sure that the center of the pulley is on the left of the mounting bolt and the pulley flange is nearest the engine.
14 Hold the tension pulley and move it in the direction of the arrow until the belt is tight. While tightening the tensioner, make sure that the tensioner pulley does not rotate any further, because this will result in the belt being overtightened. A belt which is too tight will cause excessive noise and one which is too loose will result in excessive belt wear, possibly resulting in the belt coming out of mesh.
15 Check that the two sprockets are still opposite their timing marks and that when the tight side of the belt is pushed with a forefinger it

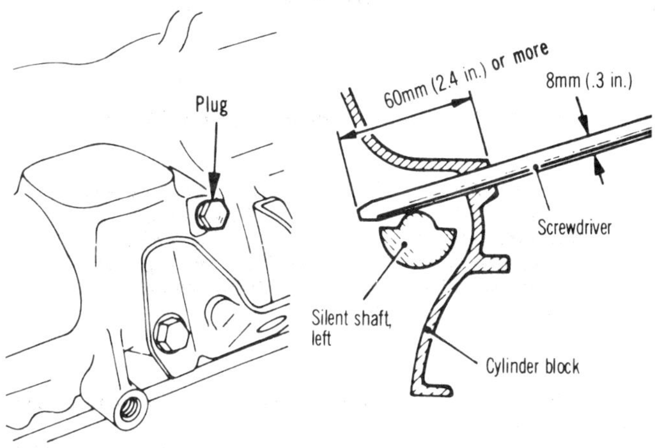

Fig. 2.29 Removing oil pump sprocket (Sec 22)

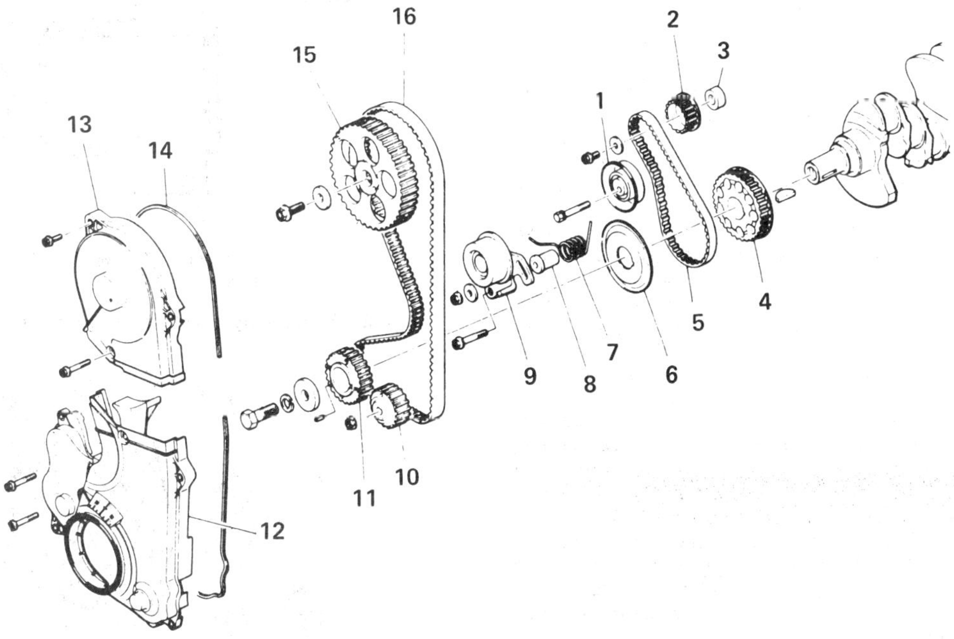

Fig. 2.30 Timing/Silent Shaft belt components – exploded view (Sec 22)

1 Silent Shaft belt tensioner
2 Right Silent Shaft sprocket
3 Spacer
4 Crankshaft sprocket (large)
5 Silent Shaft belt
6 Flange
7 Tensioner spring
8 Tensioner spacer
9 Timing belt tensioner
10 Oil pump sprocket
11 Crankshaft sprocket (small)
12 Front lower cover
13 Front upper cover
14 Gasket
15 Camshaft sprocket
16 Timing belt

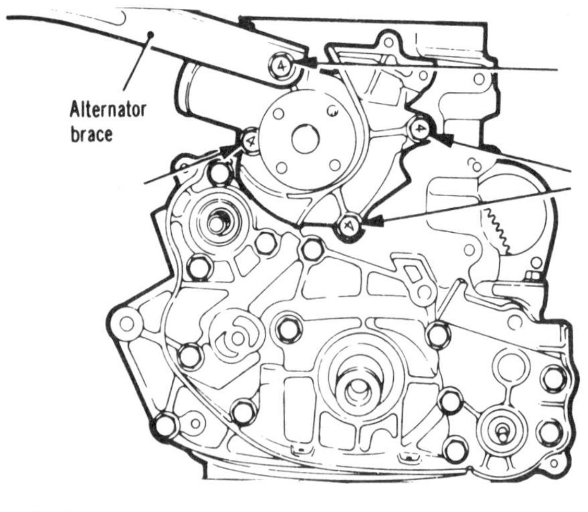

Fig. 2.31 Water pump installation. Securing bolts arrowed (Sec 22)

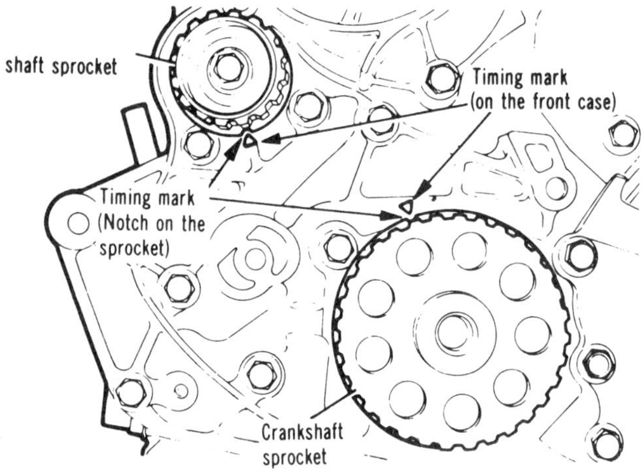

Fig. 2.32 Silent Shaft belt sprocket installation (Sec 22)

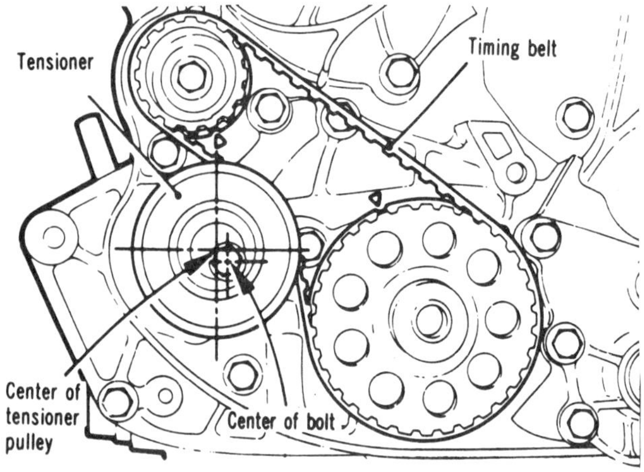

Fig. 2.33 Installing the belt tensioner (Sec 22)

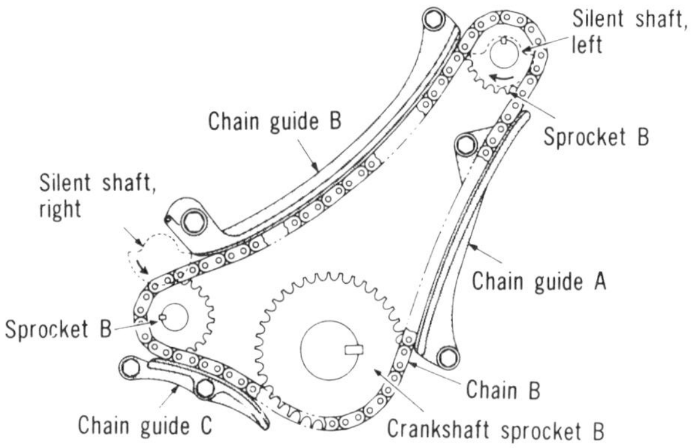

Fig. 2.34 Silent Shaft chain system (Sec 23)

can just be deflected to the far side of the front case mounting bolt.
16 Tighten the mounting bolt of the right Silent Shaft sprocket to Specifications.
17 Install the oil pump sprocket, tighten its nut to the specified torque and align the mark on the sprocket flange with the mark on the front cover of the pump. It is now necessary to check that the left Silent Shaft, which is meshed with the oil pump, is in the correct phase and this is done as follows.
18 Remove the plug on the left-hand side of the cylinder block and insert a screwdriver. If the screwdriver can be inserted more than about $2\frac{1}{2}$ in (60 mm), the alignment is correct. If it can only be inserted about 1 in (25 mm), rotate the oil pump pulley 360° to align with the timing mark again. Insert the screwdriver fully and leave it in place until installation of the timing belt has been completed.
19 Proceed to Section 21 to install the timing belt. When the belts are all in place correctly you can remove the screwdriver and replace the plug.

23 Silent Shaft chain/sprockets – removal and installation

Removal

1 Before attempting to remove the Silent Shaft chain and sprockets, remove the cylinder head and the oil pan by referring to the appropriate Sections.
2 Remove the large bolt at the front of the crankshaft and slide the pulley off.
3 Remove the bolts attaching the timing chain case to the engine block. Draw a simple diagram showing the location of each of the bolts so they can be returned to the same holes they were removed from.
4 Tap the timing chain case with a soft-faced hammer, to break the gasket seal, and remove the case from the engine block. Do not pry between the case and the engine block, as damage to the gasket sealing surfaces will result.
5 Remove the chain guides labeled A, B and C. They are held in place with two bolts each. Again, draw a simple diagram showing the location of each of the bolts (so they can be returned to the same holes they were removed from).
6 Reinstall the large bolt in the end of the crankshaft and hold it with a wrench (to keep the engine from turning) while loosening the bolt in the end of the right (lower) Silent Shaft, the bolt attaching the right Silent Shaft drive sprocket to the oil pump shaft and the bolt in the end of the left (upper) Silent Shaft. If the bolt in the end of the right Silent Shaft is difficult to loosen, remove the oil pump and Silent Shaft as an assembly (see Section 25), then remove the bolt with the Silent Shaft securely clamped in a vise.
7 Slide the crankshaft sprocket, the Silent Shaft sprockets and the chain off the engine as an assembly. Leave the bolt in the end of the right (lower) Silent Shaft in place. Do not lose the keys that index the sprockets to the shafts.

Installation

8 Before installing the Silent Shaft chain and sprockets, the timing chain must be properly installed and the number 1 piston must be at

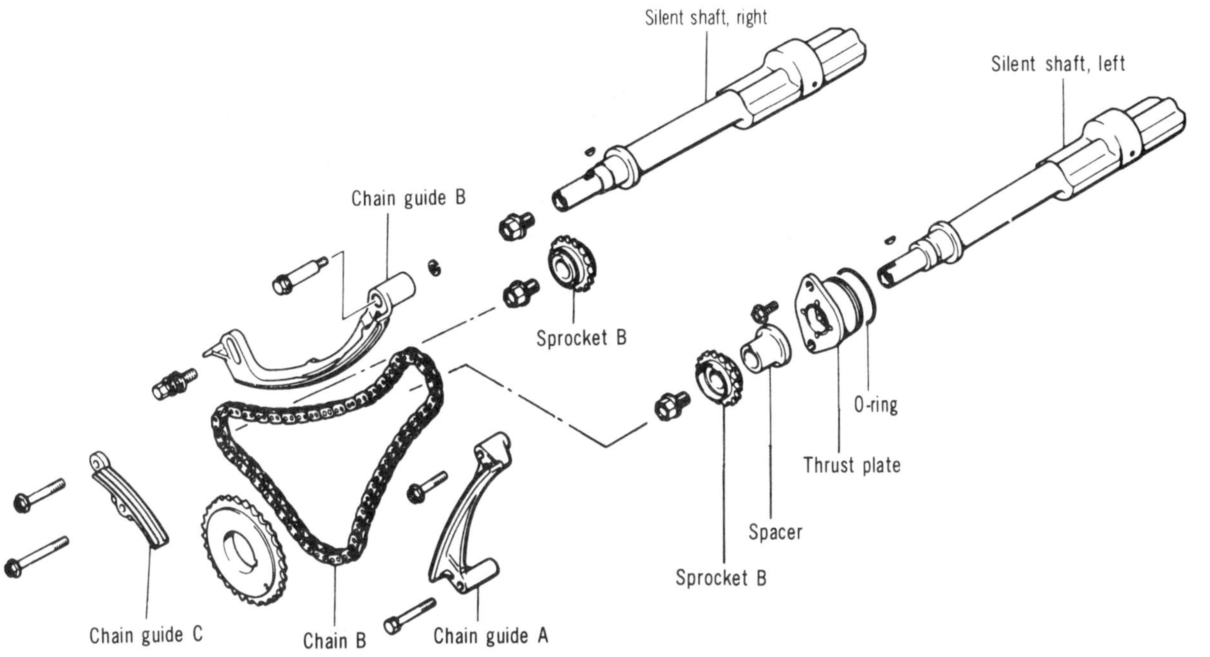

Fig. 2.35 Silent Shaft drive system – exploded view (Sec 23)

TDC on the compression stroke. It is assumed that both Silent Shafts and the oil pump are also in place.

9 Slide the crankshaft sprocket part-way onto the front of the crankshaft (by lining up the key-way in the sprocket with the key on the shaft).

10 Install the Silent Shaft chain onto the crankshaft sprocket and the left Silent Shaft sprocket. The dished or recessed side of the left Silent Shaft sprocket must face out. Line up the plated links on the chain with the mating marks stamped into the sprockets.

11 With the dished or recessed side facing in, install the right Silent Shaft sprocket onto the chain. Line up the plated link on the chain with the mating mark on the sprocket. Slide the Silent Shaft sprockets onto their respective shafts, lining up the key-ways in the sprockets with the keys on the shafts. Simultaneously, push the crankshaft sprocket back until it bottoms on the crankshaft timing chain sprocket. Recheck the position of the mating marks on the chain and sprockets, then install the Silent Shaft sprocket attaching bolts and tighten them to the specified torque.

12 Install the chain guides labeled A, B and C and tighten the mounting bolts for chain guides A and C securely (photo). Leave the mounting bolts for chain guide B finger tight. Note the difference between the upper and lower chain guide B mounting bolts. Make sure they are installed in the proper location.

13 Adjust the chain slack as follows: Rotate the right Silent Shaft clockwise and the left Silent Shaft counterclockwise so that the chain slack is collected at point P. Pull the chain with your finger tips in the direction of arrow F, then move the lower end of the chain guide B up or down, as required, until the clearance between the chain and the guide (chain slack) is as specified (photo). Tighten the chain guide B mounting bolts securely, then recheck the slack to make sure it has not changed. If the chain is not tensioned properly, engine noise will result.

14 Apply a coat of clean multi-purpose grease to the chain and chain guides.

15 Using a hammer and punch, drive the old seal out of the timing chain case (photo).

16 Lay a new seal in place (with the lip facing in) and tap around its entire circumference, with a block of wood and a hammer, until it is properly seated.

23.12 Adjust the Silent Shaft chain guides

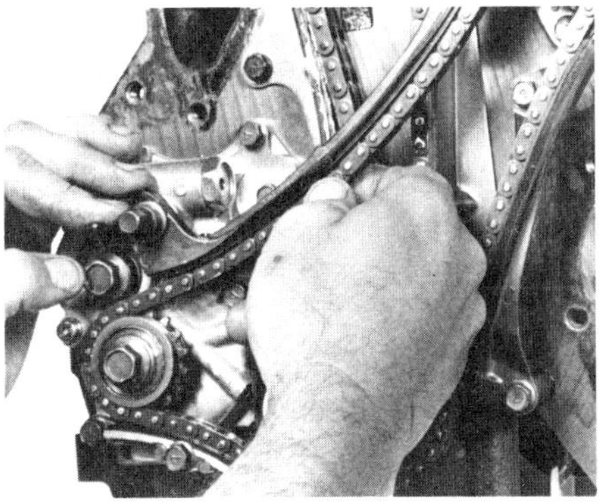

23.13 Adjust the Silent Shaft chain slack

23.15 Drive the old oil seal out of the timing case cover

23.18 Apply grease to the seal surface of the crankshaft pulley

24.4 Install the camshaft sprocket holder onto the engine block

24.5 Install the timing chain tensioner plunger into the oil pump bore

24.6 Install the timing chain sprocket (wide shoulder facing out)

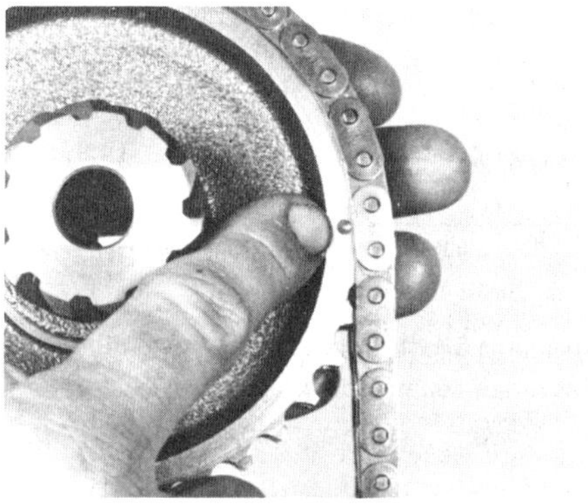

24.7 Match the camshaft sprocket mark to the plated link on the chain

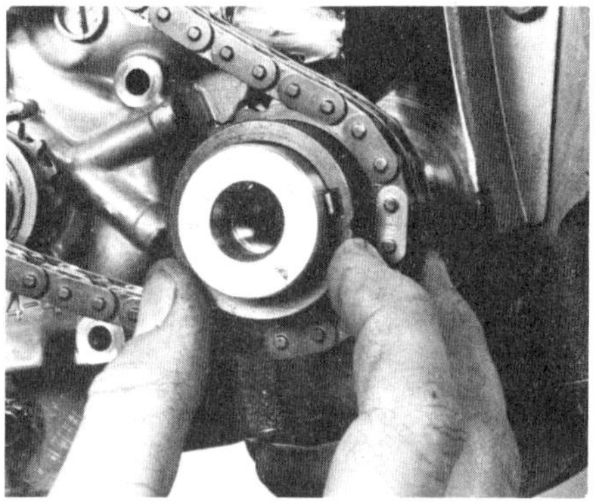

24.8 Match the crankshaft sprocket mark to the plated link on the chain

17 Using a new gasket and silicone-type gasket sealer, fit the timing chain case onto the front of the engine. Install the bolts and tighten them securely, using a criss-cross pattern. If the gasket protrudes beyond the top or bottom of the case and engine block, trim off the excess with a razor blade.
18 Apply a thin layer of clean multi-purpose grease to the seal contact surface of the crankshaft pulley (photo), then slide it onto the crankshaft. Install the bolt and tighten it finger tight only. The bolt should be tightened to the specified torque only after the cylinder head and camshaft have been installed.

24 Timing chain/sprockets – removal and installation

Removal

1 Since the Silent Shaft chain and sprockets must be dismantled to gain access to the timing chain assembly, refer to Section 23 and remove the Silent Shaft chain and sprockets.
2 Depress the timing chain tensioner plunger (on the oil pump) and slide the camshaft sprocket, the crankshaft sprocket and the timing chain off the engine as an assembly. Do not lose the key that indexes the crankshaft sprocket in the proper place. Remove the timing chain tensioner plunger and spring from the oil pump.
3 Remove the camshaft sprocket holder and the right and left timing chain guides from the front of the engine block.

Installation

4 Install the sprocket holder (photo) and the right and left timing chain guides onto the engine block. Tighten the attaching bolts securely. The upper bolt in the left timing chain guide should be installed finger tight only. Coat the entire length of the chain contact surfaces of the guides with clean, high-quality multi-purpose grease.
5 Turn the crankshaft with a wrench on the large bolt at the front until the number 1 piston is at top dead center. When it is flush with the top of the engine block, it is at top dead center. Apply a layer of clean multi-purpose grease (or engine assembly lube) to the timing chain tensioner plunger and install the tensioner spring and plunger loosely into the oil pump body (photo).
6 Position the timing chain sprocket on the end of the crankshaft with the wide shoulder facing out (photo). Line up the key-way in the sprocket with the key on the crankshaft.
7 Install the camshaft sprocket onto the chain, lining up the plated link on the chain with the marked tooth on the sprocket (photo).
8 Slip the chain over the crankshaft sprocket, lining up the plated link on the chain with the marked tooth on the sprocket (photo). Slide the crankshaft sprocket all the way onto the crankshaft while depressing the chain tensioner so that the chain fits into place in the guides. Rest the camshaft sprocket on the sprocket holder. Do not rotate the crankshaft for any reason until the cylinder head and camshaft have been properly installed.

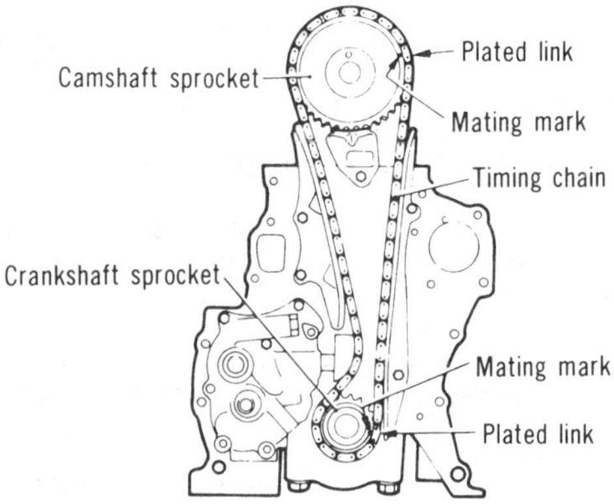

Fig. 2.36 Timing chain installation (Sec 24)

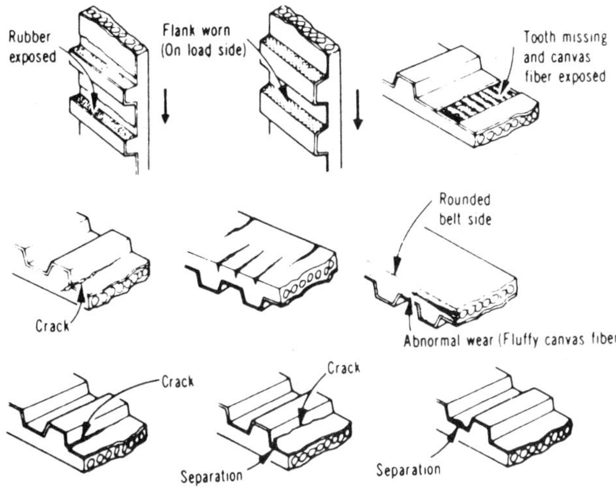

Fig. 2.37 Inspect the cogged-type belts (Sec 25)

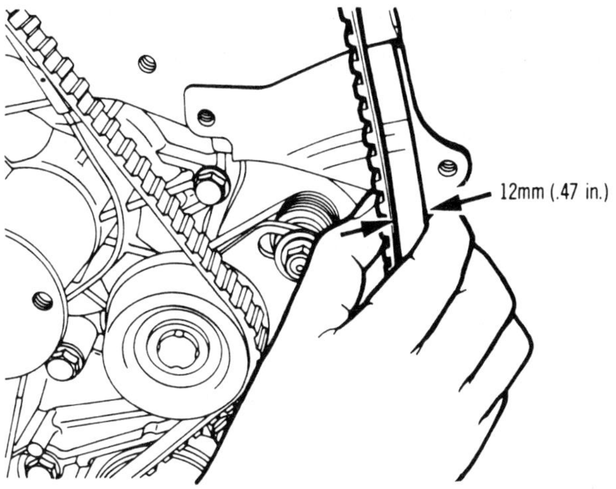

Fig. 2.38 Timing belt adjustment (Sec 26)

25 Timing belt/chain and sprockets – inspection

Belt

1 Check the belt carefully for oil and dirt deposits. Slight deposits can be removed with a shop towel. Do not clean the belt with solvent.
2 Whenever the belt is removed or the tension is adjusted, check the belt for hardened or cracked back surface rubber, cracked or separated plies, worn, cracked or missing teeth and cracked or worn sides.
3 Check the sprockets and tensioner for cracks, damage and abnormal wear. The surfaces of the oil pump sprocket and camshaft spacer that contact the oil seals should also be checked for wear. Check the tensioner pulley for smooth rotation. Replace any worn or damaged parts with new ones.

Chain

4 Inspect the sprocket teeth for wear and damage. Check the chain for cracked plates and pitted or worn rollers. Check the chain tensioner rubber shoe for wear and the tensioner spring for cracks or deterioration. Measure the tensioner spring free length. It should be 2.587 in (65.7 mm) long. Check the chain guides for wear and damage. Replace any defective parts with new ones.

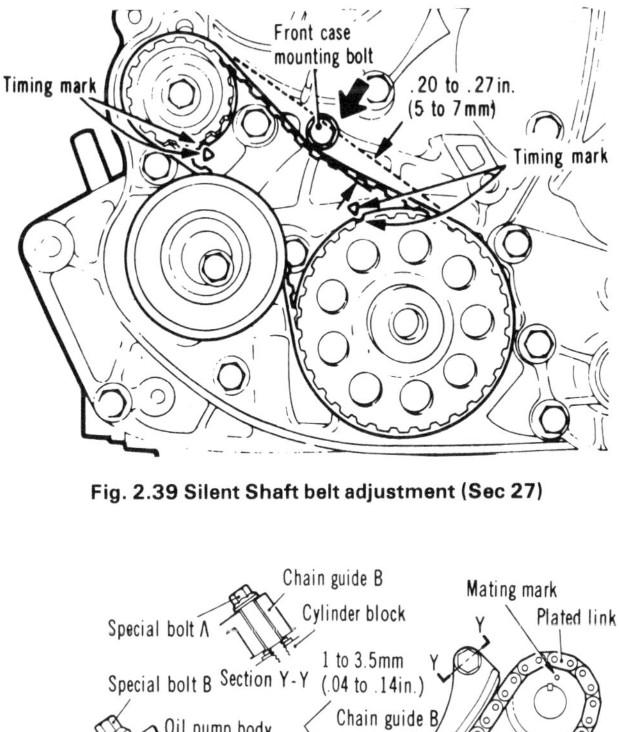

Fig. 2.39 Silent Shaft belt adjustment (Sec 27)

26 Timing belt/chain and sprockets – adjustment

Belts

1 By releasing the tensioner nut and bolt, the spring will cause the tensioner pulley to apply the correct tension to the belt. Tighten the nut to the specified torque and then the bolt. If the bolt is tightened first there is a danger of the tensioner moving and making the belt too tight. At no time during belt tensioning must the belt be touched, or the crankshaft will be turned in the reverse direction.
2 On completion of tensioning, check that the timing marks are still aligned and then grip the tension side of the belt between the thumb and forefinger to check that the clearance between the outer surface of the belt and the seal line of the under cover is $\frac{1}{2}$ in (12 mm). Re-adjust the belt tension if necessary (see illustrations).

Chain

3 There is no adjustment of the timing chain because of the spring and hydraulic-type tensioner.

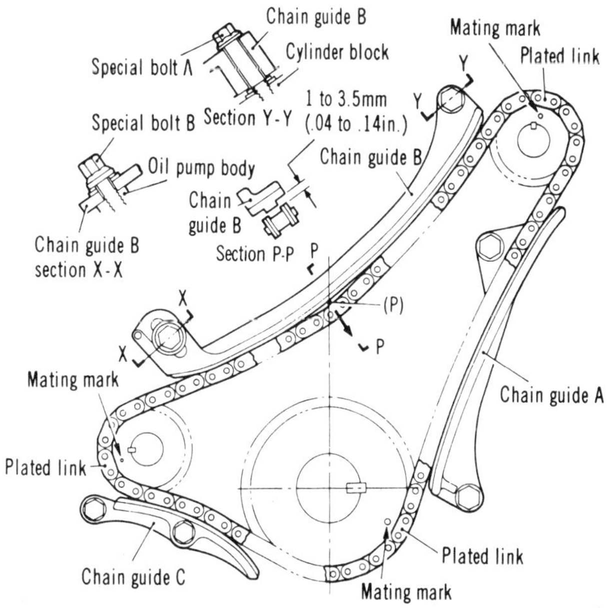

Fig. 2.40 Silent Shaft chain adjustment (Sec 27)

27 Silent Shaft belt/chain and sprockets – inspection and adjustments

1 For inspection of the belts or chain, refer to Section 27.
2 For adjustments of the Silent Shaft belts, refer to Section 22.
3 Adjust the chain slack as follows: rotate the right Silent Shaft clockwise and the left Silent Shaft counterclockwise so that the chain

slack is collected at point P. Pull the chain with your finger tips in the direction of arrow F, then move the lower end of the chain guide B up or down, as required, until the clearance between the chain and the guide (chain slack) is as specified. Tighten the chain guide B mounting bolts securely, then recheck the slack to make sure it has not changed. If the chain is not tensioned properly, engine noise will result.

4 Apply a coat of clean multi-purpose grease to the chain and chain guides.

28 Oil pump (1600 only) – removal and installation

Engines without Silent Shafts

Removal

1 Remove the bolts holding the oil pump cover and remove the pump cover.

2 Remove the front case and trochoid-type oil pump as an assembly. The front case may be hard to loosen. If so, insert a screwdriver in the case groove and pry on it. To avoid damage, do not apply any strong shock to the case.

Installation

3 Install a new front case gasket on the surface of the cylinder block. Install the case and tighten the bolts to Specifications and in the order shown in the illustration.

4 Install the oil pump inner and outer rotors onto the front case. Coat each one lightly with oil and make sure that the triangle marks are pointing in the same direction.

5 Install a new pump gasket and install the pump cover. Torque the bolts to Specifications.

Engines with Silent Shafts

Removal

6 Remove the bolts holding the oil pump cover and remove the pump cover.

7 Again, insert the screwdriver in the plug hole in the side of the cylinder block to hold the left Silent Shaft in position.

8 Loosen the pump-driven gear mounting bolt until it can be loosened by hand and leave it there.

9 Remove the front case with the left Silent Shaft still attached to it. If the front case is hard to remove, insert a screwdriver in the driver slot of the case and pry on it. Do not apply any shock to the case to avoid any damage.

10 Separate the pump gear and left shaft from the case.

Installation

11 Install the oil pump driven gear and the left Silent Shaft into the front case. Temporarily tighten the drivegear bolt to the shaft.

12 Install the front case, with gear and shaft attached, into the cylinder block. Be sure to replace the case gasket with a new one.

13 Install the case mounting bolts but do not tighten them. Install the oil pump drive gear. Coat both pump gears with engine oil and make sure that the timing marks line up.

14 Insert a screwdriver into the access hole and keep the left Silent Shaft in position and torque the bolt to Specification.

15 Install the pump cover and torque the retaining bolts to Specifications.

16 Now, tighten the case bolts to the specified torque.

17 Finally, install the rear upper and lower covers and tighten their bolts to the correct torque.

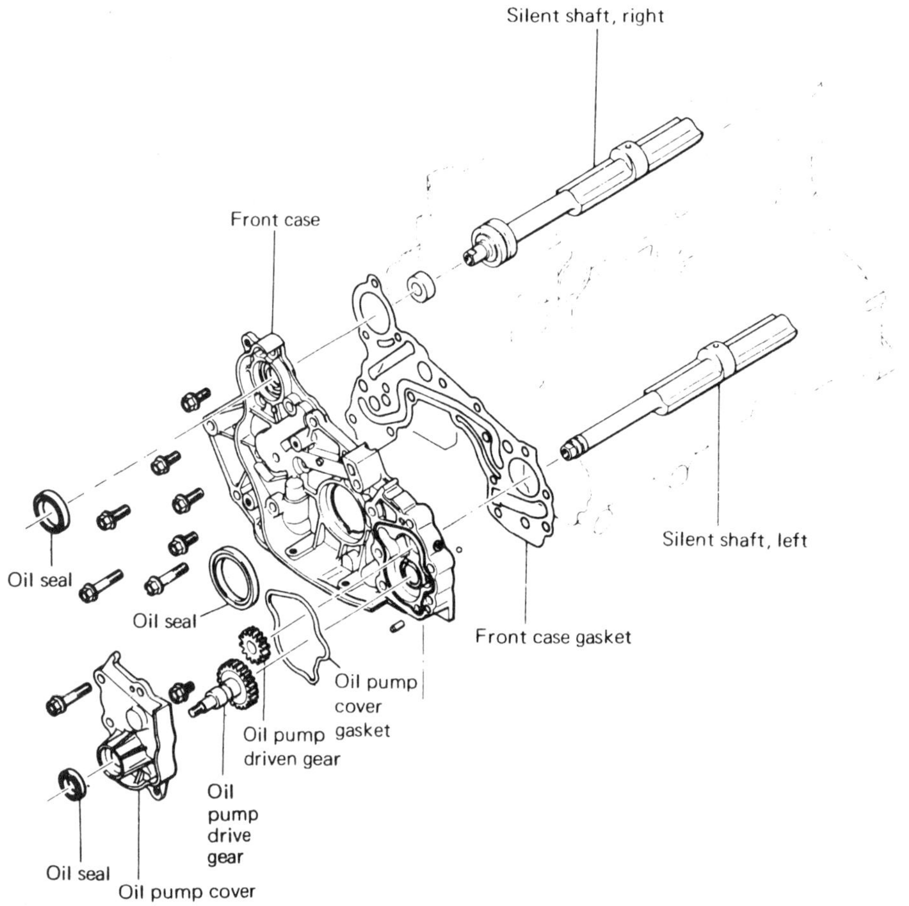

Fig. 2.41 Oil pump and case with Silent Shafts (1600 cc only) – exploded view (Sec 28)

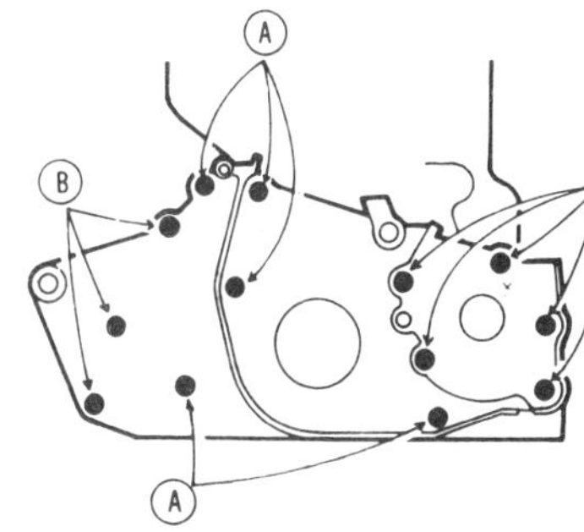

Fig. 2.42 Front case bolt tightening sequence (Sec 28)

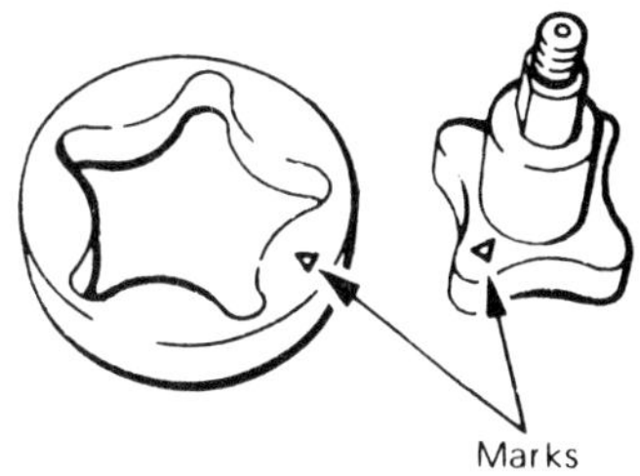

Fig. 2.43 Correct oil pump rotor installation (Sec 28)

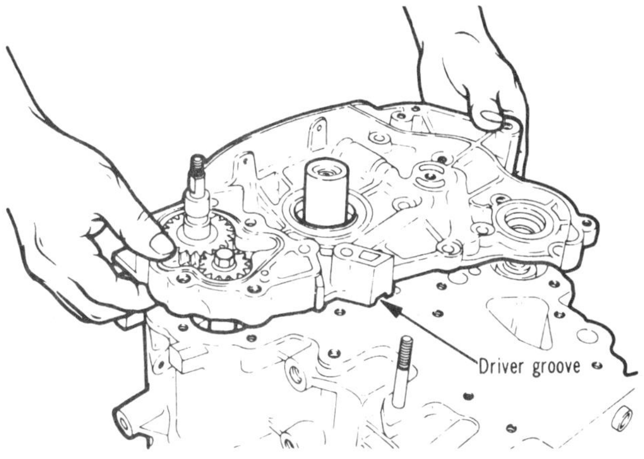

Fig. 2.44 Front case driver pry groove (Sec 28)

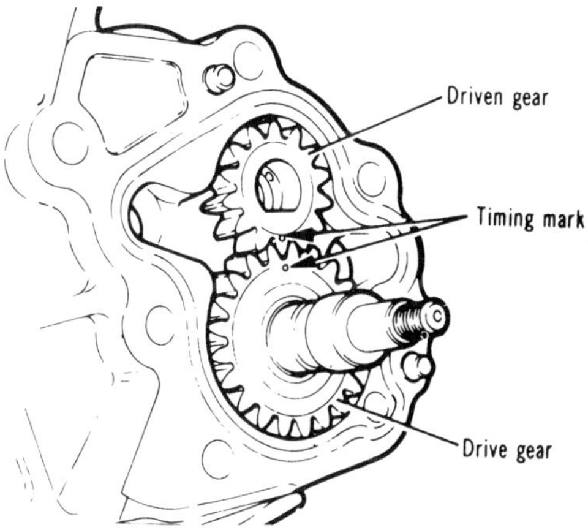

Fig. 2.45 Oil pump drive gear alignment (Sec 28)

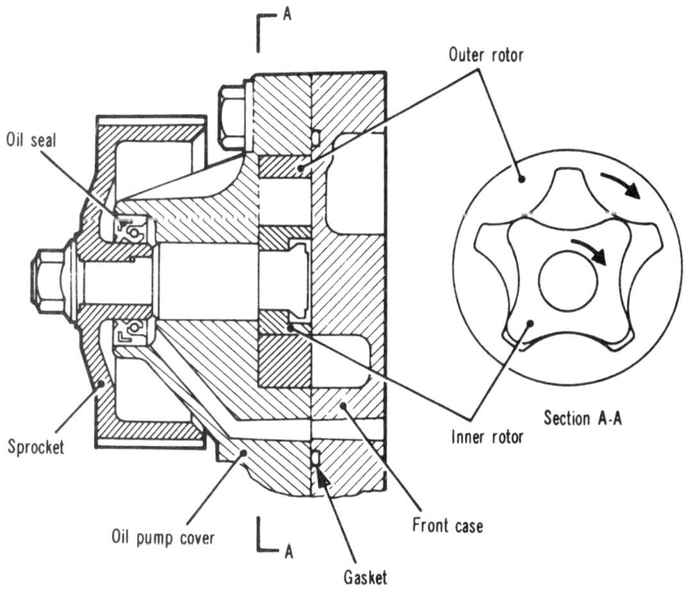

Fig. 2.46 Trochoid pump components – sectional view (Sec 29)

29 Oil pump (1600 only) – inspection and overhaul

1 Remove the cover retaining bolts, take off the cover and then remove and discard the gasket.
2 If it is necessary to renew the rotor assembly or the gear, drill away the peened section of the gear retaining pin and drive the pin out.
3 Check that the rotor-to-cover clearance does not exceed 0.008 in, that the outer rotor-to-body clearance is not more than 0.012 in and that the inner rotor clearance is not more than 0.010 in. Check that the relief plunger slides freely and that the oil passage and plunger bore are undamaged. Examine the spring to see that it is not bent or broken.
4 Reassemble the pump, using a new gasket. If the gear has been removed, install it with the mating marks aligned. Install the gear locking pin and peen it at both ends.
5 If clearances in the pump and mating parts are beyond the Specifications, replace the pump as a unit with a new one.

2

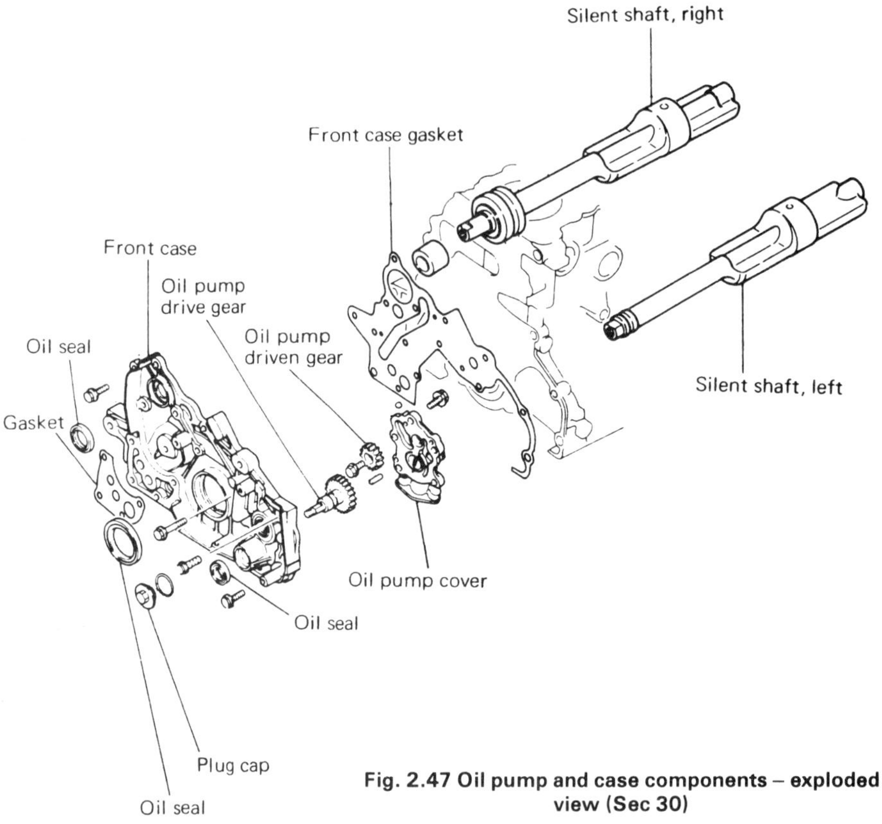

Fig. 2.47 Oil pump and case components – exploded view (Sec 30)

30 Oil pump – removal and installation

Removal

1 The oil pump and right Silent Shaft are removed from the engine as an assembly.

2 Remove the bolt attaching the oil pump to the engine block. Some of the Silent Shaft chain guide mounting bolts also serve as oil pump mounting bolts; they have already been removed. Leave the Phillips head screw in the left side of the pump in place.

3 Carefully pull straight ahead on the oil pump and remove it, along with the right Silent Shaft, from the engine block. You may have to tap gently on the oil pump body with a soft-faced hammer to break the gasket seal. Do not pry between the oil pump and engine block, as damage to the pump body could result.

4 Remove the bolt from the end of the right Silent Shaft and pull the shaft out of the oil pump from the rear. Do not lose the key in the end of the shaft. Refer to Section 33 for Silent Shaft inspection procedures.

5 Remove the plug from the upper side of the pump body and withdraw the relief spring and plunger. You may have to mount the pump body in a vise equipped with soft jaws to loosen the plug. If so, do not apply excessive pressure to the pump body.

6 Remove the Phillips head screw from the left side of the pump. Separate the oil pump cover from the body and lift out the two pump gears. Do not lose the key in the lower gear shaft. Do not pry between the cover and body, as damage to the pump may result.

Installation

7 Lay a new gasket in place on the cover (no sealer is required). The dowel pins should align it properly and hold it in place.

8 Make sure the key is in place in the front of the shaft, then slip the right Silent Shaft through the oil pump driven gear as you line up the key in the shaft with the key-way in the gear. Once the shaft and gear are properly mated, clamp the counterweight end of the shaft in a vise equipped with soft jaws, install the bolt in the front end of the shaft and tighten it to the specified torque.

9 Apply a thin layer of clean multi-purpose grease (or engine assembly lube) to the rear bearing journal of the right Silent Shaft.

30.10 Fill the oil pump with 10 cc of oil before installing

10 Hold the pump upright and fill it with a minimum of 10 cc of engine oil (photo). Insert the Silent Shaft into the engine block and through the rear bearing. Be careful not to scratch or gouge the bearing as the shaft is installed.

11 Make sure the pump is seated on the engine block, then install the mounting bolts and tighten them evenly and securely. Do not forget to tighten the Phillips head screw. The remaining pump mounting bolts will be installed with the chain guides.

12 Temporarily slip the Silent Shaft drive sprocket onto the lower pump gear shaft and use it to rotate the pump gears/Silent Shaft. Check for any obvious binding.

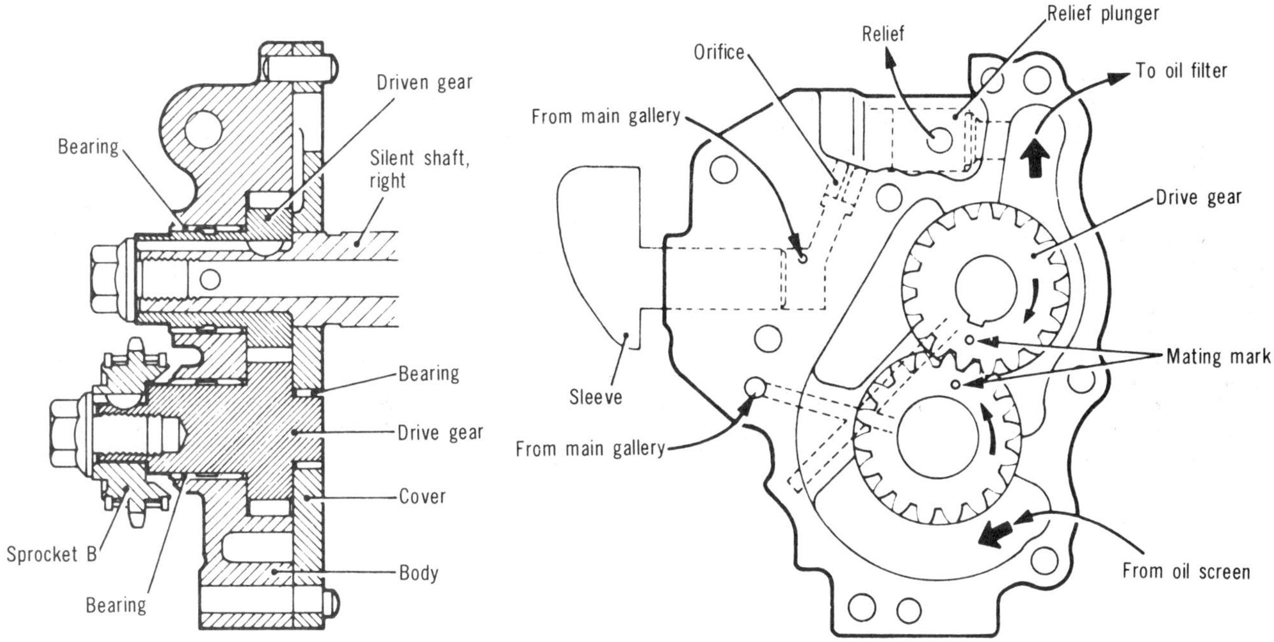

Fig. 2.48 Gear pump components – sectional view (Sec 31)

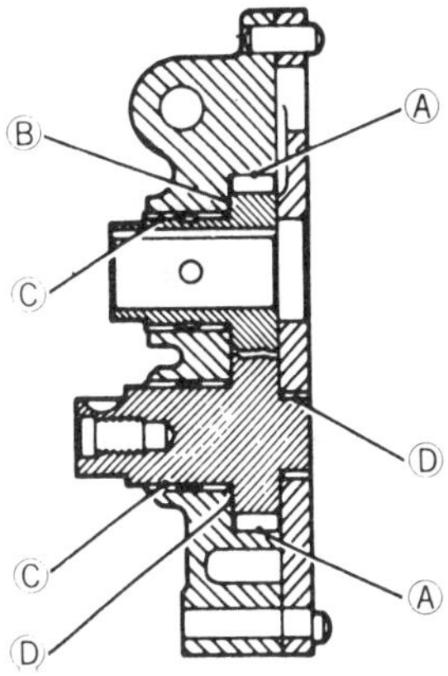

Fig. 2.49 Gear pump clearance check – see text and specifications for letter designations (Sec 31)

31 Oil pump – inspection and overhaul

1 Remove the plug from the upper side of the pump body and withdraw the relief spring and plunger. You may have to mount the pump body in a vise equipped with soft jaws to loosen the plug. If so, do not apply excessive pressure to the pump body.
2 Remove the Phillips head screw from the left side of the pump. Separate the oil pump cover from the body and lift out the two pump gears. Do not lose the key in the lower gear shaft. Do not pry between the cover and body, as damage to the pump may result.
3 Clean the parts with solvent and dry them thoroughly. Use compressed air to blow out all of the oil holes and passages.
4 Check the entire pump body and cover for cracks and excessive wear. Look closely for a ridge where the gears contact the body and cover.
5 Insert the relief plunger into the pump body and check to see if it slides smoothly. Look for cracks in the relief spring and measure its free length. Inspect the timing chain tensioner plunger sleeve for noticeable wear and the rubber pad for cracks and excessive wear. Measure the tensioner spring free length.
6 With the gears in place in the pump body, measure the top clearance A between the gears and the pump body with a feeler gauge. Measure the inside diameter of the bearing surfaces and the outside diameter of the gear shaft at C and D. Subtract the gear shaft diameters from their matching bearing surface diameters to obtain the gear-to-bearing clearance. With the pump assembled, check the gear end play B using a dial indicator set. Compare the measured clearances to the Specifications.
7 If the oil pump clearances are excessive or if excessive wear is evident, replace the oil pump as a unit.
8 Coat the oil pump relief plunger with clean multi-purpose grease and insert the plunger and spring into the oil pump body. Install the cap and tighten it securely.
9 Apply a layer of multi-purpose grease to the gear teeth, the sides of the gears and the bearing surfaces in the pump body and cover. Lay the gears in place in the body with the mating marks lined up (photo). If the mating marks are not properly aligned, the right Silent Shaft will be out of phase and engine vibration will result.
10 Lay the cover in place using the dowel pins to align it properly. Install the Phillips head screw in the left side of the pump, but do not tighten it completely at this time. Make sure the gears rotate smoothly without binding.

31.9 Line up the mating marks on the oil pump gears

2

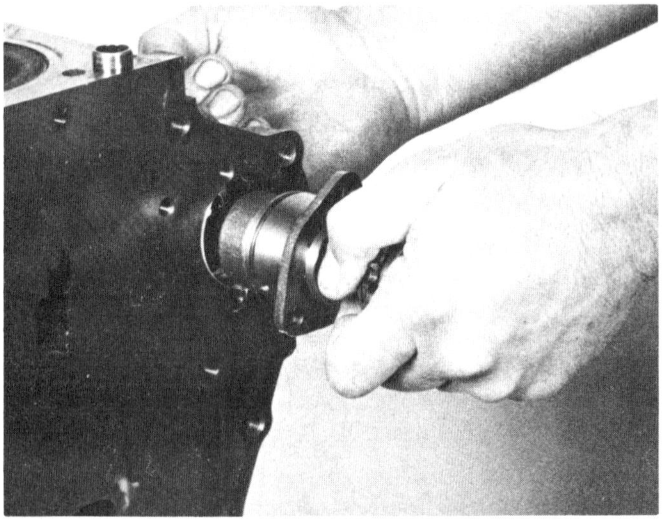

32.3 Remove the left Silent Shaft thrust plate assembly

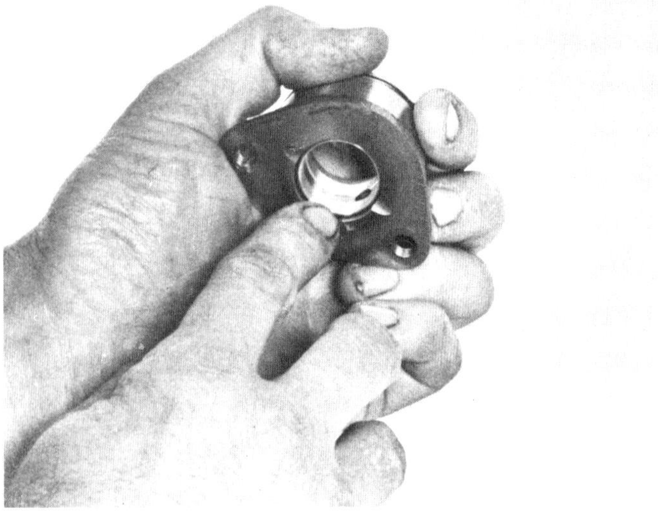

33.2 Check the bearing in the left Silent Shaft thrust plate

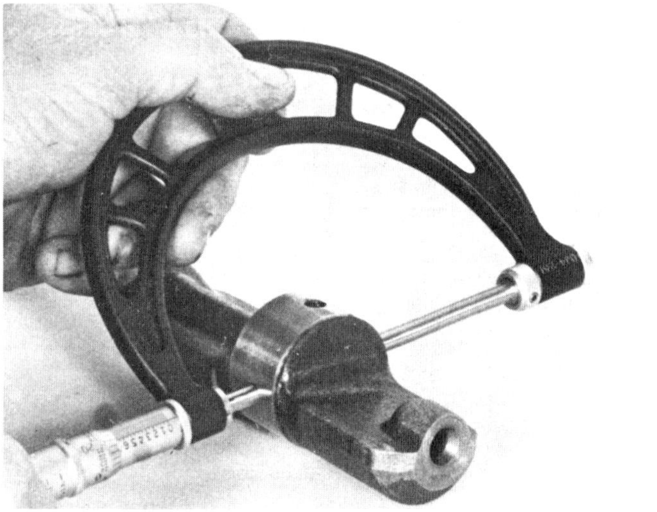

33.3 Measure the Silent Shaft bearing journal outside diameter

32 Silent Shafts – removal and installation

Removal

1 During engine disassembly, the Silent Shaft chain and sprockets, the timing chain and sprockets and the oil pump should be removed before the Silent Shafts.

2 Remove the left Silent Shaft chamber cover plate from the engine block. It is held in place with two bolts. You may have to tap the cover with a soft-faced hammer to break the gasket seal.

3 Remove the bolts attaching the left Silent Shaft thrust plate to the engine block, then carefully pull out the thrust plate and the Silent Shaft as an assembly. Support the rear of the shaft by reaching through the access hole to prevent damage to the rear bearing as the shaft is withdrawn from the engine (photo). If the thrust plate proves to be difficult to pull out, screw the appropriate size bolt into each of the threaded holes in the thrust plate flange until they bottom on the engine block. Continue turning them with a wrench, one turn at a time, alternating between the two, until the thrust plate is backed out of the engine block. Remove the bolts from the thrust plate flange.

4 The right Silent Shaft is removed with the oil pump (refer to Section 30).

5 To disassemble the left Silent Shaft, slip off the spacer and the thrust plate/bearing assembly. Do not lose the key in the end of the shaft. Remove the O-ring from the thrust plate.

Installation

6 Apply a thin layer of clean multi-purpose grease (or engine assembly lube) to the bearing journals on the left Silent Shaft, then carefully insert it into the engine block. Support the rear of the shaft so that the rear bearing is not scratched or gouged as the shaft passes through it.

7 Install a new O-ring onto the outside of the thrust plate and lubricate it with clean multi-purpose grease. Also, apply a layer of grease to the thrust plate Silent Shaft bearing.

8 Cut the heads off two 6 x 50 mm bolts and install the bolts in the thrust plate mounting bolt holes. Using the bolts as a guide, carefully slide the thrust plate into position in the engine block. The guides are necessary to keep the bolt holes in the thrust plate aligned with the holes in the engine block. If the thrust plate is turned to align the holes, the O-ring could be twisted or damaged.

9 Remove the guide bolts, install the mounting bolts and tighten them securely.

10 Slip the spacer onto the end of the Silent Shaft. Make sure that the key is in place.

11 Turn the shaft by hand and check for smooth operation.

12 Using a new rubber gasket and silicone-type gasket sealer, as well as new O-rings on the bolts, install the left Silent Shaft chamber cover plate and tighten the bolts to the specified torque.

13 The right Silent Shaft is installed with the oil pump.

33 Silent Shafts – inspection

1 Clean the components with solvent and dry them thoroughly. Make sure that the oil holes in the shafts and thrust plate are clean and clear.

2 Check both Silent Shafts and the thrust plate for cracks and other damage. Check the bearings in the engine block and the thrust plate (photo) for scratches, scoring and excessive wear. Check the bearing journals on the Silent Shafts for excessive wear and scoring.

3 Measure the outside diameter of each bearing journal (photo) and the inside diameter of each bearing. Subtract the journal diameter from the bearing diameter to obtain the bearing oil clearance. Compare the measured clearance to the Specifications. If it is excessive, have an automotive machine shop or dealer service department replace the bearings with new ones. If new bearings do not restore the oil clearance, or if the bearing journals on the shafts are damaged or worn, replace the shafts also. If the bearing in the left Silent Shaft thrust plate is bad, replace the bearing and thrust plate as an assembly.

34 Pistons and connecting rods – removal and installation

Removal

1 Prior to removing the piston/connecting rod assemblies remove

the cylinder head, the oil pan, the timing chain case, the Silent Shaft chain and sprockets and the timing chain and sprockets by referring to the appropriate Sections.

2 Using a ridge reamer, completely remove the ridge at the top of each cylinder. Follow the manufacturer's instructions provided with the ridge reaming tool. Failure to remove the ridge before attempting to remove the piston/connecting rod assemblies will result in piston breakage.

3 With the engine in the upside-down position, remove the oil pick-up tube and screen assembly from the bottom of the engine block (photo). It is held in place with bolts.

4 Mark each of the connecting rods and connecting rod bearing caps to ensure that they are properly mated during reassembly.

5 Loosen each of the connecting rod cap nuts approximately $\frac{1}{2}$-turn each. Remove the number 1 connecting rod cap and bearing insert. Do not drop the bearing insert out of the cap. Slip a short length of plastic or rubber hose over each connecting rod cap bolt to protect the crankshaft journal when the piston is removed (photo) and push the connecting rod/piston assembly out through the top of the engine. Use a wooden tool to push on the upper bearing insert in the connecting rod. If resistance is felt, double-check to make sure that all of the ridge was removed from the cylinder.

6 Repeat the procedure for cylinders 2, 3 and 4. After removal, reassemble the connecting rod caps and bearing inserts to their respective connecting rods and install the cap nuts finger tight. Leaving the old bearing inserts in place until reassembly will help prevent the connecting rod bearing surfaces from being accidentally nicked or gouged.

7 Do not clean or inspect any parts until the engine block is cleaned and inspected.

Installation

8 Before installing the piston/connecting rod assemblies, the cylinder walls must be perfectly clean, the top edge of each cylinder must be chamfered, and the crankshaft must be in place.

9 Remove the connecting rod cap from the end of the number 1 connecting rod. Remove the old bearing inserts and wipe the bearing surfaces of the connecting rod and cap with a clean, lint-free cloth (they must be spotlessly clean).

10 Clean the back side of the new upper bearing half, then lay it in place in the connecting rod. Make sure that the tab on the bearing fits into the recess in the rod. Also, the oil holes in the rod and bearing insert must line up. Do not hammer the bearing insert into place, and be very careful not to nick or gouge the bearing face. Do not lubricate the bearing at this time.

11 Clean the back side of the other bearing insert half and install it in the rod cap. Again, make sure the tab on the bearing fits into the recess in the cap, and do not apply any lubricant. It is critically important to ensure that the mating surfaces of the bearing and connecting rod are perfectly clean and oil-free when they are assembled together.

12 Position the piston ring gaps as shown, then slip a section of plastic or rubber hose over the connecting rod cap bolts.

13 Lubricate the piston and rings with clean engine oil and install a piston ring compressor on the piston. Leave the skirt protruding about $\frac{1}{4}$ in to guide the piston into the cylinder. The rings must be compressed as far as possible.

14 Rotate the crankshaft so that the number 1 connecting rod journal is as far from the number 1 cylinder as possible (bottom dead center), and apply a uniform coat of engine oil to the number 1 cylinder walls.

15 With the arrow on top of the piston pointing to the front of the engine, gently place the piston/connecting rod assembly into the number 1 cylinder bore (photo) and rest the bottom edge of the ring compressor on the engine block. Tap the top edge of the ring compressor to make sure it is contacting the block around its entire circumference.

16 Clean the number 1 connecting rod journal on the crankshaft and the bearing faces in the rod.

17 Carefully tap on the top of the piston with the end of a wooden hammer handle while guiding the end of the connecting rod into place on the crankshaft journal. The piston rings may try to pop out of the ring compressor just before entering the cylinder bore, so keep some downward pressure on the ring compressor. Work slowly, and if any resistance is felt as the piston enters the cylinder, stop immediately, find out what is hanging up and fix it before proceeding. Do not, for

34.3 Remove the oil pick-up tube mounting bolts

34.5 Install short lengths of old hose over the connecting rod cap bolts to prevent damage to the crankshaft journal during removal of the piston/connecting rod assembly

34.15 Install the piston/connecting rod assembly into the cylinder bore with the ring compressor

2

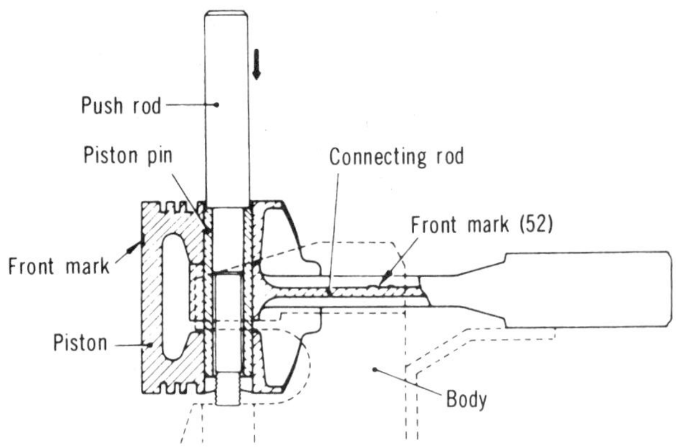

Fig. 2.50 Piston pin removal (Sec 34)

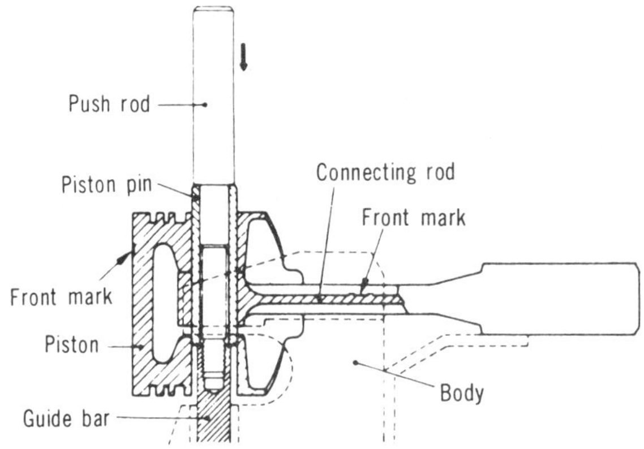

Fig. 2.51 Piston pin installation (Sec 34)

any reason, force the piston into the cylinder, as you will break a ring and/or the piston.

18 Once the piston/connecting rod assembly is installed, the connecting rod bearing oil clearance must be checked before the rod cap is permanently bolted in place.

19 Trim a piece of the appropriate type Plastigage so that it is slightly shorter than the width of the connecting rod bearing and lay it in place on number 1 connecting rod journal, parallel with the journal axis. It must not cross the oil hole in the journal.

20 Clean the connecting rod cap bearing face, remove the protective hoses from the connecting rod bolts and gently install the rod cap in place. Make sure the mating mark on the cap is on the same side as the mark on the connecting rod. Install the nuts and tighten them to the specified torque, working up to it in three steps. Do not rotate the crankshaft at any time during this operation.

21 Remove the rod cap, being very careful not to disturb the Plastigage. Compare the width of the crushed Plastigage to the scale printed on the Plastigage container (photo) to obtain the oil clearance. Compare it to the Specifications to make sure the clearance is correct. If the clearance is not correct, double-check to make sure that you have the correct size bearing inserts. Also, recheck the crankshaft connecting rod journal diameter and make sure that no dirt or oil was between the bearing inserts and the connecting rod or cap when the clearance was measured.

22 Carefully scrape all traces of the Plasigage material off the rod journal and/or bearing face. Be very careful not to scratch the bearing. Make sure the bearing faces are perfectly clean, then apply a uniform layer of clean, high quality multi-purpose grease (or engine assembly lube) to both of them. You will have to push the piston into the cylinder to expose the face of the bearing insert in the connecting rod. Be sure to slip the protective hoses over the rod bolts first.

23 Slide the connecting rod back into place on the journal, remove the protective hoses from the rod cap bolts, install the rod cap and tighten the nuts to the specified torque. Again, work up to the torque in three steps.

24 Without turning the crankshaft, repeat the entire procedure for the number 4 piston/connecting rod assembly. Keep the back sides of the bearing inserts and the inside of the connecting rod and cap perfectly clean when assembling them. Make sure you have the correct piston for the cylinder and that the arrow on the piston points to the front of the engine when the piston is installed. Remember, use plenty of oil to lubricate the piston before installing the ring compressor, and be sure to match up the mating marks on the connecting rod and rod cap. Also, when installing the rod caps for the final time, be sure to lubricate the bearing faces adequately.

25 After completing the procedure for piston number 4, turn the crankshaft 180° and repeat the entire operation for pistons number 2 and 3.

26 After all the piston/connecting rod assemblies have been properly installed, rotate the crankshaft a number of times by hand and check for any obvious binding.

27 As a final step, the connecting rod big end side clearances must be

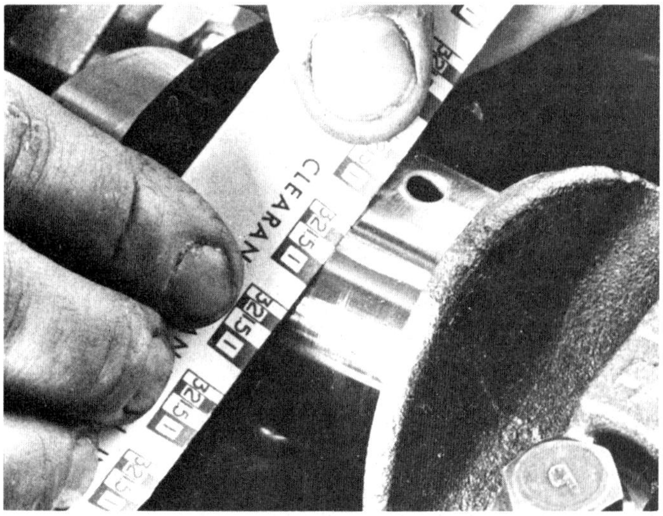

34.21 Compare the width of the crushed Plastigage to the container scale to obtain the connecting rod bearing oil clearance

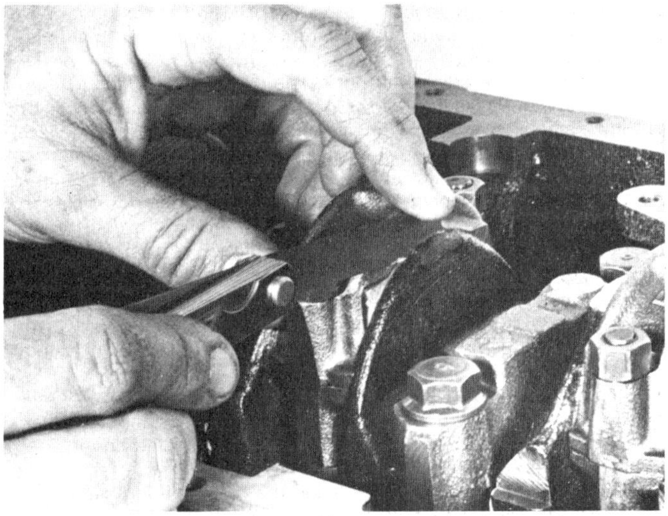

34.27 Check the connecting rod big-end side clearance

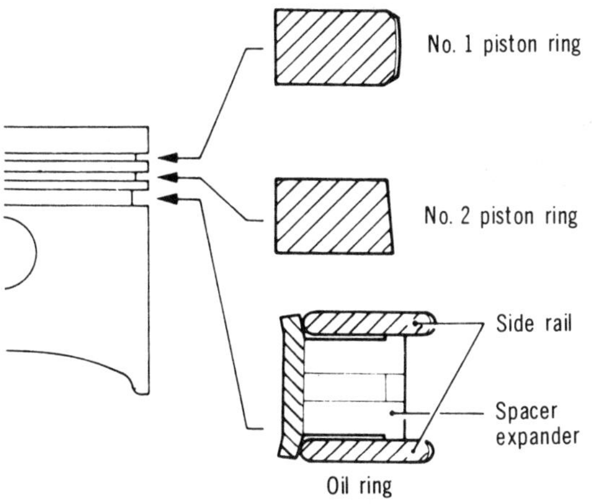

Fig. 2.52 Piston ring installation sequence (Sec 34)

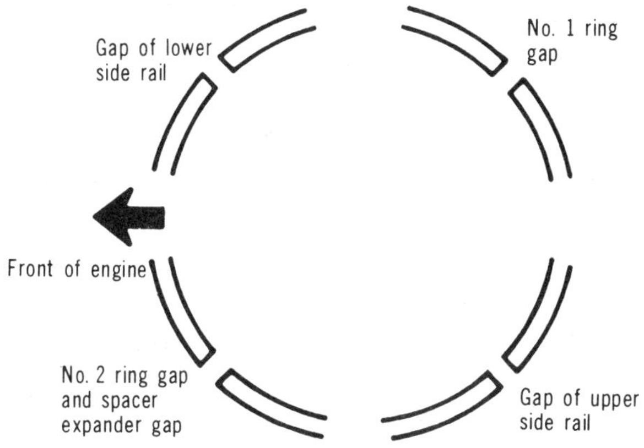

Fig. 2.53 Piston ring end gap positions (Sec 34)

checked. Slide the number 1 connecting rod all the way to one end of its journal and slip a feeler gauge between the side of the connecting rod and the crankshaft throw (photo). Be sure to compare the measured clearance to the Specifications to make sure it is correct. Repeat the procedure for the other three connecting rods.

35 Crankshaft – removal and installation

Removal

1 Before removing the crankshaft, you must remove the flywheel, the rear oil seal housing, the cylinder head, the oil pan, the timing chain case, the Silent Shaft chain and sprockets and the timing chain and sprockets, by referring to the appropriate Sections.
2 With the engine upside-down, remove the oil pick-up tube and screen assembly from the bottom of the engine block. It is held in place with two bolts.
3 Remove the piston assemblies from the engine block, as described in Section 34. Be sure to mark each connecting rod and bearing cap so that they will be properly mated during reassembly.
4 Loosen each of the main bearing cap bolts $\frac{1}{4}$ of a turn at a time, in sequence, starting at the center of the engine, until they can be removed by hand.
5 Gently tap the main bearing caps with a soft-faced hammer, then remove them from the engine block. If necessary, use the main bearing cap bolts as levers to remove the caps. Try not to drop the bearing shell, if it comes out with the cap. The main bearing caps are marked at the factory with a number (1 through 5, starting at the front of the engine) and an arrow (indicating the front of the engine) so you do not have to mark them.
6 Carefully lift the crankshaft out of the engine. It is a good idea to have an assistant available, as the crankshaft is quite heavy. With the bearing inserts in place in the engine block and the main bearing caps, return the caps to their respective location on the engine block and tighten the bolts finger tight.
7 Do not clean or inspect any parts until the engine block is cleaned and inspected.

Installation

8 Crankshaft installation is generally one of the first steps in engine reassembly. It is assumed at this point that the engine block and crankshaft have been cleaned and inspected and repaired or reconditioned.
9 Position the engine so that the bottom is facing up.
10 Remove the main bearing cap bolts and lift out the caps. Lay them out in the proper order to help ensure they are installed correctly.
11 If they are still in place, remove the old bearing inserts from the block and the main bearing caps. Wipe the main bearing surfaces of the block and caps with a clean, lint-free cloth. They must be kept spotlessly clean.
12 Clean the back side of the new main bearing inserts and lay one bearing half in each main bearing saddle (in the block) and the other

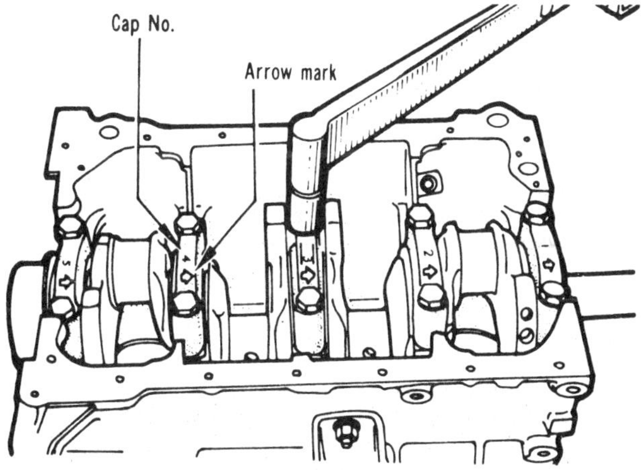

Fig. 2.54 Main bearing cap installation (Sec 35)

2

bearing half from each bearing set in the corresponding main bearing cap. Make sure the tab on the bearing insert fits into the recess in the block or cap. Also, the oil holes in the block and cap must line up with the oil holes in the bearing insert. Do not hammer the bearing into place and do not nick or gouge the bearing faces. No lubrication should be used at this time.
13 The flanged thrust bearing must be installed in the number 3 (center) cap and saddle.
14 Clean the faces of the bearings in the block and the crankshaft main bearing journal with a clean, lint-free cloth. Check or clean the oil holes in the crankshaft, as any dirt here can only go one way – straight through the new bearings.
15 Once you are certain that the crankshaft is clean, carefully lay it in position (an assistant would be very helpful here) in the main bearings with the counterweights lying sideways.
16 Before the crankshaft can be permanently installed, the main bearing oil clearance must be checked.
17 Trim 5 pieces of the appropriate type of Plastigage (so that they are slightly shorter than the width of the main bearings) and place one piece on each crankshaft main bearing journal, parallel with the journal axis. Do not lay them across any oil holes.
18 Clean the faces of the bearings in the caps and install the caps in their respective positions (do not mix them up) with the arrows pointing toward the front of the engine. Do not disturb the Plastigage.
19 Starting with the center main and working out toward the ends, tighten the main bearing cap bolts, in three steps, to the specified torque. Do not rotate the crankshaft at any time during this operation.
20 Remove the bolts and carefully lift off the main bearing caps. Keep them in order. Do not disturb the Plastigage or rotate the crankshaft. If any of the main bearing caps are difficult to remove, tap gently from side to side with a soft-faced hammer to loosen them.

21 Compare the width of the crushed Plastigage on each journal to the scale printed on the Plastigage container (photo) to obtain the main bearing oil clearance. Check the Specifications to make sure it is correct.
22 If the clearance is not correct, double-check to make sure that you have the right size bearing inserts. Also, recheck the crankshaft main bearing journal diameters and make sure that no dirt or oil was between the bearing inserts and the main bearing caps or the block when the clearance was measured.
23 Carefully scrape all traces of the Plastigage material off the main bearing journals and/or the bearing faces. Do not nick or scratch the bearing faces.
24 Carefully lift the crankshaft out of the engine. Clean the bearing faces in the block, then apply a thin, uniform layer of clean, high-quality multi-purpose grease (or engine assembly lube) to each of the bearing faces. Be sure to coat the thrust flange faces as well as the journal face of the thrust bearing in the number 3 (center) main. Make sure the crankshaft journals are clean, then carefully lay it back in place in the block. Clean the faces of the bearings in the caps, then apply a thin, uniform layer of clean, high-quality multi-purpose grease to each of the bearing faces and install the caps in their respective positions with the arrows pointing toward the front of the engine. Install the bolts and tighten them to the specified torque, starting with the center main and working out toward the ends. Work up to the final torque in three steps.
25 Rotate the crankshaft a number of times by hand and check for any obvious binding.
26 The final step is to check the crankshaft endplay. This can be done with a feeler gauge or a dial indicator set (photo).
27 If a feeler gauge is used, gently pry the crankshaft all the way toward the back of the engine with a large screwdriver. Slip a feeler gauge between the crankshaft thrust face and the bearing thrust face at the rear side of the number 3 (center) main bearing. Compare the measured endplay to the Specifications.
28 If a dial indicator is used, mount it at the rear of the engine with the indicator stem touching the end of the flange on the crankshaft. Gently pry the crankshaft all the way to the back of the engine, then zero the dial indicator. Carefully pry the crankshaft as far as possible in the opposite direction and observe the needle movement on the dial indicator, which will indicate the amount of endplay. Compare it to the Specifications.

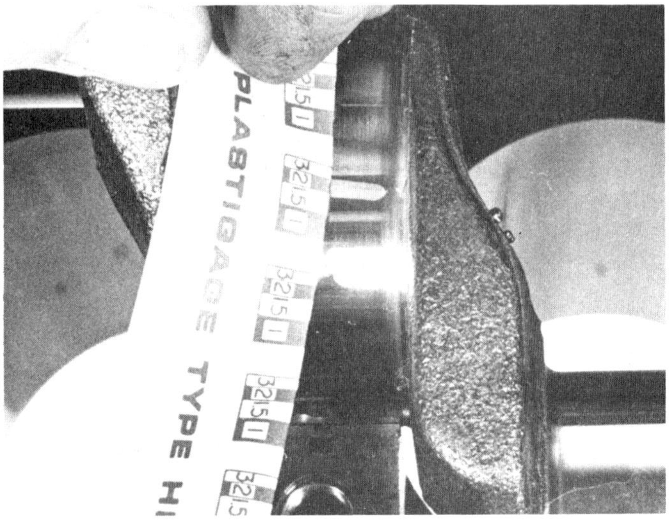

35.21 Compare the width of the crushed Plastigage to the container scale to obtain the main bearing oil clearance

35.26 Check the crankshaft endplay with a dial indicator

36 Engine block – cleaning and inspection

Cleaning

1 Remove the soft plugs from the engine block. To do this, knock the plugs into the block (using a hammer and punch), then grasp them with a large pliers and pull them back through the hole.
2 Using a gasket scraper, remove all traces of gasket material from the engine block. Be very careful not to nick or gouge the gasket sealing surfaces.
3 Remove the main bearing caps and separate the bearing shells from the caps and the engine block. Tag the bearing shells according to which cylinder they were removed from (and whether they were in the cap or the block) and set them aside.
4 Using a hex wrench of the appropriate size, remove the threaded oil gallery plugs from the front and back of the block.
5 If the engine is extremely dirty, it should be taken to an automotive machine shop to be steam cleaned or hot tanked. Any bearings left in the block (such as the Silent Shaft bearings) may be damaged by the cleaning process, so plan on replacing them.
6 After the block is returned, clean all oil holes and oil galleries one more time (brushes for cleaning oil holes and galleries are available at most auto parts stores). Flushing the passages with warm water (until the water runs clear), dry the block thoroughly and wipe all machined surfaces with a light rust-preventative oil. If you have access to compressed air, use it to speed the drying process and to blow out all of the oil holes and galleries.
7 If the block is not extremely dirty or sludged up, you can do an adequate cleaning job with warm soapy water and a stiff brush. Take plenty of time and do a thorough job. Regardless of the cleaning method used, be very sure to thoroughly clean all oil holes and galleries, dry the block completely and coat all machined surfaces with light oil.

36.10 Install the soft plugs in the engine block

36.15 Measure the cylinder diameter with a bore gauge

36.18 Hone the cylinder with a surface hone

8 The threaded holes in the block must be clean to ensure accurate torque readings during reassembly. Run the proper size tap into each of the holes to remove any rust, corrosion, thread sealant or sludge and to restore any damaged threads. If possible, use compressed air to clear the holes of debris produced by this operation. Now is a good time to thoroughly clean the threads on the head bolts and the main bearing cap bolts as well.
9 Reinstall the main bearing caps and tighten the bolts finger tight.
10 After coating the sealing surfaces of the new soft plugs with a good quality gasket sealer, install them in the engine block (photo). Make sure they are driven in straight and seated properly, or leakage could result. Special tools are available for this purpose, but equally good results can be obtained using a large socket (with an outside diameter slightly larger than the outside diameter of the soft plug) and a large hammer.
11 If the engine is not going to be reassembled right away, cover it with a large plastic trash bag to keep it clean.

Inspection

12 Thoroughly clean the engine block as described above and double check to make sure that the ridge at the top of the cylinders has been completely removed.
13 Visually check the block for cracks, rust and corrosion. Look for stripped threads in the threaded holes. It is also a good idea to have the block checked for hidden cracks by an automotive machine shop that has the special equipment to do this type of work. If defects are found, have the block repaired, if possible, or replaced.
14 Check the cylinder bores for scuffing and scoring.
15 Using the appropriate precision measuring tools, measure each cylinder's diameter at the top (just under the ridge), center and bottom of the cylinder bore, parallel to the crankshaft axis (photo). Next, measure each cylinder's diameter at the same 3 locations across the crankshaft axis. Compare the results to the Specifications. If the cylinder walls are badly scuffed or scored, or if they are out-of-round or tapered beyond the limits given in the Specifications, have the engine block rebored and honed at an automotive machine shop. If a rebore is done, oversized pistons and rings will be required as well.
16 If the cylinders are in reasonably good condition and not worn to the outside of the limits, and if the piston-to-cylinder clearances can be maintained properly, then they do not have to be rebored; honing is all that is necessary.
17 Before honing the cylinders, install the main bearing caps (without the bearings) and tighten the bolts to the specified torque.
18 To perform the honing operation, you will need the proper size flexible hone (with fine stones), plenty of light oil or honing oil, some rags and an electric drill motor. Mount the hone in the drill motor, compress the stones and slip the hone into the first cylinder. Lubricate the cylinder thoroughly, turn on the drill and move the hone up and down in the cylinder at a pace which will produce a fine cross-hatch pattern on the cylinder walls with the cross-hatch lines intersecting at approximately a 60° angle. Be sure to use plenty of lubricant and do not take off any more material than is absolutely necessary to produce the desired finish. Do not withdraw the hone from the cylinder while it is running. Instead, shut off the drill and continue moving the hone up and down in the cylinder until it comes to a complete stop, then compress the stones and withdraw the hone. Wipe the oil out of the cylinder and repeat the procedure on the remaining cylinders. Remember, do not remove too much material from the cylinder wall. If you do not have the tools or do not desire to perform the honing operation, most automotive machine shops will do it for a reasonable fee (photo).
19 After the honing job is complete, chamfer the top edges of the cylinder bores with a small file so that the rings will not catch when the pistons are installed. 2
20 Next, the engine block must be thoroughly washed again with warm soapy water to remove all traces of the abrasive grit produced during the honing operation. Be sure to run a brush through all oil holes and galleries and flush them with running water. After rinsing, dry the block and apply a coat of light rust preventive oil to all machined surfaces. Wrap the block in a plastic trash bag to keep it clean and set aside until reassembly.

37 Engine rebuilding alternatives

1 At this point in the engine rebuilding process, the home mechanic is faced with a number of options for completing the overhaul. The decision to replace the cylinder block, piston/rod assemblies and crankshaft depend on a number of factors with the number one consideration being the condition of the cylinder block. Other considerations are: cost, competent machine shop facilities, parts availability, time available to complete the project and experience.
2 Some of the rebuilding alternatives are as follows:

Individual parts – If the inspection procedures prove that the engine block and most engine components are in reusable condition, this may be the most economical alternative. The block, crankshaft and piston/rod assemblies should all be inspected carefully. Even if the block shows little wear, the cylinder bores should receive a finish hone.

Master kit (crankshaft kit) – This rebuild package usually consists of a reground crankshaft and a matched set of pistons and connecting rods. The pistons will come already installed with new piston pins to the connecting rods. Piston rings and the necessary bearings may or may not be included in the kit. These kits are commonly available for standard cylinder bores, as well as for engine blocks which have been bored to a regular oversize.

Short block – A short block consists of a cylinder block with a crankshaft and piston/rod assemblies already installed. All new bearings are incorporated and all clearances will be within tolerances. Depending on where the short block is purchased, a guarantee may be included. The existing camshaft, valve mechanism, cylinder head and ancillary parts can be bolted to this short block with little or no machine shop work necessary for the engine overhaul.

Long block – A long block consists of a short block plus oil pump, oil pan, cylinder head, valve cover, camshaft and valve mechanism, camshaft gear, timing chain and crankcase front cover. All components are installed with new bearings, seals and gaskets incorporated throughout. The installation of manifolds and ancillary parts is all that is necessary. Some form of guarantee is usually included with purchase.

3 Give careful though to which method is best for your situation and discuss the alternatives with local machine shop owners, parts dealers or dealership partsmen.

38 Engine components – cleaning and storing

1 When the engine has been dismantled, thoroughly clean all components with a cleaning solvent. Remove any traces of gasket material which is still adhering, using a blunt scraper, but take care not to score any of the sealing faces.

2 Once the components have been cleaned, both before and after inspection, keep them wrapped or covered so that they stay clean. Replace all badly worn components.

39 Crankshaft – inspection

1 Clean the crankshaft with solvent (be sure to clean the oil holes with a stiff brush and flush them with solvent) and dry it thoroughly. Check the main and connecting rod bearing journals for uneven wear, scoring, pitting and cracks. Check the remainder of the crankshaft for cracks and damage.

2 Using an appropriate size micrometer, measure the diameter of the main and connecting rod journals (photo) and compare the results to the Specifications. By measuring the diameter at a number of points around the journal's circumference, you will be able to determine whether or not the journal is worn out-of-round. Take the measurement at each end of the journal, near the crank throw, to determine whether the journal is tapered.

3 If the crankshaft journals are damaged, tapered, out-of-round or worn beyond the limits given in the Specifications, have the crankshaft reground by a reputable automotive machine shop. Be sure to use the correct undersize bearing inserts if the crankshaft is reconditioned.

39.2 Measure the main bearing journal diameter

40.4 Clean the piston ring grooves with a groove cleaning tool

40 Pistons and connecting rods – inspection

1 Before the inspection process can be carried out, the piston/connecting rod assemblies must be cleaned and the old piston rings removed from the pistons.

2 Using a piston ring installation tool, carefully remove the rings from the pistons. Do not nick or gouge the pistons in the process.

3 Scrape all traces of carbon from the top (or crown) of the piston. A hand-held wire brush or a piece of fine emery cloth can be used once the majority of the deposits have been scraped away. Do not, under any circumstances, use a wire brush mounted in a drill motor to remove deposits from the pistons. The piston material is soft and will be eroded away by the wire brush.

4 Use a piston ring groove cleaning tool to remove any carbon deposits from the ring grooves (photo). If a tool is not available, a piece broken off the old ring will do the job. Be very careful to remove only the carbon deposits. Do not remove any metal and do not nick or scratch the sides of the ring grooves.

5 Once the deposits have been removed, clean the piston/rod assemblies with solvent and dry them thoroughly. Make sure that the oil hole in the big end of the connecting rod and the oil return holes in the back side of the ring groove are clear.

6 If the pistons are not damaged or worn excessively, and if the engine block is not rebored, new pistons will not be necessary. Normal piston wear appears as even vertical wear on the piston thrust surfaces and slight looseness of the top ring in its groove. New piston rings, on the other hand, should always be used when an engine is rebuilt.

7 Carefully inspect each piston for cracks around the skirt, at the pin bosses and at the ring lands.

8 Look for scoring and scuffing on the thrust faces of the skirt, holes in the piston crown and burned areas at the edge of the crown. If the skirt is scored or scuffed, the engine may have been suffering from overheating and/or abnormal combustion, which caused excessively high operating temperatures. The cooling and lubrication systems should be checked thoroughly. A hole in the piston crown, an extreme to be sure, is an indication that abnormal combustion (pre-ignition) was occurring. Burned areas at the edge of the piston crown are usually evidence of spark knock (detonation). If any of the above problems exist, the causes must be corrected or the damage will occur again.

9 Corrosion of the piston (evidenced by pitting) indicates that coolant is leaking into the combustion chamber and/or the crankcase. Again, the cause must be corrected or the problem may persist in the rebuilt engine.

10 Measure the piston ring side clearance by laying a new piston ring in the ring groove and slipping a feeler gauge in beside it (photo). Check the clearance at 3 or 4 locations around the groove. Be sure to use the correct ring for each groove; they are different. If the side clearance is greater than specified, new pistons will have to be used and the block rebored to accept them.

40.10 Measure the piston ring side clearance with a feeler gauge

40.11 Measure the piston diameter to determine the piston-to-bore clearance

11 Check the piston-to-bore clearance by measuring the bore (see Section 36) and the piston diameter (photo). Make sure that the pistons and bores are correctly matched. Measure the piston across the skirt, on the thrust faces (at a 90° angle to the piston pin), about 0.100 in (2 mm) up from the bottom of the skirt. Subtract the piston diameter from the bore diameter to obtain the clearance. If it is greater than specified, the block will have to be rebored and new pistons and rings installed. Check the piston pin-to-rod clearance by twisting the piston and rod in opposite directions. Any noticeable play indicates that there is excessive wear, which must be corrected. The piston/connecting rod assemblies should be taken to an automotive machine shop to have new piston pins installed and the pistons and connecting rods rebored.
12 If the pistons must be removed from the connecting rods, such as when new pistons must be installed, or if the piston pins have too much play in them, they should be taken to an automotive machine shop. While they are there, it would be convenient to have the connecting rods checked for bend and twist, as automotive machine shops have special equipment for this purpose.
13 Check the connecting rods for cracks and other damage. Temporarily remove the rod cap, lift out the old bearing inserts, wipe the rod and cap bearing surfaces clean and inspect them for nicks, gouges and scratches. After checking the rods, replace the old bearings, slip the caps in place and tighten the nuts finger tight. Unless new pistons or connecting rods must be installed, do not disassemble the pistons from the connecting rods.

41 Main and connecting rod bearings – inspection

1 Even though the main and connecting rod bearings should be replaced with new ones during the engine overhaul, the old bearings should be retained for close examination, as they may reveal valuable information about the condition of the engine.
2 Bearing failure occurs mainly because of lack of lubrication, the presence of dirt or other foreign particles, overloading the engine and/or corrosion. Regardless of the cause of bearing failure, it must be corrected before the engine is reassembled to prevent it from happening again.
3 When examining the bearings, remove them from the engine block, the main bearing caps, the connectng rods and the rod caps and lay them out on a clean surface in the same general position as their location in the engine. This will enable you to match any noted bearing problems with the corresponding crankshaft journal.
4 Dirt and other foreign particles get into the engine in a variety of ways. It may be left in the engine during assembly, or it may pass through filters or breathers. It may get into the oil, and from there into the bearings. Metal chips from machining operations and normal engine wear are often present. Abrasives are sometimes left in engine components after reconditioning, especially when parts are not thoroughly cleaned using the proper cleaning methods. Whatever the source, these foreign objects often end up embedded in the soft bearing material and are easily recognized. Large particles will not embed in the bearing and will score or gouge the bearing and shaft. The best prevention for this cause of bearing failure is to clean all parts thoroughly and keep everything spotlessly clean during engine assembly. Frequent and regular changes of engine oil, and oil filters, is also recommended.
5 Lack of lubrication (or lubrication breakdown) has a number of interrelated causes. Excessive heat (which thins the oil), overloading (which squeezes the oil from the bearing face) and oil leakage or throw-off (from excessive bearing clearances, worn oil pump or high engine speeds) all contribute to lubrication breakdown. Blocked oil passages, which usually are the result of misaligned oil holes in a bearing shell, will also oil-starve a bearing and destroy it. When lack of lubrication is the cause of bearing failure, the bearing material is wiped or extruded from the steel backing of the bearing. Temperatures may increase to the point where the steel backing turns blue from overheating.
6 Driving habits can have a definite effect on bearing life. Full-throttle low-speed operation (or 'lugging' the engine) puts very high loads on bearings, which tends to squeeze out the oil film. These loads cause the bearings to flex, which produces fine cracks in the bearing face (fatigue failure). Eventually the bearing material will loosen in pieces and tear away from the steel backing. Short-trip driving leads to corrosion of bearings, as insufficient engine heat is produced to drive off the condensed water and corrosive gases produced. These products collect in the engine oil, forming acid and sludge. As the oil is carried to the engine bearings the acid attacks and corrodes the bearing material.
7 Incorrect bearing installation during engine assembly will lead to bearing failure as well. Tight-fitting bearings, which leave insufficient bearing oil clearance, result in oil starvation. Dirt or foreign particles trapped behind a bearing insert result in high spots on the bearing which lead to failure.

42 Piston rings – installation

1 Before installing the new piston rings, the ring end gaps must be checked.
2 Lay out the piston/connecting rod assemblies and the new ring sets so that the rings will be matched with the same piston and cylinder during the end gap measurement and engine assembly.
3 Insert the top (number 1) ring into the first cylinder and square it

2

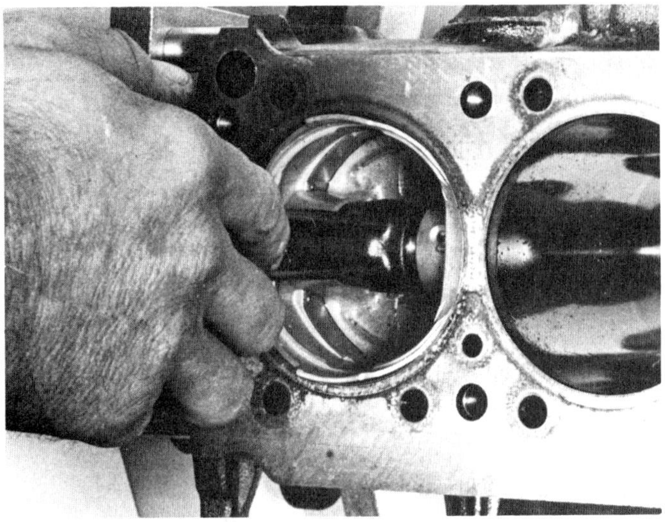

42.3a Use the piston to square up the piston ring in the cylinder before measuring the end gap

42.3b Measure the piston ring end gap with a feeler gauge

42.9a Install the spacer expander in the oil control ring groove

42.9b Install the upper side rail in the oil control ring groove

up with the cylinder walls by pushing it in with the top of the piston (photo). The ring should be at least two inches below the top edge of the cylinder. To measure the end gap, slip a feeler gauge between the ends of the ring (photo). Compare the measurement to the Specifications.

4 If the gap is larger or smaller than specified, double-check to make sure that you have the correct rings before proceeding.

5 If the gap is too small, it must be enlarged or the ring ends may come in contact with each other during engine operation, which can cause serious damage to the engine. The end gap can be increased by filing the ring ends very carefully with a fine file. Mount the ring in a vise equipped with soft jaws, holding it as close to the gap as possible. When performing this operation, file only from the outside in.

6 Excess end gap is not critical unless it is greater than 0.040 in (1 mm). Again, double-check to make sure you have the correct rings for your engine.

7 Repeat the procedure for each ring that will be installed in the first cylinder and for each ring in the remaining cylinders. Remember to keep rings, pistons and cylinders matched up.

8 Once the ring end-gaps have been checked/corrected, the rings can be installed on the pistons.

9 The oil control ring (lowest one on the piston) is installed first. It is composed of three separate components. Slip the spacer expander

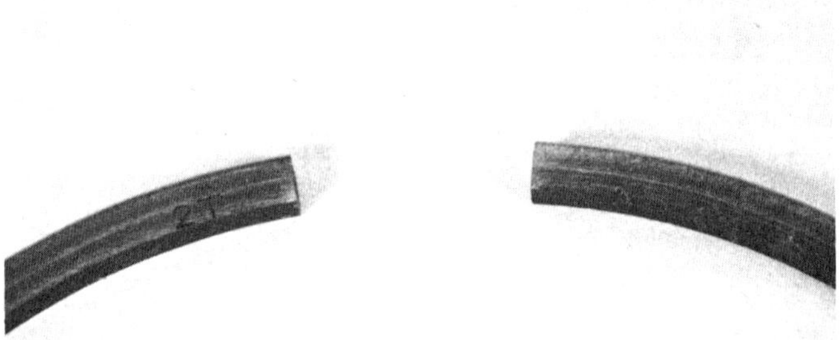

42.9c The piston rings must be installed with the marked side up

into the groove (photo) then install the upper side rail (photo) with the size mark and manufacturer's stamp facing up (photo). Do not use a piston ring installation tool on the oil ring side rails, as they may be damaged. Instead, place one end of the side rail into the groove between the spacer expander and the ring land, hold it firmly in place and slide a finger around the piston while pushing the rail into the groove (photo). Next, install the lower side rail. Again, the size mark and manufacturer's stamp must face up in the same manner.

10 After the three oil ring components have been installed, check to make sure that both the upper and lower side rails can be turned smoothly in the ring groove.

11 The number 2 (middle) ring is installed next. It is stamped with a '2' so that it can be readily distinguished from the top ring. Do not mix the top and middle rings up, as they have different cross sections.

12 Use a piston ring installation tool and make sure that the identification mark is facing up, then fit the ring into the middle groove on the piston (photo). Do not expand the ring any more than is necessary to slide it over the piston.

13 Finally, install the number 1 (top) ring in the same manner. Make sure the identifying mark is facing up.

14 Repeat the procedure for the remaining pistons and rings. Be careful not to confuse the number 1 and number 2 rings.

42.12 Install the piston ring with a piston ring tool

43 Oil pressure switch and sending unit – check

Refer to *Switches – checking* in Chapter 10 for these engine electrical checks.

44 Reconnecting the engine and transmission

1 This procedure must be done carefully to avoid any damage to the engine or the transmission.

2 Support the transmission and engine on blocks or other suitable means, and at the same time align the mounting holes.

3 Install the transmission-to-engine block mounting bolts. Torque them to the Specifications.

4 Install the starter to the left side of the bellhousing. Tighten the bolts to their Specifications.

5 Install the exhaust pipe bracket to the right side of the bellhousing and tighten the bolts to Specifications.

6 Now, install the splash shield to the bottom of the transmission bellhousing, tighten the bolts and prepare to install the engine and transmission into the vehicle.

45.16 Attach the metal insulator to the right motor mount (US only)

45 Engine – installation

1 Once the clutch components, the transmission and the starter are in place on the engine, it is ready to be reinstalled in the vehicle.

2 Raise the vehicle and set it securely on jackstands.

3 Install a short length of heavy chain between the hoisting brackets on the engine. Attach the engine hoist lifting hook to the chain and raise the engine until it clears the front of the vehicle. Do not let the engine swing freely.

4 Angle the transmission steeply toward the back of the vehicle and carefully lower the engine into place. Work slowly and use the transmission and hoist to direct the engine to its proper location on the motor mounts.

5 With the engine in place (still attached to the hoist), support the transmission with a jack and install the front motor mount bolts through the roll restrictors and insulators and into the frame holes. Tighten them finger tight only.

6 Remove the chains and move the hoist out of the way.

7 Install the transmission support crossmember by raising or lowering the supporting jack as necessary. Tighten the nuts attaching the transmission to the crossmember and the bolts holding the crossmember to the frame.

8 Tighten the motor mount bolts securely.

9 Install the speedometer cable and housing at the drive unit and tighten the fittings. Bend the retaining strap that holds the speedometer cable to the crossmember back into position.

10 Slip the emergency brake cable housing end into the frame bracket and attach the cable end of the brake pull arm.

11 Attach the emergency brake cable balancer to the brake pull arm and slip a new cotter pin through the hole in the balancer pivot pin.

12 Install the driveshaft by referring to Chapter 8.

13 Slip the clutch cable housing into place on the transmission. Push the rubber dust cover over the end of the clutch cable and hook the cable end to the clutch control lever. Refer to Chapter 8 and adjust the clutch.

14 Plug in the back-up light switch wiring connector.

15 Install the exhaust pipe and tighten the rear mounting nuts first, followed by the front mounting nuts. Don't forget to tighten the bracket and hanger bolts also.

16 Attach the fuel hose isolator strap to the left engine mount with the concave side of the washer facing out. Install the metal insulator on the right engine mount (photo).

17 Hook the battery lead to the starter motor and plug in the bayonet-type connector at the starter solenoid. The starter motor wiring bracket is attached to the engine by the rear bolt on the lower air conditioner bracket (if so equipped).

18 If your vehicle is equipped with air conditioning, position the compressor in its mounts and install the mounting bolts through the rear bracket and into the compressor. Tighten all mounting bolts securely.

19 Attach the battery ground wire (lower left) to the engine block.

45.23 Plug in the distributor primary circuit connector

20 Install the alternator and hook up the wiring. Do not tighten the mounting or pivot bolts at this time.
21 If your vehicle is equipped with power steering, position the pump in its mount and install, but do not tighten, the bolts. Install the pulley on the pump shaft with the concave side to the front. Hold the pulley carefully with a large pliers and tighten the nut securely.
22 Attach the wires to the water temperature and oil pressure sending units.
23 Insert the coil wire into the center terminal of the distributor cap and plug in the primary circuit connector on the distributor body (photo).
24 Plug in the air conditioner compressor electrical lead (if so equipped) and the 3-wire emission system electrical connector just below the carburetor.
25 Hook up the fuel hoses to the fuel pump and the carburetor. They are color-coded to decrease the possibility of mixing them up. Be sure to tighten the hose clamps securely.
26 Install the radiator and the lower fan shroud only. Tighten the shroud bolts finger-tight. Hook up the overflow tubes to the spigot at the radiator filler neck.
27 Install the water pump pulley and the fan clutch, then position the power steering pump drivebelt and adjust its tension. Be sure to tighten the pivot and adjusting bolts securely.
28 Install the alternator/water pump drivebelt and adjust its tension. Be sure to tighten the alternator pivot and adjusting bolts securely.
29 If your vehicle is equipped with air conditioning, install and adjust the drivebelt.
30 Install the upper fan shroud and fasten the shrouds together with the sheetmetal screws. Center the shroud on the fan and tighten the bolts attaching the shroud to the radiator. Rotate the fan to make sure it clears the shroud on all sides.
31 Install the upper and lower radiator hoses and tighten the hose clamps.
32 Attach the heater hose to the metal coolant transfer tube at the rear of the engine and tighten the hose clamp.
33 Attach the brake vacuum booster hose to the intake manifold and slide the hose clamp into place.
34 Attach the electrical ground strap on the exhaust manifold to the firewall heat shield.
35 Attach the purge control valve hose bracket to the valve cover.
36 Hook up the throttle linkage at the carburetor and valve cover.
37 Attach the carburetor vent hose to the metal tube on the valve cover.
38 Attach the vacuum hoses to the distributor vacuum advance unit, the CAV on the carburetor, the throttle opener (if so equipped) on the carburetor and the air cleaning housing. Install the air cleaner housing and the rubber snorkel connecting the air cleaner housing to the headlight support channel.
39 Install the shift lever assembly and the center console (if so equipped).
40 Install the hood and the battery. Attach the battery cables (positive first, then negative). If sparking occurs when the battery cables are being hooked up, make sure all switches are off and the doors closed.
41 Fill the radiator with coolant (a 50/50 mixture of water and ethylene glycol-based antifreeze). You will have to add additional coolant after the engine is started, so keep a close eye on the level.
42 Add the proper amount of the recommended lubricant to the transmission and double-check the engine oil level.
43 Double-check all nuts and bolts for tightness and make sure all hoses, electrical wiring and other connections are properly installed, then lower the vehicle to the ground.

46 Valves – check and adjustment

Refer to the appropriate section in Chapter 1 for valve adjustment.

47 Initial start-up and break-in procedure

1 Once the engine has been properly installed in the vehicle, double-check the engine oil and coolant levels.
2 With the spark plugs out of the engine and the coil high-tension lead grounded to the engine block, crank the engine over until oil pressure registers on the gauge.
3 Install the spark plugs, hook up the plug wires and the coil high-tension lead.
4 Make sure the carburetor choke plate is closed, then start the engine. It may take a few moments for gasoline to reach the carburetor, but the engine should start without a great deal of effort.
5 As soon as the engine starts, it should be set at a fast idle to ensure proper oil circulation and allowed to warm up to normal operating temperature. While the engine is warming up, make a thorough check for oil and coolant leaks.
6 After the engine reaches normal operating temperature, shut it off, remove the valve cover, retorque the head bolts and recheck the valve clearances using the hot engine Specifications.
7 Install the valve cover and recheck the engine oil and coolant levels. Also, check the ignition timing and the engine idle speed (refer to Chapter 1) and make any necessary adjustment.
8 Drive the vehicle to an area with minimum traffic, accelerate at full throttle from 30 to 50 mph, then allow the vehicle to slow to 30 mph with the throttle closed. Repeat the procedure 10 or 12 times. This will load the piston rings and cause them to seat properly against the cylinder walls. Check again for oil and coolant leaks.
9 Drive the vehicle gently for the first 500 miles (no sustained high speeds) and keep a constant check on the oil level. It is not unusual for an engine to use oil during the break-in period.
10 At approximately 500 to 600 miles, change the oil and filter, retorque the cylinder head bolts and recheck the valve clearances.
11 For the next few hundred miles, drive the vehicle normally. Do not pamper it or abuse it.
12 After 2000 miles, change the oil and filter again and consider the engine fully broken in.

Chapter 3 Cooling, heating and air conditioning systems

Contents

3

Specifications

Radiator capacity ... See Chapter 1 Specifications

Coolant type ... Ethylene glycol

Thermostat

Opening temperature ... 190°F (88°C)
Full opening temperature ... 212°F (100°C)

Heater

Blower speed ... 3000 rpm
Power consumption ... 150W

Torque specifications

Water temperature sending unit ... 22 to 28 ft lbs (30 to 39 Nm)

1 General information

The cooling system used is very conventional in design, utilizing a vertical-flow radiator, an engine driven water pump, and thermostat controlled coolant flow. The fan is equipped with a clutch, which allows it to draw air through the radiator at lower speeds. At higher speeds, when the fan is not needed for cooling, the clutch automatically lowers the fan speed and reduces the engine power required for fan operation.

The water pump is located on the right front side of the engine and is driven by a belt from the pulley mounted on the front of the crankshaft. This belt is also used to drive the alternator.

The heater utilizes the heat produced by the engine and contained in the coolant to warm the interior of the vehicle. It is manually controlled from inside by the driver or passenger.

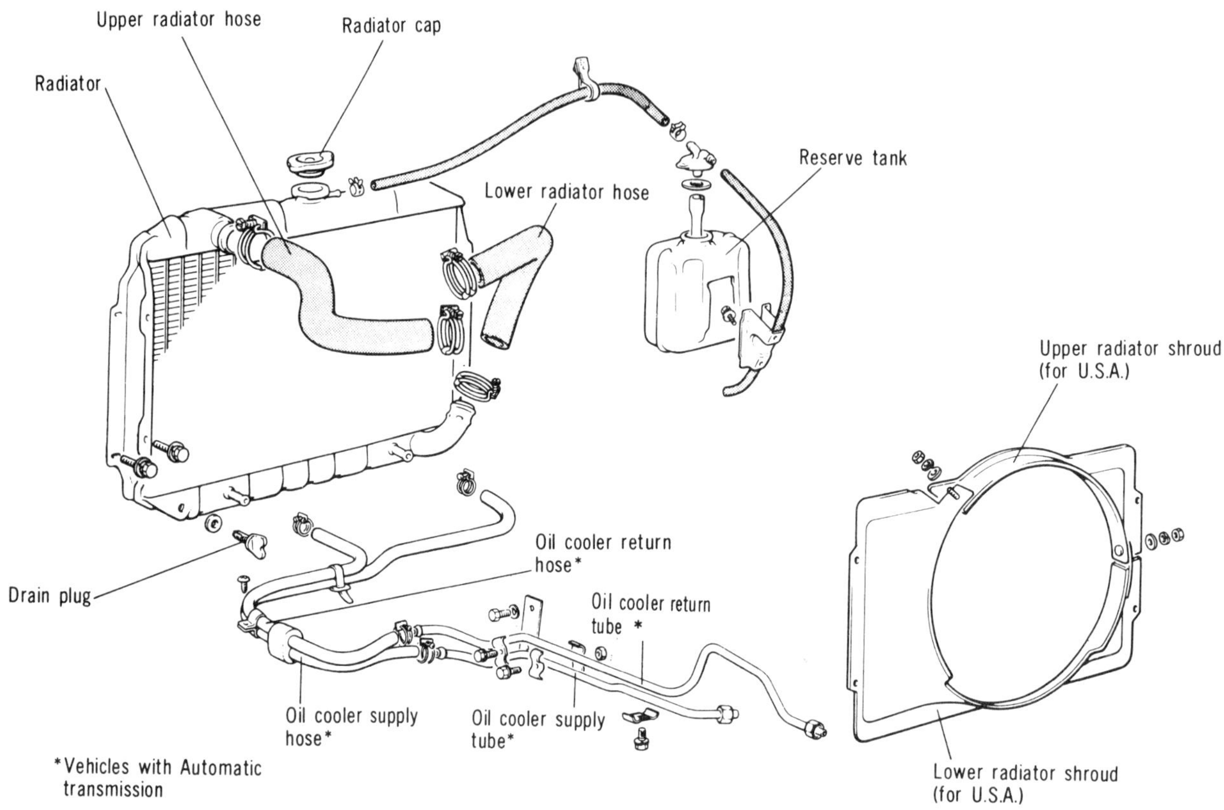

Fig. 3.1 Cooling system components – exploded view (Sec 21)

Air conditioning is available as an option. All components of the system are mounted in the engine compartment and the system is driven by a belt from the pulley mounted on the front of the crankshaft. Output of the system is controlled from inside the vehicle.

2 Radiator coolant – check and change

1 As part of regular routine maintenance, the coolant should be drained and the system completely flushed. Refer to Chapter 1 for the procedure.
2 Always use a mixture of 50% soft water and 50% ethylene glycol based antifreeze when refilling the cooling system. Many of the engine parts are made of aluminum, which requires the corrosion protection offered by this type of antifreeze.

3 Radiator cap – check and replacement

To check the radiator cap, refer to Chapter 1, *Cooling system checking.*

4 Radiator reserve reservoir – check

A quick test for the correct functioning of the reserve system is found in Chapter 1 with the cooling system checks.

5 Antifreeze – general note

Caution: *Children and pets may be attracted to coolant by its sweet odor and taste but a few licks of any antifreeze solution can be lethal. Keep all containers closed and wipe up any spills under your vehicle as soon as you notice them. When handling antifreeze, take care that it is not spilled on the vehicle paint, since it will invariably cause damage if not removed immediately.*
1 It is recommended that the cooling system is filled with a water/ethylene glycol based antifreeze solution which will give protection down to at least –20°F at all times. This provides protection against corrosion and increases the coolant boiling point.
2 The cooling system should be drained, flushed and refilled every alternate Fall. The use of antifreeze solutions for periods longer than two years is likely to cause damage and encourage the formation of rust and scale due to the corrosion inhibitors gradually losing their efficiency.
3 Before adding antifreeze to the system, check all hose connections and the tightness of the cylinder head bolts.
4 The exact mixture of antifreeze to water which you should use depends upon the relative weather conditions. The mixture should contain at least 50 percent antifreeze, offering protection to –20°F. Under no circumstances should the mixture contain more than 70 percent antifreeze.

6 Radiator hoses – check and replacement

1 Checking is a scheduled maintenance item and can be found in Chapter 1.
2 To replace the radiator hoses, first drain the coolant from the radiator.
3 Make sure you have the correct hose replacements for your vehicle. Compare the new ones with the old ones before removal to make sure.
4 Remove the hoses by first loosening the hose clamps. Work them loose and off the metal tubes with a twisting action.
5 In some cases, the clamps will be destroyed when removing the hoses. If this occurs, make sure you have replacements. You may want to replace any spring-type hose clamps with worm drive-type ones because they give a more reliable seal on the hoses, especially on the main (large) hoses.

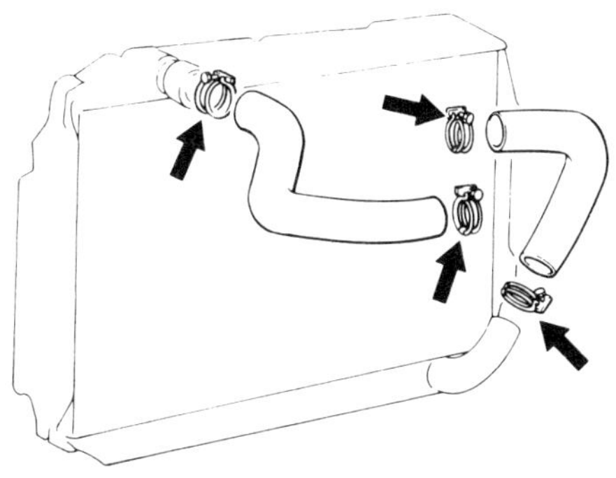

Fig. 3.2 Disconnecting upper and lower main radiator hoses (Sec 6)

6 For vehicles with automatic transmissions, it may be necessary to replace the oil cooler hoses due to deterioration.
7 Remove the clamps from the oil cooler supply and return hoses from the bottom of the radiator and the ends of their respective metal tubes.
8 You will also have to remove some routing clamps in order to completely remove the hoses from the vehicle. Make sure these clamps are returned to their original positions.
9 When replacing any cooling system hoses, make sure that all connections are tight. Run the engine to normal operating temperature and double-check for leaks before making any trips.

7 Fan drivebelt – check, adjustment and replacement

1 All drivebelt checks and adjustments can be found in Chapter 1.
2 Removing the drivebelt is a fairly simple task. Slightly loosen the alternator support bolt and the alternator brace bolt.
3 Push the alternator all the way toward the engine and then remove the belt. Work the belt around the fan blades in order to remove it.
4 Install the new belt in the opposite order of removal. Make sure you have the correct belt for your vehicle.
5 Adjust the belt referring to the appropriate section in Chapter 1.

8 Thermostat – testing and replacement

1 The thermostat is located at the front of the engine inside a housing just to the rear of the distributor (photo). The thermostat allows for quick warm-ups and governs the normal operating temperature of the engine.
2 If the thermostat is functioning properly, the temperature gauge should rise to the normal operating temperature quickly and then stay there, only rising above the normal position occasionally when the engine gets unusually hot. If the engine does not rise to normal operating temperature quickly, or if it overheats, the thermostat should be removed and checked or replaced.
3 The engine must be cool when removal is performed.
4 Place a suitable container under the radiator and drain some of the coolant into the container by opening the radiator drain valve.
5 Loosen and slide back the hose clamp, then pull the upper radiator hose off the thermostat housing cover.
6 Remove the bolts (photo) and lift off the housing cover (photo). You may have to tap the cover with a soft-faced hammer to break the gasket seal.
7 After the cover has been removed, note how the thermostat is installed and lift it out. If it is open when it is removed, it is defective and must be replaced with a new one.
8 To check the thermostat, submerge it in a container of water along with a thermometer. The thermostat should be suspended so it does not touch the container.
9 Gradually heat the water in the container with a hotplate or stove and check the temperature when the thermostat first starts to open.

8.1 Thermostat housing (arrow)

8.6a Remove the thermostat housing bolts

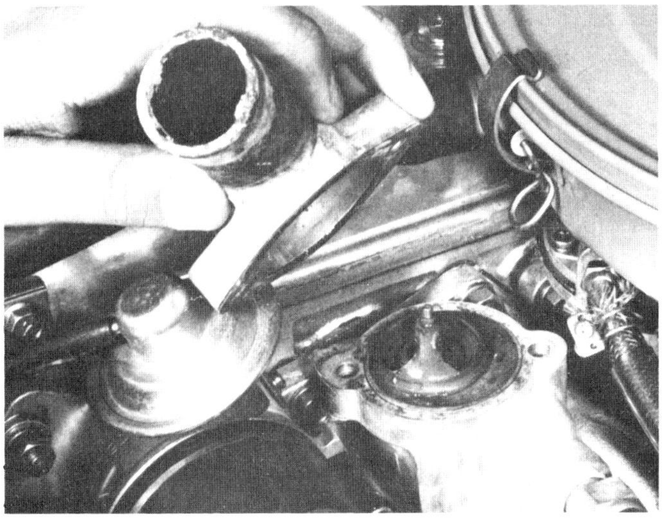

8.6b Lift off the housing cover. Notice which way the thermostat is installed

3

8.15 This end of the thermostat should face into the engine

10 Continue heating the water and check the temperature when the thermostat is fully open.
11 Lift the fully open thermostat out of the water and allow it to cool.
12 Compare the opening temperature and the fully open temperature to the Specifications.
13 If these Specifications are not met, or if the thermostat does not open while the water is heated, replace it with a new one.
14 Scrape all traces of the old gasket from the thermostat housing and cover. Do not nick or gouge the gasket sealing surfaces.
15 To install the thermostat, lay it in place in the housing with the proper end facing up. Each thermostat is marked as to which end should face into the engine, so examine yours carefully before installing it (photo). Make sure that the thermostat flange is properly seated in the recessed area of the housing.
16 Apply a thin, even layer of silicone-type gasket sealer to both sides of a new gasket and lay it in place on the housing.
17 Next, carefully position the housing cover, install the bolts and tighten them securely.
18 Slip the upper radiator hose onto the housing cover spigot, install the hose clamp and tighten it securely.
19 Pour the drained coolant back into the radiator. Start the engine and check for leaks around the thermostat housing and the upper radiator hose.

9 Cooling system – pressure test

A test of the cooling system pressure is an important preventive maintenance item. Refer to Chapter 1, *Cooling system checking.*

10 Temperature sending unit – check

Refer to Chapter 10 for electrical switch checks.

11 Radiator fan/clutch – removal and installation

1 The fan clutch can fail in one of two ways; it can either slip excessively, which would prevent the fan from cooling the engine sufficiently at low speeds, or the drive can seize, causing noise and wasting engine power because the fan is turning with the engine no matter what the engine speed.
2 If your vehicle is equipped with a fan shroud, it must be removed first. The air conditioner belt should also be removed by loosening the idler pulley.
3 Loosen the alternator pivot and adjusting bolts and slip the drivebelt off the water pump pulley.
4 Remove the four nuts attaching the fan clutch/pulley to the water pump flange. Pull the fan clutch assembly forward and out of the

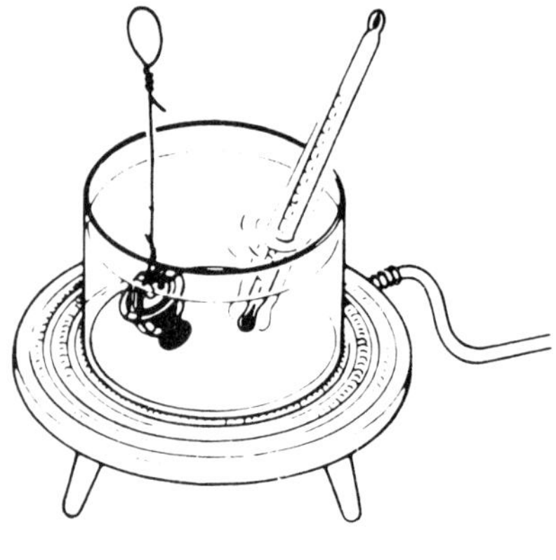

Fig. 3.3 Thermostat function test (Sec 8)

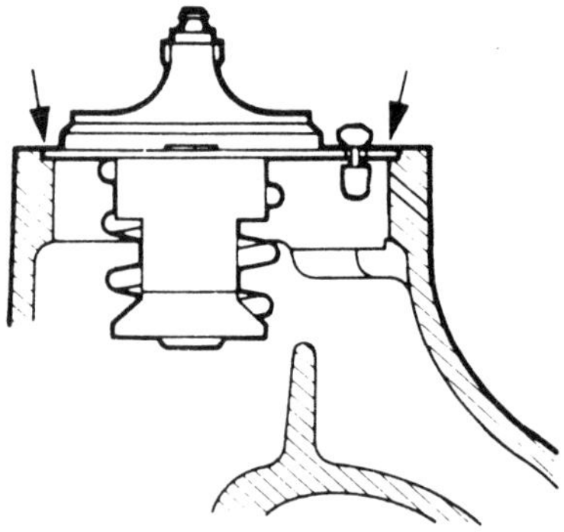

Fig. 3.4 Correct thermostat installation (Sec 8)

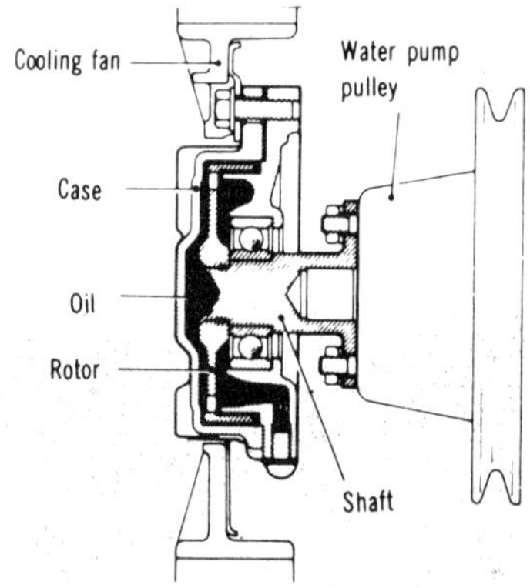

Fig. 3.5 Fan clutch components – sectional view (Sec 12)

engine compartment. Be very careful not to gouge the radiator with the fan blades or clutch.
5 The fan is attached to the clutch assembly with four bolts.
6 Check the fan blades for cracks and evidence of damage.
7 If it was removed, attach the fan to the clutch assembly and tighten the bolts securely. Install the water pump pulley and the fan clutch in place on the water pump flange. Install the lock washers and nuts and tighten them evenly and securely.
8 Replace the drivebelt and adjust the tension by referring to Chapter 1. Be sure to tighten the alternator pivot and mount bolts securely.
9 Reinstall the fan shroud (if so equipped).

12 Fan clutch – inspection

1 Check for evidence of leaks where the two halves of the fan clutch are joined and where the input shaft enters the clutch case. If leaks are present, replace the clutch assembly.

2 Rotate the input shaft and check for obvious binding and noise. Also, check for side-to-side play between the shaft and case. If the shaft will not rotate, the drive mechanism is seized and a new clutch assembly should be obtained.

13 Water pump – removal and installation

1 The water pump is mounted on the front of the engine and is driven by a belt from the crankshaft. Water pump problems can generally be narrowed down to failed bearings or leaking seals.
2 The most common problem with water pumps is a leaking seal, evidenced by coolant leakage from behind the drive pulley. Bearing failure may appear as a squealing noise or too much free movement. Noises can be pinpointed with a length of hose held to the ear while moving the other end around the water pump itself. If this is done, be very careful of the fan and other moving parts of the engine, which can cause serious injury. Free play can be felt by moving the drive pulley back and forth.
3 To gain access to the water pump, disconnect the battery ground cable and remove the fan shroud (if so equipped), the fan/fan clutch assembly (see Section 11) and the water pump drive pulley. Place a suitable container under the vehicle to catch the coolant (it can be reused) and remove the radiator pressure cap. Drain the coolant from

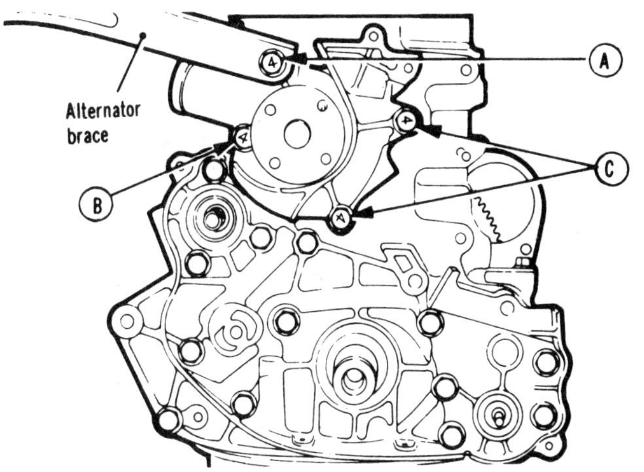

Fig. 3.6 Water pump installation (Sec 13)

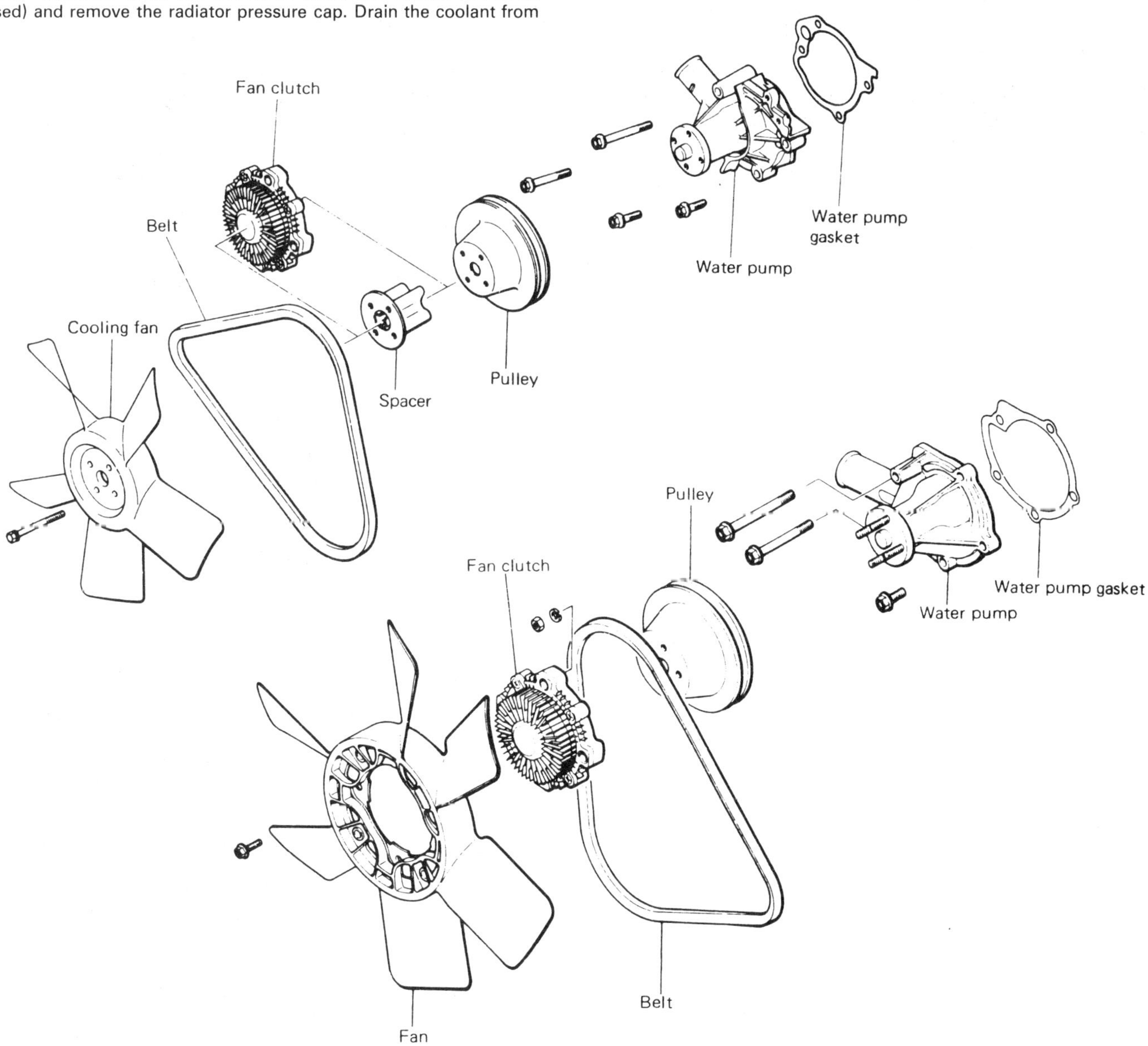

Fig. 3.7 Fan, clutch and water pump components – exploded view (1600 cc top, 2000 and 2600 cc bottom) (Sec 13)

the radiator and the engine by opening the radiator drain petcock and removing the block drain plug on the right side of the engine. After the coolant has drained, close the radiator petcock and install the block drain plug. Use silicone-type gasket sealer or thread tape on the drain plug threads.
4 Loosen and slide back the hose clamp and remove the lower radiator hose from the radiator and water pump. Loosen and slide back the hose clamp attaching the rubber heater hose to the water pump.
5 Remove the bolts attaching the pump to the front of the engine and lift out the pump. You may have to tap gently on the pump with a soft-faced hammer to break the gasket seal. Be careful not to gouge the radiator when removing the bolts or the pump.
6 Scrape all traces of the old gasket and gasket sealer off the engine. Do not nick or gouge the gasket sealing surfaces.
7 Coat both sides of a new gasket with silicone-type gasket sealer and install the new pump. Be sure to line up the bolt holes on the pump body and the new gasket before placing the pump in position on the engine. Slip the rubber heater hose over the pump's spigot as the pump is installed.
8 Install the pump mounting bolts and tighten them evenly and securely. Slip the heater hose clamp into place and tighten it securely.
9 Install the lower radiator hose and tighten the hose clamps. Install the drive pulley, the fan/fan clutch assembly and the fan shroud. Install and adjust the drivebelt and hook up the battery ground cable.
10 Fill the radiator with a 50/50 mixture of soft water and ethylene glycol based antifreeze.
11 Start the engine and check for leaks around the water pump mounting area, the heater hose and the lower radiator hose. Keep an eye on the coolant level, as it will drop. More coolant should be added as required.

14 Radiator – removal, inspection and installation

1 Remove the radiator pressure cap and drain the coolant from the radiator and the engine block. The radiator drain petcock is located on the lower left side of the radiator. The engine block drain is located on the lower right side of the engine underneath the exhaust manifold.
2 Once the coolant has been drained, remove the radiator hoses by loosening and sliding back the hose clamps and pulling the hoses off the radiator and engine.
3 If your vehicle is equipped with an automatic transmission, disconnect and plug the transmission oil cooling lines at the bottom of the radiator. Do not allow any dirt to enter the lines or fittings.
4 If your vehicle is equipped with a fan shroud, remove both the upper and lower sections. Each section is held in place by two bolts and the two sections are fastened together with a sheet metal screw on each side.
5 Pull the overflow tube off the spigot at the radiator filler neck. Remove the bolts attaching the radiator to the vehicle and carefully lift the radiator out of the engine compartment. Do not gouge the radiator coolant tubes or cooling fins with the fan blades.
6 Carefully examine the radiator for evidence of leaks and damage. It is recommended that any necessary repairs be performed by a reputable radiator repair shop.
7 If the radiator is clogged or if large amounts of rust or scale have formed, the repair shop will also do a thorough cleaning job.
8 Make sure the spaces between the cooling tubes and fins are clear. If necessary, use compressed air or running water to remove anything that may be clogging them.
9 Carefully lower the radiator into place in the engine compartment. Again, be very careful not to gouge the cooling fins and coolant tubes with the fan blades.
10 Install the four bolts attaching the radiator to the vehicle and tighten them securely. Slip the overflow tube over the spigot on the radiator filler neck.
11 Attach the fan shrouds to the radiator and center the shroud on the fan. Tighten the mounting bolts securely. Rotate the fan and check for adequate clearance around the entire shroud hole.
12 Unplug and hook up the automatic transmission fluid cooling lines at the bottom of the radiator. Tighten the fittings securely.
13 Install both radiator hoses and tighten the hose clamps securely. Make sure the radiator drain petcock is closed and the engine block drain is in place, then add coolant until the radiator is full.
14 Install the radiator cap. Start and run the engine and check for leaks. Add additional coolant as the engine is running.

15 Heater controls – adjustment

1978 through 1980 vehicles

1 The heater control should be periodically checked and adjusted to ensure optimum heater performance.
2 The Recirc/Vent air control is adjusted first. Place the control lever in the Recirc position and check to make sure that the damper lever is down and the outside air intake is closed. If it is not, move the cable housing in its securing clip until the intake is closed.

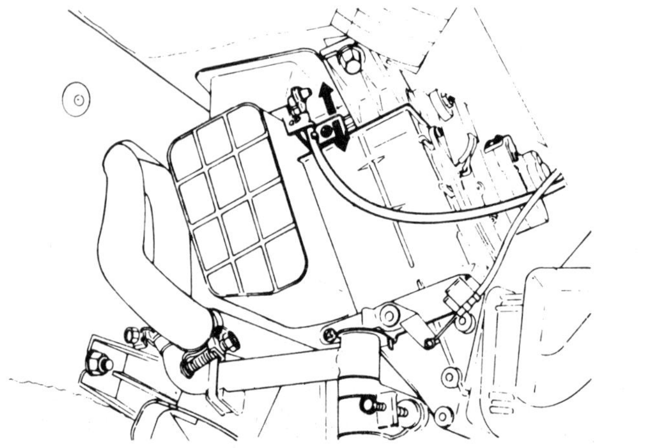

Fig. 3.8 1978 thru 1980 Recirc-Vent control wire adjustment (Sec 15)

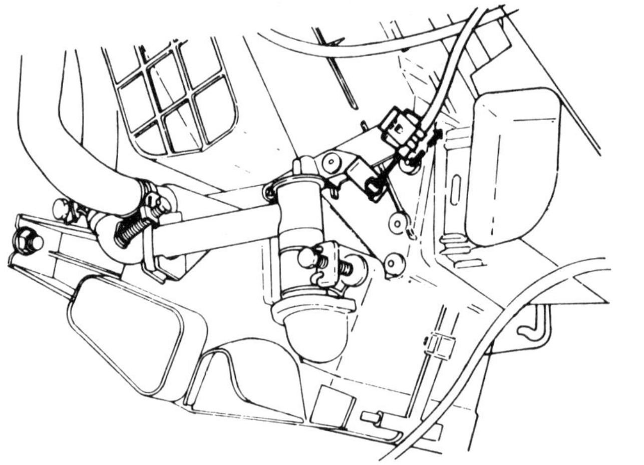

Fig. 3.9 1978 thru 1980 Hot water flow control wire adjustment (Sec 15)

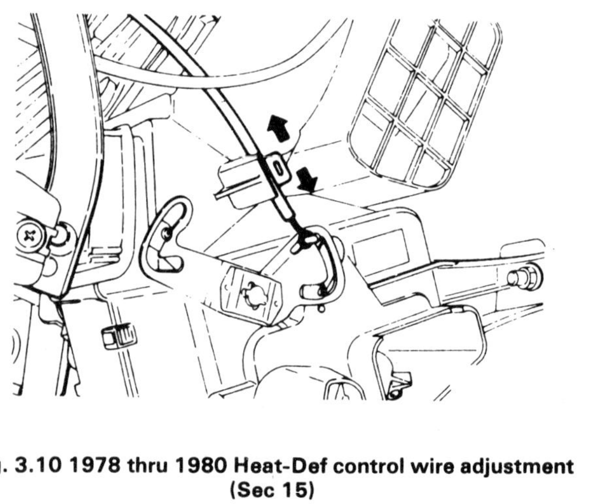

Fig. 3.10 1978 thru 1980 Heat-Def control wire adjustment (Sec 15)

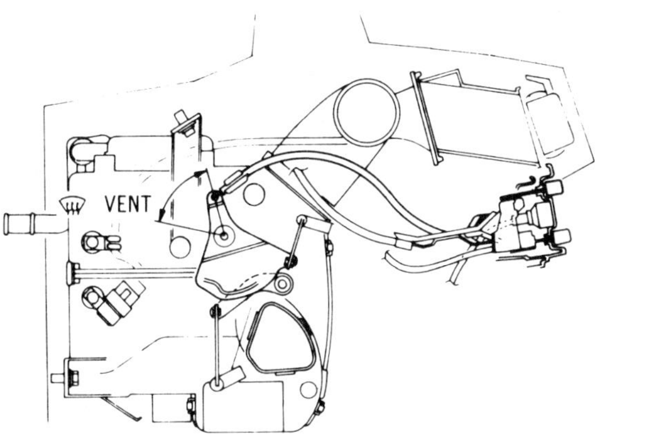

Fig. 3.11 1981 thru 1983 outlet control wire adjustment (Sec 15)

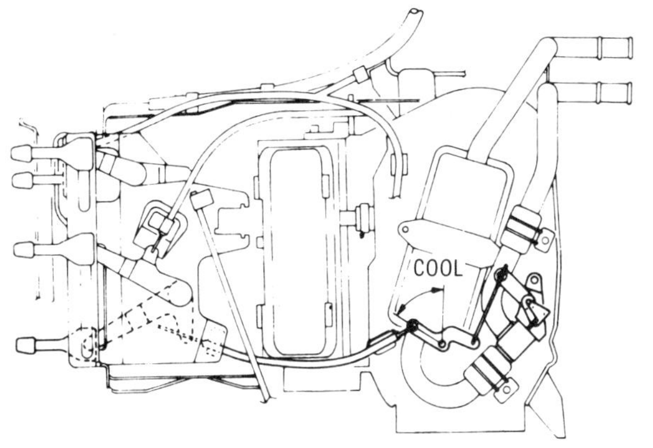

Fig. 3.12 1981 thru 1983 temperature control wire adjustment (Sec 15)

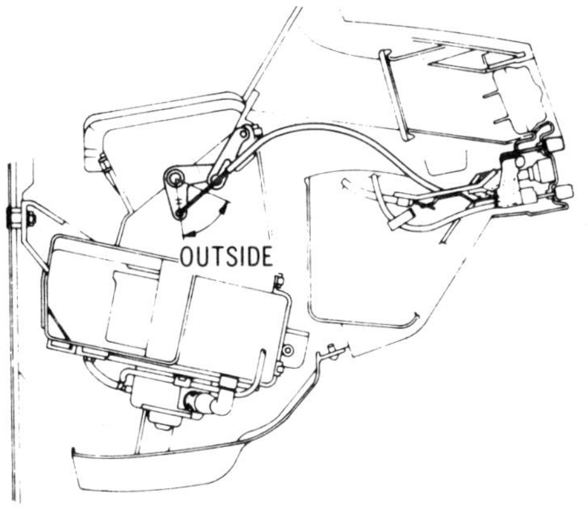

Fig. 3.13 1981 thru 1983 inside/outside air control wire adjustment (Sec 15)

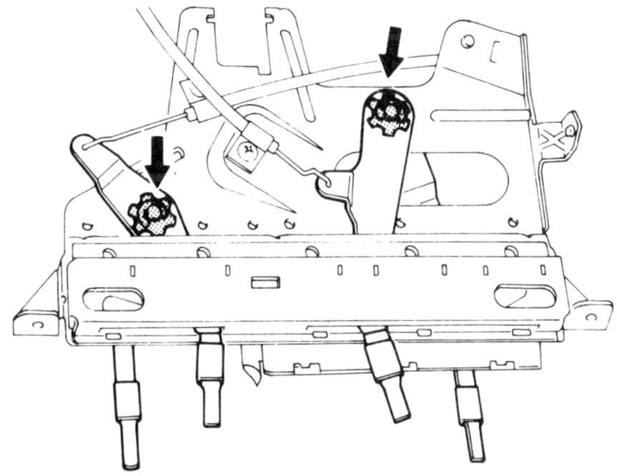

Fig. 3.14 Typical lever greasing points (Sec 15)

3 Move the control lever to the Vent position and make sure the air intake is open.

4 The heater temperature control is adjusted next. With the control lever in the Off position, check to see if the control valve is fully closed. The lever on the valve should be in the up position.

5 If it is not, move the cable housing in its securing clip until the valve is fully closed with the control lever in the Off position. Move the control lever to the Hot position and check for smooth and complete operation of the control valve. With the engine running at normal operating temperature, check for proper operation of the temperature control.

6 If the heater control valve binds and does not operate properly, it should be replaced with a new one.

7 The last control to be adjusted is the Def-Heat-Vent selector lever. Place the control lever in the Def position. The damper lever should be in the up position.

8 With the engine running at normal operating temperature, turn on the heater fan switch and feel for air being forced out of the defroster duct at the base of the windshield. Move the control lever to the Heat position. The air should no longer flow from the defroster duct or the vent ducts. If air movement is felt, move the cable housing in its clip to adjust the damper.

1981 through 1983 vehicles

9 The outlet control lever is adjusted first. Place the control lever to the farthest left (Vent) position and the temperature control lever to the farthest left (Cool) position.

10 Make sure that the damper plate is in an almost horizontal position. If it is not, then adjust the cable until it is.

11 The temperature control lever is adjusted next with the controls in the same position as step 9.

12 The best way to check if the damper plates are positioned correctly is to turn the fan on Fast. Warm the engine to operating temperature. The damper should completely direct the air flow around the heater core and you should get cool air from the vents. If not, some air may be passing through the heater core. If adjustment is necessary, loosen the cable and physically move the lever linkage until the coolest amount of air is felt. Make sure the lever is in the Cool position and tighten the cable again.

13 Finally, adjust the inside/outside air control lever. Set the outlet control lever all the way to the right (Vent) position and the inside/outside air control lever all the way to the left (Outside) position.

14 With the lever in this position, the damper plate should be at its farthest position upward, shutting off the defroster ducts and cool air should be felt coming into the vehicle through the vents when you are in motion.

15 A further check would be to drive the vehicle and close the damper plate by moving the lever all the way to the right (Inside) position. No air movement should be felt; if it is, adjust the cable accordingly.

16 On all cables, check for excessive bending and interference with other parts. For smoother operation, add grease to any contact pivot points.

16 Heater assembly – removal and installation

1978 through 1980 vehicles

Removal

1 In order to gain access to the heater core (in case of leaks or other damage) the heater assembly should be removed from the vehicle.

2 Disconnect the negative battery cable from the battery.

3 Place the heater controlled lever in the Off position, then drain the coolant from the engine and radiator (see Section 14).

4 Remove the centre console and the side panels of the parcel tray.

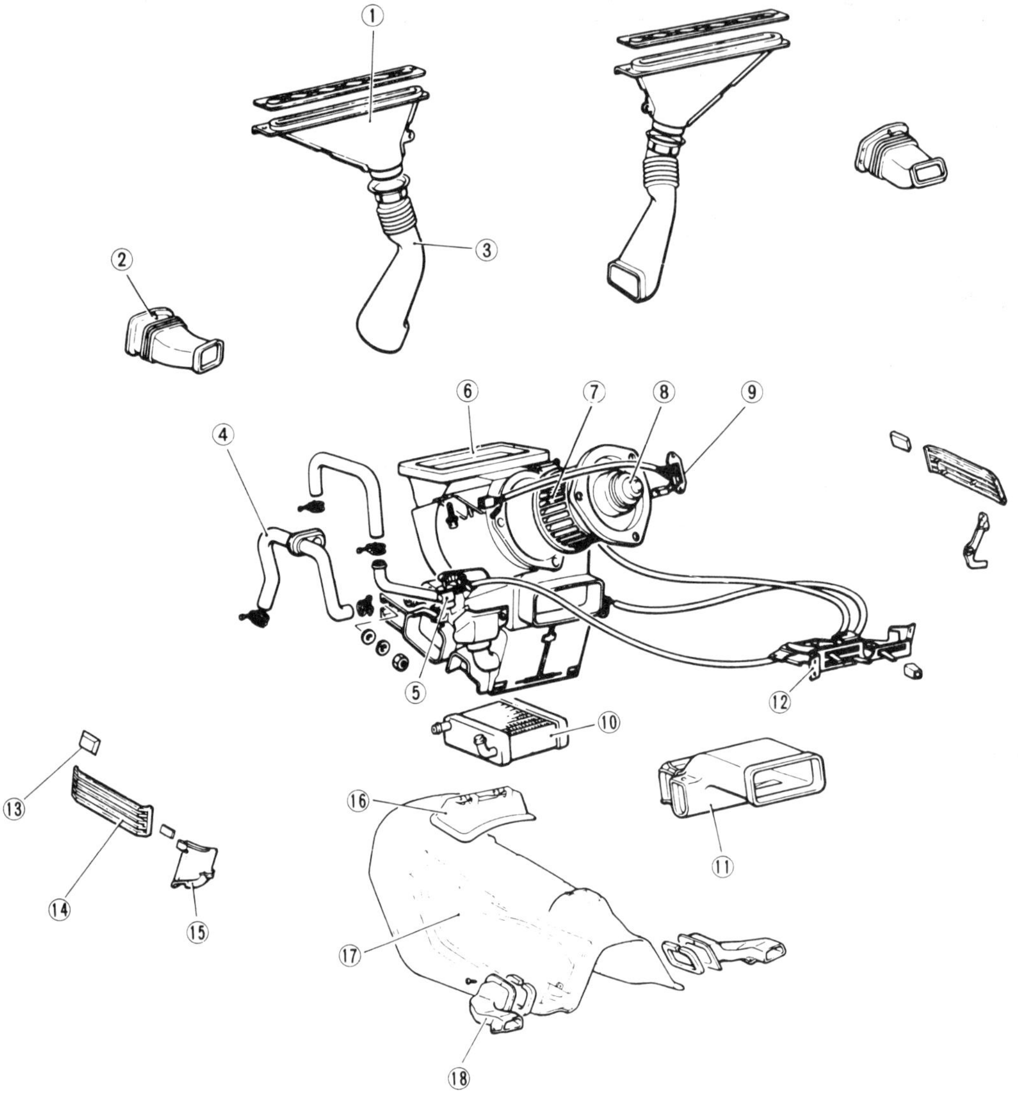

Fig. 3.15 1978 thru 1980 heater/ventilation components – exploded view (Sec 14)

1 Defroster nozzle
2 Side duct
3 Air duct
4 Water hose
5 Water valve
6 Heater assembly
7 Fan
8 Motor
9 Heater resistor
10 Heater resistor
11 Center duct
12 Heater control levers
13 Pad
14 Outlet covering
15 Rear vent duct
16 Rear heat duct
17 Rear heat cover
18 Rear heat nozzle

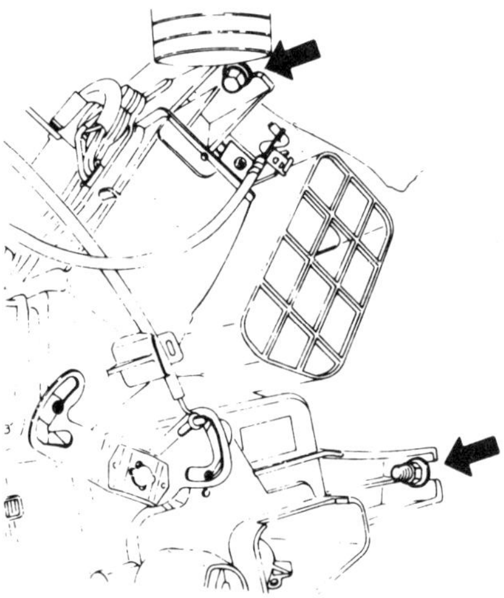

Fig. 3 16 Heater assembly removal (Sec 16)

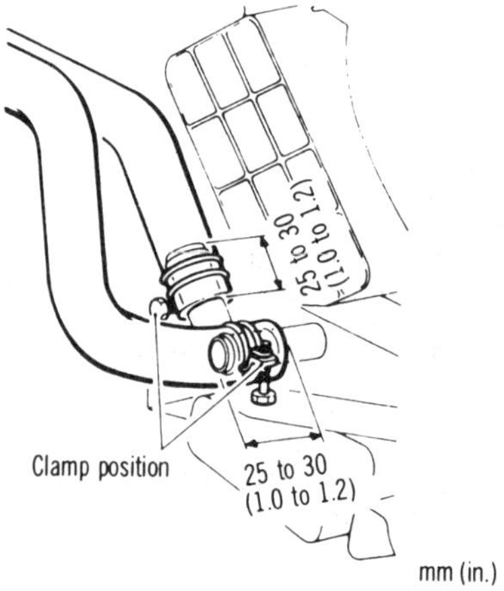

Fig. 3.17 Heater hose installation (Sec 16)

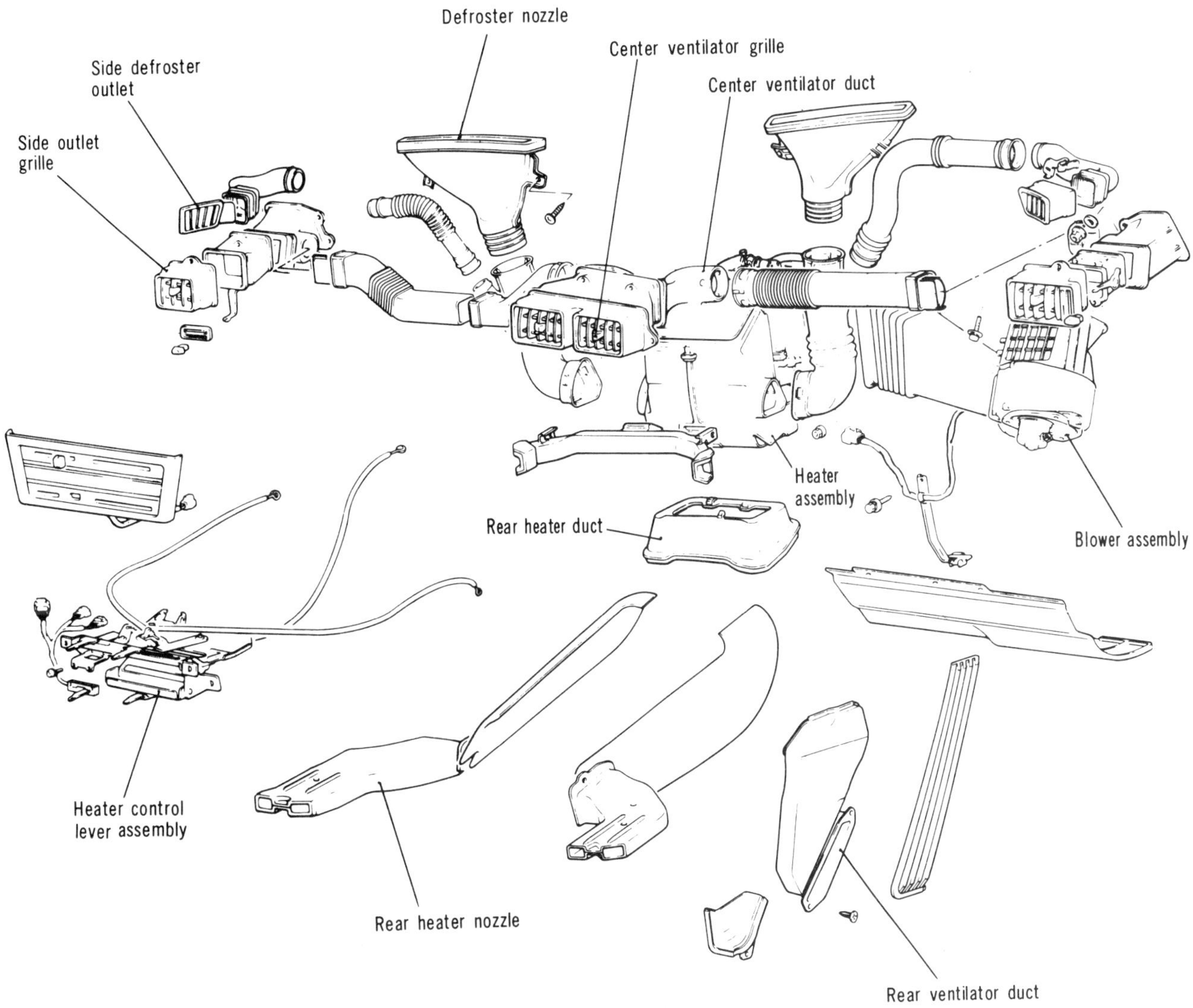

Fig. 3.18 1981 thru 1983 heater/ventilation components – exploded view (Sec 16)

5 Remove the center panel, the center ventilator grill and duct and the defroster ducts.
6 Disconnect the heater control cables at the heater (not at the control assembly). Hold a shallow container or some rags near the hoses and disconnect the heater hoses from the inlet and outlet spigots of the heater core. Catch any coolant that may run out of the hoses and plug the hoses and the heater core spigot.
7 Unplug the heater fan motor wiring connectors.
8 Remove the mounting bolts from the top and the mounting nuts from the center of the heater assembly.
9 Carefully lift the heater assembly out of its mounting position.

Installation

10 Installation is the reverse of removal. Be sure the heater hoses are properly seated on the heater core inlet and outlet spigots, then tighten the hose clamps securely.
11 Adjust the heater control cables by referring to Section 15.
12 After the heater assembly is in place, fill the radiator with a 50/50 mixture of soft water and ethylene glycol based antifreeze. Place the heater control in the Hot position. Start the engine and allow it to run for a while to circulate the coolant and eliminate any air from the heater assembly and cooling system.
13 Keep an eye on the coolant level and add more coolant as the level drops. Once the level has stabilized, shut off the engine and install the radiator pressure cap.

1981 thru 1983 vehicles

Removal

Note: *This procedure is very involved (but not complicated). You may want to read through the section step-by-step to decide whether you want to attempt a repair yourself or let your dealer or a service center handle it.*

14 Disconnect the negative battery cable from the battery. Remove the steering wheel referring to the appropriate Section in Chapter 11.
15 Loosen the tilt lock lever and fully lower the steering column. Remove the bolts holding the meter cover in place and remove the meter cover.
16 Remove the instrument meter assembly by referring to the appropriate Section in Chapter 10.
17 Remove the remote control mirror switch referring to Chapter 10.
18 Remove the inner box from the lower console accessory box. Remove the accessory box and disconnect the harness.
19 Pull the heater control knobs off, remove the panel and disconnect the illumination harness.
20 Pull the radio control knobs off, remove the panel mounting nuts and the radio panel.
21 Remove the under-dash cover and the center console side covers.
22 Remove the shift knob and the center console.
23 Remove the instrument panel pads on both sides and remove the

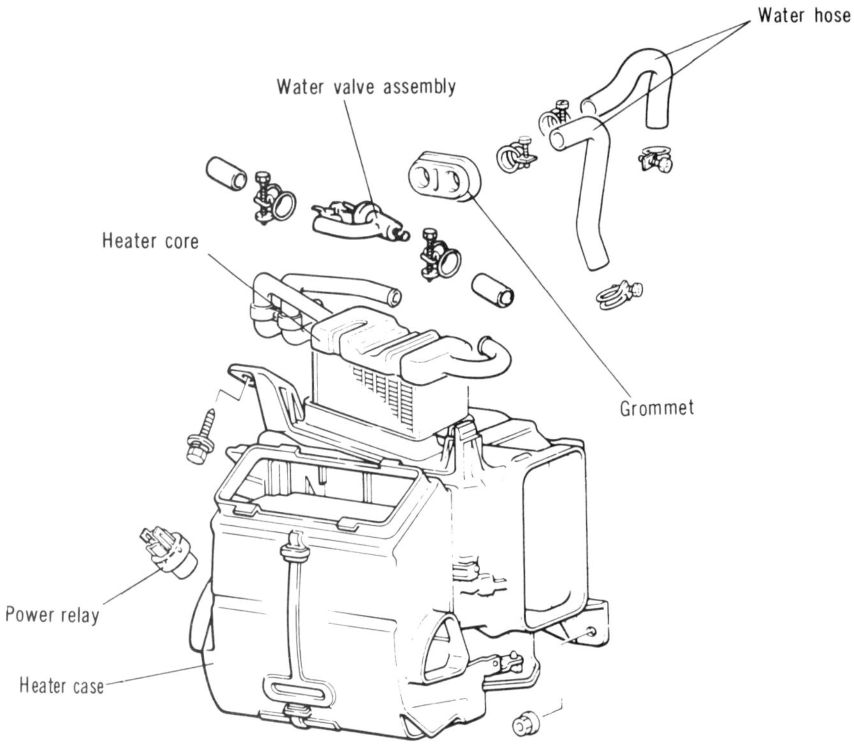

Fig. 3.19 1981 thru 1983 outside heater components – exploded view (Sec 16)

Fig. 3.20 Remove lower console accessory box (Sec 16)

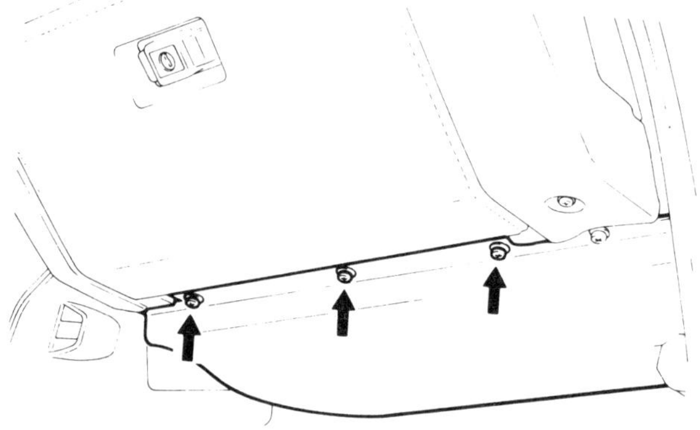

Fig. 3.21 Under-dash cover removal (Sec 16)

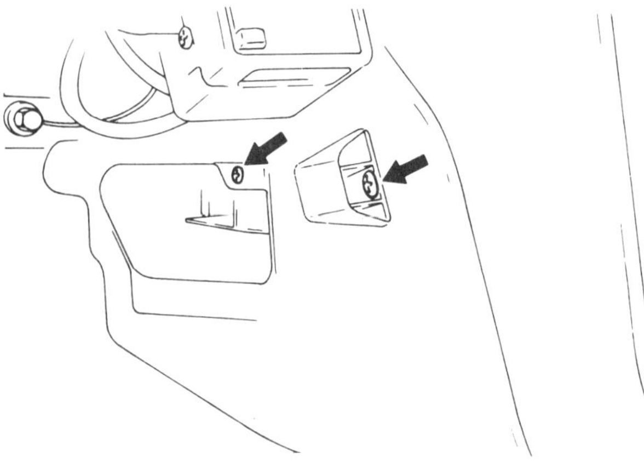

Fig. 3.22 Center console side cover removal (Sec 16)

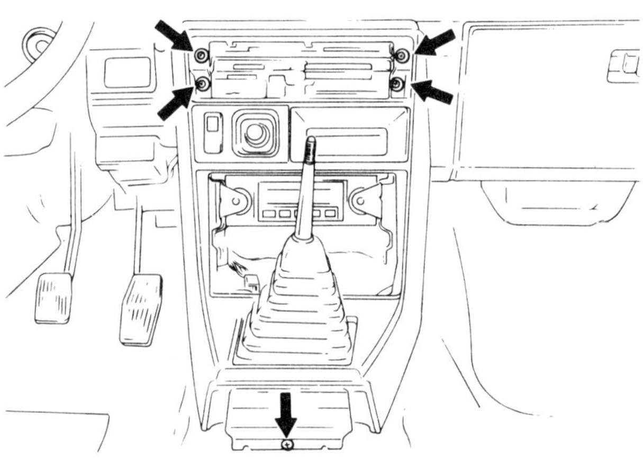

Fig. 3.23 Centre console removal (Sec 16)

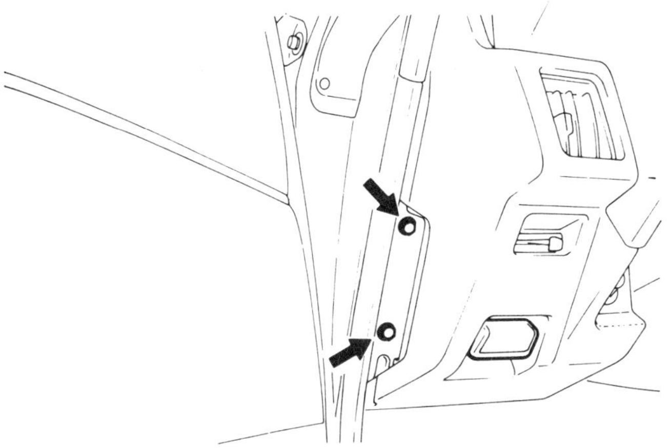

Fig. 3.24 Instrument panel cover removal (Sec 16)

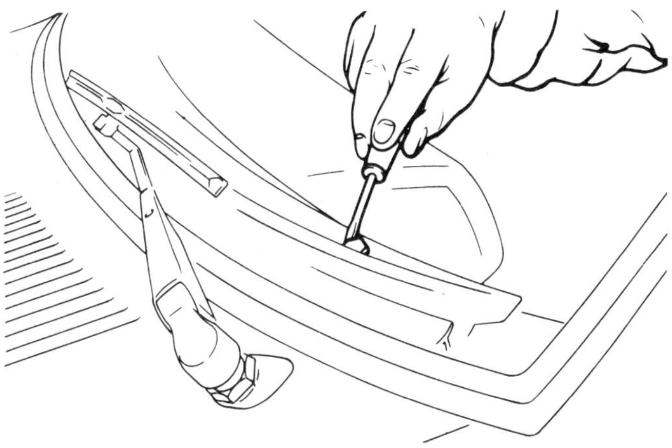

Fig. 3.25 Defroster trim removal (Sec 16)

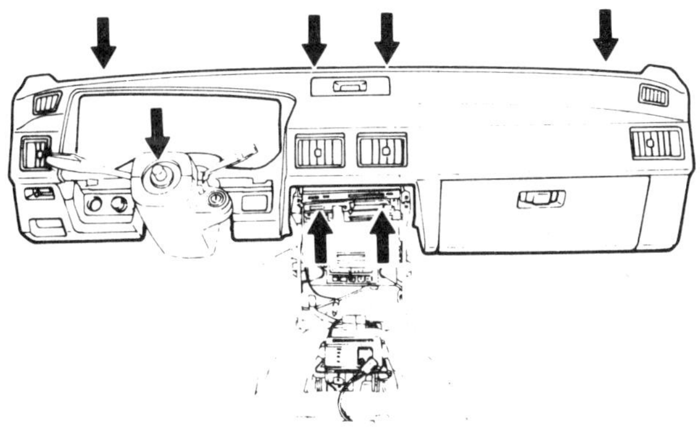

Fig. 3.26 Instrument panel removal (Sec 16)

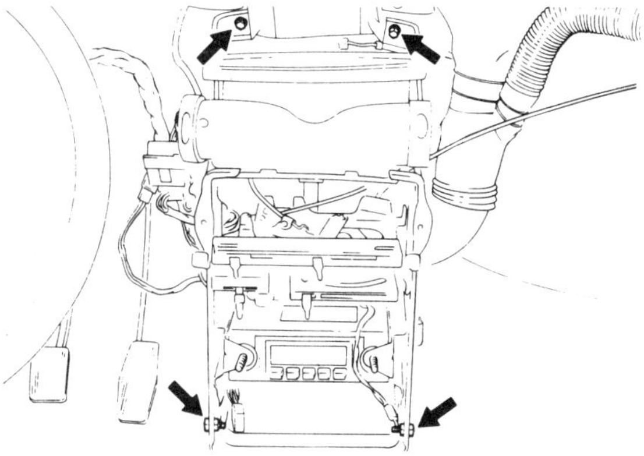

Fig. 3.27 Center console reinforcement removal (Sec 16)

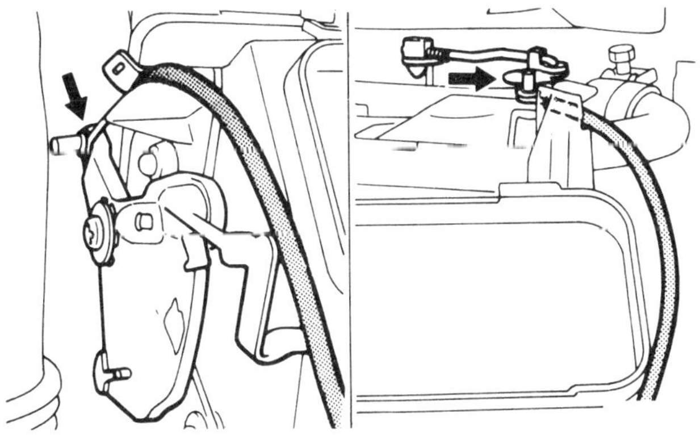

Fig. 3.28 Removal of the air mix and bypass damper cables (Sec 16)

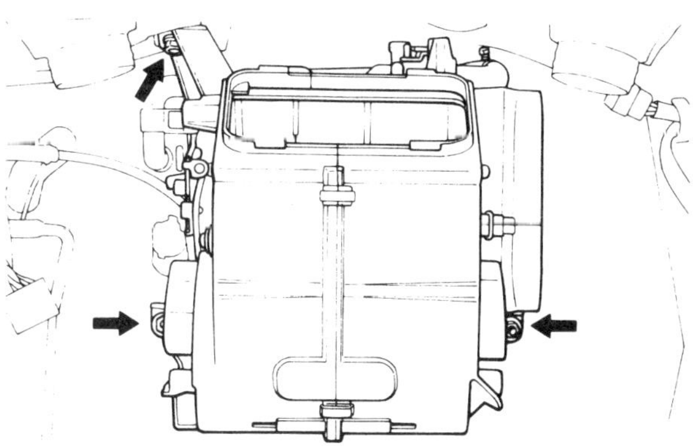

Fig. 3.29 Heater unit removal (Sec 16)

mounting nuts. Take off the hood lock release knob and the screws attaching the release cable to the instrument panel.

24 Remove the defroster trim by removing its attaching screws. Remove the screws attaching the glove compartment plate to the center reinforcement.

25 Remove the instrument panel mounting nuts and bolts. Remove the instrument panel and disconnect the connectors for the clock, glove compartment, chime and dimmer control. You may want to label these as you disconnect them for easier reassembly.

26 Remove the center console reinforcement bolts as shown. Remove the console reinforcement and disconnect the connectors for the defogger switch, radio, chime driver, defogger relay and the antenna feeder. Again, you may want to label these as you disconnect them for easier reassembly.

27 Set the heater temperature control lever to the Warm position, open the radiator drain plug and drain the cooling system. From inside the engine compartment, disconnect the water hoses from the heater unit.

28 Disconnect and remove the rear heater duct by unsnapping the clips out of the slots. Remove the air mix control cable and the bypass damper control cable from the heater unit.

29 Disconnect the heater power relay connection and remove the heater unit by removing its mounting bolts.

Installation

30 Installation is the reverse of removal. Be sure the heater hoses are properly seated on the heater core inlet and outlet spigots, then tighten the hose clamps securely.

3

31 Make sure all electrical connections are made and tight. Tighten all mounting bolts securely.
32 After the heater assembly is in place, fill the radiator with a 50/50 mixture of soft water and ethylene glycol based antifreeze. Place the heater control in the Hot position. Start the engine and allow it to run for awhile to circulate the coolant and eliminate any air from the heater assembly and cooling system.
33 Keep an eye on the coolant level and add more coolant as the level drops. Once the level has stabilized, shut off the engine and install the radiator pressure cap.
34 Adjust the heater control cables by referring to Section 15.

17 Heater power relay (1981 through 1983) – check

1 The heater power relay can easily be removed from the heater unit. Remove the relay harness and the mounting screw.
2 To check the function of the relay, refer to Chapter 10.
3 Installation is the reverse of removal.

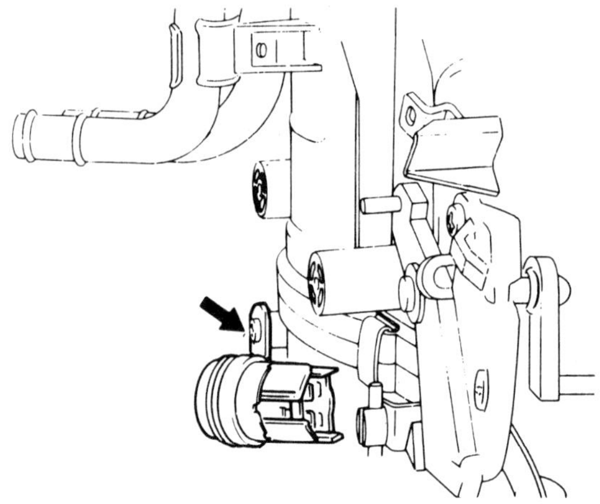

Fig. 3.30 Heater power relay removal (Sec 17)

18 Heater core – removal and installation

1 Refer to Section 16 and remove the heater assembly.
2 Once the heater assembly is out of the vehicle, remove the screws holding the core in place in the heater. Carefully lift the core out of the heater unit.
3 Remove the heater water valve by loosening the hose clamps and using a pulling and twisting action.
4 Inspect the heater core for any visible leakage or crushing of the cooling fins or of the core itself. Repair and cleaning of the core is best left to a radiator repair shop. If it is in questionable condition, replace it with a new core.
5 Inspect the heater water valve for visible clogging, crushed casing and whether it operates smoothly. If it is in a doubtful condition, replace the valve with a new one.
6 Installation is the reverse of removal. Make sure that the mounting bolts are tightened securely and all hose connections are tight.
7 Now is the time to check the heater hoses. Replace them with new ones if they appear cracked or brittle.

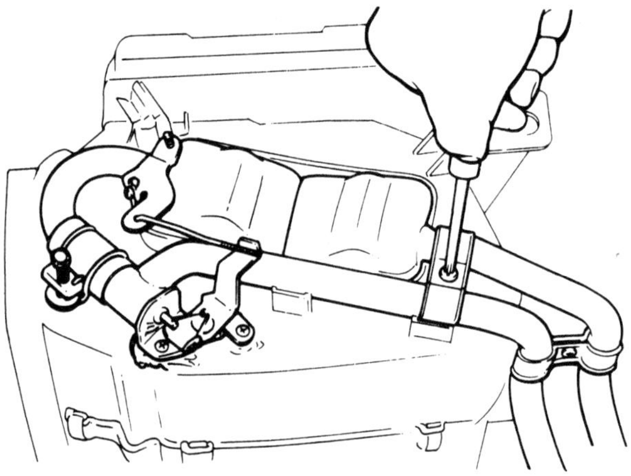

Fig. 3.31 Heater core removal (Sec 18)

19 Heater motor/fan – removal, testing and installation

1978 through 1980 vehicles

1 The heater motor is attached to the heater assembly so it is automatically removed when the heater assembly is removed. It can also be taken out as a separate unit.
2 Remove the center console (if so equipped), the center panel and the center ventilator grille and duct.
3 Unplug the motor electrical connectors.
4 Remove the bolts attaching the motor and fan assembly to the heater, then lift out the motor and fan separately.
5 Refer to Chapter 10 for heater motor testing procedures.
6 Position the fan and motor in place in the heater assembly, install the mounting bolts and tighten them evenly and securely.
7 Plug in the motor electrical connectors.
8 Install the center ventilator grill and duct, the center panel and the console.

1981 through 1983 vehicles

9 The heater motor/fan (blower) assembly can be removed with the complete heater assembly out (skip steps 10 through 14). It can also be removed as a separate unit without removing the heater assembly as follows:
10 Remove the under-dash cover assembly.
11 Remove the center console side covers.
12 Remove the bolt holding the glove compartment to the center reinforcement.
13 Loosen the stops on both sides of the glove compartment so it will be free. Disconnect the glove compartment illumination switch.
14 Remove the screws holding the glove compartment plate to the instrument panel. Remove the glove compartment.
15 Disconnect any heat ducts, the heater fan switch connector and the inside/outside air control cable from the blower assembly.
16 Remove the blower assembly by removing its mounting bolts and nut.
17 To separate the motor and fan from the blower assembly, remove the bracket and mounting screws.
18 Disconnect the motor connector. Remove the motor retaining screws and the motor from the blower.
19 The fan is attached to the motor by a nut. Remove the nut and the fan from the motor.
20 Remove the heater resistor by removing its retaining screws. To check the resistor, refer to Chapter 10.
21 To check the motor, refer to Chapter 10.
22 Inspect the fan for any deformation of the fan fins. Replace with a new one if damaged.
23 Installation is the reverse of removal. Make sure all connections are made and tight and that the ground wire is hooked up.

20 Heater and fan switches – check

1 On 1978 through 1980 vehicles, refer to Chapter 10 to check the fan switch.
2 On 1981 through 1983 vehicles, to gain access to the heater and fan switches, first remove the instrument panel and the center console panel. (Section 16).
3 To remove the heater/fan switch, disconnect the switch assembly connector and remove the mounting screws.
4 To check the heater/fan switch, the heater mode switch and the heater microswitch, refer to Chapter 10.
5 Installation is the reverse of removal.

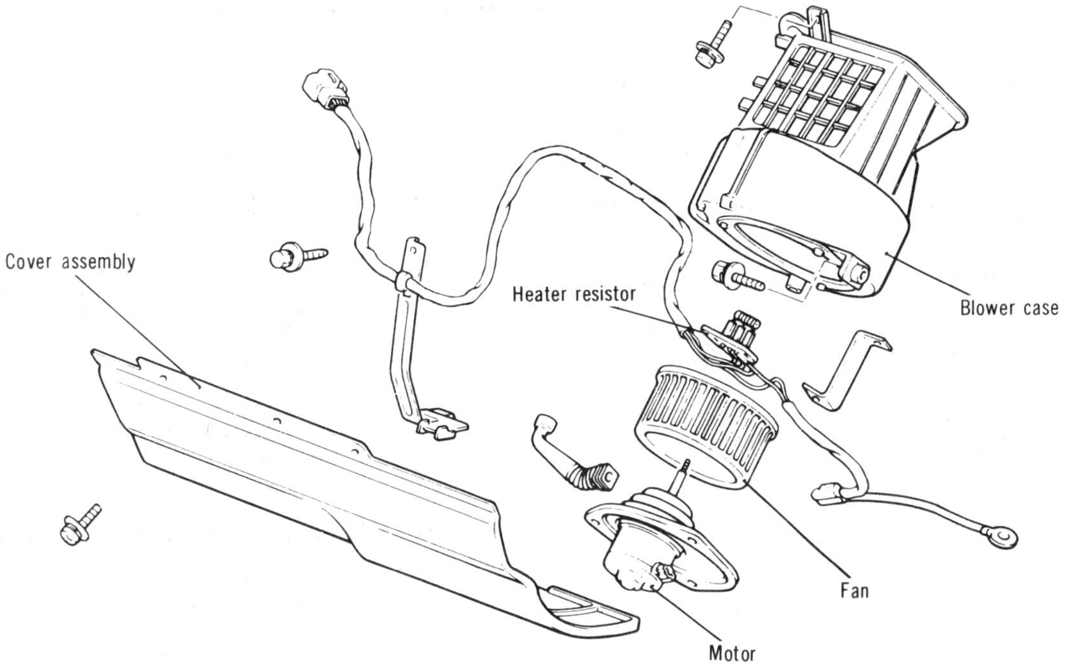

Fig. 3.32 1981 thru 1983 heater fan/motor assembly – exploded view (Sec 19)

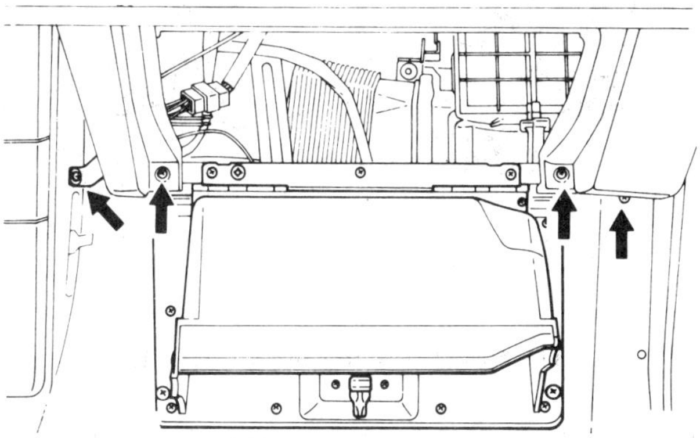

Fig. 3.33 Glove compartment removal (Sec 19)

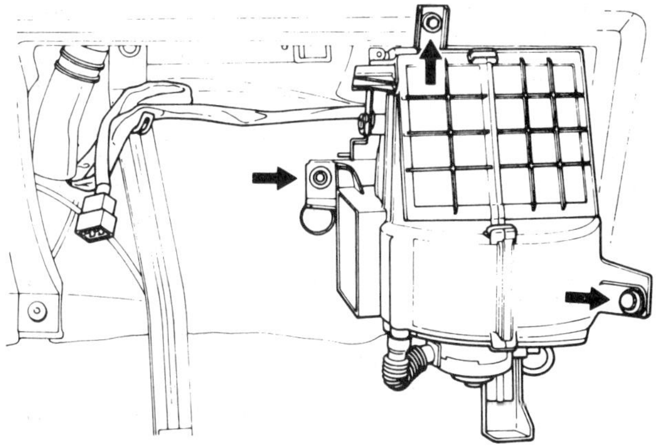

Fig. 3.34 Blower assembly removal (Sec 19)

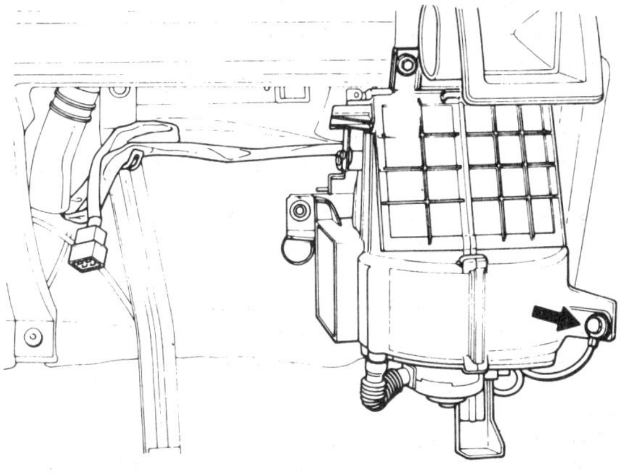

Fig. 3.35 Motor ground wire installation (Sec 19)

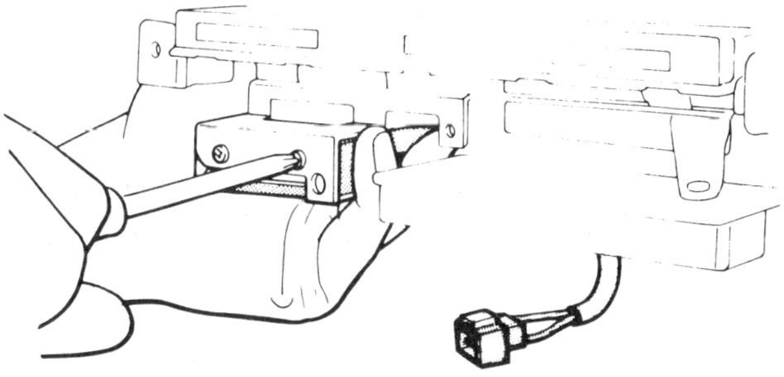

Fig. 3.36 Heater/fan switch removal (Sec 20)

21 Air conditioning system – general servicing

Caution: *In view of the toxic nature of the chemicals and gases employed in the system, no part of the system should be disconnected by the home mechanic. Due to the need for the specialized evacuating and charging equipment such work should be left to your dealer or a refrigeration specialist.*

Because of the special tools, equipment and skills required to service air conditioning systems and the differences between the various systems that may be installed on vehicles, air conditioner servicing cannot be covered in this manual. We will cover component removal, as the home mechanic may realize a substantial savings in repair costs if he removes components himself, takes them to a professional for repair and/or replaces them with new ones.

Problems in the air conditioning system should be diagnosed and the system refrigerant evacuated by an air conditioning technician before component removal/replacement is attempted. Once the new or reconditioned component has been installed, the system should then be charged and checked by an air conditioning technician.

Before indiscriminately removing air conditioning system components, get more than one estimate or repair cost from reputable air conditioning service centers. You may find it to be cheaper and less trouble to let the entire operation be performed by someone else.

22 Air conditioner compressor fluid – check and change

Caution: *In view of the toxic nature of the chemicals and gases employed in the system, no part of the system should be disconnected by the home mechanic. Due to the need for the specialized evacuating and charging equipment such work should be left to your dealer or a refrigeration specialist.*

1 To check or change the air conditioner fluid, refer to the appropriate sections in Chapter 1.

23 Air conditioner drivebelt – checking, adjustment and replacement

1 To check or adjust the air conditioner drive-belt, refer to the air conditioning system checks in Chapter 1.

2 To replace the air conditioner drivebelt, loosen the idler pulley and move to the side. Remove the old belt and replace it with a new one.

3 Adjust the belt according to procedures in Chapter 1.

24 Air conditioner hoses – checking and replacement

Caution: *In view of the toxic nature of the chemicals and gases employed in the system, no part of the system should be disconnected by the home mechanic. Due to the need for the specialized evacuating and charging equipment such work should be left to your dealer or a refrigeration specialist.*

1 To check the air conditioner hoses, refer to the air conditioning system checks in Chapter 1.

25 Air conditioner evaporator – removal and installation

Caution: *In view of the toxic nature of the chemicals and gases employed in the system, no part of the system should be disconnected by the home mechanic. Due to the need for the specialized evacuating and charging equipment such work should be left to your dealer or a refrigeration specialist.*

1 The air conditioner evaporator is combined with the heater assembly and is mounted under the right side of the vehicle instrument panel.

2 Before removing the evaporator, the system must be evacuated by an air conditioning technician.

3 Loosen the hose clamps and remove the hoses from the evaporator fittings inside the engine compartment.

4 Disconnect the control cable from the damper control lever at the right side of the evaporator.

5 Slide back the hose clamp and remove the drain hose from the spigot at the rear of the evaporator.

6 Peel off the sealing compound around the evaporator inlet and outlet tubes at the vehicle fire wall.

7 Remove the bolts attaching the evaporator to the instrument panel and fire wall and carefully move it down and out from under the instrument panel. Do not misplace the plastic duct that fits between the heater assembly and the evaporator.

8 Installation is basically the reverse of removal. Be sure to position

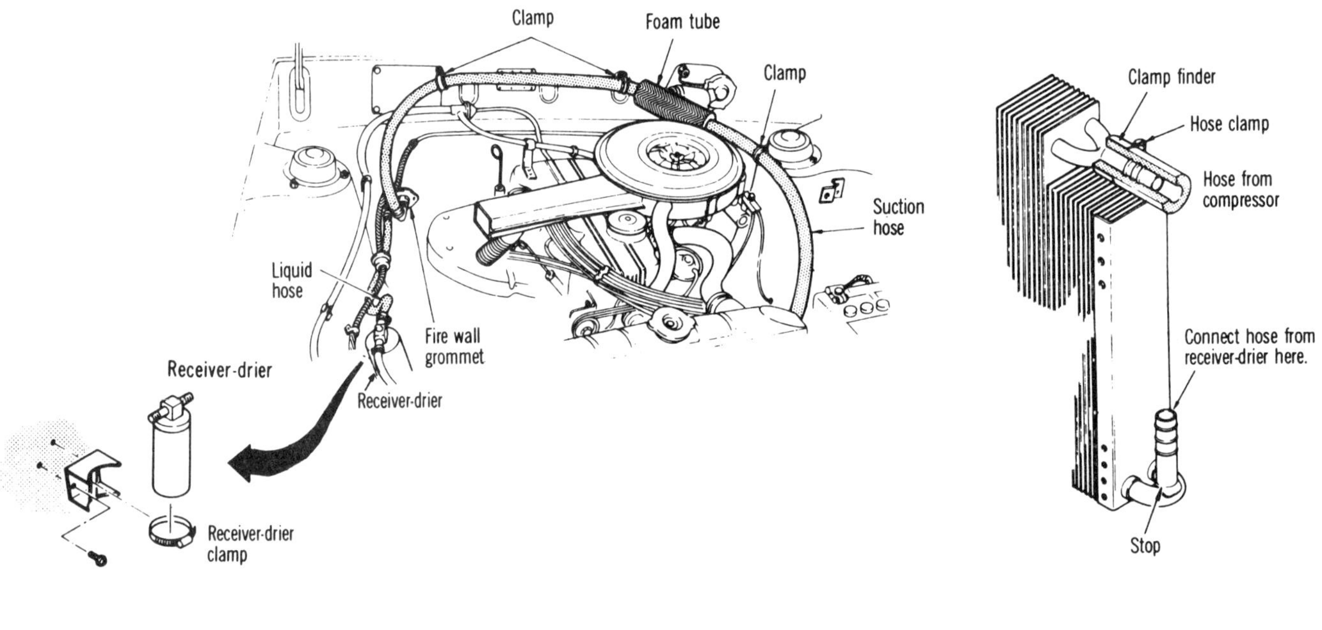

Fig. 3.37 Air conditioner hoses and receiver – dryer location (Sec 24)

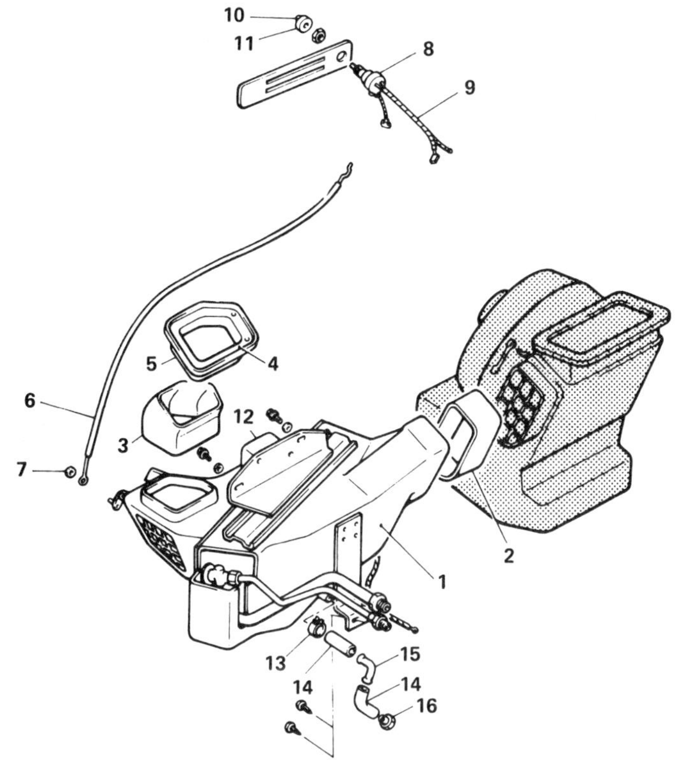

Fig. 3.38 Air conditioner evaporator components – exploded view (Sec 25)

1 Evaporator
2 Duct sleeve
3 Fresh air duct
4 Fresh air duct gasket
5 Fresh air cover
6 A/C control cable
7 Clip
8 Fan and temperature switch
9 Wiring harness
10 Fan knob
11 Temperature knob
12 Thermistor control box
13 Drain clamp
14 Drain hose
15 90° elbow
16 Drain restrictor

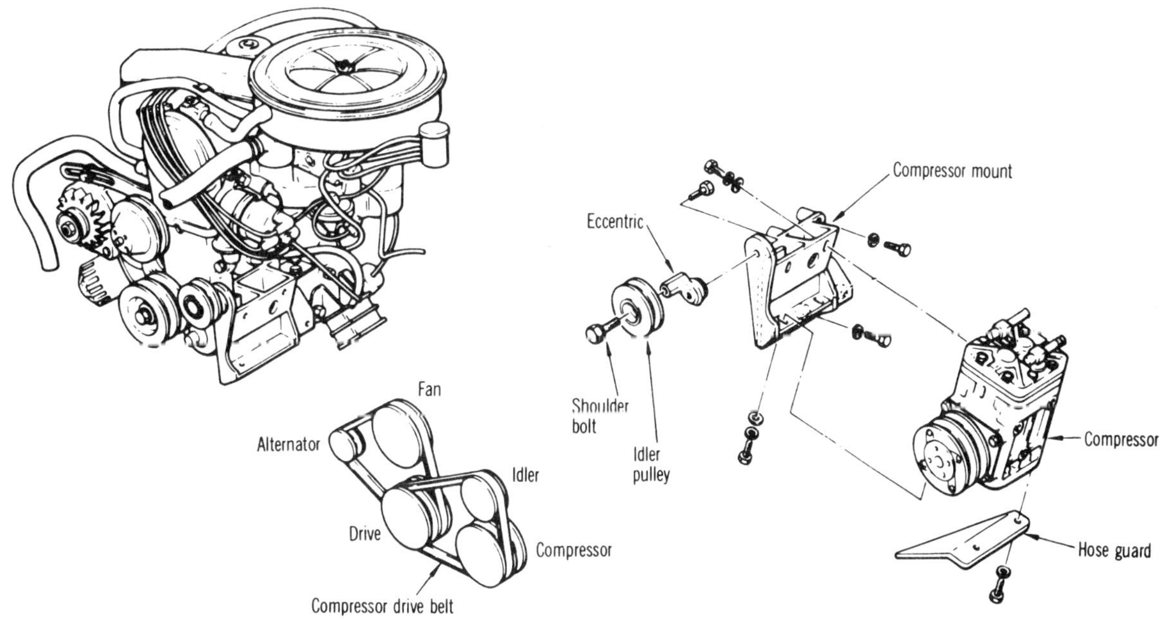

Fig. 3.39 Air conditioner drivebelt and compressor components – exploded view (1600 cc engine) (Sec 26)

the plastic ducts before slipping the evaporator into place. When installing the hoses, lubricate the inside surfaces and the outside of the fittings with refrigerant oil. The hose clamps must be positioned properly with the clamp finders and tightened securely. Do not forget to install the drain hose and the sealing compound.

26 Air conditioner compresser – removal and installation

Caution: *In view of the toxic nature of the chemicals and gases employed in the system, no part of the system should be disconnected by the home mechanic. Due to the need for the specialized evacuating and charging equipment such work should be left to your dealer or a refrigeration specialist.*

1 The air conditioner compresser is mounted at the front of the engine at the upper left side and is driven by a belt from the crank shaft.

2 Before removing the compresser, the system must be evacuated by an air conditioning technician.

3 Loosen the drive belt idler pulley and slip the drivebelt off the compressor clutch pulley.

4 Loosen the hose clamps and remove the hoses from the compressor.

5 Unplug the air conditioner compressor clutch electrical connector.

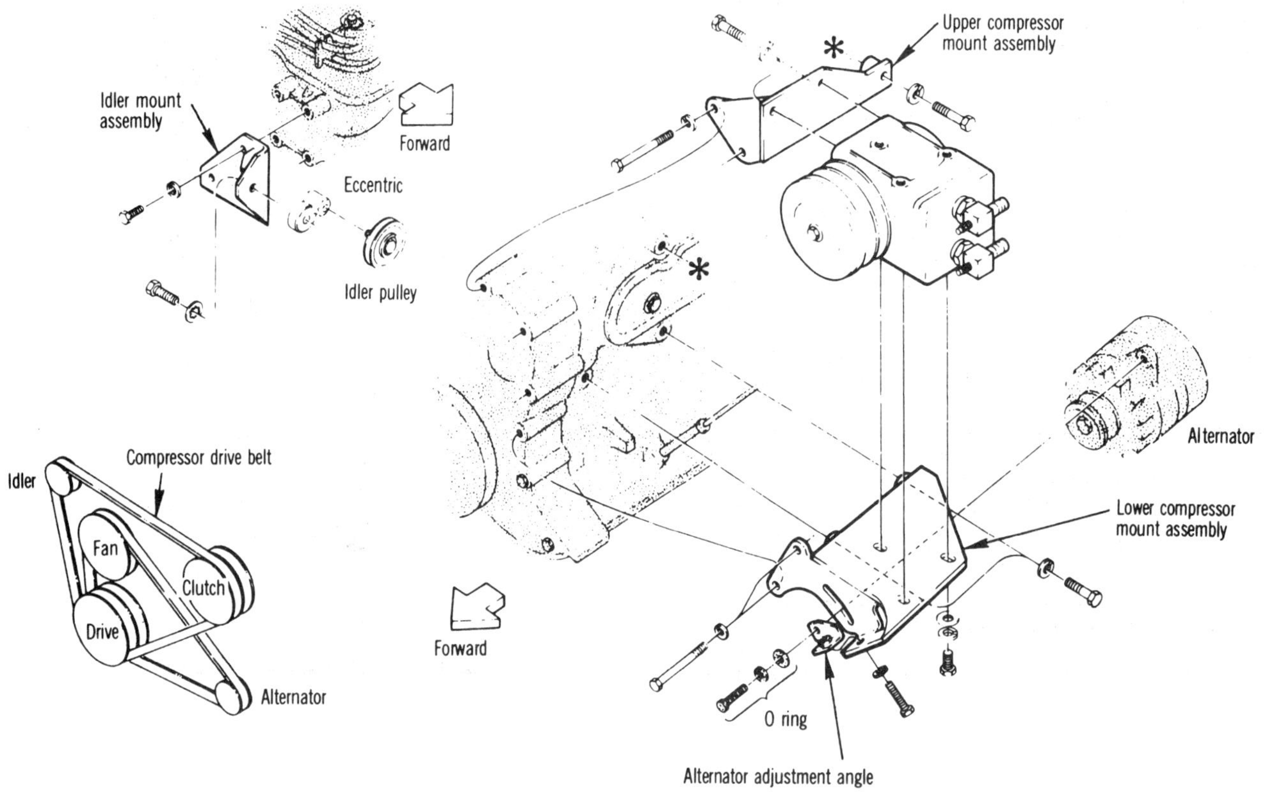

Fig. 3.40 Air conditioner drivebelt and compressor – exploded view (2000 cc and 2600 cc engine) (Sec 26)

6 Remove the bolts attaching the compressor to the mounts and the compressor can be lifted out of the vehicle. The bolts on the bottom are accessible only from under the vehicle.
7 Installation is basically the reverse of removal. Lubricate the inside of the hoses and the outside of the fittings with refrigerant oil before installing the hoses. Be sure to carefully seat the hoses on the compressor fittings and install the hose clamps securely. Locate the hose clamps the correct distance from the hose end with the hose clamp finder. The belt must be correctly tensioned for proper air conditioner operation.

27 Air conditioner receiver/dryer – removal and installation

Caution: *In view of the toxic nature of the chemicals and gases employed in the system, no part of the system should be disconnected by the home mechanic. Due to the need for the specialized evacuating and charging equipment such work should be left to your dealer or a refrigeration specialist.*
1 The receiver/dryer, which acts as a reservoir for the refrigerant, is the canister-shaped object mounted on the right fender well in the engine compartment.
2 Before removing the receiver/dryer, the system must be evacuated by an air conditioning technician.
3 Loosen the hose clamps and remove both hoses from the receiver/dryer.
4 Loosen the clamp and pull up on the receiver/dryer to remove it from its mount.
5 When installing the receiver/dryer, lubricate the inside surfaces of the hoses and the outside of the fittings with refrigerant oil. Be sure the hose clamps are properly lcoated by the clamp finders and securely tightened.

28 Air conditioner condenser – removal and installation

Caution: *In view of the toxic nature of the chemicals and gases employed in the system, no part of the system should be disconnected by the home mechanic. Due to the need for the specialized evacuating and charging equipment such work should be left to your dealer or a refrigeration specialist.*

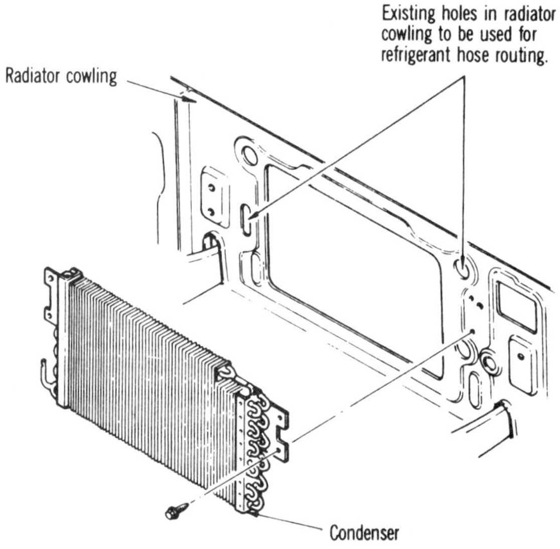

Fig. 3.41 Condenser location (Sec 28)

1 The air conditioner condenser is mounted in front of the radiator.
2 Before removing the condenser, the system must be evacuated by an air conditioning technician.
3 Loosen the hose clamps and remove the hoses leading from the

compresser and receiver/dryer to the condenser. Do not remove the hoses from the condenser.

4 Remove the grill (by referring to Chapter 12) and the vertical hood latch supprt.

5 Remove the bolts attaching the condenser to the front panel. Carefully lift the condenser out of the vehicle; do not bend the cooling fins or coil.

6 Loosen the hose clamps and remove the hoses from the condenser.

7 Installation is the reverse of removal. When installing the hoses, lubricate the inside surfaces of the hoses and the outside of the fittings with refrigerant oil. Be sure to install the hoses onto the condenser before mounting the condenser in the vehicle. Support the hose fittings against a solid surface, such as a work bench, when pushing the hoses onto them. This will prevent bending of the fittings or the coils, which could cause leaks. Be sure to locate the clamps properly with the clamp finders and tighten them securely.

29 Throttle opener system – checking and adjustment

1 To check or adjust the throttle opener, refer to the air conditioning system checks in Chapter 1.

2 An illustration of the system is given.

30 Air conditioner switches – checking

1 Refer to Chapter 10 for checking the air conditioning switches.

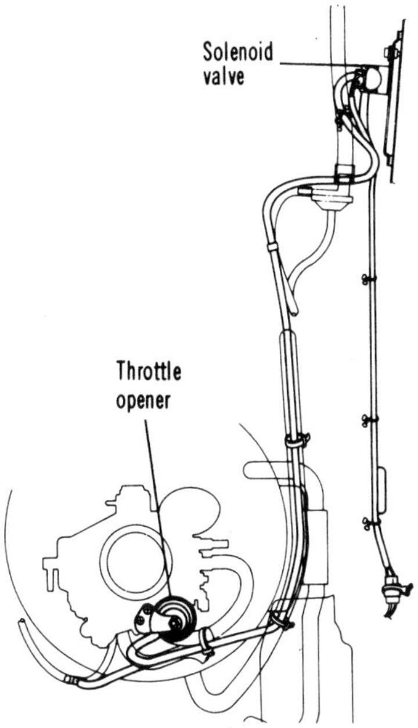

Fig. 3.42 Throttle opener system (Sec 29)

Chapter 4 Fuel and exhaust systems

Contents

Specifications

Accelerator stopper bolt length	0.75 in (19 mm)	
Fuel pump		
Type	Mechanical diaphragm	
	1600 cc	**2000 cc & 2600 cc**
Discharge rate at engine speed	0.43 gal/min (1.6 lit/min)	0.53 gal/min (2.0 lit/min)
Discharge pressure	3.7 to 5.1 psi (22 to 29 kPa)	4.6 to 6.0 psi (26 to 35 kPa)
Fuel filter	Replaceable cartridge type	
Carburetor		
Type	Downdraft 2-barrel	
	USA	**Canada**
Throttle bore size		
Primary	1.26 in (32 mm)	1.18 in (30 mm)
Secondary	1.38 in (35 mm)	1.26 in (32 mm)
Torque specifications	**ft-lb**	**Nm**
Accelerator rod-to-yoke nut	11 to 14	15 to 19
For USA		
Front pipe-to-catalytic converter nuts	21 to 28	29 to 39
Front pipe-to-heat insulator nuts	5 to 10	7 to 14
Front pipe-to-center pipe bolts	14 to 21	19 to 29
Center pipe-to-main muffler bolts	14 to 21	19 to 29
For Canada		
Front pipe-to-manifold nuts	14 to 21	19 to 29
Front pipe-to-pre-muffler nuts	21 to 28	29 to 39
Front pipe-to-bellhousing bolts	14 to 21	19 to 29
Pre-muffler-to-heat insulator nuts	5 to 10	7 to 14
Pre-muffler-to-center pipe bolts	14 to 21	19 to 29

1 General information

The fuel system is very conventional, utilizing a rear mounted fuel tank, a mechanical diaphragm-type fuel pump which is driven off the engine camshaft, and a 2-barrel down-draft carburetor. The fuel is routed through a cartridge-type filter, mounted on the fuel tank, before entering the fuel line and pump.

Additions to the system provide facilities for preventing vapor locking. On the 1600 cc engine, this is done by installing a thermostatically controlled non-return valve in the fuel return hose from the carburetor to the fuel tank. On the 2000 cc and 2600 cc engines, a vapor separater is installed to achieve the same result.

Since many of the emission control systems' components and parts of the fuel system are interrelated, the material covered in this Chapter should be used in conjunction with the material in Chapter 6.

The extra system consists of a front exhaust pipe, a main muffler assembly and the various brackets and hangers that support them.

2 US Federal regulations – emission control

The fuel system is designed so that the vehicle will comply with all US Federal regulations covering emission hydrocarbons and carbon monoxide. To achieve this, the ignition system must be accurately set using the proper equipment. Proper ignition timing is a must before attempting any other emission-related adjustments. The information in this Chapter is given to assist the reader to clean and/or replace certain components before taking the vehicle to your local dealer or repair shop for final adjustments. Failure to do this could mean that the vehicle will not comply with the regulations.

3 Air cleaner filter – check and replacement

To check or replace the air cleaner filter, refer to Chapter 1.

4 Air cleaner assembly – removal and installation

1 The air cleaner assembly must be removed in order to perform many maintenance repair and adjustment procedures. It is very important to remove and install it carefully and correctly to ensure proper engine operation.
2 Remove the snorkel tube (connected between the air cleaner and the headlight brace) from the air cleaner.
3 Pull off the crankcase breather hose from the front of the air cleaner housing.
4 Remove the large hose leading to the secondary air supply system valve.
5 Slide back the hose clamp and remove the hose that leads to the purge control valve from the air cleaner housing.
6 Remove the top cover. It is held in place with spring clips and a wing nut. Lift out the filter element.
7 Remove the nuts, lock washers and flat washers attaching the air cleaner housing to the valve cover.
8 Carefully lift up on the housing and disconnect the hot-air duct between the exhaust manifold and air cleaner housing and the vacuum hose leading to the air bleed valve in the housing. The hose is color coded white.
9 Install the air cleaner by reversing the removal procedure. Be sure to line up the arrows on the top cover and the housing before setting the cover in place.

5 Fuel filter – check and replacement

To check the fuel filter, refer to the fuel system checks in Chapter 1. To replace the filter, refer to the appropriate Section in Chapter 1.

6 Automatic choke – check and adjustment

1 To check the automatic choke, refer to Chapter 1.
2 The choke is automatically operated by a wax element that senses the coolant temperature. This element allows the choke valve to close under spring pressure at low coolant temperatures and opens it through a set lever and a rack and pinion gear setup as the coolant temperature increases.
3 The wax element plunger pushes against an adjustable screw on the choke set lever. This screw is preset at the factory to provide for proper choke closing and opening and sealed with white paint. Do not tamper with it, as choke operation will be adversely affected.
4 The choke should not require any adjustment as long as the rack and pinion gears are properly oriented and the choke pinion gear

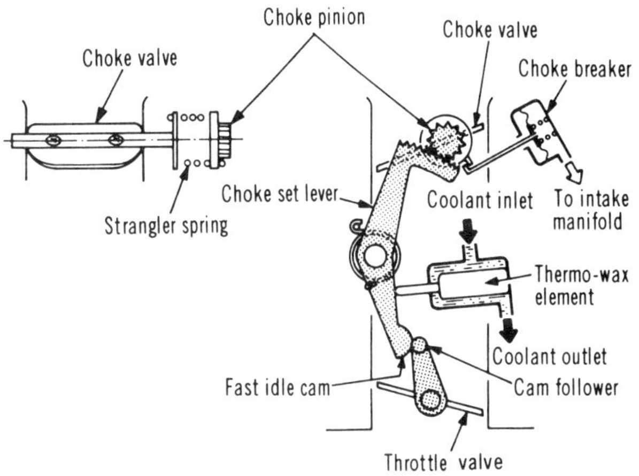

Fig. 4.1 Choke mechanism and linkage (Sec 6)

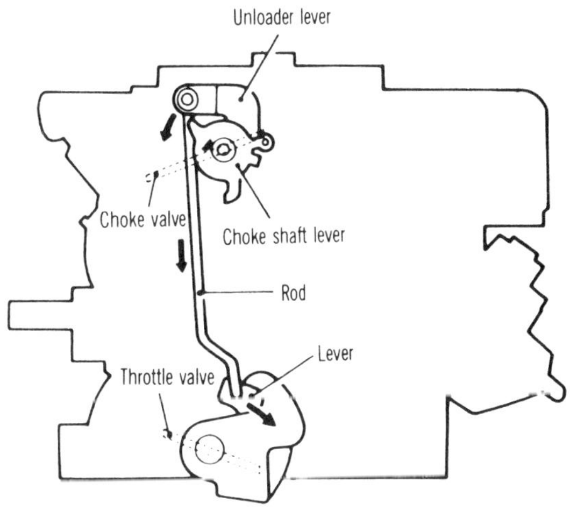

Fig. 4.2 Choke unloader mechanism (Sec 6)

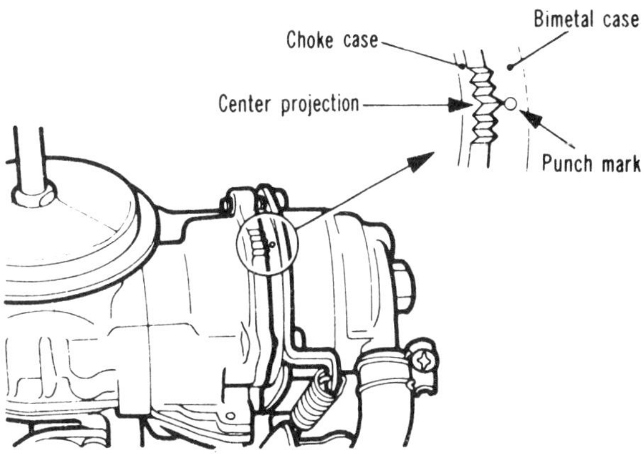

Fig. 4.3 Mating mark of automatic choke (Sec 6)

4

assembly is adjusted so that the choke plate is lightly seated in the closed position when the choke linkage is installed.

5 If the choke mechanism is suspected of malfunctioning, before you take it apart or try to adjust it, cleaning off its parts may be all it needs.

6 Spray a carburetor cleaning solvent into the end of the auto-choke and (with the air cleaner assembly removed) onto the choke and throttle valve plates and pivot points.

7 Also, spray the throttle linkage and the fast idle cam and link to remove any dirt build-up.

8 Cleaning gum deposits off these parts may free-up the choke and it will work again.

7 Accelerator linkage (1978 thru 1980) – adjustment

1 Make sure that the accelerator pedal stopper bolt meets the specifications to define the floor clearance of the pedal.

2 Now, see if the lip of the rubber grommet in the firewall, that the accelerator rod goes through, is in the groove on the accelerator rod. If it is not, position it there. If it is, make sure it is in line with the outer edge of the grommet without any distortion towards the front or the rear.

3 If there is any distortion, it has to be adjusted accordingly. Back off or tighten the nut on the carburetor end of the accelerator rod in order to position the rubber grommet so that there is no distortion.

4 Apply multi-purpose grease to all pivot points to assure smooth operation.

8 Accelerator cable (1981 thru 1983) – adjustment

1 The adjustment is made by loosening the cable housing clamps on the valve cover and carburetor and moving the housing toward or away from the carburetor, as necessary.

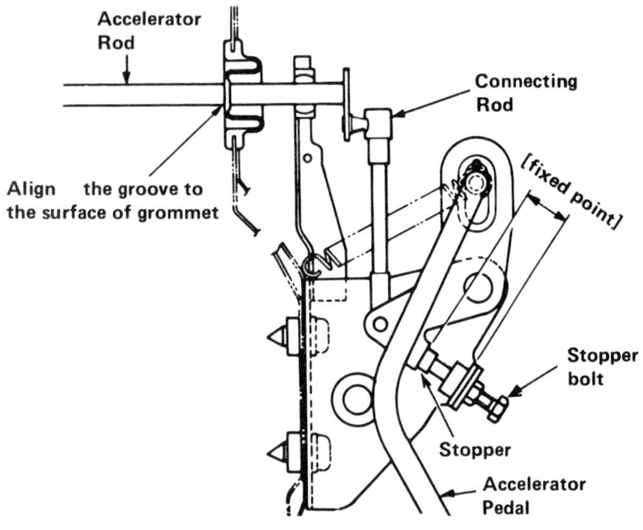

Fig. 4.4 Accelerator linkage adjustment (Sec 7)

2 The free play of the accelerator should be within the limits specified. If it is not, change it by moving the cable housing. Remember to tighten the clamps if adjustments are made.

3 The accelerator pedal must operate smoothly and the throttle valve must be fully open when the accelerator pedal is depressed as far as possible.

4 Periodically apply a thin coat of multi-purpose grease to the accelerator pedal pivot points.

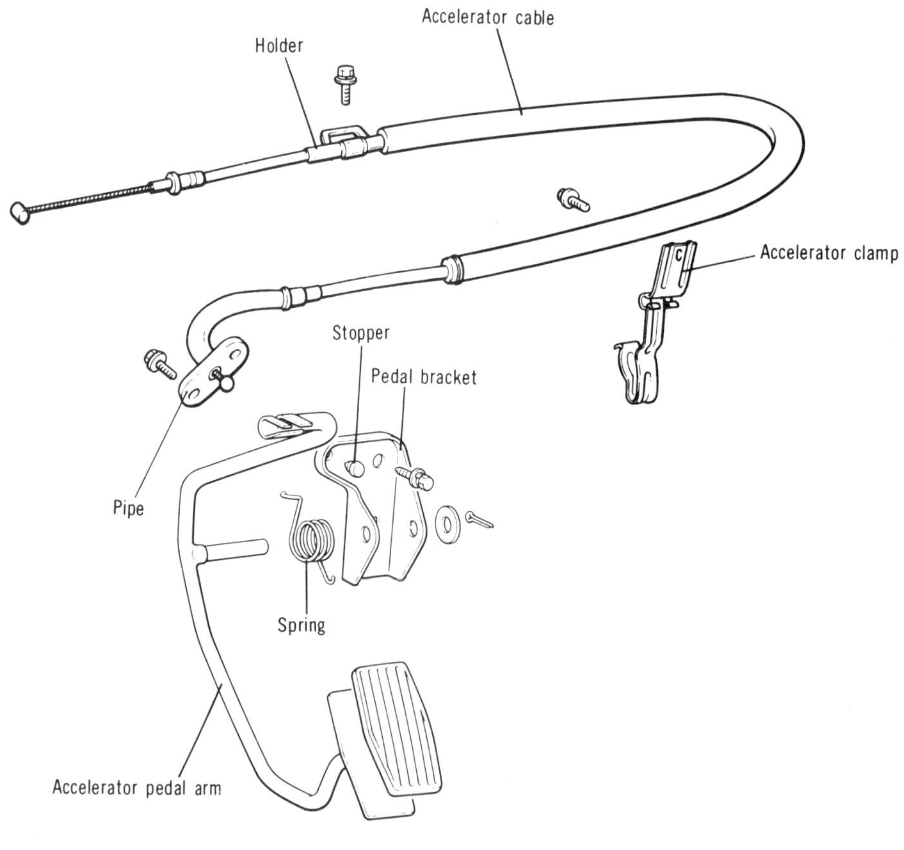

Fig. 4.5 1981 thru 1983 accelerator components (Sec 8)

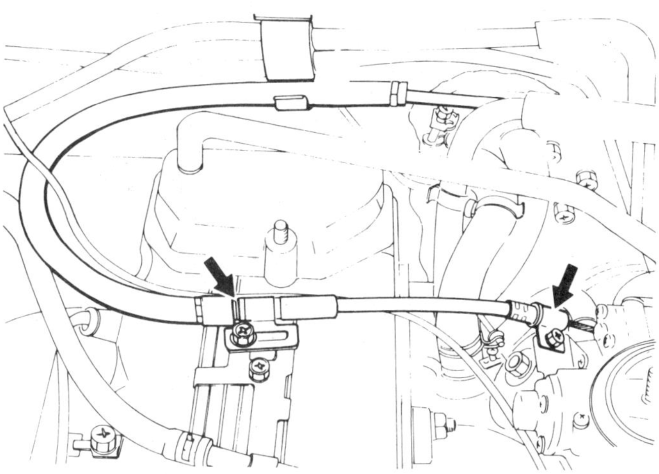

Fig. 4.6 Accelerator cable adjustment points (Sec 8)

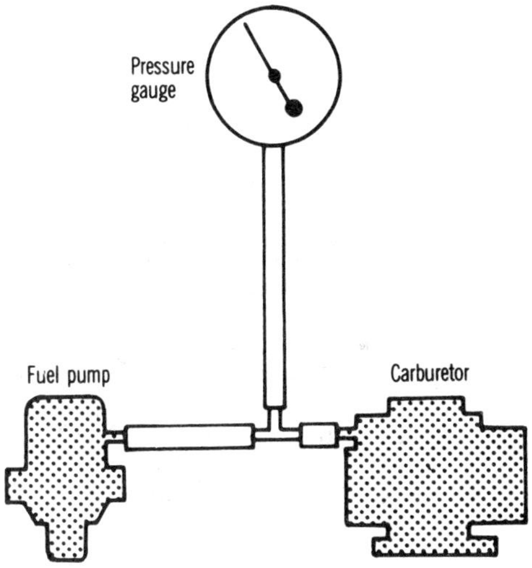

Fig. 4.7 Pressure testing fuel pump (Sec 9)

9 Fuel pump – testing

1 Before deciding that the fuel pump is defective, it should be tested for correct pressure while still in the vehicle.

2 To check the fuel pump pressure, you will need a T fitting, a length of hose (with the same inside diameter as the fuel hoses), a fuel pressure gauge and a tachometer.

3 Loosen the hose clamp and pull the fuel hose off the fuel pump outlet fitting. Insert one end of the T fitting into the hose that was disconnected from the pump and tighten the hose clamp. Cut a short length of hose, slip one end over the T fitting and the other end onto the fuel pump outlet fitting.

4 Connect another length of hose (approximately 6 inches long) between the fuel pressure gauge and the remaining end of the T fitting. Install hose clamps on all the connections.

5 Loosen the hose clamp and disconnect the fuel return hose, which returns fuel to the fuel tank from the carburetor. Slip a short length of hose, which has been plugged, onto the fitting and install the hose clamp.

6 Connect the tachometer according to the instructions provided by the manufacturer.

7 Start the engine and allow it to run for a few minutes before taking the pressure reading. This will allow any air in the pump to be vented, which will ensure an accurate reading.

8 Make sure that the engine idle speed is correct, then note the pressure reading on the gauge and compare it to the Specifications.

9 Stop the engine and observe the gauge. The pressure should remain constant or return to zero slowly.

10 If the pressure was higher or lower than specified or if it dropped to zero instantly when the engine was shut off, the fuel pump is defective and should be replaced with a new one.

10 Fuel pump – removal and installation

1 The fuel pump is mounted on the cylinder head immediately in front of the carburetor.

2 Pull the coil high-tension lead out of the distributor and ground it on the engine block. Remove the spark plugs and place your thumb over the number one cylinder spark plug hole.

3 Rotate the crankshaft in a clockwise direction (with a wrench on the large bolt attaching the pulley to the front of the crankshaft) until

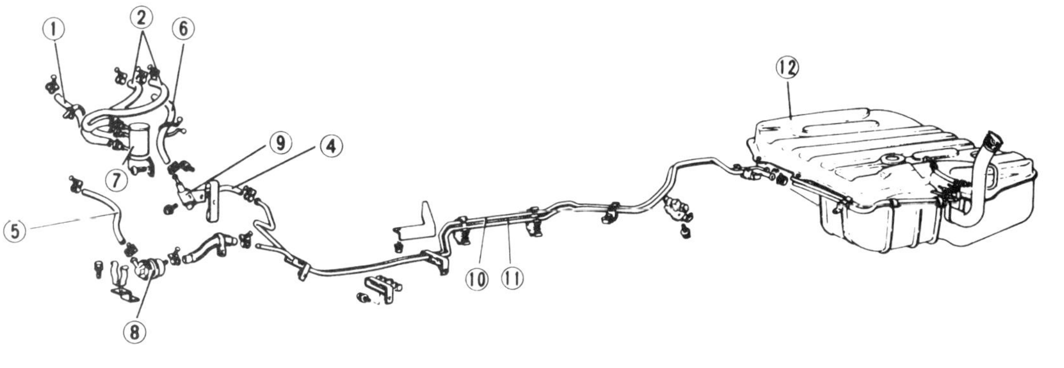

Fig. 4.8 1978 thru 1980 fuel system – exploded view (Sec 10)

1 Fuel hose, separator-to-pump
2 Fuel hose, separator-to-carburetor
3 Fuel hose, pump-to-return pipe
4 Fuel hose, carburetor-to-return pipe
5 Fuel hose, filter-to-pump
6 Fuel hose, carburetor-to-return valve
7 Vapor separator tank
8 Fuel filter
9 Fuel return valve
10 Fuel return pipe
11 Fuel main pipe
12 Fuel tank

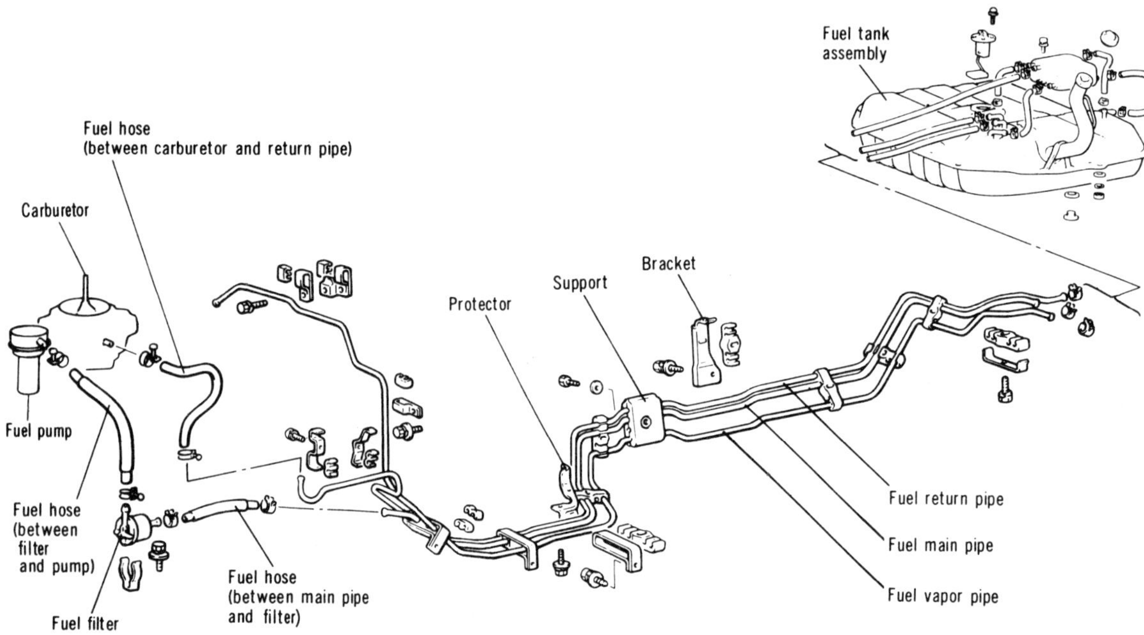

Fig. 4.9 1981 thru 1983 fuel system – exploded view (Sec 10)

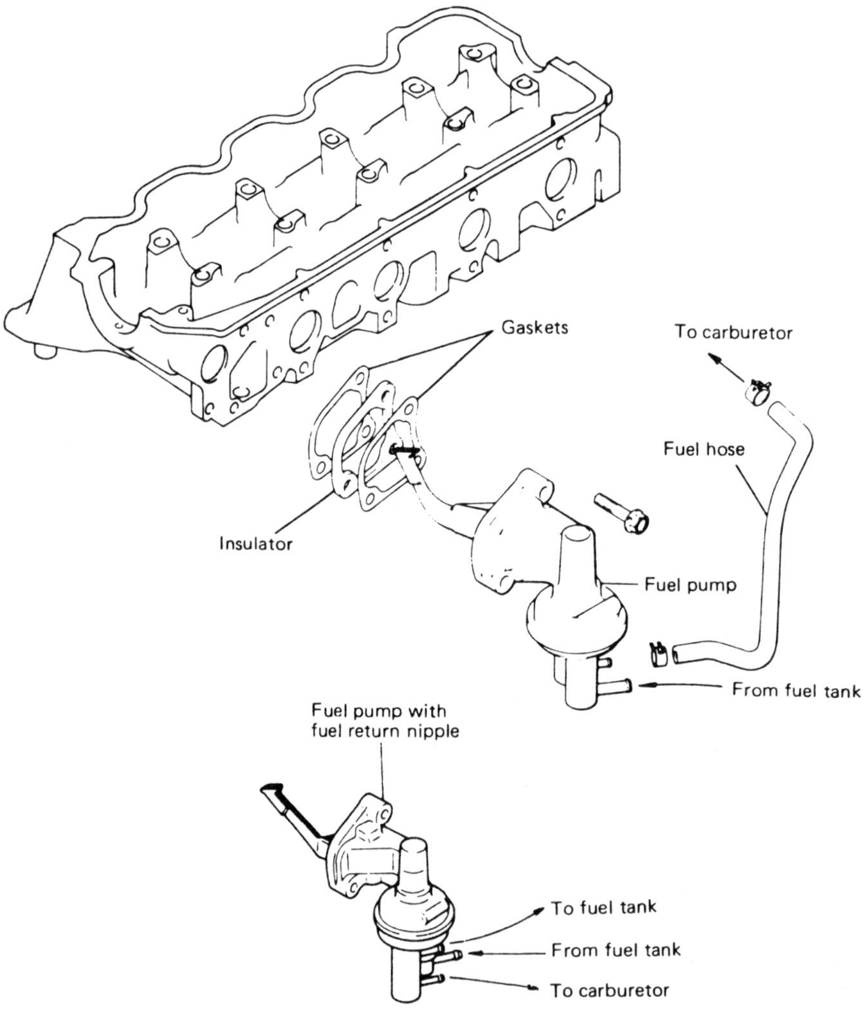

Fig. 4.10 1600 cc engine fuel pump – exploded view (Sec 10)

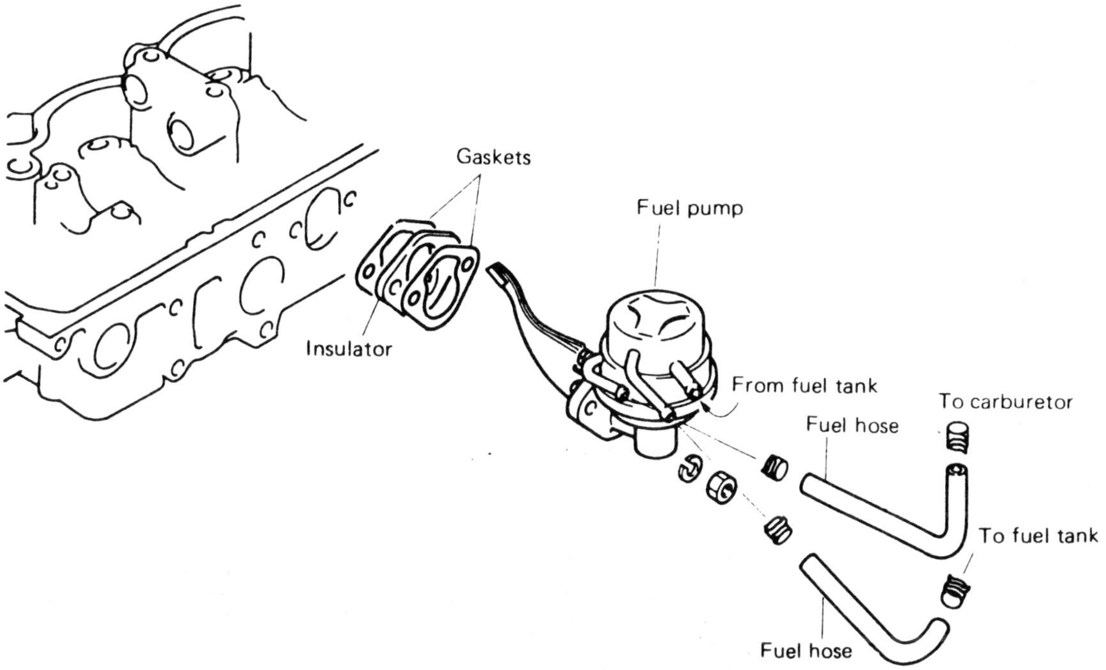

Fig. 4.11 2000 cc and 2600 cc fuel pump – exploded view (Sec 10)

you can feel the compression pressure rising in the number one cylinder.

4 Continue rotating the crankshaft until the notch on the crankshaft pulley lines up with the T on the timing mark tab on the timing chain case. At this point, the lift of the fuel pump drive cam is reduced to a minimum, which will make the pump easier to remove.

5 Install the spark plugs and hook up the wires. Do not forget the coil high-tension lead.

6 Loosen the hose clamps and remove the fuel hoses from the pump fittings. Plug the ends of the hoses.

7 Remove the fuel pump mounting nuts and pull the pump off the engine. You may have to tap the pump body with a soft-faced hammer to break the gasket seal.

8 If the pump is difficult to remove, take off the valve cover (see Chapter 1, *Valve clearance adjustment*) and guide the pump rocker arm out of the head from the inside.

9 Remove the insulator block and scrape off all traces of the old gaskets and sealer.

10 Before installing the new pump, ensure that the rocker arm moves up and down without binding or sticking.

11 Coat both sides of the new gaskets with silicone-type gasket sealer before installation.

12 Slip the first gasket, the insulator block and the second gasket (in that order) onto the fuel pump mounting studs.

13 Install the fuel pump. It may be necessary to guide the rocker arm into place from inside the head. Work slowly; there is not much clearance between the rocker arm and the valve gear.

14 Once the fuel pump is properly seated, install the mounting nuts and tighten them evenly. Do not overtighten them or the insulator block may crack.

15 Install the valve cover if it was removed.

16 Install the hoses (after inspecting them for cracks) and the hose clamps.

17 Start the engine and check for fuel leaks at the hose fittings. Check for oil leaks where the fuel pump mounts on the cylinder head.

11 Fuel lines and hoses – check and replacement

1 To check or replace any fuel lines or hoses, refer to the fuel system checks in Chapter 1.

2 Also, you can refer to illustrations 4.8 and 4.9 for routing of lines and hoses.

12 Carburetor – servicing

1 A thorough road test and check of carburetor adjustments should be done before any major carburetor service. Specifications for some adjustments are listed on the vehicle emission control information label found in the engine compartment.

2 Some performance complaints directed at the carburetor are actually a result of loose, misadjusted or malfunctioning engine or electrical components. Others develop when vacuum hoses leak, are disconnected or are incorrectly routed. The proper approach to analyzing carburetor problems should include a routine check of the following areas:

3 Inspect all vacuum hoses and actuators for leaks and proper installation (see Chapter 6, *Emission control systems*).

4 Tighten the intake manifold nuts and carburetor mounting nuts evenly and securely.

5 Perform a cylinder compression test.

6 Clean or replace the spark plugs as necessary.

7 Test the resistance of the spark plug wires (refer to Chapter 1).

8 Inspect the ignition primary wires and check the vacuum advance operation. Replace any defective parts.

9 Check the ignition timing with the vacuum advance line disconnected and plugged.

10 Set the carburetor idle mixture as described in Section 16.

11 Check the fuel pump pressure as described in Section 9.

12 Inspect the heat control valve in the air cleaner for proper operation (refer to Chapter 6).

13 Remove the carburetor air filter element and blow out any dirt with compressed air. If the filter is extremely dirty, replace it with a new one.

14 Inspect the crankcase ventilation system (see Chapter 6).

15 Carburetor problems usually show up as flooding, hard starting, stalling, severe backfiring, poor acceleration and lack of response to idle mixture screw adjustments. A carburetor that is leaking fuel and/or covered with wet-looking deposits definitely needs attention.

16 Diagnosing carburetor problems may require that the engine be started and run with the air cleaner removed. While running the engine without the air cleaner it is possible that it could backfire. A backfiring situation is likely to occur if the carburetor is malfunctioning, but removal of the air cleaner alone can lean the air/fuel mixture enough to produce an engine backfire.

17 Once it is determined that the carburetor is indeed at fault, it

should be disassembled, cleaned and reassembled using new parts where necessary. Before dismantling the carburetor, make sure you have a carburetor rebuild kit, which will include all necessary gaskets and internal parts. You will also need some carburetor cleaning solvent and some means of blowing out all the internal passages of the carburetor. To do the job properly, you will also need a clean place to work and plenty of time and patience.

13 Carburetor – removal and installation

Removal

1 Remove the negative battery cable from the battery.
2 Remove the air cleaner assembly by referring to Section 3.
3 Remove the throttle cable clamps from the carburetor and the valve cover, then disconnect the cable from the throttle shaft.
4 Remove the float bowl vent tube from the carburetor.
5 Remove the coolant hose from the rear of the carburetor.
6 Disconnect the electrical lead at the left side of the carburetor.
7 Note the color-code on the various vacuum hoses connected to the carburetor and to avoid confusion later, draw a simple diagram showing how they are connected.
8 Remove the vacuum hoses from the carburetor body, the ASV and the throttle opener (air conditioner-equipped vehicles only).
9 Remove the 3 fuel hoses from the carburetor and plug them.
10 Remove the 5 nuts and lock washers attaching the carburetor to the intake manifold. Removal of the idle speed adjusting screws (SAS) from the carburetor body will make access to the left rear mounting nut less restricted.
11 Carefully lift the carburetor off the intake manifold. You may have to tap gently on the carburetor body with a soft-faced hammer to break the gasket seal. Do not pry between the carburetor and intake manifold, as damage to the gasket sealing surfaces may result. Remove the insulator block and all traces of gasket material or gasket sealer from the manifold.
12 Cover or plug the intake ports with clean rags to keep out dirt and foreign objects. Also, plug the coolant passage in the intake manifold so coolant does not get into the intake ports.

Installation

13 Inspect the mating surfaces of the carburetor and intake manifold. They must be clean and free of nicks, burrs and other damage.
14 Hold the new carburetor base gasket in place on the carburetor to make sure that all the holes match up. It is possible to install the gasket upside down or backward so make sure it is properly oriented before laying it in place on the intake manifold.
15 Lay the new gasket in place then carefully set the carburetor on top of it.
16 Install the five mounting nuts and tighten them evenly and securely. Work slowly and make sure that each nut is tightened the same amount or vacuum leaks may occur between the carburetor and manifold. Removal of the idle-speed adjusting screw will make access to the left rear mounting nut easier. Attach the vacuum hoses to the ASV, the throttle opener (if so equipped) and the carburetor body. Refer to the diagram that you drew during carburetor removal (or the vacuum hose routing diagram on the underside of the hood) to ensure proper installation of the vacuum hoses.
17 Unplug and slip the fuel hoses into place on the carburetor. Tighten the hose clamps securely; the hoses and fittings are color coded so installation is quite simple.
18 Plug in the electrical lead on the left side of the carburetor.
19 Slip the coolant hose onto the spigot at the rear of the carburetor and tighten the hose clamp securely.
20 Install the float bowl vent tube and slip the hose clamp into place.
21 Hook the end of the throttle cable to the throttle shaft and install the cable clamps on the carburetor and valve cover. Adjust the cable as described in Section 4. Make sure the throttle plate opens completely when the accelerator is depressed. The choke plate must also be free to close and open completely.
22 Connect the battery cable to the battery.
23 **Caution**: *The practice of priming an engine by pouring gasoline into the carburetor air horn should be strictly avoided.* Cranking the engine and depressing the accelerator pedal several times should provide enough fuel for the engine to start.
24 Start the engine and adjust the idle-speed and mixture as described in Section 14.

14 Carburetor (1978 thru 1980) – overhaul

Disassembly

1 Remove the air cleaner hold-down stud (photo) and the air cleaner gasket from the top of the carburetor. Pull back the hose clamp and remove the coolant hose from the back of the carburetor (photo).
2 Remove the spring clip and carefully pry the throttle opener actuating rod out of the primary shaft lever (air conditioner-equipped model only) (photo). Remove the throttle opener from the carburetor body.
3 Disconnect the fuel cut-off solenoid ground wires from the carburetor body. Remove the solenoid retaining screw and lift the solenoid away from the carburetor (photos). Do not lose the O-ring on the solenoid body.
4 Unscrew and remove the idle mixture screw, the spring, the washer and rubber seal (photos).
5 Disconnect the linkage at the sub-EGR valve by prying off the spring clip and removing the pin. Slide the linkage out of position and remove the spring and ball from the end of the sub-EGR plunger. Using a screwdriver, unsnap the accelerator pump linkage from the throttle shaft arm and remove the accelerator pump from the carburetor body. It is held in place with four screws (photos).
6 Remove the four screws holding the ASV housing in place and lift off the housing. Remove the spring, the spring cap, the spring guide and the diaphragm. Lay the parts out on a clean surface in the order of disassembly (photos).
7 Remove the screw attaching the ASV body to the carburetor and carefully lift off the ASV body (photo).

14.1a Remove the air cleaner hold-down stud

14.1b Slide back the hose clamps and remove the coolant hose

14.2 Remove the spring clip, then pry the throttle opener rod out of the throttle lever (air conditioner-equipped vehicles only)

14.3a Remove the fuel cut-off solenoid ground wire

14.3b Remove the solenoid retaining screw

14.3c Carefully lift the solenoid away from the carburetor

14.4a Remove the idle mixture screw

14.4b Idle mixture screw, spring, washer and rubber seal

14.5a Pry the spring clip off the sub-EGR valve linkage pin

14.5b Unsnap the accelerator pump linkage from the throttle shaft arm

14.5c Remove the accelerator pump from the carburetor body

14.5d Accelerator pump components

14.6a Remove the ASV housing screws

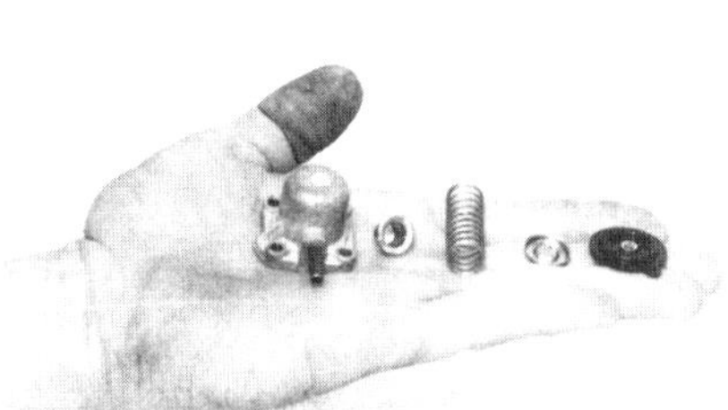

14.6b ASV components

14.7 Remove the ASV body attaching screws

8 Remove the vent system ground wire and the screws holding the solenoid to the carburetor body (photos). Carefully lift the solenoid and the spring inside it away from the carburetor (photo).
9 Remove the remaining screw holding the vent system body to the carburetor (photo) and lift it off. Do not forget to remove the rubber gasket from the carburetor body.
10 To disassemble the vent valve, remove the spring clip, the washer, and the valve seal from the end of the plunger. Slip the O-ring off the body. The diaphragm and plunger (one piece) can now be withdrawn from the valve body. Lay the parts out on a clean surface in the order of disassembly (photo).
11 Remove the enrichment system diaphragm housing. It is held in place by three screws. Remove the gasket, separate the two halves of the housing, and lift out the spring and the diaphragm (photo).
12 Remove the CAV housing. It is held in place by three screws (photo). Lift out the spring guide, the springs, the spring cap and the diaphragm. Lay the parts out on a clean surface in the order of disassembly (photo). Remove the three screws holding the choke unloader diaphragm plate to the carburetor body (photo). Lift off the plate and remove the spring (photo).
13 Carefully pry the secondary diaphragm link out of the secondary throttle lever (photo) and pull the hose off the carburetor body (photo). Remove the two mounting screws and lift off the diaphragm assembly (photo).
14 Disconnect the throttle return spring from the primary throttle lever (photo). The upper choke pinion gear assembly mount has a series of lines scribed on it. Note which one is lined up with the dot on the body (photo).
15 Remove the screws holding the choke pinion gear assembly to the carburetor body and carefully pull it free (photo).
16 Separate the choke plate from the choke shaft. It is held in place with two small screws (photo).
17 Remove the spring clip and carefully pry the manual choke unloader linkage out of the choke lever (photo).

14.8a Remove the vent system ground wire

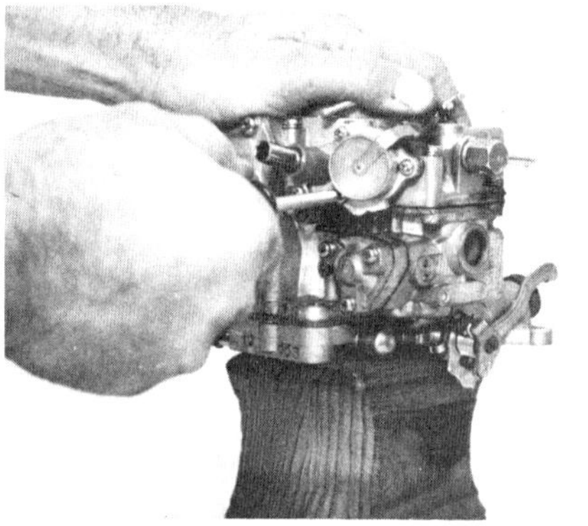
14.8b Remove the screws attaching the solenoid to the carburetor body

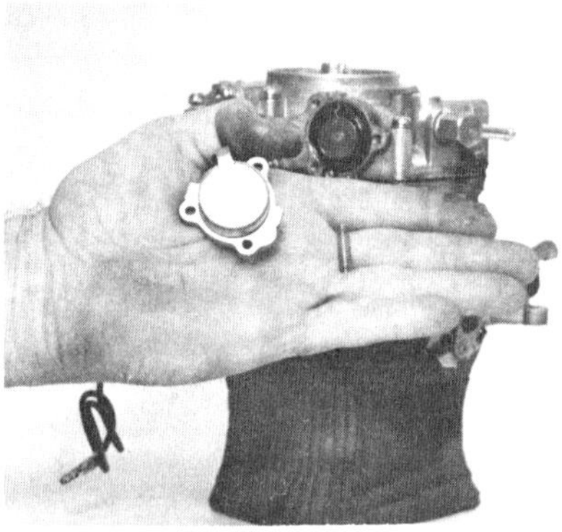
14.8c The solenoid and spring

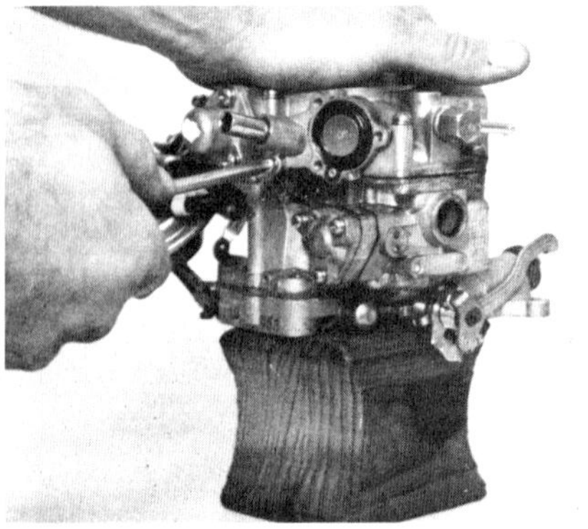
14.9 Remove the screw holding the vent system body to the carburetor

14.10 Vent system components

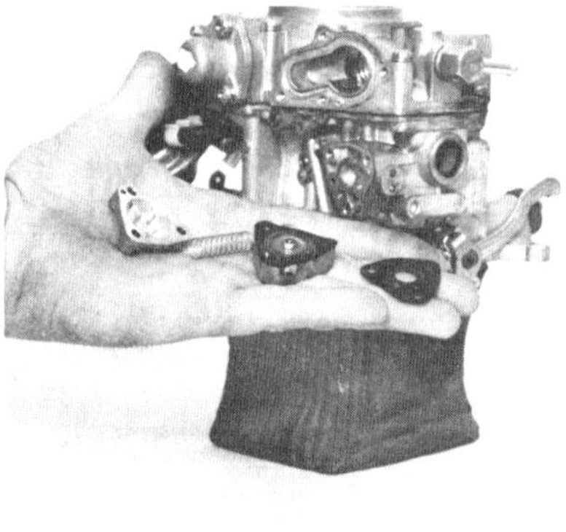
14.11 Enrichment system components

14.12a Remove the CAV housing screws

14.12b CAV components

14.12c Remove the choke unloader diaphragm plate screws

14.12d Choke unloader diaphragm plate and spring

14.13a Pry the secondary diaphragm link out of the secondary throttle lever

14.13b Pull the hose off the carburetor body

14.13c Remove the secondary diaphragm mounting screws

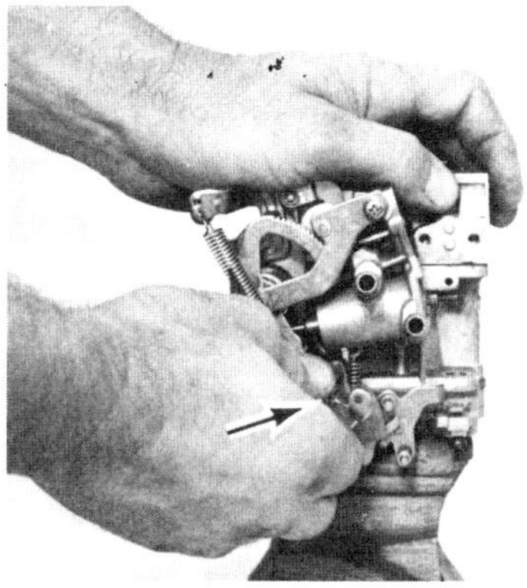

14.14a Disconnect the throttle return spring (arrow) from the primary throttle lever

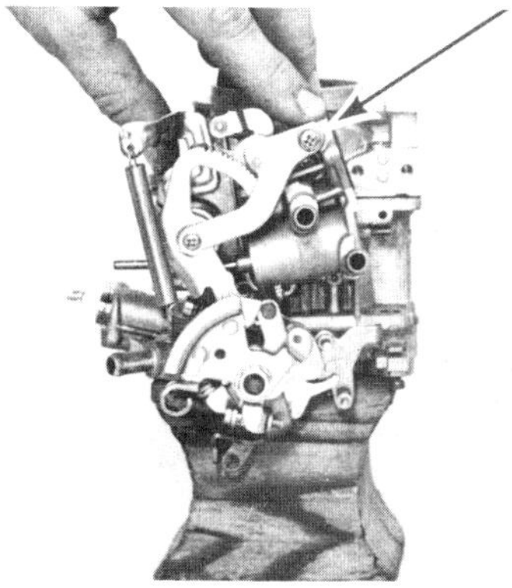

14.14b Note the reference lines on the upper choke pinion gear assembly mount (arrow)

14.15 Remove the screws holding the choke pinion gear assembly to the carburetor

14.16 Remove the screws attaching the choke plate to the choke shaft

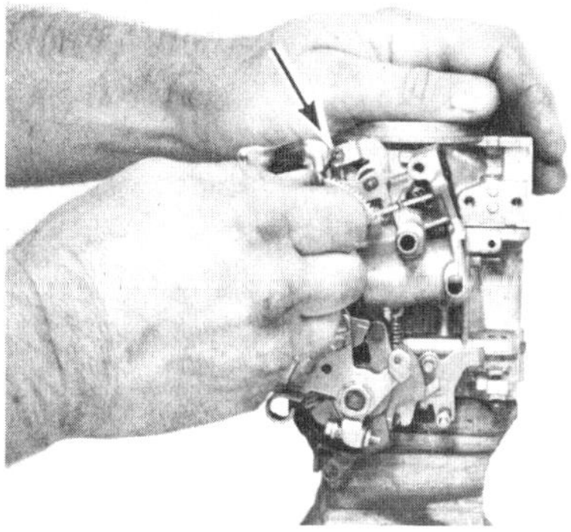

14.17 Remove the spring clip (arrow) from the manual choke unloader linkage rod

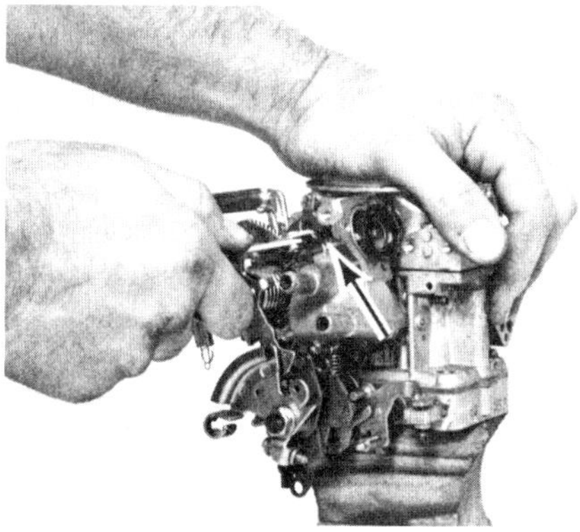

14.18 Pull out the pin (arrow) while holding the choke unloader diaphragm in alignment

14.19 Remove the throttle return spring mount

14.20a Pull out the choke unloader diaphragm and linkage

14.20b Withdraw the choke shaft

14.21a Unhook the secondary return spring

14.21b Remove the two choke mechanism housing screws

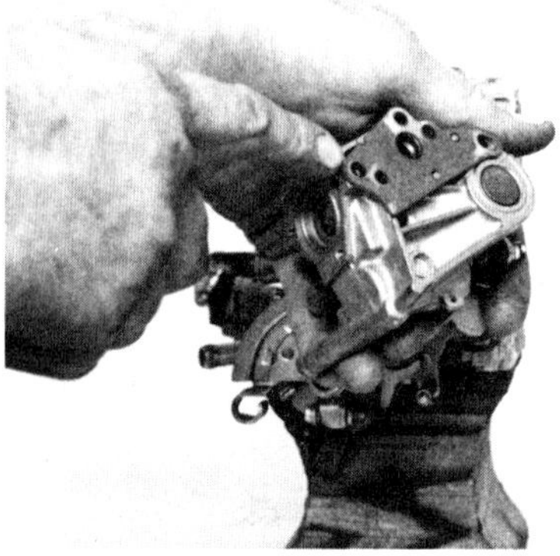

14.21c Separate the spacer and the O-ring from the housing

14.22a Remove the top cover screws

14.22b Lift off the cover without bending the float arm

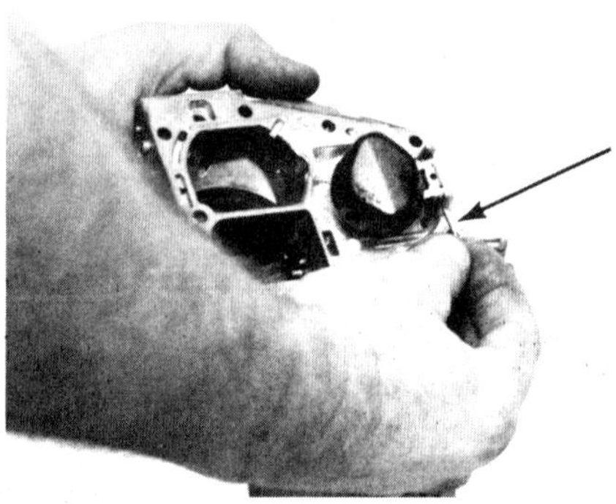

14.24a Slide out the pivot pin (arrow)

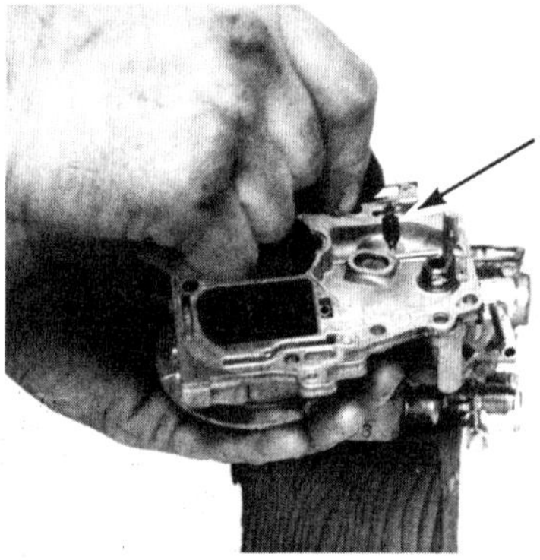

14.24b Separate the float and needle (arrow) from the top cover

14.24c Remove the inlet needle seat

18 Using small pliers, pull out the pin holding the choke unloader diaphragm in alignment (photo).

19 Remove the throttle return spring mount. It is held in place with one bolt (photo).

20 Pull out the choke unloader diaphragm and linkage (photo), then withdraw the choke shaft from the carburetor body (photo).

21 Unhook the secondary return spring from the choke mechanism housing (photo). Remove the two screws (photo) and lift the choke mechanism housing away from the carburetor body. Separate the spacer and small O-ring from the housing (photo).

22 Remove the four remaining screws (photo) and lift the top cover off the carburetor. Be careful not to bend or otherwise damage the float mechanism (photo).

23 Before removing the float, invert the top cover and measure the distance from the float seam to the gasket surface of the top cover (see Fig. 4.12). Record the measurement for future reference.

24 Carefully slide out the pivot pin and separate the float and inlet needle from the top cover (photo). Slip the needle out of its mount on the float. Unscrew and remove the inlet needle seat and washer (photo).

25 Remove the top cover gasket from the carburetor body.

26 Hold your finger over the accelerator pump discharge plunger bore (photo). Tip the carburetor upside down and let the steel ball from the anti-overflow mechanism in the bottom of the float bowl fall out. Next, remove the accelerator pump steel check ball and weight. Draw a simple diagram showing the sizes (stamped on the jets) of the primary and secondary main jets and the primary and secondary jets, then unscrew and remove them from the carburetor body (photos).

27 Remove the two attaching screws (photo) and separate the throttle body from the carburetor body (photo). **Note:** *Do not remove any plugs or fittings from the carburetor body that have been sealed with white paint.*

28 Slip off the rubber boot and slide the sub-EGR valve plunger out of the throttle body (photo).

14.26a Accelerator pump discharge plunger bore

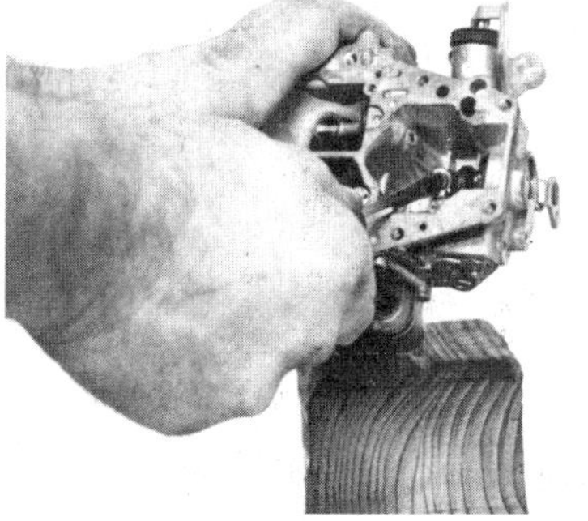
14.26b Remove the primary main jet

14.26c Remove the secondary main jet (arrow)

14.26d Remove the idle jets

14.27a Remove the two screws attaching the throttle body to the carburetor body

14.27b Separate the throttle body from the carburetor body. Do not disassemble the throttle shafts or linkages

14.28 Slide the sub-EGR plunger out of the throttle body

Inspection

29 Once the carburetor has been completely disassembled, the parts should be thoroughly cleaned and inspected. There are many commercial carburetor cleaning solvents available which can be used with good results.

30 The diaphragms and some plastic parts of the carburetor can be damaged by solvents; avoid placing these parts in any liquid. Clean the external surfaces of these parts with a clean cloth or soft brush. Shake or wipe dirt and other foreign material from the stem plunger side of the diaphragm. Compressed air can be used to remove loose dirt, but should not be connected to the vacuum diaphragm fitting.

31 If the commercial solvent or cleaner recommends the use of water as a rinse, hot water will produce the best results. After rinsing, all traces of water must be blown from the passages using compressed air. Never clean jets with a wire, drill bit or other objects. The orifices may be enlarged, making the mixture too rich for proper performance.

32 When checking parts removed from the carburetor, it is often difficult to be sure they are serviceable. It is therefore recommended that new parts be installed, if available, when the carburetor is disassembled. The required parts should be included in the carburetor rebuild kit.

33 After all the parts have been cleaned and dried, check the throttle valve shaft and choke shaft for proper operation. If sticking or binding occurs, clean the shafts with solvent and lubricate them with engine oil.

34 Check the jets for damage or clogging. Replace them if damage is evident.

35 Inspect the idle mixture adjusting screw. The tapered portion of the screw must be straight and smooth. If the tapered portion is grooved or ridged replace the screw with a new one.

36 Check the strainer screen for clogging and damage.

37 Check the vacuum chamber. Push the vacuum chamber rod in, seal off the nipple and release the rod. If the rod does not return, the

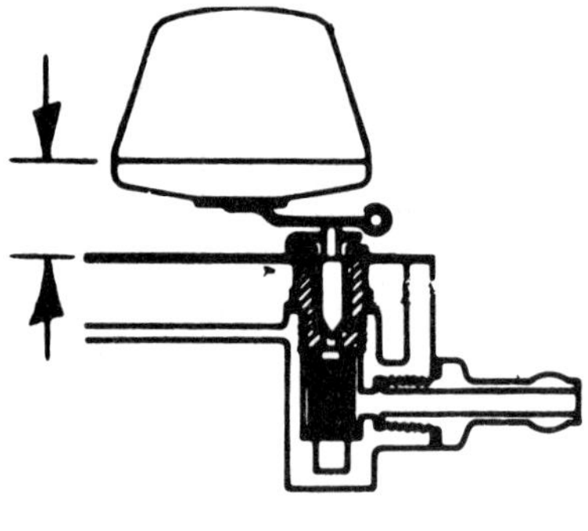

Fig. 4.12 Float seam-to-gasket surface measurement (Sec 14)

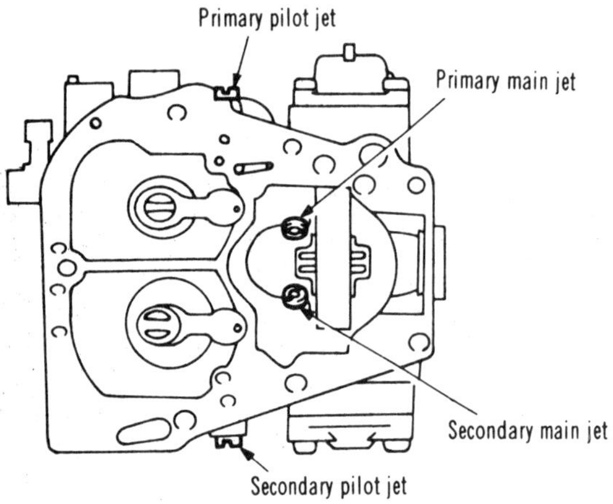

Fig. 4.13 Jet locations (Sec 14)

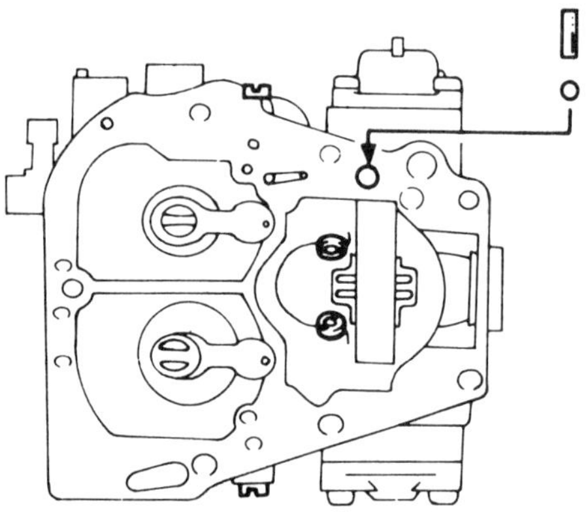

Fig. 4.14 Accelerator steel ball and weight location (Sec 14)

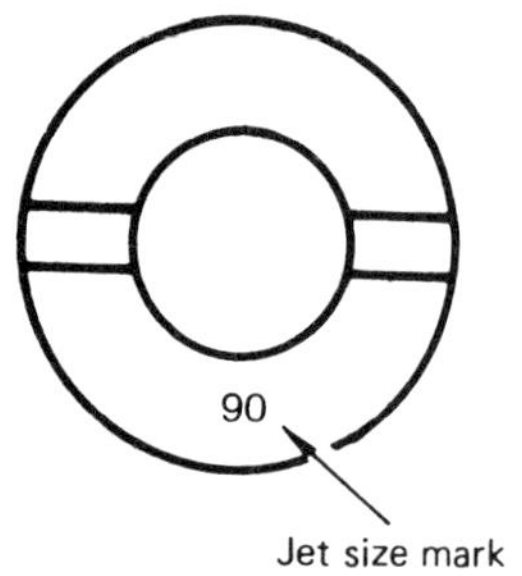

Fig. 4.15 Jet size indicator (Sec 14)

vacuum chamber is most likely in good condition. If the rod returns when released, the diaphragm is defective. The vacuum chamber should be replaced with a new one if this condition exists.

38 To check the fuel cut-off solenoid, connect a jumper lead to the positive (+) terminal of a 12 volt battery and the wire lead of the solenoid. Connect a second jumper lead to the negative (–) terminal of the battery and the solenoid ground wire. The needle should move in toward the solenoid when the battery is connected and out when the battery is disconnected. If it does, the fuel cut-off solenoid is good.

Reassembly

Note: *The reassembly process will be easier if the sequenced photos in the disassembly section are followed in reverse.*

39 Using a new gasket, assemble the throttle body to the carburetor body and tighten the mounting screws securely.

40 Install the main and pilot jets in the carburetor body. The primary main jet, the secondary main jet, the primary pilot jet and the secondary pilot jet are each stamped with a different number that denotes their size.

41 Place the anti-overflow ball in place in the bottom of the float bowl and insert the accelerator pump steel check ball and weight into the accelerator pump bore.

42 Install the new inlet needle seat in place in the carburetor top cover using a new washer. Assemble the new inlet needle to the float and attach the float to the top cover.

43 Invert the top cover and measure the distance from the float seam to the gasket surface of the top cover. If the measured distance is more or less than it was during reassembly, remove the float from the top cover, unscrew the inlet needle seat and add or remove washers (as necessary) to change the float height. Reassemble the inlet needle and float and recheck the measurement. Repeat the procedure as required until the distance is the same as it was during disassembly.

44 Gently lay the top cover in place using a new gasket and install the mounting screws. Tighten them evenly and securely.

45 Install the choke mechanism housing and tighten the screws securely. Make sure the manual choke unloader rod is facing in the proper direction.

46 Slide the choke shaft into place and install the choke plate. It is a very good idea to use a thread locking compound on the choke plate attaching screws.

47 Insert the manual choke unloader rod into the choke lever.

48 Install the choke unloader/diaphragm and push the pin into place.

49 Install the throttle return spring mount and tighten the screw securely.

50 Engage the spring loop on the choke pinion gear assembly, hold the choke plate closed and engage the plastic teeth of the choke pinion gear with the gear teeth on the choke set lever. Install the screws, move the pinion gear assembly to line up the marks exactly as they were before disassembly, then tighten the screws securely.

51 Install the secondary diaphragm assembly and hook up the hose. Slip the diaphragm link into the secondary throttle lever.

52 Install the choke unloader diaphragm plate and tighten the screws.

53 Install the CAV internal parts and housing then tighten the mounting screws evenly and securely.

54 Assemble the enrichment system components and install the housing in place on the carburetor body. The wire clamp fits over the upper left mounting screw. Tighten the mounting screws securely.

55 Assemble the vent valve. Lubricate the O-ring on the valve body and slide the valve into place in the carburetor body. Tighten the mounting screws securely.

56 Install the vent valve solenoid and tighten the mounting screws. Attach the ground wire to the carburetor body.

57 Install the ASV housing (with the wire clamp on the longest screw) and tighten the mounting screws finger tight. Assemble the ASV internal parts, install the housing and tighten the mounting screws.

58 Install the accelerator pump and hook the linkage to the throttle shaft arm.

59 Slip the small steel ball and spring into place in the end of the sub-EGR valve plunger. Install the rubber boot and push the plunger into place in the throttle body. Hold the linkage in place, install the pin and snap the spring clip into place on the end of the pin.

60 Make sure the O-ring is in place on the fuel cut-off solenoid body, then install the solenoid and tighten the mounting screws. Remove the short screw on the ASV body. Install the fuel cut-off solenoid ground wire and tighten both ASV body mounting screws securely.

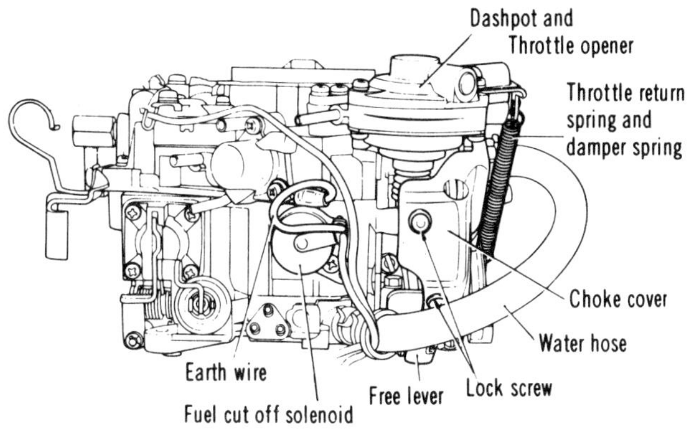

Fig. 4.16 1981-1983 carburetor – left side (Sec 15)

61 Insert the throttle opener actuating rod into the primary throttle shaft lever. Install the spring clip and mount the throttle opener on the carburetor (air conditioner-equipped models only).
62 Install the coolant hose and slide the hose clamps into place.
63 Double check all screws to make sure they are tight and the carburetor reassembly is complete.

15 Carburetor (1981 thru 1983) – overhaul

Disassembly

1 Pull the water hose off the nipple of the throttle body and off the nipple of the wax element portion.
2 Clean off the head of the choke cover lever lock screws by using a hand grinder or other instrument.
3 Disconnect the ground line of the fuel cut-off solenoid at the float chamber cover.
4 Remove the throttle return spring and the damper spring.
5 Pull off the vacuum hose connecting the depression chamber and the throttle body.
6 Remove the accelerator pump rod from the throttle lever.
7 Remove the dashpot rod (for a manual transmission) or throttle opener (for an automatic transmission) from the free lever.
8 Remove the depression chamber rod from the secondary throttle lever.
9 Remove the float chamber cover screws. **Note:** *Screws A connect the float chamber cover to the main body and screws B go through to the throttle body.*
10 Remove only the main body by lifting the float chamber cover. Do not turn the carburetor upside down during this operation. **Note:** *When lifting the chamber cover, the venturi retaining spring may drop down.*
11 Remove the E ring at the lower end of the choke unloaded rod and disconnect the rod from the lever.
12 No device should be removed without necessity. Especially, do not disassemble the auto-choke system.
13 The float can be removed by pulling off the pin.
14 The needle valve can be removed by removing the screw and the retainer.
15 Remove the accelerator pump and fuel cut-off solenoid. **Note:** *Do not remove any parts without necessity. Do not remove the throttle valves. Do not touch the adjusting screws (except for the SAS and dashpot adjusting screws).*

Reassembly

16 Reassembly is the reverse of disassembly. Pay attention to the following items.
17 Install the parts after cleaning them in a suitable cleaning solution. Check to be sure that there is no clogging in any of the air or fuel passages.
18 Check for smooth operation of the throttle and choke linkages. If

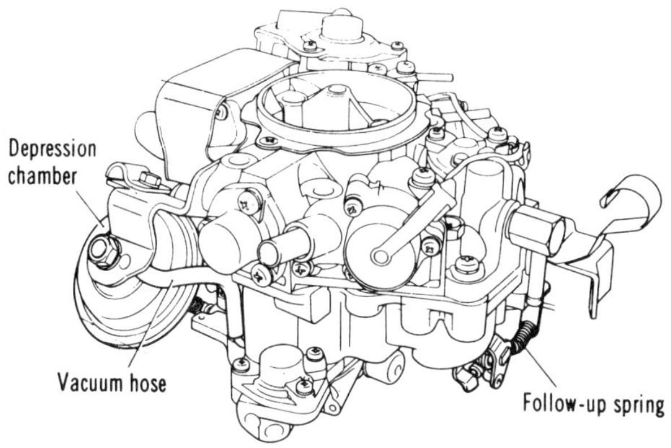

Fig. 4.17 1981-1983 carburetor – right side (Sec 15)

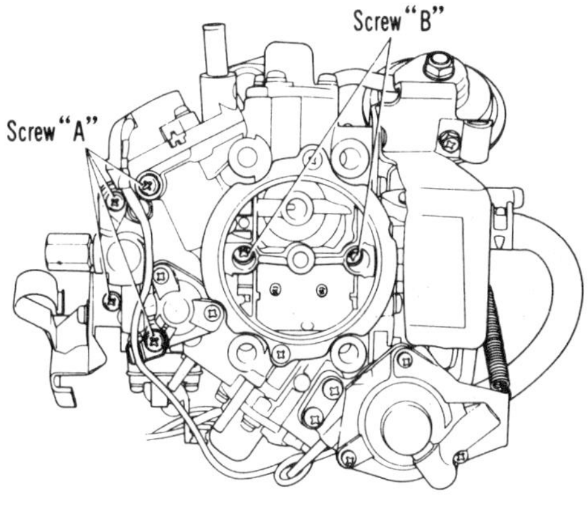

Fig. 4.18 1981-1983 carburetor – top (Sec 15)

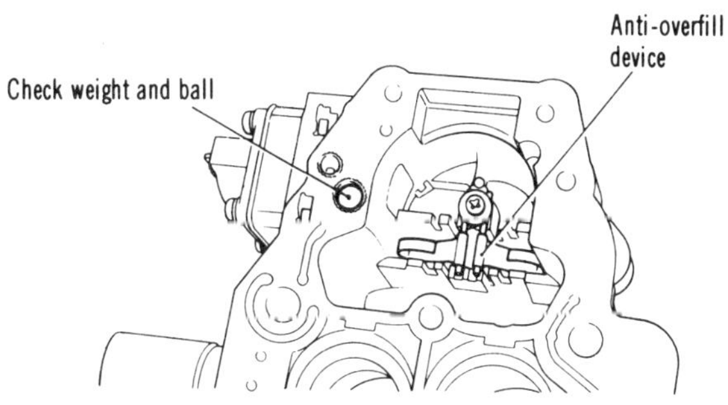

Fig. 4.19 Check weight and steel ball location (Sec 15)

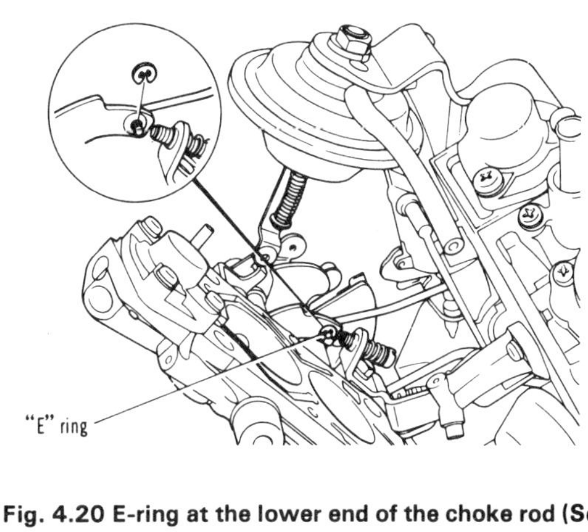

Fig. 4.20 E-ring at the lower end of the choke rod (Sec 15)

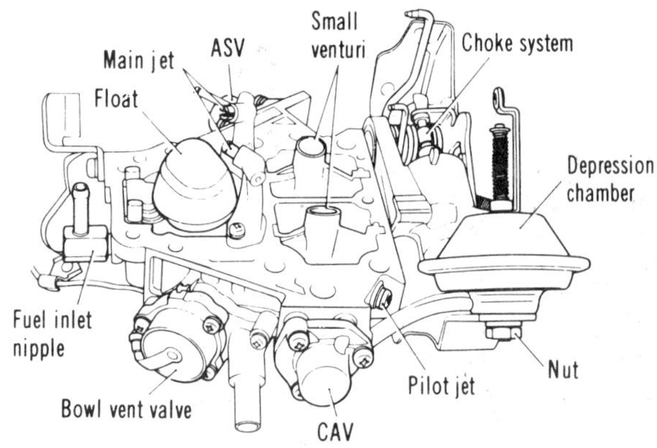

Fig. 4.21 Float chamber cover (Sec 15)

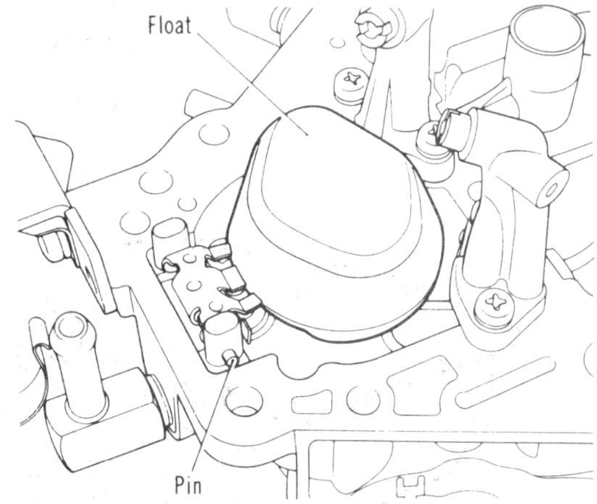

Fig. 4.22 Float pivot/retaining pin (Sec 15)

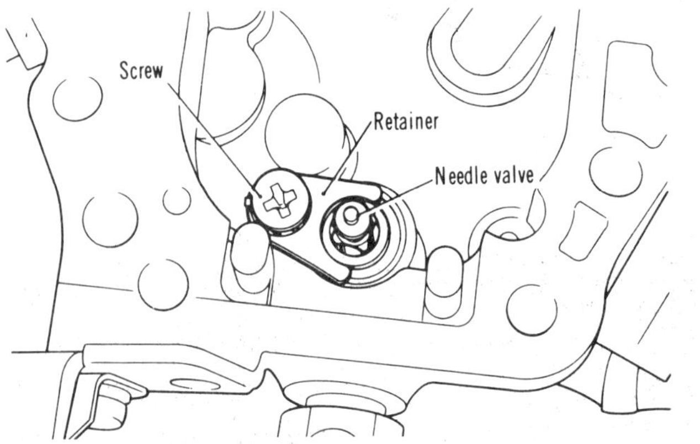

Fig. 4.23 Needle valve location (Sec 15)

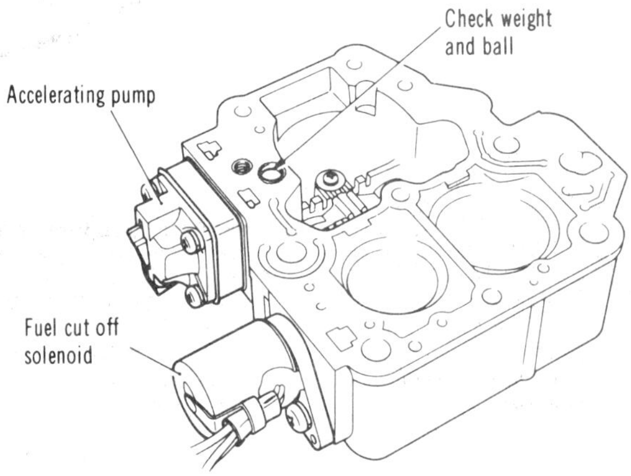

Fig. 4.24 Accelerator pump and fuel cut-off solenoid removal (Sec 15)

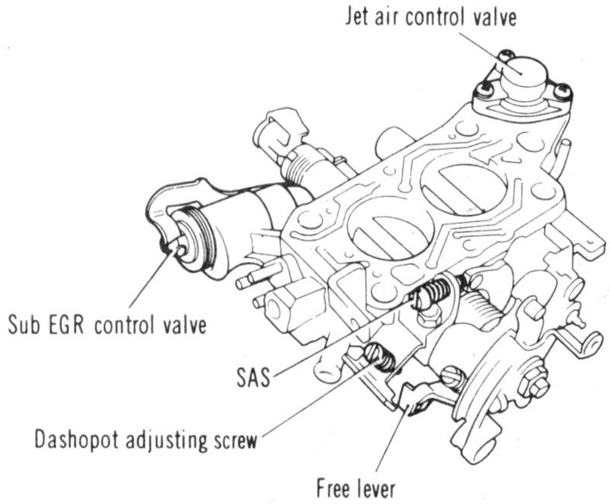

Fig. 4.25 Do not remove throttle valves or adjusting screws (Sec 15)

they catch or are sticky, apply a small amount of lubricant after cleaning and also after installation.

19 Be sure that the sub-EGR valve operates smoothly.

20 When replacing a main or pilot jet, the old jet and the new one must be the same size. A number is stamped onto each jet.

16 Idle speed and fuel/air mixture – adjustments

These carburetor adjustments can be found in the appropriate Section in Chapter 1.

17 Fuel tank – removal and installation

Caution: *Before doing any work around the fuel tank, be sure that the ignition switch is off and remove the key from the ignition lock. Gasoline and its vapor is highly explosive. Do not allow any spark or flame in or near the work area.*

1 Block the front wheels to keep the vehicle from rolling, then raise the rear of the vehicle and set it on jackstands.

2 Remove the tank filler cap so any pressure in the tank can escape.

3 Position a suitable container (large enough to hold the fuel that is in the tank) under the tank. Remove the drain plug and allow the fuel to drain into the container. After the fuel has drained completely, reinstall the drain plug.

4 Loosen the hose clamps on the main, return and vapor fuel hoses then pull the hoses off the tank.

5 Unplug the electrical wire from the fuel level sending unit.

6 Remove the filler neck mud shield from the inside of the left rear wheel well.

7 Loosen the hose clamps on the filler connecting hose (large) and the breather hose (small) where they attach to the tank. Pull the hoses off the tank. Be careful not to damage them in the process.

8 Support the fuel tank, preferably with a portable jack and block of wood. Remove the mounting bolts, lower the tank carefully and move it out from under the vehicle.

9 Check the tank interior for rust and corrosion. If the tank is not extremely corroded, it can be cleaned and reused. Special solvents made for cleaning fuel tanks are available. If you use one, be sure to follow the directions on the container. The inside of the tank is plated with zinc, so be sure to use a cleaner that will not harm it in any way.

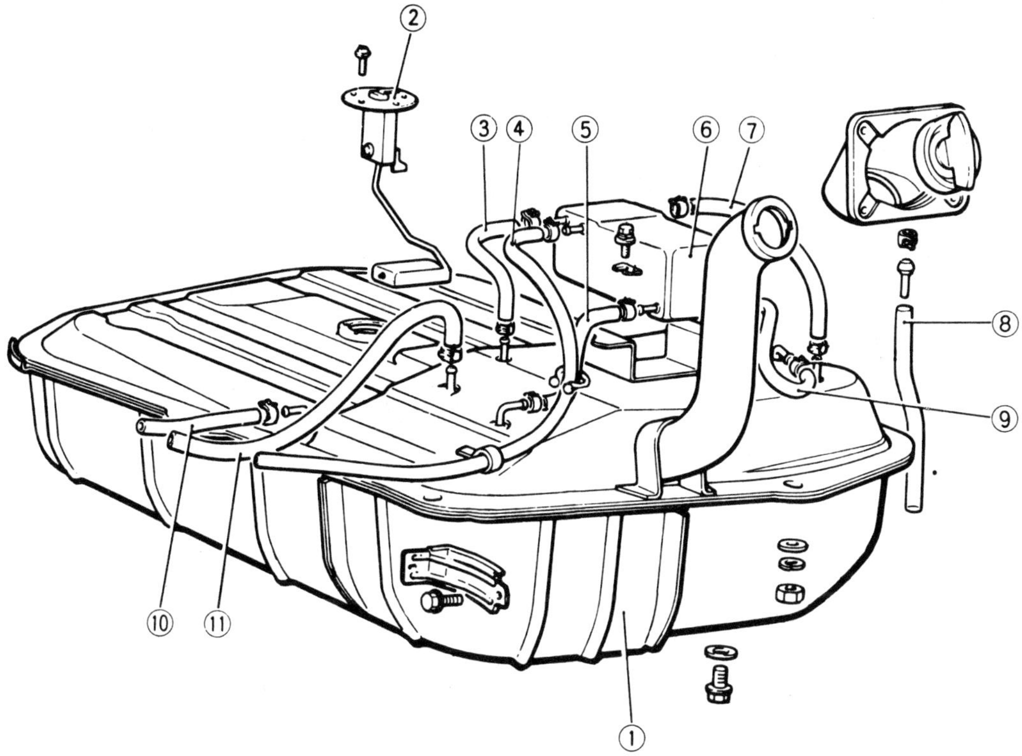

Fig. 4.26 1978-1980 fuel tank components – exploded view (Sec 17)

1 *Fuel tank*
2 *Fuel level sending unit*
3 *Separator tank-to-fuel pipe tube*
4 *Separator tank-to-vapor pipe tube*
5 *Separator tank-to-fuel tank tube*
6 *Separator tank*
7 *Separator tank-to-fuel tank tube*
8 *Drain tube*
9 *Separator tank-to-fuel tube*
10 *Fuel tank-to-fuel return pipe tube*
11 *Fuel tank-to-fuel main pipe tube*

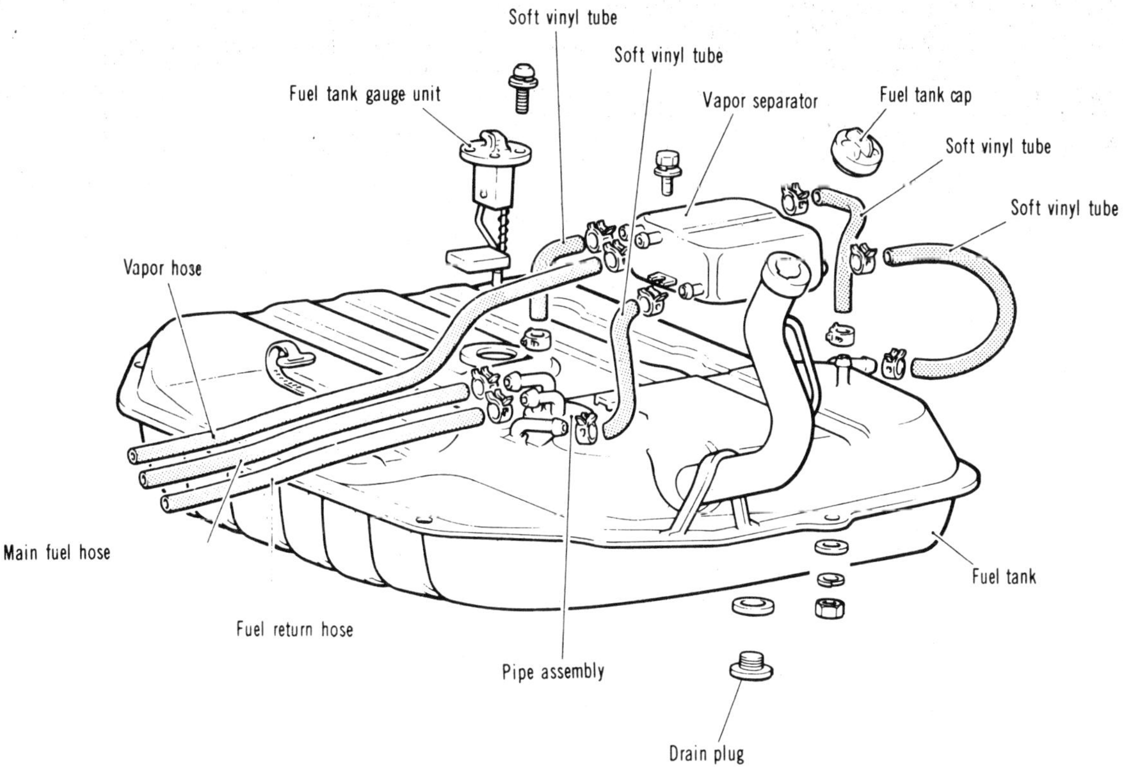

Fig. 4.27 1981-1983 fuel tank components – exploded view (Sec 17)

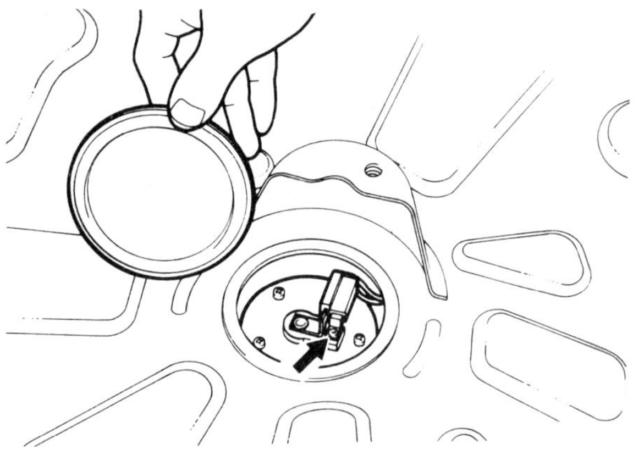

Fig. 4.28 Remove plug and disconnect fuel sending unit (Sec 17)

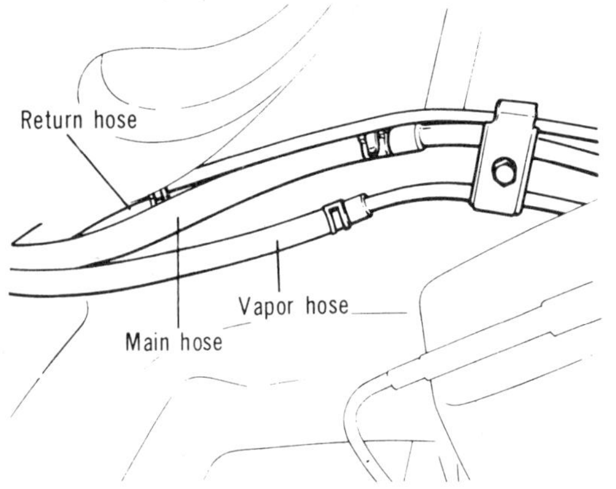

Fig. 4.29 Disconnect fuel hoses (Sec 17)

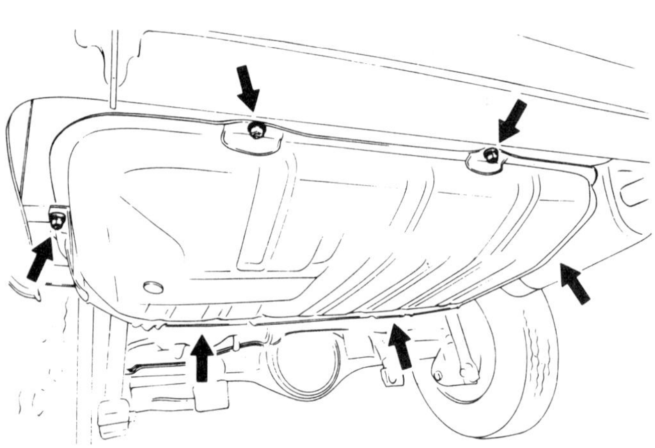

Fig. 4.30 Fuel tank mounting hardware (Sec 17)

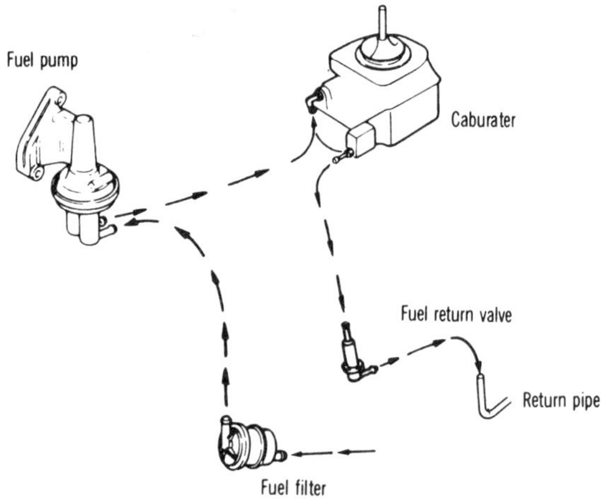

Fig. 4.31 Fuel return valve hose routing (Sec 18)

10 If the tank is severely corroded, replace it with a new one or a clean used one.
11 Look for evidence of leaks and cracks. If any are found, take the tank to a repair shop to have it fixed.
12 Inspect all fuel and breather hoses for cracks and deterioration. Check all hose clamps for damage and proper operation.
13 Installation of the tank is the reverse of removal. Be sure to double-check all hoses for proper routing. Also, if you have not already done so, be sure to tighten the drain plug securely.
14 Fill the tank with fuel and check for leaks. After the engine has been run, make a second check for leaks, particularly at the hose fittings that were removed.

18 Fuel return valve (1600 cc) – general note

1 The fuel return valve is installed in the return hose coming from the carburetor to the return pipe. The unit contains a valve and a spring which is operated by a bi-metal sensor.
2 The temperature of the fuel return from the carburetor is picked up by the bi-metal sensor, which controls the fuel return valve to restrict the fuel flow passing the valve thereby preventing vapor lock.
3 The fuel flow is fixed with the valve closed. The rise in the temperature of the fuel from 108°F to 127°F (42 to 53°C) triggers the valve to open, allowing the fuel to flow.

19 Vapor separator (2000 cc and 2600 cc) – general note

1 The vapor separator is the small canister mounted high on the left front fender well. It is mounted in the fuel system between the fuel pump and the carburetor and is designed to prevent vapor lock caused by high underhood temperatures.
2 The main fuel line from the fuel pump is connected to the middle fitting (color-coded green) on the separator. The hose connected at the top fitting (color-coded red) leads to the carburetor accelerator pump housing (which is also color-coded red). The hose connected to the bottom fitting (color-coded yellow) leads to the carburetor fuel inlet (also color-coded yellow).
3 The color-coded lines and fittings reduce the possibility of incorrect installation during carburetor servicing.
4 If the vapor separator is somehow damaged or begins to leak, it must be replaced with a new one. When installing a new vapor separator, position it so that the red fitting is at the top.

20 Fuel tank – cleaning and repair

Caution: *Never weld, solder or bring a flame close to an empty fuel tank. Repairs should be done by a professional due to the extremely hazardous conditions.*
1 With time, it is likely that sediment will collect in the bottom of the fuel tank. Condensation, resulting in rust and other impurities, will usually be found in the fuel tank of any car more than three or four years old.
2 When the tank is removed, it should be vigorously flushed out with hot water and detergent and, if facilities are available, steam cleaned.

21 Exhaust system – check

Refer to the appropriate Section in Chapter 1 for any exhaust system checks.

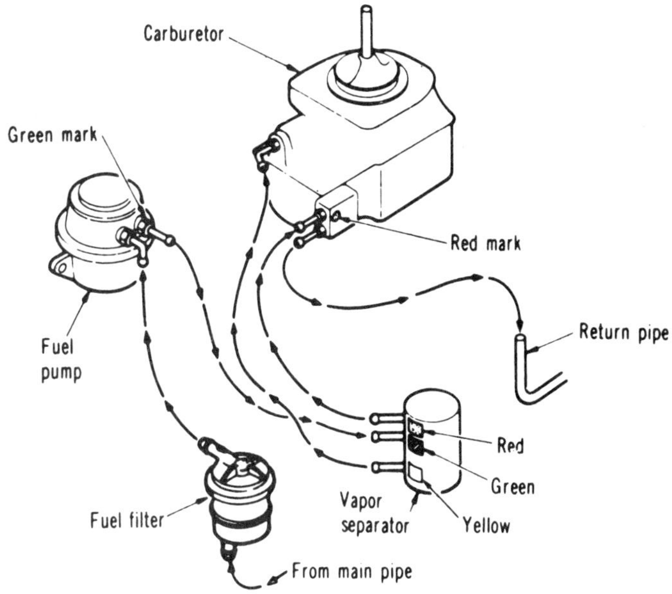

Fig. 4.32 Vapor separator hose routing (Sec 19)

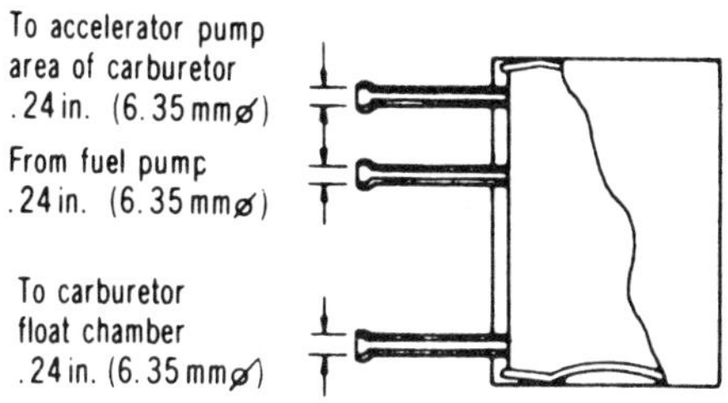

22 Main muffler assembly – removal and installation

1 Raise the vehicle and support it on jackstands.
2 Remove the bolts attaching the main muffler assembly to the front exhaust pipe.
3 Support the muffler and remove the hanger bracket bolts.
4 Lower the muffler and remove it from under the vehicle.
5 If the hanger brackets are cracked or otherwise deteriorated, replace them with new ones.
6 Lubricate all bolt threads with a small amount of oil.
7 To install the muffler, hold it in place and install the hanger bracket bolts. Do not tighten them completely.
8 Install the exhaust pipe-to-main muffler assembly attaching bolts and tighten them evenly, in steps, to the specified torque.
9 Check the clearance between the main muffler assembly and the other parts of the vehicle. If the clearance is adequate, tighten the hanger bracket bolts.
10 Lower the vehicle to the ground, start the engine and check for exhaust gas leaks where the front exhaust pipe attaches to the main muffler assembly.
11 Test drive the vehicle. If the clearances between the exhaust system components and the other parts of the vehicle are inadequate, noise and vibration may occur during vehicle operation.

23 Front and center exhaust pipes – removal and installation

Front pipe

1 Raise the vehicle and support it on jackstands.
2 Remove the bolt attaching the front exhaust pipe to the center pipe.

Fig. 4.33 1978-1980 exhaust components – exploded view (Sec 23)

1 Front pipe
2 Protector
3 Center pipe (US)
4 Center pipe (Canada)
5 Heat insulator
6 O-ring
7 Main muffler assembly

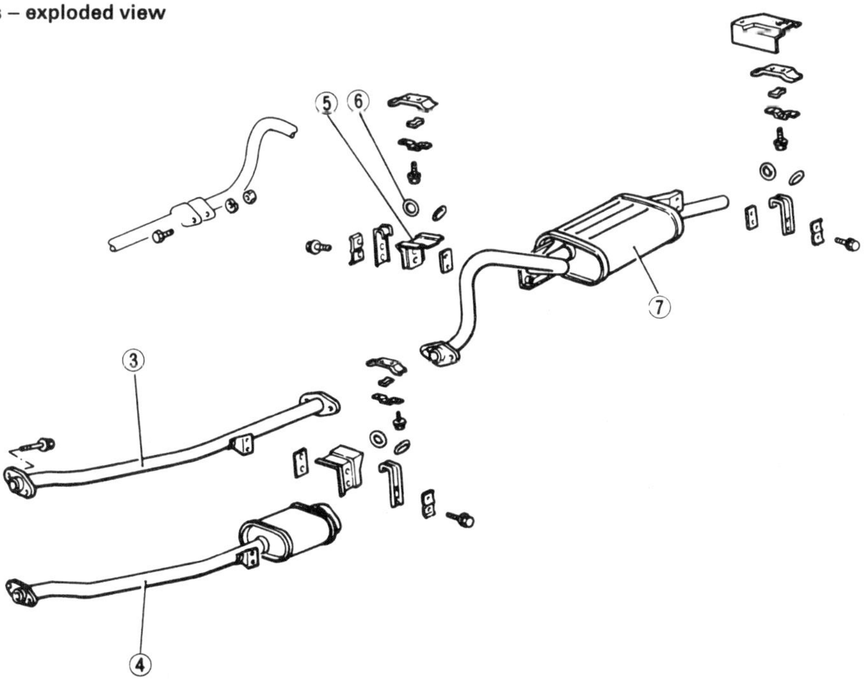

4

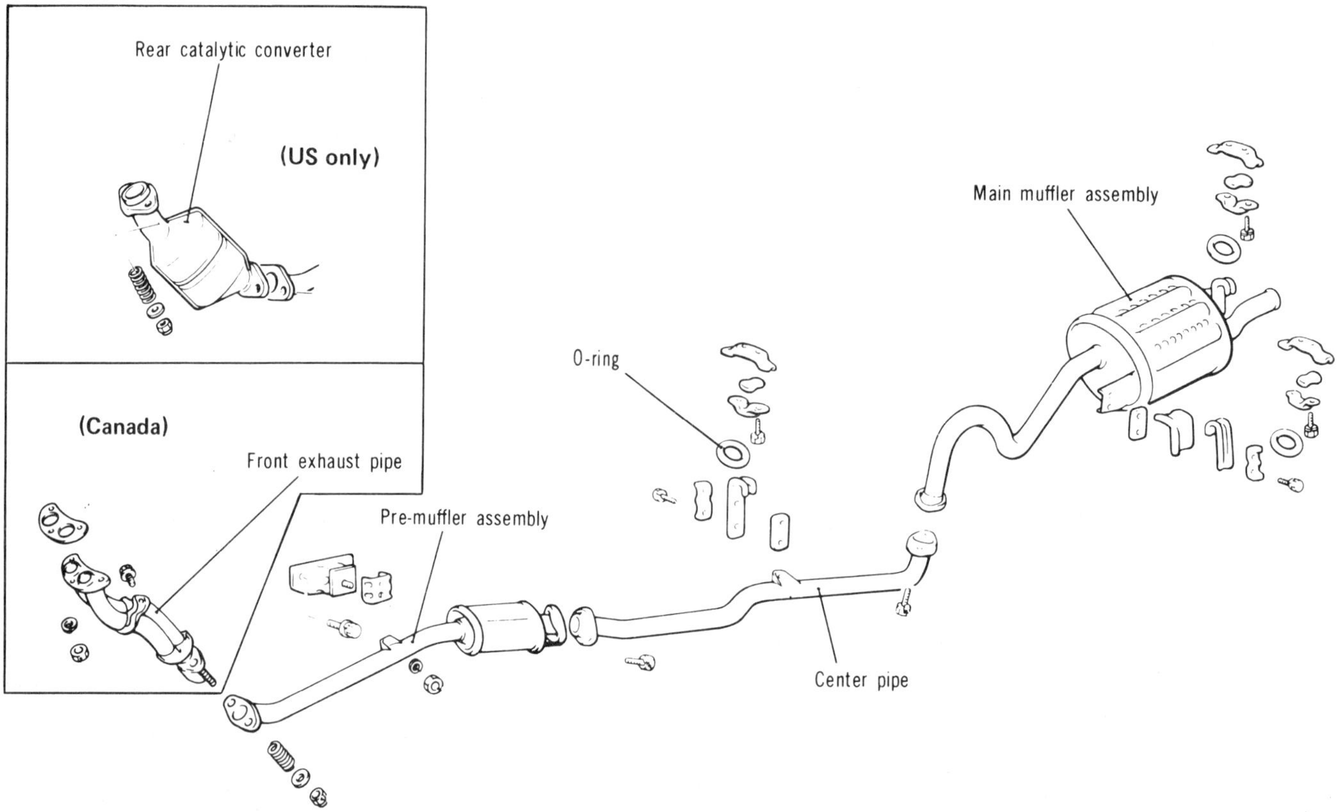

Fig. 4.34 1981-1983 exhaust components – exploded view (Sec 23)

3 Remove the nuts attaching the front exhaust pipe to the exhaust manifold. It may be necessary to spray the threads extending beyond the nut with a penetrating oil to make removal of the nuts easier. If a penetrating oil is used, let the threads 'soak' for a few minutes before attempting to remove the nuts.

4 Remove the front exhaust pipe-to-bellhousing clamp bolt.

5 Support the pipe, then remove the rear hanger bracket bolt. The pipe can now be pulled free from the center pipe and exhaust manifold and removed from under the vehicle.

6 If the exhaust pipe hanger is cracked or otherwise deteriorated, replace it with a new one.

7 Lubricate all bolt and stud threads with a small amount of oil.

8 Position the front exhaust pipe under the vehicle. Slip the front end into place on the exhaust manifold and the rear end into place on the center pipe. The main muffler assembly can be pushed slightly to the rear to provide clearance for installation of the front exhaust pipe. Install the rear hanger bracket bolt and the exhaust pipe-to-bellhousing clamp bolt. Do not tighten them completely.

9 Install the pipe-to-exhaust manifold nuts and the pipe-to-center pipe bolts. Tighten them evenly, in steps, to the specified torque.

10 Check the clearance between the pipe and the other parts of the vehicle. If the clearance is adequate, tighten the exhaust pipe-to-bell-housing clamp bolt and the hanger bracket bolt securely.

11 Start the engine and check for exhaust gas leaks where the front exhaust pipe attaches to the exhaust manifold and the center pipe.

12 Test drive the vehicle. If the clearance between the exhaust system components and the other parts of the vehicle are inadequate, noise and vibration may occur during operation.

Center pipe

13 The center pipe removal and installation is very similar to the front pipe, except where the ends connect together.

14 Refer to the illustrations given for your vehicle.

24 Exhaust manifold – removal and installation

1 Refer to Chapter 2 for this procedure.

Chapter 5 Engine electrical systems

Contents

Specifications

Note: *Additional specifications for the engine electrical system can be found in Chapter 1*

5

Battery

Voltage	12V
Electrolyte specific gravity @ 68°F (20°C)	
Fully charged	1260
Half charged	1220
Discharged	1100
Maximum charging temperature	113°F (45°C)
Freezing point	
Fully charged	- 76°F (- 60°C)
Discharged	18°F (- 8°C)

Ignition system

Distributor firing order	1-3-4-2	
Centrifugal advance (crankshaft degrees @ rpm)	**1600 cc**	**2000 & 2600 cc**
Initial	0/1000	0/1200
Final	20/4400	20/6000
Vacuum advance @ in Hg (kPa)		
Initial	0/3.15 (10.7)	0/3.15 (10.7)
Final	23/11.02 (37.3)	10/12.20 (41.3)
Contact point gap	0.018 to 0.021 in (0.45 to 0.55 mm)	
Dwell angle	52° ± 3°	
Condenser	0.22 uF	
Ignition coil resistance (ohms)	**US**	**Canada**
Primary	1.05	1.4
Secondary	17 000	10 200
Spark plug gap		
US	0.039 to 0.043 in (1.0 to 1.1 mm)	
Canada	0.028 to 0.031 in (0.7 to 0.8 mm)	

Pick up coil resistance	820 to 1,120 ohms

Starting system

	1600 cc M/T	1600 & 2000 cc A/T M/T	2000 & 2600 cc A/T M/T
Starter motor output	0.7 kW -12V	0.9 kW -12V	1.2 kW -12V
Terminal voltage	10.5V	11V	11V
Brush length (minimum)	0.453 in (11.5 mm)		
Brush spring-load	3.3 ft-lb (1.5 kg/m)		
Pinion gap	0.020 to 0.079 in (0.5 to 2.0 mm)		
Current (no load)	Less than 50A		

Charging system

Alternator output	50A – 12V
Current rating (@ 2500 rpm -14V)	More than 42A
Exposed brush length (limit)	0.22 in (5.5 mm)
Regulator voltage @ 68°F (20°C)	14.5V to 15.3 V

Torque specifications

	ft lb	Nm
Starter motor mounting bolt	16 to 23	22 to 31
Alternator support bolt	15 to 18	21 to 24
Alternator brace bolt	9 to 10	12 to 13
Spark plug	18 to 23	25 to 28

1 General information

The ignition system is designed to ignite the fuel/air charge entering the cylinder at just the right moment. It does so by producing a high-voltage electrical spark between the electrodes of the spark plug. The timing of the spark (when it occurs in the engine cycle) is automatically varied to meet the requirements of engine load and speed.

The system consists of a switch, the ignition coil, the distributor, an electronic control unit, spark plugs and wires and the battery.

The distributor used in 1978 thru 1980 vehicles incorporates contact breaker points, while the vehicles made in 1981 thru 1983 have an electronic ignition system which is very trouble and maintenance-free.

The starting system consists of a switch, solenoid, starter motor, battery cables and wiring and the battery. Two different types of starter motors are in use on this vehicle. Models with manual transmissions are equipped with a 0.9 kW motor, while those with automatic transmissions are equipped with a 1.2 kW motor. They can be identified by a model number which is stamped on the nameplate attached to the front bracket.

2 Battery electrolyte – checking

Refer to the appropriate Section in Chapter 1 to check the battery electrolyte.

3 Battery – maintenance

Refer to the appropriate Section in Chapter 1 for any maintenance of the battery.

4 Battery – removal and installation

1 The battery is located at the left front corner (driver's side) of the engine compartment and held in place by clamps at the base.
2 Hydrogen gas is proauced by the battery and open flames or lighted cigarettes should be kept away from the battery at all times.
3 Always disconnect the negative (-) battery cable first, followed by the positive (+) cable.
4 After the cables are disconnected, unbolt the battery retaining clamp.
5 When removing the battery, use a battery lifting device or pick it up by the corners because the molded plastic case can flex inward, forcing electrolyte and/or fumes out the vents.
6 Installation is the reverse of removal. Be careful not to overtighten the securing clamp bolt as this may damage the battery case.

5 Spark plugs – removal and inspection

Refer to the appropriate Section in Chapter 1 for spark plug removal and inspection.

6 Spark plug wires/distributor cap – checking and replacement

Refer to the appropriate Section in Chapter 1 for checking or replacing the spark plug wires or the distributor cap.

7 Ignition (electronic) – on vehicle test

1 Some problems you may run into due to a defective ignition system include: poor engine performance due to incorrect ignition timing, poor engine performance due to misfiring or hard engine starting due to a defective ignition system.

Vehicle will start

2 The last problem is the most difficult to find the cause of and correct. The spark would be the first place to check.
3 Disconnect the secondary cable from the distributor cap tower. Have an assistant hold the end of the cable with an insulated pliers about 0.25 to 0.38 in from the cylinder block of the engine.
4 As he is doing this, crank the engine with the starter motor and check the spark condition. If a spark is produced, the IC igniter and the ignition coil may be in good condition. The vehicle needs a thorough checking to include the distributor cap, rotor, spark plugs, spark plug cables and the ignition timing.
5 If there is no spark produced, check the voltage of the ignition coil negative terminal.
6 With the ignition switch in the On position, check the voltage with a voltmeter at the negative terminal of the ignition coil. If you do not get a voltage reading, there is an open circuit in the ignition coil and it needs to be replaced with a new one or, the ignition coil wiring is defective and needs to be replaced.
7 If you get a reading of 3 volts or less, the IC igniter in the distributor is defective and needs to be replaced with a new one.
8 If you get battery voltage (12 volts) during this check, you will need to test the ignition coil with a little more depth. Remove the coil and have it tested for continuity by a reputable service department.
9 If the ignition coil checks out to be OK, then the pick-up coil in the distributor is defective and needs to be replaced by a new one.

Vehicle will not start

10 Have an assistant follow the procedure in step 3.
11 Remove the distributor cap, turn the rotor by hand in the normal turning direction (clockwise) and then back to its original position.

Repeat this process several times to determine the sparking condition.
12 If a spark is produced, the IC igniter and the ignition coil may be in good condition. The vehicle needs a thorough checking to include the distributor cap, rotor, spark plugs, spark plug wires, and the ignition timing.
13 If there is no spark produced, and while your assistant is maintaining his position with the coil, remove the distributor from the engine and hold it in your hand.
14 Turn the distributor shaft by hand while grounding the circuit by keeping the distributor housing in contact with the engine cylinder block.
15 If there is a spark after this procedure, refer to step 12.
16 If there is still no spark, follow the procedures outlined in steps 6 through 9 after placing the distributor back into the engine.

Checking the centrifugal advance

17 After bringing the engine to operating temperature, run the engine at idle speed and remove the vacuum hose (non-striped hose) from the vacuum controller.
18 Slowly accelerate the engine to check for any changes in the advance.
19 If you experience a gradual increase in the advance, the governor spring is deteriorated or stretched and needs to be replaced with a new one.
20 A sudden increase in the advance means a broken governor spring which needs to be replaced.
21 If the advance is not up to what is specified, the governor weight or the cam operation is not functioning properly and needs to be corrected.

Checking the vacuum advance

22 A gradual increase in the advance will be caused by a deteriorated or stretched vacuum controller spring which needs to be replaced with a new one.
23 A sudden increase in the advance is caused by a broken vacuum controller spring which needs to be replaced.
24 If the advance is lower than the Specifications or there is no advance at all, the breaker plate is not working correctly or you have a broken diaphragm that needs to be replaced with a new one.

8 Ignition timing – checking and adjustment

Refer to the appropriate Section in Chapter 1 for checking and adjustment of the ignition timing.

9 Breaker points and dwell angle – checking and replacement

Refer to the appropriate Section in Chapter 1 to check or adjust the breaker points or dwell angle.

10 Ignition coil – checking and replacement

1 Mark the wires and terminals with pieces of numbered tape, then remove the primary wires and high-tension lead from the coil.
2 Remove the coil from its mount, clean the outer case and check it for cracks and other damage.
3 Clean the primary coil terminals and check the coil tower terminal for corrosion. Clean it with a wire brush if any corrosion is found.
4 Check the primary coil resistance by attaching the leads of an ohmmeter to the positive and negative primary terminals. Compare the measured resistance to the Specifications.
5 Check the secondary coil resistance by hooking one of the ohmmeter leads to one of the primary terminals and the other ohmmeter lead to the high-tension coil tower terminal. Compare the measured resistance to the Specifications.
6 If the measured resistances are not as specified, the coil is probably defective and should be replaced with a new one.
7 It is essential for proper ignition system operation that all coil terminals and wire leads be kept clean and dry.
8 Install the coil in the vehicle and hook up the wires.

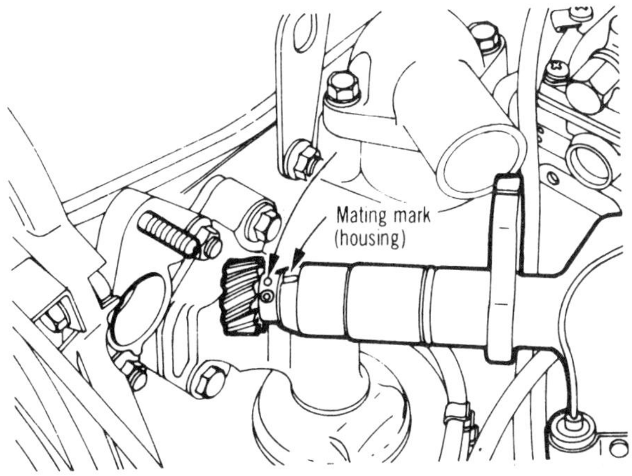

Fig. 5.1 Align the mating marks of distributor housing and drive gear (Sec 11)

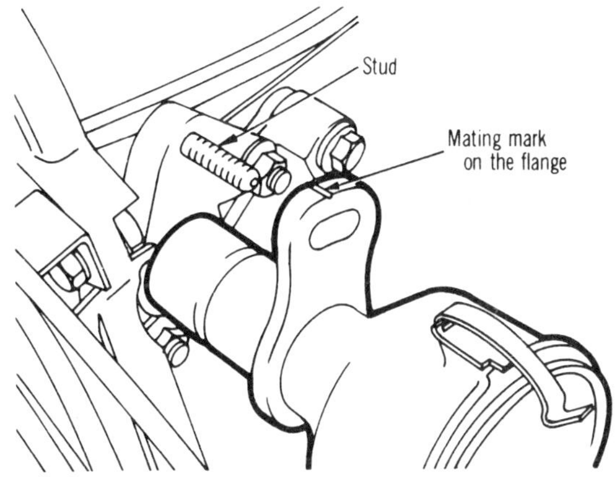

Fig. 5.2 Align the mating marks of distributor flange and mounting stud (Sec 11)

11 Distributor – removal and installation

1 Disconnect the negative battery cable from the battery.
2 On pointless distributors (electronic), unplug the wiring harness from the distributor control unit and remove the distributor cap by depressing and turning the spring-loaded screws.
3 On contact-breaker point distributors, unplug the primary and the high-tension wires from the distributor cap and remove the cap by depressing and turning the spring-loaded screws.
4 Disconnect the vacuum hose from the vacuum advance control unit on the distributor.
5 Pull the spark plug wires off the spark plugs. Pull only on the rubber boot or damage to the spark plug wire could result.
6 Remove the spark plugs, then place your thumb over the No. 1 cylinder's spark plug hole and turn the crankshaft in a clockwise direction (looking at it from the front) until you can feel the compression pressure in the No. 1 cylinder. Continue to slowly turn the crankshaft until the notch in the crankshaft pulley lines up with the T on the timing mark tab. At this point, the No. 1 piston is at TDC on the compression stroke.
7 Remove the distributor attaching nut and pull straight out on the distributor.
8 Do not allow the engine to be cranked until the distributor has been reinstalled.
9 To install the distributor, line up the mating marks on the distributor housing (line) and the distributor-driven gear (punch marks). Slide the distributor into place in the cylinder head while lining up the mark on the distributor hold-down flange with the center of the stud. Make sure the distributor is completely seated, then install the nut and tighten it finger tight.

5

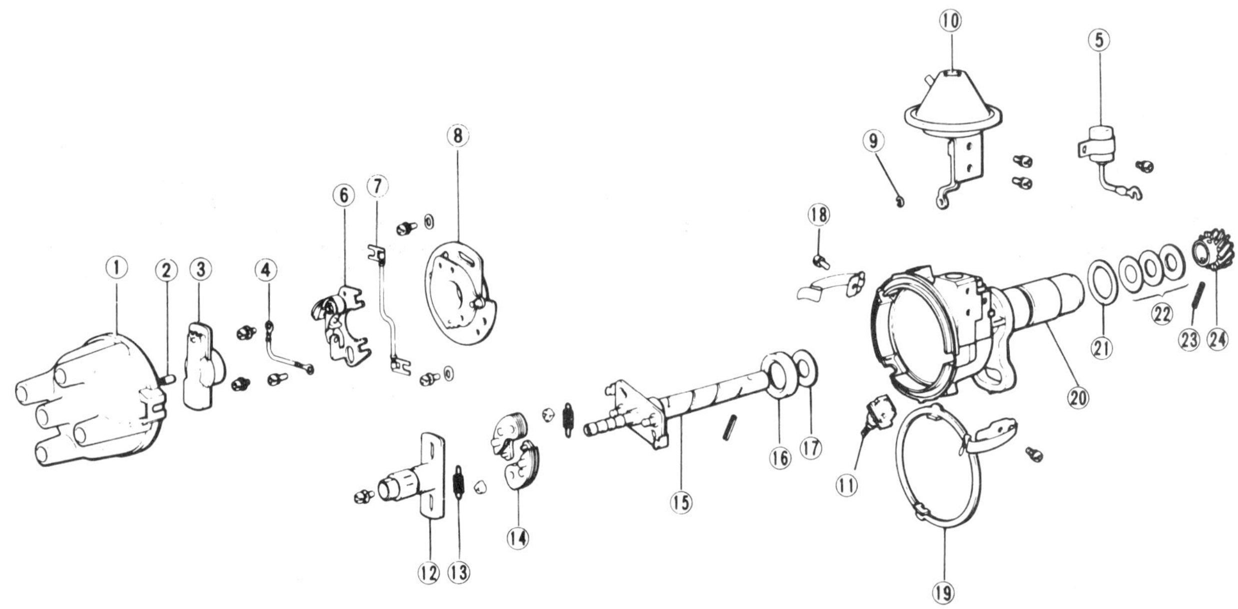

Fig. 5.3 Contact breaker point distributor – exploded view (Sec 12)

1	*Distributor cap*	*7*	*Lead wire A*	*13*	*Governor spring*	*19*	*Packing*
2	*Metal contacts*	*8*	*Breaker base*	*14*	*Governor weight*	*20*	*Housing*
3	*Rotor*	*9*	*Snap ring*	*15*	*Shaft assembly*	*21*	*O-ring*
4	*Lead wire E*	*10*	*Vacuum control unit*	*16*	*Oil seal*	*22*	*Washer*
5	*Condenser*	*11*	*Terminal*	*17*	*Washer*	*23*	*Lock pin*
6	*Arm support*	*12*	*Cam*	*18*	*Cap clamp*	*24*	*Gear*

10 Replace the spark plugs and install the plug wires.
11 Install the distributor cap, plug in the control unit wiring harness and connect the vacuum hose to the vacuum control unit.
12 Connect the negative battery cable to the battery and check the ignition timing as described in Chapter 1. Do not forget to tighten the distributor attaching nut securely when finished.

12 Distributor (mechanical) – overhaul

1 Pull on and remove the rotor from the shaft.
2 Remove the snap-ring from the spindle of the breaker base.
3 Remove the mounting screws of the vacuum control unit and remove the control unit.
4 Disconnect the lead wires E and A from the terminal and remove the terminal.
5 Remove the arm support and the breaker base.
6 Remove the cam assembly.
7 Remove the governor springs and weights.
8 Remove the lock pin from the gear and remove the gear and shaft assembly.
9 Check the breaker point faces for roughness or irregularities and replace then with new ones if necessary. If there is any dirt or oil on any distributor components, wipe them off with a clean cloth.
10 Check the distributor cap and rotor carefully. If there are any cracks or excessive wear, replace them with new parts.
11 A faulty condenser will cause points to fail prematurely so check it with an ohmmeter. If the reading is 5M ohm or better, it is good; if it is less, replace it with a new one.
12 Check the gear for wear and replace it with a new one if necessary.
13 Reassembly is the reverse of disassembly. Be sure to apply a small amount of multi-purpose grease to the shaft and moving parts before reassembly.

13 Distributor (electronic) – overhaul

1 Remove the two mounting screws (photo) and lift the rotor off the governor assembly.
2 Remove the two screws attaching the control unit to the distributor (photo) and pull straight out on the control unit to separate

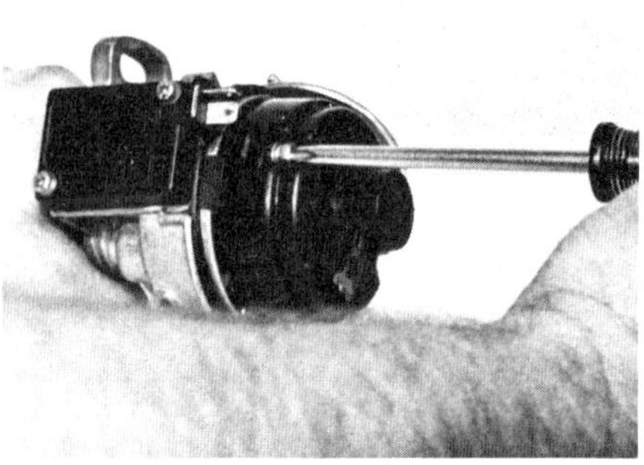

13.1 Remove the rotor mounting screws

13.2a Remove the control unit mounting screws

13.2b The mating surfaces of the control unit and the distributor are coated with silicone grease

13.3a Remove the governor/reluctor assembly mounting bolt

13.3b Remove the governor/reluctor assembly

13.4 Lift out the pickup coil and cap gasket

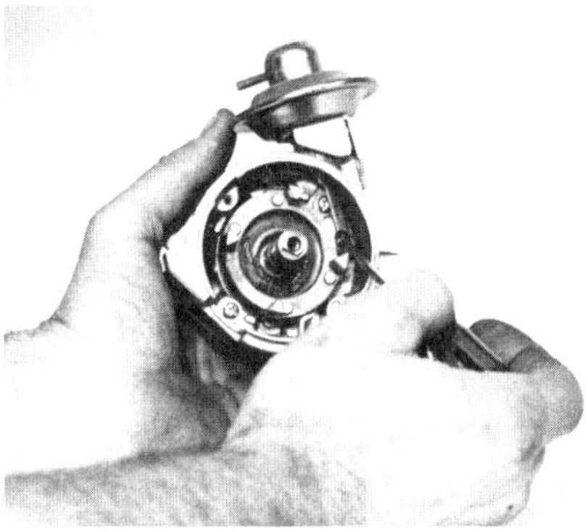
13.5a Remove the vacuum link circlip

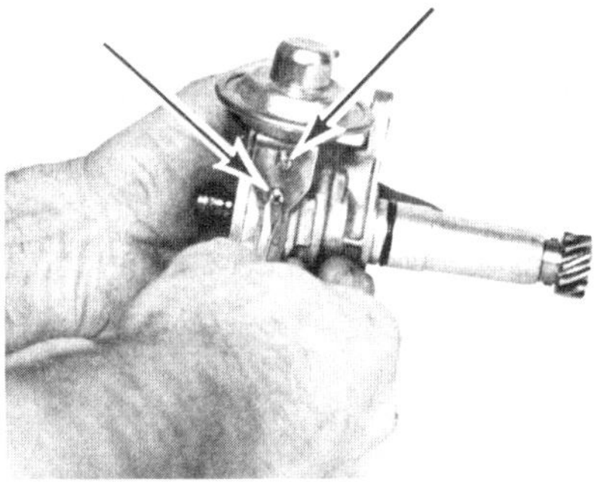
13.5b Remove the vacuum advance control unit mounting screws

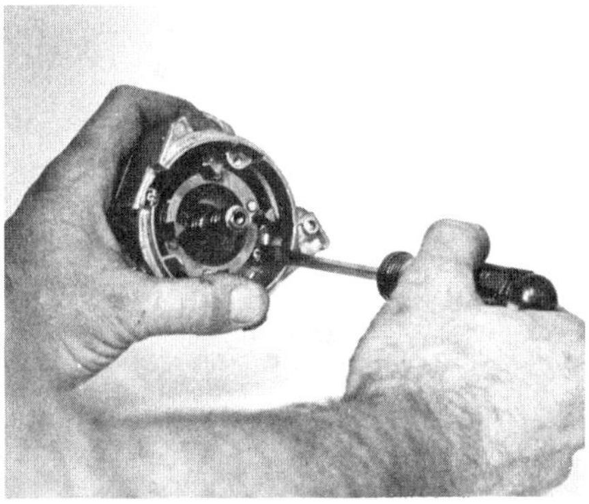
13.6a Remove the breaker assembly mounting screws

13.6b Remove the bearing retaining plate

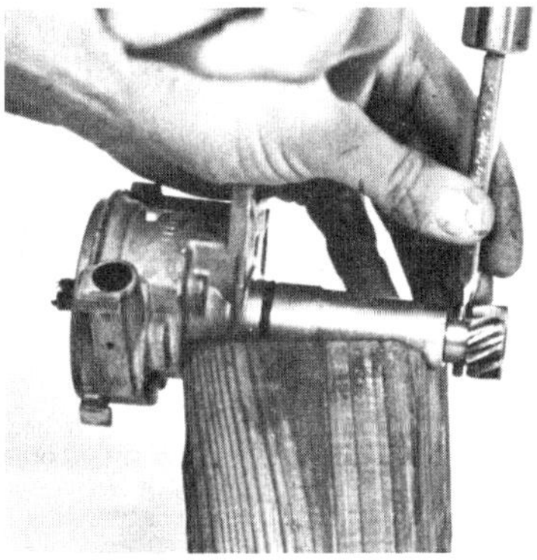
13.7 Remove the distributor drive gear retaining pin

13.8 Withdraw the shaft from the distributor body

it from the distributor. The mating surfaces of the control unit and the distributor are coated with silicone grease; do not wipe it off (photo).

3 Remove the bolt from the shaft (photo) and pull off the governor/reluctor assembly (photo).

4 Remove the two screws attaching the pickup coil to the distributor. The coil and cap gasket can now be lifted out (photo).

5 Remove the retaining clip that holds the vacuum link to the breaker assembly (photo). Remove the two screws attaching the vacuum advance control unit to the distributor (photo) and lift it off.

6 Remove the breaker assembly (photo) and the bearing retainer plate (photo).

7 Support the distributor shaft and gear, then drive out the pin that attaches the gear to the shaft (photo).

8 Slide the gear off the shaft and withdraw the shaft from the distributor (photo).

9 Do not remove the bearing and seal from the shaft unless they require replacement.

10 Using an ohmmeter, measure the resistance of the pickup coil. Compare the measured resistance to the Specifications.

11 Check for continuity between terminal C and the back side (bare metal) of the control unit. Reverse the lead and repeat the test. If there is continuity or an open circuit in both test lead positions, the control unit is defective and should be replaced with a new one. **Note:** *This test evaluates only the transistors in the control unit. Even if the results of the test are positive, the control unit could still be defective.*

12 Check the distributor gear for excessive wear and damage.

13 Check the shaft and bearing for end-to-end and side play. If excessive play is noted, replace the bearing, the seal and the shaft with new parts.

14 Check the governor springs for cracks and damage. Make sure the governor weights can move freely on their pivots.

15 Check the vacuum advance control unit by applying a vacuum at the fitting. The linkage should move in and remain in as long as a vacuum is applied to the fitting.

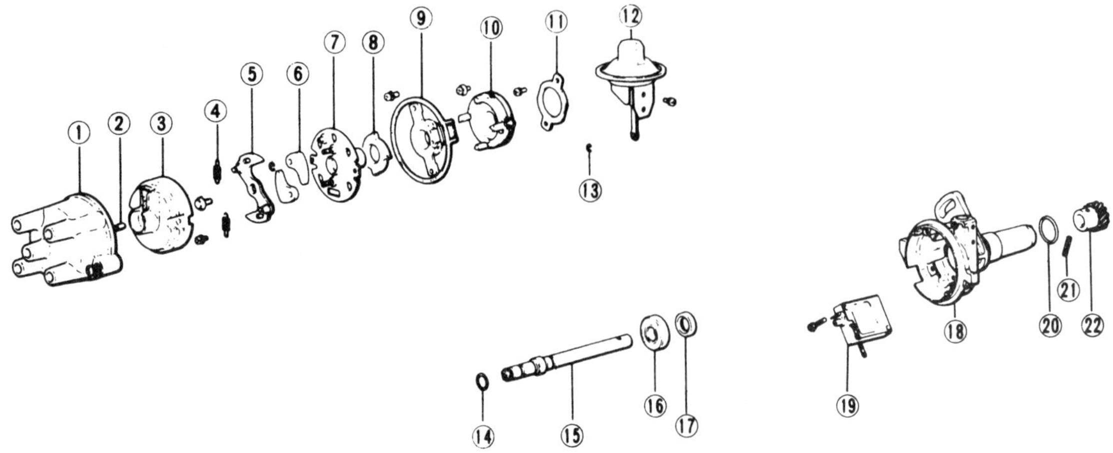

Fig. 5.4 Electronic distributor – exploded view (Sec 13)

1 Distributor cap
2 Metal contacts
3 Rotor assembly
4 Governor spring
5 Governor plate
6 Governor weight
7 Governor base
8 Reluctor
9 Pickup coil
10 Breaker
11 Plate
12 Vacuum control unit
13 E-ring
14 Washer
15 Shaft
16 Ball bearing
17 Oil seal
18 Housing
19 Control unit
20 O-ring
21 Spring pin
22 Drive gear

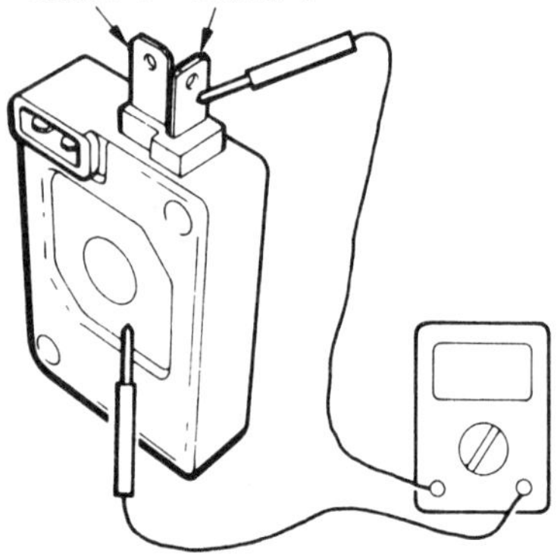

Fig. 5.5 Control unit check (Sec 13)

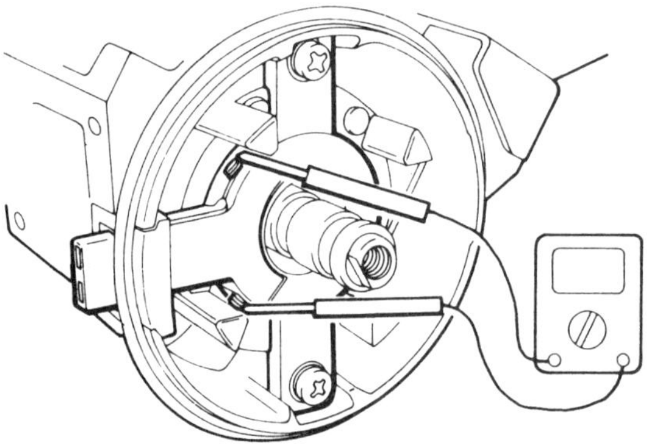

Fig. 5.6 Pick-up coil check (Sec 13)

16 Check the distributor cap and rotor for cracks, carbon tracks and deposits on the metal terminals. If any of these conditions exist, replace them with new parts. The cost is minimal.
17 Lubricate the shaft with a small amount of multi-purpose grease, then insert the shaft into the distributor.
18 Slide the gear onto the end of the shaft and install the pin. Be sure to support the gear and shaft when tapping the pin into place.
19 Install the breaker assembly. Connect the vacuum advance link, (don't forget the retaining clip) and fasten the vacuum advance control unit in place.
20 Install the pickup coil and cap gasket. Tighten the screws securely but do not overtighten them.
21 Slip the governor/reluctor assembly onto the shaft, install the bolt and tighten it securely.
22 Install the control unit ensuring that the silicone grease is in place and tighten the screws securely.
23 Install the rotor by matching the pegs on the governor assembly with the holes in the rotor and tighten the screws securely.
24 Check to make sure the distributor shaft rotates smoothly and easily.

14 Starter motor – on vehicle test

1 If the starter motor fails to operate, check the condition of the battery by turning on the headlights. If they glow brightly for several seconds and then gradually dim, the battery is in a discharged condition.
2 If the headlights continue to glow brightly and it is obvious that the battery is in good condition, check the tightness of the battery leads and all cables relative to the starting system. If possible, check the wiring with a voltmeter or test light for breaks or short circuits.
3 Check that there is current at the relay when the ignition switch is operated. If there is, then the relay should be suspect.
4 If there is no current at the relay, suspect the ignition switch. On models with automatic transmission, check the Neutral start switch.
5 Should the above checks prove negative then the starter motor brushes probably need replacement or at the worst there is an internal fault in the motor.

15 Starter motor – removal and installation

1 Before attempting to remove the starter motor, disconnect the negative battery cable from the battery.
2 Raise the vehicle and set it securely on jackstands.
3 Label the wires and terminals with pieces of numbered tape, then disconnect the starter motor wiring harness from the two terminals on the starter motor solenoid.
4 Remove the starter motor mounting bolts and separate the motor

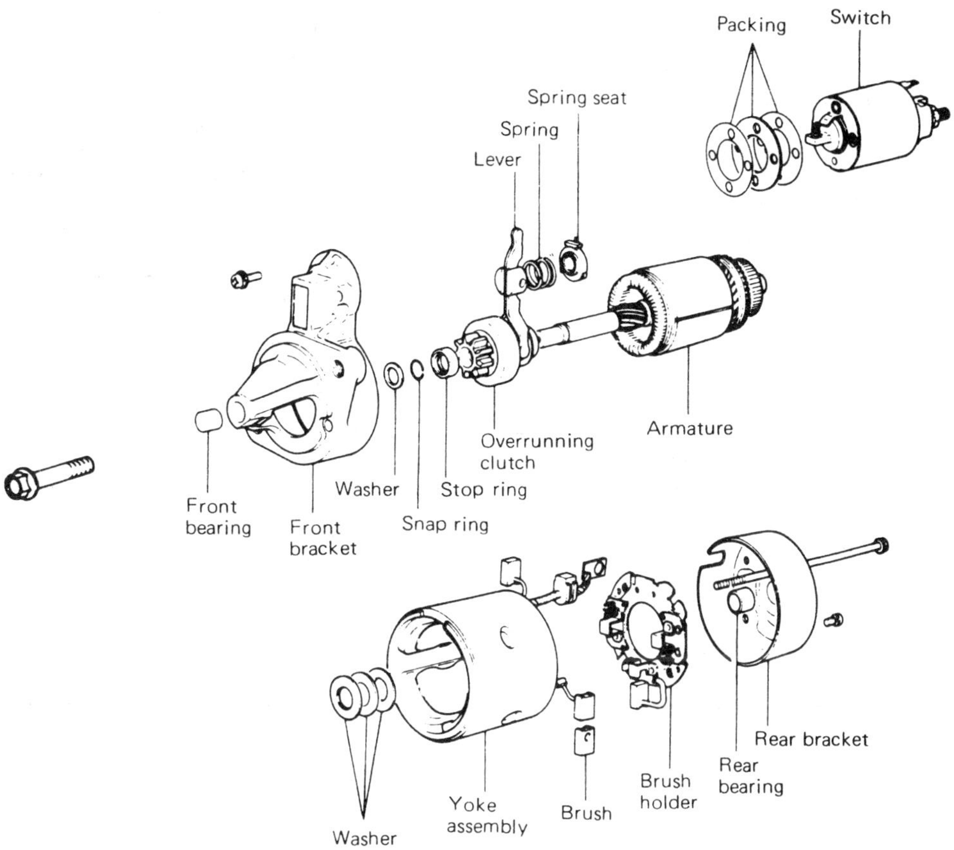

Fig. 5.7 Direct drive starter motor components – exploded view (Sec 16)

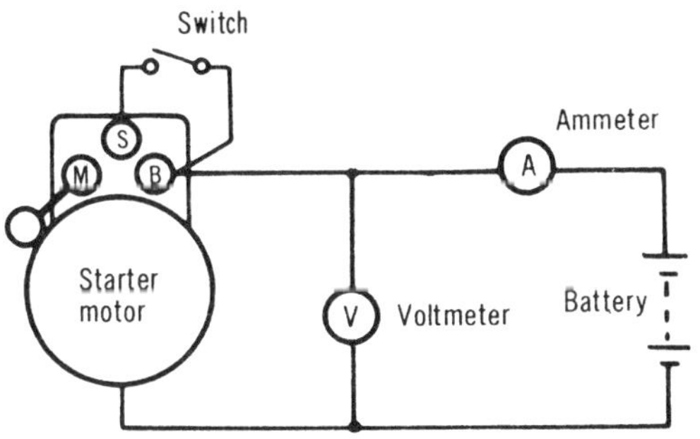

Fig. 5.8 Starter motor no-load test (Sec 16)

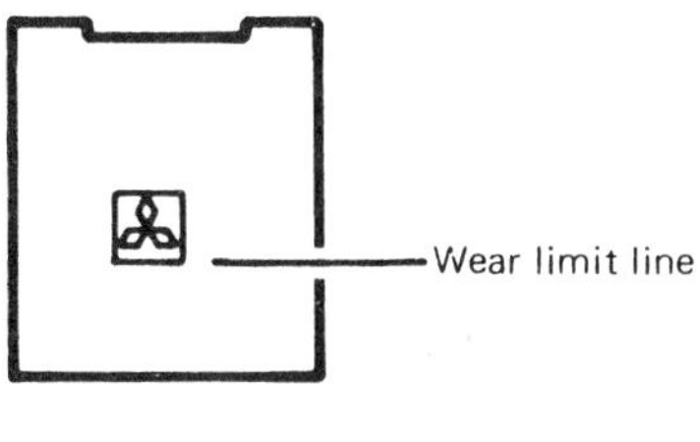

Fig. 5.9 Starter motor brush wear check (Secs 16 and 17)

from the transmission bellhousing. Work carefully, as the starter motor is quite heavy.

5 Before installing the motor, clean the mounting surfaces thoroughly. Slip the motor into place, install the mounting bolts and tighten them evenly and securely. If there is enough room to use a torque wrench, tighten the bolts to the specified torque.

6 Hook up the starter motor wiring leads (don't mix them up) and the negative battery cable.

16 Starter motor (direct drive) – brush replacement

1 When faced with starter motor problems, you must decide whether to disassemble the motor and replace the brushes (which usually cures the problem) or simply replace the motor with a new or rebuilt one. The costs involved, in terms of time and money and the availability of parts needed, are the main factors to consider.

2 Remove the connector (attached to the rear bracket) from the terminal on the solenoid.

3 The motor can be separated by removing the two through bolts. Remove the bolts carefully so the whole assembly does not fall apart because you will not separate any more than you have to.

4 Loosen the screws on the rear bracket and remove the bracket.

5 The brush holder assembly can be removed by pulling out the brushes and slipping the holder off.

6 You can now compare the brush length with the Specifications and determine if they were the cause of your problem and whether they need to be replaced.

7 On some motors, the brushes can easily be replaced by removing them from the holders and inserting the new ones with their mounting screws.

8 On most of the other motors, the only way to replace the brushes is by replacing the brush holder with a new one. This of course is still cheaper than replacing the whole motor.

9 Reassembly of the motor is the reverse of the disassembly. Make sure when you install the brushes, that the lead wires are not grounded.
10 The following tests can be performed before the motor is installed to see if the problem was solved or if there is something else malfunctioning.
11 **Note**: *The following test must be completed in less than 10 seconds to prevent damage to the solenoid:*
12 Connect a heavy jumper lead between the positive post of a 12-volt battery and terminal S on the solenoid. Connect a second heavy jumper lead between the negative post of the battery and the starter motor body. When the connection is made, the pinion gear will move out on the armature shaft.
13 Check the pinion-to-stopper clearance (pinion gap) and compare it to the Specifications. The pinion gap can be increased or decreased by adding or removing washers where the solenoid mounts to the front bracket.
14 **Note**: *This test must also be performed in less than 10 seconds.*
15 Connect terminal S to the positive post of the battery and connect terminal M to the negative post of the battery. Connect another jumper lead between terminal M and the solenoid body. If the pinion gear moves out on the armature shaft, the pull-in coil is good. If the pinion gear does not move, replace the solenoid with a new one.
16 Disconnect the wire from terminal M only. If the pinion stays out, the hold-in coil is working properly. If the pinion moves in when the wire is disconnected, the solenoid must be replaced with a new one.
17 Connect terminal M to the positive post of the battery and touch the lead from the negative post of the battery to the solenoid body. Pull the pinion out, then release it. If it quickly returns to its original position, everything is working properly. If it does not return, replace the solenoid with a new one.
18 Connect the battery to the starter motor as shown in Fig. 5.9. A voltmeter and an ammeter must be included in the circuit as well. Hold the starter motor securely while conducting this test.
19 If the motor rotates smoothly and steadily (and if the pinion gear moves out on the armature shaft) and draws less than the specified amount of current, the motor is working properly.

17 Starter motor (reduction drive) – brush replacement

1 When faced with starter motor problems, you must decide whether to disassemble the motor and replace the brushes (which usually cures the problem) or simply replace the motor with a new or rebuilt one. The costs involved, in terms of time and money and the availability of parts needed, are the main factors to consider.
2 Remove the connector (attached to the rear bracket) from the terminal on the solenoid.
3 The motor can be separated by removing the two through bolts. Remove the bolts carefully so the whole assembly does not fall apart because you will not separate any more than you have to.
4 Loosen the two screws on the rear bracket and remove the bracket. When the bracket is removed, do not lose the spring washer.
5 The brush holder assembly can be removed by pulling out the brushes and slipping off the holder.
6 You can now compare the brush length with the Specifications and determine if they were the cause of your problem and whether they need to be replaced.

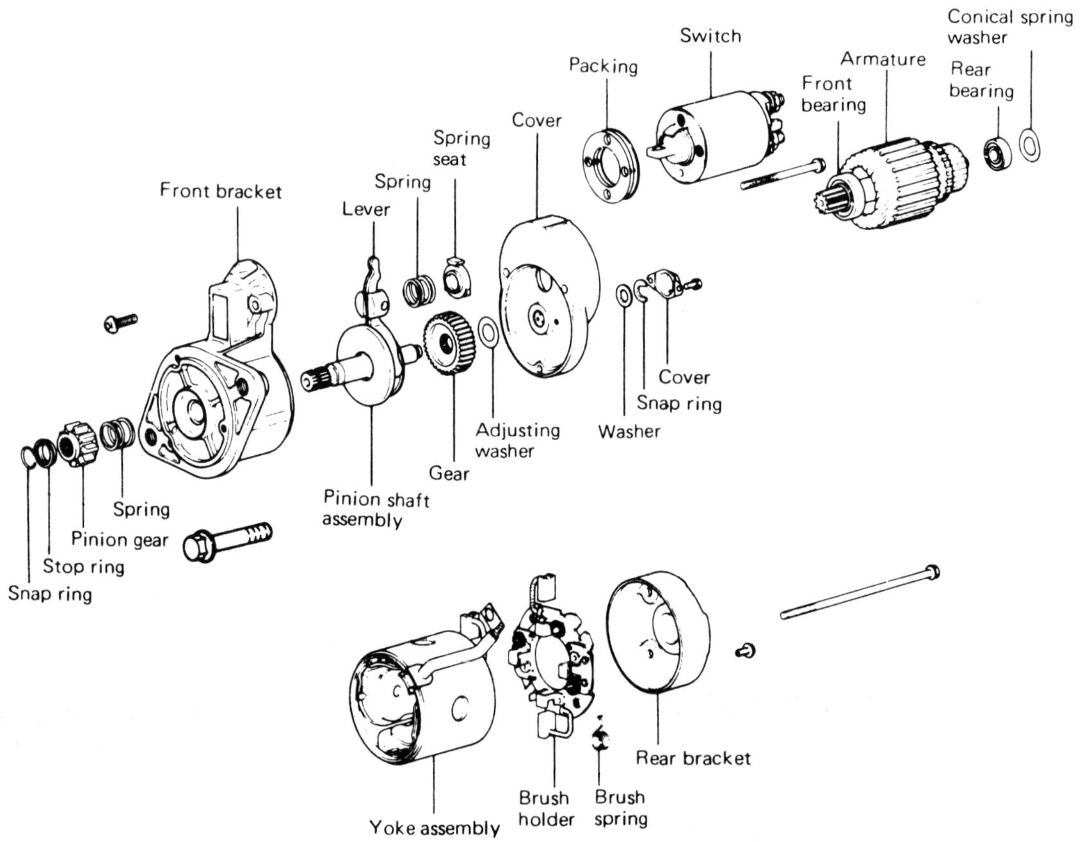

Fig. 5.10 Reduction drive starter motor components – exploded view (Sec 17)

7 The only way to replace the brushes is by replacing the brush holder with a new one. This, of course, is still cheaper than replacing the whole motor.
8 Reassembly of the motor is the reverse of disassembly. Make sure when you install the brushes, that the lead wires are not grounded.
9 The following tests can be performed before the motor is installed to see if the problem was solved or if there is something else malfunctioning.
10 Check the pinion gap as follows: **Note**: *This test must be completed in less than 10 seconds to prevent damage to the solenoid:* Connect a heavy jumper lead between the positive post of a 12-volt battery and terminal S on the solenoid. Connect another heavy jumper lead between the negative post of the battery and the starter motor body. When the connection is made, the pinion shaft and gears will move out.
11 Gently push the pinion gear back until it stops. The distance moved is the pinion gap. Compare it to the Specifications. If the gap is more or less than specified, add or remove washers from between the solenoid and the front bracket. Increasing the washers will reduce the pinion gap.
12 The remaining performance tests are the same as those for the direct-drive starter motor.

18 Charging system – on vehicle test

1 Turn the ignition switch to the Off position.
2 Disconnect the cable from the positive terminal of the battery and connect an ammeter between the cable and the terminal of the battery.
3 Connect a voltmeter between the L terminal of the alternator and ground. Check to be sure that the voltmeter reading is zero.
4 If the pointer of the meter deflects (showing the presence of voltage), a defective alternator or wiring should be suspected.
5 Set the ignition switch to the On position but do not start the engine. The voltmeter reading now should be considerably lower than the battery voltage (12 volts). If the meter reading is about the same as the battery voltage, a defective alternator should be suspected.
6 With the ammeter terminals short-circuited, start the engine. **Note**: *Be sure that there is no starting current applied to the ammeter when the engine is started or your meter will be damaged.* Bypass the meter with one jumper cable by attaching one end to the battery terminal and the other end to the battery cable (with the ammeter still hooked up). Be sure that you get good connections at both ends. Make sure that the meter leads and the jumper cable do not interfere with any moving parts when the engine is started. Attach the jumper cable to your hood with a wire in some way to keep it out of the way. Also, make sure that there are no wires or cables touching any metal parts, creating a ground.
7 After the engine is started, remove the short-circuit (jumper cable) from across the ammeter and increase the engine speed immediately to approximately 2500 rpm. An assistant will be needed for this procedure. Take the ammeter reading.
8 If the meter reading is 5A or less, take the voltmeter reading without changing the engine speed. This reading is the charging voltage.
9 Compare your reading to the standard value in the Specifications. **Note**: *The outside temperature will have an effect on a non-compensated meter reading which will make you think that your voltage regulator is bad. To compensate the meter reading with the outside temperature, at 50°F (10°C) the actual voltage reading will be -0.1V (less) than your reading.*
10 If, after you have compensated your meter reading and the charging voltage is outside the Specifications, the voltage regulator is probably faulty.
11 If the ammeter reading is more than 5A, charge the battery until the reading falls to less than 5A, or replace your battery with a new one.

19 Alternator – removal and installation

1 Disconnect the negative battery cable.
2 For clearance, raise the front of the car and support it on jackstands.

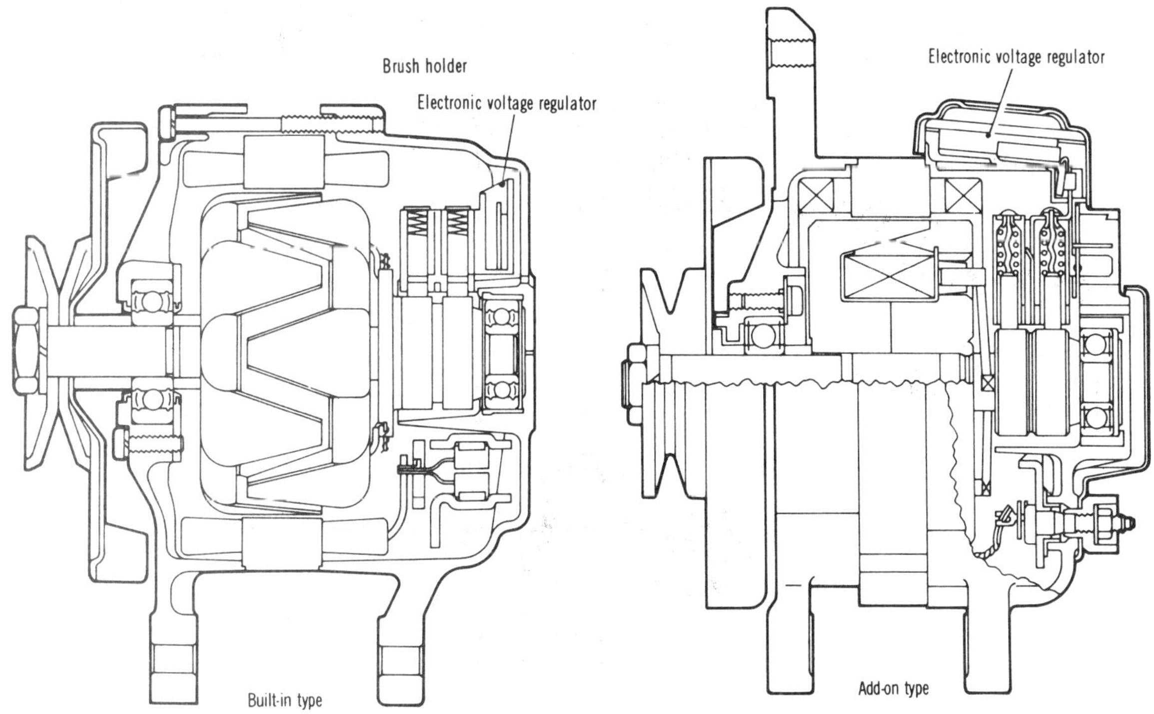

Fig. 5.11 Sectional view of both types of alternators (Sec 20)

5

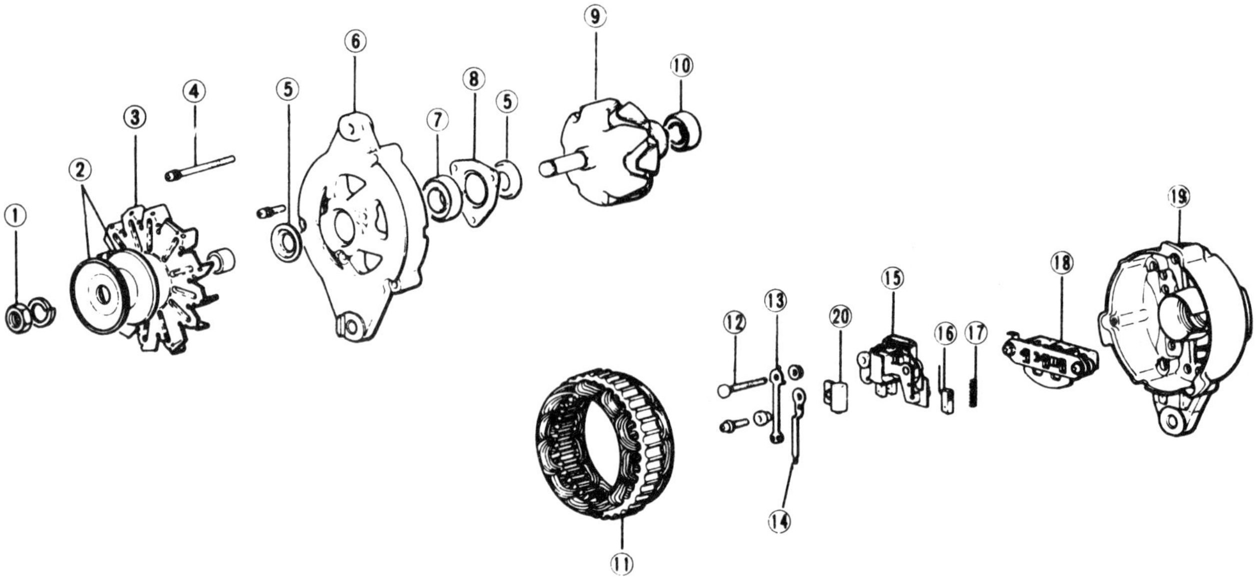

Fig. 5.12 Built-in type alternator components – exploded view (Sec 20)

1 Pulley nut
2 Pulley
3 Fan
4 Through bolt
5 Seal
6 Front bracket
7 Ball bearing
8 Bearing retainer
9 Rotor assembly
10 Ball bearing
11 Stator assembly
12 Terminal B bolt
13 Plate B
14 Plate L
15 Brush holder/electronic voltage regulator
16 Brush
17 Brush spring
18 Rectifier assembly
19 Rear bracket
20 Condenser

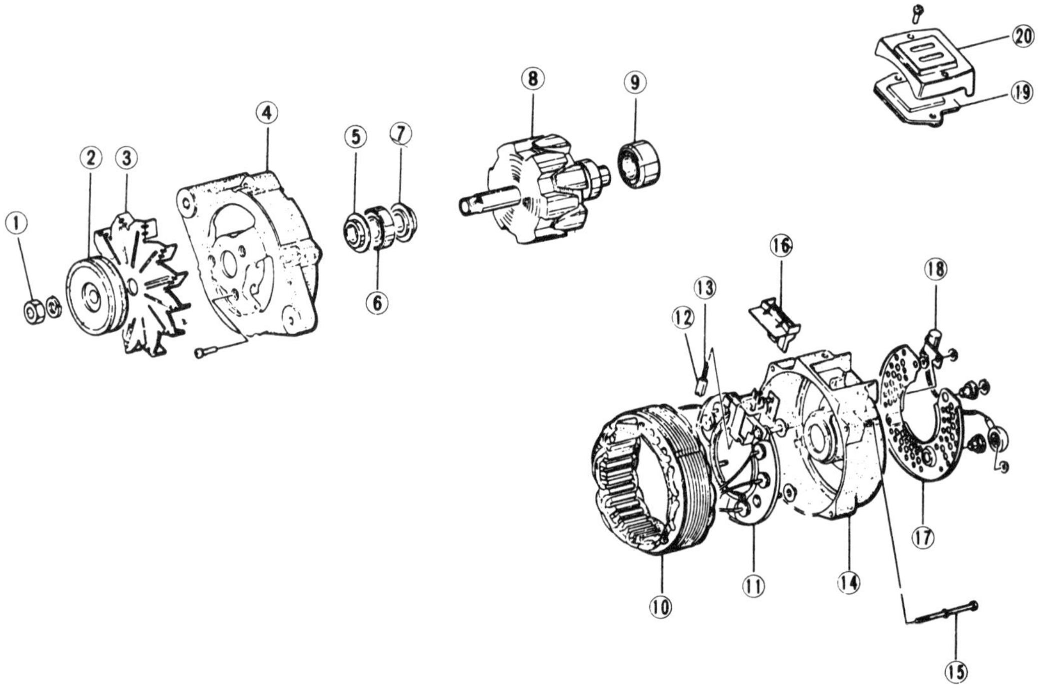

Fig. 5.13 Add-on-type alternator components – exploded view (Sec 20)

1 Pulley nut
2 Pulley
3 Fan
4 Front bracket
5 Spacer
6 Ball bearing
7 Spacer
8 Rotor assembly
9 Ball bearing
10 Stator assembly
11 Rectifier assembly with brush
12 Brush
13 Brush spring
14 Rear bracket
15 Through bolt
16 Terminal cover
17 Rear cover
18 Condenser
19 Electronic voltage regulator
20 Cover

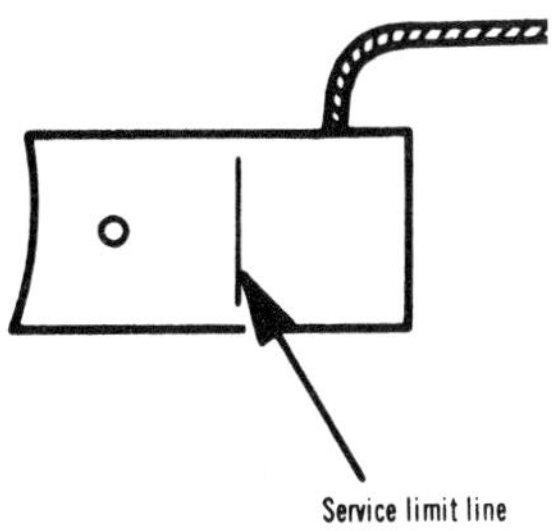

Fig. 5.14 Check brush service limit (Sec 20)

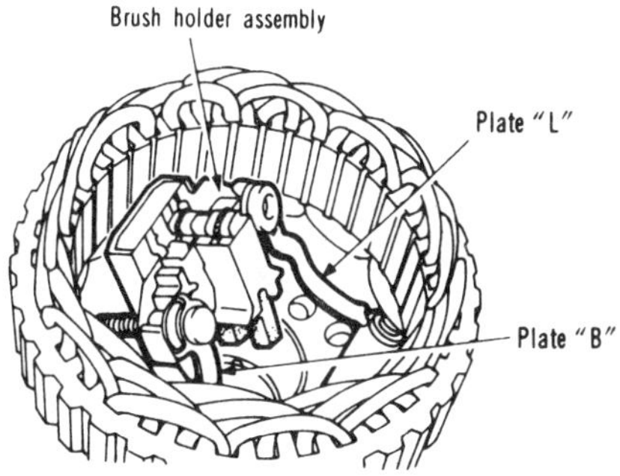

Fig. 5.15 Lift brush holder to remove the brushes (Sec 20)

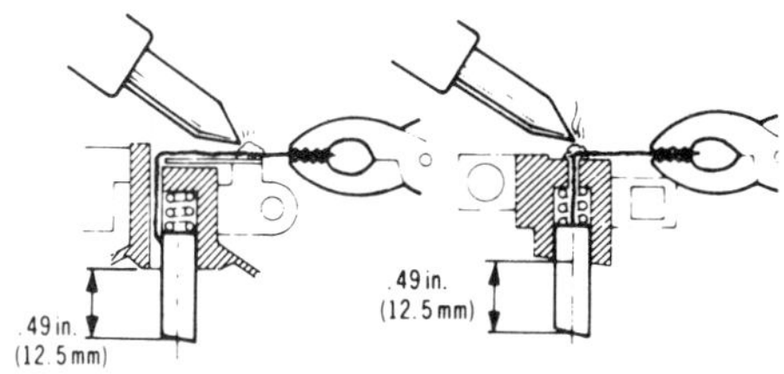

Fig. 5.16 Remove and install the brushes by soldering (Sec 20)

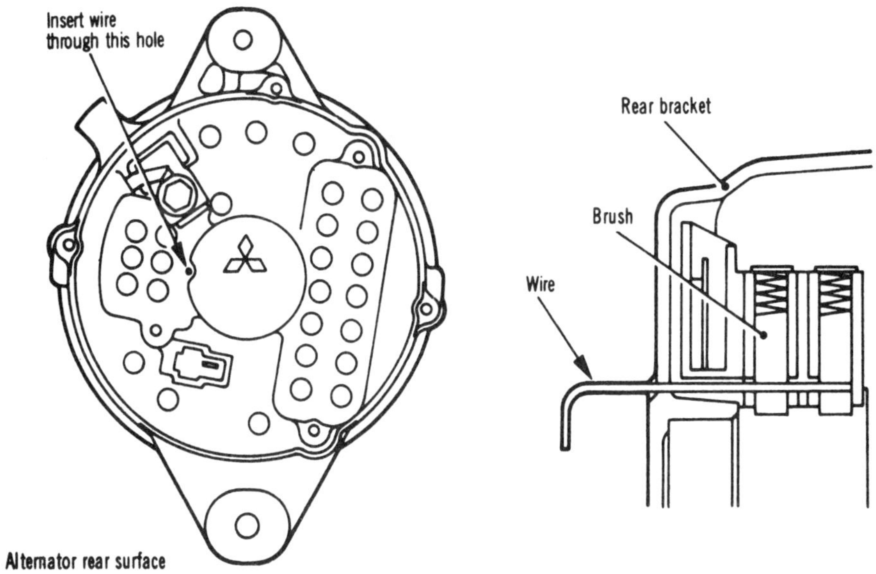

Fig. 5.17 Wire insertion location on built-in alternator (Sec 20)

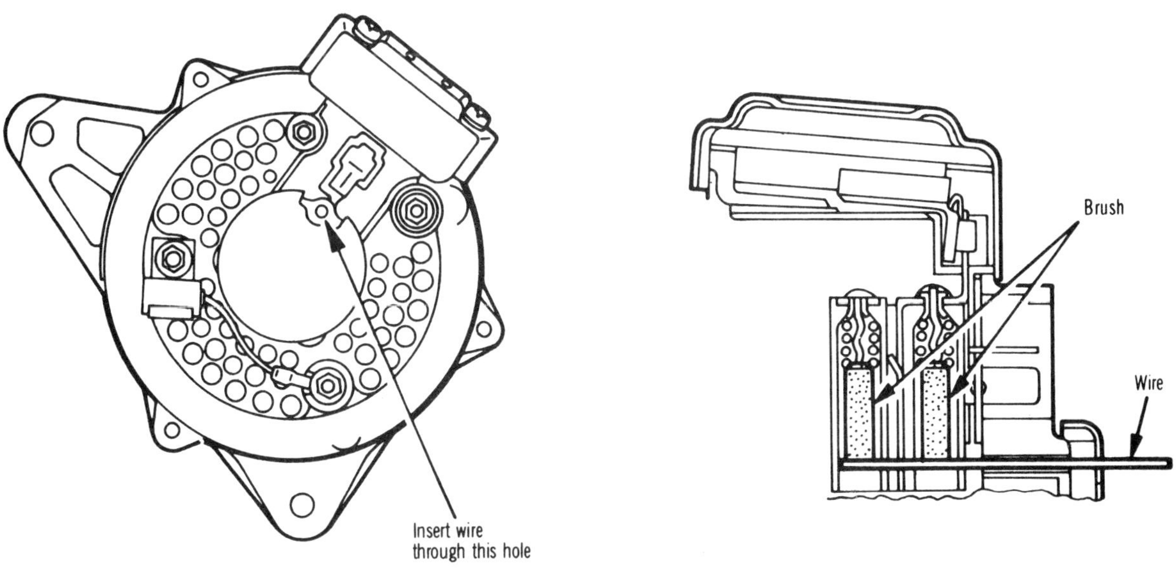

Fig. 5.18 Wire insertion location on add-on alternator (Sec 20)

3 Remove all wires from the rear of the alternator. Be sure to label them as to their locations.
4 Loosen the upper drivebelt adjusting bolt and move the alternator toward the engine until the drivebelt can be removed from the alternator pulley.
5 Remove the adjusting bolt and the alternator mounting bolts located at the bottom of the alternator.
6 Remove the alternator from the car. There is minimal clearance for removing the alternator and it must be worked out between the fan shroud, oil pump and tension rod bracket.
7 Installation is the reverse of the removal procedure.

20 Alternator – brush replacement

1 If you find that your alternator is not functioning properly, replacing the brushes is all you may have to do.
2 You must decide whether to disassemble the alternator and replace the brushes or simply replace it with a new or rebuilt one. The costs involved, in terms of money and time, and the availability of parts needed are the main items to consider.
3 To get at the brushes, remove the through bolts. Remove the bolts carefully so the whole assembly does not fall apart because you will not separate any more than you have to.
4 Use a screwdriver and carefully pry apart the rear bracket from the front bracket/stator assembly.
5 Raise the brush holder/electronic voltage regulator assembly as shown in the illustration. Unsolder the brush pig-tail and remove the brush and spring. **Note:** *Do not bend the brush holder any more than is necessary to replace the brushes, because bending the L and B plates might damage the rectifier molding.*
6 You can now compare the brush length with the Specifications and determine if they were the cause of your problems and whether they need to be replaced.
7 Reassembly is the reverse of the disassembly. Make sure the through bolts are tight.
8 In order to make the reassembly a little easier, push the brushes into the holder and insert a wire as shown in the illustration to hold the brushes in place while installing the rear bracket into the stator. Make sure that the wire is long enough to grab onto and remove when the alternator is completely reassembled.

21 Ignition switch – removal, checking and installation

Refer to the appropriate Sections in Chapter 10 for checking and in Chapter 11 for removal and installation.

Chapter 6 Emissions control systems

Contents

Specifications

Fuel filler cap valve pressure ..... – 0.640 psi (–4.413 kPa)

EGR valve control coolant temperature

Closed	Above 131°F (55°C)
Open	Below 113°F (45°C)

Torque Specifications	**ft-lb**	**Nm**
Exhaust manifold-to-catalyst case bolts	22 to 25	30 to 34
Exhaust manifold mounting nuts	11 to 14	15 to 19

1 General information

To prevent pollution of the atmosphere, a number of emission control systems are required. The combination of systems used depends on the year in which the vehicle was manufactured and the locality to which it was originally delivered.

The Sections in this Chapter include general descriptions, checking procedures (where possible) and component replacement procedures (where applicable) for each of the systems.

Before assuming that an emission control system is malfunctioning, check the fuel and ignition systems carefully. In some cases, special tools and equipment, as well as specialized training, are required to accurately diagnose the causes of a rough running or difficult to start engine. If checking and servicing become too difficult, or if a procedure is beyond the scope of the home mechanic, consult your Chrysler dealer service department.

This does not mean, however, that all the emission control systems are difficult to maintain or repair. You can quickly and easily perform many checks (if not all) of the regular maintenance at home with common tune-up and hand tools. The most frequent cause of emission control problems is simply a loose or broken vacuum hose or wiring connection. Therefore, always check hose and wiring connections first.

Pay close attention to any special precautions outlined in this Chapter (particularly the catalytic converter). Also, be aware that the illustrations of the various systems may not be *exactly* like yours due to manufacturing changes made from year-to-year.

2 Positive Crankcase Ventilation system (PCV)

6

General description

This system is designed to reduce hydrocarbon emissions (HC) by routing blow-by gases (fuel/air mixture that escapes from the combustion chamber past the piston rings into the crankcase) from the crankcase to the intake manifold and combustion chamber where they are burned during engine operation.

The system is very simple and consists of rubber hoses and a small replaceable metering valve (PCV valve) for vehicles made from 1980 through 1983. Vehicles made from 1978 through 1980 have a fixed orifice installed in the intake manifold.

Checking and component replacement

1 Checking, cleaning and replacement of the PCV system components is a routine maintenance procedure. Refer to Chapter 1 for details.

3 Evaporative Emission Control system (EEC)

General description

This system is designed to prevent the escape of fuel vapors from the carburetor and the fuel tank, which would normally enter the atmosphere and contribute to hydrocarbon (HC) emissions.

Two canisters are at work in this system. Canister A collects all vapors while the engine is not running. Canister B draws all the stored vapors in canister A, through the purge control valve and into the intake manifold, when the engine is running, where it burns these vapors off.

The purge control valve simply stops vaporized fuel from the canisters entering the intake manifold until the engine is warmed-up enough to handle it.

The carburetor bowl vent valve controls the carburetor bowl vapors and is activated (open) by turning the ignition key On. The bowl vapors are directed to the intake manifold where they are burned off. The valve is closed when the engine is turned Off.

A carbon element is placed in the air cleaner to store any vapors generated in the carburetor.

A thermo valve is incorporated into the system to sense the coolant temperature of the intake manifold. It closes the purge control valve when the temperature drops to below its pre-set value and opens the purge control valve when the temperature rises.

The fuel filler cap is equipped with a relief valve to prevent the escape of fuel vapors into the atmosphere. If the pressure in the tank drops below the specified negative pressure, the valve will open to adjust the pressure.

The vapor separator tank temporarily accomodates an increased volume of gasoline caused by expansion at high ambient temperatures. It also prevents liquid fuel from entering the vapor line during extreme cornering of the vehicle.

The fuel overfill limiter (two-way valve) consists of a pressure valve designed to open when the fuel tank internal pressure has increased over the normal pressure. It also has a vacuum valve which opens when a vacuum has been produced in the fuel tank.

The fuel check valve (roll-over valve) is used to prevent fuel leaks should the vehicle suddenly roll over. It contains two check balls that are normally open but, if a roll over should take place, either of the balls closes the fuel passage to prevent any leaks.

Checking

1 There are no checks for the canisters, the carbon element, the bowl vent, the vapor separator tank or the fuel check valve. Refer to Chapter 1 for maintenance intervals in replacing the canisters and the carbon element.

2 To check the purge control valve, make sure the coolant temperature is between 180 and 190°F (80 and 90°C). Disconnect the purge hose from the air cleaner and blow into it. If the valve is not open, the condition of it is normal. Now, start the engine and increase engine speed to 1500 to 2000 rpm and blow into the hose. If it is open, its condition is normal. If not, check for clogged or broken vacuum hose or a malfunctioning thermo valve. Replace with new parts as necessary.

3 Check the valve opening pressure of the fuel filter cap by referring to Specifications. Replace it with a new one if it fails to meet the opening pressure specified.

4 Check the overfill limiter body for cracks, leaks, and operating condition by referring to Specifications for the individual valves within it. Replace it with a new one if necessary.

Component replacement

5 Replace all rubber hoses leading to the canisters at the time of canister replacement.

6 Replace the canisters by referring to Chapter 1.

7 Replacing the purge control valve, the fuel check valve and the over fill limiter is straightforward enough by referring to the illustration in Chapter 1.

4 Jet air system (Jet Valves)

General description

The jet air system utilizes an additional inlet valve (Jet Valve) which provides for air, or a super lean mixture, to be drawn from the air intake into the cylinder. The Jet Valve is operated by the same cam as the inlet valve. They use a common rocker arm so that the Jet Valve and the inlet valve open and close simultaneously.

On the intake stroke of the engine, fuel/air mixture flows through the intake ports into the combustion chamber. At the same time, jet air is forced into the combustion chamber because of the pressure difference between the jet intake in the throttle bore and the Jet Valve in the cylinder as the piston moves down.

At small throttle openings, there is a large pressure difference, giving the jet air high velocity. This scavenges the residual gases around the spark plug and creates good ignition conditions. It also produces a strong swirl in the combustion chamber, which lasts throughout the compression stroke and improves flame propagation after ignition, assuring high combustion efficiency and lowering exhaust emissions. As the throttle opening is increased, less jet air is forced in and jet swirl diminishes but the increased flow through the intake valve ensures satisfactory combustion.

Adjustments

1 Incorrect Jet Valve clearances will affect the emission levels and could also cause engine troubles.

2 Refer to Chapter 1 for Jet Valve clearance adjustment procedures.

Component replacement

3 Jet Valve removal, inspection and installation procedures are covered in detail in Chapter 2.

5 Catalytic converters

General description

The catalytic converters provide for the oxidizing of hydrocarbons and carbon monoxide in the exhaust system, which reduces the levels of these pollutants in the exhaust.

Its ceramic monolithic element, coated with a catalytic agent, is pressed into the engine lower exhaust manifold. The catalyst cannot be replaced independently, as the catalyst and lower exhaust manifold are an assembly.

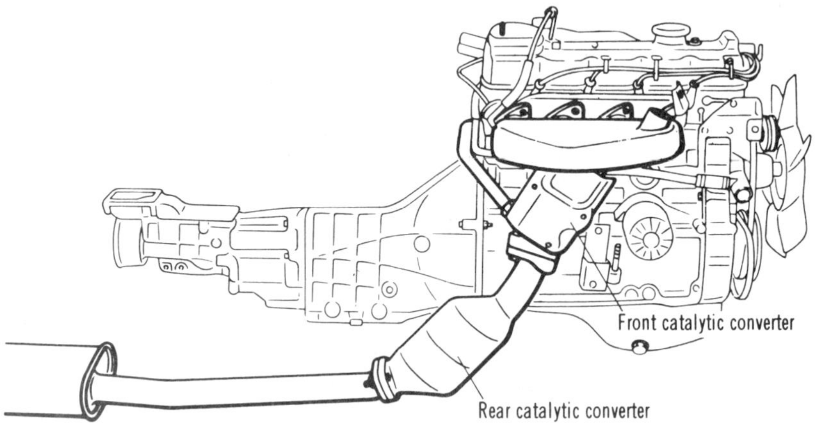

Fig. 6.1 Location of the catalytic converters (Sec 5)

The catalytic converter requires the use of unleaded fuel only. Leaded gasoline will destroy the effectiveness of the catalyst as an emission control device.

Under normal operating conditions, the catalytic converters will not require maintenance. However, it is important to keep the engine properly tuned. If the engine is not properly tuned, engine misfiring may cause overheating of the catalyst, which may damage the converters or other vehicle components. Heat damage can also occur during diagnostic testing if spark plug wires are removed and the engine is allowed to idle for a prolonged period of time. **Note:** *If large amounts of unburned gasoline enter the catalyst, it may overheat and cause a fire. Always observe the following precautions:*

Use only unleaded gasoline
Avoid prolonged idling
Do not prolong engine compression checks
Do not run the engine with a nearly empty fuel tank
Avoid coasting with the ignition turned off
Do not dispose of a used catalytic converter along with oily or gasoline soaked parts

The converters are located in the exhaust system and closely resemble mufflers, a monolithic type, mounted just past the exhaust manifold pipe, and a pelletized type mounted further downstream (see illustration).

Checking

Note: *Vehicles made in 1978 through 1980 have only one catalytic converter but the same procedures also apply to these vehicles.*

1 The catalytic converters require little if any maintenance and servicing at regular intervals. However, the system should be inspected whenever the vehicle is raised on a lift or if the exhaust system is checked or serviced.

2 Check all connections in the exhaust pipe assembly for looseness or damage. Also check all the clamps for damage, cracks, or missing fasteners. Check the rubber hangers for cracks.

3 The lower converter itself should be checked for damage or dents (maximum $\frac{3}{4}$ in deep) which could affect its performance and/or be hazardous to your health. At the same time the converter is inspected, check the metal protecter plate under it as well as the heat insulator above it for damage or loose fasteners.

Component replacement

4 Do not attempt to remove the catalytic converters until the complete exhaust system is cool. Raise the vehicle and support it securely on jackstands. Apply some penetrating oil to the clamp bolts and allow it to soak in.

5 Remove the bolts and the rubber hangers, then separate the converters from the exhaust pipes. Remove the old gaskets if they are stuck to the pipes.

6 Installation of the converters is the reverse of removal. Use new exhaust pipe gaskets and tighten the clamp bolts to the specified torque. Replace the rubber hangers with new ones if the originals are deteriorated.

6 Secondary Air Supply system (SAS)

General description

The main component of the SAS system is the Pulse Air Feeder (PAF). Its function is supplying secondary air into the exhaust system between the front and rear catalytic converters to promote oxidation of the exhaust emissions in the rear converter.

The PAF consists of a main reed valve and a sub reed valve.

The main reed valve is actuated by the movement of a diaphragm caused by pressure pulses generated in the No. 3 cylinder. These pulses are created by the piston reciprocating motion due to the crankcase being sealed by a seal cover. This seal cover has a little hole in it for discharging engine oil and blow-by gas.

The sub reed valve is actuated by the exhaust vacuum generated from the pulses in the exhaust system between the front and rear catalytic converters.

Checking

Note: *Vehicles made in 1978 to 1980 have only one reed valve that is located in the air pipe line from the top of the catalytic converter. The same procedures also apply to these vehicles.*

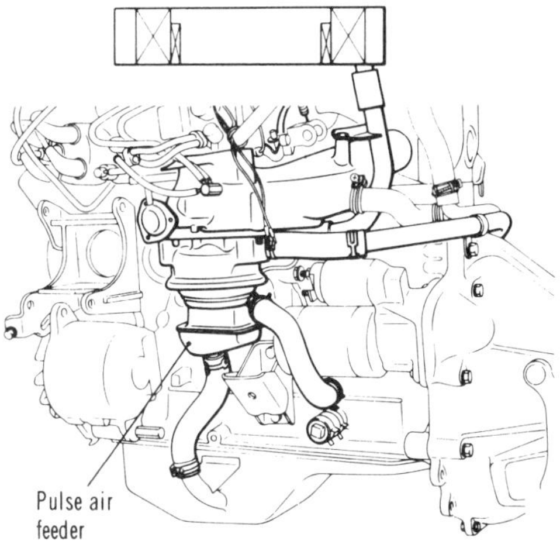

Fig. 6.2 Location of the Pulse Air Feeder (PAF) (Sec 6)

1 With the engine running, remove the hose connected to the air cleaner. Check the vacuum generated at the opening of the hose by plugging it with your finger or hand. If there is not a significant amount of vacuum present, check the hose for air or oil leaks. If no leaks are detected, the PAF should be replaced with a new one.

Component replacement

2 Remove the air cleaner and disconnect the hoses from the PAF. Remove the PAF mounting bracket bolts. Now, remove the PAF with the bracket from the intake manifold.

3 Installation is the reverse of the removal. Remember to tighten each clamp so that there is no chance of air or oil leakage. Replace any defective hoses at this time with new ones.

7 Exhaust Gas Recirculation system (EGR)

General description

The Chrysler vehicles utilize an Exhaust Gas Recirculation system (EGR) to reduce oxides of nitrogen in the exhaust.

The stringent oxides of nitrogen emission standards require high rates of EGR flow, which adversely affects driveability of the vehicle. To solve this problem, it is necessary to increase EGR flow during high load vehicle operation and decrease EGR flow to improve driveability during low load operation.

To accomplish this, two different systems are in use; one for vehicles sold in California and one for vehicles sold in the remaining 49 states. Both systems utilize an EGR control valve, a sub-EGR control valve and a thermal valve.

The California system has a dual EGR control valve (primary and secondary), which is controlled by different carburetor vacuums in response to throttle valve openings. The primary EGR valve controls EGR flow during relatively narrow throttle valve openings, while the secondary EGR valve takes over as the throttle valve is opened wider. EGR flow is suspended completely at idle and wide open throttle conditions. The thermal valve, which senses coolant temperature, controls the vacuum applied to the EGR control valve.

The 49-state EGR system utilizes a conventional-type EGR valve that is controlled by carburetor vacuum in response to various throttle valve openings. Again, EGR flow is suspended at idle and wide open throttle conditions. The thermal valve controls the vacuum applied to the EGR valve.

In both systems, the sub EGR control valve is opened and closed by a linkage connected to the throttle valve. This enables the sub-EGR valve to closely modulate the EGR flow according to the size of the throttle valve opening.

Checking

1 To check the EGR system properly, you will need a hand-held vacuum pump.

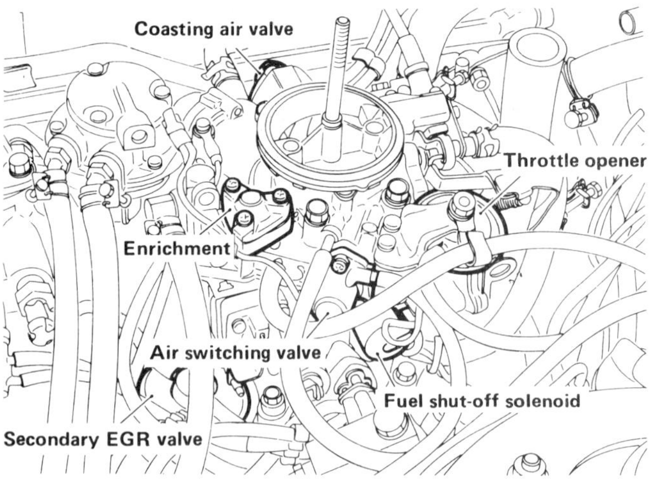

Fig. 6.3 Locations of emission control devices (Sec 7)

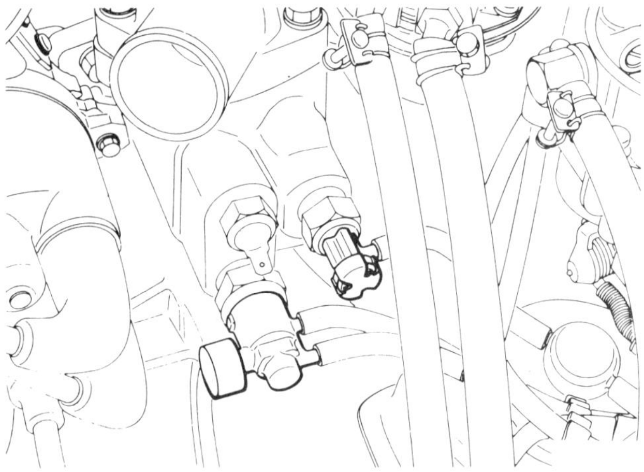

Fig. 6.4 Location of thermal valves (Sec 7)

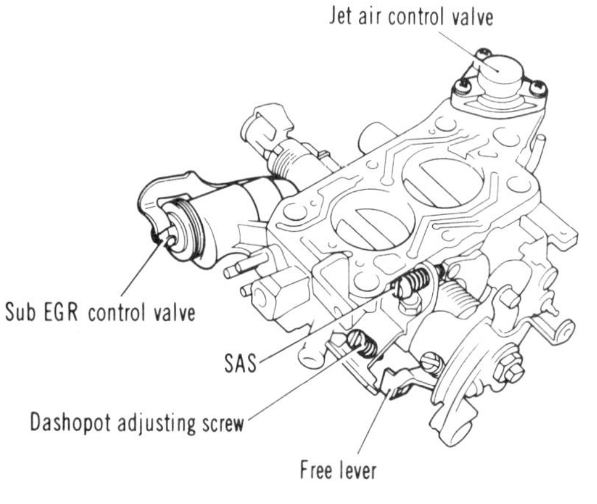

Fig. 6.5 Location of the sub-EGR valve (the carburetor does not have to be dismantled to gain access to valve) (Sec 7)

2 Check all vacuum hoses for cracks and correct installation.
3 Start the engine (it must be completely cool) and run it at idle speed.
4 Touch the underside of the secondary EGR valve diaphragm and increase the engine speed from idle to approximately 2500 rpm. No movement of the secondary EGR diaphragm should be felt. If it does move, which means the secondary EGR valve is opening, replace the thermo valve with a new one.
5 Allow the engine to warm up until the coolant temperature exceeds 131°F.
6 Again, touch the underside of the secondary EGR valve diaphragm and increase the engine speed from idle to approximately 2500 rpm. This time, the secondary EGR diaphragm should move. If it does not move, which remains the secondary EGR valve is not opening, inspect the EGR control valve and the thermo valve.
7 To check the thermo valve, disconnect the green-striped hose from the valve.
8 Connect the hand-held vacum pump to the thermo valve and apply a vacuum. If no vacuum can be held, the thermo valve is good.
9 To check the EGR control valve, disconnect the green-striped hose from the nipple on the carburetor and connect it to the hand-held vacuum pump.
10 Open the sub-EGR valve (by pulling on it by hand) and apply a vacuum to the EGR control valve with the pump.
11 If the idle speed becomes unstable, the EGR valve is operating properly. If the idle speeds remain the same, the valve is not operating properly and it should be replaced with a new one.
12 Pull on the sub-EGR valve and check for smooth operation. If the valve binds, it should be removed from its bore, cleaned thoroughly, lubricated with a small amount of light oil and reinstalled. If it still does not operate smoothly, replace it with a new one.

Component replacement

13 The EGR valve is attached to the lower part of the intake manifold, directly under the carburetor.
14 Mark the vacuum hose and fittings with pieces of numbered tape, then disconnect the vacuum hoses from the EGR valve.
15 Remove the bolts attaching the EGR valve to the intake manifold and the valve can be lifted away. You may have to tap gently on the EGR body with a soft-faced hammer to break the gasket seal.
16 When installing the EGR valve, use a new gasket and tighten the mounting bolts evenly and securely. Also, be sure to install the vacuum hoses properly.
17 The sub-EGR valve is located on the base of the carburetor and is connected by a linkage to the throttle valve.
18 Carefully pry off the spring clip and remove the pin attaching the sub-EGR valve plunger to the linkage.
19 Hold the end of the linkage up and remove the spring and the steel ball from the end of the plunger. These parts are small and easily lost, so don't drop them.
20 Slip off the rubber boot and slide the plunger out of the carburetor throttle body.
21 Before installing the plunger, clean it with solvent to remove any deposits.
22 Lubricate the plunger with a small amount of light oil, slide it into place in the carburetor throttle body and install the rubber boot.
23 Install the steel ball and spring, hold the linkage in place and insert the pin. Carefully slide the spring in place, then check for smooth operation of the valve plunger.
24 The sub-EGR adjusting screw (located on the valve linkage) has been preset at the factory and should not be disturbed.
25 The thermal valve is located just in front of the carburetor and is threaded into the coolant passage in the intake manifold.
26 Removal of the thermal valve is quite simple. Pull off the vacuum hoses that are connected to the thermal valve fittings, then unscrew the valve from the manifold.
27 When installing the thermal valve, be sure to use thread-sealing tape on the threads.

8 Heated Air Intake system (HAI)

General description

The Chrysler vehicles are equipped with a temperature-regulated air cleaner so that the carburetor can be calibrated leaner to reduce carbon monoxide and hydrocarbon emissions. Improved engine warm-up characteristics and minimized carburetor icing can also be attained with this system.

The air cleaner is equipped with an air control valve inside the snorkel to modulate the temperature of carburetor intake air which flows through the intake. The air control valve is controlled by a vacuum motor/temperature sensor combination system which responds to the intake manifold vacuum and temperature inside the air cleaner.

When the bi-metal senses a temperature inside the air cleaner below about 84°F, the air bleed valve of the temperature sensor assembly remains closed, causing intake manifold vacuum to be applied to the diaphragm of the vacuum motor. This in turn opens the air control valve and allows the preheated intake air to flow through the heat cowl and air duct into the air cleaner.

When the bi-metal senses that the temperature inside the air cleaner is above about 113°F, the air bleed valve is fully open. As a result, the intake air to the carburetor comes directly through the fresh air duct, since the air control valve is positioned at B, as shown, regardless of the intake manifold vacuum.

At intermediate temperatures, the air entering the carburetor is a blend of fresh and preheated air as regulated by the thermostatically actuated air control valve.

Checking

1 Refer to Chapter 1 for preliminary checks and an illustration to show the location of the air control valve.

2 Make sure all vacuum hoses and the heat cowl-to-air cleaner air duct are properly attached and in good condition.

3 With the engine completely cold, and the outside air temperature less than 84°F, remove the rubber tube from the end of the air cleaner snorkel. Start the engine and look into the snorkel. **Note:** *Be careful when working around moving engine parts.* The air control valve should be in the up (Heat on) position.

4 With the engine running at normal operating temperatures, check the temperature of the air entering the end of the air cleaner snorkel. If the temperature is 113°F or higher, the air control valve should be in the down (Heat off) position.

5 To check the operation of the sensor and vacuum motor, you will need a hand-type vacuum pump.

6 Remove the air cleaner from the engine (see Chapter 4) and allow it to cool to below 84°F. Hook the vacuum pump to the sensor hose and apply a vacuum to the sensor. The air control valve should be in the up (Heat on) position. If it is not, check the vacuum motor for proper operation.

7 To check the vacuum motor, apply a vacuum directly to the motor inlet fitting. The air control valve should be in the up (Heat on) position. If it is not, check to be sure it is not sticking. If the valve moves freely but will not operate properly when a vacuum is applied, the air cleaner housing will have to be replaced.

8 If the vacuum motor operates properly but the valve does not operate when vacuum is applied to the sensor, the sensor should be removed and replaced with a new one.

Component replacement

9 To replace any of these components, a complete new air cleaner housing will have to be purchased.

9 Deceleration device

General description

The deceleration device decreases hydrocarbon emissions during vehicle deceleration. It includes the Coasting Air Valve (CAV), the Air Switching Valve (ASV) and the fuel cut-off solenoid, which are built into the carburetor (some 1979 models are not equipped with a CAV).

The CAV, which is activated by carburetor ported vacuum, supplies additional air into the intake manifold, leaning the fuel/air mixture.

The ASV, which is also activated by carburetor ported vacuum, improves fuel economy by supplying additional air into the idle circuit slow passage.

In order to maintain smooth vehicle deceleration, and to prevent stalling, operation of the CAV and ASV is suspended by opening the solenoid valve (when the engine speed sensor detects engine speed at or below a specified value).

Checking

1 Start and run the engine at idle speed. It must be at normal operating temperature.

2 Disconnect the solenoid valve connector to deactivate the solenoid valve. Manifold vacuum will act on the air switching valve, causing the valve to open. If the idle speed falls excessively, or if the engine stalls, the air switching valve and solenoid valve are operating properly. If the idle speed does not change, check the vacuum passages for clogging and check the condition of the air switching valve and solenoid valve.

3 With the engine at idle, battery voltage should be present at the solenoid connector.

4 Increase the engine speed to 1500 rpm. Battery voltage should again be present at the solenoid valve connector. If there is no voltage present, the engine speed sensor is defective.

5 Increase the engine speed to 2500 rpm. Battery voltage should no longer be present at the solenoid valve connector. If voltage is present, the engine speed sensor is defective.

Component replacement

6 These valves are attached to the outside of the carburetor and removal/replacement is fairly straightforward. Reference can be made to Chapter 4.

7 Individual parts within these valves can be replaced by seeing your dealer parts department.

10 High Altitude Compensation system (HAC)

General description

This system is installed to maintain the appropriate fuel/air mixture in higher altitude areas where the available air entering the intake is too low to allow the smooth operation of the engine.

The component in this system is a small cylindrical bellows attached to a valve. It is mounted on the body panel in the engine compartment and connected to the carburetor with hoses and vented to the atmosphere at the top of the carburetor.

The small valve regulates air flow when it is raised off its seat by expanding the bellows.

When the preset bellows encounters a higher altitude, it starts to open allowing additional air to enter the main air passages. This extra air combines with the existing air to provide the system with the proper amount necessary to maintain the correct fuel/air mixture.

This system supplies varying amounts of air, depending on the altitudes it encounters. When sufficient atmosperic pressure is again restored, the valve closes and the system returns to its normal operation.

Checking

1 Check the hoses leading to the carburetor from the HAC valve for any signs of cracking or deterioration and replace them with new ones if necessary.

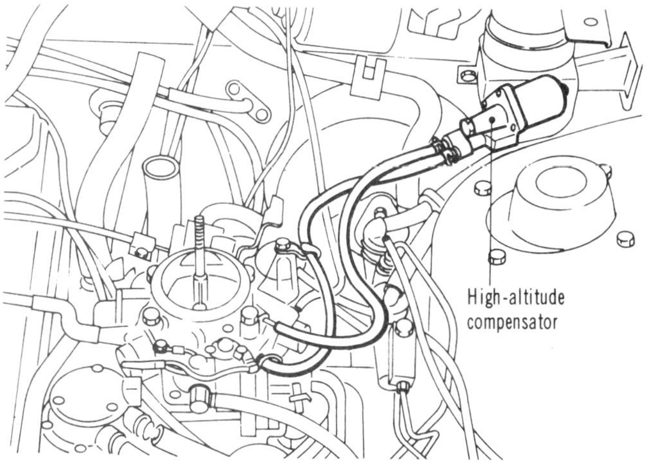

Fig. 6.6 Location of the High Altitude Compensator (Sec 10)

2 Any checks to verify the condition of the valve itself will have to be done by your dealer service department.

Component replacement

3 To replace the valve, if it is found defective, label the hoses and remove the valve mounting screws.
4 Installation is the reverse of the removal procedure. Make sure all connections are secure and mounting hardware is tight.

11 Throttle opener system

General description

This system consists of a throttle opener assembly, a solenoid valve, an engine speed sensor and a compressor switch for the air conditioning unit.

When the air conditioning is turned on and the engine speed sensor detects the decrease in engine speed, the solenoid valve opens to transfer the intake manifold vacuum to the throttle opener.

This action in turn opens the throttle valve via the throttle opener valve lever which is freely movable on the throttle valve shaft.

Consequently, the engine runs at a speed resulting from the setting of the new throttle valve opening against the air conditioner's load.

When the air conditioning is turned off, the throttle opener system stops working, and the engine runs at the original idling speed.

Checking

1 The only component to be concerned with in this system is the throttle opener assembly itself. To check and adjust the throttle opener, refer to the engine idle adjustment section in Chapter 1 because it is virtually the same thing.

Component replacement

2 The only part that may need replacing is the linkage should it get bent in some way. To do this, refer to the appropriate Section in Chapter 4.

12 Ignition timing control system

General description

Refer to the appropriate Section in Chapter 5 for the descriptions of both the contact breaker and electronic distributors.

Checking

1 Refer to the appropriate Sections in Chapters 1 and 5 to check and adjust the ignition timing.

Component replacement

2 Refer to the appropriate Section in Chapter 5 to replace or repair the contact breaker or electronic distributors.

Chapter 7A Manual transmission

Contents

Specifications

Shift fork-to-sleeve clearance	
1-2 and 3-4 speed	0.004 to 0.012 in (0.1 to 0.3 mm)
Overdrive and reverse	0.006 to 0.014 in (0.15 to 0.35 mm)
Change lever-to-selector clearance	0.004 to 0.012 in (0.1 to 0.3 mm)
Poppet spring free length	0.744 in (18.9 mm)
Neutral return spring free length	1.638 in (41.6 mm)
Resistance spring free length	1.091 in (27.7 mm)
Snap-ring-to-main drive pinion bearing clearance	0 to 0.002 in (0 to 0.06 mm)
Main drive pinion bearing snap-ring thicknesses	
White	0.091 in (2.3 mm)
No color-code	0.092 in (2.35 mm)
Red	0.094 in (2.4 mm)
Blue	0.096 in (2.45 mm)
Yellow	0.098 in (2.5 mm)
3-4 speed synchronizer hub endplay	0 to 0.003 in (0 to 0.08 mm)
3-4 speed synchronizer hub snap-ring thicknesses	
No color-code	0.085 in (2.15 mm)
Yellow	0.087 in (2.22 mm)
Green	0.090 in (2.29 mm)
White	0.093 in (2.36 mm)
Third-speed gear endplay	0.002 to 0.008 in (0.04 to 0.20 mm)
First- and second-speed gear endplay	0.002 to 0.008 in (0.04 to 0.20 mm)

Front bearing retainer-to-bearing clearance	0 to 0.004 in (0 to 0.1 mm)
Bearing spacer thicknesses	
Black	0.033 in (0.84 mm)
No color-code	0.037 in (0.93 mm)
Red	0.040 in (1.02 mm)
White	0.044 in (1.11 mm)
Yellow	0.047 in (1.2 mm)
Blue	0.051 in (1.29 mm)
Green	0.054 in (1.38 mm)
Counter reverse gear snap-ring thicknesses	
No color-code	0.059 in (1.5 mm)
Red	0.063 in (1.6 mm)
Blue	0.067 in (1.7 mm)
Green	0.073 in (1.85 mm)
Yellow	0.079 in (2.0 mm)
Reverse idler gear endplay	0.005 to 0.011 in (0.12 to 0.28 mm)
Overdrive gear endplay	0.004 to 0.010 in (0.1 to 0.25 mm)

Torque specifications	**ft-lb**	**Nm**
Transmission-to-crossmember nuts	15 to 17	20 to 24
Crossmember-to-frame bolts	30 to 37	40 to 50
Transmission mounting bolts	22 to 30	30 to 41
Mainshaft locknut	73 to 94	98 to 127
Countershaft gear locknut	50 to 72	68.6 to 98.0
Idler shaft locknut	14.5 to 43	19.6 to 58.8
Bottom cover plate bolts	6 to 7	7.8 to 9.8
Control lever housing bolts	4 to 5	4.9 to 6.9

1 General information

There are two different 5-speed manual transmissions used in these vehicles covering the years 1978 through 1983.

Both are conventional in design and nearly identical. Therefore, the various repair procedures are combined in this Chapter.

Any variations in the assemblies will be noted in the text.

2 Fluid level – checking and replacement

Refer to the appropriate Sections in Chapter 1 for checking or replacing the fluid.

3 Planning major transmission work

Before beginning the transmission disassembly, read through the entire procedure to familiarize yourself with the scope and requirements of the job.

One of the biggest problems a beginner will face when dismantling an assembly as complex as a transmission is trying to remember exactly where each part came from. To help alleviate this problem, it may be helpful to draw your own simple diagram or take instant photos during the disassembly process. Laying each part out in the order in which it was removed and tagging parts may also be useful.

Try to anticipate which parts may have to be replaced and have them available before beginning. Regardless of broken or badly worn components, there are certain items which must be replaced as a matter of course when the transmission is reassembled. These include gaskets, snap-rings, oil seals and sometimes bearings. You will also need some multi-purpose grease and a silicone-type gasket sealer to properly reassemble the transmission.

Cleanliness is extremely important when working on a precision piece of equipment such as a transmission. The work area should be kept as clean and free of dirt and dust as possible. Also, adequate space should be available to lay out the various parts as they are removed.

4 Shifter mechanism – removal and installation

1 If your vehicle is equipped with a center console, remove the screws that attach it to the vehicle. Loosen the jam nuts on the shift lever and unscrew the shift knob. Lift the console away from the lever and unplug the electrical connector behind the console.
2 Remove the screws that attach the shifter boot retainer plate to the tunnel. Lift off the retainer plate and pull back the rubber boot. It has a lip that fits over the sheet metal of the tunnel; take care not to tear it as you pull the boot back.
3 At this point, place the shift lever in the First gear position.
4 Remove the bolts attaching the shift lever assembly to the transmission and carefully lift out the lever. Plug or cover the hole with a clean rag.
5 Installation is the reverse of removal.
6 When installing the shift lever assembly, the lever must be in the First gear position.
7 Be sure to adjust the clutch as described in Chapter 8.

5 Removal

1 Disconnect the negative batttery cable from the battery.
2 Remove the air cleaner assembly by referring to Chapter 4, then disconnect the starter motor wiring and remove the starter.
3 Raise the vehicle and set it on jackstands. Place a drain pan under the transmission, remove the drain plug and allow the transmission oil to drain.
4 Remove the driveshaft as described in Chapter 8.
5 Disconnect the speedometer cable where it enters the transmission. Bend back the retaining strap that holds the speedometer cable housing to the frame crossmember and pull the speedometer cable away from the engine and transmission. Lay it on top of the left frame rail to keep it out of the way.
6 Push forward on the parking brake lever and disengage the cable from the lever. Loosen the parking brake cable housing clamp in front of the frame crossmember and slide the cable housing forward to free it from the support bracket on the crossmember. Lay the cable on top of the left frame rail to keep it out of the way. Remove the pin attaching the rear parking brake cable balancer to the parking brake lever.
7 Unplug the back-up light switch wiring harness (just behind the

steering box). Disconnect the clutch cable from the clutch control lever at the transmission bellhousing. Back off the clutch cable-adjustor and put as much free play as possible in the cable. Pull the rubber dust cover from the end of the clutch cable and slip the cable through the mounting boss on the transmission bellhousing. Lay the clutch cable on top of the left frame rail to keep it out of the way.

8 Remove the splash shield from the front of the transmission. It is attached to the engine and to the transmission.

9 Remove the bolt attaching the exhaust pipe bracket to the transmission.

10 Securely support the rear of the engine and then remove the bolts that attach the transmission bellhousing to the engine block.

11 Remove the nuts that attach the transmission to the transmission support crossmember.

12 Support the transmission with a sturdy jack (preferably one equipped with wheels or castors). Remove the bolts that attach the transmission support crossmember to the frame and lift the crossmember out from under the vehicle.

13 Carefully withdraw the transmission straight back and away from the engine by moving the transmission supporting jack toward the rear of the vehicle. It would be helpful to have an assistant at this point. You must pull the transmission straight back until it is completely free from the engine or damage to the input shaft may result.

14 Slowly lower the jack and move the transmission out from under the vehicle.

6 Disassembly

1 Before starting to disassemble the transmission, clean the exterior with a water-soluble degreaser. This will make it easier to handle and will reduce the possibility of getting dirt and other contaminants inside the transmission.

2 Remove the clutch release mechanism from the transmission bellhousing by referring to Chapter 8.

3 Release the back-up light switch wiring loom from the retaining clips and unscrew the back-up light switch from the extension housing (photo). When turning the switch, take care that the wiring harness is not twisted or damaged. There is a metal crush-type seal between the switch and the extension housing that should also be removed. There is a steel ball in the switch hole; if it does not fall out, remove it with a pencil-type magnet or other suitable tool (photo).

4 Scribe a line across the speedometer drive gear case and the extension housing (or record the position of the factory-supplied marks), then remove the locking plate and the speedometer-driven gear from the housing (photo).

5 Remove the bolts attaching the intermediate shifter cover to the extension housing (photo) and lift off the cover. You may have to tap it gently with a soft-faced hammer to break the gasket seal. Remove the sealant covering the neutral return plunger plugs (photo). Back out the plugs (by turning them in a counterclockwise direction) to release the neutral return plungers. Withdraw the spring protruding from the top right side of the extension housing. Beneath the spring is a small steel ball, which may fall into the extension housing when the right-side neutral return plunger is removed from the case.

6 Remove the bolts attaching the extension housing to the main transmission body (photo). Pull the change shifter back, and to the left, and remove the extension housing from the main transmission body (photo). You may have to tap gently with a soft-faced hammer to break the gasket seal.

7 The major difference between the 5-speed transmissions involve the components installed at the reverse idler gear.

8 Remove the snap-ring (photo) from the back side of the rear bearing on the transmission mainshaft. Remove the bearing, slip it off the mainshaft (photo) and remove the snap-ring from the front of the bearing.

9 Peel off the sealant covering the poppet spring plug holes on the right rear side of the main transmission case (photo) and remove the poppet spring plugs. Withdraw the springs and the steel balls from the poppet spring hole (photo).

10 Turn the transmission upside down, remove the bolts attaching

6.3a Carefully unscrew the back-up light switch from the extension housing

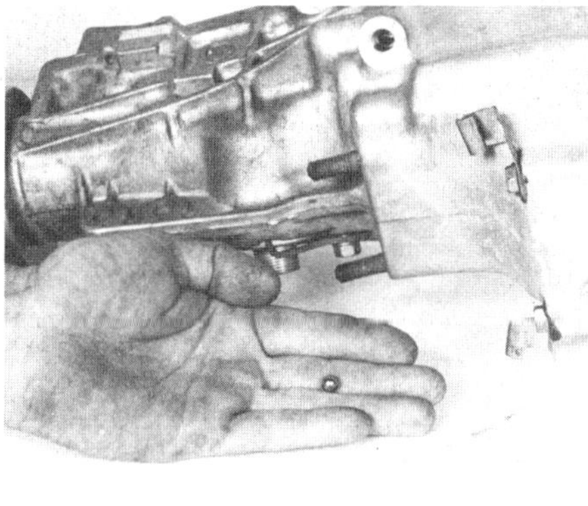

6.3b Don't forget to remove the steel ball from the back-up light switch hole

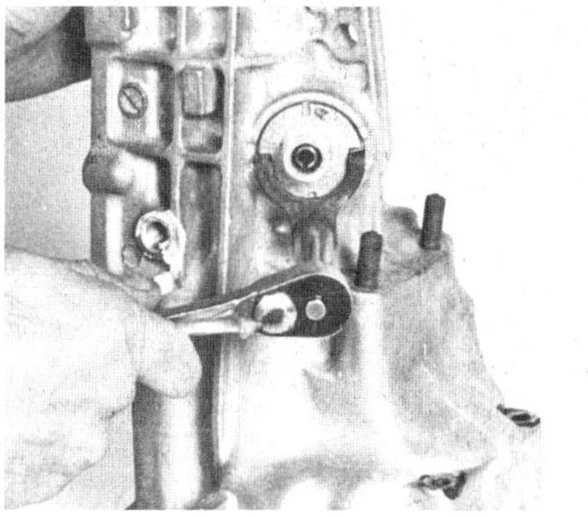

6.4 Note the position of the marks, then remove the speedometer drive gear

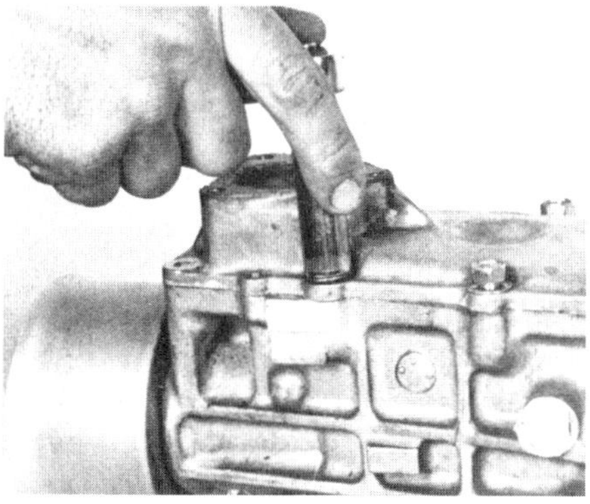

6.5a Remove the eight bolts attaching the intermediate shifter gear to the extension housing

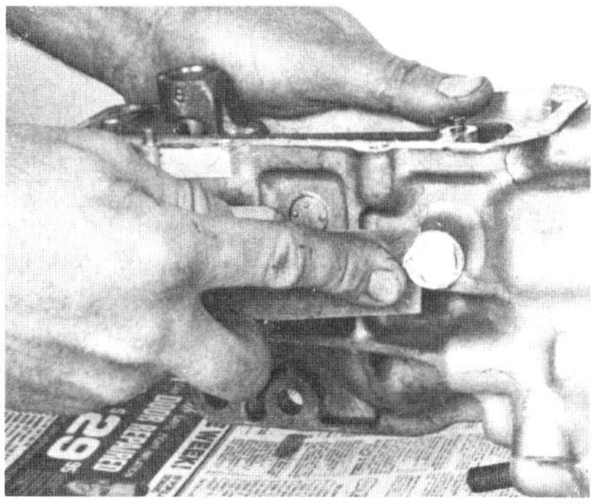

6.5b Remove the sealant covering the two Neutral-return plunger plugs

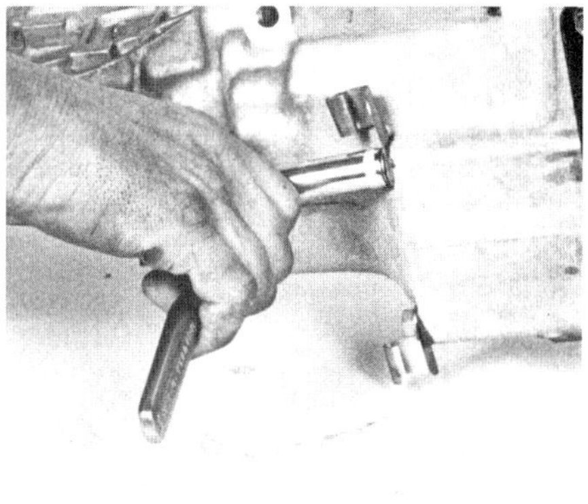

6.6a Remove the eight bolts attaching the extension housing to the main transmission body

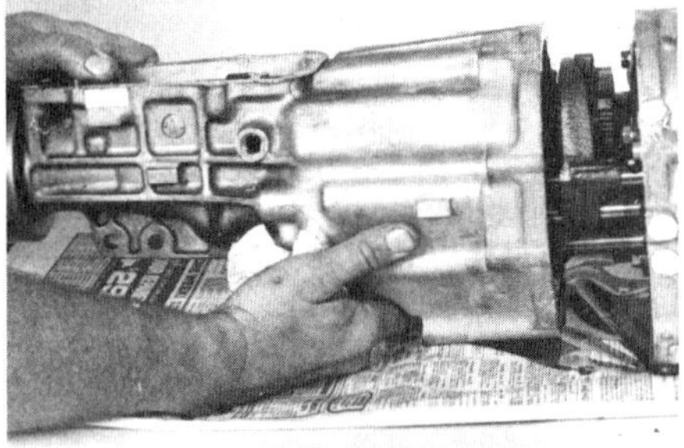

6.6b Pull straight back on the extension housing to separate it from the transmission (don't forget to pull the change shifter back and to the left first)

6.8a Remove the snap-ring from the backside of the rear bearing on the mainshaft

6.8b Slip the rear bearing off the mainshaft

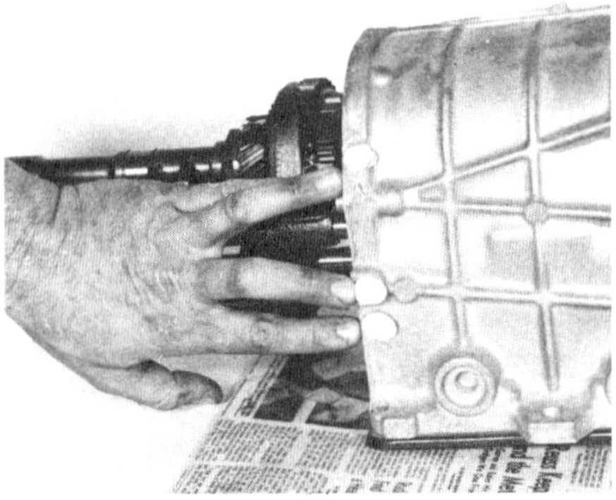

6.9a Peel off the sealant covering the poppet-spring plug holes on the right side of the case

6.9b Remove the plug, spring and steel ball from each hole

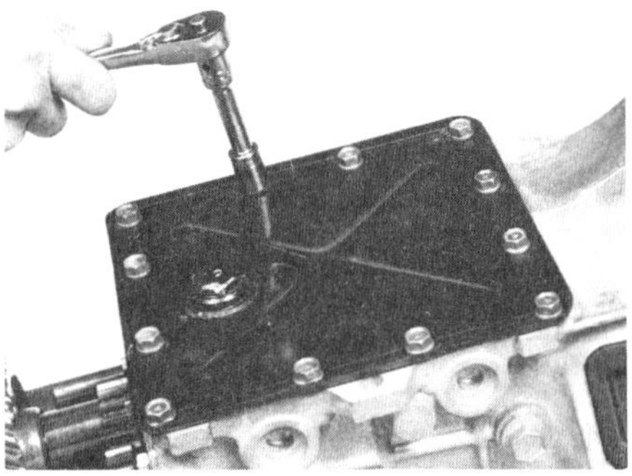

6.10 Remove the 12 bolts attaching the bottom cover plate to the transmission

6.11a Release the locking tabs before attempting to remove the nuts

6.11b Remove the large nuts from the ends of the main and countershafts

6.12 Remove the counter overdrive gear and the bearing from the countershaft with a gear puller

6.13a Using a $\frac{3}{16}$ in pin punch, drive out the 1-2 and 3-4 speed shift fork roll pins

6.13b Pull out the 1-2 and 3-4 speed shift rails

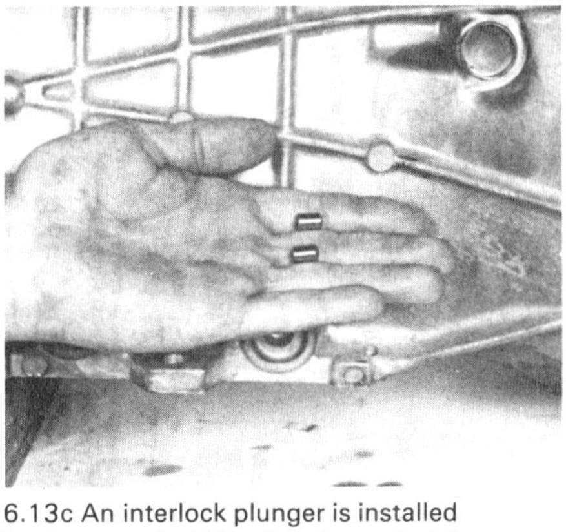

6.13c An interlock plunger is installed between each shift rail in the wall of the transmission case

the bottom cover plate to the main transmission housing (photo) and lift off the plate.

11 Remove the large nuts at the rear ends of the main and countershafts (photo). You will have to release the locking tab from the keyways in the slots before these nuts can be turned. In order to keep the shafts from turning while the nuts are loosened, you must simultaneously engage Second gear and Reverse gear (by pushing forward on the upper and lower shift rails).

12 Using an approved puller, simultaneously remove the counter overdrive gear and the ball bearing from the countershaft (photo). Then remove the spacer and the counter reverse gear.

13 Using a $\frac{3}{16}$ in pin punch, drive out the 1-2 and 3-4 speed shift fork roll pins (photo). Pull out the 1-2 and 3-4 speed shift rails through the rear of the transmission case (photo). An interlock plunger is installed between each shift rail in the wall of the transmission case; do not forget to remove them (photo).

14 Noting their position to ease reassembly, remove the 1-2 and 3-4 shift forks from the main transmission case.

15 Using a $\frac{3}{16}$ in pin punch, drive out the overdrive and reverse shift fork roll pin (photo). Pull out the overdrive and reverse shift rail with the shift fork attached (photo).

16 Remove the overdrive gear bearing and sleeve assembly from the mainshaft. You will have to use a hammer and punch to tap gently on the outer circumference of the sleeve, as you rotate the shaft, until the sleeve bearing and gear assembly can be slipped off (photos). Remove the overdrive gear synchronizer ring and slide the overdrive synchronizer assembly, the large washer and the spacer off the splines on the mainshaft (photos).

17 Remove the cotter key and nut from the end of the reverse idler gear shaft (photo) and slip the washer, the gear and the roller bearing off the shaft.

18 Remove the rear bearing retainer and the reverse idler gear plate

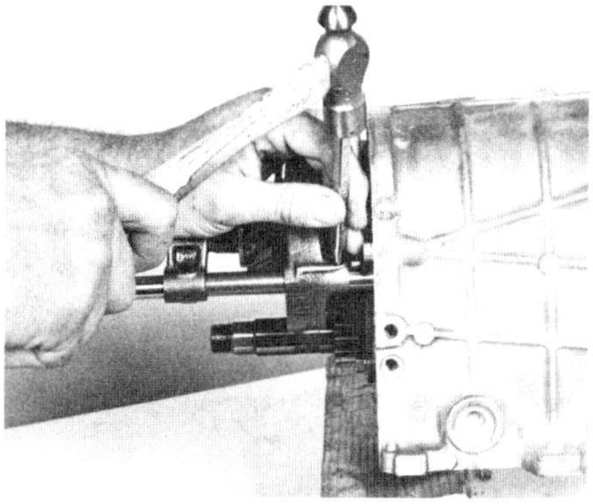

6.15a Using a $\frac{3}{16}$ in pin punch, drive out the overdrive and reverse shift fork roll pins

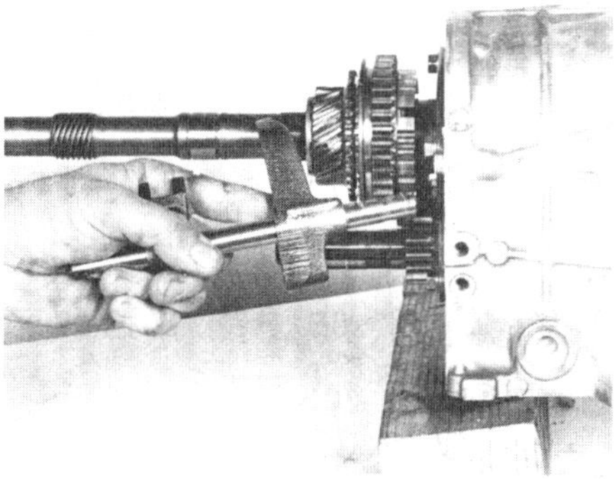

6.15b Pull out the shift rail with the fork attached

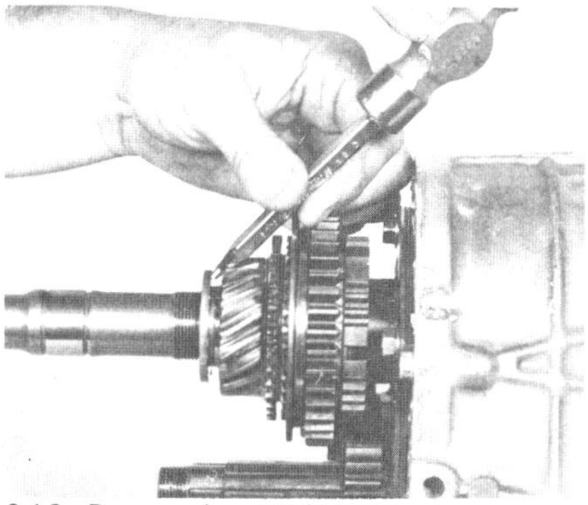

6.16a Remove the overdrive gear bearing and sleeve assembly from the mainshaft by tapping gently on the outer circumference of the sleeve

6.16b The overdrive gear assembly

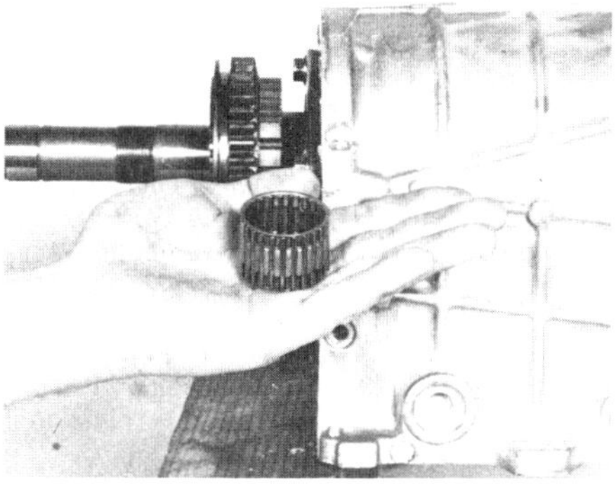

6.16c The overdrive bearing

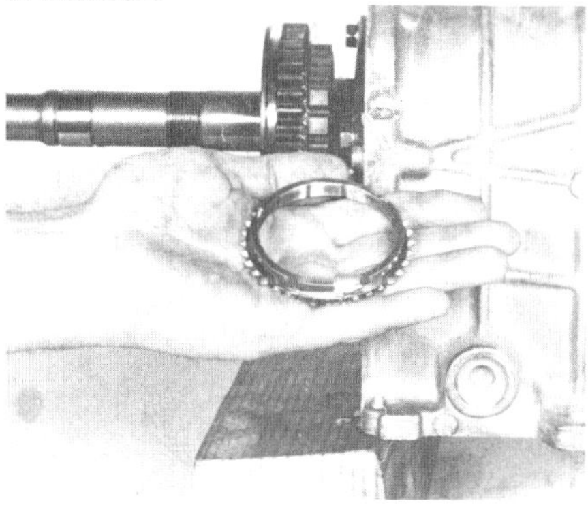

6.16d The overdrive gear synchronizer ring

6.16e The overdrive synchronizer assembly

6.17 Remove the cotter key and nut from the end of the reverse idler gear shaft

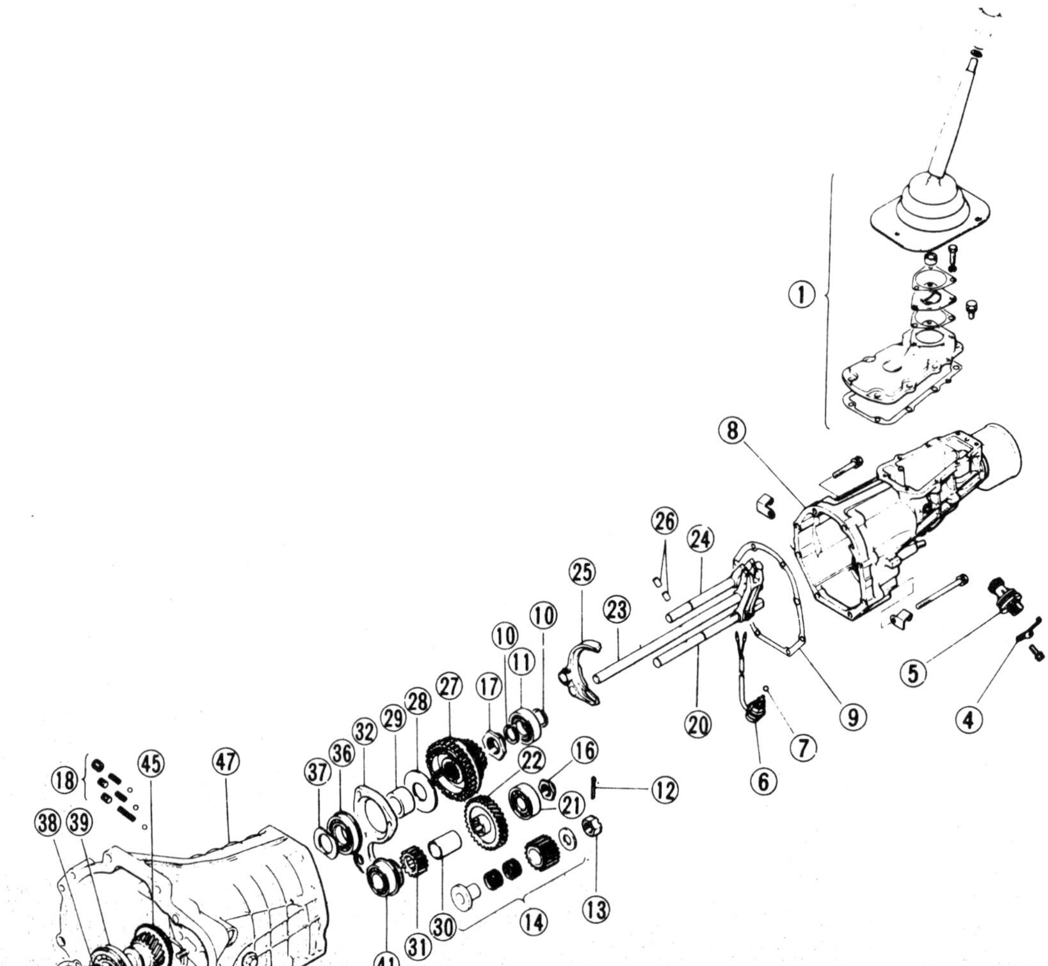

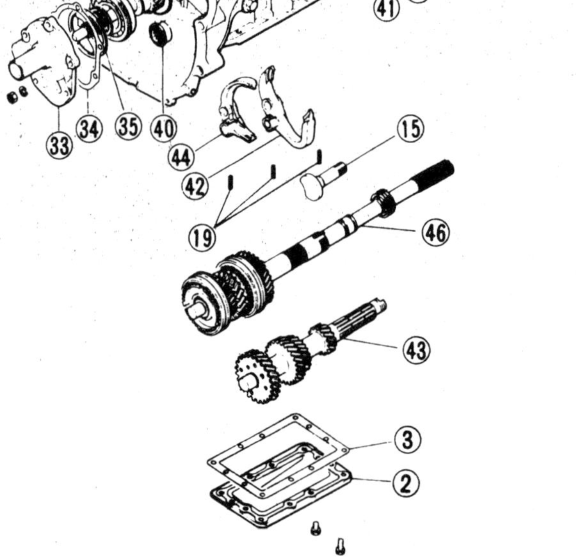

Fig. 7.1 Manual transmission components – exploded view (1600 cc engine) (Sec 6)

1 *Control lever assembly*
2 *Under cover*
3 *Under cover gasket*
4 *Sleeve clamp*
5 *Speedometer sleeve assembly*
6 *Back-up light switch*
7 *Steel ball*
8 *Extension housing*
9 *Extension housing gasket*
10 *Snap-ring*
11 *Ball bearing*
12 *Split pin*
13 *Lock nut*
14 *Reverse idler gear and bearing*
15 *Reverse idler gear shaft*
16 *Countershaft lock nut*
17 *Mainshaft lock nut*
18 *Poppet plugs, springs and balls*
19 *Spring pins*
20 *1-2 speed shift rail*
21 *Ball bearing*
22 *Overtop gear*
23 *3-4 speed shift rail*
24 *Overdrive – reverse shift rail*
25 *Overdrive – reverse shift fork*
26 *Inter lock plungers*
27 *Overtop pinion and synchronizer*
28 *Stop plate*
29 *Spacer*
30 *Spacer*
31 *Countershaft reverse gear*
32 *Front bearing retainer*
33 *Front bearing retainer*
34 *Front bearing retainer gasket*
35 *Waved washer*
36 *Mainshaft bearing*
37 *Bearing spacer*
38 *Snap ring*
39 *Main drive gear bearing*
40 *Counter front bearing*
41 *Counter rear bearing*
42 *1-2 speed shift fork*
43 *Countershaft gear*
44 *3-4 speed shift fork*
45 *Main drive gear*
46 *Mainshaft assembly*
47 *Transmission case*

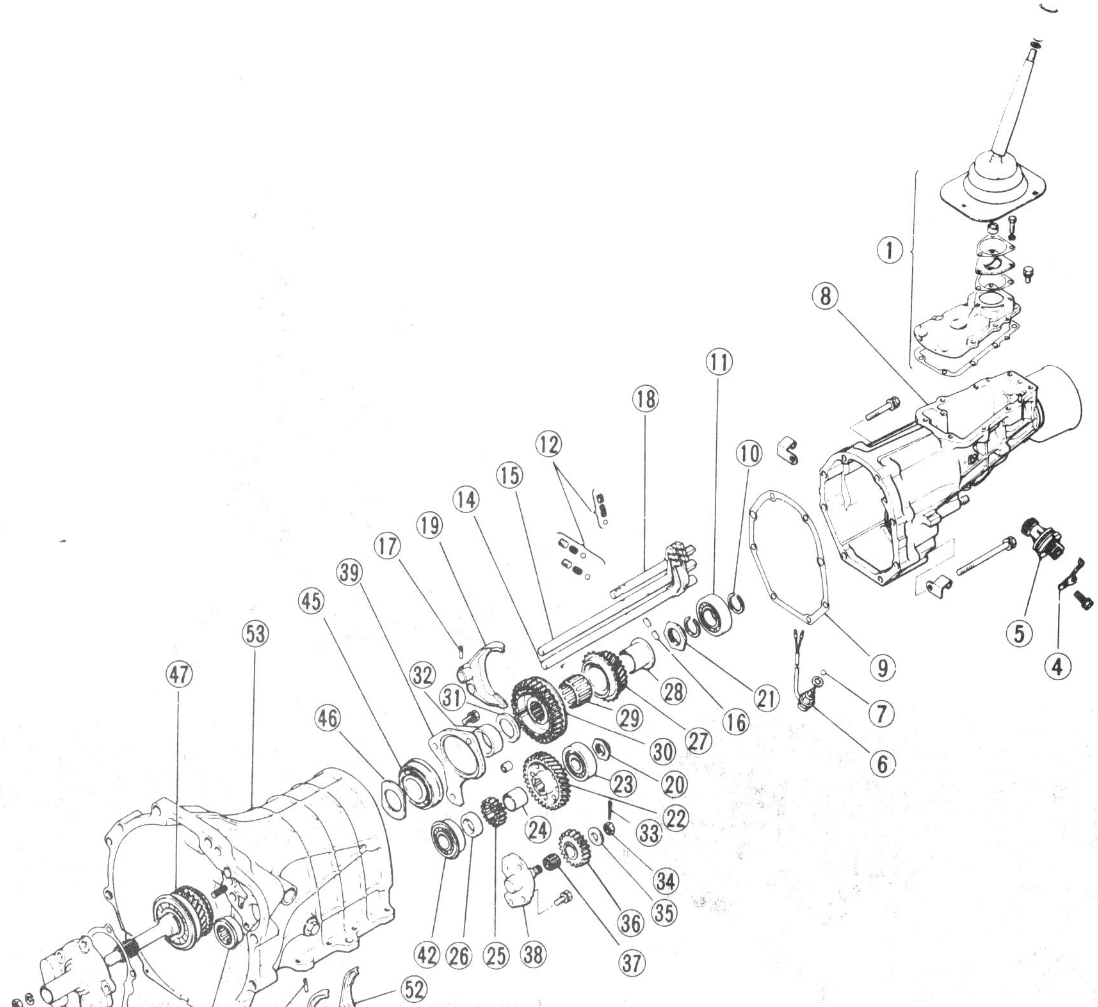

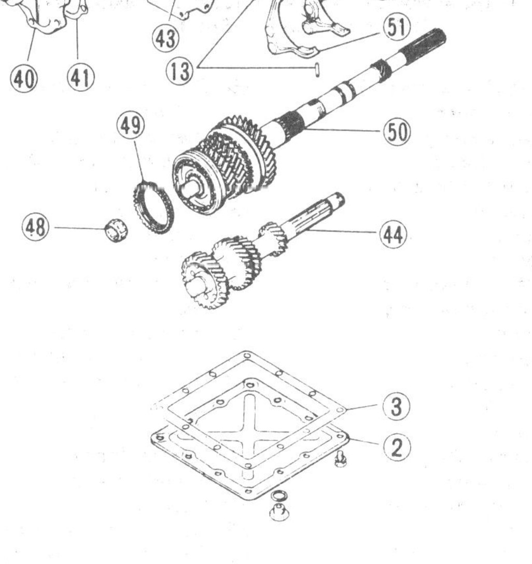

Fig. 7.2 Manual transmission components – exploded view (2000 cc and 2600 cc) (Sec 6)

1 *Control lever assembly*
2 *Under cover*
3 *Under cover gasket*
4 *Sleeve clamp*
5 *Speedometer sleeve assembly*
6 *Back-up light switch*
7 *Steel ball*
8 *Extension housing*
9 *Extension housing gasket*
10 *Snap-ring*
11 *Mainshaft rear bearing*
12 *Poppet plug, spring and ball*
13 *Spring pin*
14 *1-2 speed shift rail*
15 *3-4 speed shift rail*
16 *Interlock plunger*
17 *Spring pin*
18 *Overdrive – reverse shift rail*
19 *Overdrive – reverse shift fork*
20 *Countershaft lock nut*
21 *Mainshaft lock nut*
22 *Counter overdrive gear*
23 *Counter rear bearing*
24 *Spacer*
25 *Counter reverse gear*
26 *Spacer*
27 *Overdrive gear*
28 *Bearing sleeve*
29 *Needle bearing*
30 *Overdrive – reverse synchronizer assembly*
31 *Stop plate*
32 *Spacer*
33 *Split pin*
34 *Slotted nut*
35 *Thrust washer*
36 *Reverse idler gear*
37 *Needle bearing*
38 *Reverse idler gear shaft*
39 *Rear bearing retainer*
40 *Front bearing retainer*
41 *Front bearing retainer gasket*
42 *Counter center bearing*
43 *Counter front bearing*
44 *Countershaft gear*
45 *Mainshaft center bearing*
46 *Spacer*
47 *Main drive gear*
48 *Needle bearing*
49 *Synchronizer ring*
50 *Mainshaft assembly*
51 *3-4 speed shift fork*
52 *1-2 speed shift fork*
53 *Transmission case*

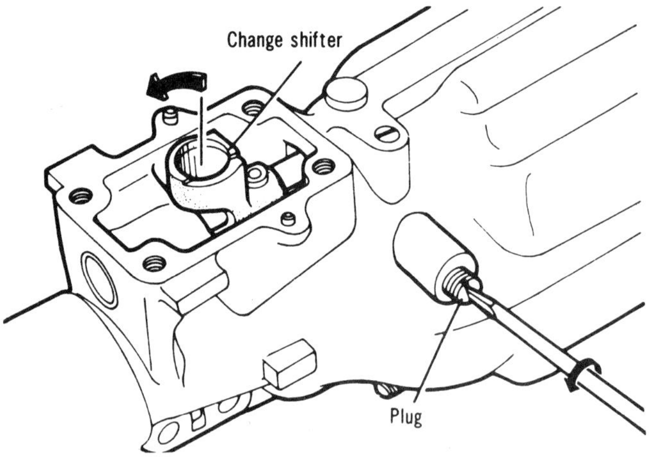

Fig. 7.3 Remove the plugs holding the neutral-return plungers and springs in place (Sec 6)

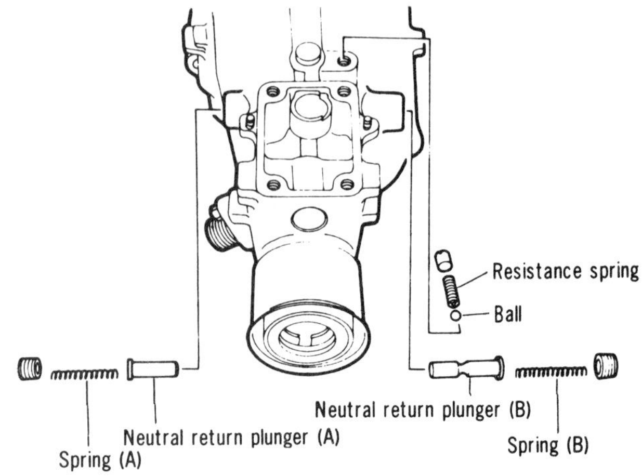

Fig. 7.4 Neutral-return plunger and spring components – exploded view (Sec 6)

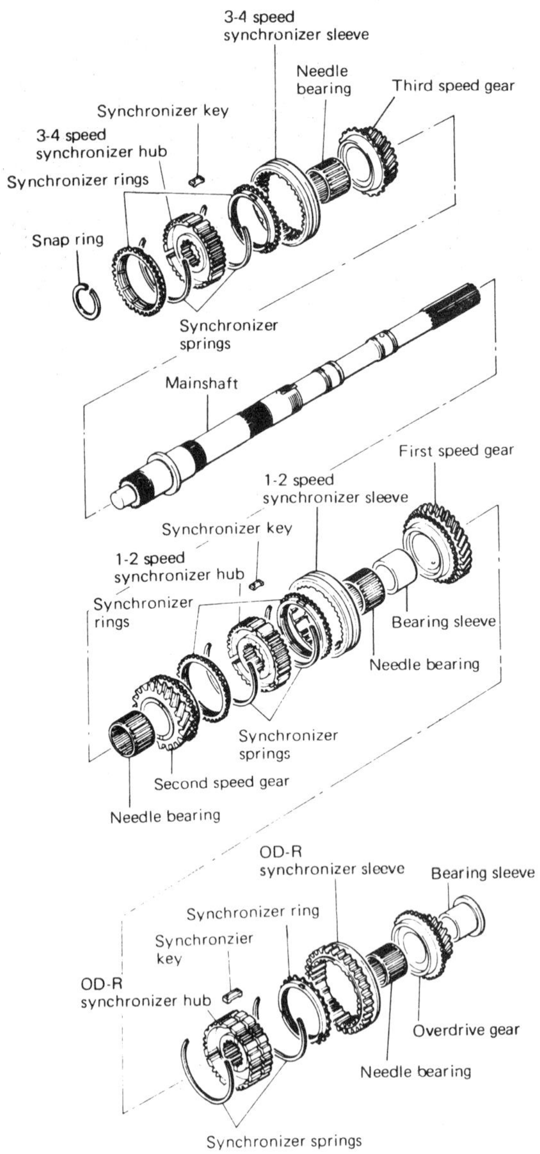

Fig. 7.5 Mainshaft components – exploded view (Sec 6)

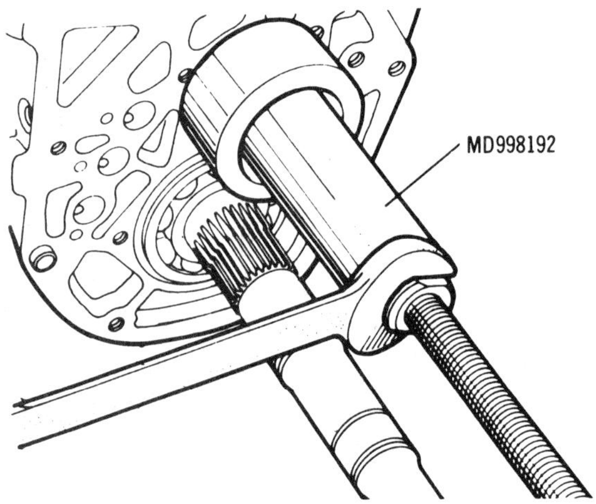

Fig. 7.6 Remove the counter rear bearing (Sec 6)

from the main transmission case (photos). Using a suitable punch, carefully drive the reverse idler gear shaft out of the main transmission case (photo).

19 Remove the nuts attaching the front bearing retainer to the main transmission case (photo). Remove the retainer and slip the spacer off the shaft (photo).

20 With the counter gear pressed to the rear, remove the rear bearing snap-ring (photo). Using the bearing puller (special tool No MD-998192), or other suitable bearing puller, remove the counter rear bearing. Remove the snap-ring from the countershaft front bearing. Using the same bearing puller, pull out the front countershaft bearing (photo) and slip the counter gear out of the main transmission case toward the front (photo).

21 Remove the main drive pinion and bearing assembly through the front of the main transmission case (photo). To separate the bearing from the main drive pinion, remove the snap-rings and pull the bearing using special tool No MD-998056, or another suitable puller. Pull off the main drive pinion-to-mainshaft bearing (photo). Remove the synchronizer ring from the mainshaft (photo). Using special tools numbered MD-998056 and MD-998056-10, remove the mainshaft ball-bearing from the rear of the main transmission cases. Remove the mainshaft assembly from the case, toward the front (photo).

22 Disassemble the mainshaft gears and bearings in the following order: using the previously mentioned puller, remove the first-speed gear. This will also remove the inner row of ball-bearings and their race from the rear of the mainshaft. Slip off the 1-2 speed synchronizer, the

6.18a Remove the rear bearing retainer

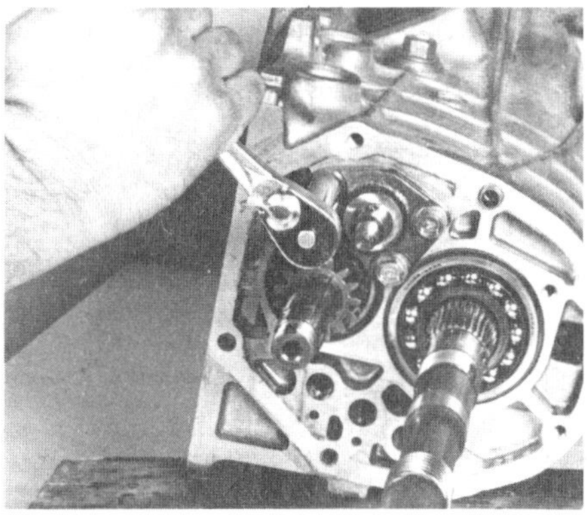

6.18b Remove the reverse idler gear plate

6.18c Using a large punch, and working from inside the case, carefully drive out the reverse idler gear shaft

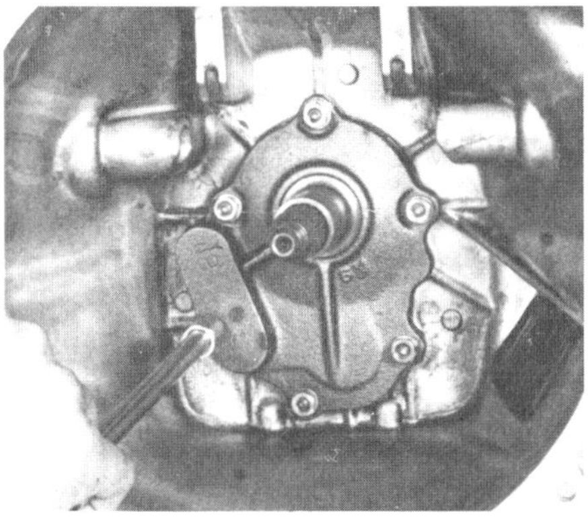

6.19a Remove the six nuts attaching the front bearing retainer to the case

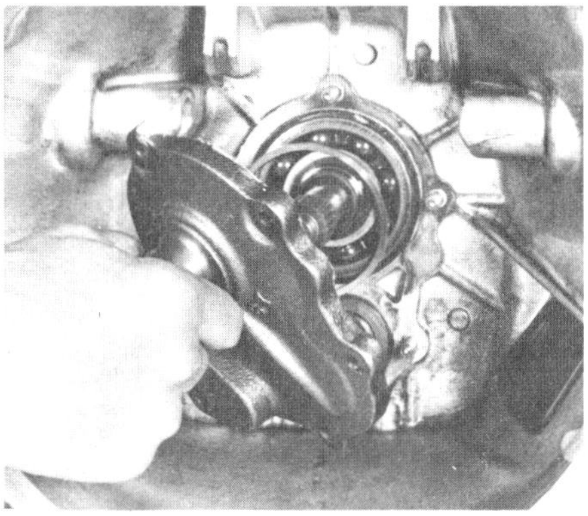

6.19b Remove the retainer and the spacer

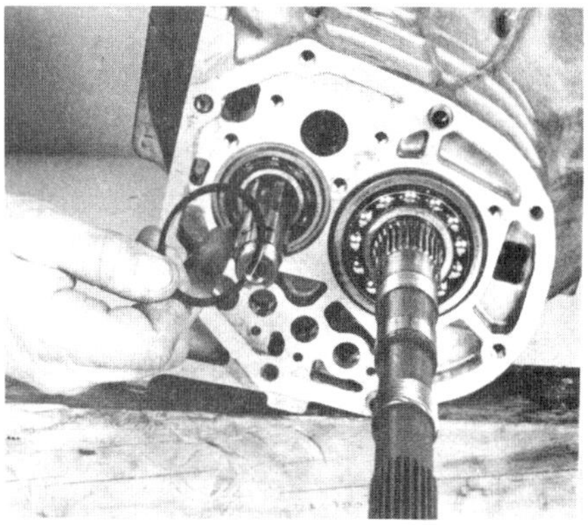

6.20a With the counter gear pressed to the rear, remove the rear bearing snap-ring

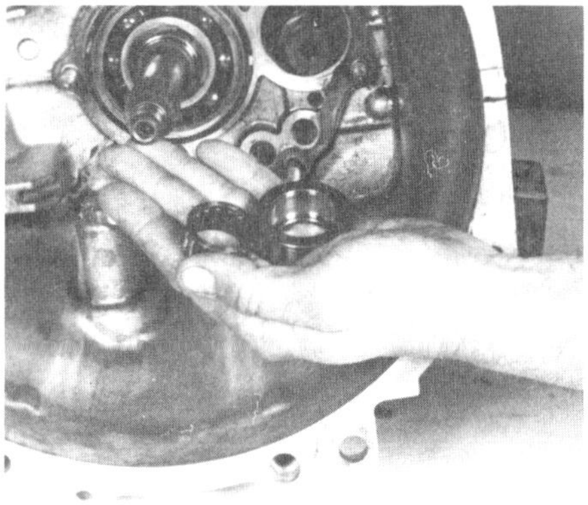

6.20b The countershaft front bearing

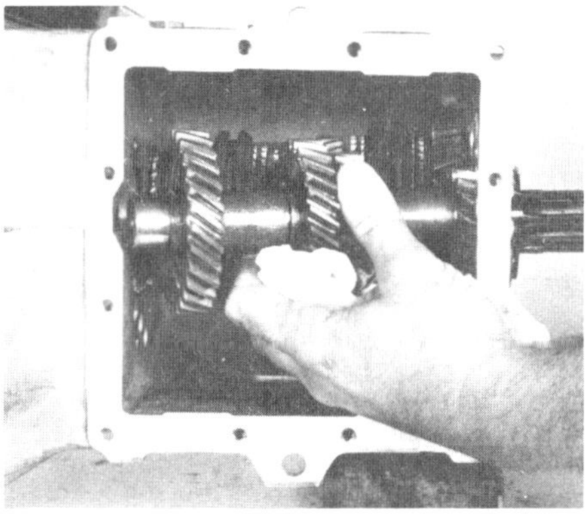

6.20c Slip the counter gear out of the case toward the front

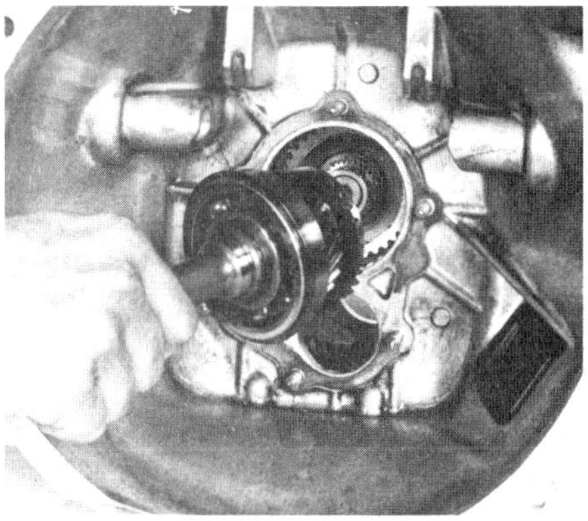

6.21a Remove the main drive pinion and bearing assembly through the front of the case

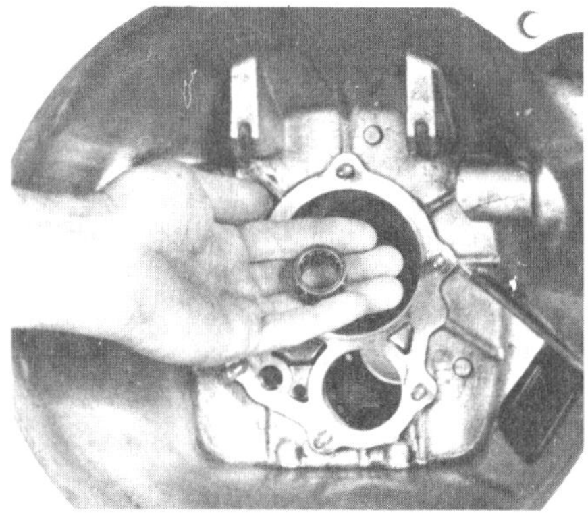

6.21b Pull off the main drive pinion-to-mainshaft bearing

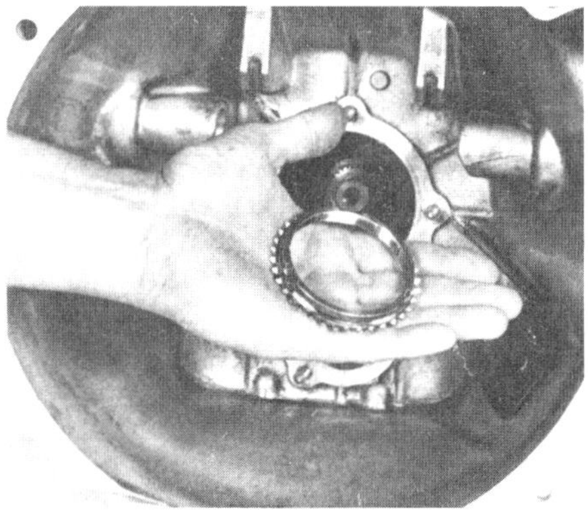

6.21c Remove the synchronizer ring from the mainshaft

6.21d Remove the mainshaft assembly from the case toward the front

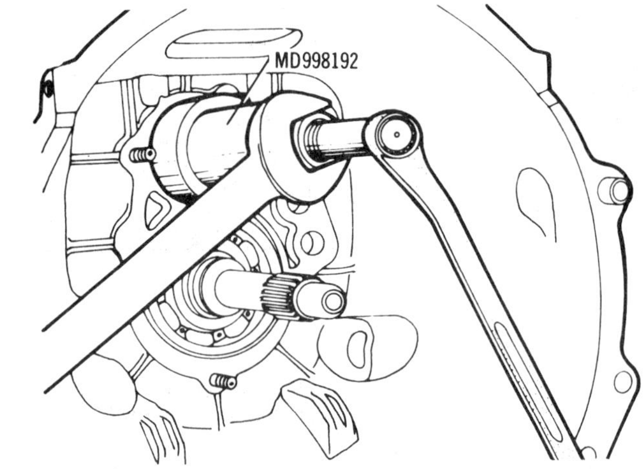

Fig. 7.7 Remove the counter front bearing (Sec 6)

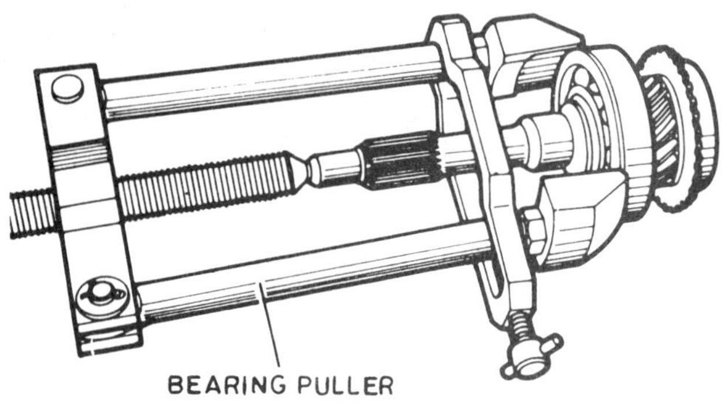

Fig. 7.8 Remove the bearing from the main drive pinion (Sec 6)

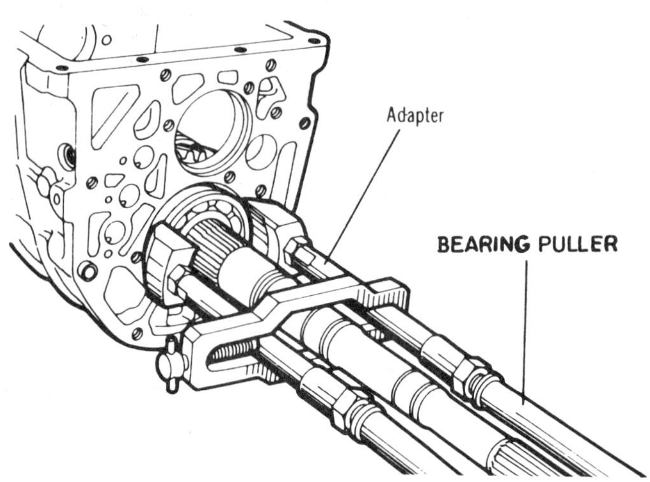

Fig. 7.9 Remove the mainshaft bearing from the rear of the case (Sec 6)

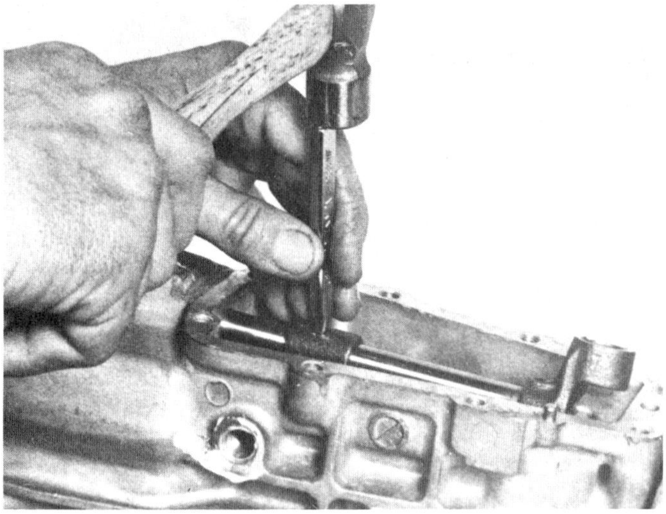

6.23 Drive the roll pins out of the control shaft stabilizer tabs and the shifter receiver

second speed gear and the roller bearing from the rear of the mainshaft. Remove the snap-ring from the forward end of the mainshaft, then remove the 3-4 speed synchronizer, the third speed gear, the roller bearing and the sleeve.

23 From the top of the extension housing (using a $\frac{3}{16}$ in pin punch) drive the roll pins out of the control shaft stabilizer tabs and the control shaft shifter receiver (photo). Pull the control shaft forward and out of the extension housing.

7 Inspection

1 Inspect the diassembled parts after cleaning them with solvent and drying them thoroughly. Repair or replace any parts that are found to be defective.

Transmission case and extension housing

2 Check the transmission case and extension housing for cracks and damage, especially at the bearing outer race bosses. Small nicks and burrs can be removed with a fine file.

Mainshaft

3 Check the mainshaft for worn or damaged gear mounting areas and worn or damaged splines. Check the first speed gear and overdrive gear spacer bushing for damage and wear.

Main drive gear

4 On the main drive gear assembly, check the front end outer diameter and the inner diameter of the needle bearing contact areas for damage and wear. Check the synchronizer cone surfaces for wear and damage. Check the splines for wear and damage and check the fit of the clutch disc on the shaft. It should move freely on the splines, but must not be excessively loose.

Gears

5 Check all gears for worn and damaged teeth. Check the inner diameter and both ends of each gear for wear and damage. Also, check the contact surface of the synchronizer cone for wear and damage.

Synchronizer rings

6 Check the gear teeth and cone inside diameter for wear and damage (photo). With the synchronizer rings assembled to their mating gears, check the synchronizer ring-to-gear clearance. If the clearance is greater than specified, replace the synchronizer ring.

Synchronizer sleeve and hub

7 With the hub and sleeve assembled, see if the sleeve slides smoothly. Also, check for excessive looseness in the direction of rotation. If either part is defective, both the hub and sleeve must be replaced as an assembly.

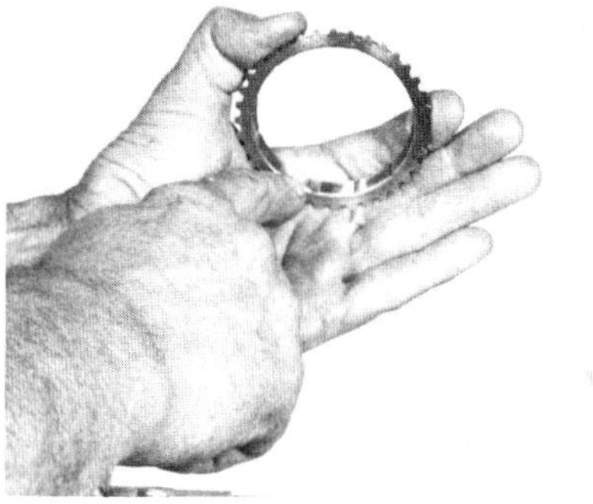

7.6 Check the inside diameter of the synchronizer rings for evidence of wear

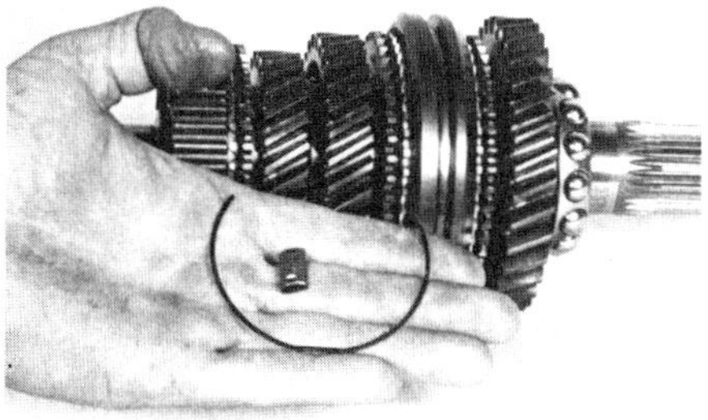

7.8 Synchronizer piece and spring

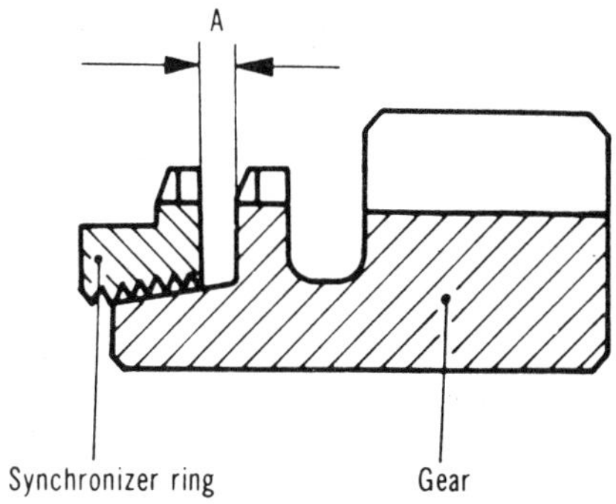

Fig. 7.10 Check the synchronizer ring-to-gear clearance (A) (Sec 7)

Synchronizer piece and spring

8 Check the synchronizer piece for wear and damage, especially at the projection. Check the springs for deterioration and cracks (photo).

Reverse idler gear and shaft

9 Inspect the teeth and both sides of the gear for wear and damage. Check the shaft for cracks, evidence of seizure and wear.

Shift forks, rails and selectors

10 Check the clearance between the shift fork and the groove in the synchronizer and compare it to the Specifications. Inspect the poppet ball slots in the rails for wear. Check the change lever-to-selector clearance and compare it to the Specifications.

Needle and ball bearings

11 Check the needle bearings for roller surface damage such as pitting, cracks and scoring. Assemble the needle bearings and gears on their respective shafts and check to see if they rotate smoothly and quietly. Inspect all ball-bearings for wear and damage. See if they rotate smoothly and quietly. If there is any doubt as to the condition of a bearing, replace it.

Poppet springs and plungers

12 Inspect the interlock plungers for wear and damage. Check the forward end of the neutral return plunger for wear. Also, check the resistance ball slot for wear. Check the poppet and neutral return springs for cracks. Measure the springs and compare the results to the Specifications.

Control lever

13 Check the upper and lower levers for chatter marks and the stop plate for wear. Inspect the plastic bushing in the lower end of the lever. If it is deformed or worn, replace it. Check the rubber boot for damage and make sure the lever operates smoothly.

8 Reassembly

1 As was previously mentioned, be sure to wash all parts in solvent and dry them thoroughly before beginning reassembly. Be sure to use new gaskets, seals and roll pins. It is not advisable to reuse snap-rings. When an old snap-ring must be reused, make certain it is not bent. Straighten it, if necessary, so that it can be installed securely. Lubricate all bearings and any other sliding and rotating parts with multi-purpose grease before reassembly. Also, apply a layer of grease to all oil seal lips.

2 Install the ball-bearings onto the main drive pinion using the main drive gear bearing installer (special tool No. MD-998029) or other suitable bearing driver. Do not hammer on the outer bearing race, as damage to the bearing will result.

3 After installing the bearing, select a snap-ring that will provide the specified clearance between the snap-ring and the bearing (a list of available snap-ring thicknesses is included in the Specifications Section) and install it into place on the main drive pinion. Measure the clearance by slipping a feeler gauge between the snap-ring and the inner race of the bearing (photo).

4 Install the mainshaft components in the following order: assemble the 3-4 speed and 1-2 speed synchronizers. The front and rear ends of the synchronizer sleeve and hub can be identified as shown. The synchronizer spring can also be installed as shown. Slip the needle bearing, the third speed gear, the synchronizer ring and the 3-4 speed synchronizer assembly onto the mainshaft from the front end. Be careful not to confuse the front and rear ends of the synchronizer assembly. Install a snap-ring of the proper size, so that the 3-4 speed synchronizer hub endplay will be within the specified tolerance (photo). A list of available snap-ring thicknesses is included in the Specifications Section. Check the third speed gear endplay with a feeler gauge. Install the needle bearing, the second speed gear, the synchronizer assembly, the bearing sleeve, the needle bearing, the first speed gear and the bearing spacer onto the mainshaft from the rear end. With the bearing spacer pushed forward, check the second and first speed gear end-play with a feeler gauge (photo). 7A

8.3 Measure the clearance between the snap-ring and inner race when installing the bearing on the main drive pinion

8.4a Check the 3-4 speed synchronizer hub endplay by slipping a feeler gauge between the snap-ring and hub

8.4b With the bearing spacer pushed forward, check the second and the first speed gear endplay with a feeler gauge

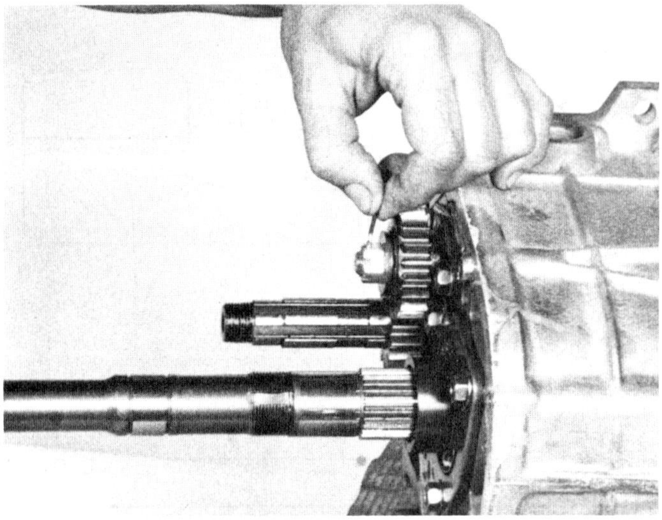

8.18 Install a new cotter pin in the reverse idler gear locknut and shaft

8.19 Check the reverse idler gear endplay with a feeler gauge

5 Slide the mainshaft assembly into the transmission case and insert the main center bearing outer race into place in the case. Assemble the rear ball-bearings and inner race onto the mainshaft.
6 Install the needle bearing assembly and the synchronizer ring into place on the front of the mainshaft (make sure that the synchronizer pieces line up with the slots in the synchronizer ring).
7 Install the main drive pinion into place in the front of the main transmission case.
8 Install the countershaft into the transmission case. It may be necessary to slide the rear part of the mainshaft to the back of the case to provide enough clearance to install the countershafts.
9 Place the snap-ring in the groove of the countershaft front bearing outer race.
10 Slip the needle bearing into the countershaft front bearing outer race, then install the outer race into the transmission case. Drive it into place by tapping carefully with a soft-faced hammer.
11 Install the snap-ring on the countershaft rear bearing outer race, then seat the countershaft rear bearing in place in the transmission case using the bearing installer (special tool No MD-998199) or other suitable tool. Push the countershaft to the rear of the case as the bearing is installed.
12 Remove the lip seal from the front bearing retainer housing and install a new seal using special tool No MD-998200, or other suitable seal driver.
13 The front bearing retainer must be installed temporarily to check the retainer-to-front bearing clearance.
14 Lay a small piece of type PB-1 Plastigage across the outer race of the bearing. Install the spacer and the retainer, using a new gasket. A small amount of grease should hold the spacer in place in the retainer. Tighten the retainer mounting nuts to the specified torque, then remove the retainer and compare the width of the Plastigage material to the chart on the Plastigage package to obtain the clearance.
15 Compare the measured clearance to the Specifications. If the clearance is greater than specified, replace the spacer with a thicker one (a list of available spacer thicknesses is included in the Specifications Section).
16 Once the bearing-to-retainer clearance has been checked and properly adjusted, coat both sides of the gasket with a silicone-type gasket sealer, lubricate the lip seal and install the retainer. Use new lock washers and tighten the mounting nuts to the specified torque.
17 Install the rear bearing retainer in place on the main transmission case and tighten the attaching bolts securely.
18 Slide the reverse idler gear shaft, using the bolts as a guide, into the main transmission case and tighten the bolts securely. Slip the reverse idler gear needle bearing, the reverse idler gear and the thrust washer (with the ground side toward the gear) onto the reverse idler gear shaft. Thread on the locknut and tighten it to the specified torque. Line up the hole in the shaft with one of the slots in the nut and install a new cotter pin (photo).

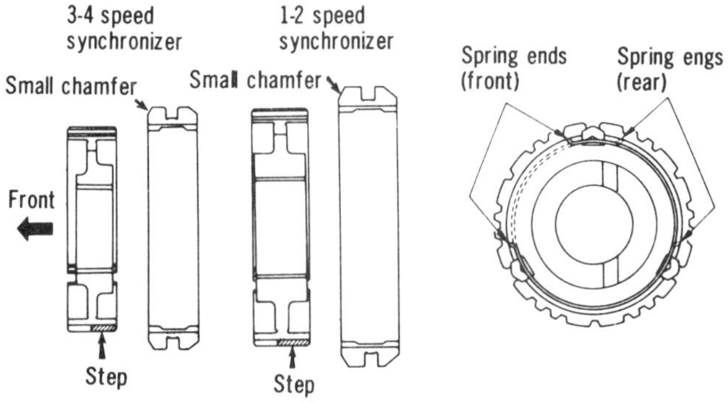

Fig. 7.11 Synchronizer sleeve and hub identification and spring installation (Sec 8)

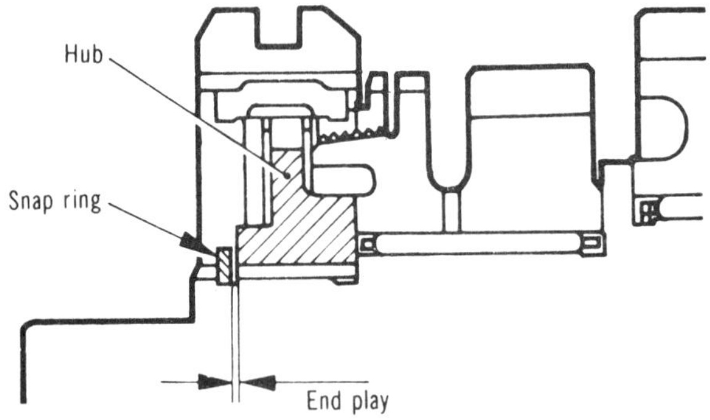

Fig. 7.12 Synchronizer hub endplay (Sec 8)

19 Check the reverse idler gear endplay with a feeler gauge and compare it to the Specifications (photo).
20 Assemble the over drive synchronizer. The long flat on the synchronizer piece must be facing forward. Make sure that the synchronizer piece engages the slot in the synchronizer ring. The spring can be installed in a manner similar to the installation of the 3-4 and 1-2 speed synchronizer spring.
21 Install the spacer, the stop plate, the overdrive synchronizer assembly, the overdrive gear bearing sleeve, the needle bearing, the synchronizer ring and the overdrive gear onto the mainshaft from the rear end. Thread the locknut onto the mainshaft and tighten it to the specified torque.

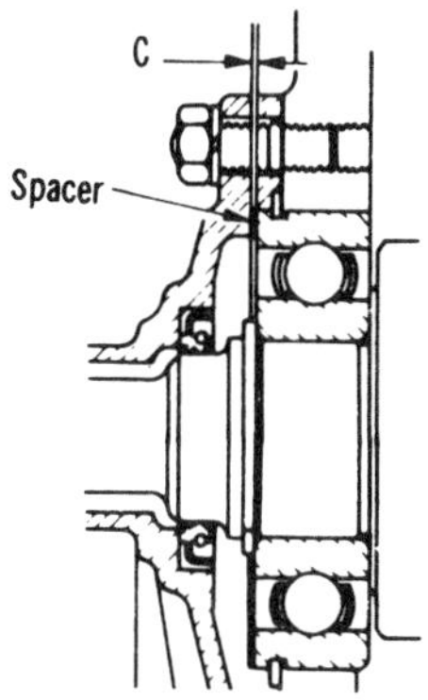

Fig. 7.13 Front bearing retainer-to-bearing clearance (C) (Sec 8)

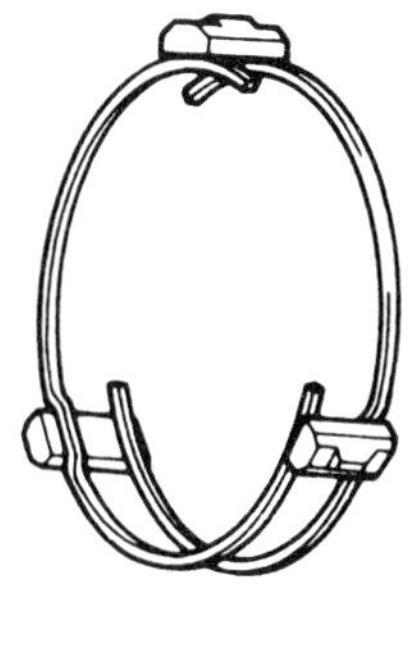

Fig. 7.14 When installing the synchronizer springs, make sure that the front and rear ones are not faced in the same direction (Sec 8)

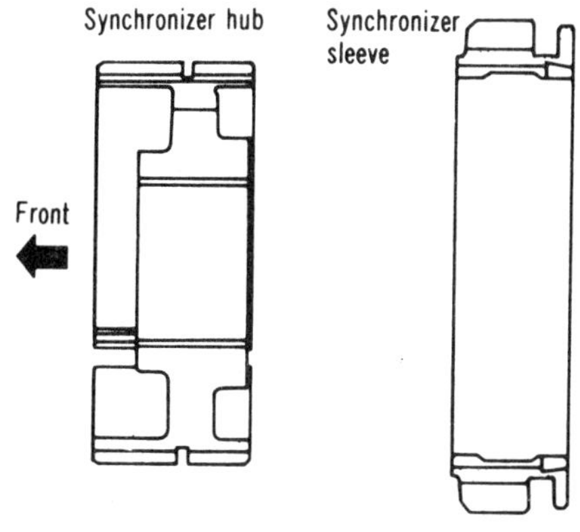

Fig. 7.15 Synchronizer hub and sleeve identification (Sec 8)

22 Check the overdrive gear endplay with a feeler gauge and compare it to the Specifications. Stake the locking collar on the locknut into the keyway on the mainshaft with a centerpunch.

23 Install the first spacer, the counter reverse gear and the second spacer onto the countershaft. Slip the 1-2 speed and the 3-4 speed shift forks into their respective synchronizer sleeves inside the main transmission case.

24 Slide the 1-2 shift rail into the main transmission case from the rear as you simultaneously slide the counter overdrive gear onto the countershaft from the rear. The counter overdrive gear must fit into the notch ground into the shift rail.

25 Slip the 1-2 shift rail through the holes in the shift fork and into the recess in the front of the transmission case. Install the roll pin through the 1-2 speed shift fork and the 1-2 shift rail. Make sure that the slot in the roll pin is installed axially to the shift rail.

26 Slip the reverse/overdrive shift fork into place on its synchronizer sleeve. Slide the reverse/overdrive shift rail through the shift fork and into the hole in the transmission case. Install the roll pin into the shift fork and reverse/overdrive shift rail. Again, make sure that the slot in the roll pin is installed axially to the shift rail.

27 Slide the interlock plungers into position in the transmission case end (between the shift rails). You may have to use some light grease to hold them in position.

28 Slip the 3-4 shift rail through the reverse/overdrive shift fork, the rear of the transmission case, the two inside shift forks and into the recess in the front of the transmission case. Install the roll pin into the 3-4 speed shift fork and the 3-4 shift rail.

29 Install the counter rear bearing on the end of the countershaft. Thread on the retaining nut and tighten it to the specified torque. Remember that the transmission must be in reverse and second gear simultaneously in order to tighten the nut on the end of the countershaft.

30 Using a center punch, stake the locking collar on the locknut into the keyway on the countershaft.

31 Insert the 3 balls and the 3 poppet springs into each shift rail. The small end of the spring must be against the steel ball. Thread the plugs into the transmission case and tighten them until the head of the plug is at the specified distance below the end of the hole in the transmission case. After installation, seal the plug head with silicone-type gasket sealer.

32 Install the inner snap-ring, the ball-bearings and the outer snap-rings onto the rear end of the mainshaft. Use special tool No MD-998199, or a similar type bearing installer.

33 Using a new gasket and gasket sealant, install the extension housing onto the rear of the main transmission case. When installing the housing, turn the change shifter down and to the left. Apply a thread sealant to each bolt, then install and tighten them to the specified torque.

34 Apply a thin coat of silicone-type gasket sealer to the outside of the speedometer drive gear sleeve. Install the speedometer drive gear assembly into the extension housing. Be sure to line up the mating marks. Make sure the gears are properly meshed before installing the lock plate and tightening the bolts.

35 Install the neutral-return plungers, the springs and the plugs in each side of the extension housing. The short plunger must be installed

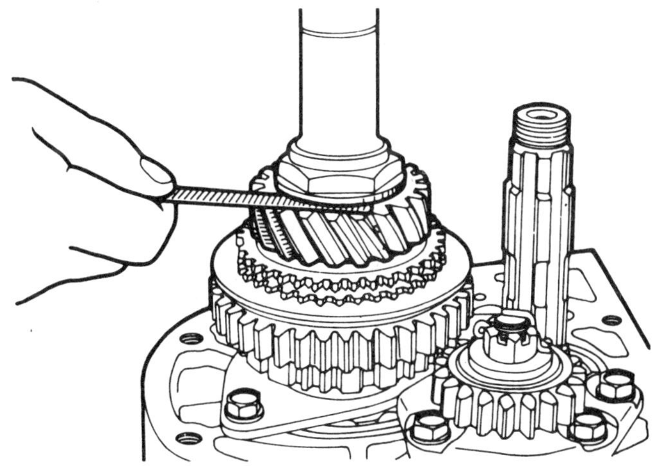

Fig. 7.16 Check the overdrive gear endplay with a feeler gauge

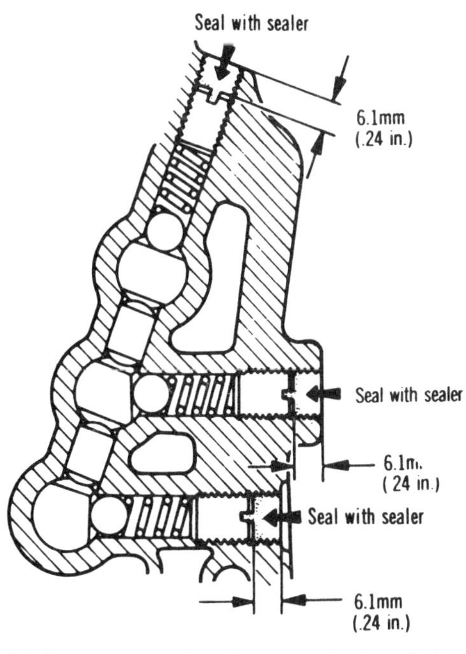

Fig. 7.17 The poppet-spring plugs must be installed until the distance from the plug head to the top of the hole is exactly as specified

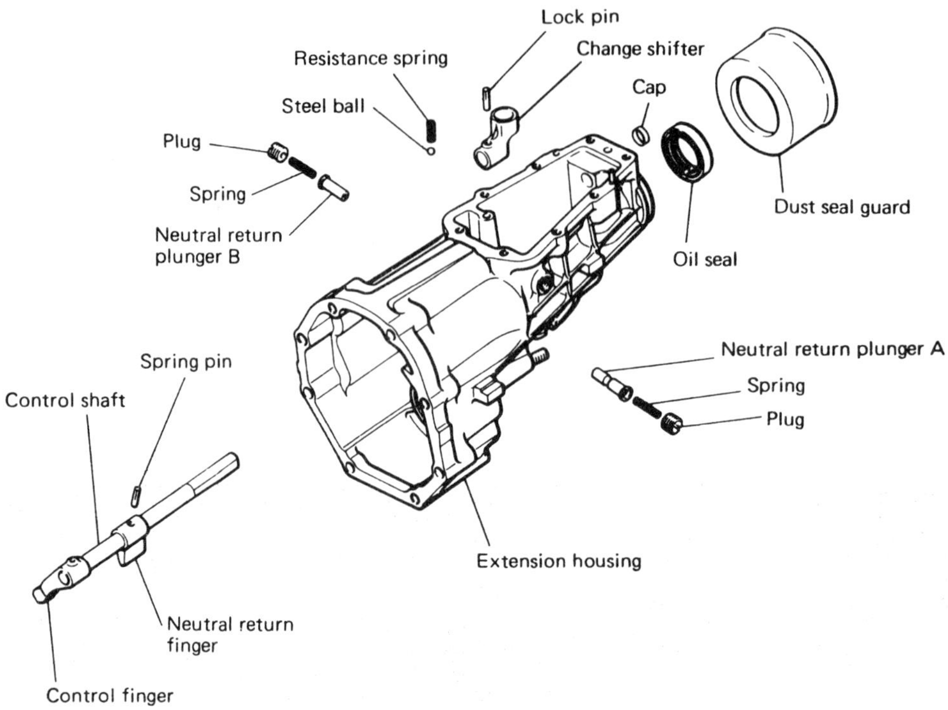

Fig. 7.18 Rear extension housing components – exploded view (Sec 8)

on the left side. Tighten the plugs until the ends are flush with the surface of the extension housing, then seal the plug heads with a silicone-type gasket sealer.
36 Install the resistance spring and ball into position from the top of the extension housing. **Caution**: *The spring and ball are held in place by the top cover and will fall out if the transmission is turned upside down before the cover is installed.*
37 Using a new gasket and gasket sealant, install the top cover onto the extension housing. Tighten the attaching bolts securely.
38 Insert the steel ball into the back-up light switch hole. Use grease to hold it in place. Apply sealant to its threads, then install the back-up light switch into the bottom of the extension housing. Take care not to damage the wiring as you thread the switch into the case and tighten it in position.
39 Place the back-up light switch wiring harness into the retaining clips on the the bottom of the transmission case.
40 At this point, it is recommended that you temporarily install the transmission shift lever assembly and check to make sure that the transmission shifts and operates in all forward gears and reverse. Remove the shift lever assembly before proceeding.
41 Plug the hole that the transmission shift lever assembly fits into with a clean rag or paper towel to guard against dropping anything into the transmission.
42 Using a new gasket and gasket sealant, install the transmission bottom cover plate. Tighten the attaching bolts to the specified torque, using a criss-cross pattern. Be very careful not to over-tighten the bolts or the gasket will be crushed out and oil leaks will result.
43 Install the clutch release mechanism and release bearing by referring to Chapter 8.
44 Don't forget to fill the transmission to the proper level with the recommended lubricant.

9 Installation

1 Installation would basically be the reverse of removal. Be sure to check the clutch disc to make sure it is centered (see Chapter 8) before sliding the transmission into place. Also, before installation, apply a coat of lithium-based grease to the end of the transmission input shaft and the splines.
2 With the help of an assistant, line up the clutch with the transmission input shaft. Make sure the engine and transmission are in a straight line, not angled in relation to each other. Carefully slide the transmission forward until the bellhousing contacts the engine block. To properly engage the clutch disc and the transmission input shaft, you may have to rotate the crankshaft slightly (with a wrench on the bolt holding the pulley to the front of the crankshaft). Do not force the input shaft into the clutch. If the transmission does not move forward smoothly, either the clutch disc/input shaft splines are not lined up, or the transmission is cocked at an angle.
3 Once the transmission is in place, support it securely and tighten all of the mounting bolts to the specified torque.
4 Don't forget to fill the transmission to the proper level with the recommended lubricant.

Chapter 7B Automatic transmission

Contents

Specifications

Pump clearances

Outer rotor-to-case bore	0.004 to 0.008 in (0.10 to 0.20 mm)
Outer-to-inner tip	0.005 to 0.010 in (0.13 to 0.25 mm)
Rotor end clearance	0.001 to 0.003 in (0.026 to 0.076 mm)

Gear train end play	0.006 to 0.033 in (0.16 to 0.83 mm)
Input shaft end play	0.022 to 0.091 in (0.56 to 2.3 mm)
Rear clutch snap-ring thicknesses	0.060 to 0.062 in (1.53 to 1.57 mm)
	0.068 to 0.070 in (1.73 to 1.77 mm)
	0.076 to 0.078 in (1.93 to 1.98 mm)
Output shaft (forward end) snap-ring thicknesses	0.040 to 0.044 in (1.02 to 1.11 mm)
	0.048 to 0.052 in (1.22 to 1.32 mm)
	0.059 to 0.065 in (1.50 to 1.65 mm)

Clutch plate clearances

Front clutch	0.077 to 0.122 in (1.96 to 3.09 mm)
Rear clutch	0.032 to 0.055 in (0.82 to 1.39 mm)

Band adjustments

Kickdown (front)	3* turns
Low/reverse (internal)	7.5** turns
	*Backed off from 6.0 ft-lbs (8.1 Nm)
	**Backed off from 3.5 ft-lbs (4.6 Nm)

Thrust washer thicknesses

Reaction shaft support-to-front clutch retainer (1)	0.061 to 0.063 in (1.55 to 1.60 mm)
Front clutch-to-rear clutch (2)	0.061 to 0.063 in (1.55 to 1.60 mm)
Input shaft-to-output shaft (3)	
No color-code	0.052 to 0.054 in (1.32 to 1.37 mm)
Red	0.068 to 0.070 in (1.73 to 1.77 mm)
Black	0.083 to 0.085 in (2.11 to 2.15 mm)
Front annulus support-to-front carrier (4)	0.121 to 0.125 in (3.08 to 3.17 mm)
Front carrier-to-driving shell thrust plate (5)	0.048 to 0.050 in (1.22 to 1.27 mm)
Driving shell thrust plate (6 and 7)	0.034 to 0.036 in (0.87 to 0.91 mm)
Rear carrier-to-driving shell (8)	0.048 to 0.050 in (1.22 to 1.27 mm)

Governor pressure

20 to 21 mph	15 psi (103.4 kPa)
35 to 40 mph	40 psi (275.8 kPa)
52 to 57 mph	60 psi (413.7 kPa)

Shift speeds

Shift points (WOT)	
1 – 2 upshift	35 to 45 mph
2 – 3 upshift	65 to 75 mph
Kickdown limit (WOT)	
3 – 2 downshift	52 to 68 mph
3 – 1 downshift	24 to 34 mph

Converter stall speed

Converter stall speed	2200 to 2650 rpm

Torque specifications

	ft-lbs	Nm
Control rod adjusting locknut	9.4	12.7
Control arm-to-selector lever locknut	13 to 17	18 to 24
Transmission mounting bolts	22 to 30	30 to 41
Starter motor mounting bolts	15 to 22	20 to 29
Drive plate-to-torque converter bolts	25 to 30	34 to 41
Extension housing bolts	24	32.3
Transmission-to-rear crossmember bolts	50	67.6
Governor body-to-support bolts	8.3	11.3
Kickdown band adjusting screw		
With adapter	3.9 to 4.1	5.4 to 5.6
Without adapter	6.0	8.1
Kickdown band locknut	35	47.0
Kickdown lever shaft plug	12.5	16.9
Oil pan bolts	12.5	16.9
Oil pump housing bolts	14.6	19.8
Output shaft support bolt	12.5	16.9
Pressure test take-off plug	9.1	12.4
Reaction shaft support bolt	13.3	18.0
Reverse band adjusting screw	3.5	4.6
Reverse band locknut	30	40.2
Speedometer drive clamp screw	8.3	11.3
Valve body screw	3.0	3.9
Valve body mounting bolt	8.3	11.3

10 General information

The automatic transmission is conventional, in that it combines a torque converter and a fully automatic 3-speed gear system.

The torque converter is attached to the crankshaft through a flexible driving plate. Cooling of the converter is accomplished by circulating the transmission fluid through an oil-to-water type cooler, located in the lower tank of the radiator. The torque converter assembly is a sealed unit which cannot be disassembled.

The transmission fluid is filtered by an internal dacron-type filter attached to the lower side of the valve body assembly.

Due to the fact that the transmission receives lubrication only when the engine is running, it is a good practice to always tow a disabled vehicle with a suitable rear-end-supporting dolly or with the driveshaft removed.

11 Fluid level – checking and replacement

Refer to the appropriate Sections in Chapter 1 to check or replace transmission fluid.

12 Filter – checking and replacement

Refer to the appropriate Section in Chapter 1 to check or replace the transmission filter.

13 Pre-overhaul – road check

1 A road check can give you some idea as to how your transmission is operating or in what area it may be malfunctioning. **Note**: *Prior to performing a road test, be certain that the fluid level, the throttle control linkage and the shift linkage have been checked and agree with the Specifications.* Refer to the appropriate Sections in this Chapter.

2 During the road test, the transmission should be operated in each shiftable position to check for any slipping or variations in shifting between each of the positions.

3 Note whether the shifts are harsh and spongy and check the vehicle's speeds where the upshifts and downshifts occur.

4 Observe closely for slipping and engine speed flareup. Transmission slipping or engine flareup in any gear usually indicates clutch, band or overrunning clutch problems.

5 In most cases, the clutch or band that is slipping can be determined by noting the transmission operation in all of the selector positions and by comparing which internal units are applied to those positions.

6 The rear clutch and the overrunning clutch are applied in D first gear and the rear clutch, and low-reverse band are applied in L first gear.

7 If the transmission slips in D range first gear, but does not slip in L first gear, the overrunning clutch must be the unit that is slipping. Similarly, if the transmission slips in any two forward gears, the rear clutch is the slipping unit.

8 Using the same procedure, the rear clutch and front clutch are applied in D third gear.

9 If the transmission slips in third gear, either the front or rear clutch is slipping. By selecting another gear which does not use one of these units, the unit which is slipping can be determined.

10 If the transmission also slips in reverse, the front clutch is slipping. If the transmission does not slip in reverse, the rear clutch is the one that is slipping.

11 This process of elimination can be used to detect any unit which is slipping and to confirm proper operation of good units.

12 However, although road test analysis can usually diagnose slipping units, the actual cause of the malfunction usually cannot be determined.

13 Unless the malfunction is obvious (ie: no drive in D range first gear) the transmission should not be removed from the vehicle until a hydraulic pressure test can be made by competent personnel.

14 Removal and installation

Note: *You may be able to realize considerable cost-savings by removing and installing your transmission if it is in need of rebuilding. The following steps will help.*

1 Disconnect the negative battery cable from the battery.
2 Remove the air cleaner assembly by referring to Chapter 2, then disconnect the starter motor wiring and remove the starter.
3 Place a drain pan under the transmission, then remove the fluid filler tube by pulling up on it.
4 Raise the vehicle and set it on jackstands.
5 Loosen the transmission oil pan mounting bolts (do not remove them completely) and allow the transmission fluid to drain into the drain pan. You may have to tap the pan with a soft-faced hammer to break the gasket seal. When the transmission fluid is finished draining, remove the oil pan from the transmission.
6 Remove the driveshaft by referring to Chapter 8.
7 Disconnect the speedometer cable and the exhaust pipe from the transmission.
8 Unhook the throttle rod from the throttle lever on the left side of the transmission.
9 Disconnect and plug the transmission oil cooler feed and return tubes and remove the linkage bellcrank, the control rod and the bellhousing cover from the transmission.
10 Mark the torque converter and driveplate so that they can be installed in the same position, then remove the torque converter attaching bolts. Use a wrench on the large bolt at the front of the crankshaft to rotate the engine clockwise so that all the bolts can be removed.
11 Securely support the rear of the engine with a jack or other suitable device.
12 Carefully support the transmission on a portable jack, then remove the rear engine support bracket.
13 Remove all the bolts attaching the transmission bellhousing to the engine.
14 Slowly withdraw the transmission from the engine by moving the jack toward the rear of the vehicle. Be very careful not to let the torque converter fall.
15 Carefully lower the jack and move the transmission out from under the vehicle. To remove the torque converter, slide it out of the transmission bellhousing.
16 Installation is basically the reverse of removal. Be sure to line up the marks on the torque converter and driveplate and do not forget to fill the transmission to the proper level with the recommended fluid (see *Recommended lubricants and fluids* at the front of the book).

15 Disassembly and repair – general note

1 Due to the complexity of the clutches and the hydraulic control system and because of the special tools and expertise required to perform an automatic transmission overhaul, it should not be undertaken by the home mechanic.
2 If the transmission requires major repair work, it should be left to an authorized dealer service department or a reputable automotive or transmission repair shop specializing in this type of work.

16 Throttle control linkage – adjustment

1 The throttle control linkage adjustment is very important to proper transmission operation. This adjustment positions a valve which controls shift speed, shift quality and part throttle downshift sensitivity. If the linkage is adjusted so that it is too short, early shifts and slippage between shifts may occur. If the linkage is adjusted so that it is too long, shifts may be delayed and part-throttle downshifts may be very erratic.
2 Start and run the engine until it reaches normal operating temperature. With the carburetor automatic choke disengaged from

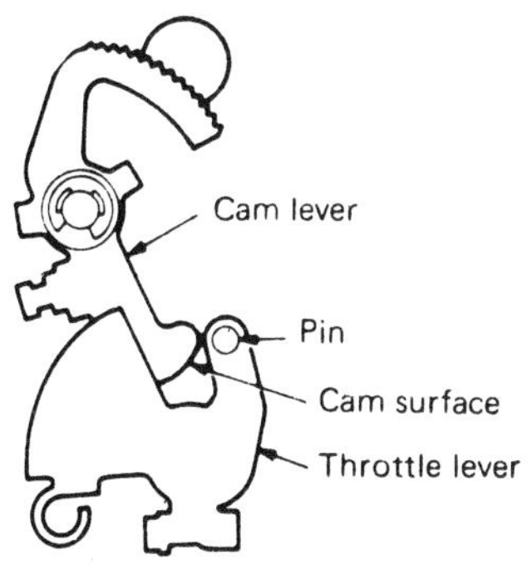

Fig. 7.19 Make sure the automatic choke is fully disengaged before making the throttle control linkage adjustments (Sec 16)

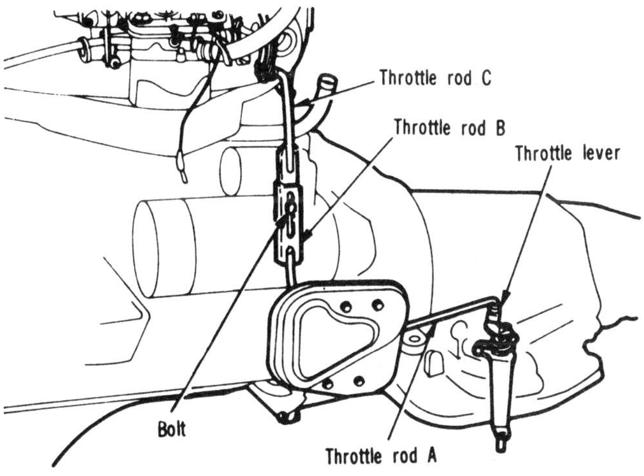

Fig. 7.20 Throttle rod adjustment (Sec 16)

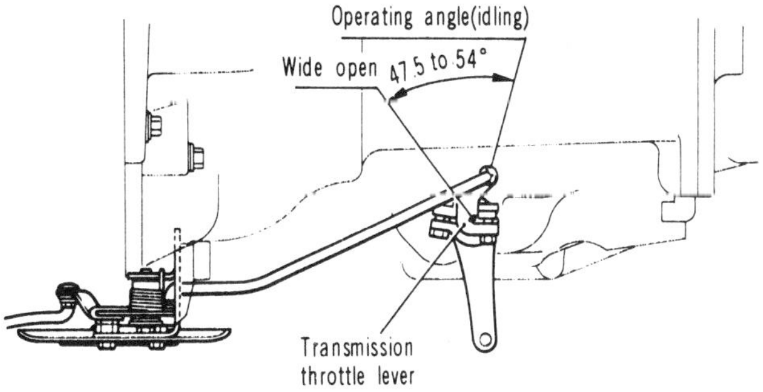

Fig. 7.21 The transmission throttle lever should move from idle to wide-open in a 47.5° to 54° arc (Sec 16)

the fast idle cam, adjust the engine idle speed (by turning the speed adjusting screw) to the specified rpm. Turn off the engine.
3 Loosen the bolt so that rods B and C can slide back and forth easily.
4 Gently push rod A all the way to the rear. Push rod C up so that the throttle is against the stop, then tighten the bolt so that rods B and C cannot move in relation to each other.
5 Open the throttle valve in the carburetor completely and observe the transmission throttle lever. It should move from the idle position to the wide open position in an arc of from 47.5 degrees to 54 degrees.
6 Make sure that when the throttle linkage is returned to the fully closed position (idle) the throttle lever on the transmission also returns to the idle position by the force of its return spring.

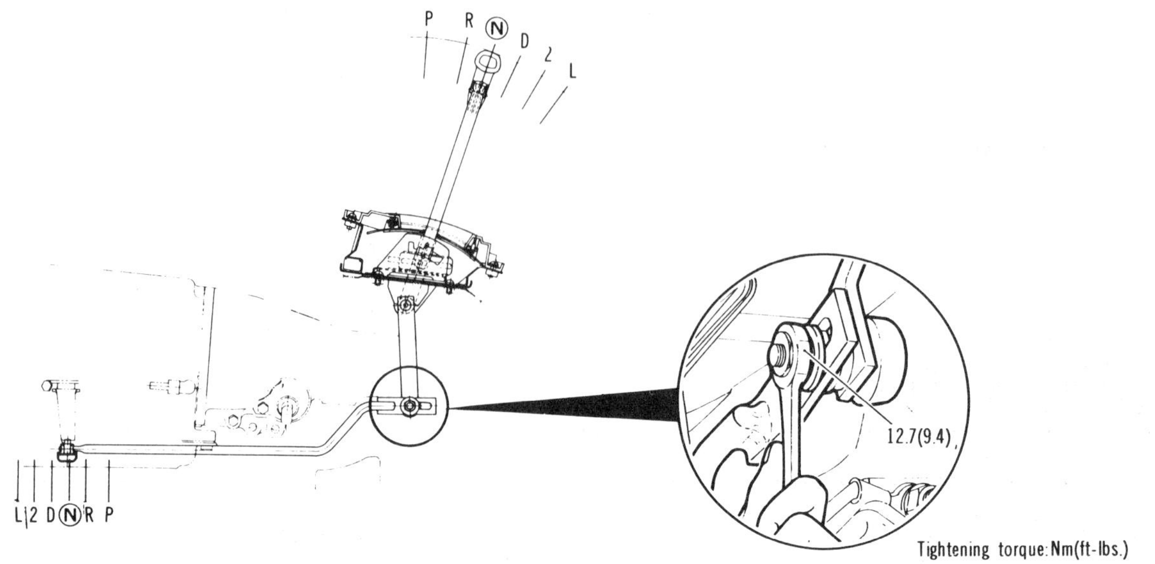

Fig. 7.22 Shift linkage control rod adjustment (Sec 17)

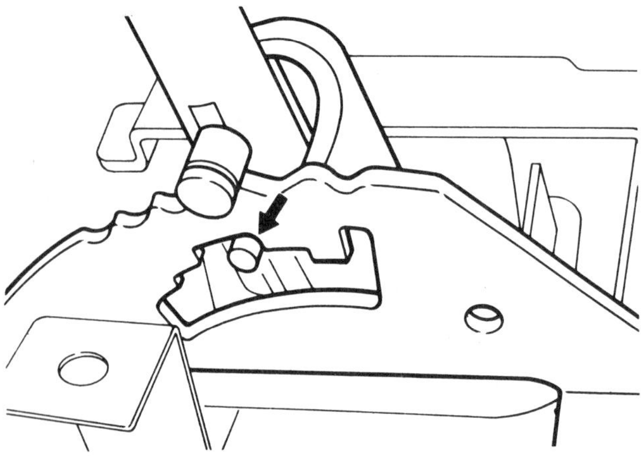

Fig. 7.23 Position shift lever in the N position (Sec 18)

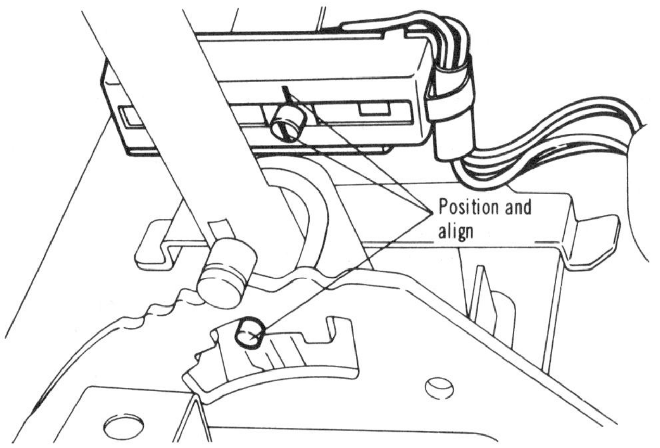

Fig. 7.24 Position and align the safety switch with the shift lever rod pin (Sec 18)

17 Shift linkage control rod – adjustment

1 The control rod is adjusted where it connects to the control arm.
2 Loosen the adjusting locknut on the control rod-to-control arm joint.
3 Place the gearshift control lever (on the left side of the transmission) in the Neutral position. Place the selector lever (inside the vehicle) in the Neutral position also.
4 At this point, the control rod adjustment is made automatically. Tighten the control rod-to-control arm adjusting locknut to the specified torque.

18 Neutral safety switch – adjustment and replacement

1 Refer to the appropriate Section in Chapter10 to check the switch.
2 To replace the safety switch, first loosen the set screw on the shift handle and remove the handle.
3 Remove the center console and remove the screws holding the indicator panel down. Disconnect the indicator lamp connector and pull the panel upward and remove it.
4 Remove the Neutral safety switch and check it for continuity.
5 To install the switch, push the shift lever to the N position so that the rod pin will be in the detent plate (see illustration).
6 Align the mating mark on the switch with that of the rod pin position and temporarily install the switch so that the clearance between the switch and the shift lever is held to 0.06 in (1.5 mm).
7 Set the shift lever to the positions P, R and N and check the switch terminals at each position for continuity. If everything checks out, tighten the switch to the shift lever bracket. If continuity does not register, readjust the position of the switch until it does.
8 Reassembly is the reverse of the removal procedure.

Fig. 7.25 Install safety switch while maintaining the specified distance of 0.06 in (1.5 mm) (Sec 18)

Chapter 8 Driveline

Contents

Specifications

Clutch

Pedal free play	
1978 thru 1979 models	0.4 to 0.6 in (10 to 15 mm)
1980 thru 1983 models	0.6 to 0.8 in (15 to 20 mm)
Cable adjusting wheel-to-insulator clearance	0.12 to 0.16 in (3 to 4 mm)
Pedal distance (A)	
1600 cc and 2000 cc	0.9 in (22 mm)
2600 cc	0.8 in (20 mm)
Pedal Height	
1600 cc and 2000 cc	6.5 in (166 mm)
2600 cc	6.9 in (176 mm)
Pedal stroke	
1600 cc and 2000 cc	5.5 in (140 mm)
2600 cc	5.9 in (150 mm)
Disc rivet sink	0.012 in (0.3 mm) minimum

Driveshaft

U-joint journal endplay	0 to 0.001 in (0 to 0.03 mm)
Snap-ring thicknesses	
MA 180905 (no color-code)	0.050 ± 0.0006 in (1.28 ± 0.015 mm)
MA 180906 (yellow)	0.516 ± 0.0006 in (1.31 ± 0.015 mm)
MA 180907 (blue)	0.0528 ± 0.0006 in (1.34 ± 0.015 mm)
MA 180908 (purple)	0.0539 ± 0.0006 in (1.37 ± 0.015 mm)
Runout	0.020 in (0.5 mm) maximum
Imbalance	0.18 oz (5.0 g) maximum

Rear axle

Standard rear-wheel bearing case-to-axle housing clearance	0.002 to 0.008 in (0.05 to 0.20 mm)
Wheel bearing preload adjusting shim thicknesses	
MB 092491	0.002 in (0.05 mm)
MB 092492	0.004 in (0.10 mm)
MB 092493	0.0079 in (0.20 mm)
MB 092494	0.0118 in (0.30 mm)
MB 092495	0.0197 in (0.50 mm)
MB 092496	0.0394 in (1.00 mm)
MB 092497	0.0591 in (1.50 mm)
MB 092498	0.0787 in (2.00 mm)
Axle shaft axial play	0.002 to 0.008 in (0.05 to 0.20 mm)
Side gear-to-axle shaft spline clearance	0.0021 to 0.0067 in (0.054 to 0.171 mm)
Spyder gear-to-spyder shaft clearance	0 to 0.0025 in (0 to 0.063 mm)

Drive pinion height-adjusting shim thicknesses	
MB 092160	0.0543 in (1.38 mm)
MB 092161	0.0555 in (1.41 mm)
MB 092162	0.0567 in (1.44 mm)
MB 092163	0.0579 in (1.47 mm)
MB 092164	0.0591 in (1.50 mm)
MB 092165	0.0603 in (1.53 mm)
MB 092166	0.0614 in (1.56 mm)
MB 092167	0.0626 in (1.59 mm)
MB 092168	0.0638 in (1.62 mm)
MB 092169	0.0650 in (1.65 mm)
MB 092170	0.0118 in (0.30 mm)
Pinion shaft bearing preload adjusting shim thicknesses	
MB 092130	0.0118 in (0.30 mm)
MB 092131	0.0787 in (2.00 mm)
MB 092132	0.0799 in (2.03 mm)
MB 092133	0.0811 in (2.06 mm)
MB 092134	0.0823 in (2.09 mm)
MB 092135	0.0835 in (2.12 mm)
MB 092136	0.0846 in (2.15 mm)
MB 092137	0.0858 in (2.18 mm)
MB 092138	0.0870 in (2.21 mm)
MB 092139	0.0882 in (2.24 mm)
MB 092140	0.0894 in (2.27 mm)
MB 092141	0.0906 in (2.30 mm)
MB 092142	0.0917 in (2.33 mm)
Pinion spacer lengths	
MB 092346(no color-code)	2.2311 + 0 in (56.67 + 0 mm) - 0.0016 - 0.14
MB 092347 (white)	2.2445 + 0 in (57.01 + 0 mm) - 0.0016 - 0.14
Backlash between differential spyder gear and side gear	0.002 to 0.005 in (0.051 to 0.127 mm)
Side gear thrust spacer thicknesses	
MB 092034	0.0315 + 0.0031 in (0.8 + 0.08 mm) - 0.0067 - 0.17
MB 092035	0.0315 + 0.0071 in (0.8 + 0.18 mm) - 0.0106 - 0.27
MB 092036	0.0315 + 0 in (0.8 + 0 mm) - 0.0028 - 0.07
Backlash between ring-and-pinion gear	0.005 to 0.007 in (0.13 to 0.18 mm)
Ring gear runout	Less than 0.002 in (0.05 mm)

Torque specifications

	ft-lb	Nm
Clutch		
Clutch cover bolts	11 to 15	15 to 21
Driveshaft		
Center bearing bracket nuts	22 to 29	29 to 39
Flange yoke bolts		
1979 models	22 to 25	30 to 34
1980 models	33 to 39	45 to 53
Center yoke nut	116 to 159	157 to 216
Rear axle		
Rear wheel bearing case-to-rear axle housing attaching nuts	36 to 43	49 to 59
Rear axle housing drain plug	43 to 50	59 to 69
Rear axle housing filler plug	29 to 43	39 to 59
Differential end yoke-to-pinion shaft nut		
1978 thru 1979 models	120 to 160	160 to 210
1980 thru 1983 models	137 to 180	186 to 245
Drive pinion bearing preload		
Without seal in place	6 to 9	0.7 to 1.0
With seal in place	9 to 11	1.0 to 1.2
Ring gear mounting bolts	58 to 65	78 to 88
Differential carrier cap bolts	40 to 47	54 to 64
Lock plate bolts	11 to16	15 to 22
Differential carrier assembly-to-axle housing nuts	18 to 22	25 to 30

1 General information

The clutch is conventional in design and is composed of a single clutch disc and a Belleville-type diaphragm spring pressure assembly. Due to the fact that access to the clutch components is difficult and time consuming, the clutch disc, clutch cover (pressure plate) assembly and release bearing should be carefully inspected or replaced whenever either the engine or the transmission is removed.

Power is transmitted from the transmission to the rear axle by a two-piece driveshaft. Universal joints are located at the front, rear and center bearing to allow for vertical movement of the rear axle and slight movement of the engine/transmission unit. A slip-joint is used to allow for fore-and-aft movement of the drivetrain.

The rear axle assembly is also conventional in design, utilizing a separable differential carrier, hypoid final drive gears and semi-floating rear axles.

Most rear-end component problems reveal themselves in the form of some sort of noise. The noise may be caused by gears (in the differential carrier assembly) or bearings (in the differential and the outer ends of the rear axle housing).

Gear noise is usually a high-pitched whine, which may be more pronounced at certain speeds or when the vehicle is under load.

Bearing noise is generally a lower-pitched, steady growl. It tends to get louder when accelerating under load. Swerving the vehicle from side-to-side on a flat, level road may help to pinpoint faulty wheel bearings. This practice throws additional side loads on the bearings, which should increase any noise coming from them. A bad bearing could show up in the differential assembly, although bearing failure in this area is much less likely than in the wheel bearings.

Although a differential overhaul section is included in this Chapter, major repair work on the differential (and other rear-end components) requires many special tools and a high degree of expertise and therefore should not be attmpted by the home mechanic. Should major repairs be necessary, we recommend that they be performed by a dealer-authorized service department or a reputable repair shop.

2 Fluid level – check and replacement

Refer to Chapter 1 to check or replace the differential fluid.

3 Clutch and pedal – check and adjustment

1 Refer to the appropriate Section in Chapter 1 for any clutch or pedal checks.

2 The clutch pedal adjustments affect the pedal height, the pedal stroke and the pedal free play. Correct clutch pedal height is important because it ensures complete clutch engagement and prevents slippage and overheating, which will lead to clutch failure. The pedal stroke indicates whether or not the clutch disengages properly (when the pedal is depressed) and provides for smooth, trouble-free gear shifts. Clutch pedal free play (the distance the pedal moves before the clutch release bearing contacts the clutch diaphragm spring) is necessary to prevent undue wear of the clutch release mechanism components.

3 To adjust the clutch pedal, loosen the adjusting bolt jam nut (on the pedal support member) and turn the bolt until the pedal height is as specified. Tighten the jam nut so that the adjusting bolt cannot turn. Measure distance A as shown in Figure 8.1 and compare it to the Specifications. When the pedal height is correct, distance A should also be correct.

4 Set the clutch cable adjusting wheel-to-insulator clearance (inside the engine compartment) to the specific amount by pulling out slightly on the cable housing and turning the adjusting wheel.

5 Check to make sure that the clutch pedal free play is as specified. Slowly depress the pedal until the resistance offered by the clutch release mechanism is felt, then measure how far the pedal has moved. The clutch cable may stretch during normal operation, so the correct adjusting wheel-to-insulator clearance may not ensure correct pedal free play. Always make the adjustment so that the specified free play is present.

6 Check the clutch pedal stroke and compare it to the Specifications. The transmission should shift smoothly and quietly with the pedal fully depressed.

4 Clutch cable – check and replacement

1 Refer to Chapter 1 to check the clutch cable.

2 To replace the clutch cable, pull out slightly on the clutch cable housing (inside the engine compartment) and loosen the adjusting wheel.

3 Loosen the jam nut on the clutch pedal adjusting bolt and back out the adjusting bolt.

4 Unhook the cable from the clutch pedal hook and pull the cable through the firewall from the engine compartment side.

5 Raise the front of the vehicle and set it on jackstands. Block the rear tires and set the parking brake to keep the vehicle from rolling. Remove the cotter key in the end of the clutch control lever. Push forward on the lever and unhook the clutch cable. Slide the rubber boot off the end of the cable and release the cable from its mount on the transmission bellhousing.

6 Before installing the new cable, apply a small amount of engine oil or other suitable lubricant between the cable and the cable housing.

7 Slip the lower end of the cable into position on the transmission bellhousing and slide the rubber boot over the end of the cable.

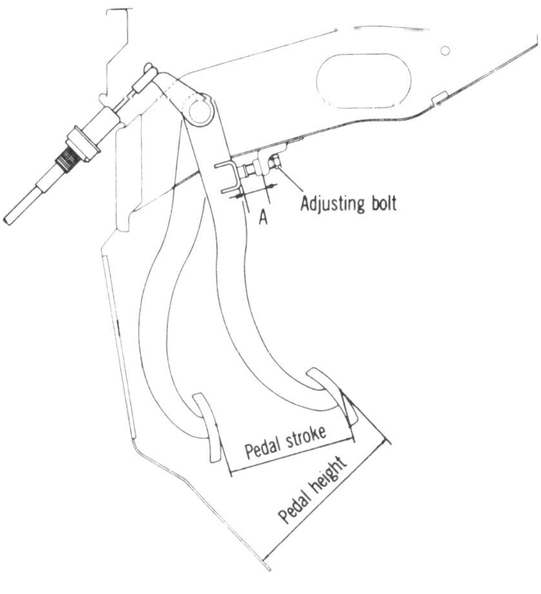

Fig. 8.1 Clutch pedal adjustments (Sec 3)

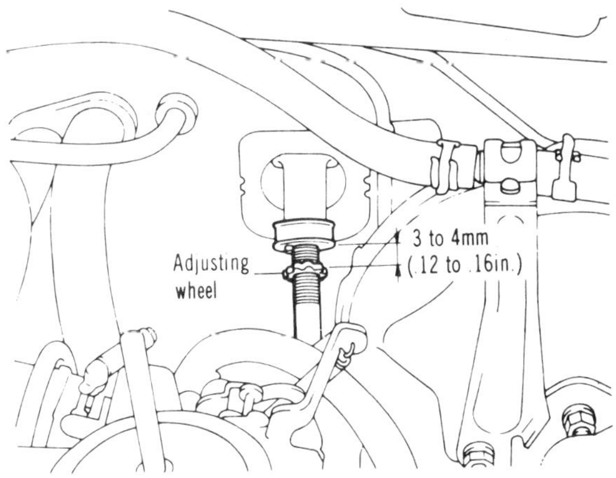

Fig. 8.2 Clutch cable adjusting wheel-to-insulator clearance (Sec 3)

8

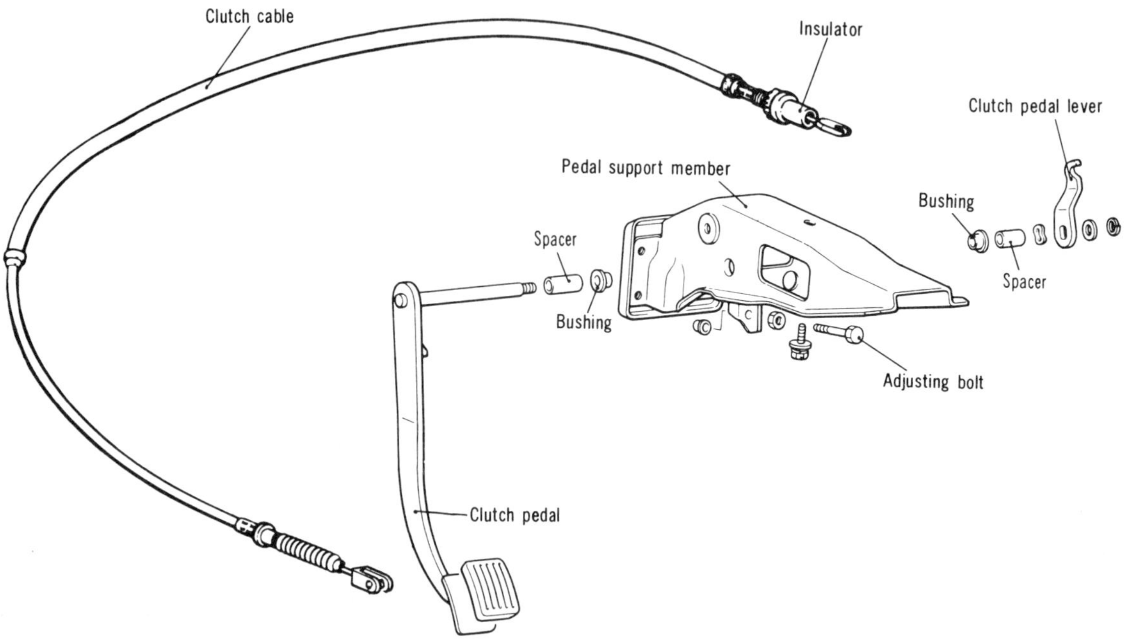

Fig. 8.3 Clutch control components – exploded view (Sec 4)

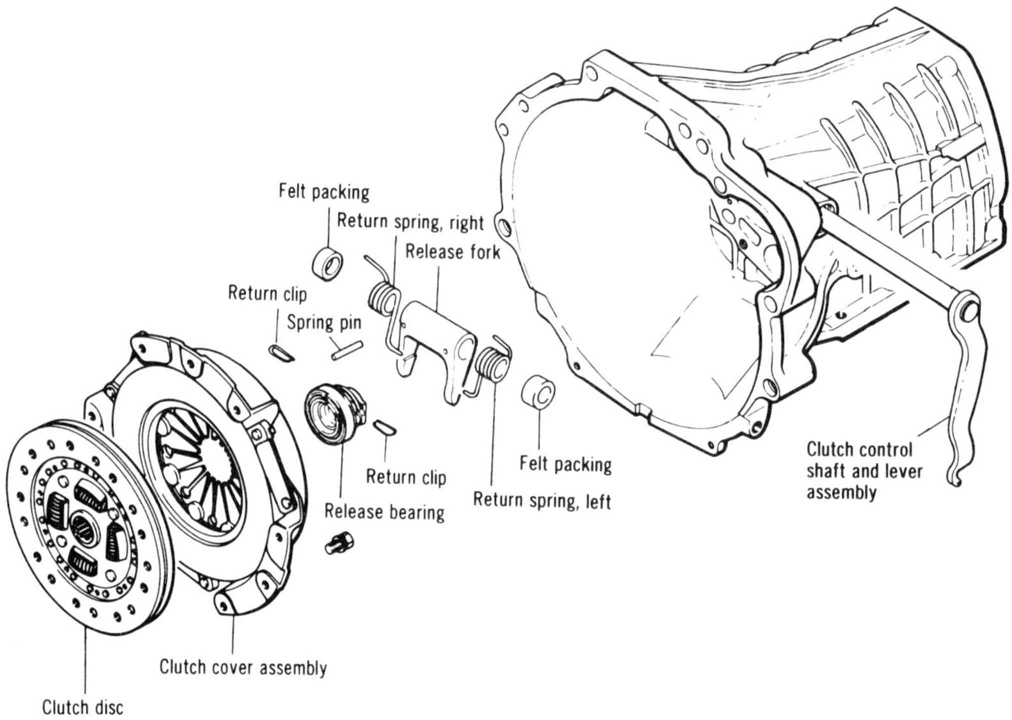

Fig. 8.4 Clutch components – exploded view (Sec 5)

8 Push forward on the clutch control lever and hook the end of the clutch cable over the lever. Remember to install the cotter key in the end of the lever.
9 Lower the vehicle to the ground and insert the upper end of the cable through the firewall and into the driver's compartment. Loosen the adjusting wheel as far as possible and hook the end of the cable onto the clutch pedal hook.
10 Adjust the clutch pedal height, the clutch pedal stroke and the pedal free play by referring to the appropriate Section.
11 After the cable has been installed, make sure that the isolating pad touches the rear side of the left engine mount insulator.

5 Clutch – removal and installation

1 Separate the transmission from the engine as described in Chapter 2.
2 Mark the clutch cover assembly and flywheel so that they can be reassembled in the same position.
3 Install a clutch alignment tool to support the clutch cover assembly and clutch disc so they do not fall when the attaching bolts are removed.
4 Remove the bolts attaching the clutch cover assembly to the

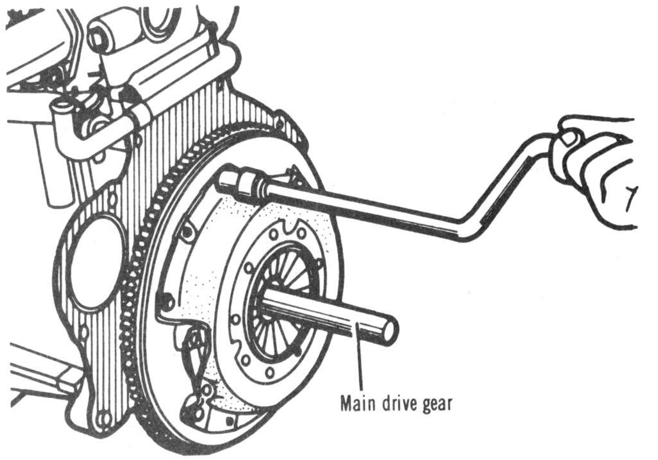

Fig. 8.5 Remove the bolts attaching the clutch cover assembly to the flywheel (Sec 5)

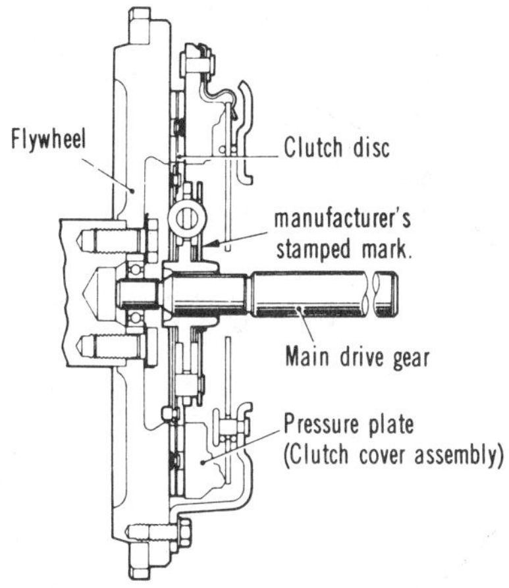

Fig. 8.6 The clutch disc must be held in alignment while installing the clutch cover assembly (Sec 5)

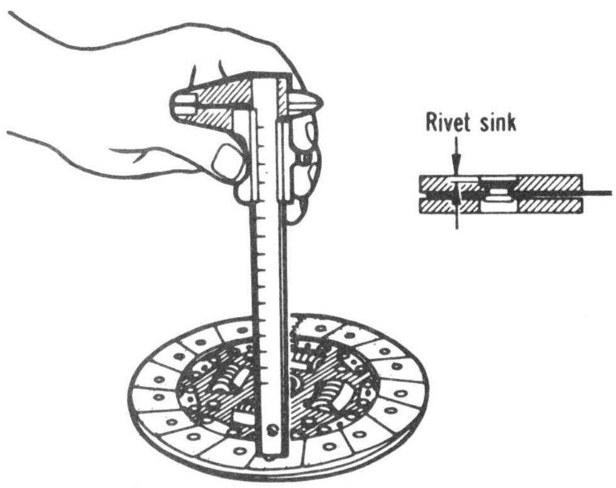

Fig. 8.7 Measure the clutch disc rivet sink with calipers or a depth micrometer (Sec 6)

flywheel. Loosen them one turn at a time each, in a diagonal or criss-cross pattern, until they are loose enough to be removed by hand.

5 Lift the clutch cover assembly and the clutch disc off the flywheel and remove the clutch alignment tool.

6 Hold the clutch disc and clutch cover assembly in place on the flywheel and loosely install the attaching bolts. Be sure to line up the marks on the flywheel and clutch cover. The manufacturer's stamped mark on the clutch disc must face away from the flywheel when the clutch is assembled.

7 Install the clutch disc alignment tool through the clutch disc and into the pilot bearing in the flywheel hub. This tool will center the clutch disc properly.

8 Tighten the clutch attaching bolts to the specified torque. Use a criss-cross pattern and tighten the bolts one turn each at a time, so that the clutch cover assembly is drawn down onto the flywheel evenly.

9 Remove the clutch disc alignment tool.

10 Install the transmission onto the engine as described in Chapter 7A.

6 Clutch – inspection

1 Check the metal parts of the clutch disc for cracks and distortion. Check carefully for broken springs. Slip the clutch disc onto the transmission input shaft and check for excessive play in the direction of rotation between the splines of the clutch disc hub and the input shaft. Inspect the clutch disc friction lining for cracks, burned spots and oil stains.

2 If oil is present on the clutch components, the engine rear oil seal or the transmission front oil seal, or both may be defective and require replacement. Minor oil stains may be removed with lacquer thinner or a similar solvent. Look for broken or loose rivets. Measure the clutch disc rivet sink (the distance from the top of the friction material to the rivet head) and compare it to the Specifications. Replace any defective parts with new ones.

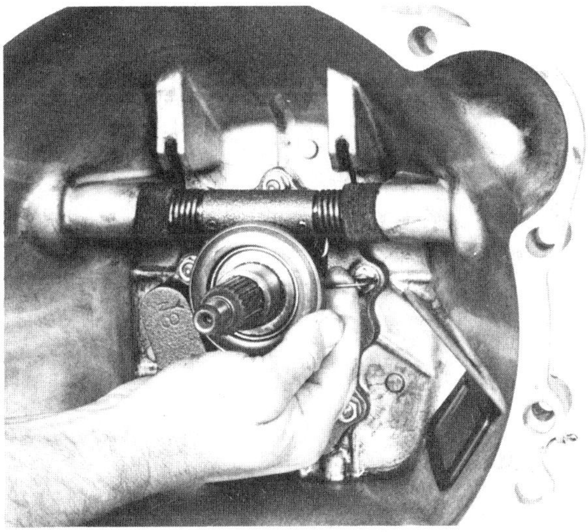

7.2 Pull forward on the spring clips and separate them from the release bearing carrier

3 Inspect the clutch cover assembly for excessive finger wear, loose strap rivets and cracks. Check the pressure plate for scoring, burn marks and ridges. Shake the clutch cover assembly and listen for noise caused by a loose pivot ring. If any noise is heard, the pivot ring is excessivly worn and the clutch cover assembly must be replaced.

4 Look for scoring, burn marks and deep ridges on the flywheel. If any of these problems exist, or if the surface is highly polished, remove the flywheel as described in Chapter 2 and have it resurfaced and balanced at a reputable automotive machine shop. Check the pilot bearing in the center hub of the flywheel. Make sure that it turns smoothly and quietly. If the transmission input shaft contact surface is worn or damaged, replace the bearing.

5 Disassemble and check the release bearing and clutch release mechanism as described in Section 7.

7 Clutch/release bearing mechanism – disassembly and reassembly

1 Refer to Chapter 2 for the procedure to follow when separating the transmission from the engine.

2 Pull forward on the spring clips retaining the bearing carrier and separate them from the release bearing carrier (photo).

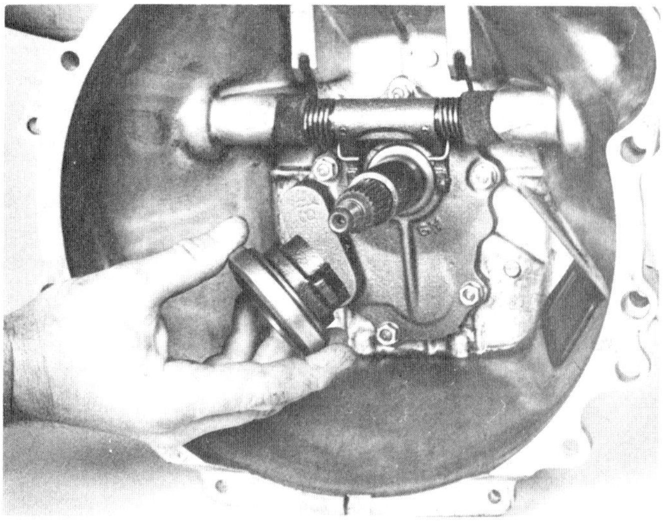

7.3 Slide the release bearing and carrier assembly off the bearing carrier

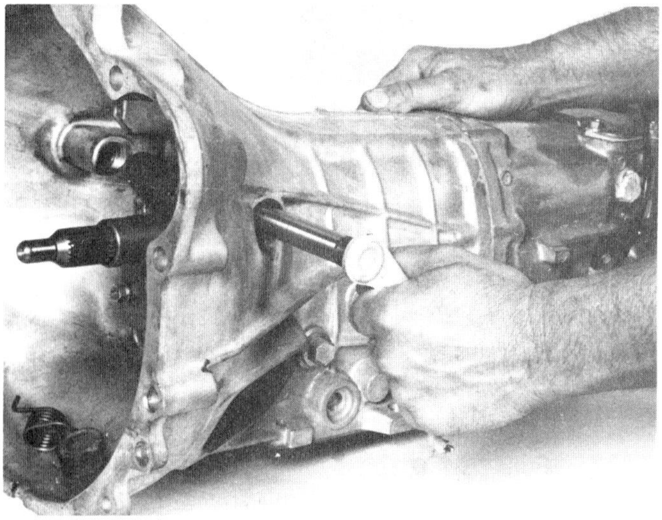

7.4 Remove the clutch lever/shaft from the transmission bellhousing by twisting and pulling on the lever

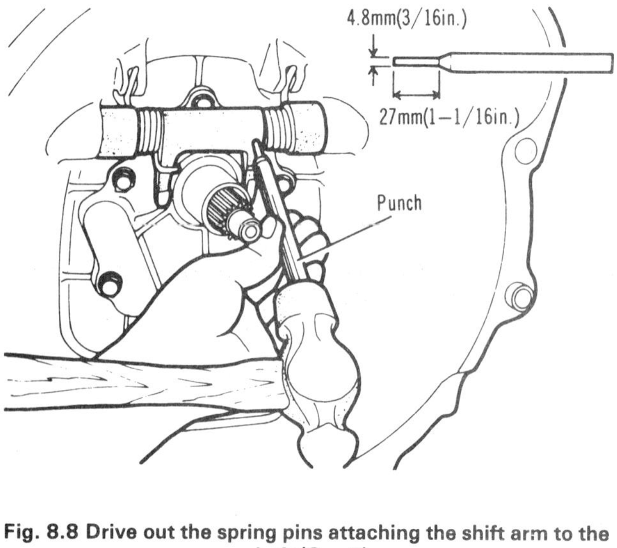

Fig. 8.8 Drive out the spring pins attaching the shift arm to the shaft (Sec 7)

3 Slide the release bearing and carrier assembly off the bearing carrier.

4 Using a $\frac{3}{16}$ in pin punch, drive out the pins attaching the clutch shift arm to the control lever shaft. Remove the clutch control lever/shaft assembly, the return springs, the felt packings and the clutch shift arm from the transmission bellhousing by twisting and pulling on the lever (photo).

5 Wipe the release bearing clean. Do not clean it in solvent, since it is packed with grease and permanently sealed. Make sure that the bearing rotates smoothly and quietly. Check the face of the bearing that contacts the diaphragm's ring fingers for excessive wear. Replace the bearing if any defects are found.

6 Clean the remaining parts with solvent and dry them thoroughly. Clean the inside of the transmission bellhousing.

7 Check the release bearing carrier for wear and damage. Inspect the clutch shift arm contact faces, the shift arm bore and the shaft assembly and bushings for wear. Replace any defective parts. Wipe clean the control lever shaft bushings in the transmission bellhousing and apply a thin coat of grease to them. Slide the control lever/shaft assembly into place with the felt packings, the return springs and the clutch shift arm installed in the proper order.

8 Engage the return spring in the clutch shift arm and install the pins that attach the arm to the control lever shaft. Make sure that the slots in the spring pins are at right angles to the control lever shaft axis. Apply a few drops of engine oil to each felt packing.

9 Slide the release bearing and carrier assembly into position and install the spring clips. Make sure they are properly engaged in the clutch shift arm and the release bearing carrier.

8 Universal joints – on vehicle inspection

Refer to Chapter 1 to check the universal joints.

9 Driveshaft/universal joints – removal and installation

1 Raise the vehicle and set it on jackstands. Drain the transmission lubricant into a suitable container.

2 Make a mark across the driveshaft flange yoke and the differential end yoke (where they come together) so that the driveshaft can be reinstalled in the exact same position (photo).

3 Remove the nuts, bolts and lock washers that attach the driveshaft to the differential assembly.

4 Remove the nuts attaching the center bearing assembly to the frame crossmember (photo).

5 Carefully lift up on the center bearing (photo), release the rear of the driveshaft from the differential (photo) and slide the driveshaft to the rear, out of the transmission housing. Be very careful not to damage the seal in the end of the transmission housing.

9.2 Make a match mark across the driveshaft flange yoke and the differential end yoke before disassembly

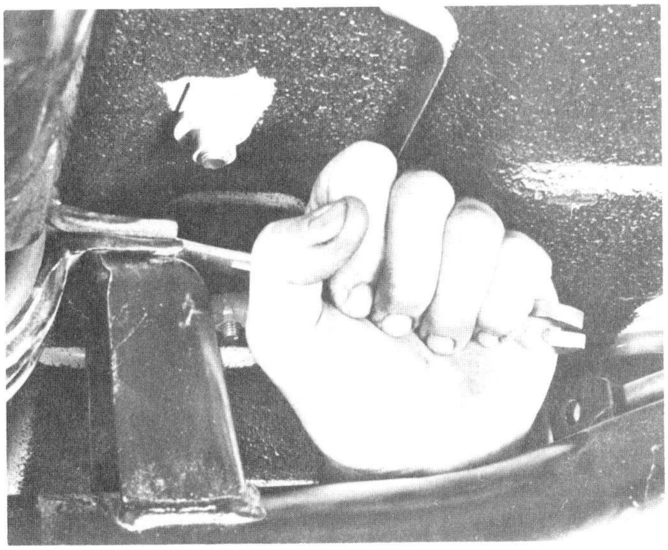

9.4 Remove the nuts attaching the center bearing to the frame

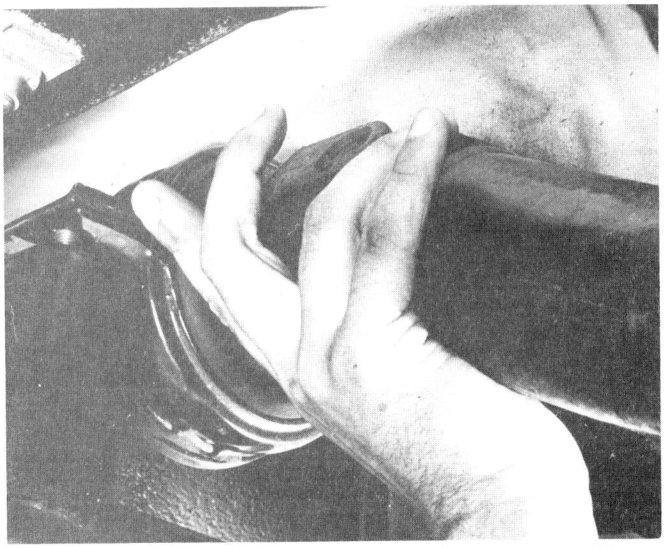

9.5a Lift up on the center bearing and drive shaft to remove the drive shaft assembly

9.5b Disengage the driveshaft from the differential

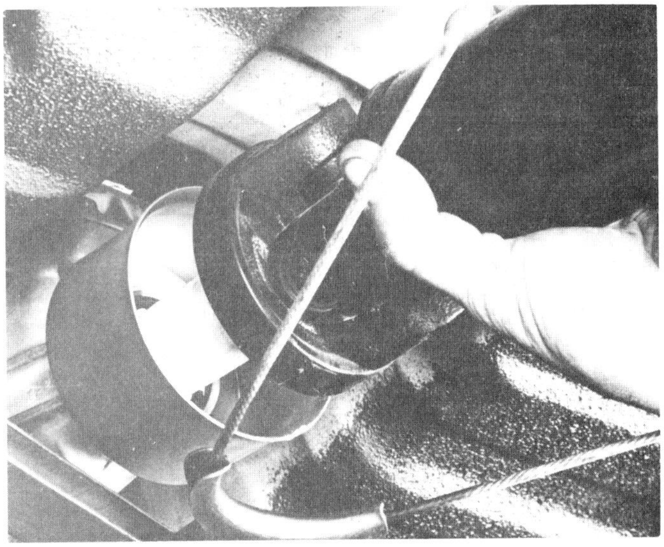

9.8a Carefully insert the sleeve yoke into the transmission housing

9.8b Install the bolts, lockwashers and nuts that hold the driveshaft to the differential end yoke

9.8c Tighten the nuts to the specified torque

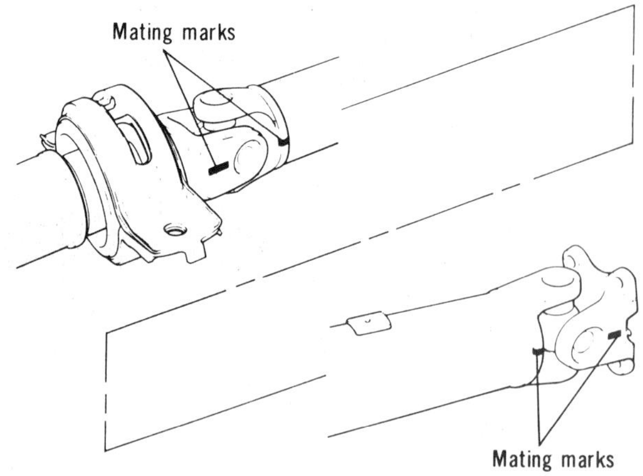

Fig. 8.9 Make match marks between the center yoke, the rear driveshaft and the flange yoke (Sec 9)

6 Refer to Section 10 for driveshaft inspection and repair procedures.
7 Before installing the driveshaft, thoroughly clean the outside surface of the sleeve yoke and apply a coat of multi-purpose grease to it. Also, check the inside of the sleeve yoke to make sure there is no foreign material present.
8 Carefully insert the sleeve yoke into the transmission housing, lining up the splines inside the sleeve yoke with the splines on the transmission output shaft (photo). Fit the driveshaft into place and install the bolts (photo), lock washers and nuts that attach it to the differential (be sure to line up the marks on the flange yoke and the end yoke). Tighten the nuts to the specified torque (photo).
9 Install the center bearing mount nuts and tighten them securely.
10 Fill the transmission to the proper level with the recommended lubricant.
11 Lower the vehicle to the ground and test drive it.

10 Driveshaft/universal joints – disassembly and reassembly

1 It is a good idea to dismantle the center universal joint first so that the driveshaft can be broken into two pieces, which makes it easier to handle and work on.
2 Support the universal joint in a vise equipped with soft jaws and remove the snap-rings from the universal joint yokes. It is recommended that each snap-ring and yoke be marked so that the snap-rings can be returned to the same position during reassembly (photo).
3 To remove the bearings from the yokes, you will need two sockets, One should be large enought to fit into the yoke where the snap-rings were installed and the other should have an inside diameter just large enough for the bearings to fit into when they are forced out of the yoke.
4 Mount the universal joint in a vise with the large socket on one side of the yoke and the small socket on the other side, pushing against the bearing. Carefully tighten the vise until the bearing is pushed out of the yoke and into the large socket. If it cannot be pushed all the way out, remove the universal joint from the vise and use a pair of pliers to finish removing the bearing (photo).
5 Reverse the sockets and push out the bearing on the other side of the yoke. This time, the small socket will be pushing against the cross-shaped universal joint journal end.
6 Before pressing out the two remaining bearings, mark the universal joint journal (the cross) so it can be installed in the same position during reassembly.
7 The two remaining universal joints can be disassembled following the same procedure. Be sure to mark all components for each universal joint so that they can be kept together and reassembled in the proper position.
8 Remove the center bearing from the front driveshaft by referring to Section 11
9 Clean the driveshaft and universal joint components with solvent and dry them thoroughly.

10.2 Remove the snap-rings from the bearing cups

10.4 Press out the trunnion (cross) using a vise and sockets (one socket slightly smaller and the other slightly larger than the bearing cup)

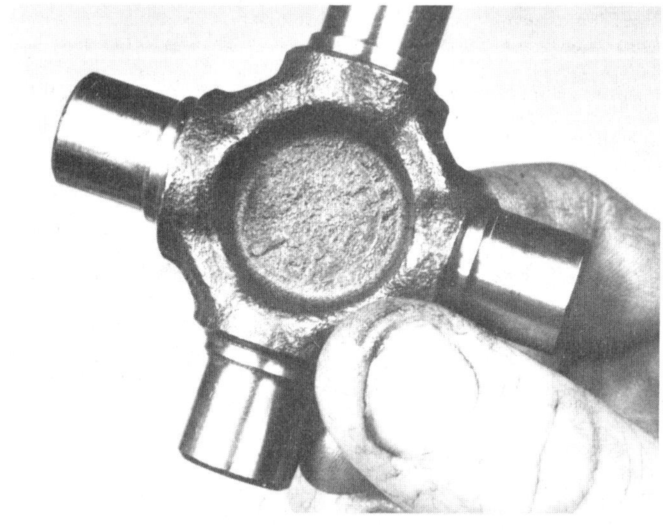

10.11 The trunnion (cross) removed from the driveshaft

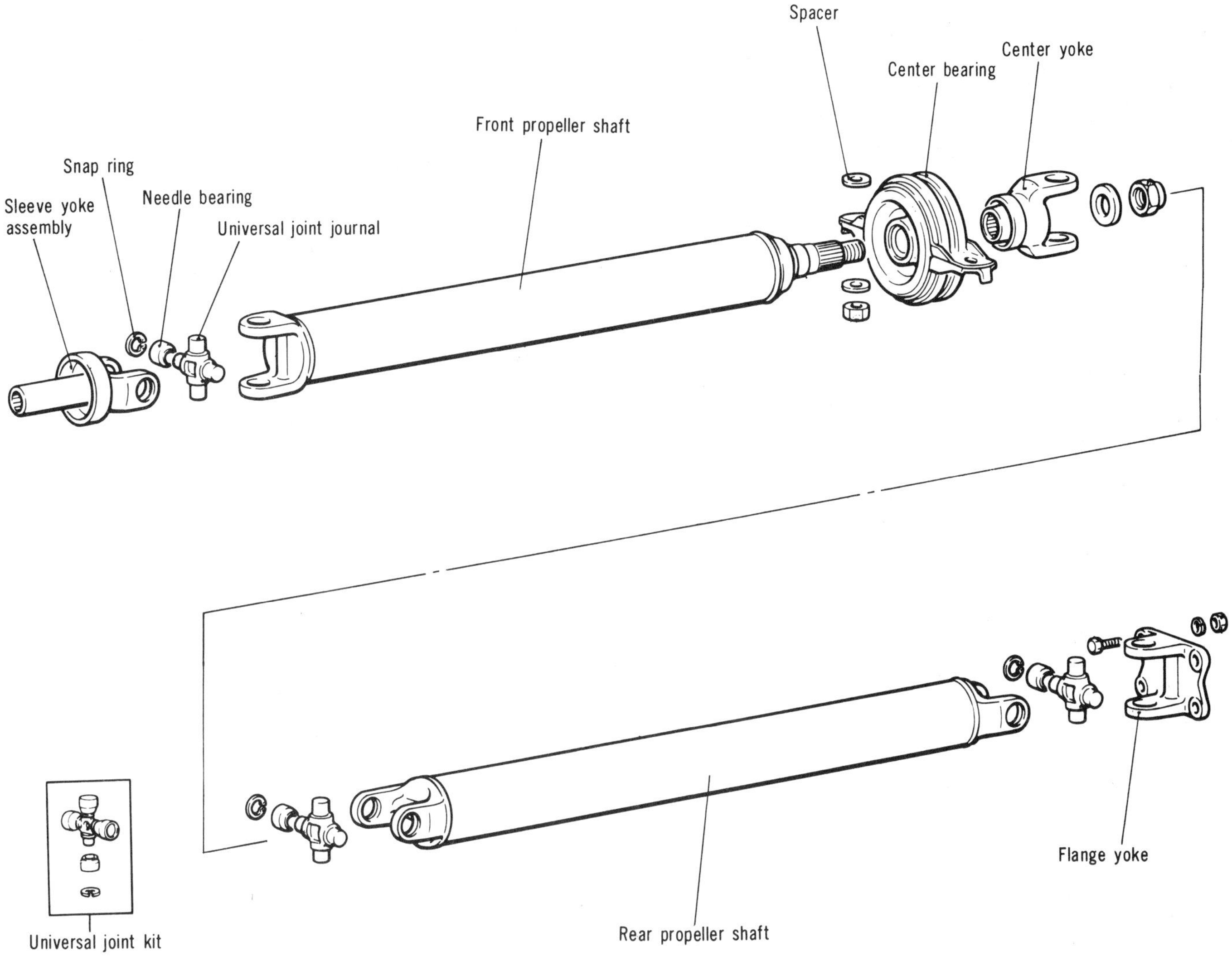

Fig. 8.10 Driveshaft components – exploded view (Sec 10)

10 Inspect each of the driveshafts for cracks and damage. If possible, check the driveshaft runout with a dial indicator. Replace both shafts if any defects are found in either one. Never replace only one of the shafts.
11 Check the universal joint journals (the crosses) for scoring, needle roller impressions, rust and pitting. Replace them if any of the above conditions exist (photo).
12 Check the sleeve yoke splines for wear and damage.
13 When reassembling the universal joints, replace all needle bearings and dust seals with new ones (photo).
14 Before reassembly, pack each grease cavity in the universal joint journals with a small amount of grease. Also, apply a thin coat of grease to the new needle bearing rollers and the roller contact areas on the universal joint journals.
15 Apply a thin coat of grease to the dust seal lips and install the bearings and universal joint journals into the yoke using the vise and sockets that were used to remove the old bearings. Work slowly and be very careful not to damage the bearings as they are being pressed into the yokes.
16 Once the bearings are in place and properly seated, install the snap-rings and check the snap-ring-to-bearing clearance (or universal joint journal endplay) with a feeler gauge. This is done with both snap-rings in place and the bearings and journal pressed toward one side of the yoke. Measure the clearance at the opposite side of the yoke. If the clearance is greater than specified, install a snap-ring of a different

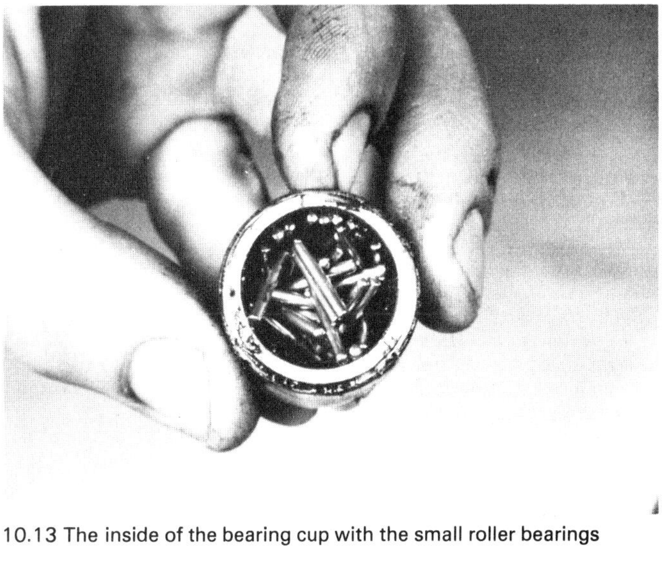

10.13 The inside of the bearing cup with the small roller bearings

8

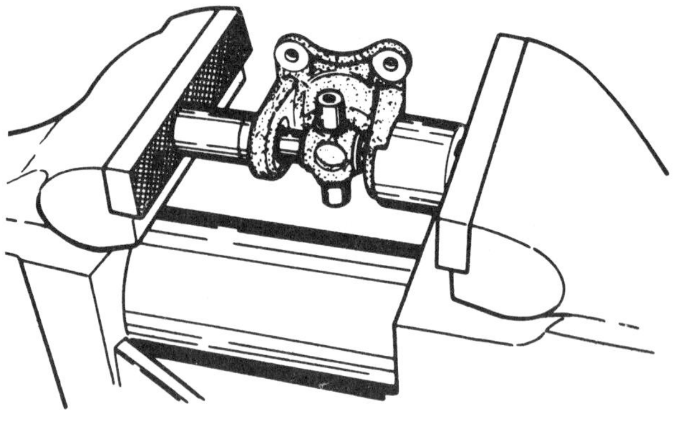

Fig. 8.11 The bearings can be removed from the universal joints with a vise and two sockets (Sec 10)

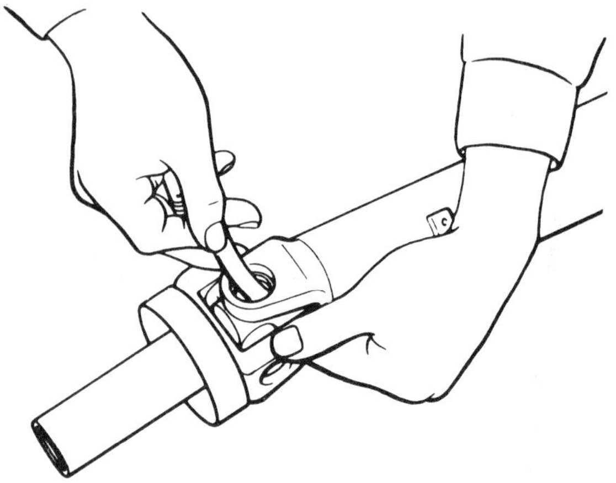

Fig. 8.12 The snap-ring-to-bearing clearance (U-joint journal endplay) is checked with a feeler gauge (Sec 10)

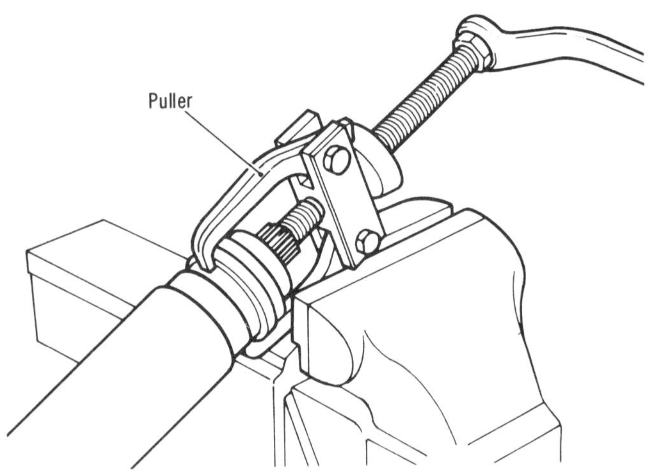

Fig. 8.13 Remove the center bearing from the shaft (Sec 11)

Fig. 8.14 Before installing the center bearing, fill the grease cavities (shaded areas) with multi-purpose grease (Sec 11)

thickness and recheck the clearance. Repeat the procedure until the correct clearance is obtained. If possible, use snap-rings of the same thickness on each side of the yoke so that driveshaft balance is not affected. A list of available snap-ring thicknesses is included in the Specifications section at the front of this Chapter.
17 Install the center bearing as described in Section 11 and assemble the center U-joint.

11 Center support bearing – disassembly, inspection and reassembly

1 Check for the presence of mating marks on the driveshafts and center yoke. If they are not visible, make some new ones to ensure correct reassembly of the driveshafts and center yoke.
2 Refer to Section 10 and disassemble the center universal joint so that the driveshaft can be separated into two pieces.
3 Support the driveshaft in a vise equipped with soft jaws and remove the center yoke attaching nut and the washer.
4 Pull the center yoke off and pry the center bearing bracket loose (be careful not to damage the rubber mount). The bearing bracket cannot be disassembled.
5 Using a suitable bearing puller, remove the center bearing from the shaft.
6 Clean the bearing parts and the yoke with solvent and dry them thoroughly.
7 Rotate the bearings and check for noise, excessive play and roughness. Replace the bearing if any defects are noted.
8 Check the center bearing bracket and mounting rubber for deterioration and damage. Replace as necessary.
9 Before installing the center bearing, fill the bearing grease cavity with multi-purpose grease.
10 Slip the bearing onto the shaft and fit the bracket to the bearing. The bracket mounting rubber should fit into the bearing groove around its entire circumference.
11 Align the mating marks on the shaft and the center yoke and slip the yoke into place on the shaft. Install the washer and a new nut and tighten the nut to the specified torque. Since the nuts are the self-locking type, the old ones should not be reused.
12 Assemble the center universal joint as described in Section 10. Be sure to align the mating marks on the shafts and yoke.

12 Axle shaft – on vehicle inspection

1 For vehicles with rear drum brakes, remove the wheel and brake drum.
2 For vehicles with rear disc brakes, remove the caliper support with the parking brake rear cable, the caliper assembly and brake hose.

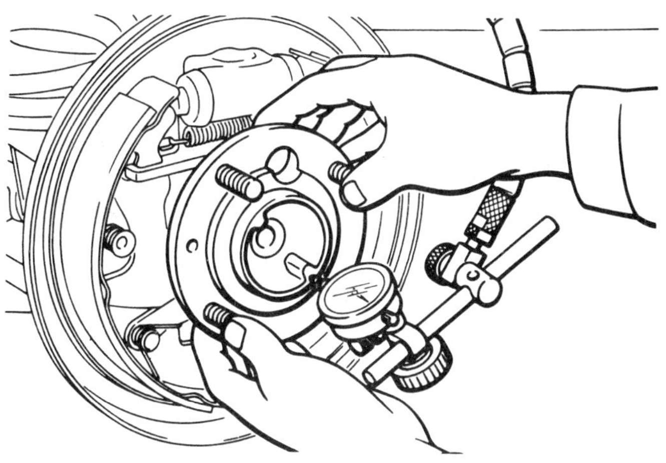

Fig. 8.15 Measuring the axial play of the rear wheel bearing (Sec 12)

Take care not to damage the hose. Hold the caliper support with wire hooks and remove the brake disc.

3 Place a dial indicator against the rear axle shaft portion (see illustration). Measure the axial play of the rear wheel bearing and see that it falls within the Specifications.

4 If your axial play does not meet Specifications, refer to the next Section in this Chapter to remove the rear axle.

13 Axle shaft – removal and installation

1 The rear axle shafts must be removed to replace leaking seals, defective wheel bearings and, obviously, broken axle shafts. Removal of the differential assembly for repair also necessitates removal of the axle shafts. Since special tools are required to properly disassemble and reassemble the rear bearing housings, it is recommended that servicing of the rear wheel bearings be left to the dealer service department or a reputable repair shop.

2 Various shims, seals and O-rings are required to properly reassemble and install the axle shafts, so be sure to read through the entire procedure before beginning the job to make sure that you have all the necessary parts.

3 Raise the vehicle and set it on jackstands. Remove the rear wheels.

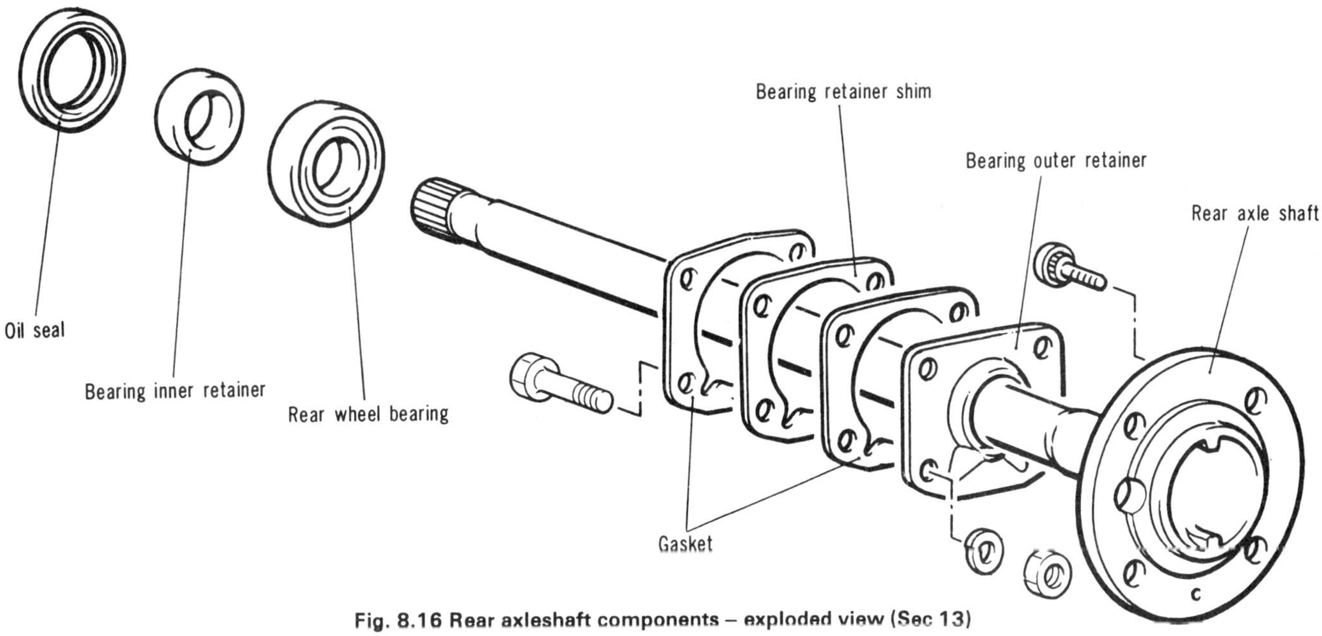

Fig. 8.16 Rear axleshaft components – exploded view (Sec 13)

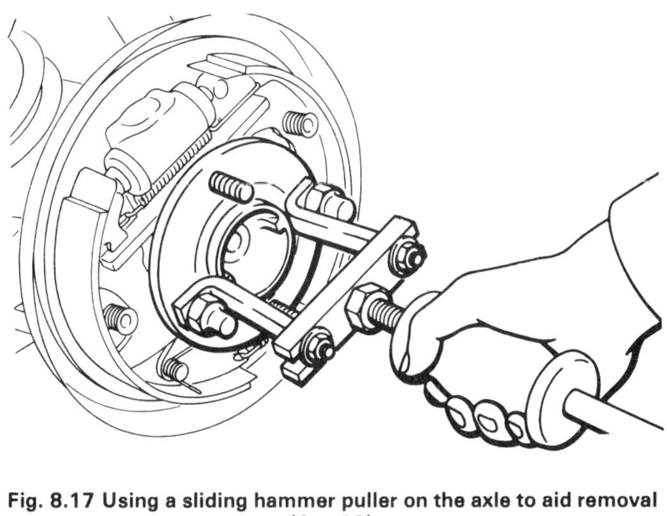

Fig. 8.17 Using a sliding hammer puller on the axle to aid removal (Sec 13)

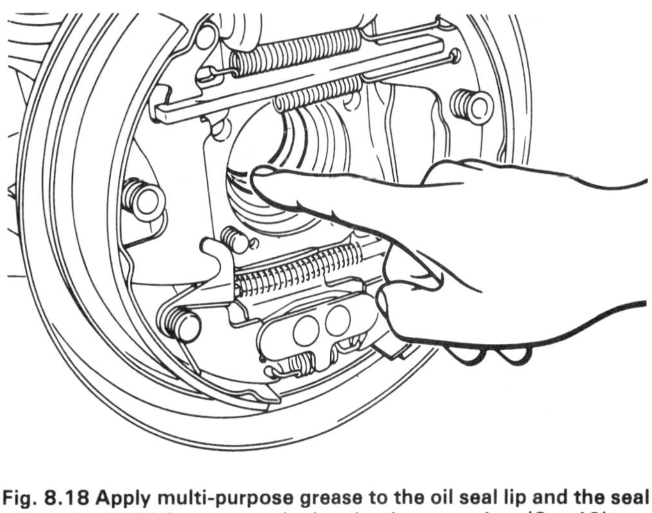

Fig. 8.18 Apply multi-purpose grease to the oil seal lip and the seal surface which contacts the bearing inner retainer (Sec 13)

8

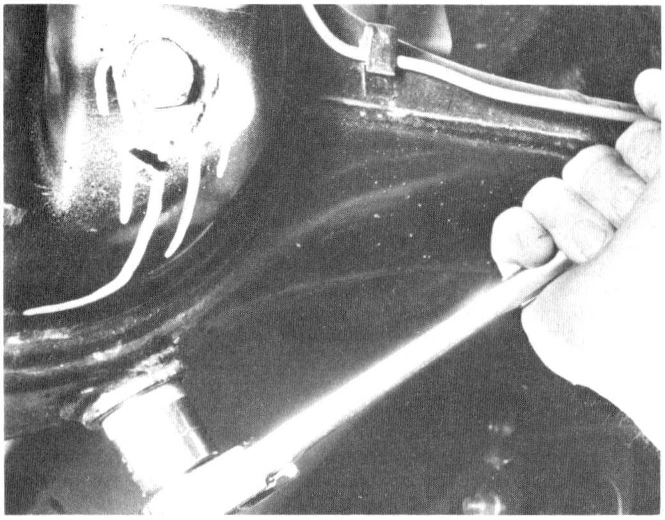

13.4 Remove the drain and fill plugs from the rear axle and drain the fluid into a suitable container

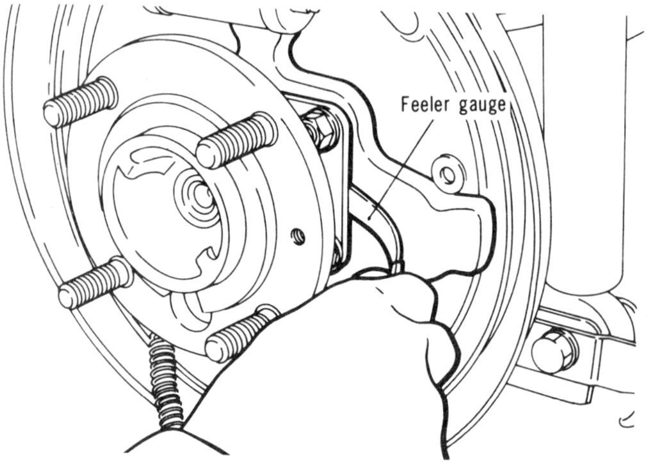

Fig. 8.19 Measure the gap between the bearing outer retainer and the backing plate to obtain shim thickness (Sec 13)

13.7 Pull the axle and brake assembly out of the axle housing

13.9 After noting which side is facing out, remove the shaft seal

4 Remove the drain and fill plugs from the rear axle housing (photo) and allow the differential lubricant to drain into a suitable container. When the draining is complete, reinstall the plugs loosely.

5 Remove the brake drum from the end of the axle and the metal brake line from the wheel cylinder by referring to Chapter 9.

6 Remove the parking brake cables from the vehicle as described in Chapter 9. Do not disconnect the cables from the levers in the rear brake assemblies. If only one axle shaft is being removed, remove only the cable on the side of the vehicle that the axle shaft is being removed from. If both axle shafts are being removed, both parking brake cables must also be removed.

7 Remove the nuts and lock washers attaching the bearing outer retainer and brake backing plate to the axle housing and withdraw the axle, the outer retainer, the brake backing plate and brake assembly from the axle housing (photo). A slide hammer-type axle puller may be required to dislodge the bearing retainer from the axle housing. Do not pry between the two flanges, as damage to the gasket sealing surfaces will result. Support the axle shaft as it is removed from the axle housing to prevent damage to the oil seal in the end of the axle housing.

8 Remove the shim (or shims) from the rear axle housing flange. Retain the shims for reassembly.

9 Inspect the oil seal inside the rear axle housing. If it is worn or damaged, or if there is any evidence of leakage, replace the seal. After noting which side of the seal is showing, pry or pull it out of the housing with a screwdriver or a slide hammer-type seal puller (photo).

10 Thoroughly clean the seal mounting area, and install a new seal (with the rubber side facing out) using a hammer and a block of wood or other suitable tool. Tap the seal carefully into place around its entire circumference and make sure it is properly seated in the axle housing.

11 Refer to the next section for the rear axle shaft oil seal and bearing replacement.

12 Inspect the axle shaft splines where the shaft mates with the differential inside the axle housing. If these splines are damaged or worn, the axle shaft should be replaced. Check the oil seal lip contact area of the shaft for wear and cracks. If any defects are noted, replace the shaft.

13 Before beginning the assembly procedure, remove all old gasket sealer and any rust from the mating surfaces of the bearing retainer and the axle housing. Also, thoroughly pack the bearing retainer and axle housing end with high-temperature wheel bearing grease and lubricate the lip of the oil seal in the axle housing.

14 If both axle shafts have been removed, the left-side shaft should be installed first during reassembly.

15 Install a 0.040 in (1.0 mm) shim into place on the left end of the axle housing.

16 Carefully install the left-side axle/brake assembly into the rear axle housing. Do not damage the oil seal in the process. It may be necessary to turn the axle slightly to engage its inner splines with the

differential. You may have to tap gently on the axle hub with a soft-faced hammer to seat the bearing retainer in the end of the axle housing.
17 Install the lock washers and nuts attaching the bearing retainer and brake backing plate to the axle housing. Tighten the nuts to the specified torque.
18 Install the right-side axle into the housing without a shim in place, and temporarily tighten the attaching nuts to a torque of 0.4 ft-lb (0.6 Nm). When the axle is installed in this manner, a gap will exist between the bearing retainer and the axle housing end flange, which must be measured with a feeler gauge.
19 Separate the axle shaft from the housing and select a shim with a thickness equal to the gap measured in the previous step. Also, select a shim with a thickness of from 0.020 to 0.079 in (0.05 to 0.20 mm). A list of available preload adjusting shims is included in the Specifications Section at the front of this Chapter.
20 Install the previously selected shims into place on the end of the axle housing.
21 Carefully install the axle assembly into the housing. Install the lock washers and nuts and tighten the nuts to the specified torque.
22 Using a dial indicator, check the axial play of the axle shaft by pulling out and pushing in on the axle shaft hub (photo). If the play is more or less than specified, remove the right-side axle again and replace the shims with shims that are thicker or thinner, as required.
23 Reinstall the axle and recheck the axial play. If necessary, repeat the procedure until the correct amount of play is obtained.
24 Install the parking brake cables, hook up the brake lines and install the brake drums by referring to Chapter 9. Also, bleed the brakes at the rear wheel cylinder as described in Chapter 9.
25 Tighten the rear axle housing drain plug to the specified torque and fill the housing to the proper level with the recommended gear lubricant. Install the filler plug and tighten it to the specified torque.
26 Install the wheels, lower the vehicle to the ground and test drive it. Check for leaks where the wheel bearing retainer attaches to the rear axle housing.

14 Axle shaft oil seal and bearing – replacement

1 At this point, the axle shaft assembly should be taken to a dealer service department or a reputable repair shop to have the outer oil seal and wheel axle bearing replaced.
2 The special tools required are out of the scope of the home mechanic.

15 Pinion oil seal – replacement

1 It is not uncommon for the pinion shaft oil seal to fail, which results in the leakage of differential gear lubricant past the seal and onto the driveshaft flange yoke. This seal is quite easily replaced without removing or disassembling the differential.
2 Raise the vehicle and set it on jackstands.
3 Remove the drain and fill plugs from the rear axle housing and allow the differential lubricant to drain into a suitable container. When the draining is complete, loosely install the drain plugs.
4 Separate the driveshaft from the differential end yoke by referring to Section 9. Be sure to tie the end of the driveshaft up, out of the way.
5 Set the parking brake, to keep the rear wheels from turning, and remove the large nut and washer from the end of the pinion gear shaft.
6 Pull off the differential end yoke, using a gear puller. Carefully pry off the dust cover and the oil seal will be visible.
7 After noting what the visible side of the oil seal looks like, carefully pry it out of the differential with a screwdriver or a pry bar. Be careful not to damage the splines on the pinion shaft.
8 Clean the seal mounting area, the outside diameter of the new seal and the pinion shaft with a clean rag.
9 Lubricate the new seal lip with molybdenum disulfide grease and carefully install it in position in the differential. Tap it into place with a hammer and a block of hardwood or other suitable tool. Work around the entire circumference of the seal, a little at a time, with the hammer and block of wood, until the seal is properly seated. Work slowly, and do not damage the rubber lip of the seal.
10 Install the dust cover on the differential.
11 Clean the sealing lip contact surface of the differential end yoke. Apply a thin coat of molybdenum disulfide grease and carefully install it onto the end of the pinion shaft. You will have to rotate the end yoke slightly, to line up the splines in the yoke and on the shaft.
12 Use a soft-faced hammer to tap the yoke into place, then install the large washer and a new self-locking nut on the end of the pinion shaft.
13 Disengage the parking brake and snug up the nut as you let the flange rotate. This will help to seat the pinion shaft bearings properly as the nut is tightened.
14 Tighten the nut to the specified torque while holding the wheel to keep the pinion shaft from turning. This torque figure is very important, as it determines the preload on the pinion shaft bearings.
15 Fasten the rear of the driveshaft to the differential end yoke by referring to Section 9.
16 Tighten the drain plug in the rear axle housing to the specified torque and fill the housing to the proper level with the recommended gear lubricant (see *Recommended lubricants and fluids* at the front of the book). Install the filler plug and tighten it to the specified torque.
17 Lower the vehicle to the ground. Test drive it and check around the differential end yoke for evidence of leakage.

16 Differential assembly – removal and installation

1 Raise the wheel and set it on jackstands. Remove the rear wheels.
2 Remove the drain and fill plugs from the rear axle housing and allow the differential lubricant to drain into a suitable container. Reinstall the plugs loosely.
3 Make a mark across the driveshaft flange yoke and the differential end yoke (where they come together) so the driveshaft can be reinstalled in exactly the same position. Remove the nuts, lock washers and bolts that attach the driveshaft to the differential. Pull the driveshaft loose from the differential and tie the end of it up out of the way so that the differential carrier assembly can be removed.
4 Remove the axle shafts as described in Section 13.
5 Remove the nuts and lock washers attaching the differential carrier assembly to the rear axle housing (photo). Tap the carrier with a soft-faced hammer, to break the gasket seal, and lift the carrier assembly out of the axle housing (photo). Do not pry between the

16.5a Remove the nuts attaching the differential carrier assembly to the rear axle

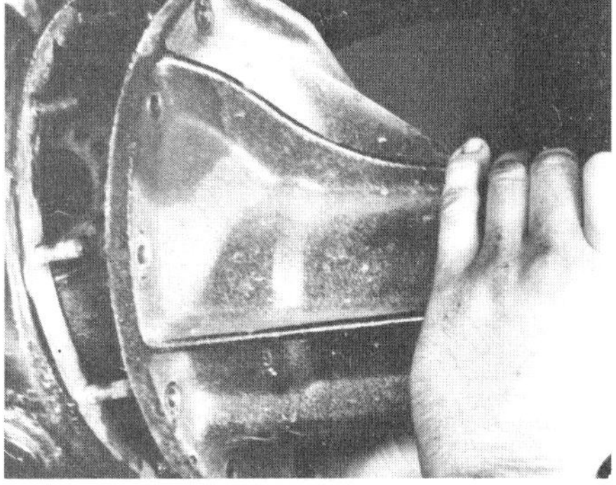
16.5b Carefully pull the differential carrier assembly off the rear axle

16.8 The tab on the gasket must face to the right

8

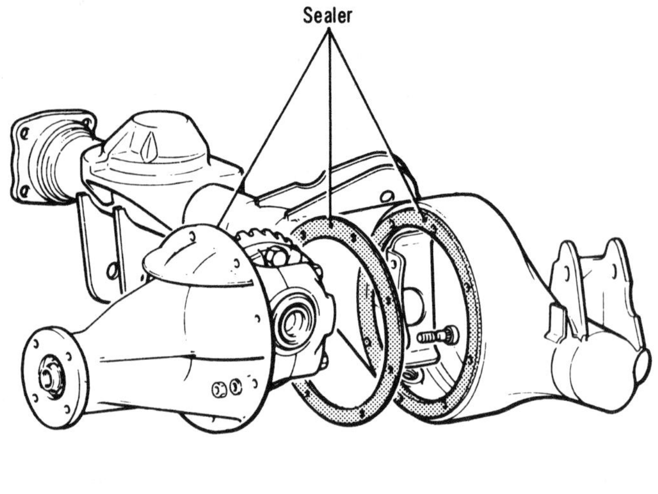

Fig. 8.20 Add sealant to both contact surfaces of the gasket, the differential and the axle housing before assembly (Sec 16)

16.9 Tighten the mounting nuts to the specified torque

carrier and the axle housing, as damage to the gasket sealing surfaces will result.

6 Scrape all traces of the old gasket and gasket sealer from the rear axle housing.

7 Before installing the differential carrier assembly into the rear axle housing, pack molybdenum disulfide grease into the ring gear teeth.

8 Apply an even coat of silicone-type gasket sealer to both sides of a new gasket and install the gasket into place on the rear axle housing with the tab to the right (photo).

9 Carefully install the differential carrier assembly into place on the rear axle housing. Install the lock washers and nuts and tighten the nuts to the specified torque, using a criss-cross pattern (photo).

10 Fit the end of the driveshaft into place on the differential assembly. Be sure to line up the marks on the driveshaft flange yoke and the differential end yoke. Install the bolts, lock washers and nuts and tighten the nut to the specified torque.

11 Install the axle shafts by referring to Section 13. Don't forget to fill the rear axle housing to the proper level with the recommended gear lubricant.

12 Install the wheels and lower the vehicle to the ground.

17 Differential assembly – overhaul

1 Problems in the differential cannot be accurately diagnosed or repaired without removing the differential from the rear axle housing.

2 As was mentioned before, major repair work on the differential is best left to a dealer-authorized service department or a reputable repair shop. The home mechanic can remove the differential, check for obvious problems, have the repair work done and then install it back in the vehicle.

3 If an overhaul is to be performed, be sure to read through the entire overhaul procedure before beginning. Also, check for availability of parts and arrange to borrow or rent any special tools that are required.

4 Remove the differential assembly from the vehicle by referring to Section 16.

5 Prior to disassembly of the differential, clean the exposed components with new, clean solvent and dry them thoroughly.

6 Check the ring gear and the drive pinion teeth for abnormal wear, scoring, pitting, cracks and other damage. A gear with damaged or broken teeth obviously must be replaced.

7 Check for correct gear tooth contact as follows: Apply a thin coat of white lead (or its equivalent) to both the drive and coast side of each of the ring gear teeth. Turn the ring gear through about 2 or 3 revolutions, then check the patterns on the gear teeth. Correct tooth contact will be indicated by a pattern of 60% to 80% contact on the drive side of the teeth (starting at the center and progressing toward the toe end) and a pattern of 40% to 60% on the coast side of the teeth, toward the toe end (see the illustration).

8 If the gears are not worn or damaged, the tooth contact can be adjusted by replacing the shims in the differential assembly, which moves the drive pinion and ring gear in relationship to each other. If correct tooth contact cannot be obtained by adjusting the gears, then excessive wear has occurred and both gears must be replaced **Note:** *Never replace only one gear.*

9 Remove the lock plate bolts and the lock plates from the carrier caps (photo).

10 Loosen the carrier cap bolts (there are two on each cap) (photo). You may have to mount the carrier assembly in a vise equipped with soft jaws to facilitate disassembly. The carrier caps should be marked, so they do not get mixed up during reassembly (photo). If they are not marked, use a punch or scribe to mark them before disassembly.

17.9 Remove the lock plate bolts and lock plates from the carrier caps

17.10a Loosen the carrier cap bolts

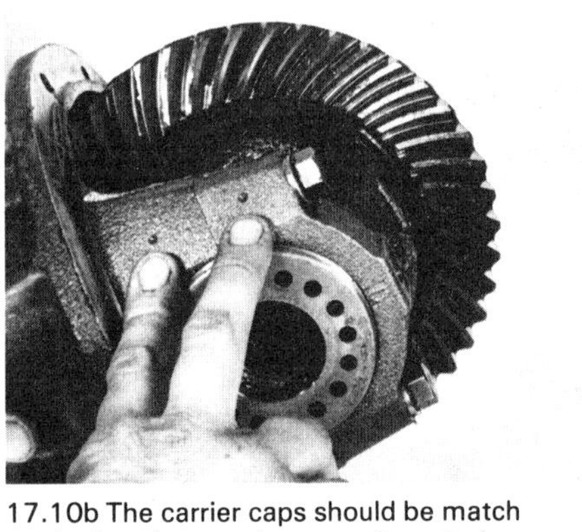

17.10b The carrier caps should be match marked so they can be properly mated during reassembly

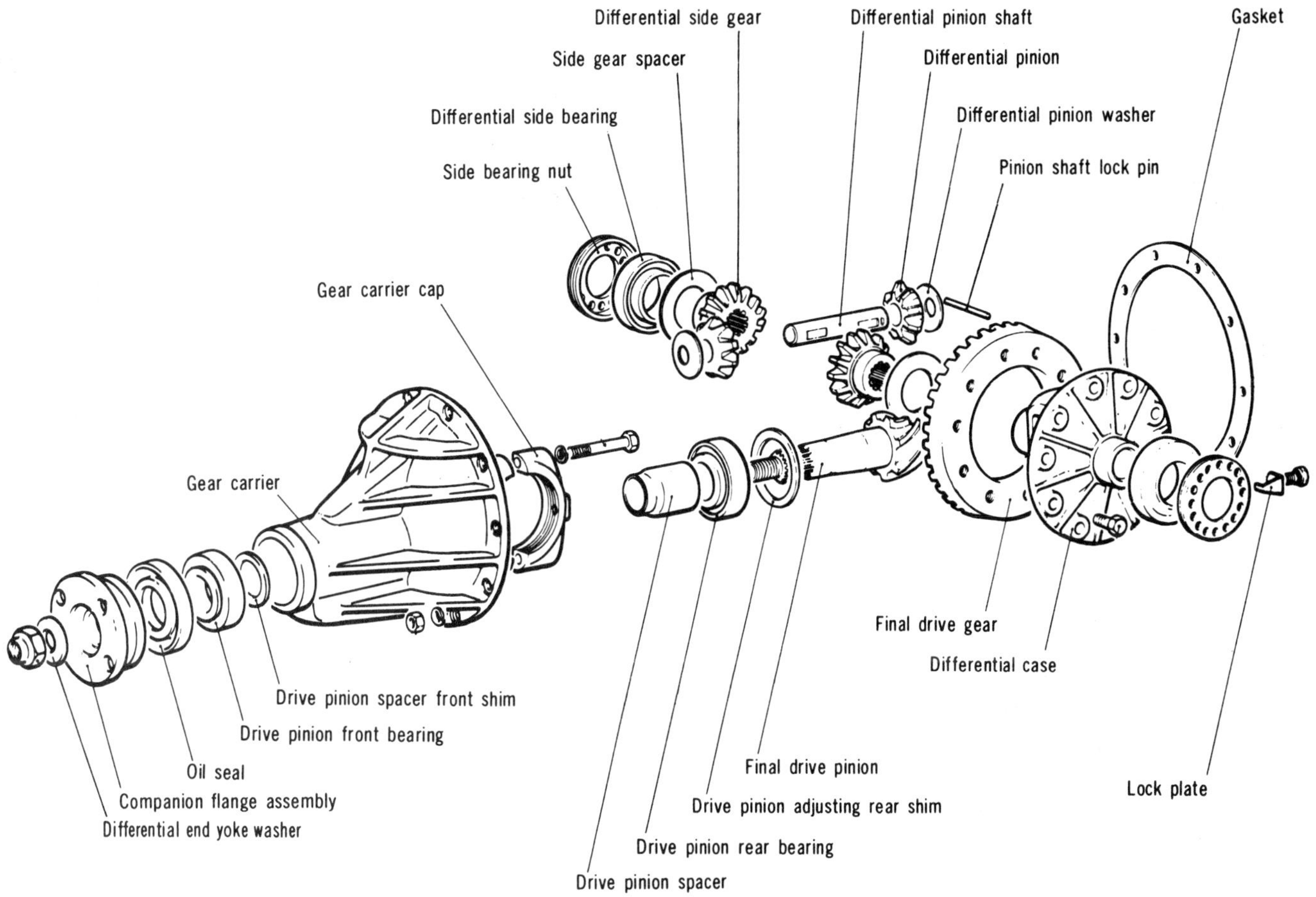

Fig. 8.21 Differential assembly components – exploded view (Sec 17)

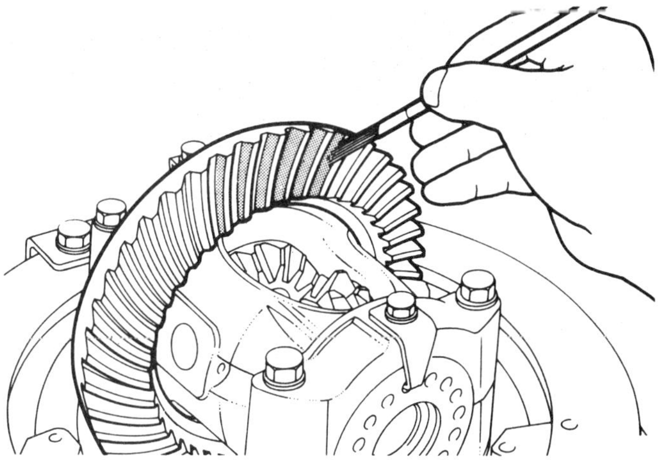

Fig. 8.22 Paint ring gear teeth for checking tooth contact (Sec 17)

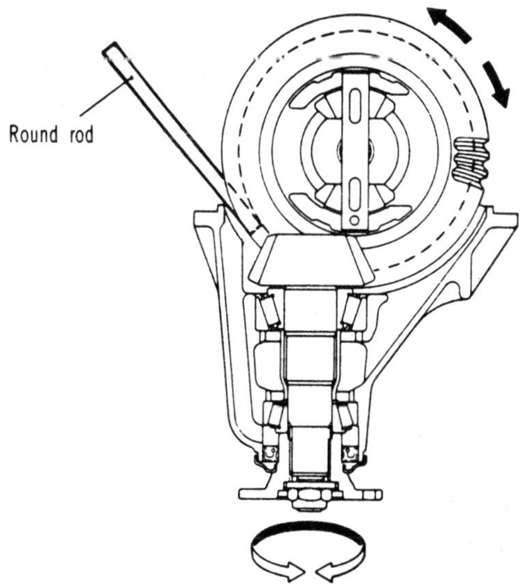

Fig. 8.23 Use a metal rod to turn ring gear two to three complete revolutions to check tooth contact (Sec 17)

11 Remove the side bearing nuts (photo).
12 Remove the carrier cap bolts completely and lift off the carrier caps (photo).
13 Lift out the differential gear case assembly, taking care not to drop the side bearing outer races (photo).
14 Using special tools numbered C-293-PA and MB990723 or an approved bearing puller, remove both differential side bearings (photo) (retain the bearings and any shims for reassembly). Lay the parts out on a clean surface in the order of disassembly.
15 Loosen the ring gear mounting bolts (photo) $\frac{1}{4}$ of a turn at a time in a crisscross pattern and dismount the ring gear. Again, it will probably be necessary to mount the differential gear assembly in a vise equipped with soft jaws to facilitate disassembly.
16 Drive out the spyder shaft lock pin from the ring gear back side (photo) and pull out the shaft, the center block, the spyder gears and the spyder washers (photo). The side gears and side gear thrust spacers can now be removed also (photo). Lay the parts out on a clean surface in the order of disassembly.
17 Loosen and remove the locknuts and large washer on the end of the drive pinion shaft (photo). You will have to hold the end yoke in a vise to keep the pinion shaft from turning.
18 Using a gear puller, remove the end yoke from the differential drive pinion shaft (photo). Drive out the pinion shaft using a soft-faced hammer (photo).

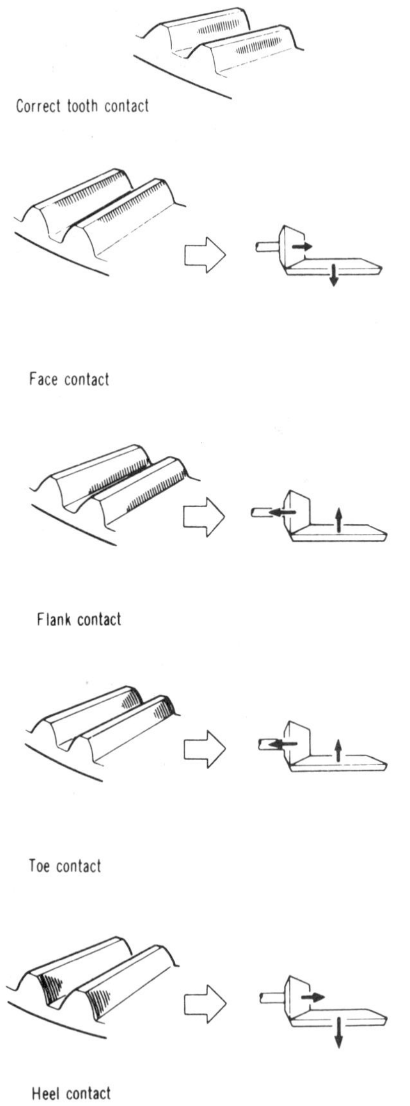

Fig. 8.24 Correct ring gear tooth contact adjustment chart (Sec 17)

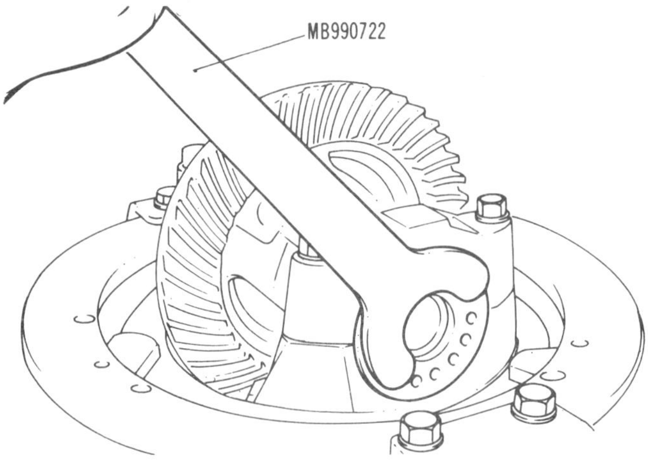

Fig. 8.25 Loosening and tightening the side bearing nuts (Sec 17)

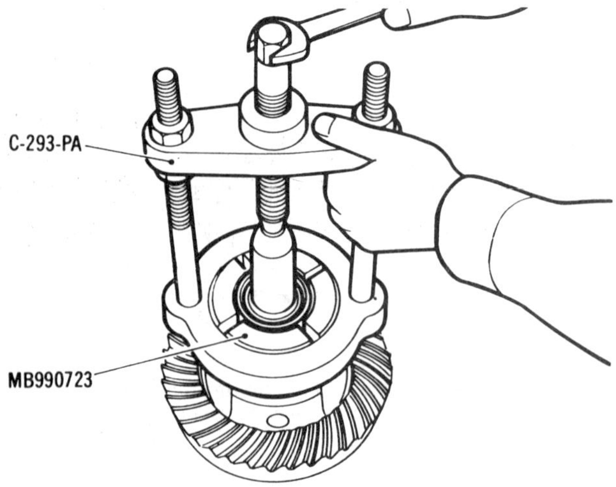

Fig. 8.26 Pulling off the differential side bearing (Sec 17)

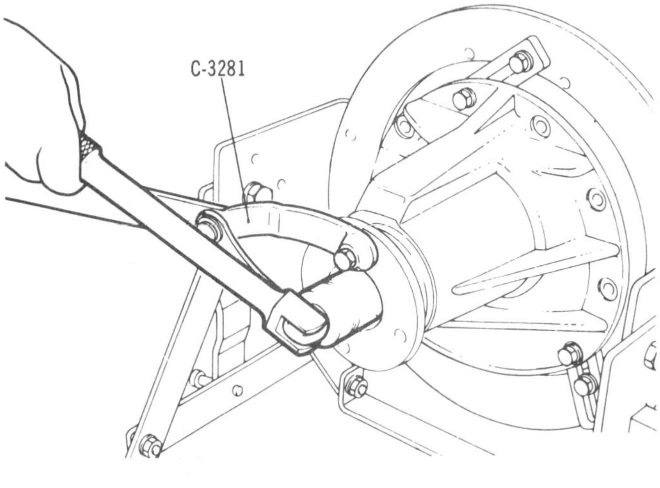

Fig. 8.27 Holding the companion flange to remove and install the locknut (Sec 17)

17.11 Remove the side bearing nuts

17.12 Lift off the carrier caps and bolts

17.13 Carefully lift out the gear case assembly

17.14 Using a bearing puller, remove the side bearings (do not pull on the outer bearing race)

17.15 Loosen the ring gear mounting bolts $\frac{1}{4}$ turn at a time and remove the gear

17.16a Drive out the spyder shaft lock pin from the ring gear backside

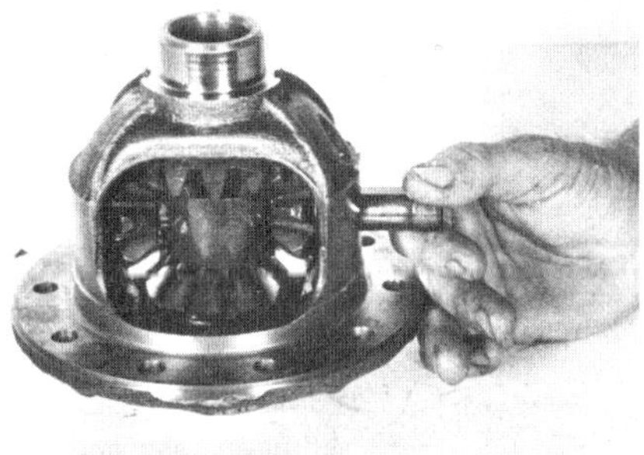

17.16b Pull out the spyder shaft

17.16c Remove the center lock, the spyder gears and the washers

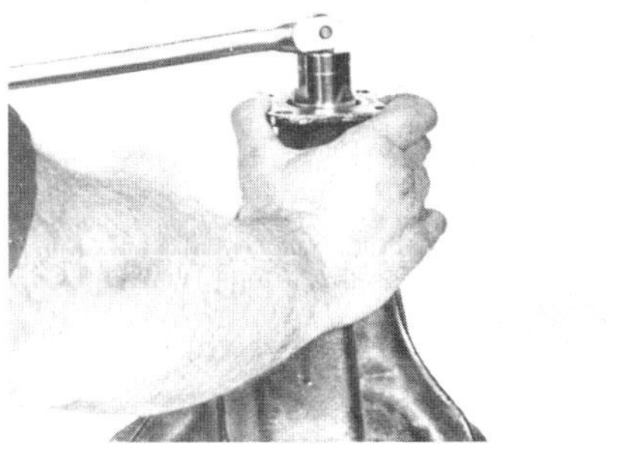

17.17 Loosen and remove the locknut and large washer at the end of the drive pinion shaft

17.18a Remove the end yoke from the differential pinion shaft with a gear puller

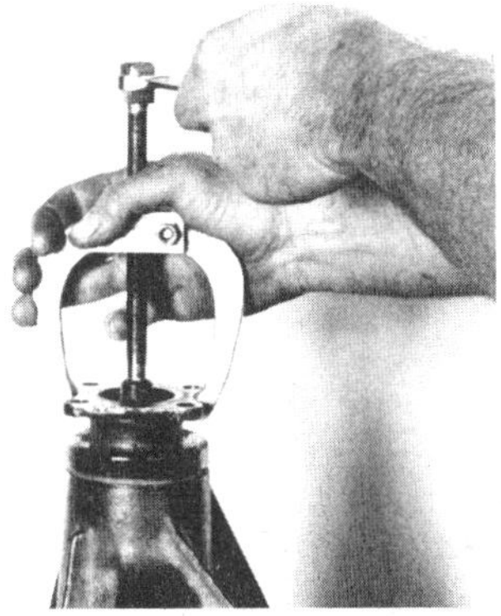

17.18b Drive out the pinion shaft with a soft-faced hammer

17.19a Remove the preload adjusting shim

17.19b Remove the drive pinion spacer

17.22 Remove the drive pinion oil seal from the differential case

17.23a Drive out the front bearing outer race

17.23b Drive out the rear bearing outer race

19 Remove the preload adjusting shim (photo) and the drive pinion spacer (photo) from the drive pinion shaft.
20 Pull the rear drive pinion bearing using special tools numbered C-293-PA and MB990723, or an approved bearing puller. Do not use a common gear puller, as damage to the bearing rollers will result.
21 Remove the drive pinion height adjusting shim.
22 Pry the drive pinion oil seal out of the differential case (photo). The forward drive pinion bearing can now be removed from the differential case.
23 Using a drift punch, remove the front and rear drive pinion bearing outer races (photo) (the differential case has grooves cast into it so that a drift punch can be placed directly on the bearing outer races) (photo). Lay the parts out on a clean surface in the order of disassembly.
24 Clean all the disassembled parts with solvent and dry them thoroughly.
25 Check all bearing races and rollers for cracks, pits and evidence of heat or seizure. Check bearing cages for deformation and cracks. Replace any defective bearings.
26 Install the differential side gears onto their respective axle shafts and check for play with a dial indicator on the spline pitch circle.
27 Check the spyder gear shaft and gear contact areas for evidence of heating or seizure. Check the differential spyder gear-to-spyder gear shaft clearance. Replace any part that is worn or damaged.

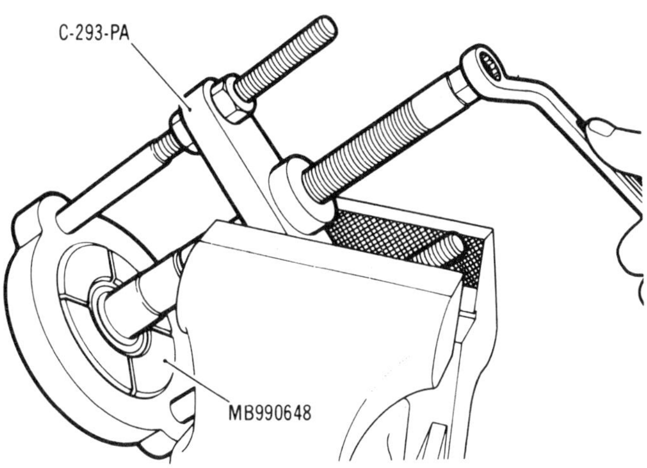

Fig. 8.28 Pulling off the drive pinion rear bearing inner race (Sec 17)

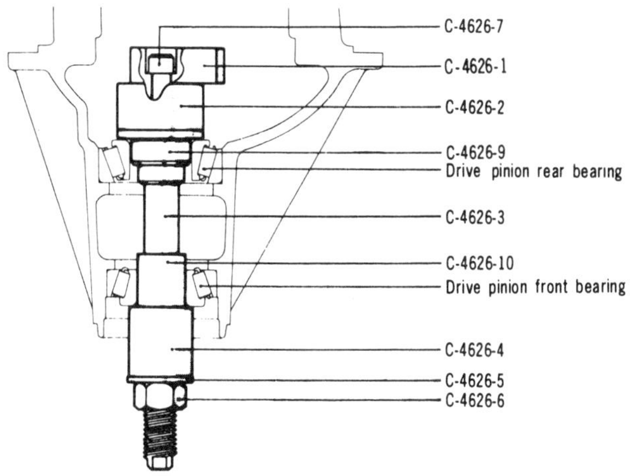

Fig. 8.29 The special tools needed to adjust the pinion height (Sec 17)

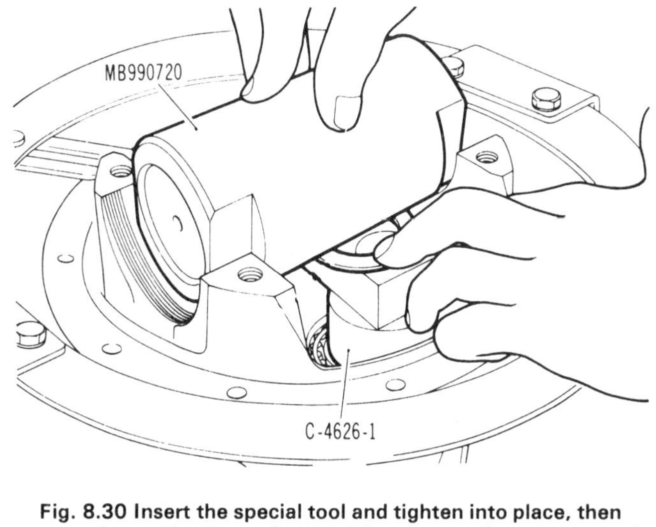

Fig. 8.30 Insert the special tool and tighten into place, then measure the gap between the special tools to arrive at a spacer for adjusting the drive pinion (Sec 17)

28 Assemble the pinion height gauge components (special tools in the illustration), and install the height gauge into the gear carrier.
29 Apply a thin coat of grease to the yoke side of the washer, then install the nut and tighten it to the drive pinion bearing preload (without the seal in place) torque with an appropriate torque wrench. This torque figure is only valid without the oil seal in place in the gear carrier.
30 Attach special tool number MB990720 to the gear carrier at the side bearing seats. Install the end cap and tighten the cap bolts to the specified torque.
31 Using feeler gauges, check the clearance between the two special tools.
32 Select a shim with a thickness equivalent to the clearance. A list of available drive pinion height adjusting shims is included in Specifications.
33 If the clearance is more than 0.0650 in (1.65 mm), select one 0.0118 in (0.3 mm) thick shim and one other shim to produce a total shim thickness equal to the clearance.
34 If the drive gear set (the ring gear and drive pinion) is being replaced, install new drive pinion height adjusting shims of the same thickness as the shims that were removed during disassembly.
35 Remove the special tools from the gear carrier.
36 Install the selected shim or shims between the drive pinion gear and the rear bearing inner race. Using special tool number MB990728, press the bearing onto the drive pinion shaft.
37 Install the drive pinion shaft, the rear bearing, the pinion spacer and the front bearing into the gear carrier. Slide the differential end yoke into place on the pinion shaft and install the large washer and nut. Tighten the nut to the specified torque.
38 Check the drive pinion bearing preload (the amount of torque required to start the drive pinion shaft turning) with an appropriate torque wrench and compare it to the Specifications.
39 If the preload is not the same as the Specifications, disassemble the drive pinion shaft, install a different thickness preload adjusting shim, reassemble the shaft and recheck the bearing preload. A list of available preload adjusting shims is included in the Specifications Section. Different length pinion spacers are also available and may be used in conjunction with the different shims to obtain the proper preload.
40 After completing the drive pinion bearing preload adjustment, remove the nut and washer from the end of the drive pinion shaft and install a new pinion seal by referring to Section 15.
41 Install the thrust spacers and side gears into the differential case.
42 Lay the spyder gear washers in position on the spyder gears. The washers have a lip on the inside diameter which must properly line up with the hole in the gear.
43 Mesh the spyder gears with the side gears exactly 180° apart and rotate them into position in the differential case.
44 Install the spyder gear shaft and check the spyder gear-to-side gear backlash with a dial indicator (photo). If the backlash is excessive, select a side gear thrust spacer of the proper thickness, install it and

17.44 Check the spyder gear-to-side-gear backlash with a dial indicator

17.53 Check the backlash between the ring and pinion gears

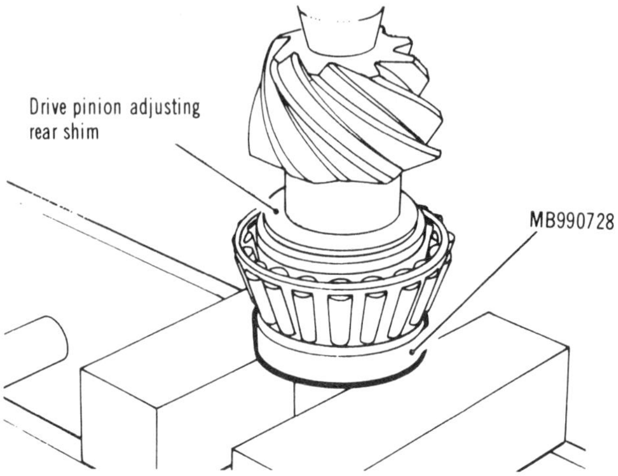

Fig. 8.31 Pressing in the drive pinion rear bearing inner race (Sec 17)

recheck the backlash. Backlash on the right and left side should be equal. A list of available side gear thrust spacers is included in the Specifications Section.

45 Disassemble the above parts, lubricate them with molybdenum disulfide grease, and reassemble them.

46 Place the center block into position. Install the spyder gear shaft and align the lock pin holes. Carefully drive the lock pin into position in the differential case and stake the differential case around the lock pin hole so that the pin will not back out.

47 Clean the ring-gear mounting bolts with a wire brush and the threaded holes in the ring-gear with the appropriate tap.

48 Apply 'Lock-tite 271', or an equivalent adhesive, to the bolt threads and install the ring-gear onto the differential case. Tighten the bolts to the specified torque, following a crisscross pattern. Set the assembly aside for approximately one-half to one hour to allow the adhesive to harden properly.

49 Press on the differential side bearings.

50 Slip the outer races into place and install the differential gear assembly into the differential case. Lay the caps in place by lining up the mating marks on the right-hand cap. Install the cap bolts and tighten them finger-tight.

51 Carefully thread the side bearing nuts into position and, using special tool number MB990722, or an equivalent homemade tool, tighten the left-hand nut until all backlash between the ring and pinion gears is removed.

52 Loosen the left-hand nut $\frac{1}{16}$ of a turn (the distance between two of the holes) tighten the right-hand bearing nut to the specified torque.

53 Using a dial indicator, check the backlash between the ring and the pinion gears (photo). If the lash is less than specified, loosen the left-hand bearing nut $\frac{1}{16}$ of a turn and tighten the right-hand bearing nut the same amount. Recheck the backlash. If it is greater than specified, loosen the right-hand bearing nut $\frac{1}{16}$ of a turn and tighten the left-hand bearing nut the same amount. Again, recheck the lash. Continue the operation until the backlash is within the Specifications.

54 Next, tighten each bearing nut $\frac{1}{32}$ of a turn ($\frac{1}{2}$ the distance between holes) to preload the bearings properly.

55 Tighten the carrier cap bolts to the specified torque (photo) and recheck the pinion and ring-gear backlash. Install the lock plates on the bearing caps and tighten the bolts to the specified torque (photo).

56 Using a dial indicator, check the ring gear run-out on the back side of the ring gear (photo). If the run-out is greater than specified, change the ring gear location relative to the differential case and recheck the run-out. If it is still greater than specified, disassemble the ring gear and check the run-out of the ring gear mounting surface on the differential case. If it is more than specified, replace the ring gear case. If it is within the Specifications, replace the ring gear with a new one.

57 Pack the ring gear teeth with molybdenum disulfide grease and install the differential assembly into the rear axle housing by referring to Section 16.

17.55a Tighten the carrier cap bolts to the specified torque

17.55b Tighten the lock plate bolts to the specified torque

17.56 Check the ring gear runout (on the backside of the gear) with a dial indicator

Chapter 9 Braking system

Contents

Specifications

Brake pedal

Free play	0.4 to 0.6 in (10 to 15 mm)
Depressed pedal-to-floorboard clearance	1 in (26 mm) or more
Height (distance between top of pedal and floorboard)	6.5 in (166 mm)
Lateral play between brake/clutch pedals	0.120 in (3 mm)

Parking brake

Hand lever lateral movement	0.24 in (6 mm)
Maximum lever stroke	4 to 6 notches

Master cylinder

Inside diameter	0.8748 to 0.8769 in (22.220 to 22.272 mm)
Piston diameter	0.8719 to 0.8732 in (22.147 to 22.180 mm)
Cylinder/piston clearance	0.0016 to 0.0049 in (0.040 to 0.125 mm)
Piston-to-power brake pushrod clearance	0 to 0.03 in (0 to 0.75 mm)

Disc brake

Pad thickness (standard)	0.41 in (10.5 mm)
Pad thickness (wear limit)	0.040 in (1.0 mm)
Disc thickness	0.79 in (20.0 mm)
Disc runout	Less than 0.006 in (0.15 mm)

Drum brake

Lining thickness (standard)	0.213 in (5.4 mm)
Lining thickness (wear limit)	0.040 in (1.0 mm)
Wheel cylinder bore	0.750 to 0.752 in (19.050 to 19.102 mm)
Piston diameter	0.7479 to 0.7492 in (18.997 to 19.030 mm)
Wheel cylinder/piston clearance	0.0008 to 0.0041 in (0.020 to 0.105 mm)
Inside diameter	9.5 to 9.579 in (241.3 to 243.3 mm)
Drum/lining clearance	0.010 to 0.016 in (0.25 to 0.40 mm)
Adjusting cable length	10.020 ± 0.006 in (254.5 ± 0.15 mm)
Primary (green) brake shoe return spring free length	4.35 in (110.5 mm)
Secondary (grey) brake shoe return spring free length	4.23 in (107.5 mm)

Torque specifications

	ft-lb	(Nm)
Master cylinder check valve cap	18 to 25	24 to 34
Master cylinder check valve case	29 to 36	39 to 49
Piston stop	1.1 to 2.2	1.5 to 3.0
Wheel cylinder bleeder screws	5 to 7	7 to 9
Disc brake caliper assembly bolts	51 to 65	69 to 88
Brake disc-to-hub nuts	30 to 35	40 to 47
Wheel cylinder attaching bolts	13 to 15	18 to 20
Power brake booster attaching nuts	6 to 9	8 to 12
Brake pedal-to-pedal support	5 to 7	7 to 9
Master cylinder	6 to 9	8 to 12
Combination valve	6 to 9	8 to 12
Porportioning valve	4 to 6	5 to 8

1 General information

The front wheels are equipped with sliding caliper disc brakes and the rear wheels with leading-trailing shoe drum brakes or sliding caliper disc brakes. All types of brakes are equipped with a self-adjusting mechanism so that the clearance between the brake shoes, linings and brake drums or the clearances between the brake pads and brake discs is automatically adjusted.

The driver's foot braking effort is assisted by a vacuum operated power servo unit.

The system is a dual-line type with a dual master cylinder and a separate hydraulic system for each of the front and rear wheels. In the event of a brake line or seal failure, half the braking system will still operate.

2 Fluid level – check and replacement

Refer to Chapter 1 to check or replace the brake fluid.

3 Brake pedal – check and adjustments

1 Refer to Chapter 1 to check the brake pedal operation.

2 Pedal height and free play are the only adjustments that may be required. Brake pedal height, or the distance from the floorboard to the pedal, should only need adjusting if the brake light switch is replaced or adjusted. If and when the brake pedal height is changed, the free play should also be checked and adjusted as necessary.

3 To adjust the pedal height, unplug the electrical connector in the wiring harness coming from the brake light switch. Loosen the jam nut and turn the brake light switch until the specified pedal height is obtained.

4 Tighten the jam nut, plug in the electrical connector and check the brake lights for proper operation. They should come on when the brake pedal is depressed and go out when it is released.

5 Check the pedal free play (the distance the pedal travels before actuating the piston in the power brake unit) and compare it to the Specifications.

6 If an adjustment is necessary, loosen the jam nut on the power brake pushrod (at the yoke that attaches the rod to the pedal) and turn the pushrod (pliers may be necessary) until the proper amount of free play is obtained. Tighten the jam nut securely.

7 Depress the pedal as far as possible and make sure that the pedal-to-floorboard clearance is as specified. If the pedal has an excessively long stroke, check the master cylinder piston-to-power pushrod clearance (see Section14) and the brake shoe lining-to-drum clearance.

4 Brake lines – inspection

Refer to Chapter 1 to inspect the brake lines.

5 Disc brake pads/disc – check

1 Refer to Chapter 1 to check the disc pads or brake disc for wear.

2 To inspect the rear disc brake pads, first remove the caliper dust cover.

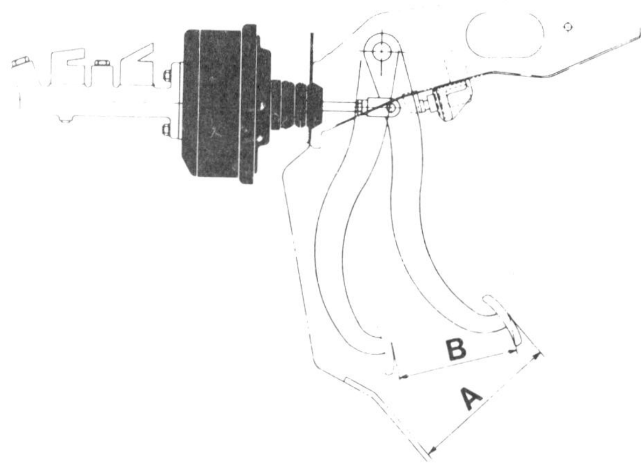

Fig. 9.1 Check pedal height (A) and pedal freeplay (B) (Sec 3)

6 Disc brake pads (front) – replacement

1 Raise the front of the vehicle and set it on jackstands. Block the rear tires and set the parking brake to keep the vehicle from rolling. Remove the wheels. It is a good idea to disassemble only one brake at a time so that the other brake can be used as a guide if difficulties are encountered during reassembly.

2 Remove the spigot pins from the stopper plugs (photo). Each caliper has two stopper plugs and each stopper plug has two spigot pins.

3 Pull out the stopper plugs and pad support plates from the caliper body. Move the caliper assembly diagonally up and down to separate it from the caliper support bracket. The upper caliper bracket bolt should be removed if it interferes with the metal brake line during caliper removal. Tie the caliper out of the way (photos).

4 Remove the pads from the caliper support bracket. Separate the anti-squeal shim from the outer pad (photo). Remove the inner and outer pad shims and the pad clips from the caliper support bracket.

5 The pads in each caliper must be replaced as a set and the pads on both front wheels must be replaced during the same servicing. Never replace the pads on one wheel only.

6 Before installing the new brake pads, check the brake disc as described in Section 10. Also check the caliper assembly around the piston for signs of brake fluid leakage. If leakage is evident, refer to Section 8 for caliper repair procedures.

7 Check the stopper plugs, the pad support plates, the anti-rattle spring, and the pad clips for damage. Replace any defective parts.

8 Install the inner and outer pad clips and the pad clips into position on the caliper support bracket.

9 Slip the new brake pads into place. Make sure the anti-squeal shim is installed on the outer pad (photo).

10 Wipe clean the exposed part of the piston in the caliper assembly and, using a hammer handle, push the piston into its bore so that the caliper assembly will fit over the new pads. If the piston does not want to slide in, loosen the bleeder screw and push again. The piston should

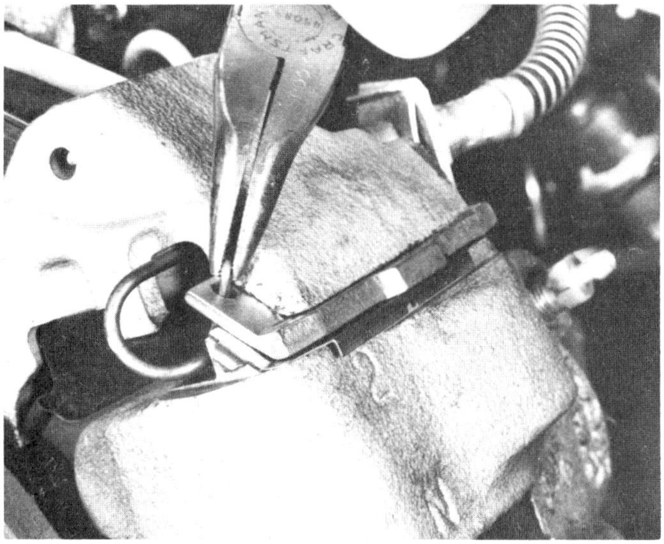

6.2 Pull the spigot pins out of the stopper plugs

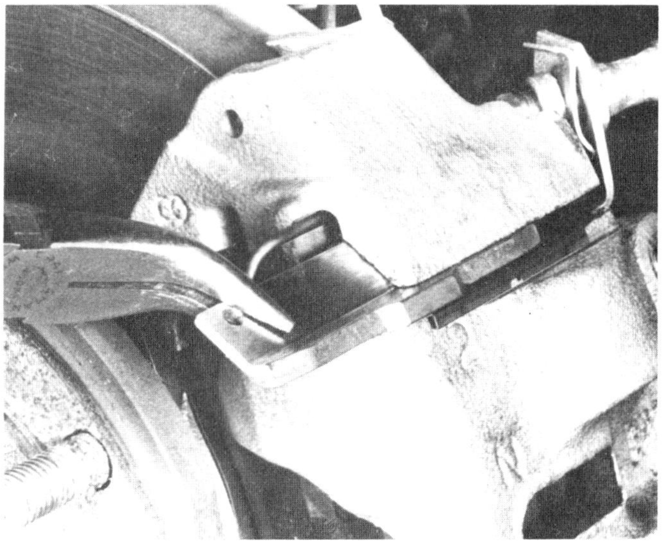

6.3a Remove the stopper plugs from the caliper

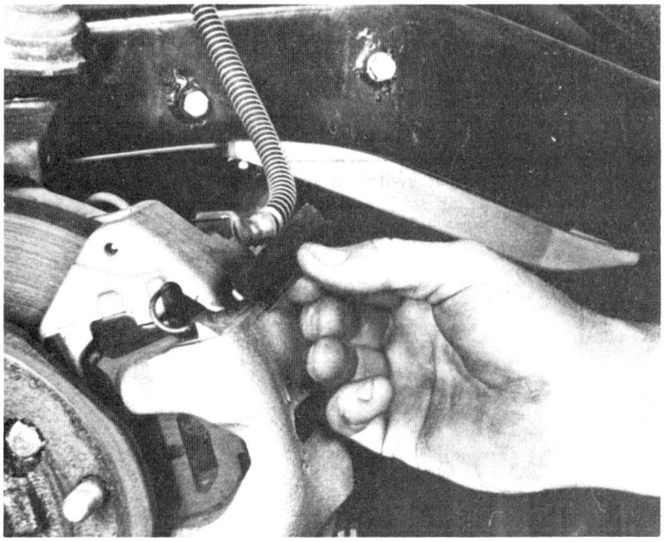

6.3b Remove the pad support plate from the caliper

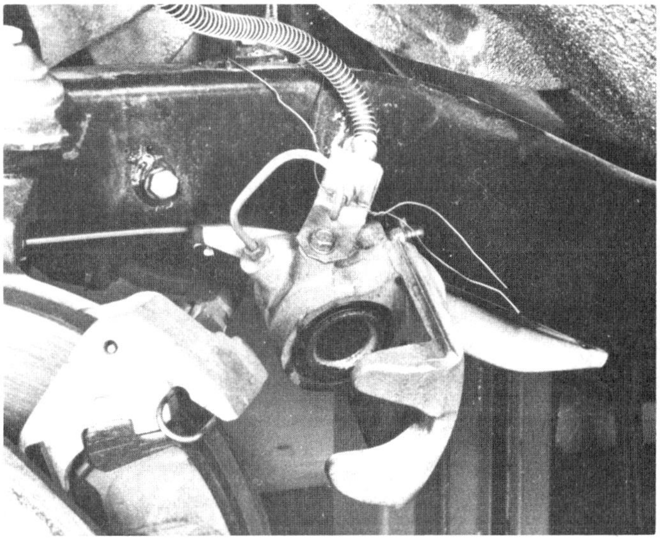

6.3c Carefully tie the caliper out of the way with a piece of wire

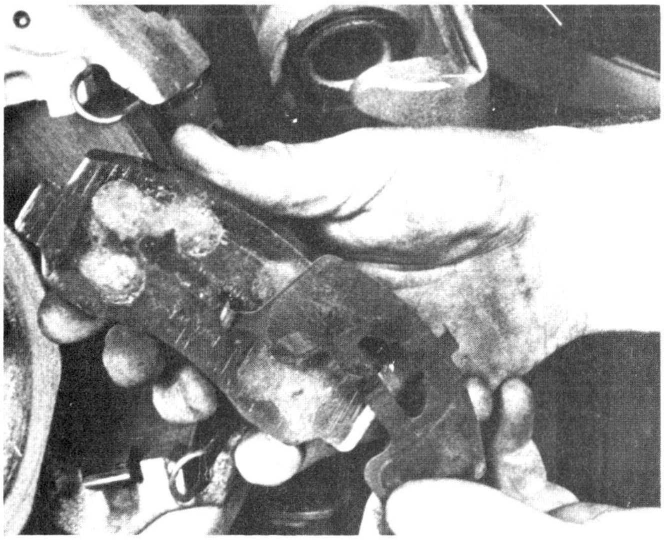

6.4 Remove the pads and separate the anti-squeal shim from the outer pad

6.9 Slip the new pads into place. Make sure the anti-squeal shim is installed on the outer pad

slide in easily. Be sure to bleed the system as described in Section 2D if you have to loosen the bleeder screw. Apply a thin layer of brake grease to the sliding surfaces of the plug plates and the stopper plugs.

11 Slide the caliper assembly over the new pads and make sure it is properly seated on the caliper support bracket. Don't forget to install and tighten the upper caliper bracket bolt if it was removed.

12 Install the pad support plates, the stopper plugs and the spigot pins.

13 Install the wheels and lower the vehicle to the ground. Be sure to bleed the brake system if the bleeder screw on the caliper assembly was loosened. Test drive the vehicle.

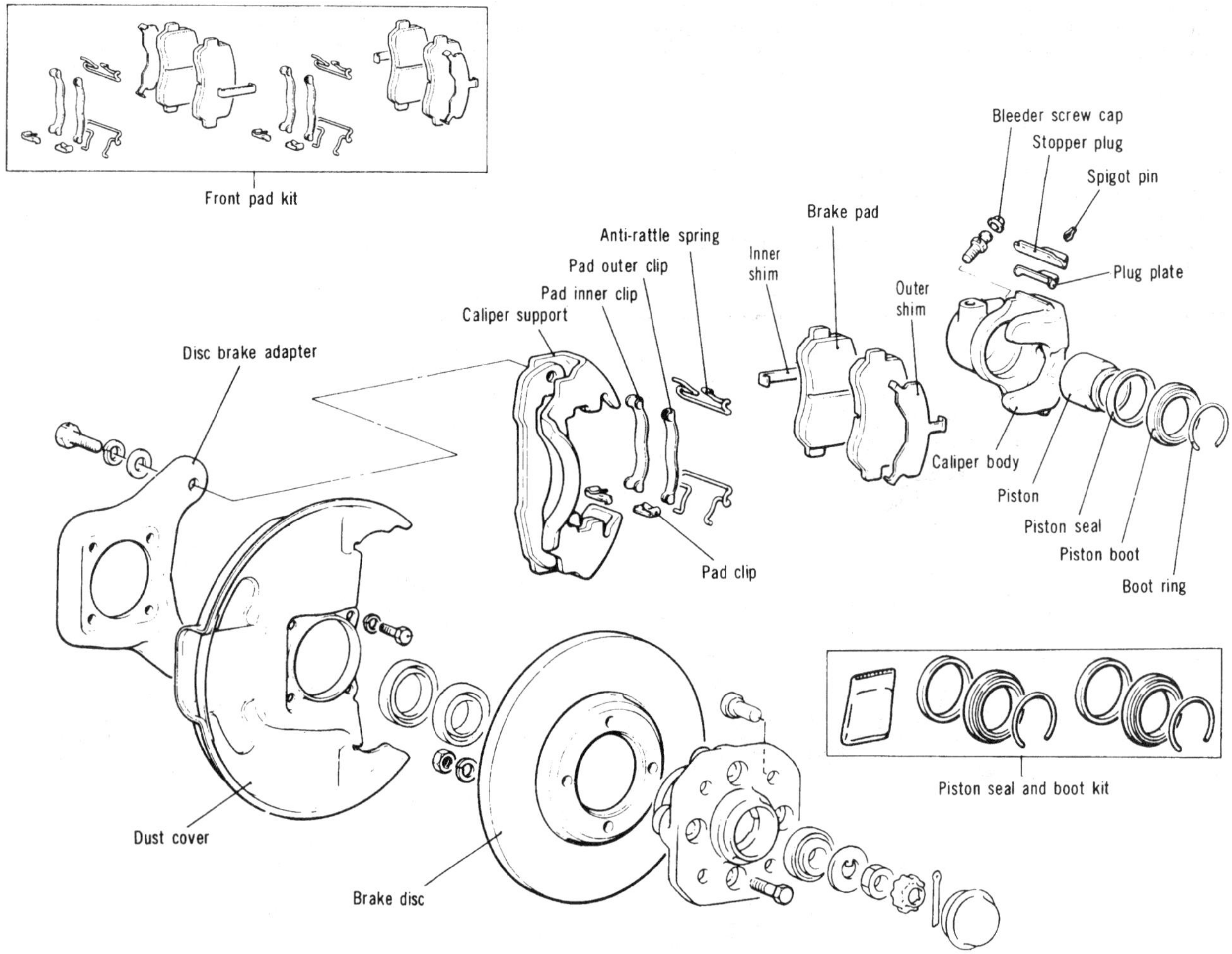

Fig. 9.2 Front disc brake assembly components – exploded view (Sec 6)

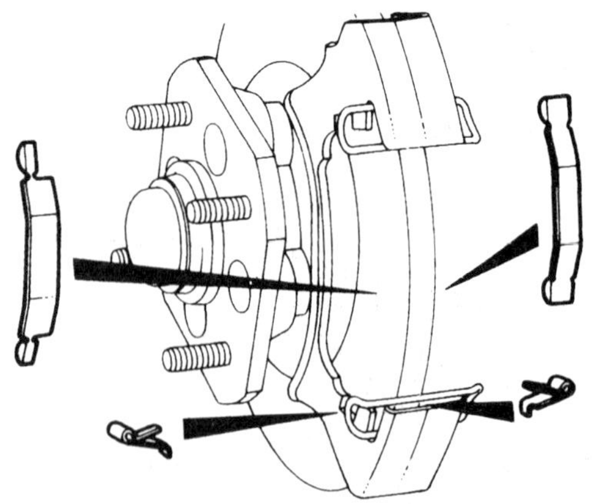

Fig. 9.3 Correct installation of springs and clips (Sec 4)

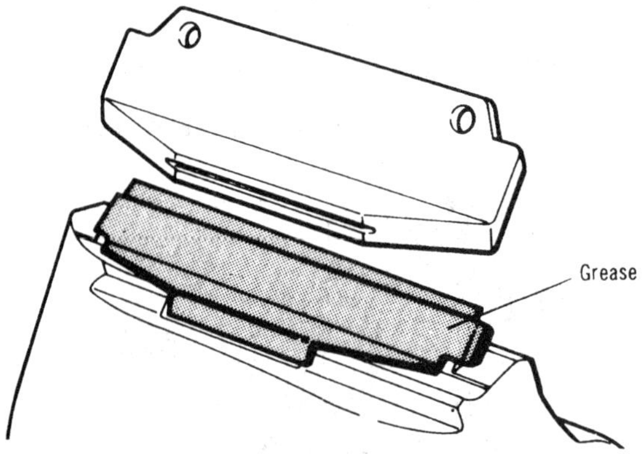

Fig. 9.4 Apply brake grease to the sliding surfaces of the plug plates and stopper plugs (Sec 6)

7 Disc brake pads (rear) – replacement

1 In order to replace the disc brake pads on the rear of the vehicle, first remove the parking brake rear cable from the parking lever and the bracket by removing the retaining clips.

2 Remove the spigot pins and the support plugs from the caliper assembly.

3 Grab the calipers with your hand and lift them diagonally upward or downward and away from the caliper support. Position the calipers and with some wire, tie them out of the way without removing them completely from your vehicle. **Note:** *Be careful not to damage the brake lines in doing this.*

4 Now you can remove the brake pads from the caliper support and physically inspect them for wear. If they do not fall within the Specifications, replace them with new ones. **Note:** *Always replace the pads on both sides of your vehicle, never only one side at a time.*

5 Inspect the anti-rattle springs, the pad clips, the stopper plugs and the plug plates for abnormal wear or damage and replace any of them with new ones.

6 Apply a light coat of brake grease to the sliding surfaces of the stopper plugs and the plug plates **(see illustration)**.

7 Install the anti-rattle springs and clips into the caliper support **(see illustration)**.

8 Mount the anti-squeak shims to the brake pads, then install the pads to the caliper supports.

9 Using special tool MB990652, screw the piston clockwise into the caliper bore until it seats **(see illustrations)**.

Note: *On some models it will be necessary to line up the groove in the piston with a projection on the back of the brake pad.*

10 Install the caliper to the caliper support.

11 Depress the brake pedal fully several times, bleed the brakes if necessary, and check for excessive drag while rotating the discs.

12 Install the wheels and lower the vehicle to the ground. Road test the vehicle in an open area and check for proper brake operation.

8 Disc brake caliper (front) - overhaul

Note: *Obtain a caliper rebuild kit before starting this procedure.*

1 Jack up the front of the vehicle and set it on jack stands. Block the rear tires to keep the vehicle from rolling. Remove the wheels.

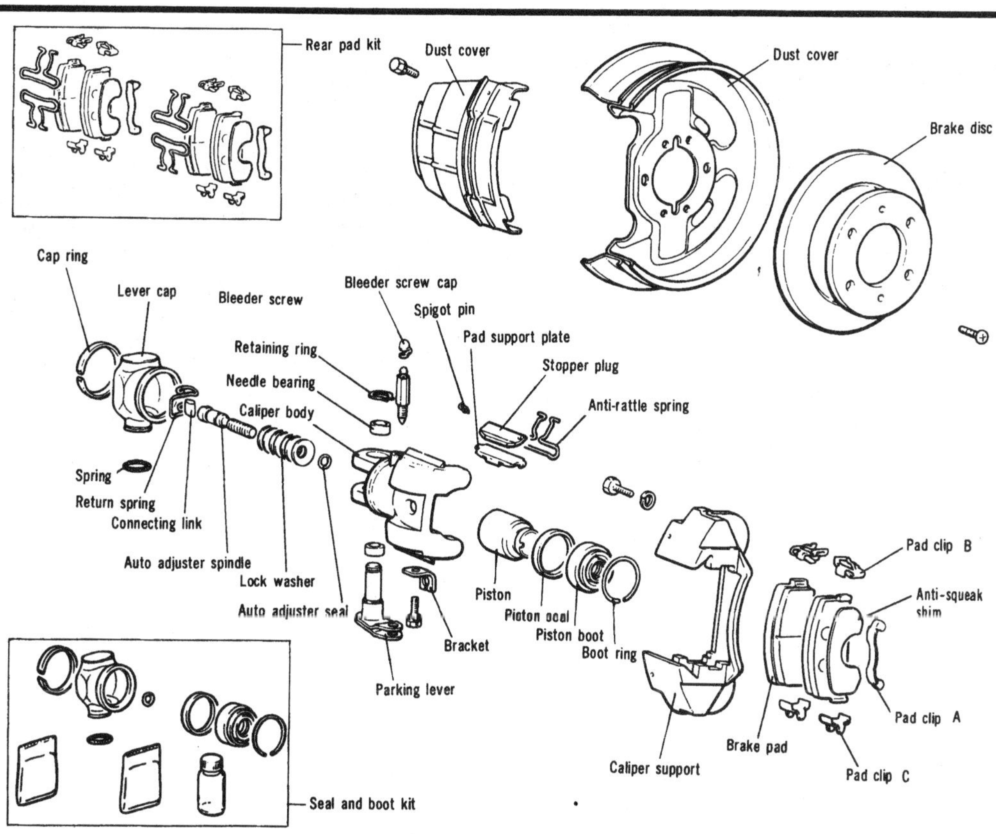

Fig. 9.5 Rear disc brake assembly components – exploded view (Sec 7)

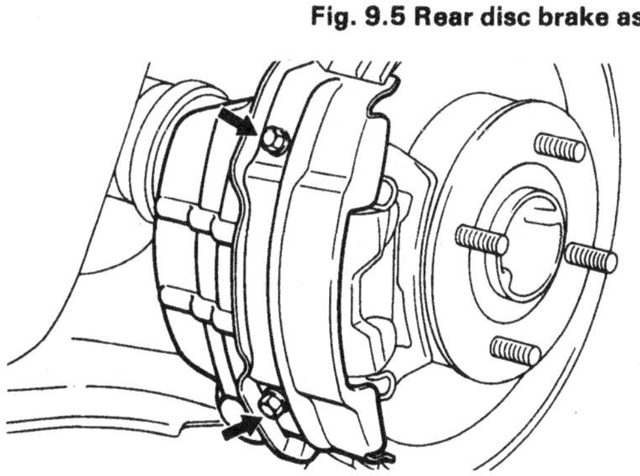

Fig. 9.6 To inspect the rear disc pads, remove the dust cover (Sec 7)

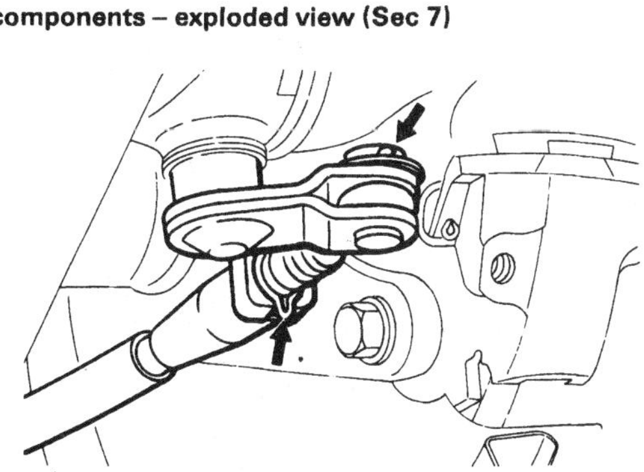

Fig. 9.7 Disconnect the parking brake rear cable from the lever and bracket (Sec 7)

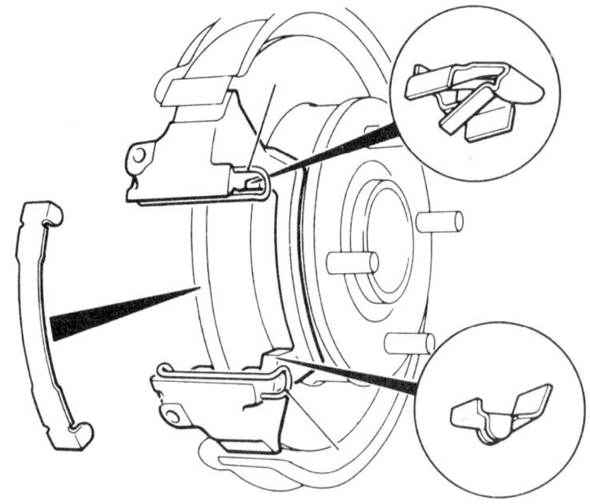

Fig. 9.8a Install the springs and clips into the caliper support (Sec 7)

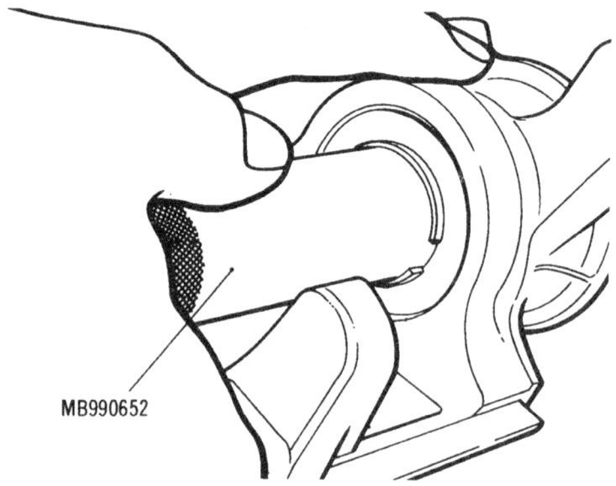

Fig. 9.8b Seat the piston into the caliper using a special tool (Sec 7)

2 Loosen the fitting which attaches the metal brake line to the flexible brake hose at the caliper bracket (photo). Pull out the spring clip holding the flexible hose to the bracket (photo) and disconnect the metal line from the flexible hose to the bracket (photo) and disconnect the metal line from the flexible hose. Place a container under the fitting to catch any brake fluid that may drip. Plug the flexible hose to keep out dirt and other contaminants.
3 Remove the caliper from the caliper support as described in Section 6 except, instead of tying them out of the way with some wire, remove the unit completely from the vehicle.
4 You must have a clean place to work, clean rags, a caliper rebuilt kit for each caliper, a container of brake fluid and some alcohol to perform the caliper overhaul.
5 Remove the pad support plates from the caliper assembly if you have not already done so. Next, remove the boot retaining snap-ring and the dust boot from around the piston (photos).
6 Loosen the fitting and remove the metal brake line from the caliper body (photo).
7 The piston must now be removed from the caliper body. This can be achieved in one of three ways, depending upon the degree of difficulty. Make sure the caliper cavity is well cushioned with rags to prevent damage to the piston or bore. Also, do not pry on the piston with metal tools.

a) First, try dislodging the piston by tapping the caliper with a wood block, or by jolting the caliper against two wood blocks.
b) If the above procedure does not work, temporarily reconnect the caliper to the brake fluid line. Have an assistant depress the brake pedal. The fluid pressure should force the piston out.
c) If compressed air is available, sometimes this air pressure can be used to move the piston. Blow the air into the brake line fitting hole (photo).

8 Remove the seal in the caliper bore with a plastic or wooden probe. Do not use a metal probe, as you may scratch or gouge the bore surface (photo).

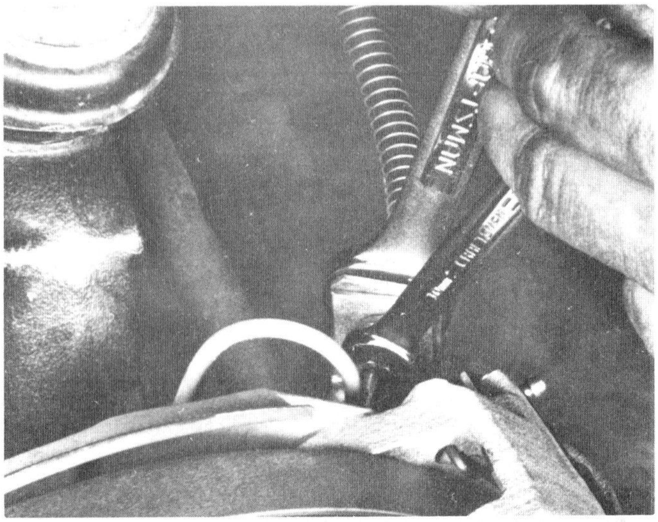

8.2a Use two wrenches to loosen the fitting which attaches the metal brake line to the flexible hose

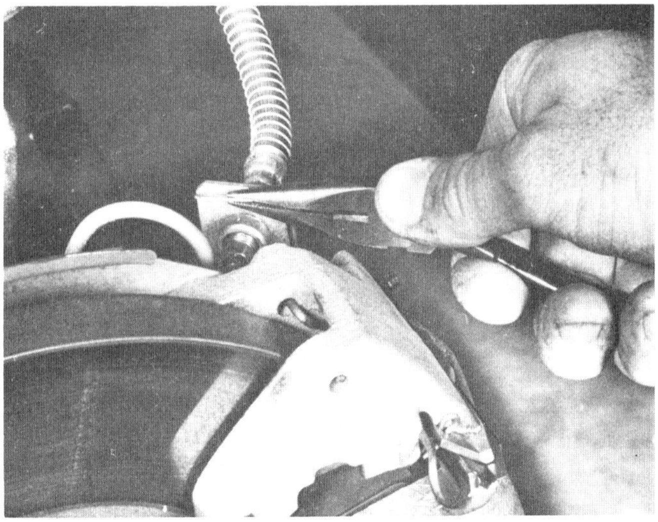

8.2b Pull out the spring clip holding the flexible hose to the bracket

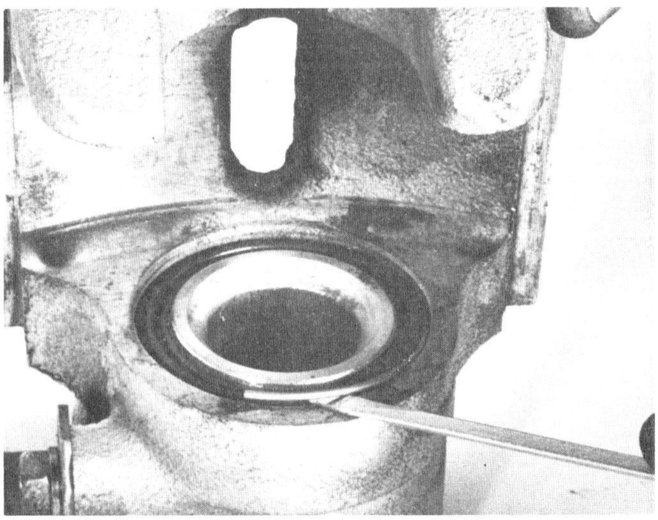

8.5a Remove the bolt retaining snap-ring

8.5b Remove the dust boot

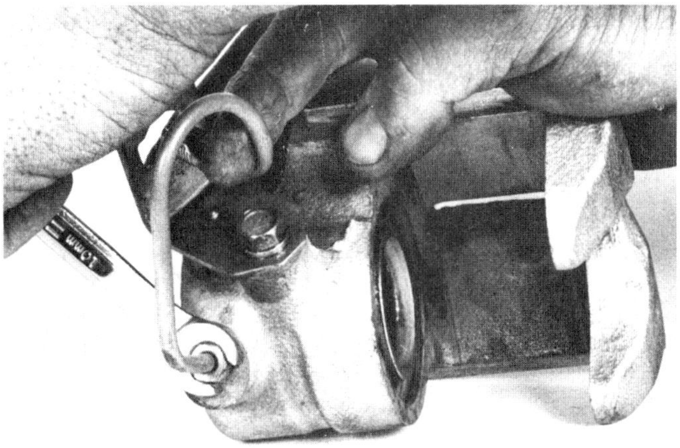

8.6 Loosen the fitting and remove the metal brake line from the caliper body

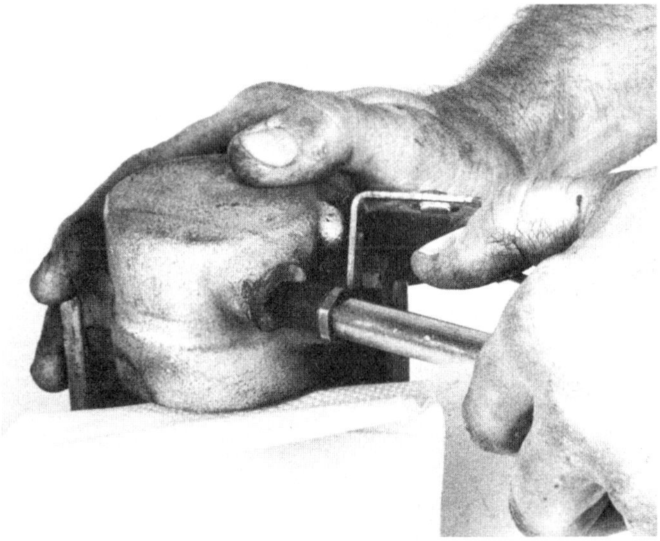

8.7 Air pressure blown into metal brake line fitting hole can be used to remove the piston

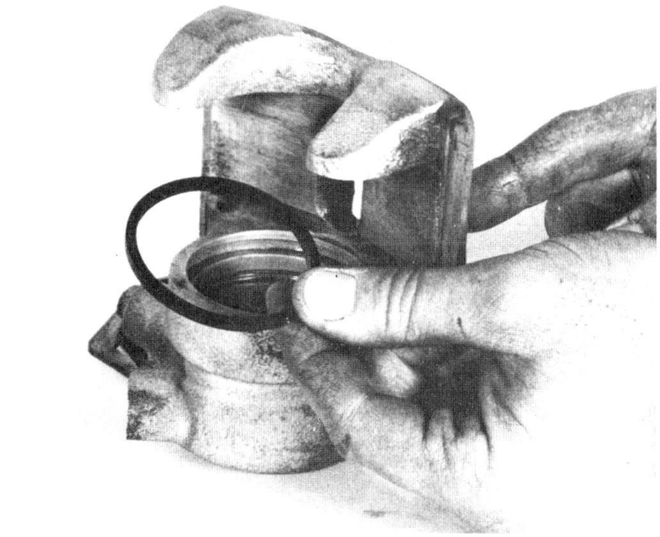

8.8 Remove the seal from the caliper bore. Do not use a metal tool for this

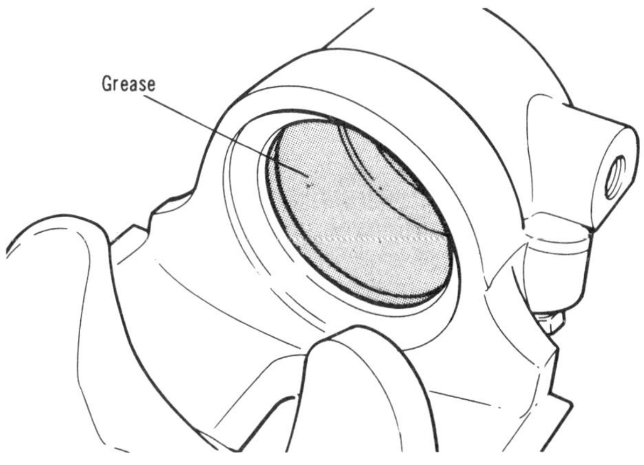

Fig. 9.9 Apply *RED* grease to the inner surface of the cylinder (Sec 8)

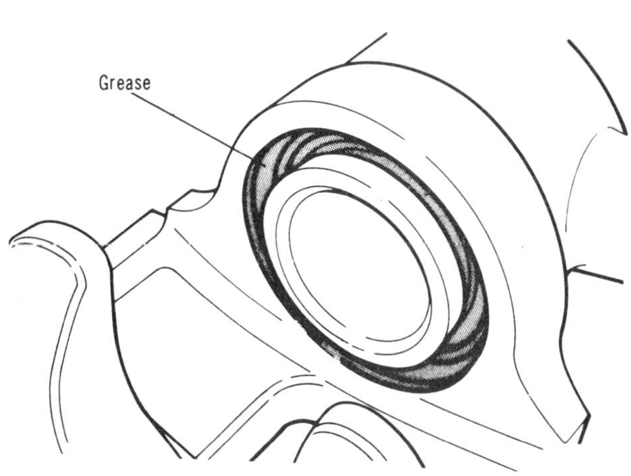

Fig. 9.10 Apply *ORANGE* grease to the piston boot groove of the caliper body (Sec 8)

9 Carefully clean the entire caliper and the piston with alcohol or clean brake fluid. Do not, under any circumstances, use a petroleum-base cleaning solvent. Dry the parts thoroughly and make sure none of the fluid passages are clogged or dirty.
10 Inspect the piston and caliper bore for signs of wear, scoring, pitting or rust. Replace any defective parts.
11 Lubricate the new piston seal with the red grease included in the rebuild kit and install the seal in the caliper bore.
12 Apply clean brake fluid to the caliper bore inside the seal and the piston. Carefully slide the piston into the caliper bore. Do not pinch or twist the seal.
13 Apply the orange grease supplied with the rebuild kit to the dust boot groove in the caliper body. Install the dust boot with the raised inner ring facing the piston. Make sure it is properly seated and install the boot retaining snap-ring.
14 Wipe off any grease or brake fluid that may have gotten on the outside of the piston, dust boot or caliper.
15 Install the metal brake line and tighten the fitting securely.
16 Install the pad support plates onto the caliper.
17 Install the caliper assembly onto the vehicle by referring to Section 4.
18 Connect the metal brake line to the flexible brake hose. Install the spring clip (photo) and securely tighten the fitting.
19 Bleed the system as described in Section 20 and install the wheels. Lower the vehicle to the ground and test drive it.

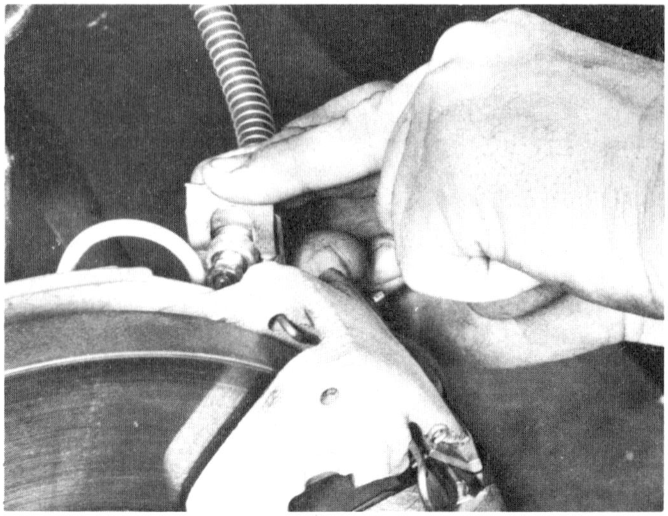

8.18 Install the spring clip that attaches the flexible hose to the bracket

9 Disc brake caliper (rear) – overhaul

Note: *Obtain a caliper rebuild kit before starting this procedure.*
1 Jack up the rear of the vehicle and set it on jackstands. Block the front tires to keep the vehicle from rolling. Remove the wheels.
2 Loosen the fitting which attaches the metal brake line to the flexible brake hose at the caliper bracket (photo). Pull out the spring clip holding the flexible hose to the bracket (photo) and disconnect the metal line from the flexible hose. Place a container under the fitting to catch any brake fluid that may drip. Plug the flexible hose to keep out dirt and other contaminants.
3 Remove the calipers from the caliper support as described in Section 7 except, instead of tying them out of the way with some wire, remove the unit completely from the vehicle.
4 You must have a clean place to work, clean rags, a caliper rebuild kit for each caliper, a container of brake fluid and some alcohol to perform the caliper overhaul.
5 Remove the cap ring and spring, and then lower the lever cap from the groove in the caliper body.
6 After removing the retaining ring, pull out the parking lever, together with the lever cap, from the caliper body.
7 Remove the automatic adjuster spindle by turning it with your hands or a pair of pliers. **Note**: *When using pliers, be careful not to damage the auto adjuster spindle.*
8 Remove the boot ring. Push the piston and the piston boot out from the caliper body by using a screwdriver.
9 Push the needle bearings out of the caliper body by using the special tool MB990665. Remove the piston seal, taking care not to damage the cylinder.
10 Carefully clean the entire caliper and the piston with alcohol or clean brake fluid. Do not, under any circumstances, use a petroleum-base cleaning solvent. Dry the parts thoroughly and make sure none of the fluid passages are clogged or dirty.
11 Inspect the piston and caliper for signs of wear, scoring, pitting or rust. Replace any defective parts.
12 Apply orange grease to the inner surface of the needle bearing, and using the special tool, press the needle bearing into place until the stamped surface of the bearing is flush with the end of the caliper.
13 Install the piston seal into the cylinder and apply the red grease to the inner surface of the cylinder. **Note**: *Be sure to use a new piston seal.*
14 Gently insert the piston by hand, being careful not to twist the piston seal.
15 Apply the orange grease to the piston boot groove of the caliper body, and install the piston boot and the boot ring.
16 Install the auto adjuster seal onto the adjuster spindle and then apply the orange grease. **Note**: *Be sure you use a new auto adjuster seal.*
17 After you install the lock washers onto the auto adjuster spindle in

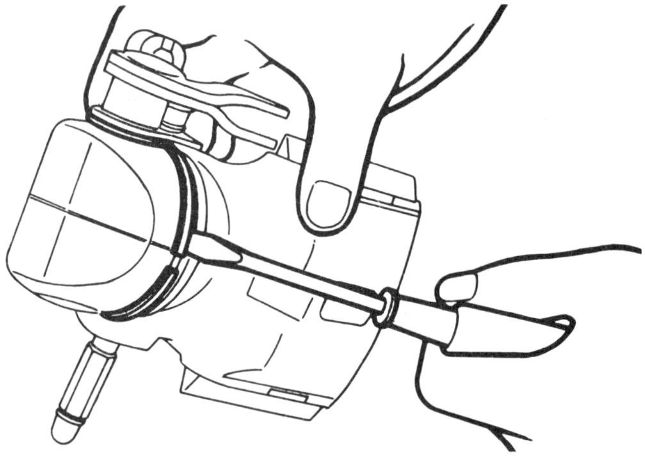

Fig. 9.11 Remove the cap ring and lever cap (Sec 9)

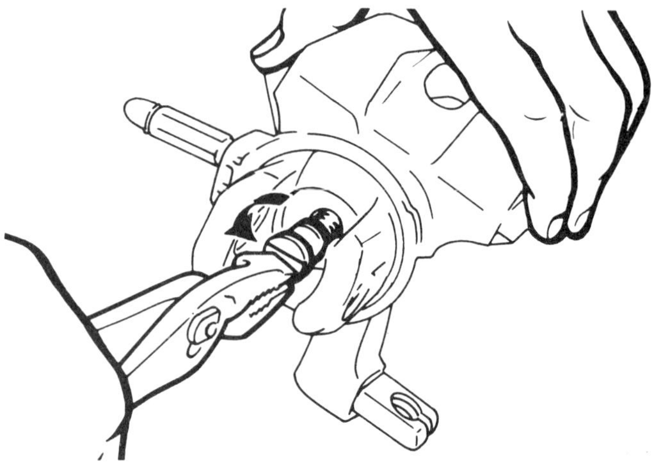

Fig. 9.12 Remove the auto adjuster spindle (Sec 9)

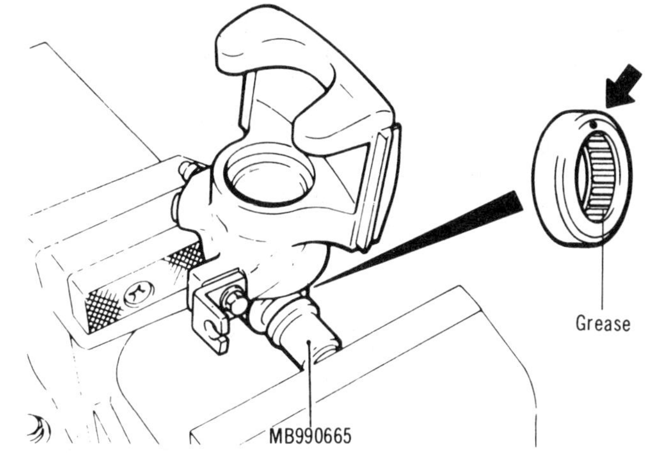

Fig. 9.13 Removal and installation of needle bearing (Sec 9)

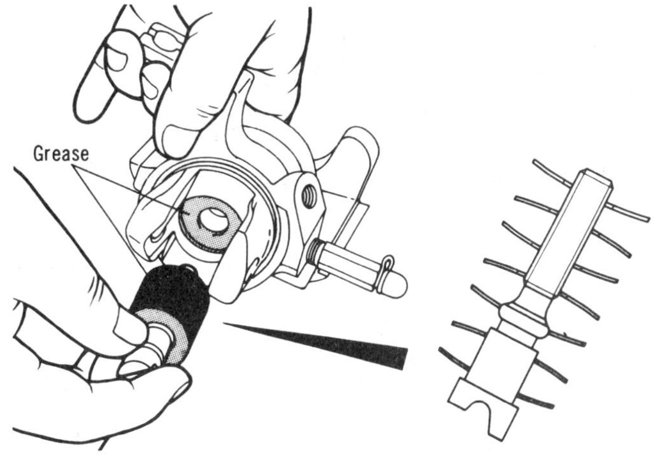

Fig. 9.14 Installation of auto adjuster spindle and lock washers (Sec 9)

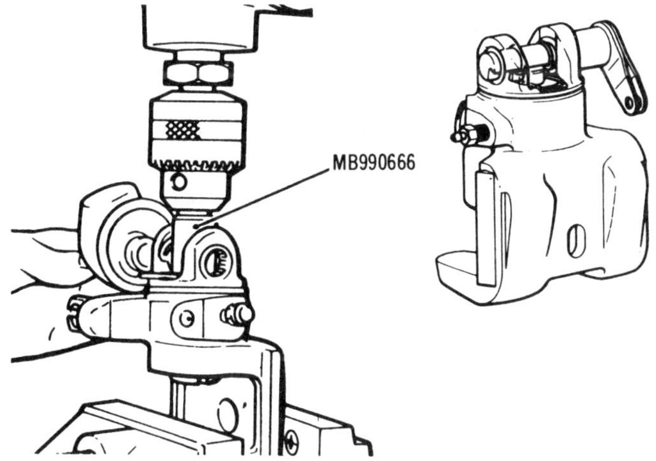

Fig. 9.15 Install the parking lever (Sec 9)

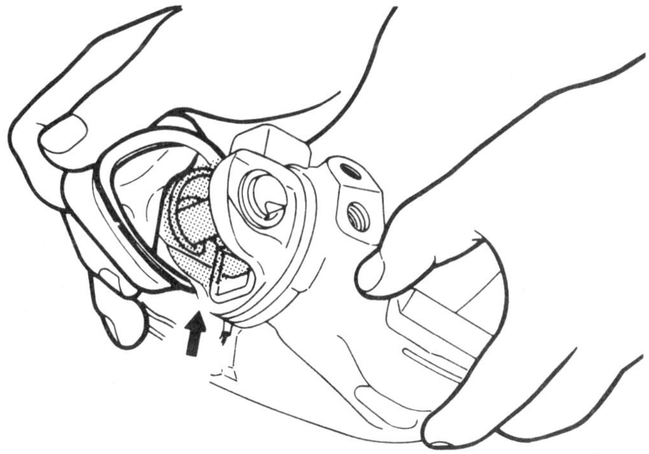

Fig. 9.16 Fill the lever cap with *ORANGE* grease and install the cap to the parking lever (Sec 9)

the direction shown in the illustration, apply the orange grease to the contacting surface of the caliper body to the lock washers. Then, screw the auto adjuster spindle into the piston up to the end of the threads.
18 Use a screwdriver to press in the spindle and tighten into place.
19 After installing the lever cap onto the parking lever, install the parking lever onto the caliper body. **Note:** *Apply the rest of the orange grease to the inside of the lever cap and install the cap ring.*
20 Install the caliper assembly onto the vehicle by referring to Section 7.
21 Connect the metal brake line to the flexible brake hose. Install the spring clip (photo) and securely tighten the fitting.
22 Bleed the system as described in Section 20 and install the wheels. Lower the vehicle to the ground and test drive it.

10 Brake disc – removal and installation

Note: *Checking or replacing the brake disc on the front or the rear of the vehicle is the same procedure.*
1 Raise the vehicle and set it on jackstands. Block the tires to keep the vehicle from rolling. Remove the wheels.
2 Remove the caliper assembly and brake pads as described in Sections 6 or 7. Tie the caliper out of the way. Be careful not to stretch or kink the flexible brake hose.
3 Remove the two bolts attaching the caliper support bracket to the spindle (photo). Remove the screw attaching the dust shield to the top

10.3a Remove the bolts attaching the caliper support bracket to the wheel spindle

9

10.3b Lift the caliper out of its mounting position

of the bracket and lift the bracket out of its mounting position (photo).
4 On the front wheels, remove the hub as described in Chapter 1. On the rear wheels, you should already be to the disc.
5 Check the brake disc for scoring, abnormal wear, cracks, and signs of brake fluid leakage. Measure the thickness of the disc and compare it to the Specifications. If the disc is slightly worn or scored, it can be resurfaced at a reputable brake repair shop. If it is worn so badly that it cannot be resurfaced and still meet the required thickness specification, then it can be removed from the hub and replaced with a new one.
6 On the front wheels, install the hub as described in Chapter 1. On the rear wheels, install the disc/hub over the wheel studs.
7 If you have access to a dial indicator, check the brake disc runout and compare it to the Specifications. The hub must be properly installed and the spindle nut (front) torqued to Specifications. If the runout exceeds the value given in Specifications, change the position of the disc relative to the hub. If the runout cannot be corrected in this manner, replace the disc with a new one.
8 Install the caliper support bracket and tighten the bolts to the specified torque.
9 Install the brake pad and caliper assembly as described in Sections 6 or 7.
10 Install the wheels and lower the vehicle to the ground.

11 Brake drum and shoes (rear) – check

1 Refer to Chapter 1 to inspect the rear brake drum or the brake shoes.

12 Drum brake shoes (rear) – replacement

1 Jack up the rear of the vehicle and set it on jackstands. Remove the wheel. It is a good idea to work on one brake at a time so that the other one can be used as a guide if difficulties occur during reassembly.

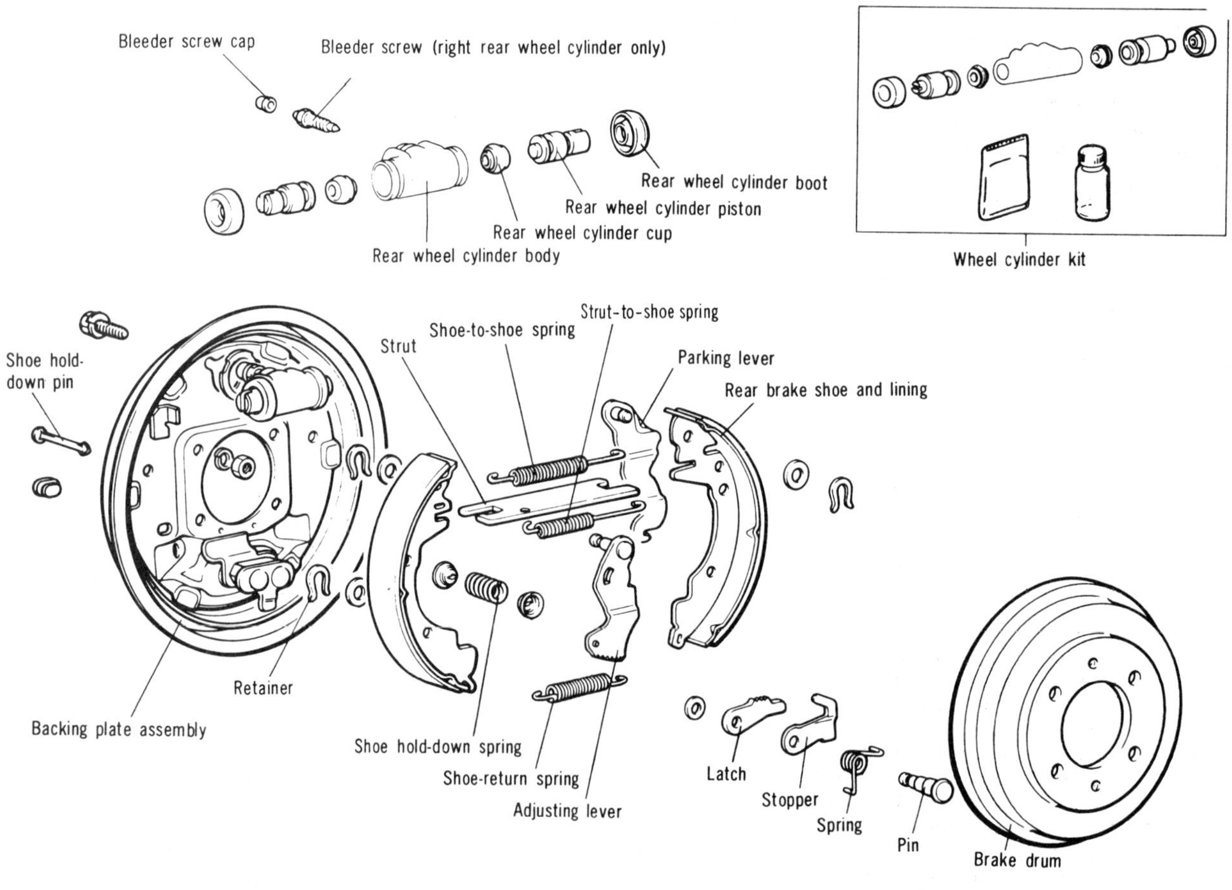

Fig. 9.17 Rear drum brake components – exploded view (Sec 12)

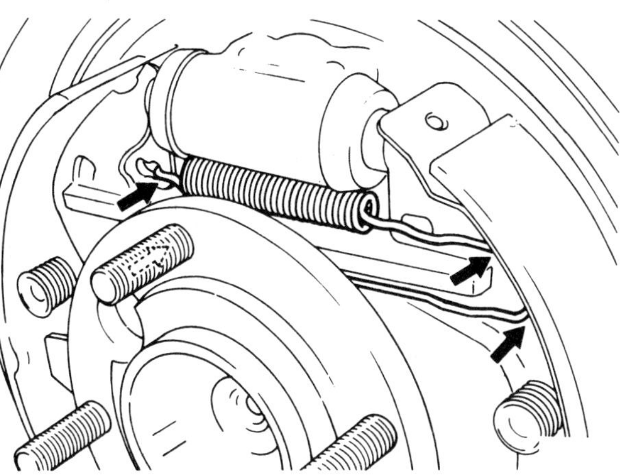

Fig. 9.18 Remove the shoe-to-shoe and the strut-to-strut springs (Sec 12)

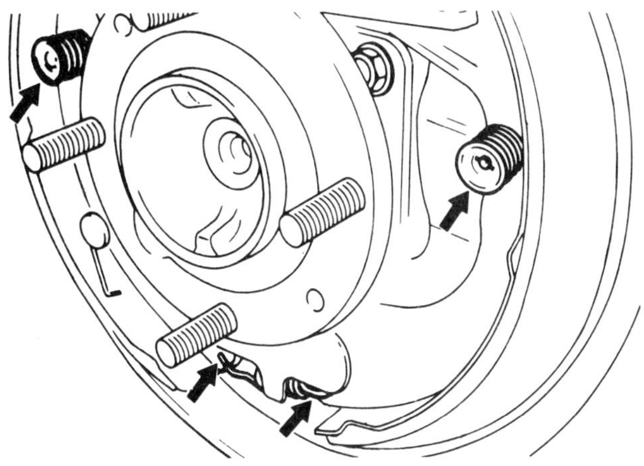

Fig. 9.19 Remove the shoe hold-down and the shoe-return springs (Sec 12)

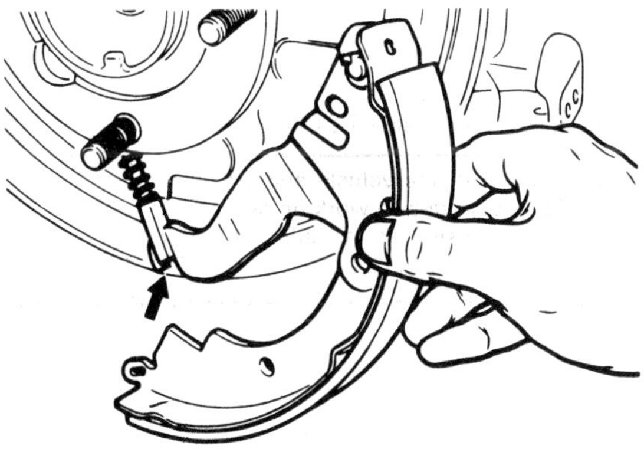

Fig. 9.20 Remove the brake cable from the rear shoe (Sec 12)

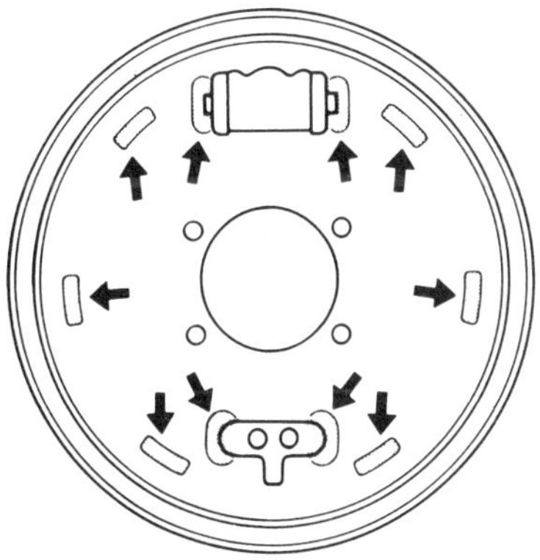

Fig. 9.21 Apply a light coat of brake grease to the areas shown (Sec 12)

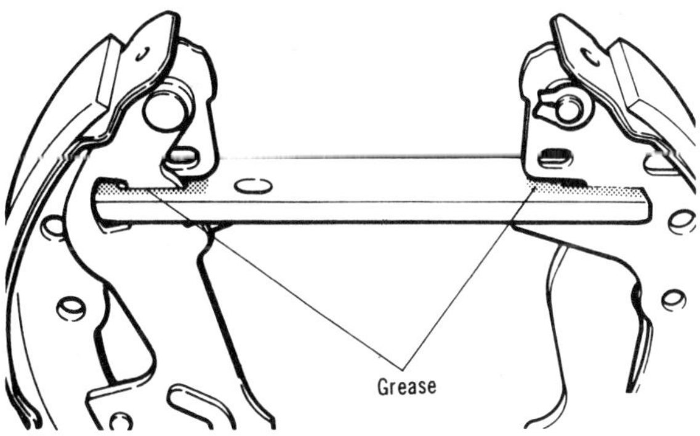

Fig. 9.22 Apply a coat of brake grease to the areas shown (Sec 12)

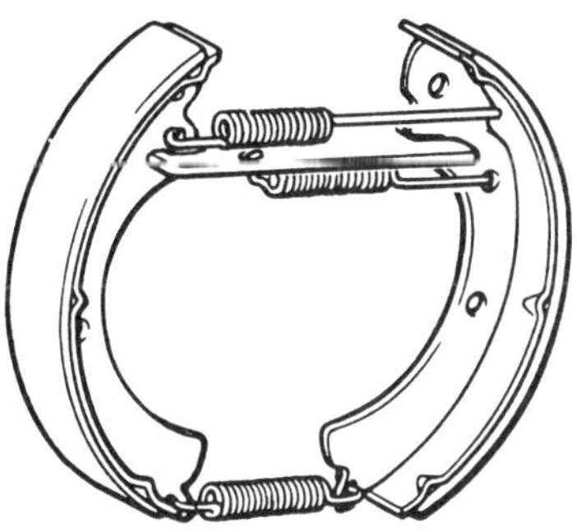

Fig. 9.23 Correct installation of springs (Sec 12)

2 Pull off the brake drum. If you have difficulty removing it, screw an 8 mm bolt into each of the two threaded holes in the drum. Tighten each bolt one-half turn at a time to back the drum off the axle flange. Take a long close look at the relationship between the parts before disassembling the brake.

3 Disconnect the shoe-to-shoe spring and the strut-to-shoe spring. Disconnect the shoe hold-down springs and the shoe return spring.

4 Separate the parking brake rear cable from the parking brake lever and remove the rear brake shoe and lining (trailing shoe).

5 Remove the front brake shoe and lining (leading shoe).

6 Disassemble the front (leading) brake shoe, if it is found in need of replacement, and reassemble the parking brake components to the new brake shoes.

7 Check the brake shoe linings for the specified thickness, abnormal wear, or oil on the linings. Check the brake drum for abnormal wear and the specified thickness. Look for any oil leaking around the brake cylinder which shows the need of an overhaul. 9

8 Check the adjusting lever and latch for abnormal wear or damage. Replace all parts with new ones if needed.

9 Installation is the reverse of removal. Make sure the retaining springs are installed correctly and apply brake grease to the areas shown in the illustrations. **Note**: *Be sure you do not get any grease on the brake linings.*

13 Rear wheel cylinder (drum brakes) – removal, overhaul and installation

1 Remove the brake shoes as described in Section 12.

2 Disconnect the brake line from the wheel cylinder by loosening the fitting.

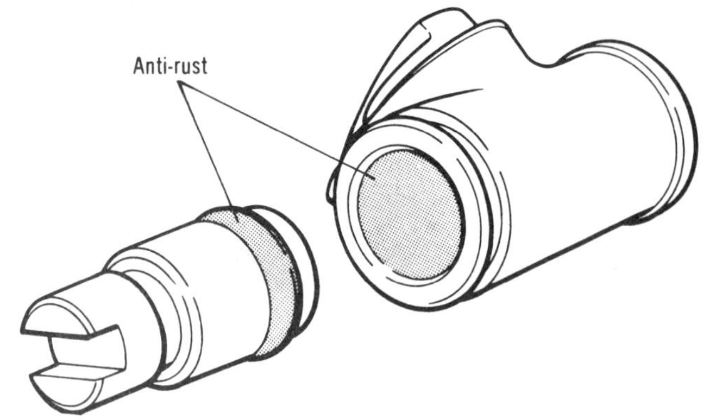

Fig. 9.24 Apply *ORANGE* (anti-rust) grease to outside of piston and interior of cylinder as shown (Sec 13)

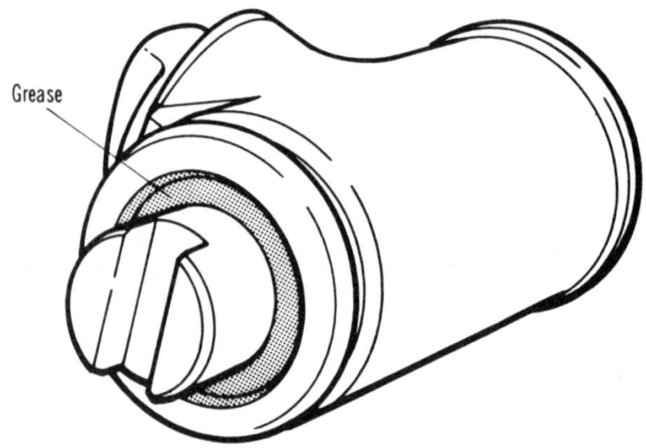

Fig. 9.25 Apply *ORANGE* grease to the area shown and install the cylinder boot (Sec 13)

3 Remove the bolts which attach the wheel cylinder to the backing plate and lift out the wheel cylinder.

4 Remove the bleeder screw from the cylinder body (photo).

5 Remove the dust boots and pistons from the cylinder body (photo). Separate the dust boots from the pistons, noting how they are installed.

6 Remove the rubber piston cups from the pistons, taking care that the pistons are not scratched or gouged in the process.

7 Check the wheel cylinder bore for wear, scoring, pitting and rust. If the bore is worn, pitted, scored or rusted, it can be honed slightly to restore it to reusable condition. Be sure to use the appropriate size hone. If a hone is not available, or if the damage is slight, polish the bore with crocus cloth.

8 Carefully clean the wheel cylinder body and the pistons with alcohol or clean brake fluid. Do not, under any circumstances, use a petroleum-base cleaning solvent. Dry the parts thoroughly with a lint-free rag or compressed air and make sure that none of the fluid passages are clogged or dirty.

9 Measure the piston diameter (photo) and compare it to the Specifications. If the pistons are smaller than the specified diameter, replace them. Measure the cylinder bore diameter and compare it to the Specifications. If it is larger than the specified diameter, the wheel cylinder must be replaced. Subtract the piston diameter from the cylinder bore diameter to obtain the piston-to-bore clearance. If the clearance is greater than specified, the pistons and wheel cylinder must be replaced.

10 Install the new piston cups onto the pistons. The widest outside diameter of the cup must be installed as shown (photo).

11 Apply the orange grease supplied with the rebuild kit to the dust boot grooves on the pistons and wheel cylinder body (photos).

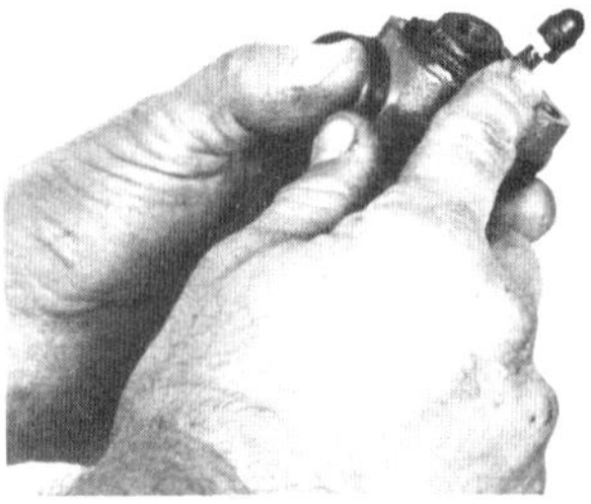

13.4 Remove the bleeder screws from the wheel cylinder body

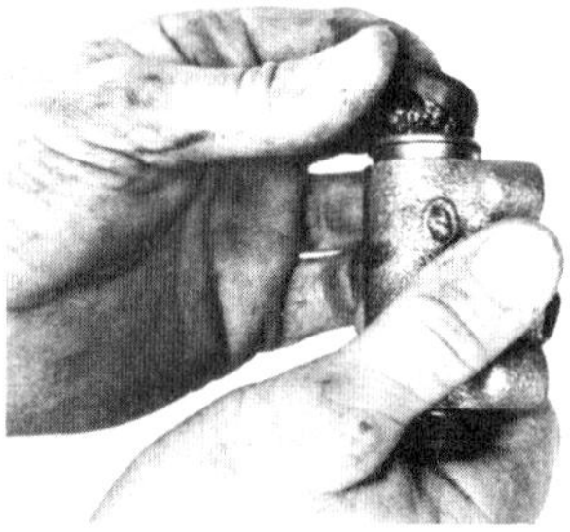

13.5 Remove the dust boots and pistons from the wheel cylinder

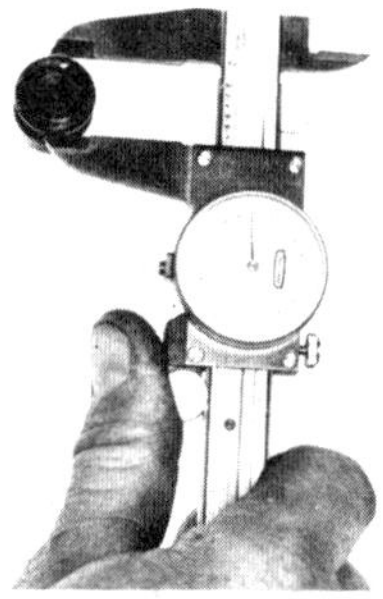

13.9 Measure the outside diameter of the pistons

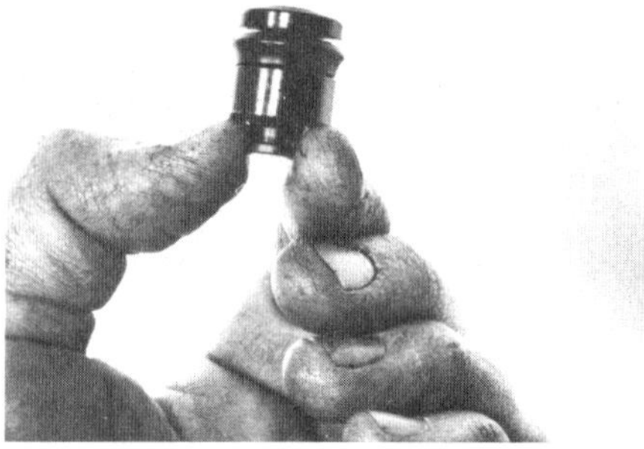

13.10 Install the new piston cups onto the pistons

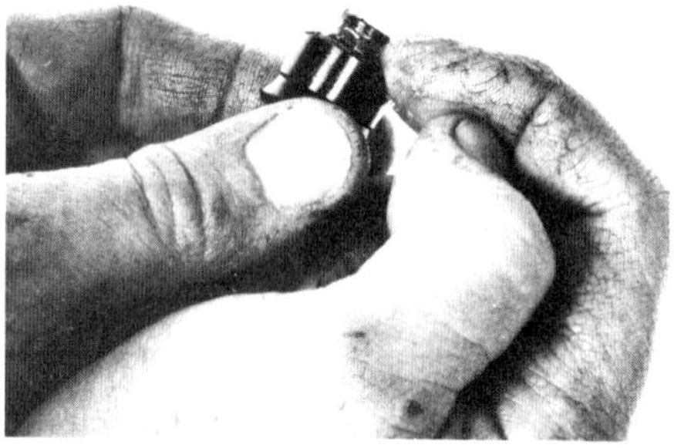

13.11a Apply the orange (anti-rust) grease supplied with the rebuild kit to the dust boot grooves on the pistons

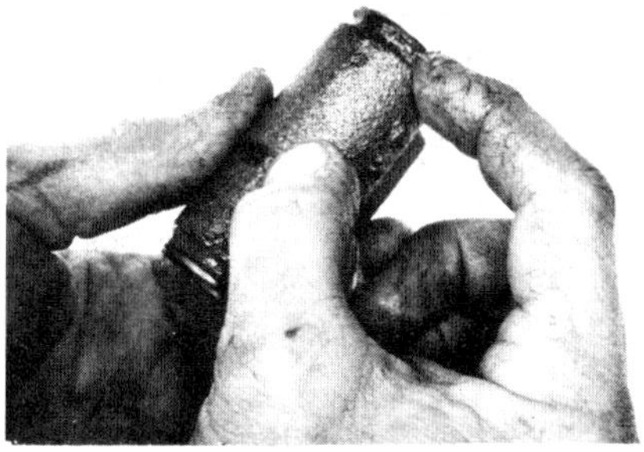

13.11b Apply orange grease to the dust boot grooves on the wheel cylinder

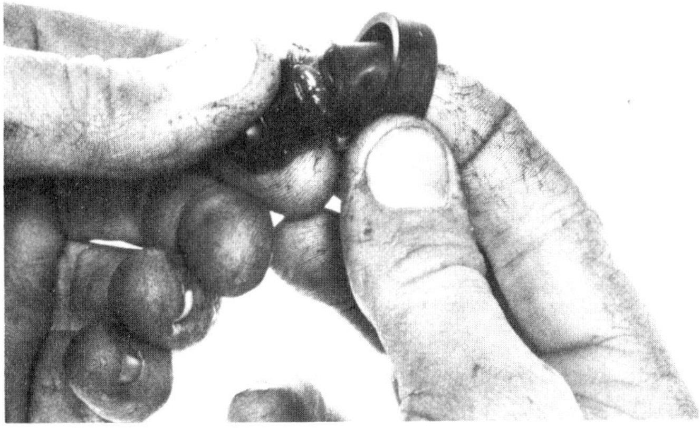

13.12 Install the dust boots onto the pistons

13.13 Lubricate the pistons and wheel cylinder bore with clean brake fluid and carefully slip the pistons into the bore

12 Install the new dust boots onto the pistons as shown (photo).
13 Lightly lubricate the wheel cylinder bore, the pistons and piston cups with clean brake fluid. Slip the pistons into the cylinder bore (photo). Be careful not to pinch or twist the piston cups as the pistons are inserted into the bore. Fit the outer edges of the dust boots into the grooves on the cylinder body.
14 Wipe off any grease or brake fluid that may have gotten on the outside surfaces of the wheel cylinder body or the dust boots.
15 Install the bleeder screw into the wheel cylinder body.
16 To install the wheel cylinder, slip it into position on the backing plate and connect the brake line to the wheel cylinder. Tighten the brake line fitting with your fingers to make sure the threads are properly engaged. Do not tighten it with a wrench at this point. Install the wheel cylinder mounting bolts and tighten them to the specified torque. Now tighten the brake line fitting securely.
17 Install the brake shoes as described in Section 12.
18 Bleed the system by referring to Section 20 and inspect carefully for fluid leakage.

14 Master cylinder – removal, overhaul and installation

1 **Note**: *The master cylinders are all the same in these vehicles. Only the reservoirs change from year to year.*
2 Place a clean rag around and under the master cylinder so that any spilled brake fluid does not get on the painted surfaces of the body or frame. Slide back the hose clamps and disconnect the two hoses leading from the brake fluid reservoir to the top of the master cylinder. Use a bolt or other suitable object to plug the hoses so that brake fluid does not leak out of them.
3 Loosen the fitting and remove the rear brake line from the master cylinder. Loosen the through-bolt attaching the front brake line adaptor to the master cylinder. Be careful not to lose the two soft metal washers on the bolt. Note their positions so that the washers can be installed properly upon reassembly.
4 Slide back the hose clamp and remove the power brake vacuum hose from the booster fitting. Remove the nut attaching the vacuum hose bracket to the master cylinder booster assembly. Reinstall the nut onto the stud after removing the bracket.
5 Remove the nuts and lock washers holding the master cylinder to the vacuum booster and withdraw the master cylinder straight ahead and out of the vehicle. Be careful not to spill any of the brake fluid onto painted surfaces.
6 Check for fluid leakage at the rear of the master cylinder. If there is evidence of fluid leakage, the master cylinder should be overhauled or replaced with a rebuilt unit. If for some reason you cannot or do not want to overhaul the master cylinder, a rebuilt unit may be purchased from your dealer or a reputable auto parts store and installed on the vehicle.
7 Loosen and remove the clamps holding the chamber covers to the master cylinder (photo). It is a good idea to somehow mark the position of the spigots before removing the chamber covers (so they can be reinstalled with the spigots facing the same direction). Pry off the chamber covers. Be very careful when removing the covers; they are made of plastic and may be brittle.
8 Remove the check valve cap, the rear line seat, the check valve and the check valve spring from the rear brake line mounting hole

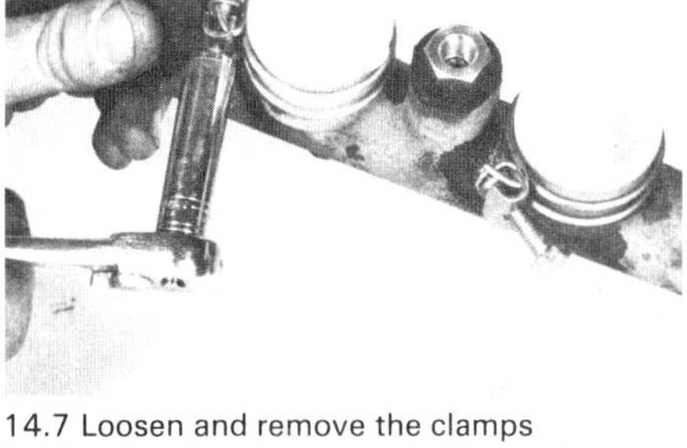

14.7 Loosen and remove the clamps holding the chamfer covers to the master cylinder

14.8a Remove the check valve cap from the rear brake line mounting hole

14.8b Lift out the rear line seat

9

14.8c Remove the check valve

14.8d Remove the check valve spring

14.8e Remove the valve case from the front brake line mounting hole

14.8f Remove the washer

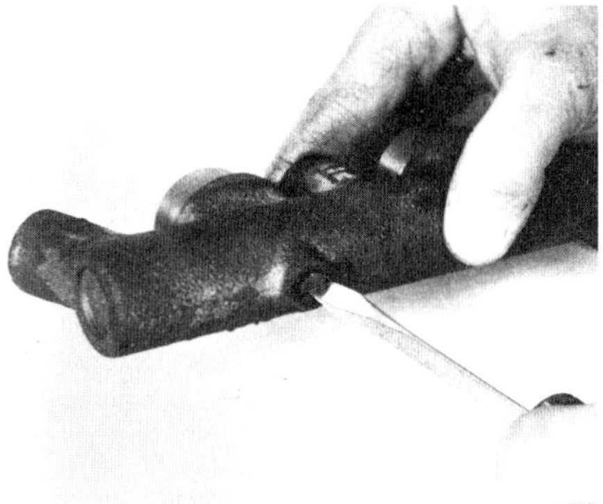
14.9 Remove the secondary piston stop and O-ring

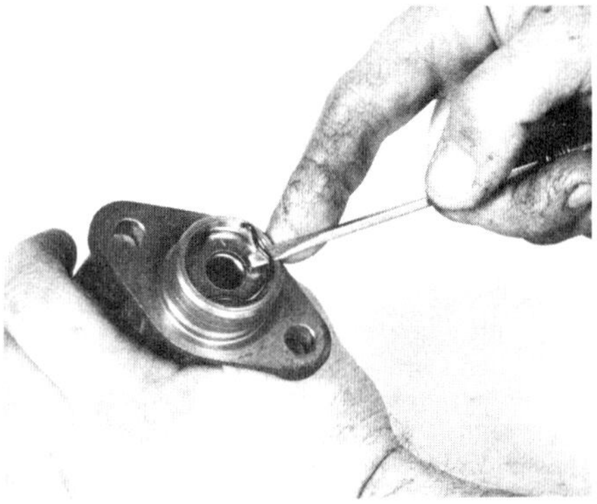
14.10a Remove the stop ring from the rear of the master cylinder bore

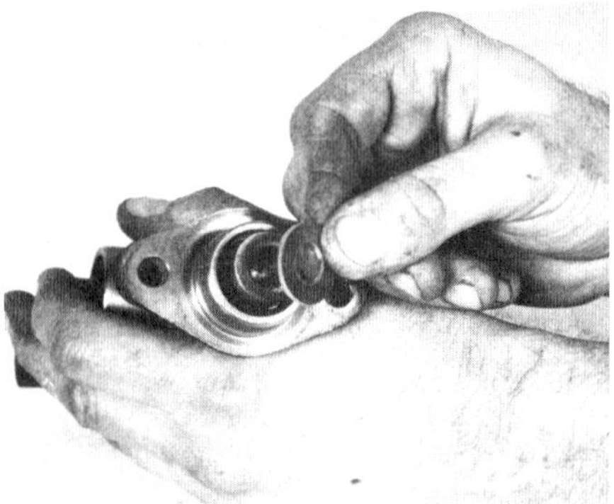
14.10b Remove the piston stop from the rear of the master cylinder

14.10c Carefully remove the primary piston assembly from the master cylinder

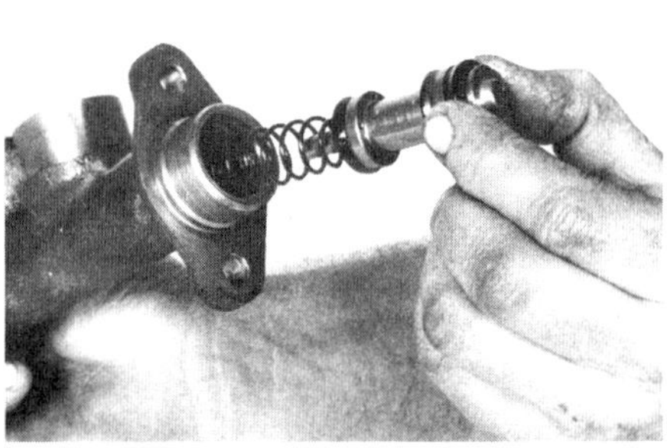
14.10d Carefully remove the secondary piston assembly from the master cylinder

(photos). Note the order in which they are removed to ensure proper reassembly. Next, remove the valve case, the washer, the check valve and the check valve spring from the front brake line mounting hole (photos). Again, note the order in which they are removed to ensure proper reassembly.

9 Remove the secondary piston stop and O-ring from the bottom of the master cylinder (photo).

10 Remove the stop ring and piston stop from the rear of the master bore (photos). Slide out the primary and secondary piston assemblies (photos). Do not disassemble the primary piston assembly, as the distance between the spring seat and the spring retainer is factory set by a screw and must not be disturbed.

11 Check the master cylinder bore for wear, scoring, pitting and rust. If it is scored, pitted or worn, it can be honed slightly to restore it to reusable condition. Check the piston contact surfaces for scoring and wear.

12 Clean the master cylinder, piston assemblies and all other parts with alcohol or clean brake fluid. Do not, under any circumstances, use a petroleum-base solvent. Dry the parts thoroughly and make sure that none of the fluid passages in the cylinder body are clogged or dirty.

13 Measure the master cylinder bore diameter with inside micrometers and compare it to the Specifications. If it is larger than the specified diameter, the master cylinder must be replaced. Measure the outside diameter of the pistons and compare to the Specifications. If they are smaller than the specified diameters, the pistons must be replaced. Subtract the piston diameter from the bore diameter to obtain the piston-to-bore clearance. If the clearance is greater than specified, the pistons and master cylinder body must be replaced.

14 Check the primary and secondary piston return springs for loss of tension and damage. If they are defective, the entire piston assembly must be replaced. It is a good practice, and highly recommended, that the piston assemblies be replaced whenever the master cylinder needs any type of repair work done on it.

15 Lightly lubricate the cylinder bore, the piston assemblies and the

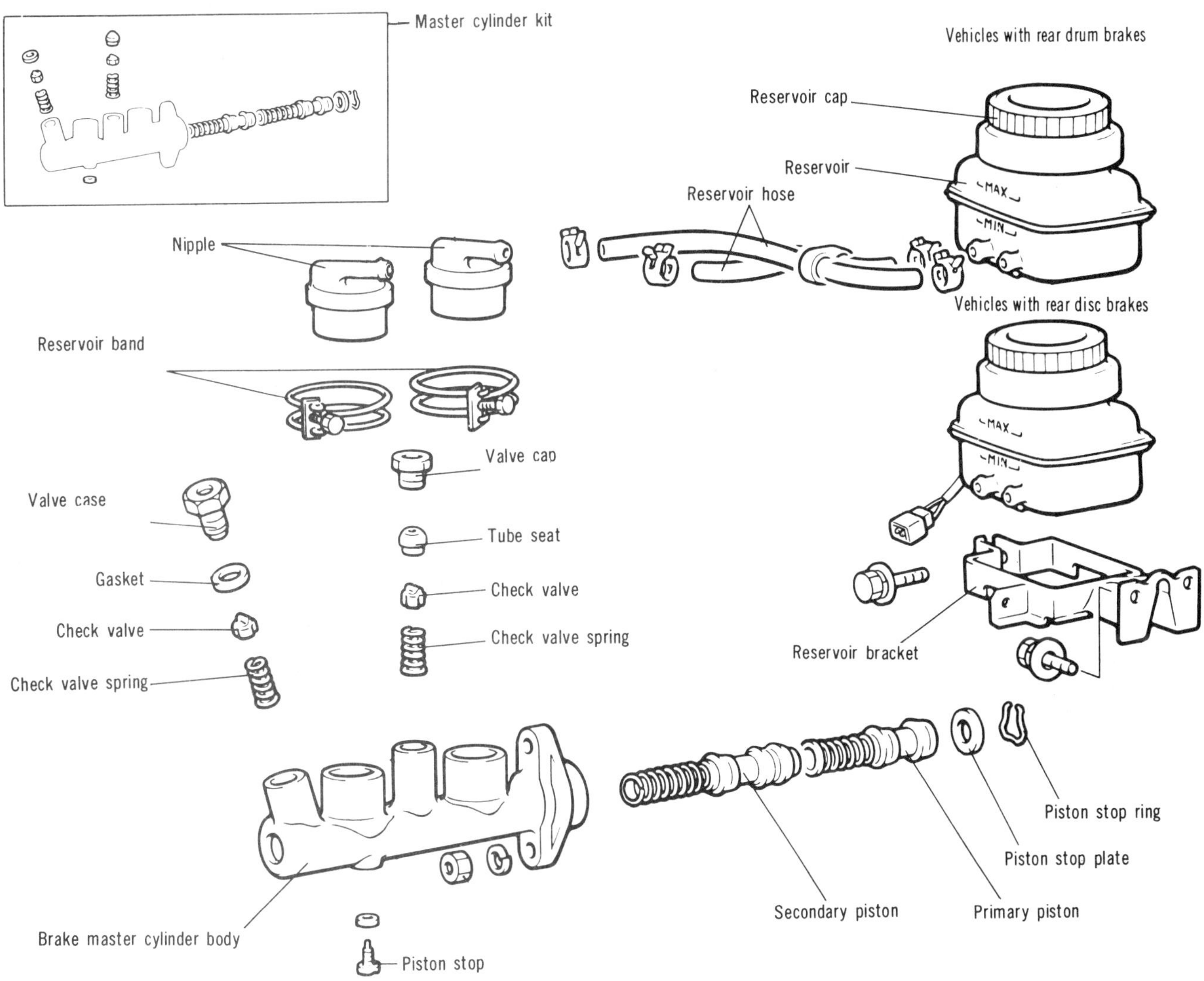

Fig. 9.26 Master cylinder components – exploded view (Sec 14)

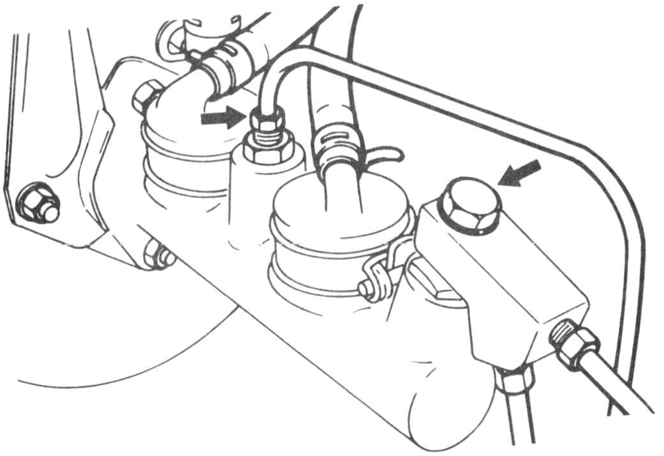

Fig. 9.27 Remove brake tube and adapter (Sec 14)

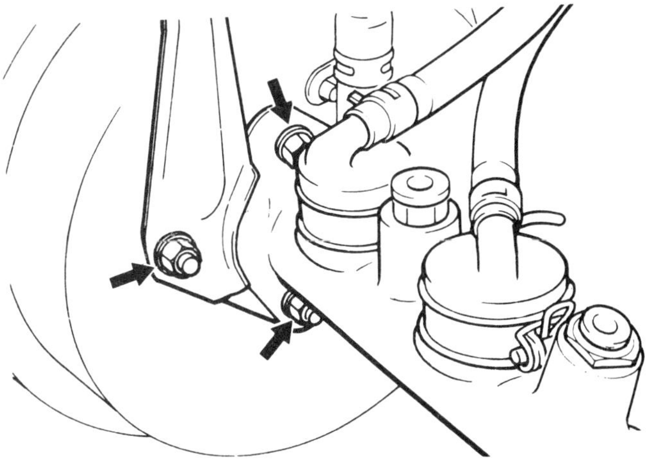

Fig. 9.28 Remove the brake master cylinder (Sec 14)

9

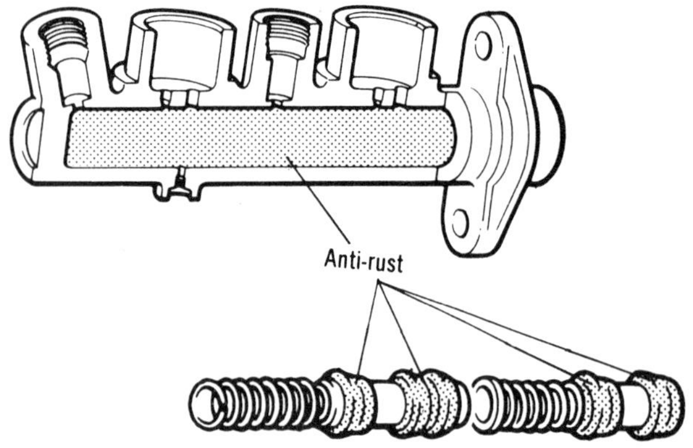

Fig. 9.29 Apply *ORANGE* (anti-rust) grease to the interior of the master cylinder and the pistons as shown (Sec 14)

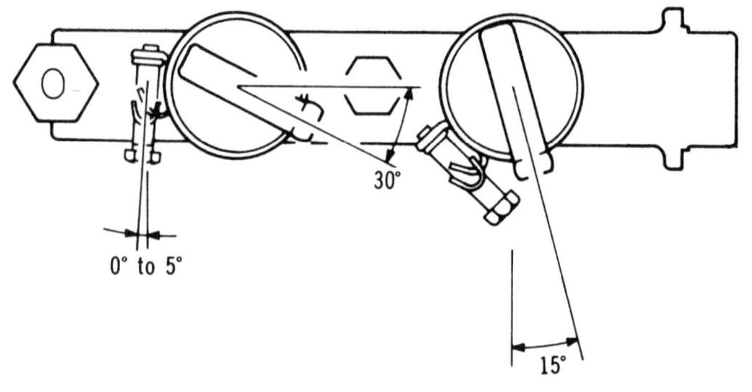

Fig. 9.30 Correct installation of the nipples and the reservoir bands (Sec 14)

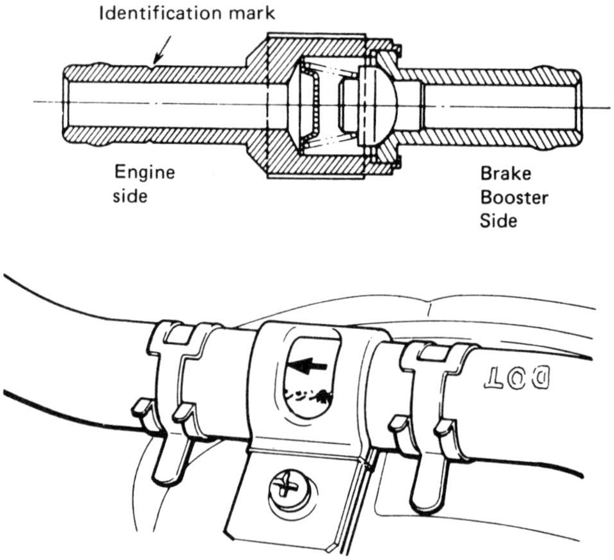

Fig. 9.31 Correct installation of the power booster check valve (Sec 15)

piston cups with clean brake fluid. Insert the new secondary piston assembly, followed by the primary piston assembly, into the cylinder bore. Be careful not to pinch or twist the piston cups in the process. Lay the piston stop in position and install the stop ring in the end of the cylinder bore. Install the piston stop and O-ring into the bottom of the cylinder.

16 Install the check valve spring, the check valve, the rear line seat and the check valve cap into the rear brake line mounting hole. Install the check valve spring, the check valve, the washer and the valve case into the front brake line mounting hole. Use the exploded view drawing to make sure they are installed in the proper order.

17 Install the chamber covers and clamps. Make sure the spigots are facing in the same direction as they were before removal.

18 If a master cylinder other than the original is being installed, such as a commercially rebuilt unit, check the clearance between the back of the piston and power brake pushrod. Using a depth micrometer, or vernier calipers, measure the distance from the piston to the master cylinder mounting flange. Next, measure the distance from the end of the power brake pushrod to the surface on the booster assembly that the master cylinder mounting flange is in contact with when installed. Subtract the two measurements to get the clearance. If the clearance is more or less than specified, turn the adjusting screw on the end of the power brake pushrod until the clearance is within the specified limit. Be sure to lock the jam nut on the adjusting screw when the adjustment is completed.

19 Hold the master cylinder in place and loosely install the brake lines to the master cylinder. Don't forget to install the soft washers on the through-bolt that attaches the front brake line. If the washers are not installed properly, leakage will result.

20 Install the lock washers and nuts that attach the master cylinder to the vacuum booster assembly. Tighten them securely.

21 Hold the power brake vacuum hose bracket in place and install the lock washer and nut that attached it to the vacuum booster assembly. Tighten the nut securely.

22 Tighten both brake line fittings securely.

23 Attach the power brake vacuum hose to the fitting on the vacuum booster assembly and slide the hose clamp into place.

24 Slip the two hoses from the brake fluid reservoir into place on the chamber caps. Install the hose clamps.

25 After installation of the master cylinder, the system must be bled as described in Section 20.

15 Power brakes – check

1 Slide back the hose clamp and remove the power brake side vacuum hose from the check valve. Place your thumb over the open end of the hose.

2 Have an assistant start the engine. Keep clear of moving engine parts.

3 A vacuum should be produced and maintained. If no vacuum is felt, the check valve is probably defective and must be replaced with a new one. When installing a new check valve, make sure the arrow on the valve body points toward the engine as shown.

4 Check the vacuum hose leading to the check valve for cracks and leaks. Replace it if any are found.

5 Shut off the engine, reconnect the vacuum hose and slide the hose clamp into place.

6 A further check of the power brake system is to physically inspect the check valve. Remove the valve from the vacuum hose and blow into both sides of it.

7 If, when blowing, air does not pass through from the engine side but does pass through from the brake booster side, the valve is OK. If, after doing this test, the valve does not function this way, replace it with a new one.

16 Brake booster – check

1 The following procedure is a manual check to find out if your booster unit is functioning properly. **Note:** *It is not designed to pinpoint the exact location of a problem, but is sufficient to attain a general knowledge of its condition. You can also remove the unit and have it checked on a brake booster tester at your dealer service department.*

2 To check the air tightness, start the engine and let it run for one to two minutes (no more), then shut it off.

3 Pump the brake pedal several times. If the pedal depresses farther

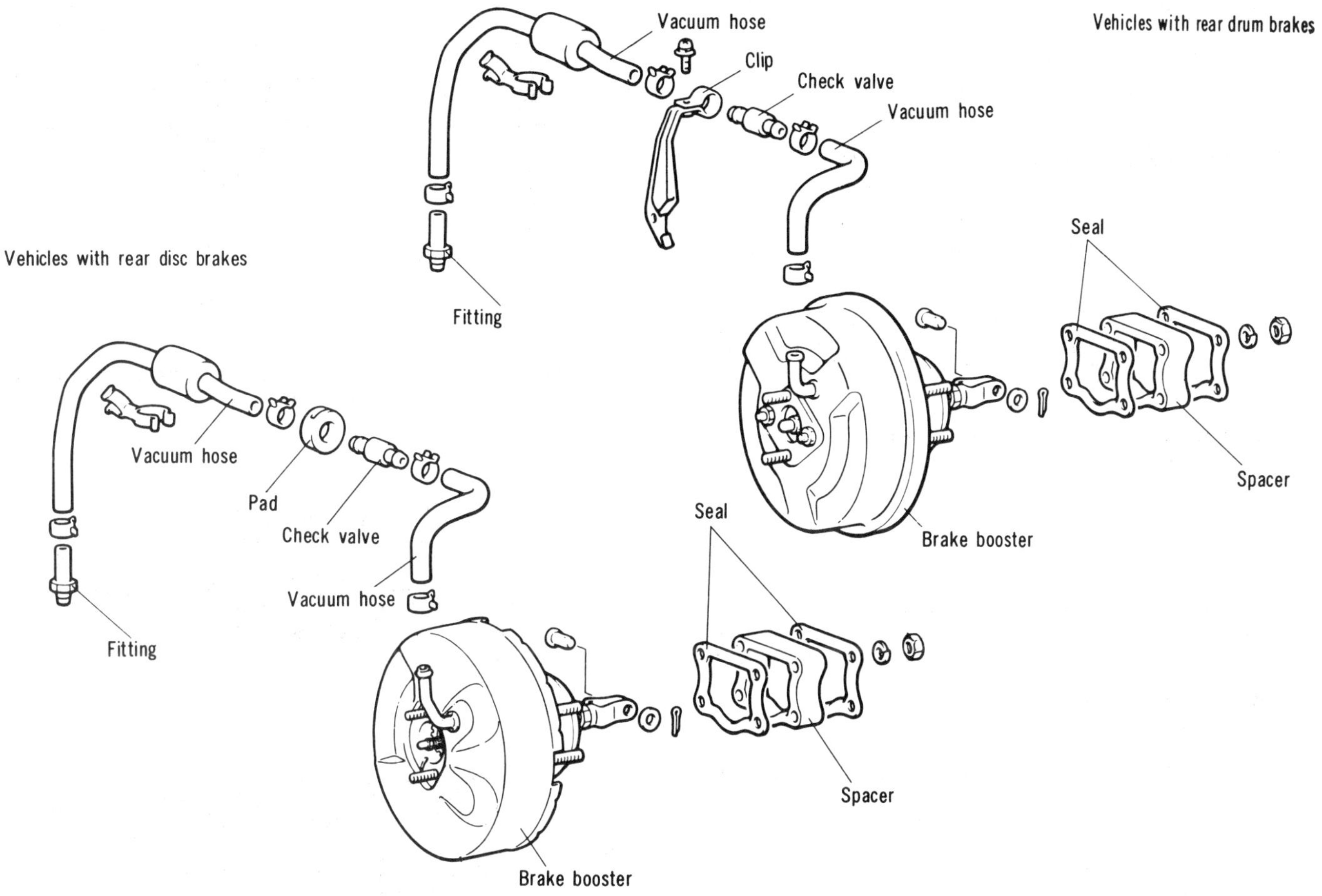

Fig. 9.32 Brake booster components – exploded view (Sec 17)

than normal the first time but gradually rises to a normal position the second and third time, it is in good condition.

4 If there is no change in the pedal height when it is depressed the second and third time, it is defective. **Note**: *If you suspect that your booster is defective because of its performance, first inspect the vacuum lines and the sealing parts and replace them if they are bad, then repeat the procedure.*

5 With the engine stopped, pump the brake pedal several times (with even pressure) and then keep it depressed.

6 With the pedal still depressed, start the engine. If the pedal goes down slightly, the booster is in good condition.

7 If there is no change in pedal height, it is defective.

8 With the engine running, check the air tightness under a load by depressing the brake pedal. Now, while keeping the pedal depressed, stop the engine.

9 Hold the pedal depressed for 30 seconds. If the pedal height does not change, it is in good condition. If it rises, the booster is defective.

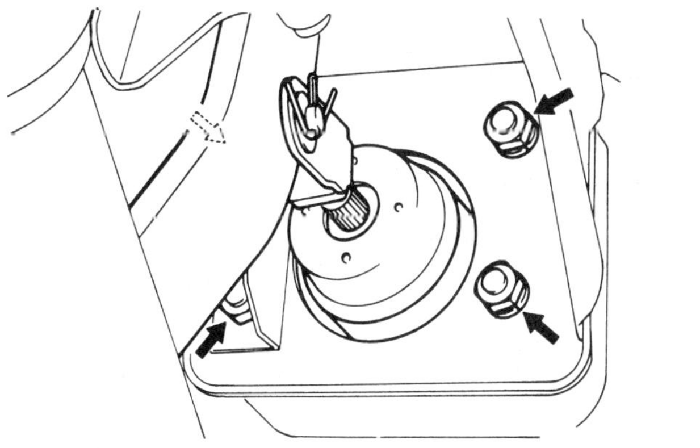

Fig. 9.33 Disconnect and remove the brake booster from inside the driver's compartment (Sec 17)

17 Brake booster – removal and installation

1 If you find that the booster is defective, it is not recommended that you overhaul it. Because of its complexity and the special tools needed to do the job, it is best to let your dealer service department overhaul it for you.

2 However, you can remove it yourself by following the procedure outlined here:

3 Remove the brake master cylinder by referring to the appropriate Section in this Chapter. Disconnect the vacuum hose from the booster unit.

4 Working on the inside of your vehicle, remove the pedal return spring, the cotter pin, the push rod clevis pin and the four booster nuts, then remove the booster from the vehicle.

5 To install the booster, reverse the removal procedure.

6 Bleed the brake system according to the bleeding procedure found in this Chapter.

18 Combination/proportioning valve – check and replacement

1 The combination valve is used on vehicles with rear drum brakes and the proportioning valve is used on vehicles with rear disc brakes. Neither one of these valves is reparable. If, through testing, they are found to be malfunctioning, they must be taken out of the vehicle and replaced with a new one.

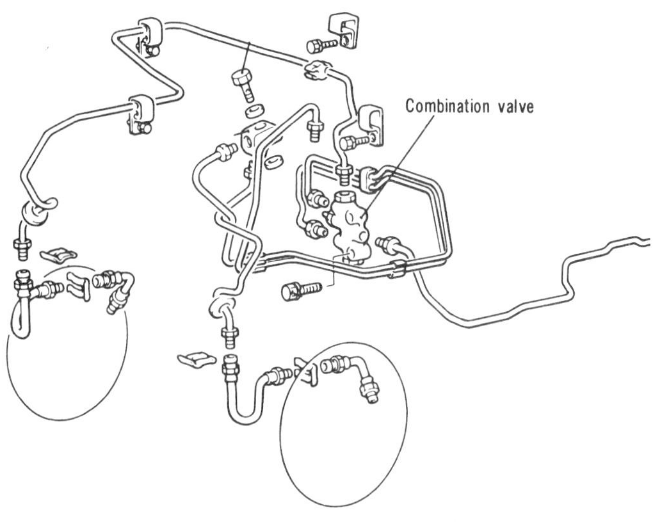

Fig. 9.34 Combination valve (rear drum brakes) (Sec 18)

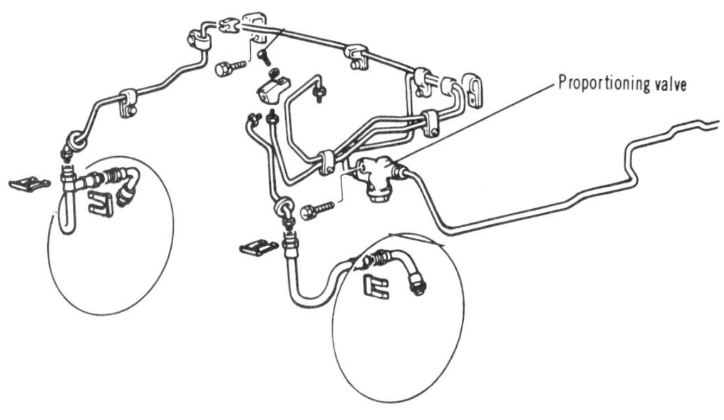

Fig. 9.35 Proportioning valve (rear disc brakes) (Sec 18)

2 Testing of these valves requires the use of gauges and should be left to your dealer service department or a reputable repair shop. However, to save money, you can remove and install the valves yourself if they are to be replaced.
3 To replace these valves, mark the brake tubes to be removed to aid in the installation of the new valve.
4 Remove all the lines to each valve and plug them as they are removed to keep out any contaminants. Place a couple of rags under the work area to catch as much spilled brake fluid as you can.
5 Carefully install the new valve and tighten the tube fittings. Refill the reservoir with new brake fluid and bleed the brake system according to the procedure in this Chapter.
6 Check all the fittings for any leakage and tighten accordingly.

19 Brake system air bleeding procedure

1 If the brake system has air in it, operation of the brake pedal will be spongy and imprecise. Air can enter the brake system whenever any part of the system is dismantled or if the fluid level in the master cylinder reservoir runs low. Air can also leak into the system through a fault too slight to allow fluid to leak out. In this case, it indicates that a general overhaul of the brake system is required.
2 To bleed the brakes, you will need an assistant to pump the brake pedal, a supply of new brake fluid, an empty glass jar, a plastic or vinyl tube which will fit over the bleed nipple, and a wrench for the bleeder screw.
3 There are five locations at which the brake system is bled: the master cylinder; the front caliper assemblies; and the rear brake wheel cylinders or calipers.
4 Check the fluid level at the master cylinder reservoir. Add fluid, if necessary, to bring the level up to the Full mark. Use only the recommended brake fluid, and do not mix different types. Never use fluid from a container that has been standing uncapped. You will have to check the fluid level in the master reservoir often during the bleeding procedure. If the level drops too far, air will enter the system through the master cylinder.
5 Raise the vehicle and set it securely on jackstands.
6 Remove the bleeder screw cap from the wheel cylinder or caliper assembly that is being bled. If more than one wheel must be bled, start with the one farthest from the master cylinder.
7 Attach one end of the clear plastic or vinyl tube to the bleeder screw nipple and place the other end in the glass or plastic jar submerged in a small amount of clean brake fluid.
8 Loosen the bleeder screw slightly, then tighten it to the point where it is snug yet easily loosened.
9 Have the assistant pump the brake several times and hold it in the fully depressed position.
10 With the pressure on the brake pedal, open the bleeder screw approximately one-half turn. As the brake fluid is flowing through the

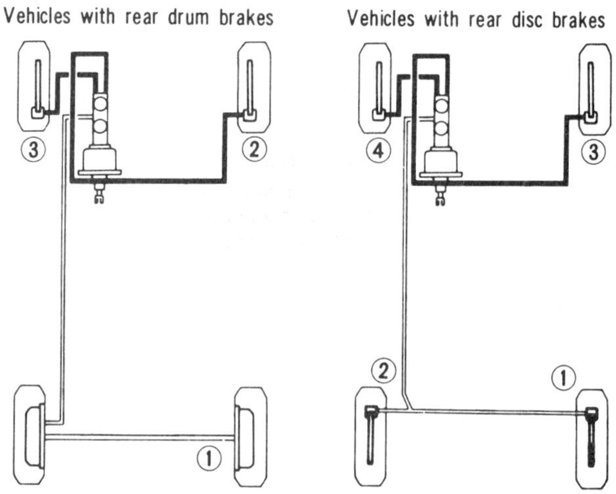

Fig. 9.36 Correct order of air bleeding (Sec 19)

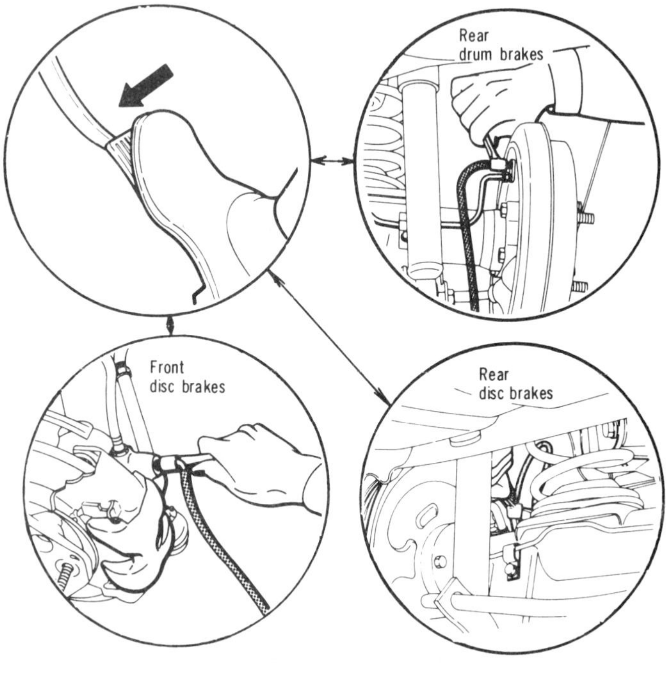

Fig. 9.37 Bleeding the brake system (Sec 19)

tube and into the jar, tighten the bleeder screw. Again, pump the brake pedal, hold it in the fully depressed position, and loosen the bleeder screw momentarily. Do not allow the brake pedal to be released with the bleeder screw in the open position.

11 Repeat the procedure until no air bubbles are visible in the brake fluid flowing through the tube. Be sure to check the brake fluid level in the master cylinder reservoir while performing the bleeding operation.

12 Fully tighten the bleeder screw, remove the plastic or vinyl tube and install the bleeder screw cap.

13 Follow the same procedure to bleed the other wheel cylinder or caliper assemblies.

14 To bleed the master cylinder, have the assistant pump and hold the brake pedal. Momentarily loosen the brake line fittings, one at a time, where they attach to the master cylinder. Any air in the master cylinder will escape when the fittings are loosened. Brake fluid will damage painted surfaces, so use paper towels or rags to cover and protect the areas around the master cylinder.

15 Check the brake fluid level in the master cylinder to make sure it is adequate, then test drive the vehicle and check for proper brake operation.

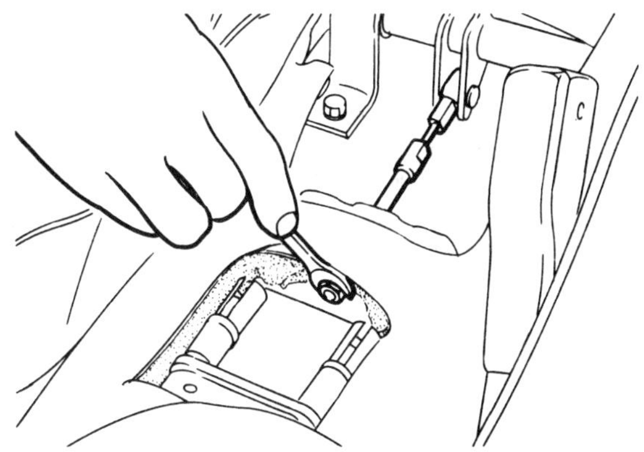

Fig. 9.38 Tightening the parking brake cable adjusting nut (Sec 20)

20 Parking brake – adjustment

1 If the parking brake needs adjustment, first remove the center console accessory box to gain access to the adjuster.

2 Refer to the illustration and tighten the adjusting nut in order to make the parking brake cable tighter. This will also change the number of clicks heard in the lever when the parking brake is applied.

3 The correct number of clicks that should be heard is from 4 to 6, which will also tell you that the brake is adjusted correctly.

4 If the number of clicks cannot be obtained by this procedure, or the brake still does not hold the vehicle on a hill, it indicates that the cables are stretched beyond adjustment and should be replaced with new ones. Refer to the appropriate Section in this Chapter.

21 Parking brake cables – inspection

Refer to the appropriate Section in Chapter 1 to inspect the parking brake cables.

22 Parking brake cables – replacement

1 The parking brake cable is slightly different in vehicles with rear disc brakes as opposed to ones with rear drum brakes. These differences will be noted.

2 First, remove the center console accessory box and the rear seat cushion.

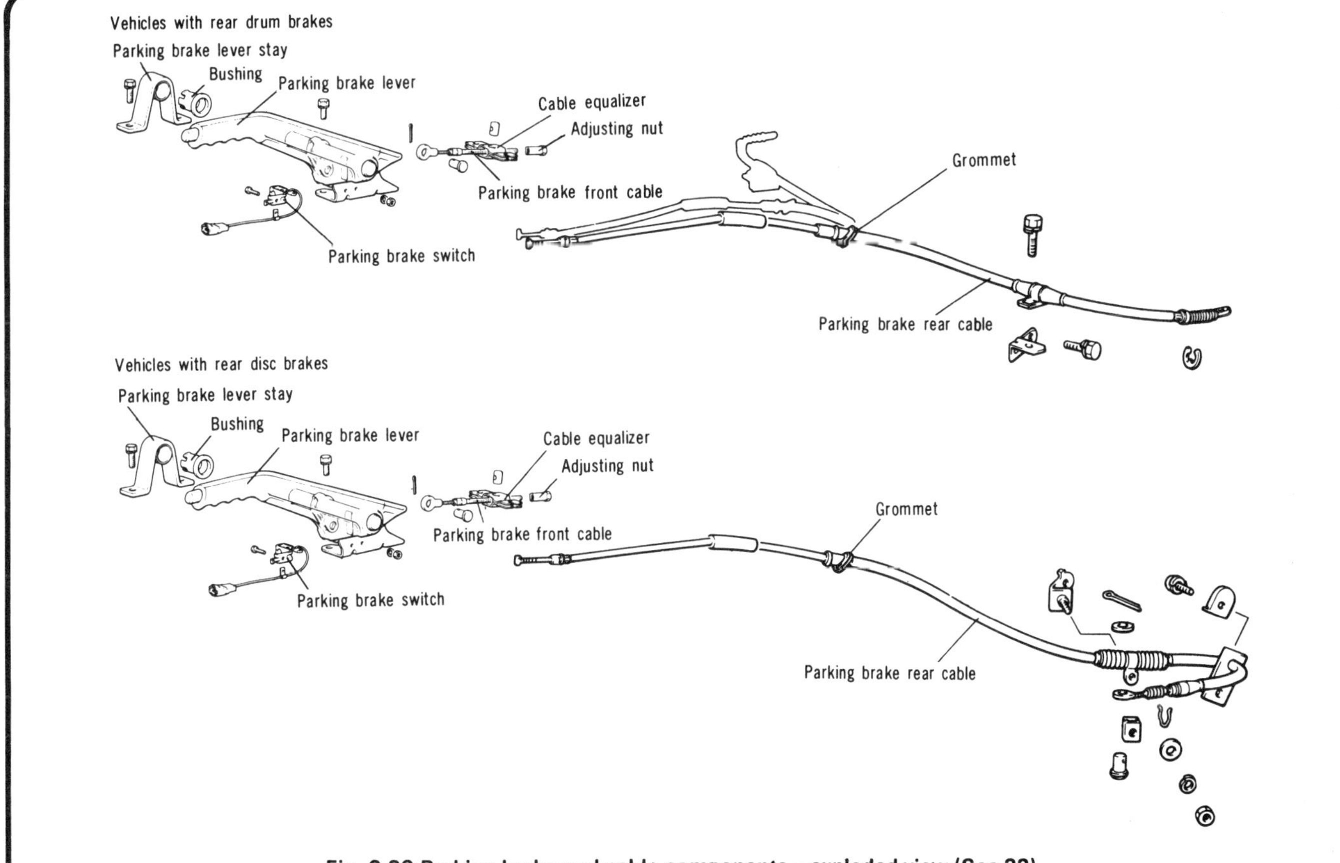

Fig. 9.39 Parking brake and cable components – exploded view (Sec 22)

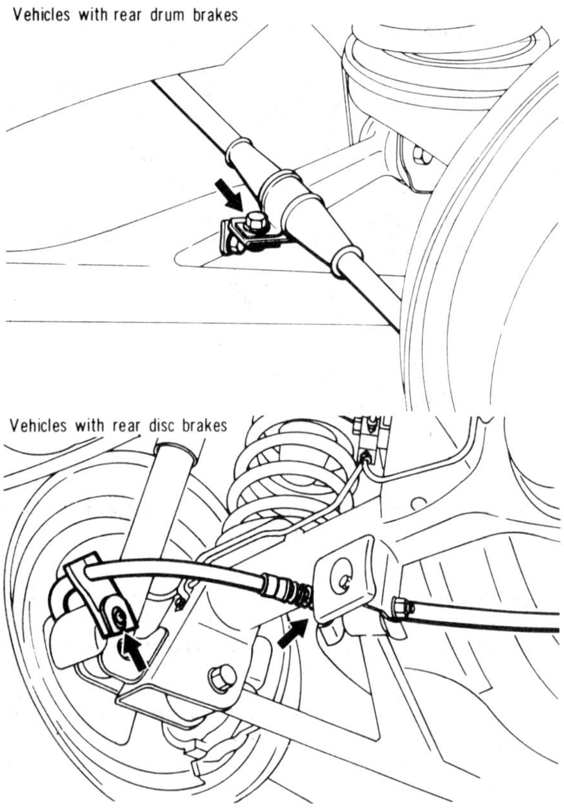

Fig. 9.40 Disconnect rear parking brake cable clamps (Sec 22)

3 Loosen and remove the adjuster nut and the rear parking brake cable from the cable equalizer.
4 On vehicles with drum brakes, disconnect the rear cable from the parking brake lever inside the rear brake drum housing by referring to Section 12 in this Chapter.
5 On vehicles with disc brakes, disconnect the rear cable from the parking brake lever that is part of the disc caliper body by referring to Section 9 in this Chapter.
6 Disconnect the cables from their retaining clamps as shown in the illustration.
7 Installation is the reverse of removal.
8 Be sure to adjust the cables after they are installed.

23 Parking brake warning light switch – check and adjustment

1 Refer to Chapter 10 to check the parking brake switch.
2 To adjust the switch, remove the center console accessory box to gain access.
3 Loosen the clamp-screws attaching the parking brake light switch to the pullrod bracket.
4 Move the switch until the brake warning light goes out when the pullrod is released and comes on when the pullrod is engaged on the first notch.
5 Tighten the clamp screws.

24 Brake pedal – removal and installation

1 Remove the cotter key and washer from the pin connecting the power brake pushrod to the brake pedal. Pull out the pin.
2 If equipped with a manual transmission, back off the clutch adjusting wheel on the clutch cable (inside the engine compartment) and unhook the end of the clutch cable from the clutch cable hook on the pedal.
3 Remove the nuts, bolts and lock washers attaching the pedal support member to the firewall and dash, and lift out the brake pedal, the clutch pedal (if equipped) and the support member as an assembly.

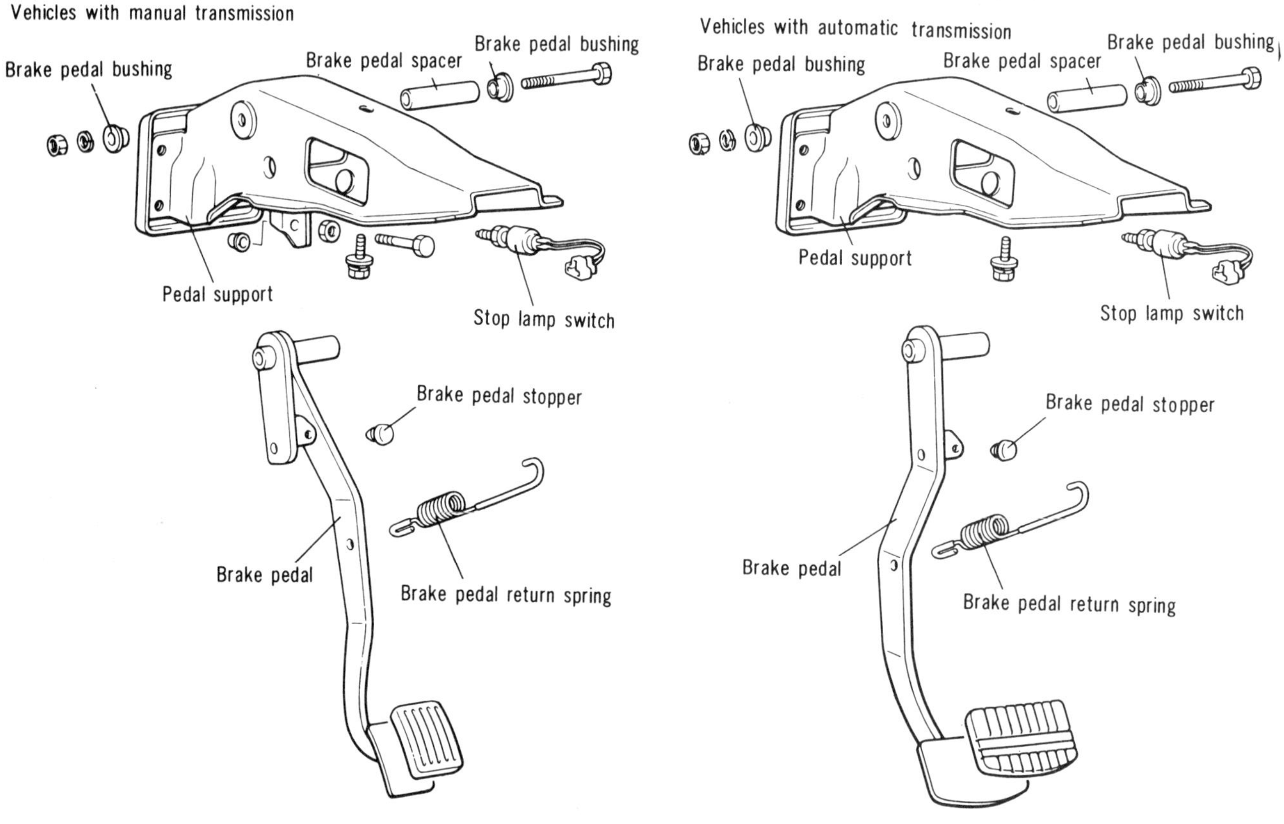

Fig. 9.41 Brake pedal components – exploded view (Sec 24)

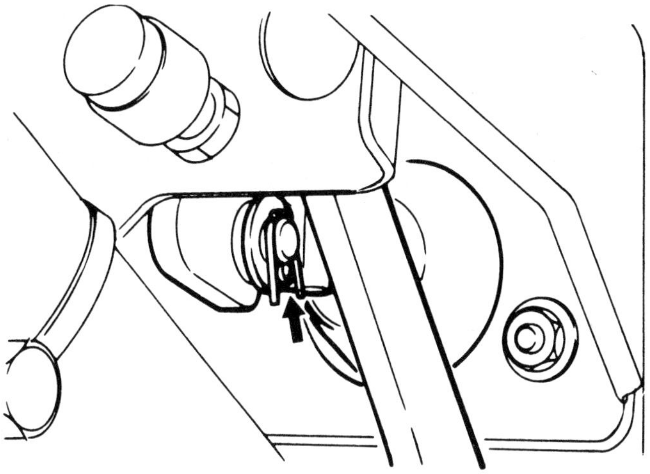

Fig. 9.42 Disconnect the brake pedal and the operating rod (Sec 24)

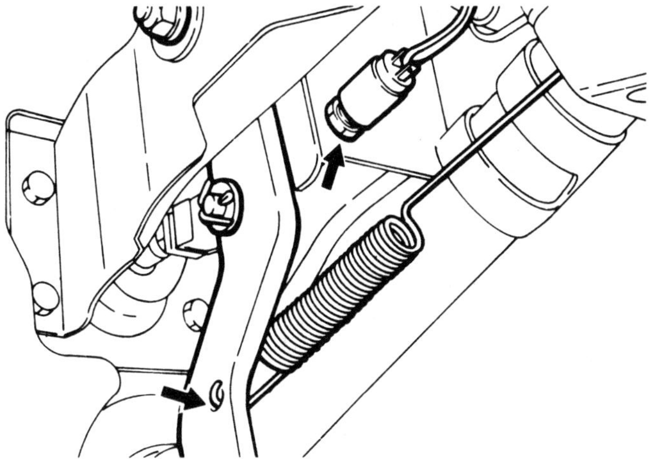

Fig. 9.43 Remove the pedal return spring and the stoplight switch (Sec 24)

4 Disengage the clutch return spring, remove the nut and washers on the end of the clutch pedal shaft and slip out the clutch pedal (if equipped). The clutch cable hook, the spacer and the spring washer will come off the pedal shaft also.
5 Disengage the return spring from the brake pedal.
6 Remove the bolt holding the brake pedal pivot rod in place. Pull out the pivot rod and the brake pedal will slip out of the support member.
7 Check the bushings, pedal shafts and pads for wear and damage. Repair or replace any defective parts. Check the pedal(s) for distortion and repair or replace as necessary.
8 Apply a thin coat of grease to the pedal bushings and pivots. Hold the brake pedal in place and slip the brake pedal pivot rod into the support member and through the brake pedal. Install the pivot rod bolt.
9 Hook up the brake pedal return spring.
10 If equipped with manual transmission, slide the clutch pedal into place and install the spring washer, the spacer, the clutch cable hook and the washers and nut on the end of the clutch pedal shaft. Tighten the nut securely and hook up the clutch pedal return spring.
11 Check the lateral (side-to-side) play at the center of the foot pads on the clutch and brake pedals. If it is greater than the specified amount, replace the bushings with new ones.
12 Install the support member/pedal assembly into the vehicle and tighten all nuts and bolts securely.
13 Connect the power brake pushrod to the brake pedal and install the pin, the washer and the cotter key.
14 If applicable, apply a thin coat of grease to the clutch cable hook, hook up the clutch cable and adjust the clutch pedal height and free play by referring to Chapter 8.
15 Adjust the brake pedal height as described in Section 3.

Chapter 10 Chassis electrical system

Contents

Specifications

Indicator lights	Bulb capacity
Turn signal	3.4W
High beam	1.4W
Fuel level failure	3.4W
Door ajar	1.4W
Fasten seat belt	1.4W
Stoplight warning	1.4W
Brake warning	1.4W
Washer liquid level	1.4W

Exterior lights	Bulb capacity
Headlight (type I)	50W
Headlight (type II)	40/60W
Rear combination	27/8W
Front and rear side marker	3.8W
Stop/tail	27/8W
Back-up	27W
License plate	8W

Interior lights	Bulb capacity
Door light	5W
Dome light	10W
Reading	6W
Glove compartment	3.4W
Courtesy	3.4W
Heater panel	1.4W
Meter illumination	1.4W
Cigarette lighter	3W
Accessory box	1.4W
Ash trays	1.4W
Shift illumination	1.7W
Defogger switch	1.4W

Oil pressure sending unit current check	
At 0 psi (0 kPa)	0 Amps
At 57 psi (393 kPa)	83.5m Amps
At 114 psi (786 kPa)	110m Amps

1 General information

This Chapter covers the repair and service procedures for the various lighting and electrical components not associated with the engine, as well as general information on troubleshooting the car's various electrical circuits. Information on the battery, generator, distributor and starter motor can be found in Chapter 5.

The electrical system is of the 12-volt, negative ground type with power supplied by a lead/acid-type battery which is charged by the generator.

Electrical components located in the dashboard do not use ground wires or straps, but rather use grounding provisions which are integrated in the printed circuit mounted behind the instrument cluster.

It should be noted that whenever portions of the electrical system are worked on, the negative battery cable should be disconnected to prevent electrical shorts and/or fires.

2 Electrical troubleshooting – general information

A typical electrical circuit consists of an electrical component, any switches, relays, motors, etc relevant to that component and the wiring and connectors that connect the component to both the battery and the chassis. To aid in locating a problem in any electrical circuit,

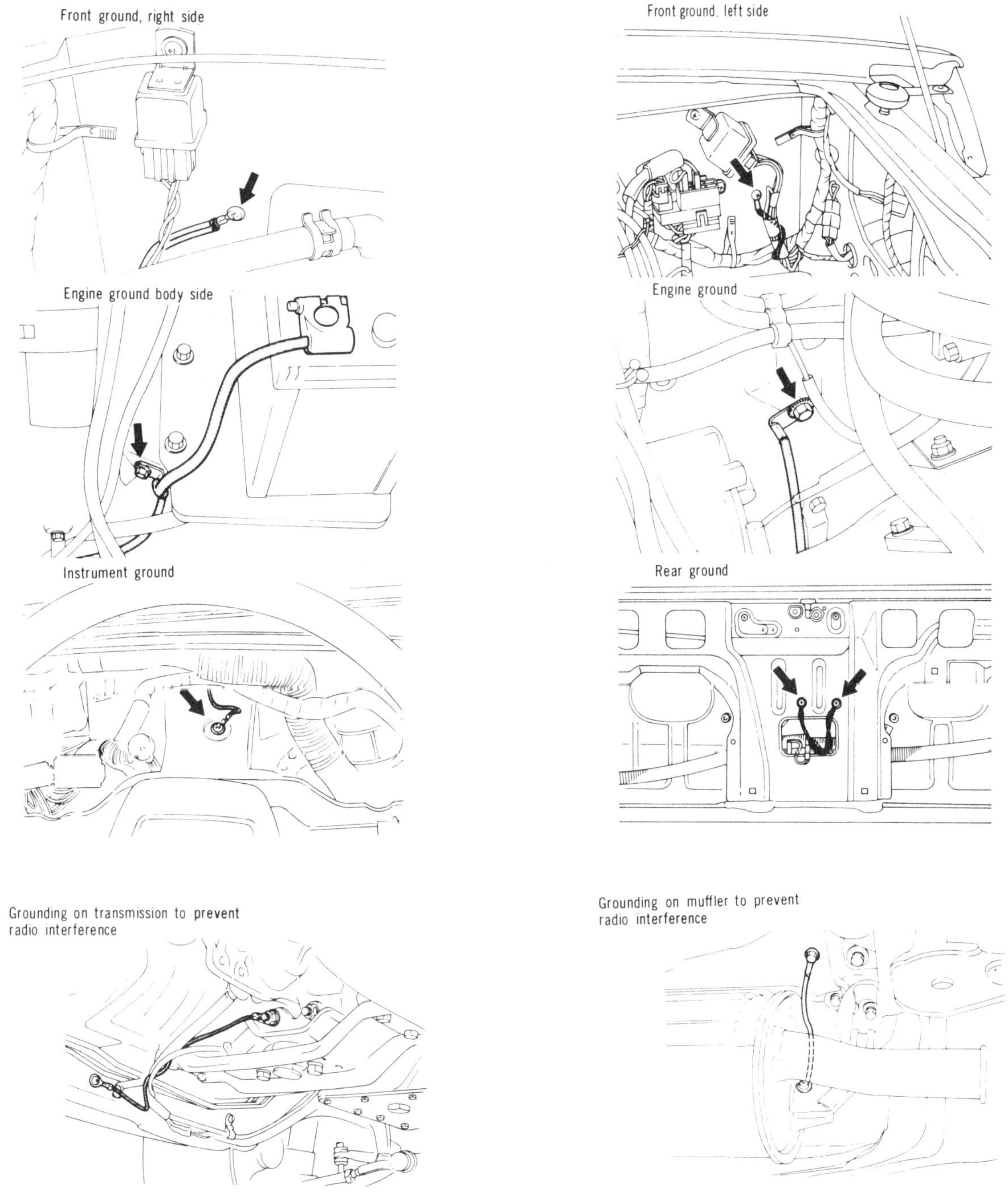

Fig. 10.1 Centralized grounding points (Sec 2)

complete wiring diagrams of each model are included at the end of this Chapter. Also of benefit in locating specific circuits on the car are wiring connector illustrations which identify all connectors used on the car. These are also found at the end of this Chapter.

Before tackling any troublesome electrical circuit, first thoroughly study the appropriate diagrams to get a complete understanding of what makes up that individual circuit. Trouble spots, for instance, can often be narrowed down by noting if other components related to that circuit are operating properly or not. If several components or circuits fail at one time, chances are the fault lies in the fuse or ground connection, as several circuits often are routed through the same fuse and ground connections. This can be confirmed by referring to the fuse box and ground distribution diagrams in this Chapter.

Often, electrical problems stem from simple causes, such as loose or corroded connections, a blown fuse or melted fusible link. Prior to any electrical trouble shooting, always visually check the condition of the fuse, wires and connections of the problem circuit.

If testing instruments are going to be utilized, use the diagrams to plan ahead of time where you will make the necessary connections in order to accurately pinpoint the trouble spot.

The basic tools needed for electrical troubleshooting include a circuit tester or voltmeter (a 12-volt bulb with a set of test leads can also be used) a continuity tester (which includes a bulb, battery and set of test leads) and a jumper wire, preferably with a circuit breaker incorporated, which can be used to bypass electrical components.

Voltage checks should be performed if a circuit is not functioning properly. Connect one lead of a circuit tester to either the negative battery terminal or a known good ground. Connect the other lead to a connector in the circuit being tested, preferably nearest to the battery or fuse. If the bulb of the tester goes on voltage is reaching that point, which means the part of the circuit between that connector and the battery is problem-free. Continue checking along the circuit in the same fashion. When you reach a point where no voltage is present, the problem lies between there and the last good test point. Most of the time the problem is due to a loose connection. **Note:** *Some circuits only receive voltage when the ignition key is in the Accessory or Run position.*

A method of finding shorts in a circuit is to remove the fuse and connect a test light or voltmeter in its place to the fuse terminals. There should be no load in the circuit. Move the wiring harness from side to side while watching the test light. If the bulb goes on, there is a short to ground somewhere in that area, probably where insulation has rubbed off a wire. The same test can be performed on other components of the circuit, including the switch.

A ground check should be done to see if a component is grounded properly. Disconnect the battery and connect one lead of a self-powered test light such as a continuity tester to a known good ground. Connect the other lead to the wire or ground connection being tested. If the bulb goes on, the ground is good. If the bulb does not go on, the ground is not good.

A continuity check is performed to see if a circuit, section of circuit or individual component is passing electricity through it properly. Disconnect the battery, and connect one lead of a self-powered test light such as a continuity tester to one end of the circuit being tested and the other lead to the other end of the circuit. If the bulb goes on, there is continuity, which means the circuit is passing electricity through it properly. Switches can be checked in the same way.

Remember that all electrical circuits are composed basically of electricity running from the battery, through the wires, switches, relays, etc to the electrical component (light bulb, motor, etc). From there it is run to the car body (ground) where it is passed back to the battery. Any electrical problem is basically an interruption in the flow of electricity from the battery and back.

3 Fuses and fusible links – general information

Fuses

The electrical circuits of the car are protected by a combination of fuses and fusible links.

The fuse box is located underneath the dash on the right side of the car. Access to the fuses is achieved by simply pulling down on the fuse cover.

Each of the fuses is designed to protect a specific circuit, as identified on the fuse cover.

If an electrical component has failed, your first check should be the

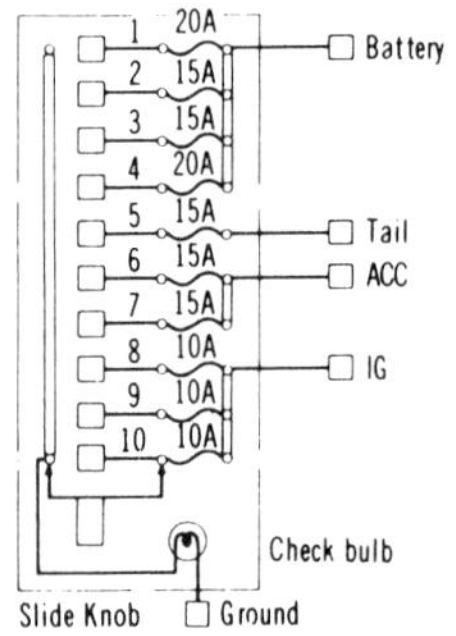

Fig. 10.2 Fuse block and capacities (Sec 3)

	Fuse capacity	Fuse label
1	*20*	*Defogger, room*
2	*15*	*Hazard*
3	*15*	*Stop*
4	*20*	*Heater*
5	*15*	*Tail, meter illum.*
6	*15*	*Wiper, washer*
7	*15*	*Radio, cigar, horn*
8	*10*	*Turn, gauge, seat belt*
9	*10*	*Back*
10	*10*	*V/Reg.*
Check bulb		*14V/1.4W*

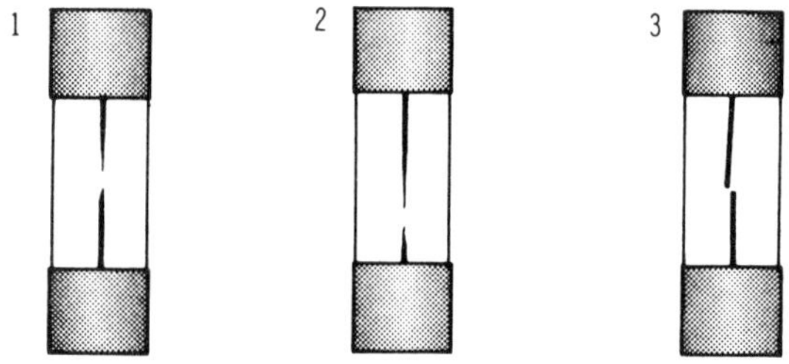

Fig. 10.3 Typical fuse breakdown and causes (Sec 3)

1 An excessive flow of current from a short-circuit, etc.
2 A contact malfunction between the fuse and fuse holder
3 Vibration of the vehicle or looseness of the fuse block

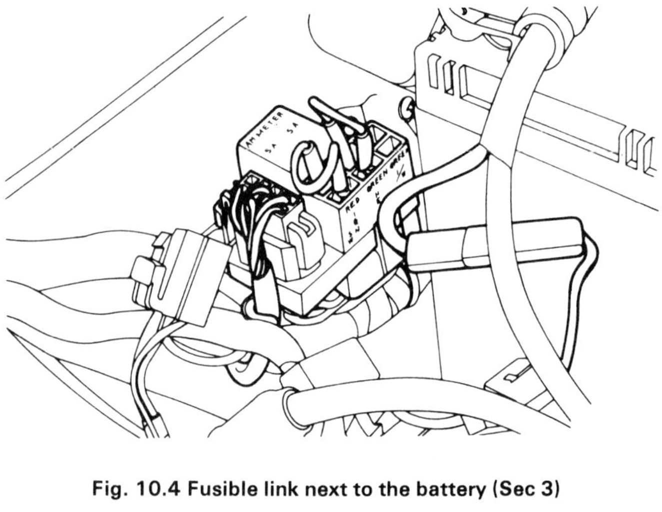

Fig. 10.4 Fusible link next to the battery (Sec 3)

fuse. A fuse which has 'blown' can be readily identified by inspecting the curved metal element inside the plastic housing. If this element is broken the fuse is inoperable and should be replaced with a new one.

Fuses are replaced by simply pulling out the old one and pushing in the new one.

It is important that the correct fuse be installed. The different electrical circuits need varying amounts of protection, indicated by the amperage rating on the fuse. A fuse with too low a rating will blow prematurely, while a fuse with too high a rating may not blow soon enough to avoid serious damage.

At no time should the fuse be bypassed by using metal or foil. Serious damage to the electrical system could result.

If the replacement fuse immediately fails, do not replace it with another until the cause of the problem is isolated and corrected. In most cases this will be a short circuit in the wiring system caused by a broken or deteriorated wire.

Fusible links

In addition to fuses, the wiring system incorporates fusible links for overload protection. These links are used in circuits which are not ordinarily fused, such as the ignition circuit and the electronic fuel injection circuit.

The fusible links are located near the positive battery terminal, and are easily removed by unplugging the connectors at either end.

If an electrical failure occurs in one of the circuits covered by a fusible link, these should be the first check. If the link is melted, the entire fusible link harness should be replaced, but only after checking and correcting the electrial fault that caused it.

4 Relays/flasher units – general information

Relays

The various electrical relays are grouped together either in the engine compartment or under the dash for convenience in the event of needed replacement.

The main relay bracket in the engine compartment is located on

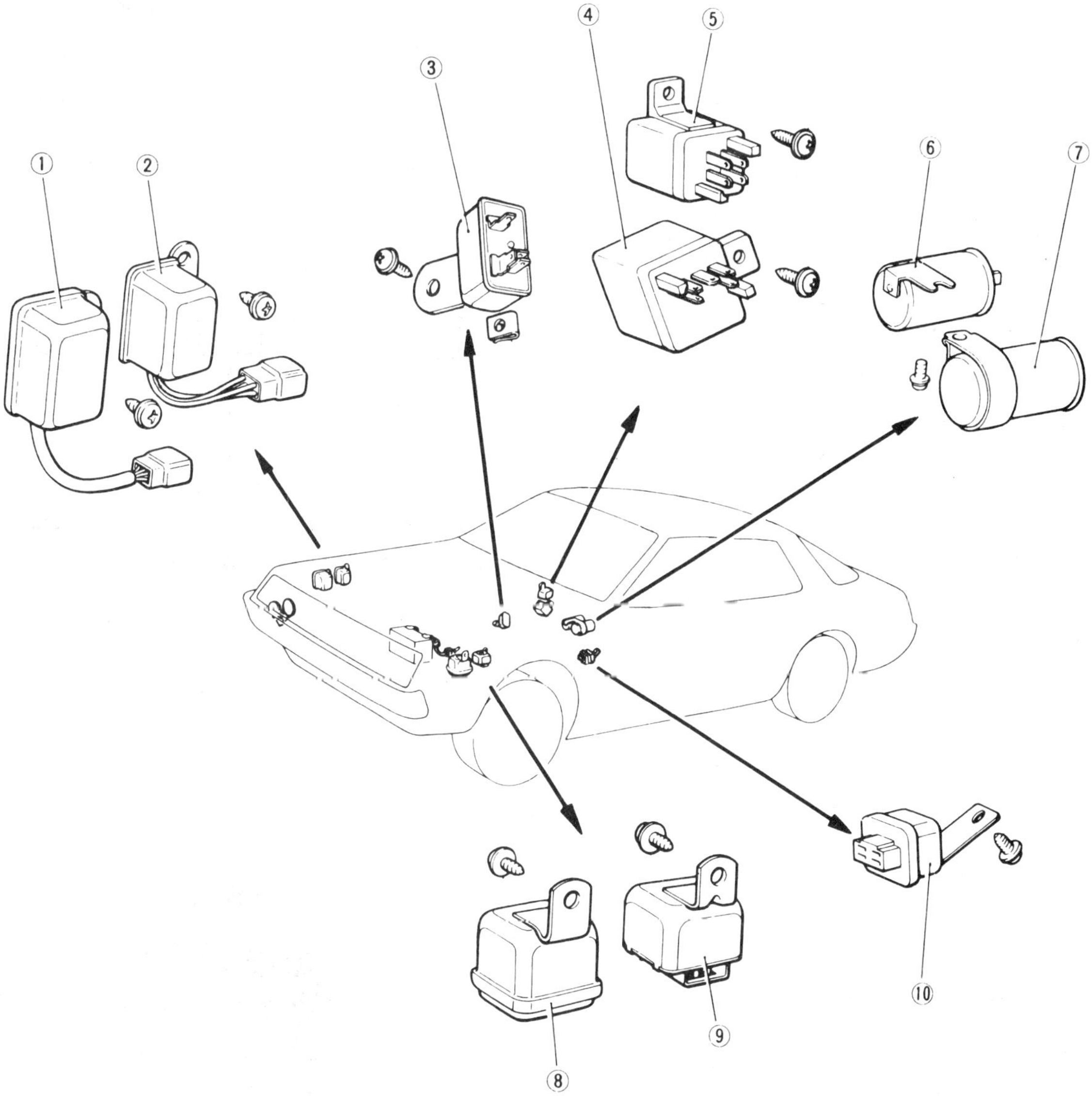

Fig. 10.5 1978 through 1980 relays and locations (Sec 4)

1 *Intermittent wiper*
2 *Power window*
3 *Defogger*
4 *Key illumination*
5 *Chime driver*
6 *Hazard warner flasher*
7 *Turn signal flasher*
8 *Light control*
9 *Wiper*
10 *Seat belt warning*

10

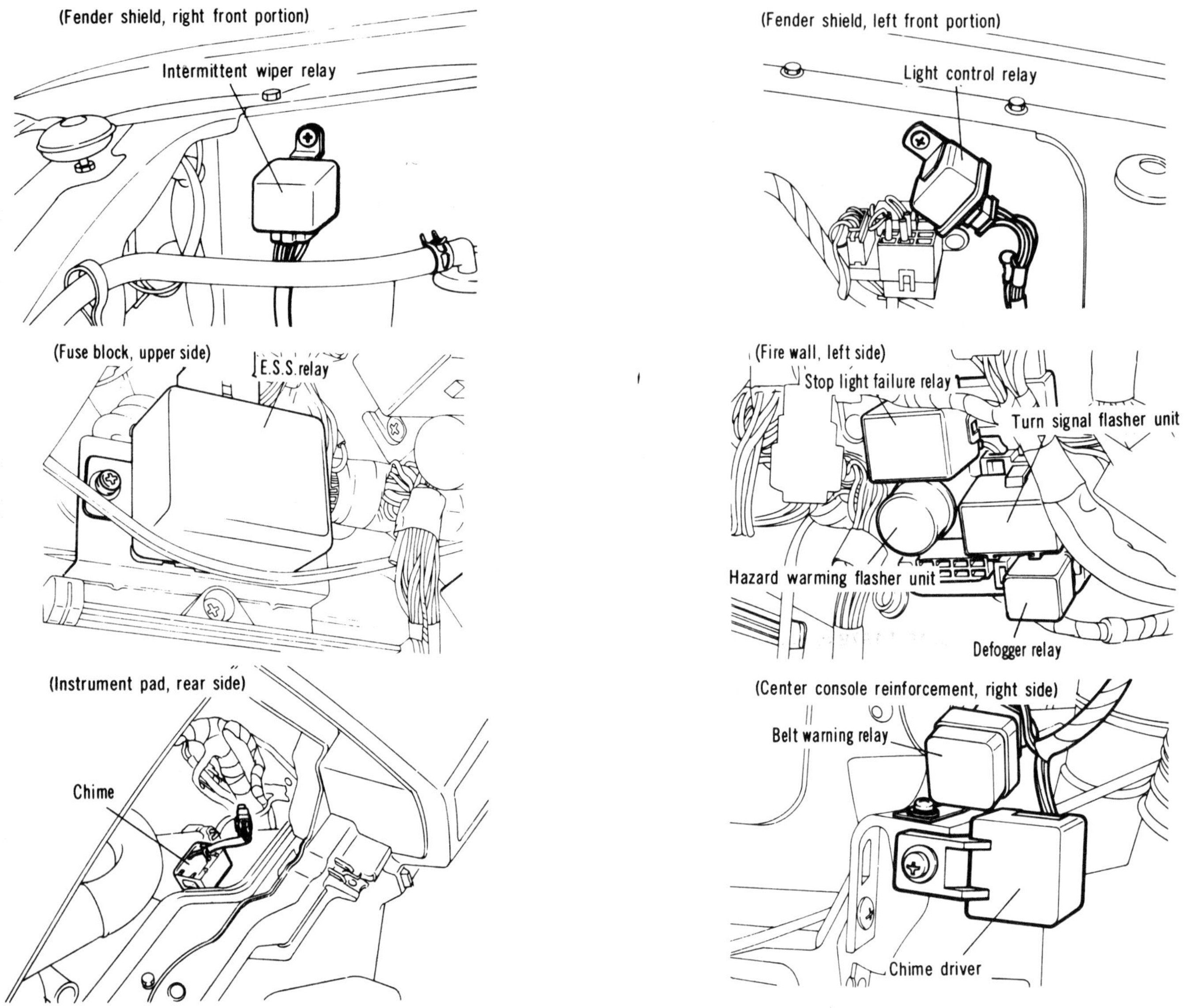

Fig. 10.6 1981 through 1983 relays and locations (Sec 4)

the right side, and has the windshield washer reservoir attached to its outer mounting case.

If a faulty relay is suspected, it can be removed and tested by a reputable dealer or other qualified shop. Defective relays must be replaced as a unit.

Flasher units

Small canister-shaped flasher units are incorporated into the electrical circuits for the directional signals and hazard warning lights.

When the units are functioning properly an audible click can be heard with the circuit in operation. If the turn signals fail on one side only and the flasher unit cannot be heard, a faulty bulb is indicated. If the flasher unit can be heard, a short in the wiring is indicated.

If the turn signal fails on both sides, the fault may be due to a blown fuse, faulty flasher unit or switch, or a broken or loose connection. If the fuse has blown, check the wiring for a short before installing a new fuse.

The hazard warning lamps are checked in the same manner as paragraph 3 above.

Both the turn signal and hazard warning flasher units are located on a single bracket underneath the dash on the driver's side (see accompanying figure).

When replacing either of these flasher units it is important to buy a replacement of the same capacity. Check the new flasher against the old one to be assured of the proper replacement.

5 Instrument cluster – removal and installation

1978 thru 1980

1 Remove the ash tray bracket and the panel just over the panel cover.

2 Disconnect the speedometer cable and remove all of the instrument cluster attaching screws. To do this, pry up the trim at point A and B using a thin tipped screwdriver or a stiff piece of wire and loosen the screws.

3 Carefully pull out the instrument cluster a little and disconnect all of the electrical connections.

4 Remove the instrument cluster.

5 At this time you can refer to the following appropriate Sections in

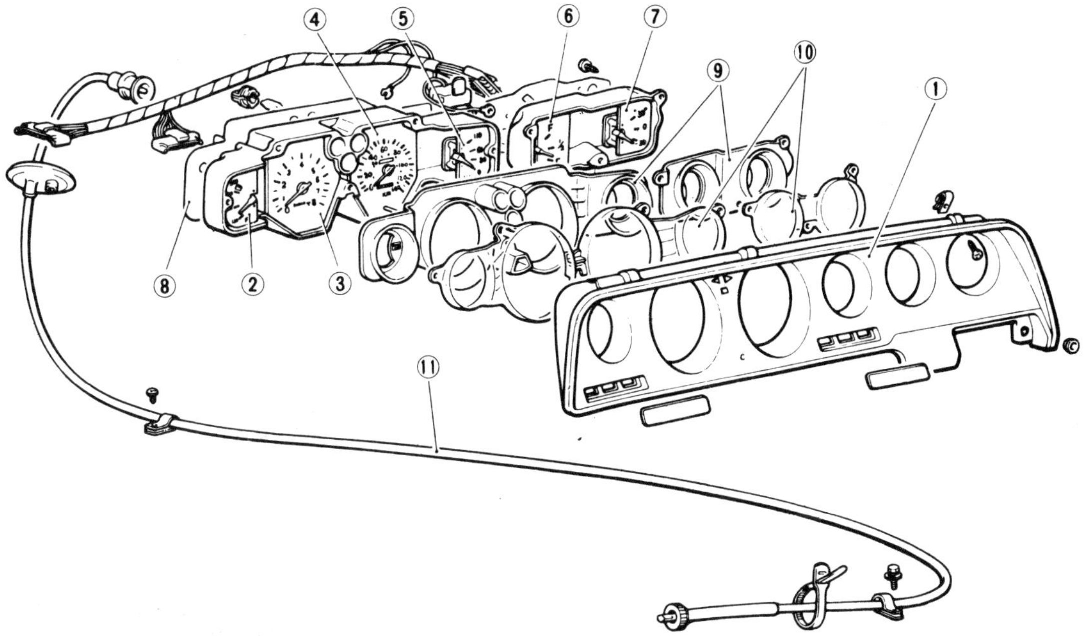

Fig. 10.7 1978 through 1980 instrument cluster components – exploded view (Sec 5)

1 *Instrument cluster panel*
2 *Water temperature gauge*
3 *Tachometer*
4 *Speedometer*
5 *Oil pressure gauge*
6 *Fuel gauge*
7 *Ammeter*
8 *Printed circuit board*
9 *Instrument cluster panel*
10 *Instrument cluster glass*
11 *Speedometer cable*

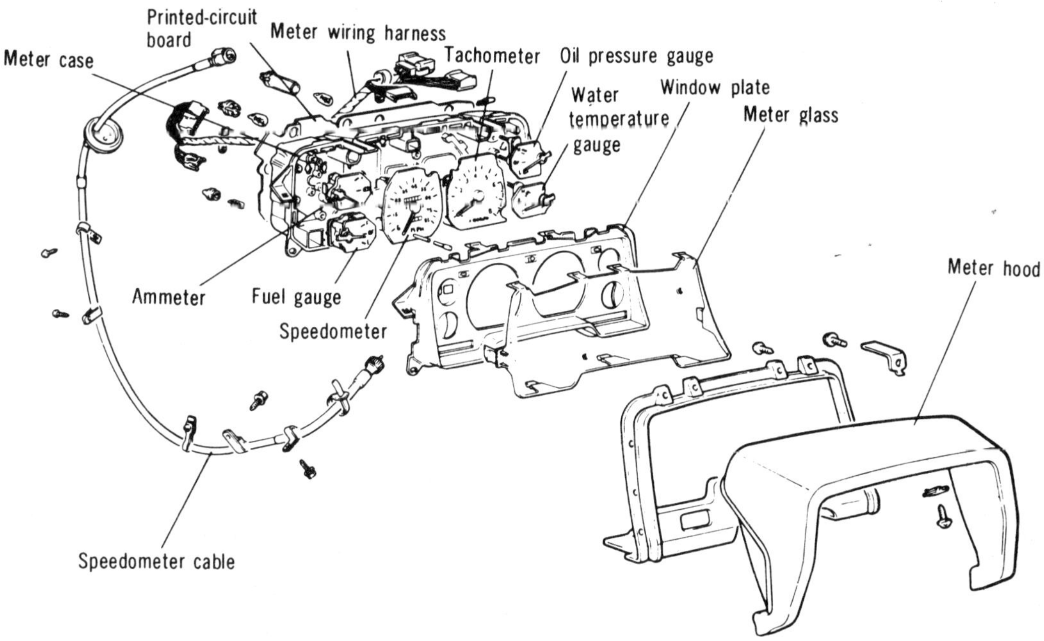

Fig. 10.8 1981 through 1983 instrument cluster components – exploded view (Sec 5)

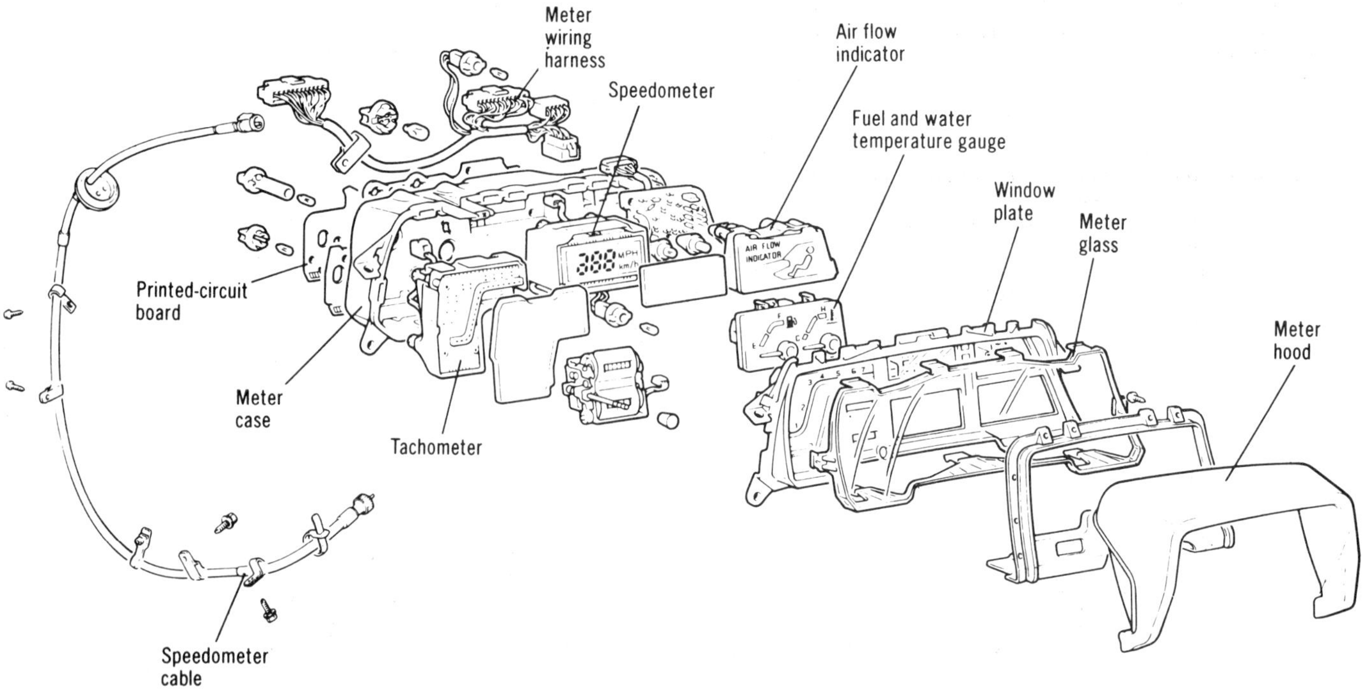

Fig. 10.9 1983 electronic instrument cluster components – exploded view (Sec 5)

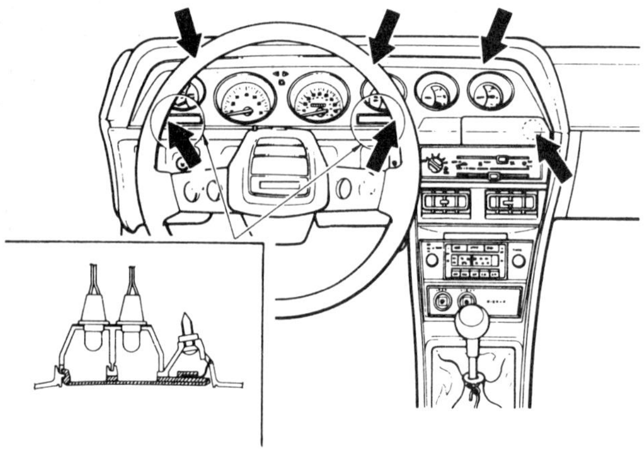

Fig. 10.10 1978 through 1980 instrument cluster removal (Sec 5)

Fig. 10.11 1981 through 1983 meter hood removal (Sec 5)

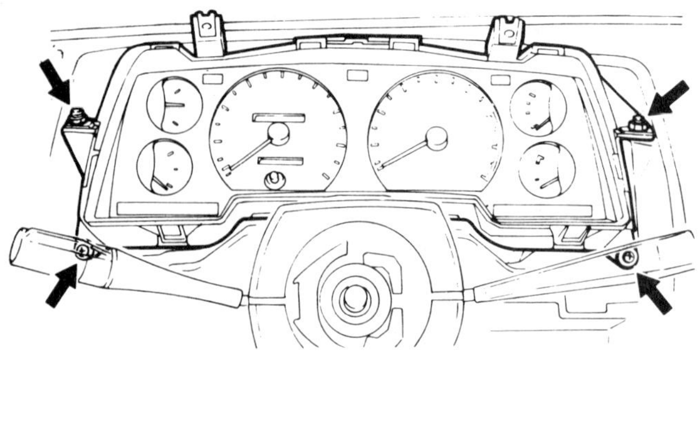

Fig. 10.12 1981 through 1983 meter assembly removal (Sec 5)

this Chapter to remove any of the defective parts that you want to replace or check.

6 Installation is the reverse of the removal procedure.

1980 thru 1983

7 Remember to disconnect the negative terminal of the battery. Remove the meter hood screws and the meter hood.

8 Remove the meter assembly mounting nuts and screws. Pull out the meter assembly a little and disconnect all of the electrical connections.

9 At this time you can refer to the following appropriate Sections in this Chapter to remove any of the defective parts that you want to replace or check.

10 Installation is the reverse of the removal procedure.

1983 (with electronic meters)

11 Disassembly of, or replacing and checking of most of the components in the electronic meter assembly is complicated and requires

special instruments to perform. To save some money, you can remove and install the unit yourself but repair should be left to your dealer service department.

12 Refer to the above Section for 1983 vehicles in order to remove and install the meter assembly.

6 Meter, gauge and bulb – checking and replacement

Note: *Handle the instrument cluster with care so that you will not damage the printed circuit board.*

1 Tachometer and speedometer checking requires the purchase of a calibrated tune-up tester and is best left to a qualified service repair department. If you know that the tach or speedometer is bad, just replace it with a new one.

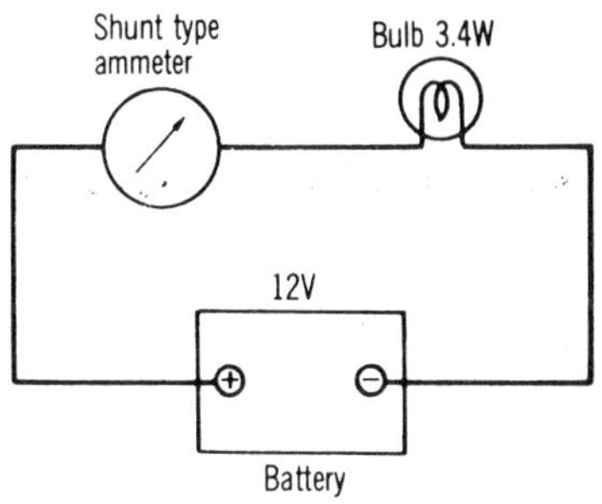

Fig. 10.13 Checking the ammeter (Sec 6)

2 Ammeter checking involves wiring a 3.4 Watt bulb in series with the ammeter. If the ammeter indicates approximately 6A, then it is in good condition; if not, then it should be replaced with a new one.

3 The fuel gauge has a number of simple checks. To check the voltage limiter, disconnect the connector at the bottom of the instrument panel and measure the voltage betwen the connector output terminal and ground with a voltmeter. If the reading is less than 7V, replace the gauge with a new one.

4 To check the gauge for continuity, use an ohmmeter and measure the resistance between the terminals shown in the illustration. If the resistance is less than 55 ohms, the coil is possibly shorted; if it is higher than 55 ohms, then the coil may be broken; in either case, replace the gauge with a new one.

5 To check the gauge indication, install a specified resistance (95 ohm-empty and 7 ohm-full) into the line between the gauge and the battery and connect the other lead to the battery. Read the gauge after the pointer has time to settle (about 2 min), replace the gauge with a new one if it does not read accurately.

6 To check the temperature gauge, disconnect the cable from the terminal of the gauge and connect a 25 ohm resistor in series to the gauge and ground it. If the gauge indicates approximately 248°F (120°C) it is in good condition; if not, replace it with a new one.

7 To check the continuity, measure the resistance between the terminals shown using an ohmmeter. The resistance measured should be 55 ohms; if not, replace the gauge with a new one.

8 To check the gauge for the correct indication, connect it to the battery and insert the specified resistance in series to the gauge. To read Hot (239°F-115°C) use a 23.8 resistor and to read Cold (158°F-70°C) use a 104 ohm resistor. If the gauge does not read accurately after this check, replace it with a new one.

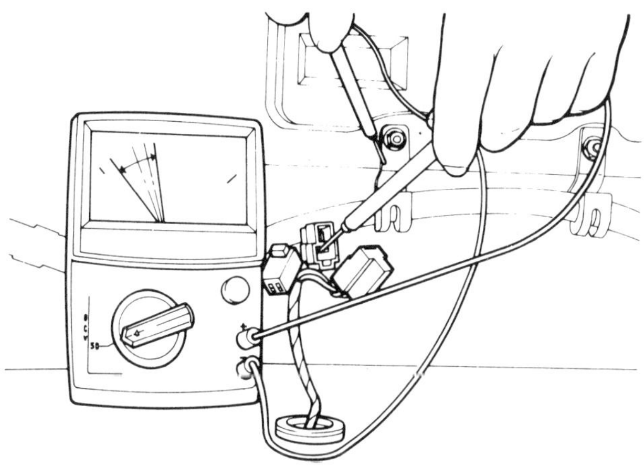

Fig. 10.14 Checking the fuel gauge voltage limiter (Sec 6)

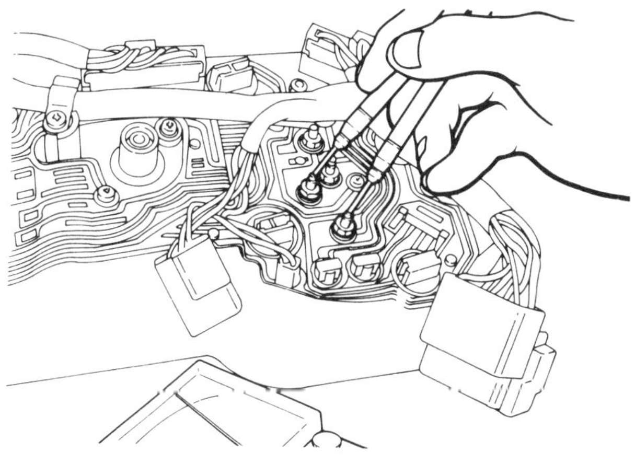

Fig. 10.15 Checking fuel gauge continuity (Sec 6)

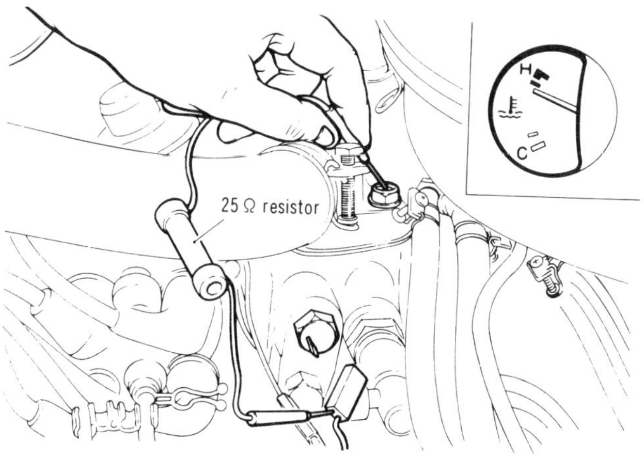

Fig. 10.16 Checking the temperature gauge (Sec 6)

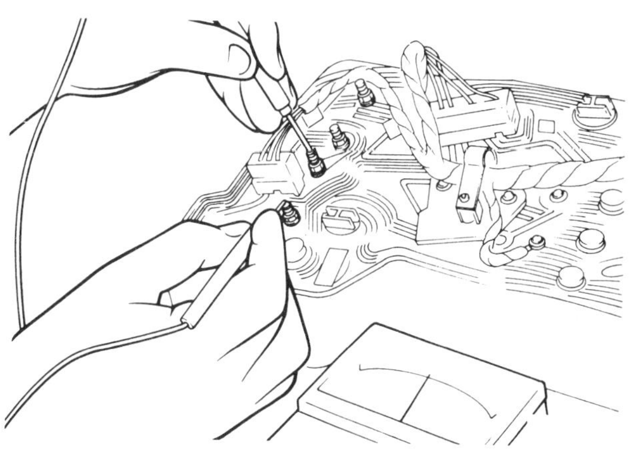

Fig. 10.17 The temperature gauge continuity check (Sec 6)

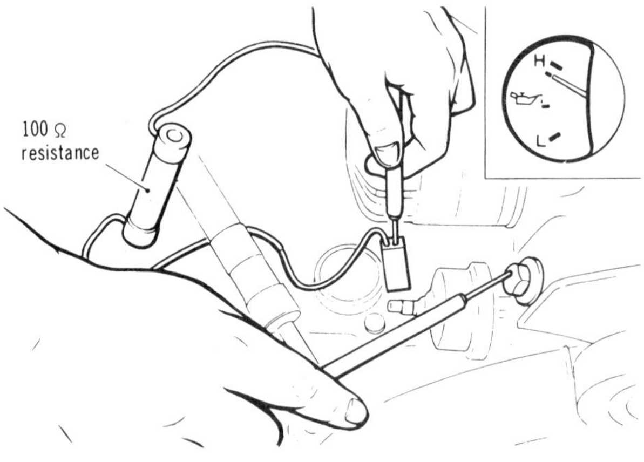

Fig. 10.18 Checking the oil pressure gauge (Sec 6)

9 The oil pressure indication test is fairly simple. Connect a 100 ohm resistor in series with the gauge and ground it. If the gauge indicates approximately 85 psi (588 kPa), it is in good condition, if not, replace it with a new one.

10 Replacing indicator bulbs is just a matter of pushing in and turning the bulb counter-clockwise to remove and clockwise to install the new one. While replacing any bulbs, be careful not to scratch or gouge the printed circuit board. **Note**: *It is possible that if you have a gauge that you thought was malfunctioning and through these checks it showed to be working OK, you may have a sending unit that is bad. Refer to Section 9 to check these.*

7 Printed circuit board and diode – checking

1 The printed circuit board in your vehicle is used for simplifying the complicated wiring that the gauges require.

2 The thin deposit of copper which comes on the board is usually burned out by overcurrent draw due to an electrical short.

3 As a general rule, if the circuit board ever becomes burned out, replace it with a new one.

4 If a new board is not immediately available, there are ways of permanently fixing it by taking it to an electronics repair shop experienced in printed circuit board repair.

5 A quick (but temporary) fix is also outlined below. It should be done by someone who is handy with a soldering iron.

6 Trace both ends of the burned (open) circuit and solder a 20 gauge covered wire to the copper deposited over a wide area around the function that is open.

7 Both ends of the wire should be soldered to within the dimensions shown in the illustration.

8 Polish the place to be soldered lightly with fine sandpaper. Coarse paper will ruin the copper film.

9 After the soldering is complete, insulate the new connections with sprayed-on clear lacquer.

10 Finally, locate the cause of the open circuit and correct it or it will repeat itself.

11 The diode on the back of the printed circuit board was installed for the purpose of checking for filament breakage in the brake warning indicator light.

12 If the parking brake and the brake failure switch are operating correctly and the indicator light illuminates faintly when the ignition key is in the On position and then goes out soon after, the diode is working correctly.

13 If, during this check, the light does not go on faintly and the

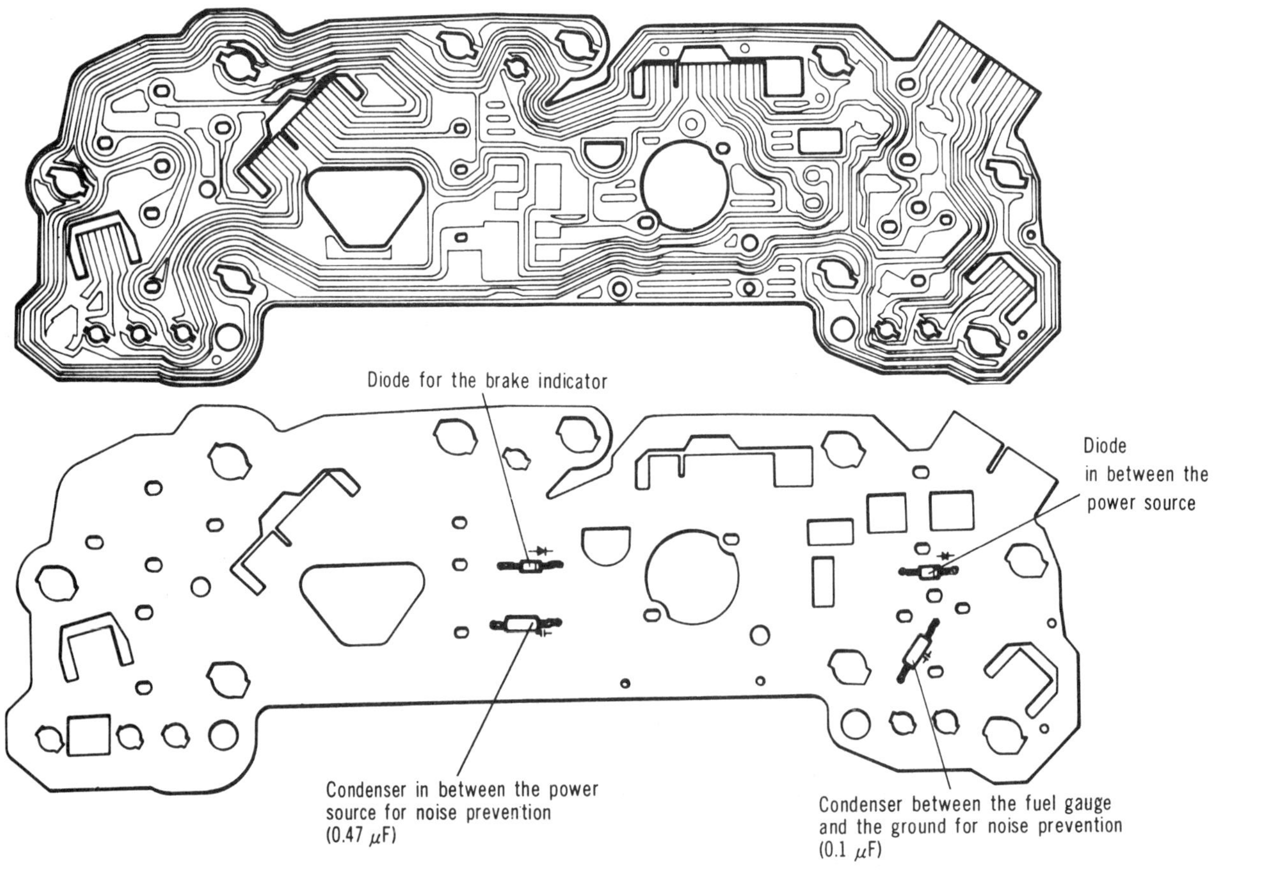

Fig. 10.19 Instrument cluster printed circuit board (Sec 7)

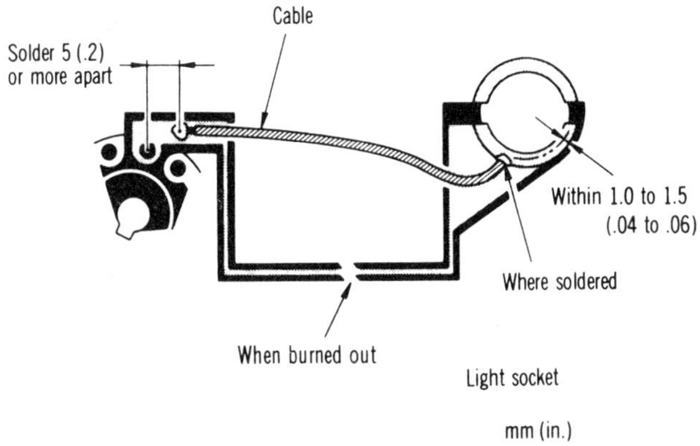

Fig. 10.20 Temporary circuit board repair (Sec 7)

parking brake light illuminates when you pull the lever, then the diode is bad and needs to be replaced with a new one.

14 If the parking light did not go on either, then there is a problem with the indicator light bulb and it needs to be replaced with a new one.

8 Speedometer cable – replacement

1 To check the operation of the speedometer, a speedometer tester is required. This procedure should be left to a qualified service department.

2 If the cable is found to be at fault, make sure that it is installed properly so that you don't have a fluctuating pointer, noise or damage to the harness inside the meter assembly itself.

3 When connecting the cable to the speedometer, insert the cable until its stopper properly fits in the speedometer side groove.

4 Pull as much of the new cable through the engine side of the engine compartment as you need in order to clearly see the color markings of the cable.

5 Connect the new cable to the transmission but be careful not to allow the inner wire of the cable to extend into the transmission. Also, make sure there is no dust or dirt on the speedometer gear.

9 Engine sensing units – checking and replacement

1 The oil pressure switch is used on vehicles with oil pressure indicator lights. The switch is found at the center of the right side of the engine. To check it for continuity, install a continuity tester in the line as shown in the illustration. Apply 4 psi or less oil pressure to the switch. If the bulb lights up, the switch is OK. If the bulb does not light up, replace the switch with a new one.

2 The oil pressure sending unit is used on vehicles with an oil pressure gauge to read. The sending unit is found at the center of the right side of the engine. To check the unit, install an ammeter into the line as shown in the illustration. Apply the specified amount of oil pressure and compare the readings to those given. If your readings are not the same as those shown, replace the unit with a new one. When installing the sending unit into the engine, make sure that you apply a sealant to the threads to prevent any leakage of oil from the engine at that point.

3 The water temperature sending unit is located in the cooling system thermostat housing. To check the unit, connect an ohmmeter to it and place the unit in hot water measuring 180°F (80°C) as shown in the illustration. Make sure that the heat sensing section of the unit and the thermometer stay away from the heated sides of the container while doing this test. Also, be sure that the heat sensing part of the unit is held .12 in (3 mm) from the surface of the water. If the check fails to register 69.4 ohms on the meter, replace the sending unit with a new one. When installing the unit back into the thermostat housing, apply some sealant to the threads to prevent coolant leakage at that point.

Fig. 10.21 Install the speedometer cable to the speedometer (Sec 8)

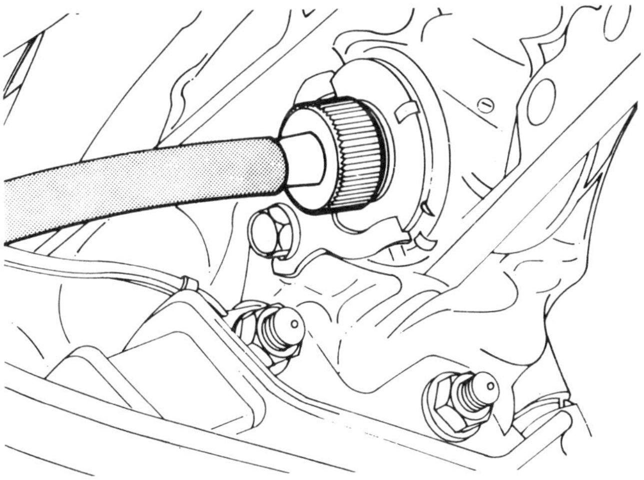

Fig. 10.22 Install the speedometer cable to the transmission (Sec 8)

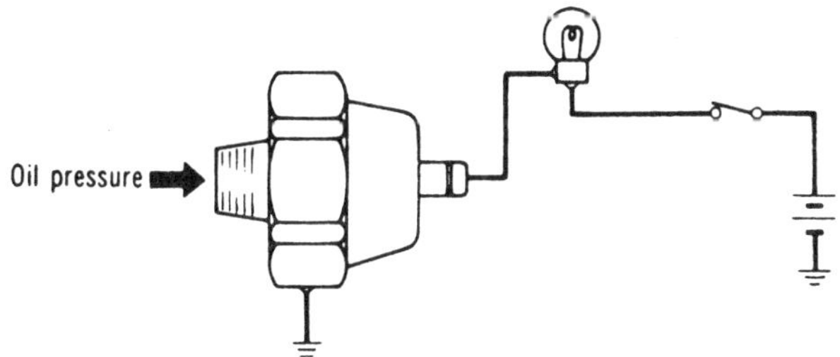

Fig. 10.23 Checking the oil pressure switch (for models having warning lights) (Sec 9)

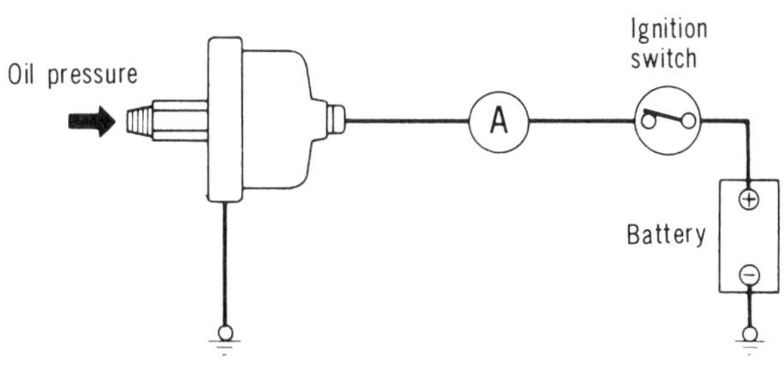

Fig. 10.24 Checking the oil pressure sending unit (for models having gauges) (Sec 9)

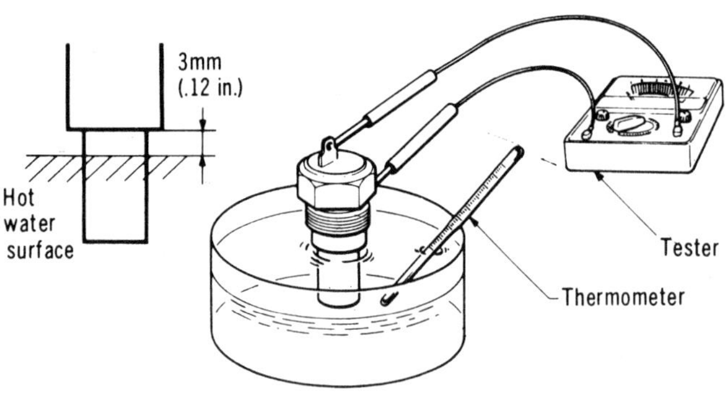

Fig. 10.25 Water temperature sending unit check (for models having gauges) (Sec 9)

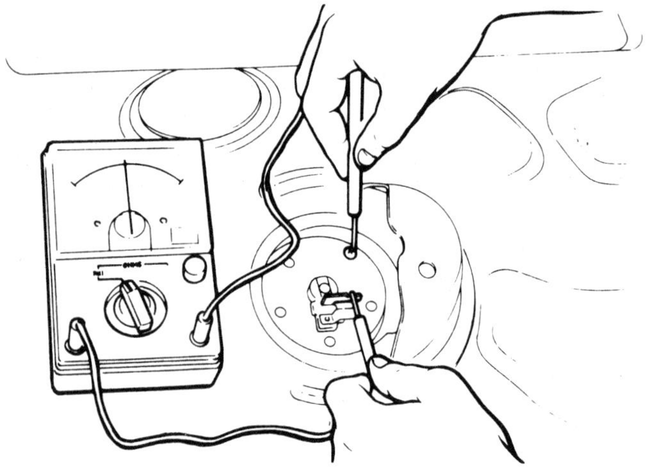

Fig. 10.26 Checking the fuel level sending unit (for models having gauges) (Sec 9)

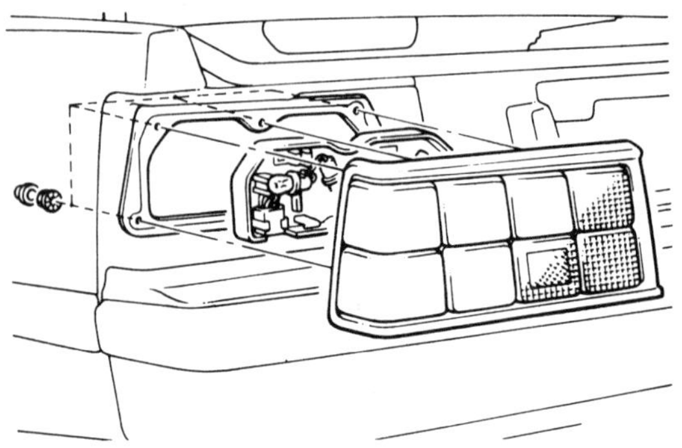

Fig. 10.27 Removing the combination light assembly (Sec 10)

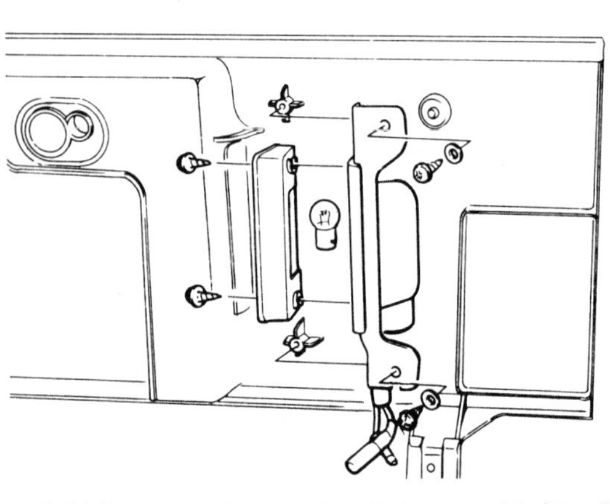

Fig. 10.28 Removing license plate light assembly (Sec 10)

4 The fuel level sending unit is on top of the fuel tank. There is no need to remove this unit in order to check it. In order to gain access to the unit, lift the trunk lid, remove the spare tire and the access cover. Disconnect the connector and with an ohmmeter measure the resistance between the unit's terminal and an unpainted surface, as shown in the illustration. The resistance measured with the tank full should be 3 ohms; with the tank empty, 110 ohms. If your readings do not agree with these, replace the sending unit with a new one.

5 If you have to replace a faulty sending unit, drain the tank before proceeding.

6 Disconnect the battery negative ground terminal and clean the area around the sending unit. Remove the screws and remove the unit from the tank. **Note**: *Make sure that you cover the access hole with a clean lintless cloth to prevent contaminants from entering the fuel tank.*

7 Before you install the new unit, coat both sides of the packing with a sealant to prevent leakage at that point. Use only a small amount of sealant and make sure the sending unit is grounded just like the one that was replaced.

10 Exterior lights – replacement

1 If any of your vehicle's lights fail to work and need to be replaced, it is an easy job to remove their respective lenses and bulbs. To remove any of the bulbs, push in on the bulb while turning it counterclockwise. To install the new bulb, push in on it while turning it clockwise.

2 The front turn signal lights are located in the lower front of the vehicle below the bumper. To gain access to the bulbs, remove the lens cover screws and then the lenses. Install the lens cover back onto the vehicle and tighten the mounting screws.

3 The front side marker lights are located on the front section of the left and right fenders. To gain access to the bulbs, remove the lens cover screws and the lenses. Install the lens cover back onto the vehicle by inserting the side tabs of the lens into the fender and tighten the mounting screws.

4 The rear side marker lights are located on the rear section of the left and right fenders. To gain access to the bulbs, open the trunk lid and look inside the fender wells of the side you want to replace. To replace the bulb, first remove the bulb socket assembly by turning it, then remove the bulb. Install the bulb and the socket assembly in the same manner.

5 The rear side marker lenses can easily be removed for replacement by removing the mounting screws, replacing the lens then tightening the mounting screws.

6 The rear turn signal, brake, back-up and running lights are found in the rear combination light assembly on both sides of the vehicle above the rear bumper. To gain access to the bulbs inside the combination light assembly, open the trunk lid and look inside toward the bottom rear of the trunk. Disconnect the connector and carefully squeeze both locking tabs and pull the assembly a short distance away from the rear of the trunk. Replace the bulb that is malfunctioning and carefully insert the assembly back into the light unit. Make sure it is securely in place.

7 The rear combination light lens can easily be removed by again opening the trunk and removing the mounting nuts and washers and then removing the lens. Install the new lens and tighten the nuts in a criss-cross pattern to avoid distorting the lens and causing it to crack.

8 The license plate light is located in the rear of the vehicle on the left side of the license plate holder. To gain access to the bulb, remove the lens cover screws and the lens cover. Install the lens back onto the vehicle and tighten the mounting screws.

9 The license plate light assembly can also be replaced by removing the lens and the rear panel of the vehicle. Disconnect the light connector and the ground wire and remove the assembly. To install the light assembly, reverse the procedure making sure the ground wire is attached correctly in the right spot and then tighten the mounting screws. Install the rear panel back onto the vehicle and tighten the mounting hardware.

10 The back-up light on some vehicles is a separate unit by itself. It is located on the left and right sides of the rear panel. To gain access to the bulb, open the trunk area and look down towards the rear of the trunk. Disconnect the connector and while pushing in on the bulb holder, turn it counterclockwise. Replace the bulb with a new one and install the holder into its place. Reconnect the connector.

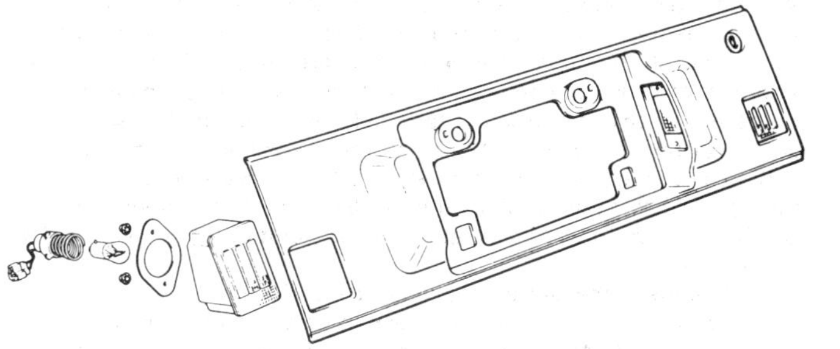

Fig. 10.29 Removing the back-up light assembly (Sec 10)

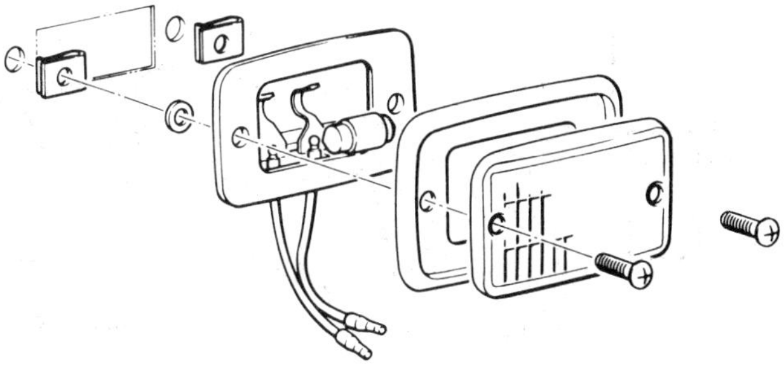

Fig. 10.30 Removing the door light assembly (Sec 11)

11 This back-up light assembly can also be replaced by disconnecting the connector and removing the rear panel. Remove the assembly mounting nuts and washers and the assembly. To install the assembly, reverse this procedure, install and tighten the screws and washers. Install the rear panel and reconnect the connector.

11 Interior lights – replacement

1 The door lights are located in the lower portion of both door panels. To gain access to the bulbs, remove the lens mounting screws and the lens. Replace the bulb by pulling out on it like a fuse. Install the lens mounting screws and the lens and tighten the screws.
2 The overhead dome light is found (in 1979 through 1980) in the overhead console. To gain access to the bulb, carefully squeeze the lens cover while you pull down on the lens. Replace the bulb by pulling it down and out like a fuse. Install the lens into place by positioning it and pushing up until it snaps into place.
3 The overhead spotlight (reading light) is also found in the overhead console. To gain access to its bulb, remove the digital cloth cover and the digital clock with its mounting screws. Now, remove the console mounting screws and pull the console down and out of its slot in the headliner. Disconnect the connector and remove the screws holding the bulb into place. Replace the bulb and install the screws tightly. Reconnect the connector and install the front part of the console into the slot and then install and tighten the mounting screws. Install the digital clock and its mounting hardware and tighten. Install the clock cover.
4 The overhead dome light is found (1981 through 1983) also in the overhead console but a little differently. To gain access to the bulb, carefully pry on the backside of the lens with a cloth-covered screwdriver. Remove the bulb from its socket and replace the lens by positioning it and pushing up on it until it snaps into place.
5 The console can also be removed by carefully prying on the access cover with a screwdriver until it comes loose. Remove the mounting screws of the console and pull the console down. Disconnect the connector and pull the console away from the headboard slot. To install the console, reverse this procedure. Install the mounting screws and tighten them. Then, install the access cover panel until it snaps into place.

12 Headlight – checking and adjustment

To check or adjust your headlights, refer to Chapter 1.

13 Headlight – replacement

1 To remove the headlights for replacement, disconnect the negative battery terminal.
2 Remove the front grille mounting screws. Pull the front grille forward. Detach the grille from the securing clips on both sides and remove it.
3 Remove the light bezel (retaining frame) of the headlight unit. Pull the headlight forward and disconnect the connector.
4 To install the new headlight, align the unit in the securing position of the lamp mounting housing and secure it with the light bezel.
5 Be sure not to tamper with the headlight adjustment screws or they will have to be realigned.
6 Attach the front grille securely to the clips on both sides and install it. Tighten the mounting screws.

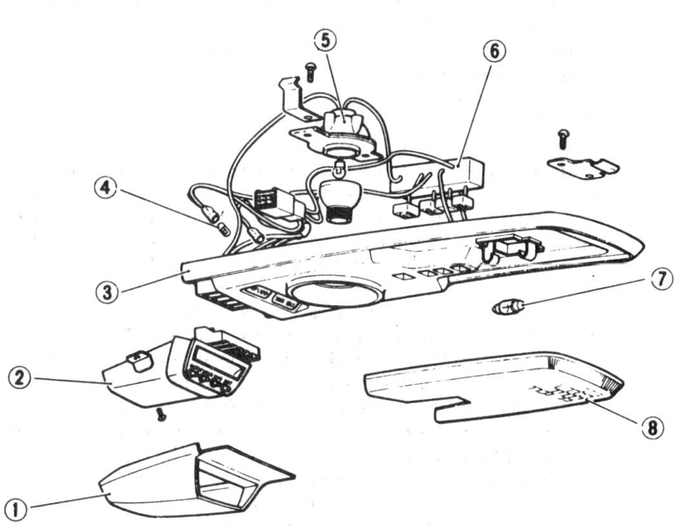

Fig. 10.31 1978 through 1980 overhead console components – exploded view (Sec 11)

1 *Digital clock cover*
2 *Digital clock*
3 *Overhead console*
4 *Indicator light bulb*
5 *Reading light*
6 *Light switch*
7 *Dome light bulb*
8 *Dome light lens*

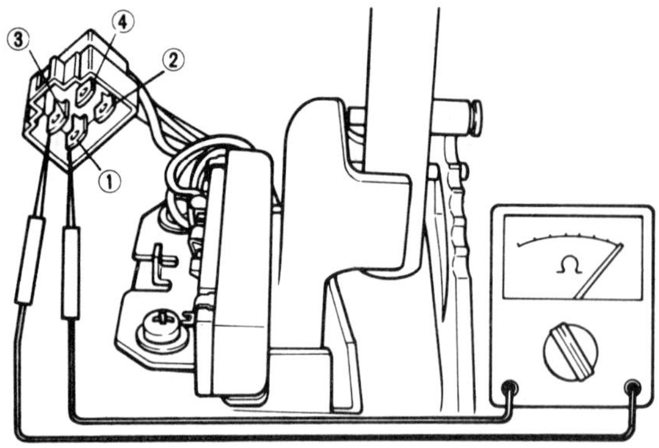

Continuity Chart

Position \ Terminal	1	2	3	4
P	O—	—O		
R			O—	—O
N	O—	—O		

Fig. 10.32 Continuity check of Neutral safety switch (Sec 14)

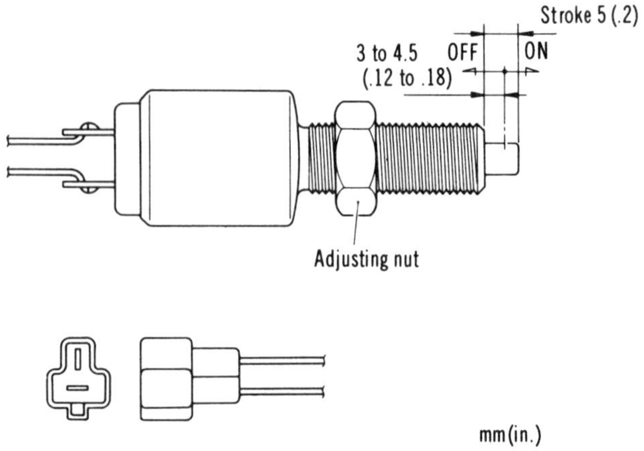

Fig. 10.33 Checking the brake light switch (Sec 14)

7 The headlight bulbs cannot be installed in the wrong position because the mounting lugs for the bulbs are offset at different angles or corners.

14 Switches – checking

1 The dome light switch is inside the door panels. Refer to the appropriate section in Chapter 12 to remove the door panels. Check the operation of the switch by use of a multimeter. The values to look for are 12V and 10A. If these values are not what you obtain, replace the switch with a new one.
2 The glove compartment light switch is located in the glove compartment hinge plate. Loosen both stoppers on the sides of the glove compartment door and let the door swing down. Disconnect the connector of the switch and remove the switch with a screwdriver. To replace the switch, reverse this procedure.
3 The Neutral safety switch is found built in near the transmission selector. To gain access to the switch, remove the selector handle and

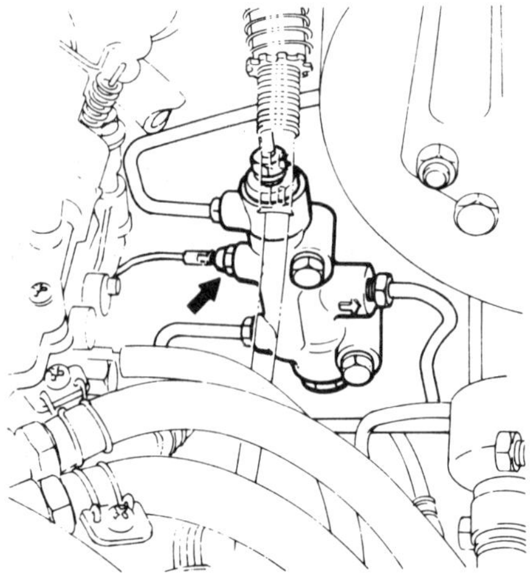

Fig. 10.34 Location of the brake failure switch (arrow) (Sec 14)

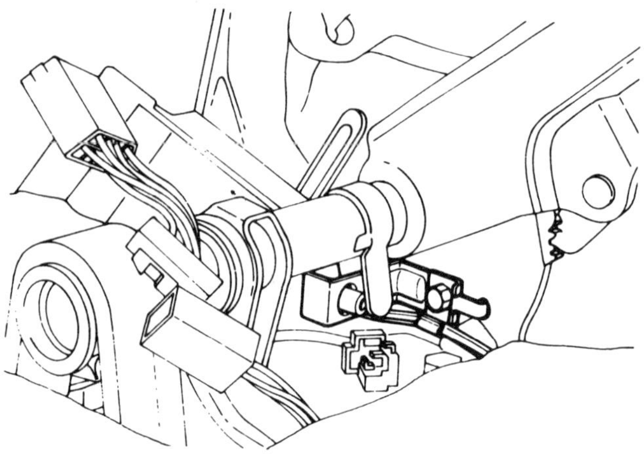

Fig. 10.35 Location of the parking brake switch (Sec 14)

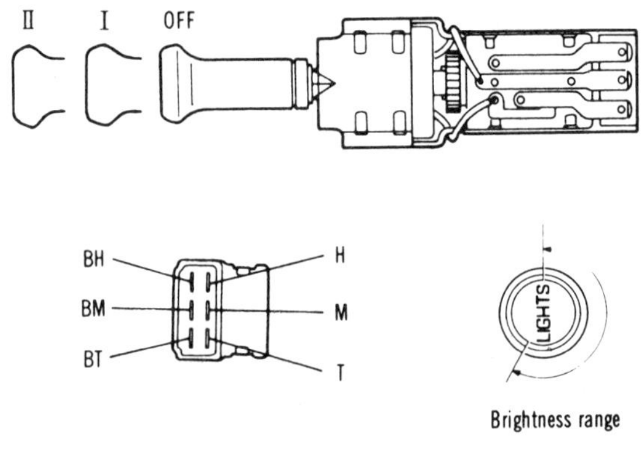

Switch position \ Terminal	Battery for tail light (BT)	Tail light (T)	Battery for Head-light (BH)	Head-light (H)	Battery for Meter illu. (M)	Ground (BM)
OFF					O—	—O
I	O—	—O			O—	—O
II	O—	—O	O—	—O	O—	—O

Fig. 10.36 Continuity check of the headlight switch (Sec 14)

the indicator panel screws and the panel. To check the switch, use a continuity tester at the points shown in the illustration to see if the switch is malfunctioning. If the switch shows no continuity in any of the positions, replace it with a new one.

4 The stoplight switch is also the brake pedal stop and is located at the upper end of the brake pedal lever under the dash. Check the operation of the switch by using a multimeter. The values to look for are 12V and 15A. If these values are not what you obtain, replace the switch with a new one. Make sure, if you replace the switch, that the brake pedal distance must be rechecked and adjusted with the switch by referring to Chapter 9.

5 The brake failure switch is incorporated into the combination valve. To check the switch, connect the leads of an ohmmeter to the terminal and the switch body. Press the plunger tip firmly against the valve body and see if the meter pointer swings. If the pointer doesn't swing, replace the switch with a new one. When replacing a switch, make sure the connections are tight so they will not leak at that point.

6 The parking brake switch is found built in near the bottom of the parking brake lever. To gain access to the switch, remove the brake dust boot and the center console. Remove the switch if it is found to be faulty. Remember to adjust it according to the procedure in Chapter 9.

7 The headlight switch is located in the instrument panel. It is accessible by going under the instrument panel. To check this switch, use a continuity tester and check for continuity by referring to the illustration. Replace the switch, if it is found to be faulty, with a new one.

15 Steering column lighting switch – checking

1 To remove the switch, refer to Chapter 11.

2 To check the switch once it is removed from the steering column, you need a continuity tester. Disconnect the connector and check the circuit according to the illustration. If the switch is found to be faulty, replace it with a new one and refer to the installation in Chapter 11.

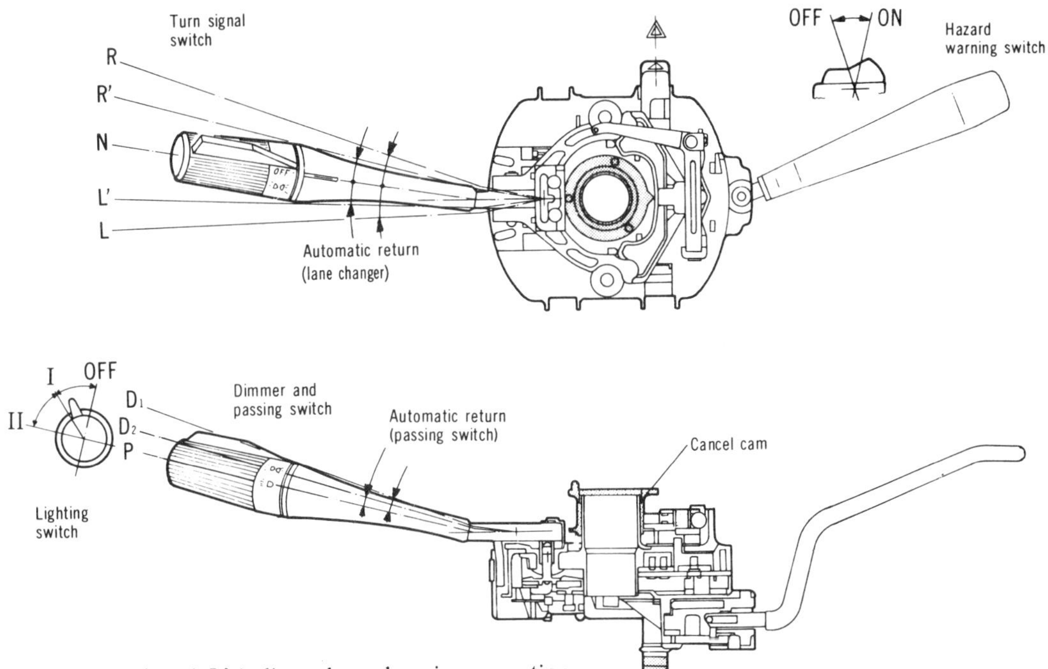

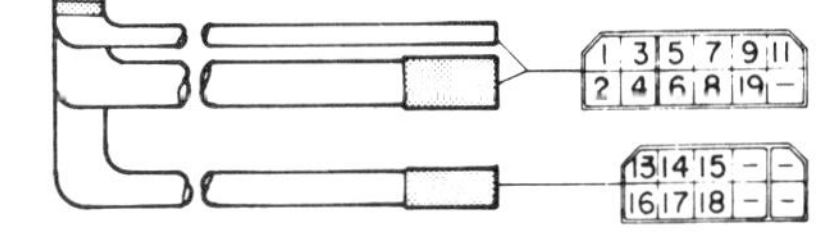

NOTE: R' and L' indicate lane-changing operation.

Dimmer and passing switch

Lever position \ Terminal	14	7	8	2
D_1	○	○		
D_2	○		○	
P	○		○	○

Turn signal and hazard warning switch

Lever position		3	5	6	4	19
OFF	L (L')	○	○			
	N					
	R (R')	○		○		
ON	L·N·R		○	○	○	○

Lighting switch

Lever position \ Terminal	1	2	9
OFF			
I	○		○
II	○	○	○

NOTE: ○—○ indicates that there is continuity between the points.

Fig. 10.37 Continuity check of the steering column lighting switch (Sec 15)

10

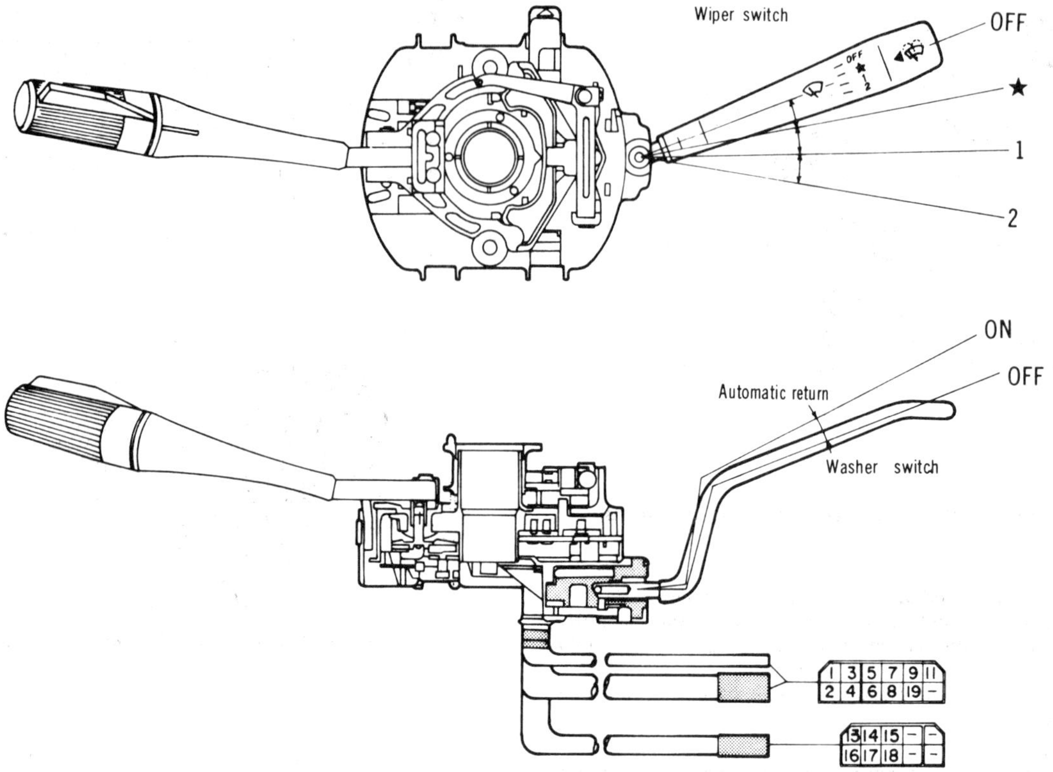

• Continuity table

Lever position \ Terminal	18	16	15	14	17	13
OFF	○		○	○		○
★	○		○	○	○	
				○		○ (dashed)
1	○			○		
				○		○ (dashed)
2		○		○		
				○		○ (dashed)

NOTE: Dashed lines indicate washer switch operational conditions.

Fig. 10.38 Continuity check of the steering column windshield wiper switch (Sec 16)

16 Steering column windshield wiper switch – checking

1 Refer to the appropriate Section in Chapter 11 to remove the switch.
2 To check the switch, you need a continuity tester. Disconnect the connector and check the switch according to the illustration. If the switch is found to be faulty, replace it with a new one according to the illustration in Chapter 11.

17 Horn and components – checking and adjustment

1 The horn is checked by removing the connector (or connectors if two horns are used) and installing a voltmeter into the circuit. Attach one of the probes of the meter to an unpainted surface (ground), and the other probe to the connector or connectors alternately, to see if you are getting 12V battery voltage. If you are getting voltage at the connectors and the horn does not work, replace the horn/horns with new ones.

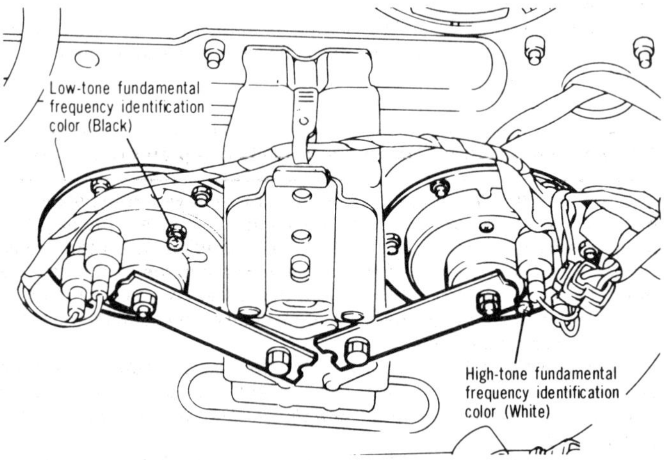

Fig. 10.39 Double-horn sound adjustment (Sec 17)

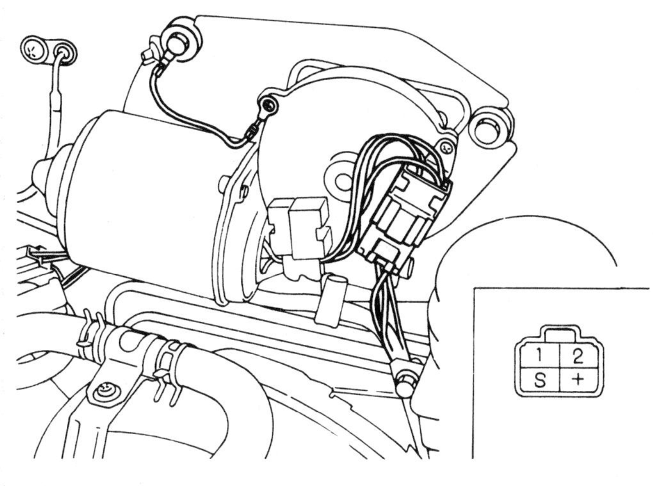

Fig. 10.40 Checking the windshield wiper motor (Sec 19)

2 The horn sound is adjusted by turning the tone frequency adjusting screw either left or right to find the best sound. Refer to the illustration for adjusting two horns. After adjusting the horn, apply lacquer to the screw to keep the sound from changing again.
3 The horn switch can be accessed by removing the steering wheel and referring to Chapter 11.

18 Windshield wiper system – checking and adjustment

Refer to Chapter 1 to check or adjust the wiper system.

19 Windshield wiper motor – checking and replacement

1 To check the wiper motor, raise the wiper arms so they are perpendicular to the windshield. Disconnect the motor connector and confirm that the motor operates when the 12V battery voltage is directed to the No. 1 terminal (low speed) and the positive terminal. Check also that voltage is present at the No. 2 terminal (high speed) and the positive terminal. If these tests do not check out, replace the motor with a new one.
2 To replace the wiper motor, first remove the wiper arms. Unhook the negative battery terminal and remove the access panel on the firewall.
3 Remove the wiper motor mounting screws and the wiper motor by pulling it towards you. Disconnect the linkage in such a manner that the motor shaft and linkage are positioned at right angles to each other. Make sure that you do not move this linkage while replacing the motor because it is positioned correctly to stop the blades in the right position on your windshield.
4 Tighten all the fastening hardware and recheck the stopping position of the blades on the windshield. If they need adjustment, refer to Chapter 1.

20 Defogger electrical components – checking and replacement

1 To check the defogger switch, it must be removed from behind the center console. To gain access to the switch, disconnect the negative battery terminal and remove the heater/air conditioning control knobs. Remove the radio knobs and the ash tray. Remove the center console mounting screws and carefully pull out the center console. Remembering which connectors go where, disconnect all of the connectors. Label them for easy reassembly.
2 Remove the defogger switch by depressing the catches on both sides of the switch. Disconnect the connector for the switch and the indicator light. **Note:** *The defogger indicator light bulb can be replaced at this time.*
3 Inspect the continuity of the switch with a circuit tester as shown in the illustration. The test must be carried out with the switch at both

• Connection table

Terminal \ Switch	OFF	ON	Connected to
1		○	IG power source
2		○	Defogger relay

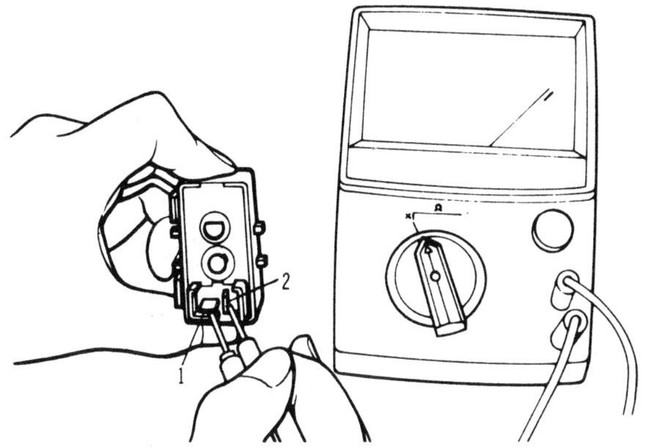

Fig. 10.41 Checking the defogger switch (Sec 20)

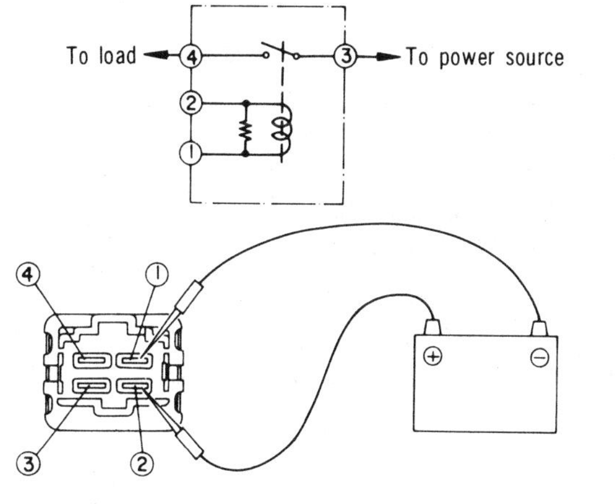

Fig. 10.42 Checking the defogger relay (Sec 20)

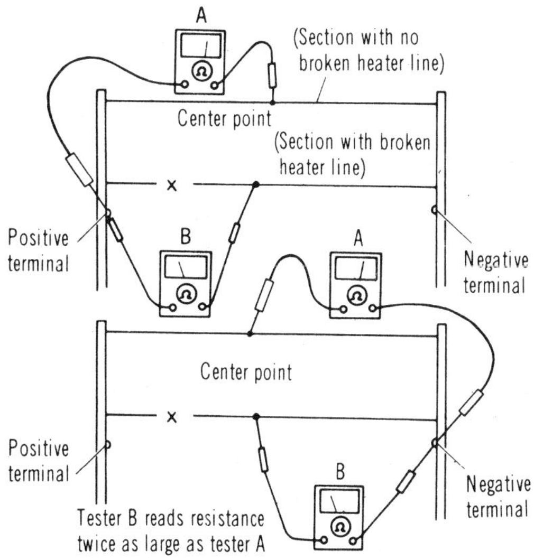

Fig. 10.43 Voltage and resistance checking of the defogger glass grid lines (Sec 20)

Connector terminal number	Standard value
Between terminals (1) and (3)	About 32Ω
Between terminals (2) and (4)	

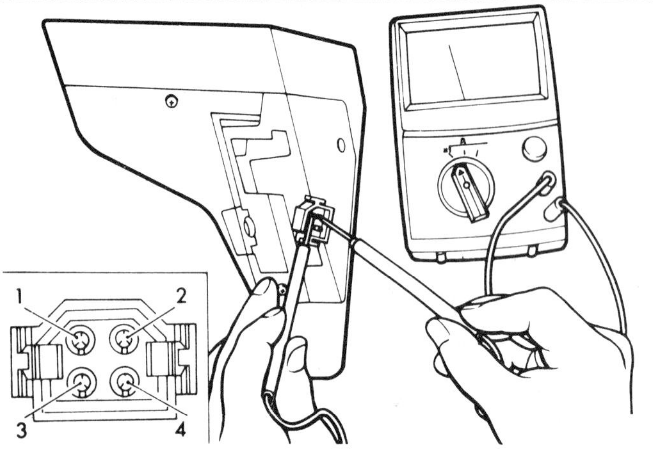

Fig. 10.44 Checking resistance in the remote control mirror motor (Sec 21)

the On and the Off positions. If the switch does not pass this test, replace it with a new one.

4 The defogger relay is located on the engine firewall. Refer to the relay section in this Chapter. To check the relay, remove it and check it with a tester.

5 Check the continuity between terminals 1 and 2. There should be about 60 ohms there. Now check between terminals 3 and 4. There should be no continuity there. Now, apply a 12V power source between terminals 1 and 2. There should now be continuity between terminals 3 and 4. If you did not achieve these results, replace the relay with a new one.

6 If the rear window defogger glass does not heat up after about 5 minutes of operation, there is a check you can perform on the glass filament itself.

7 Turn on the defogger and use a voltmeter to measure the voltage of each of the grid lines at the center. Refer to the illustration for the procedure. If the voltage at any one of the grids is 12V, then there is a broken line between the center of that grid line and the negative side of the grid. Move the tester probe towards the end of the grid and look for the voltage to drop sharply to 0V. That is where the grid is broken.

8 On the other hand, if the voltage from the center immediately drops to 0V, there is a break in the grid from the center to the positive side of the grid. Therefore, to pinpoint the exact location of the break, move the test probe towards the positive side of the grid and look for a sharp rise in voltage to 12V. That is where the grid is broken.

9 A back-up test can be performed to confirm the break using an ohmmeter. Using the same illustration as a guide, measure the resistance of each of the grid lines by measuring from the center of each grid to the right and left sides separately. The section involving a break indicates resistance twice as much as a good grid line. In the affected grid section, move the probe closer to the outside and look for the resistance to change sharply. That is the location of the break.

10 The repair of the grid lines should be left to your dealer service department.

11 **Note**: *Since grid lines can be easily damaged or scraped off with sharp instruments, take care when cleaning the glass or removing decals or stickers.*

21 Remote control mirror components – checking and replacement

1 To gain access to the mirror motor, first disconnect the negative battery terminal. Remove the cap on the lower outside of the mirror and remove the inside and outside mounting screws. Remove the mirror and disconnect the connector.

● Continuity table

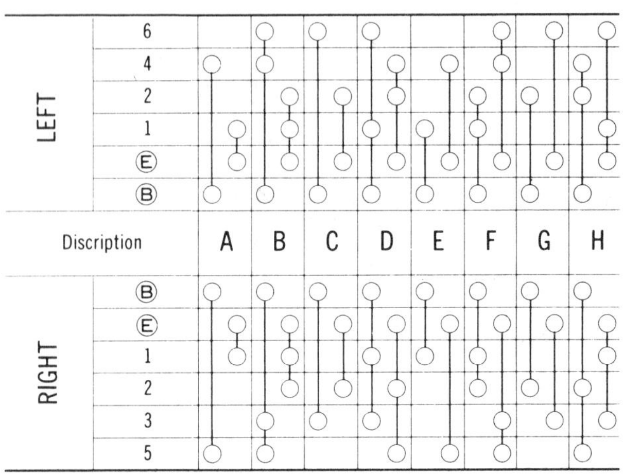

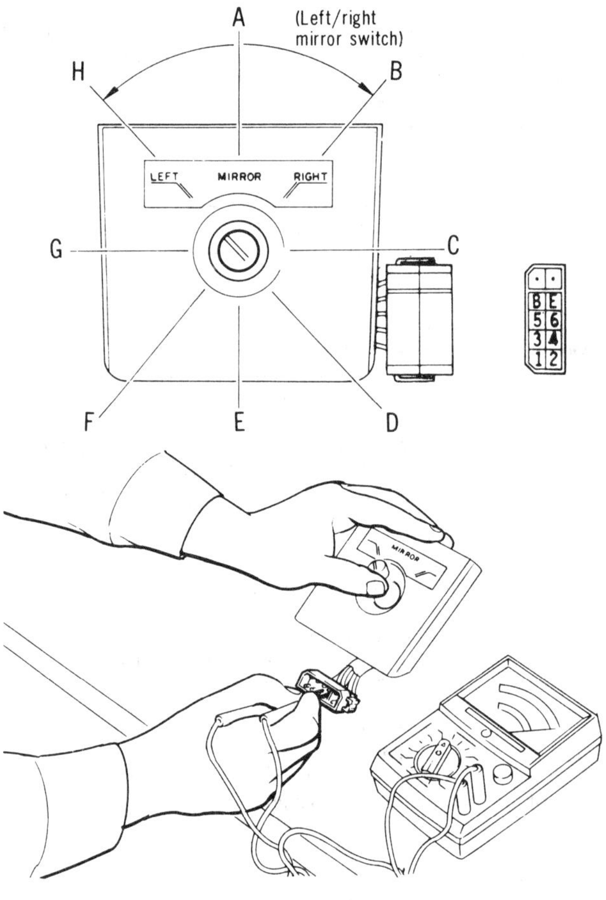

Fig. 10.45 Continuity check of the remote control mirror switch (Sec 21)

2 Using an ohmmeter, measure the resistance between the terminals as shown in the illustration. The resistance between terminals 1 and 3, and 2 and 4 should be about 32 ohms. If this is not the reading you obtain, replace the motor with a new one as a complete assembly.

3 The remote control mirror switch is located in the lower center console and can be removed by depressing the catch on the switch. **Note**: *In vehicles of years 1978 through 1980, the mirror switch is located in the upper-center console. Access to the switch is gained by*

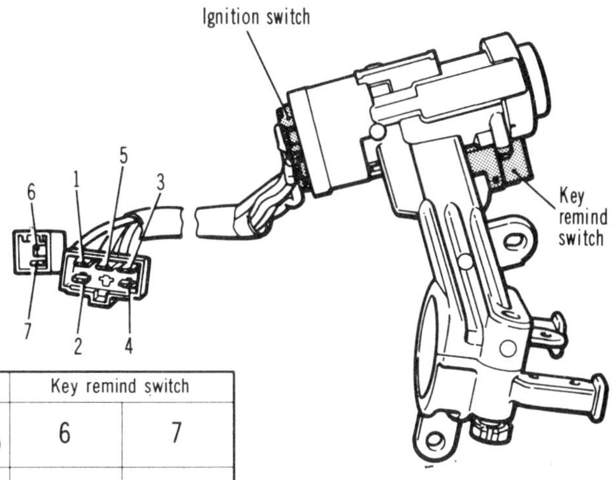

• Continuity table

Position	Key	1 Battery (AM)	2 Accessory (ACC)	3 Ignition coil (IG)	4 Resistance (R)	5 Starting motor (ST)	6	7
		Ignition switch					Key remind switch	
LOCK	Removed							
LOCK	Installed						○	○
ACC	Installed	○	○				○	○
ON	Installed	○	○	○			○	○
START	Installed	○		○	○	○	○	○

NOTE : ○–○ indicates that there is continuity between the terminals.

Fig. 10.46 Continuity check of the ignition switch (Sec 23)

completely removing the upper-center console. Refer to section 20 to remove the console. All of the switches can be checked in the same manner.

4 Remove the switch by disconnecting the connector. With the use of a continuity tester, check the switch by referring to the illustration and table. Replace the switch, if it fails the test in any way, with a new one.

22 Speed (cruise) control – checking

1 The following is a quick test if the speed control system fails to operate:

2 The entire brake light circuit must be operating for the speed control to work. Make a visible check of the brake lights and see if they come on when the brake pedal is depressed.

3 Check the fuse in the fuse block that powers the speed control system. It is the same fuse used for the voltage regulator. Replace it with a new one if necessary.

4 Check the operation of the brake and clutch safety switches by listening for a faint click when these pedals are depressed.

5 Remove the short section of hose between the vacuum reservoir and the valve body at the reservoir and check for a vacuum. Even with the engine off, there should be enough vacuum left in the reservoir. If there is no vacuum, check for loose or cracked hoses and replace or tighten them where necessary.

6 Check for smooth speedometer operation.

7 The speed control is electronically operated and any further tests or replacing of parts should be left to a qualified service department.

23 Ignition switch – checking

1 To check the ignition switch, first disconnect the negative battery terminal. Remove the steering wheel by referring to the appropriate section in Chapter 11.

2 Lower the steering tilt handle to its lowest position and remove the column covers.

3 Disconnect the ignition and key remind switch connectors. Using a continuity tester, check both of the switches by referring to the illustration.

4 If either one of the switches proves to be faulty, replace it with a new one.

5 To remove or replace the switches, refer to the steering column removal procedure in Chapter 11.

24 Power window components – checking and replacement

1 To check the power window motor, you have to remove it from the door by referring to Chapter 11.

2 A simple check of the motor to see if it is operating correctly is done by attaching it to the terminals of a 12V battery.

m3 Check to make sure the motor runs soothly, without any abnormal noise, vibration or irregular rotation. If the motor runs when out of the vehicle but not in the vehicle, the problem may be in the wiring or the switches. If the motor does not operate at all or malfunctions during this test, replace the whole unit with a new one.

4 The main power window switch is located in the lower center console and can be removed by lifting it up and out of its catches.

5 Disconnect the switch connector and, with a continuity tester, check the switch by referring to the illustration. If any or all of the switches malfunction, replace the whole unit as an assembly with a new one.

6 The sub (quarter window) switch is located under the quarter window. Remove the switch by referring to the appropriate Section in Chapter 11 for removing the quarter panel.

7 After the quarter panel is removed, the switch has to be removed

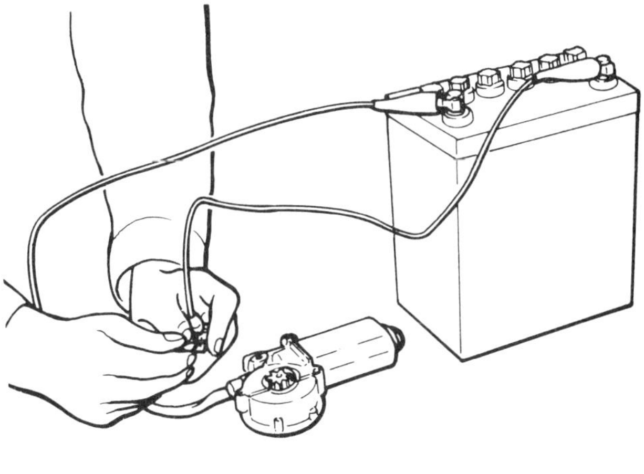

Fig. 10.47 Checking the operation of the power window motor (Sec 24)

10

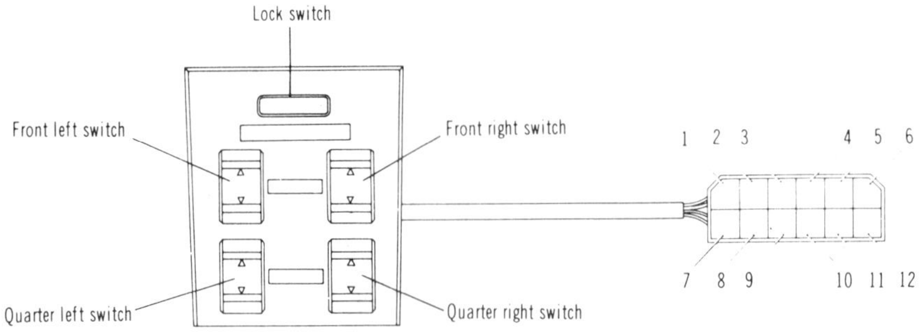

Switch operation	Terminal connection	Front left switch 2	5	8	11	Front right switch 1	5	7	11	Quarter left switch 4	5	10	11	Quarter right switch 3	5	9	11	Lock switch 5	12		11	Panel ill. lamp 6		11
Power Window Switches	UP	O–	–O	O–	–O	O–	–O	O–	–O	O–	–O	O–	–O	O–	–O	O–	–O							
	OFF	O–	—	—	–O	O–	—	—	–O	O–	—	—	–O	O–	—	—	–O							
			O–	–O			O–	–O			O–	–O			O–	–O								
	DOWN	O–	—	—	–O	O–	—	—	–O	O–	—	—	–O	O–	—	—	–O					O–	–⊗–	–O
			O–	–O			O–	–O			O–	–O			O–	–O								
Lock Switch	ON (Lock)																	O–	—	–⊗–	–O			
	OFF (Free)																	O–	–O					

Fig. 10.48 Continuity check of the main power window switch (Sec 24)

• Continuity table

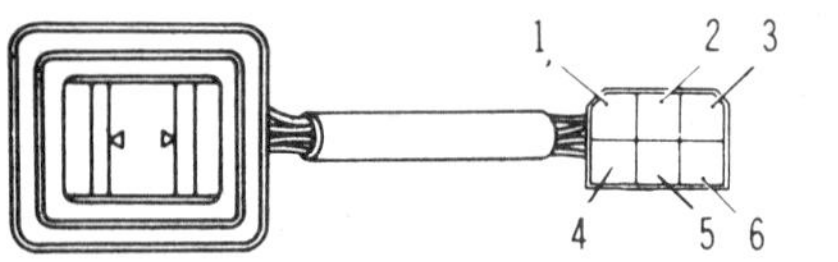

Operation \ Terminal	1	2	3	4	5	6
UP	O–	–O		O–	—	–O
OFF	O–	—	–O			
				O–	—	–O
DOWN		O–	—	–O		
	O–	—	–O			

Fig. 10.49 Continuity check of the sub-power window switch (Sec 24)

from the panel in order to check it. Refer to the illustration to check the continuity of the switch and replace it with a new one if necessary.

8 The power window relay is located in the engine compartment and on the fender well close to the windshield washer fluid reservoir.

9 Disconnect the relay connector and, with an ohmmeter, check the continuity between the terminals 2-L and 2-LR.

10 Also, check the resistance (with an ohmmeter) between the terminals 1 and 2 for 80 ohms.

11 If the results of your checks do not agree with the above, replace the relay with a new one.

25 Heater electrical components – checking

1 The heater power relay removal is covered in Chapter 3.

2 To check the relay, you will need a continuity tester. Check the continuity between terminals 1 and 2. It should be approximately 65

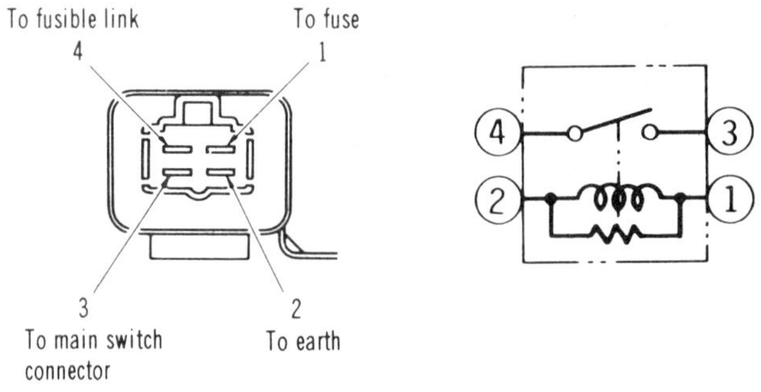

Fig. 10.50 Resistance test of the power window relay (Sec 24)

ohms. Between terminals 3 and 4 there should be no continuity.

3 If either of these checks fail to produce these results, replace the unit with a new one. As a final check, you can apply 12V to terminals 1 and 2. You should now have continuity between terminals 3 and 4.

4 The heater resistor can be checked for continuity by placing the test probes across the ends of the resistor. Replace the resistor, if necessary, with a new one.

5 To gain access to the heater motor, refer to the appropriate Section in Chapter 3. To check the motor, test the connector on the motor for continuity. Replace it, if necessary, with a new one.

6 Check the heater mode switch for continuity by referring to the illustration. Replace the switch, if necessary, with a new one.

7 Check the heater microswitch for continuity by referring to the illustration. Replace the switch, if necessary, with a new one.

26 Audible warning system – general information

The warning system on all vehicles is complicated and requires a lot of expensive electronic equipment to diagnose any problems with the system. Leave all system warning checks and repair to a qualified dealer service department.

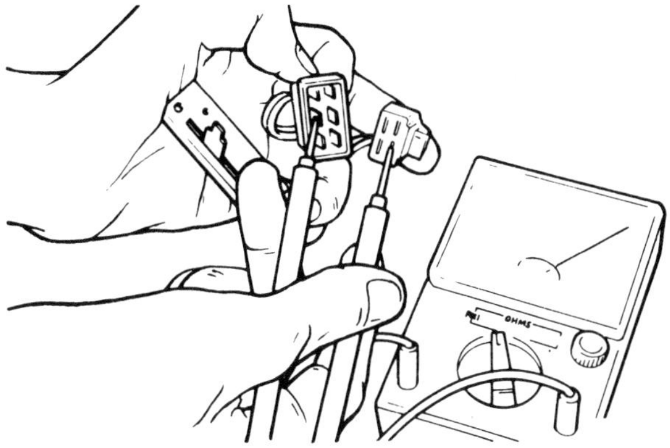

• Continuity Chart

Switch position \ Terminal No.	1	2	3	4
OFF				
• (Low)	O	O		
• (Medium)	O		O	
● (High)	O			O

NOTE: Switch is good when there is continuity between O—O positions as switch is operated.

Fig. 10.51 Continuity check of the heater fan switch (Sec 25)

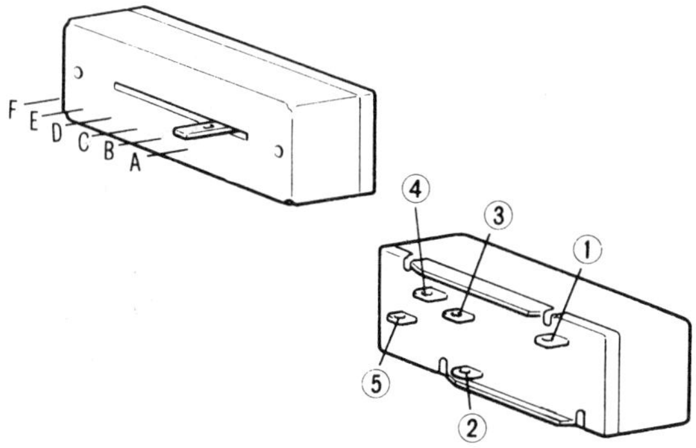

• Continuity Chart

Switch position \ Terminal No.	1	2	3	4	5
A	O				O
B	O	O			O
C		O			O
D		O	O		O
E			O		O
F			O	O	O

NOTE: Switch is good when there is continuity between O—O positions as switch is operated.

Fig. 10.52 Continuity check of the heater mode switch (Sec 25)

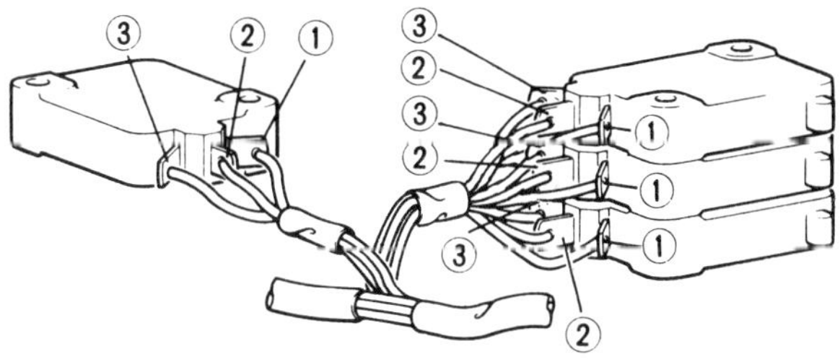

• Continuity Chart

Switch position \ Terminal No.	1	2	3
PRESSED	O	O	
NOT PRESSED		O	O

NOTE: Switch is good when there is continuity between O—O positions as switch is operated.

Fig. 10.53 Continuity check of the heater micro switch (Sec 25)

10

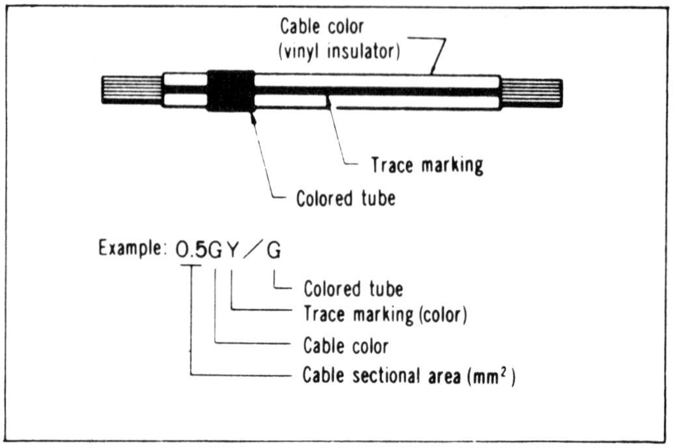

Nominal size (designated by sectional area in mm^2 of wire)	SAE gauge No.	Permissible current	
		Within engine com-Partment	Other areas
0.5	20	7A	13A
0.85	18	9A	17A
1.25	16	12A	22A
2.0	14	16A	30A
3.0	12	21A	40A
5.0	10	31A	54A

Symbol	Coloring
B	Black
BR	Black/red
BW	Black/white
BY	Black/yellow
W	White
WR	White/red
WB	White/black
R	Red
RW	Red/white
RB	Red/black
RL	Red/blue
G	Green
GW	Green/white
GY	Green/yellow
GB	Green/black
GL	Green/blue
Y	Yellow
YR	Yellow/red
YB	Yellow/black
YG	Yellow/green
YW	Yellow/white
L	Blue
LW	Blue/white
LY	Blue/yellow

Fig. 10.54 Cable color identifications for circuits

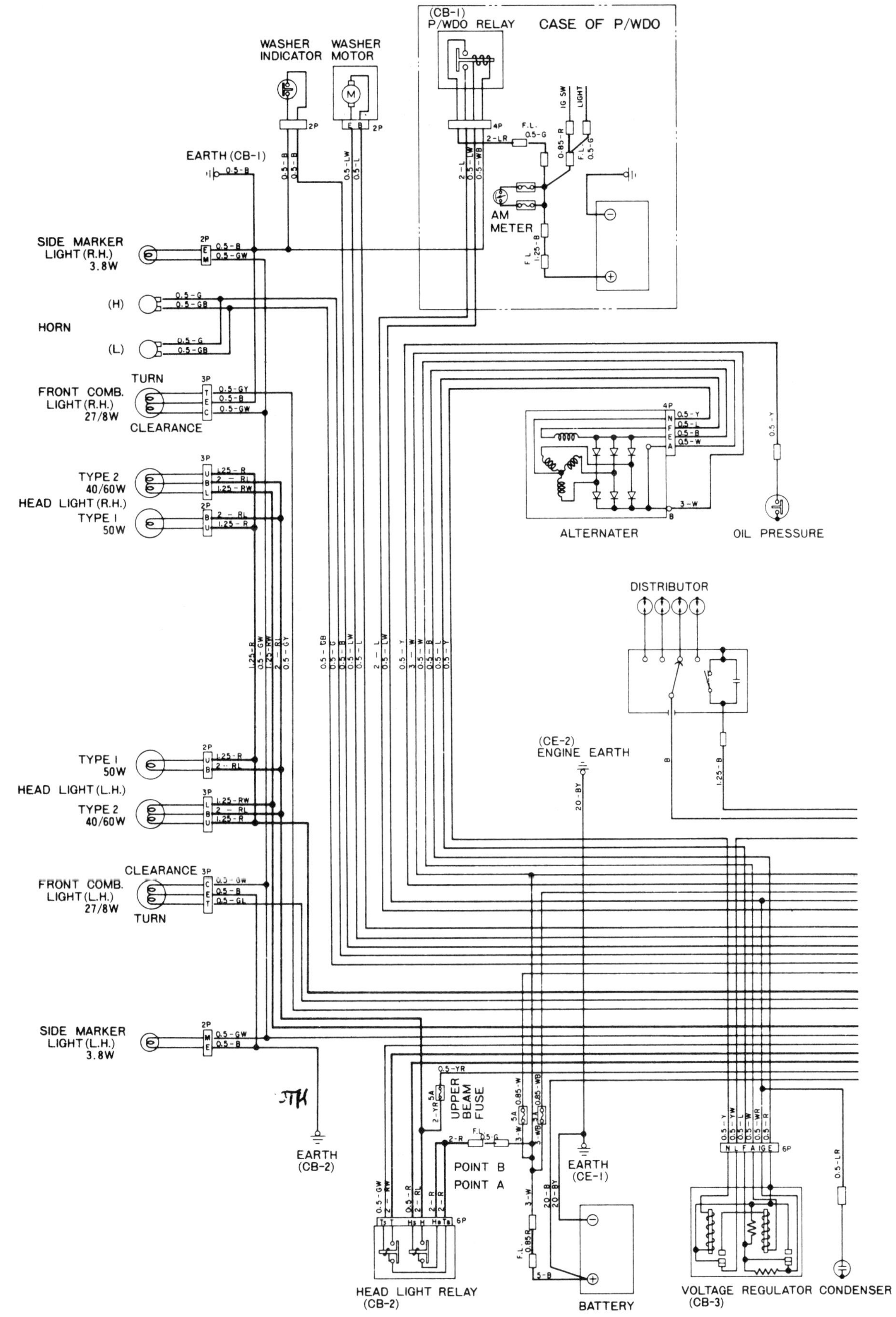

Fig. 10.55 Wiring diagram – 1978 models

10

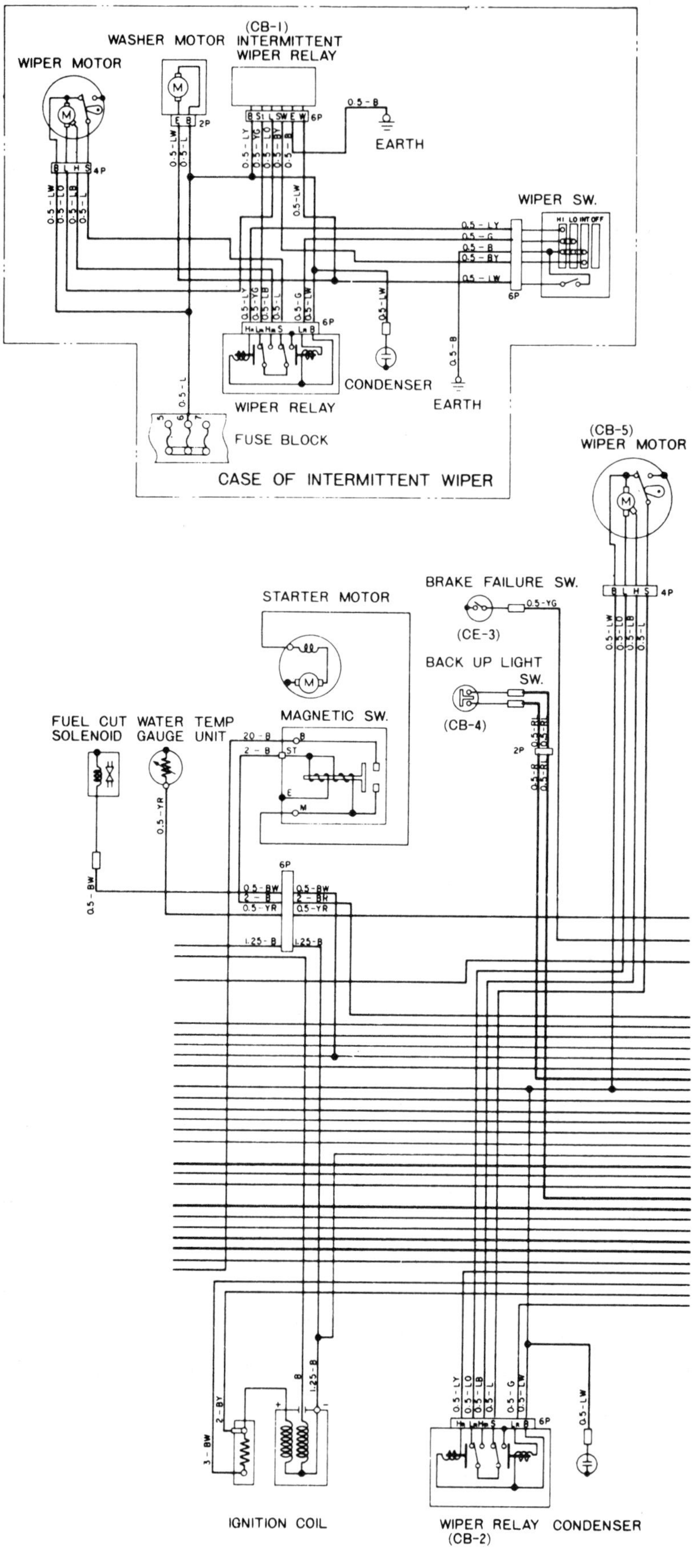

Fig. 10.56 Wiring diagram – 1978 models (continued)

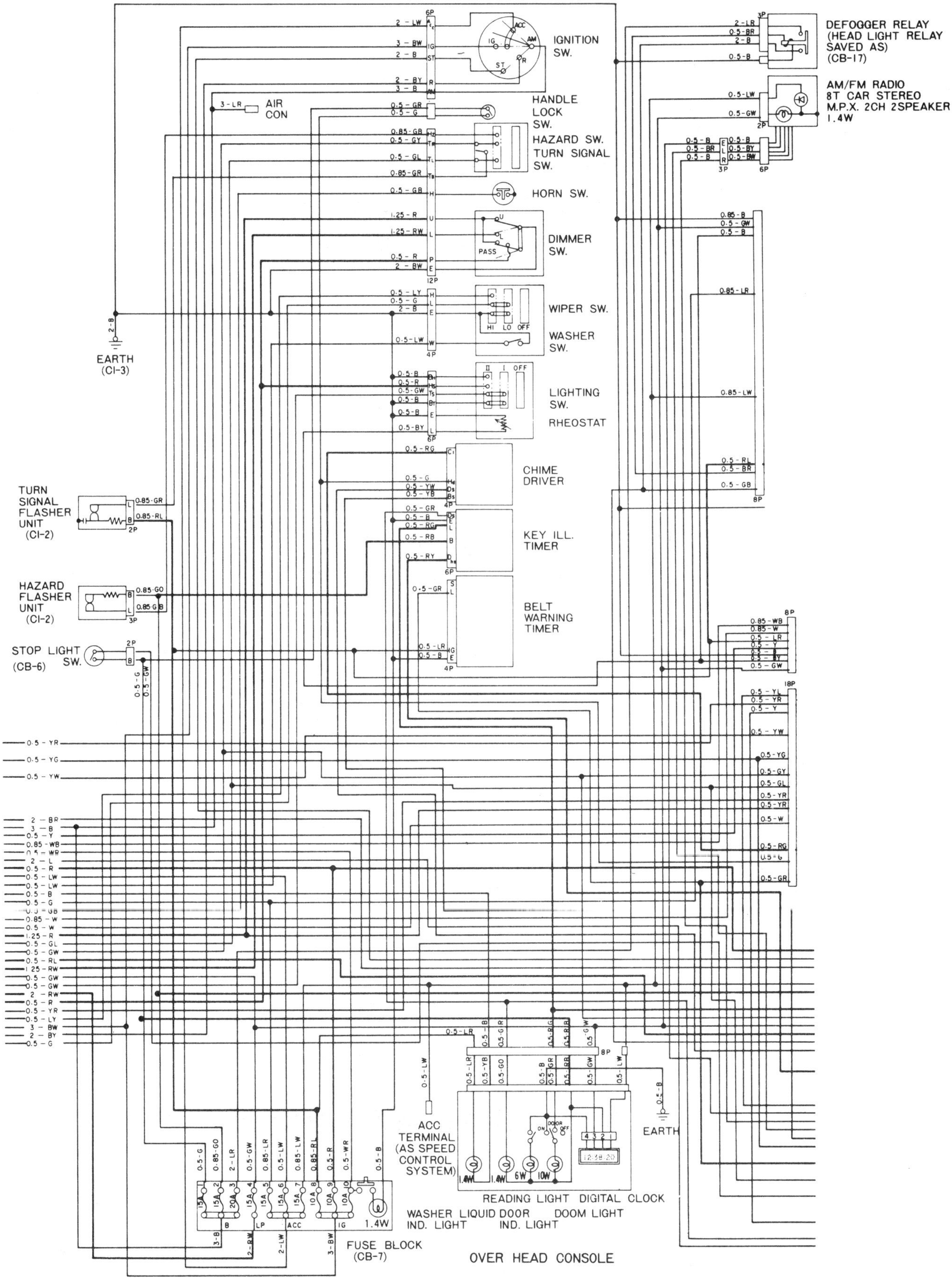

Fig. 10.57 Wiring diagram – 1978 models (continued)

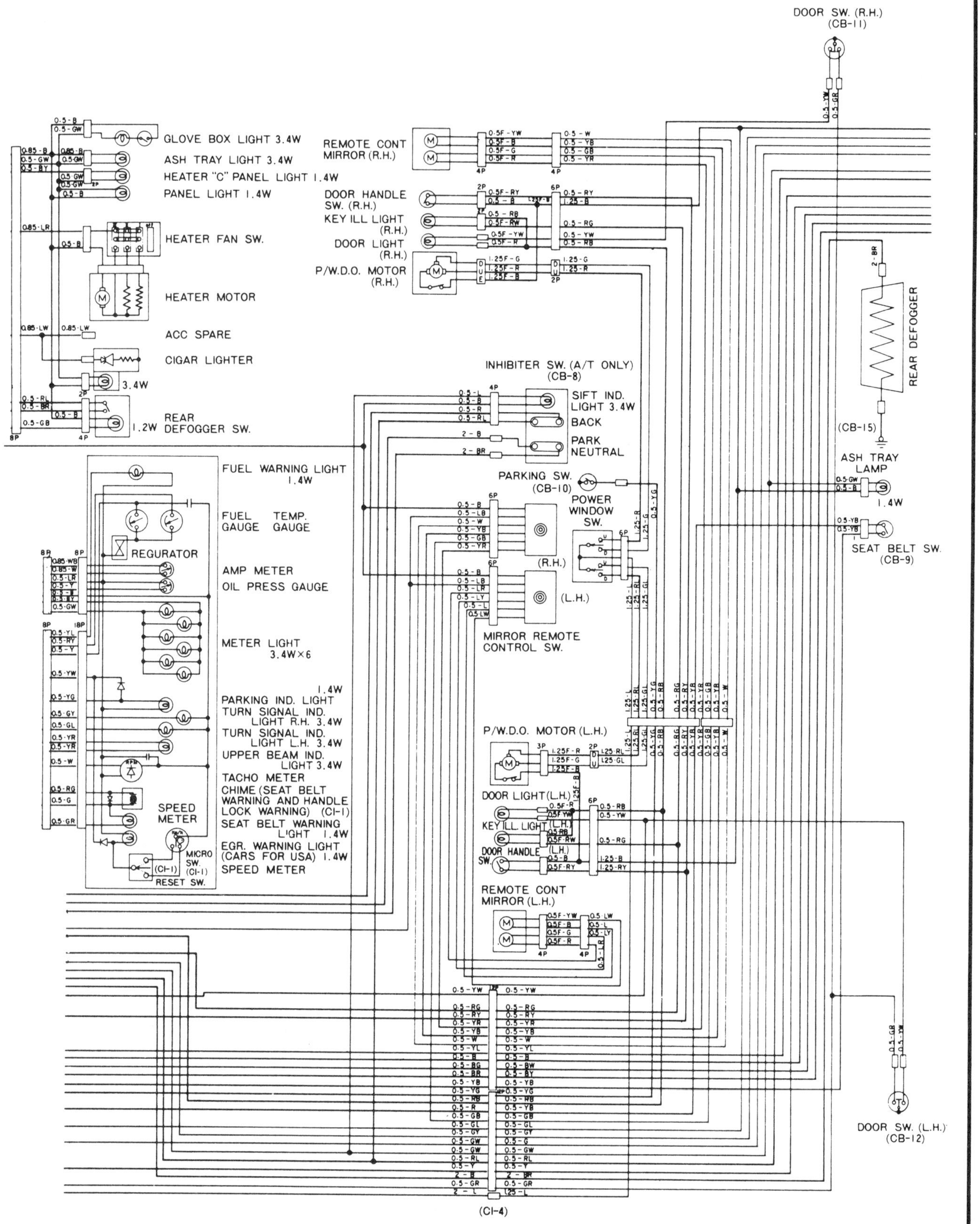

Fig. 10.58 Wiring diagram – 1978 models (continued)

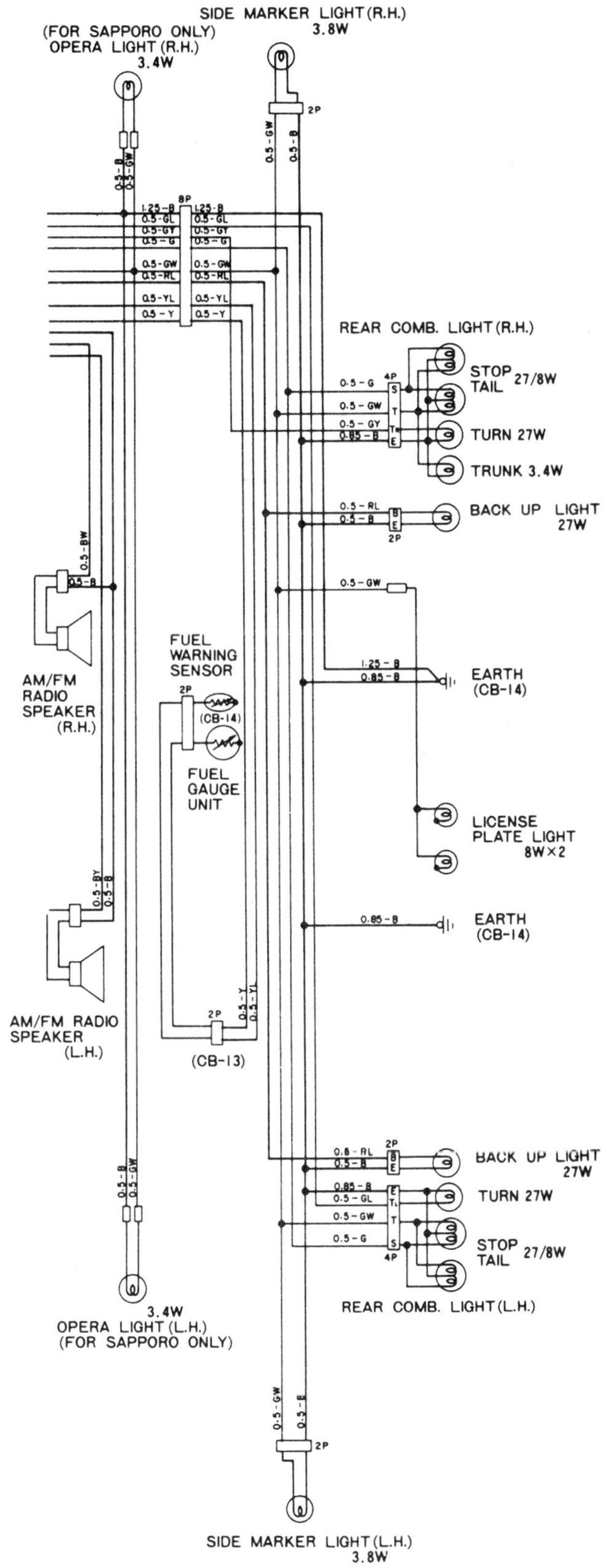

Fig. 10.59 Wiring diagram – 1978 models (continued)

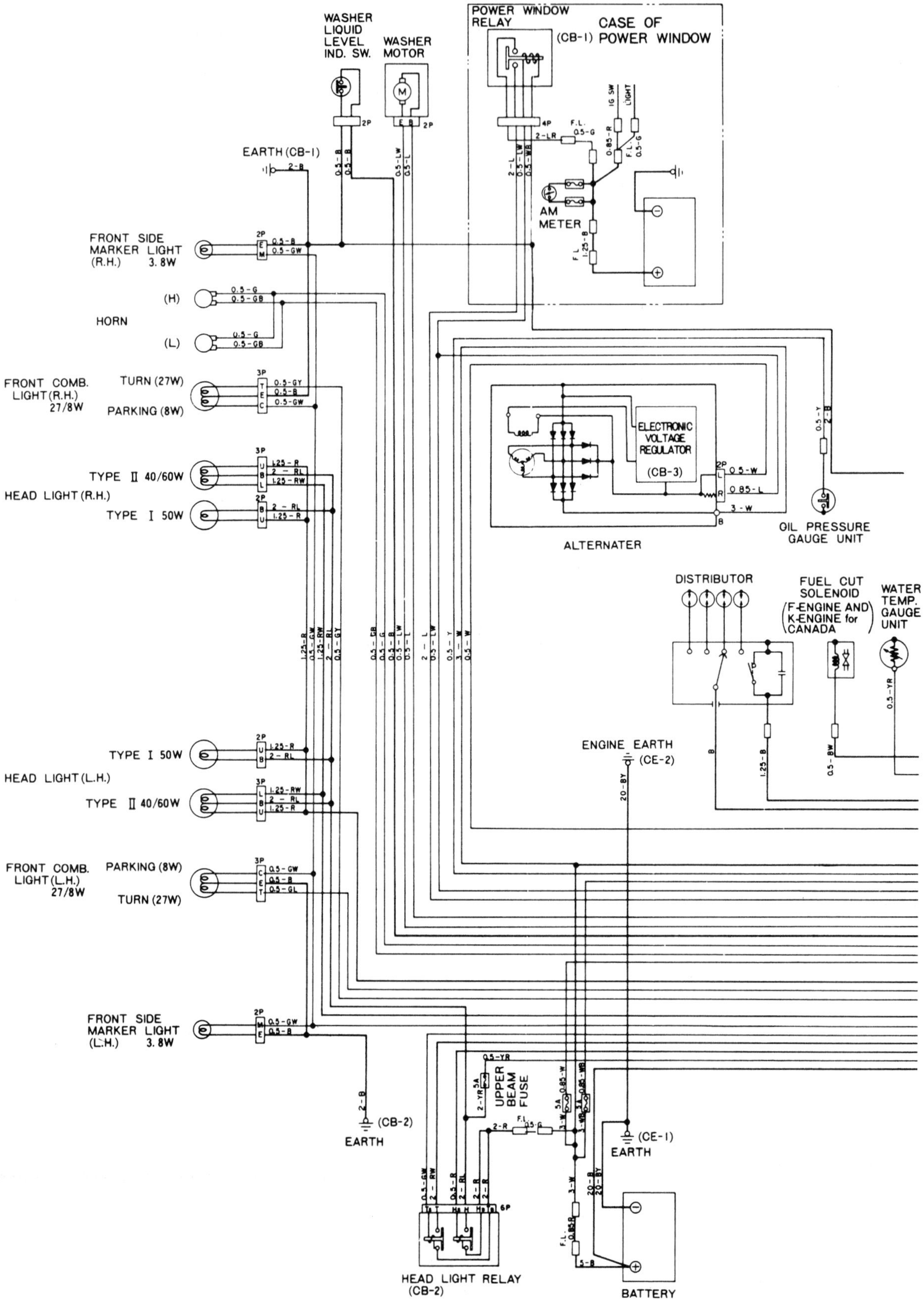

Fig. 10.60 Wiring diagram – 1979 models

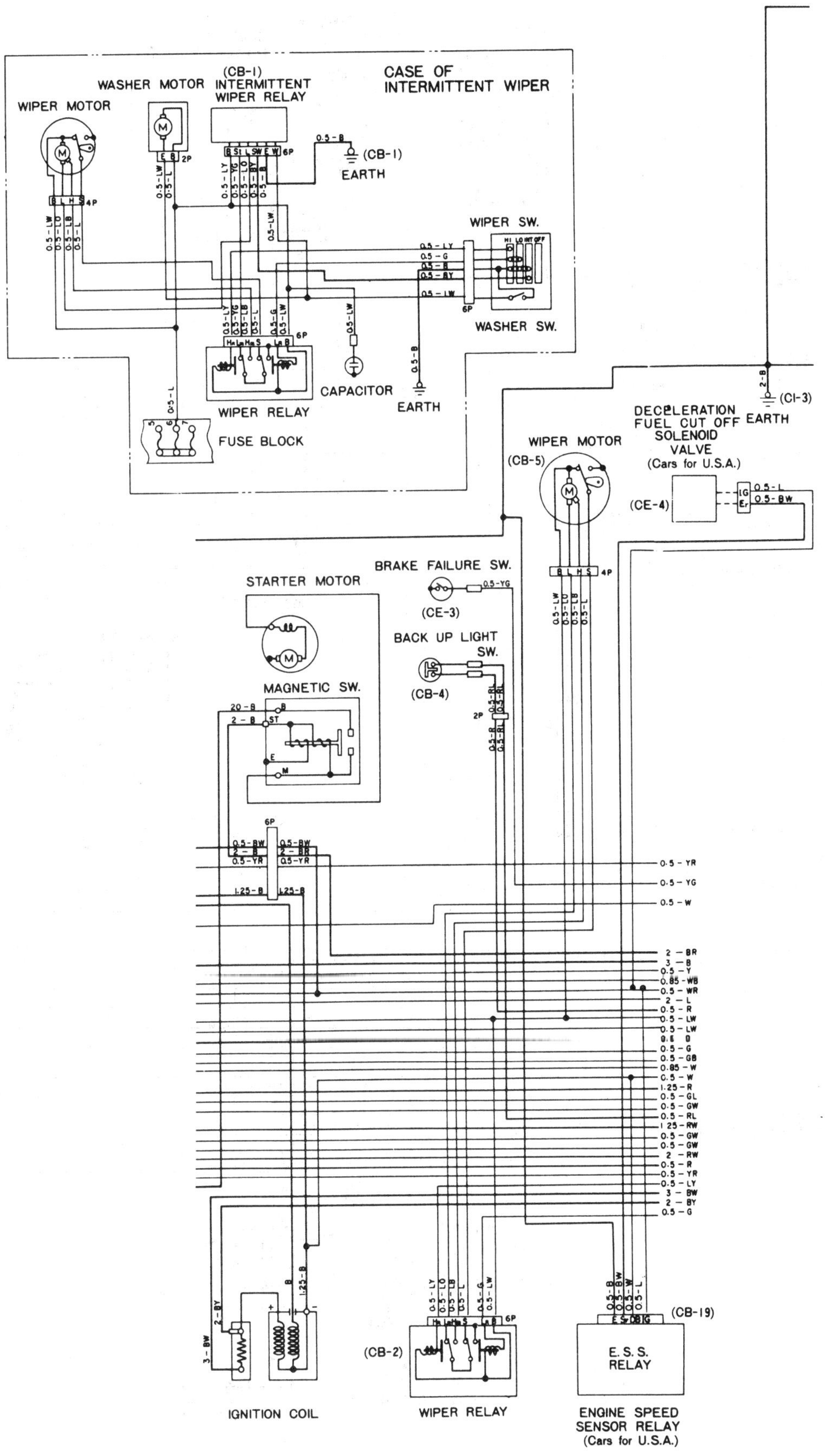

Fig. 10.61 Wiring diagram – 1979 models (continued)

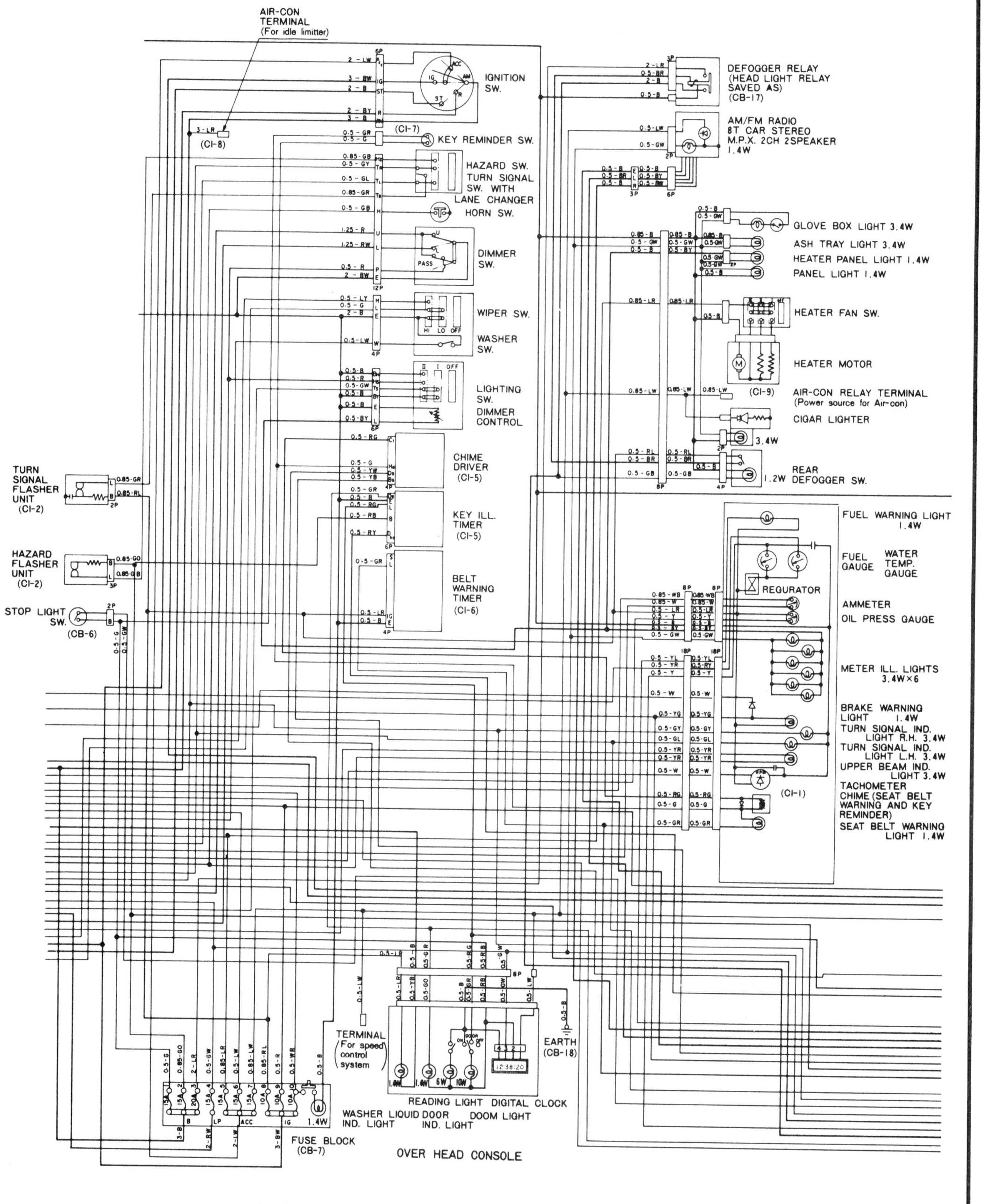

Fig. 10.62 Wiring diagram – 1979 models (continued)

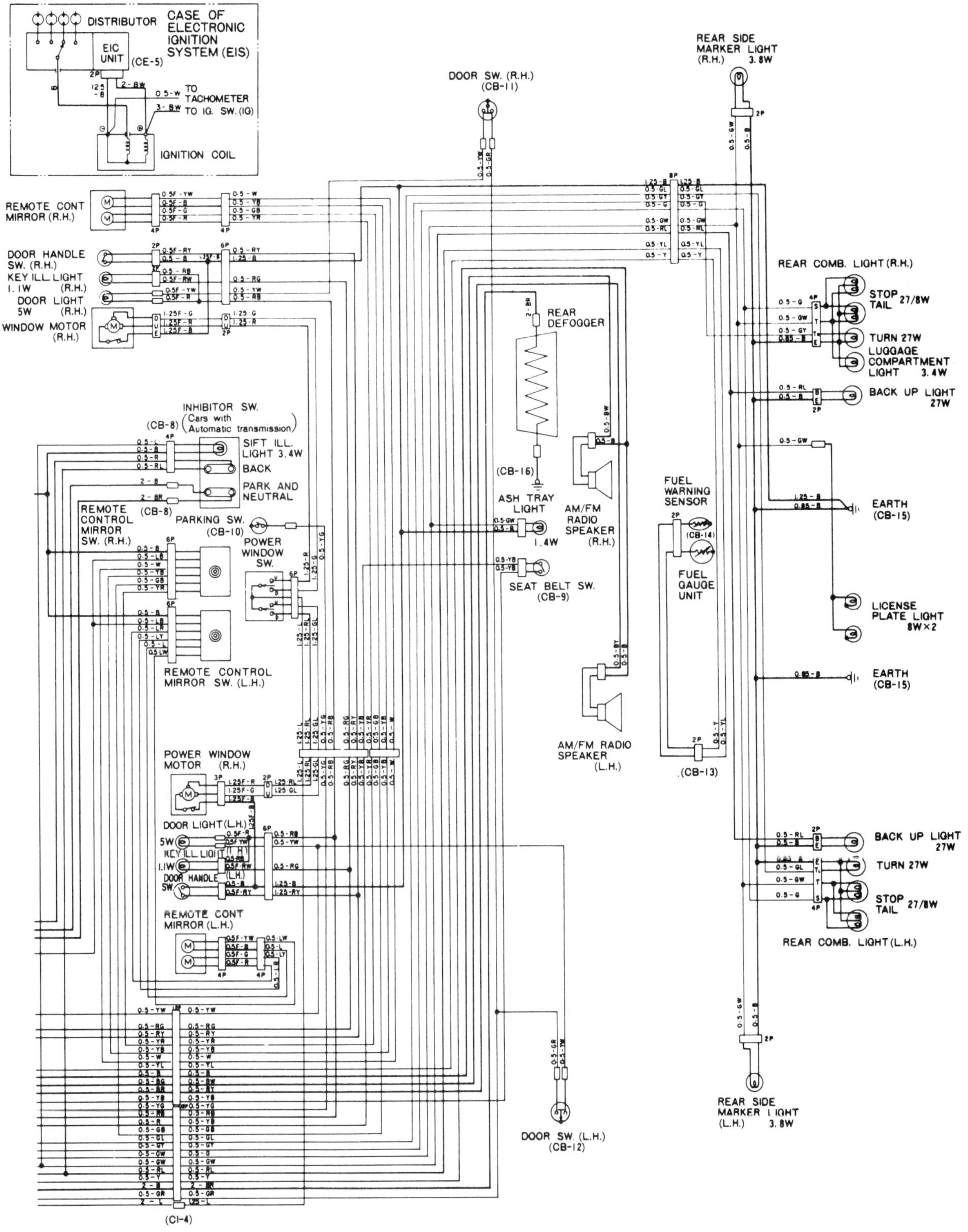

Fig. 10.63 Wiring diagram – 1979 models (continued)

10

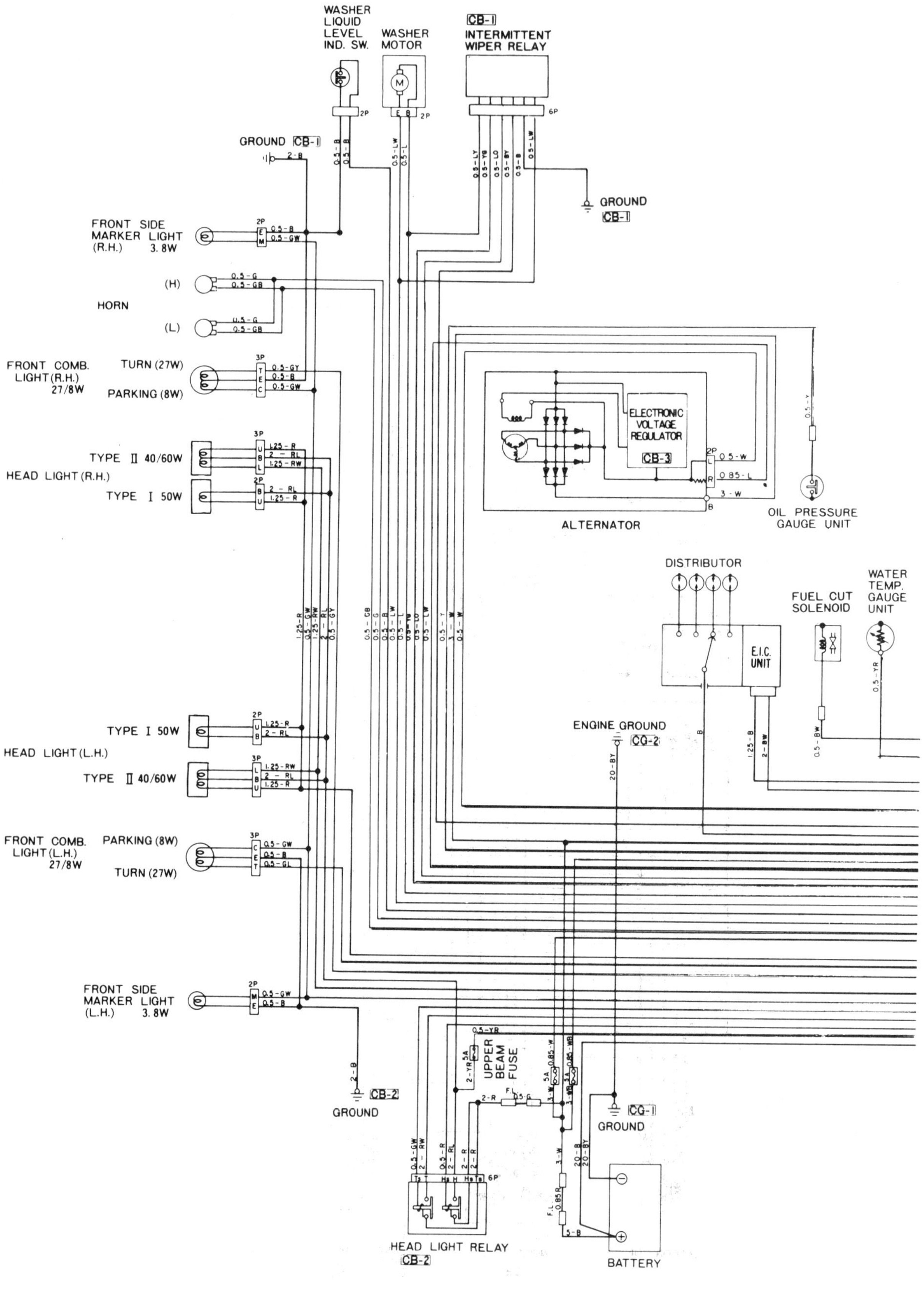

Fig. 10.64 Wiring diagram – 1980 models

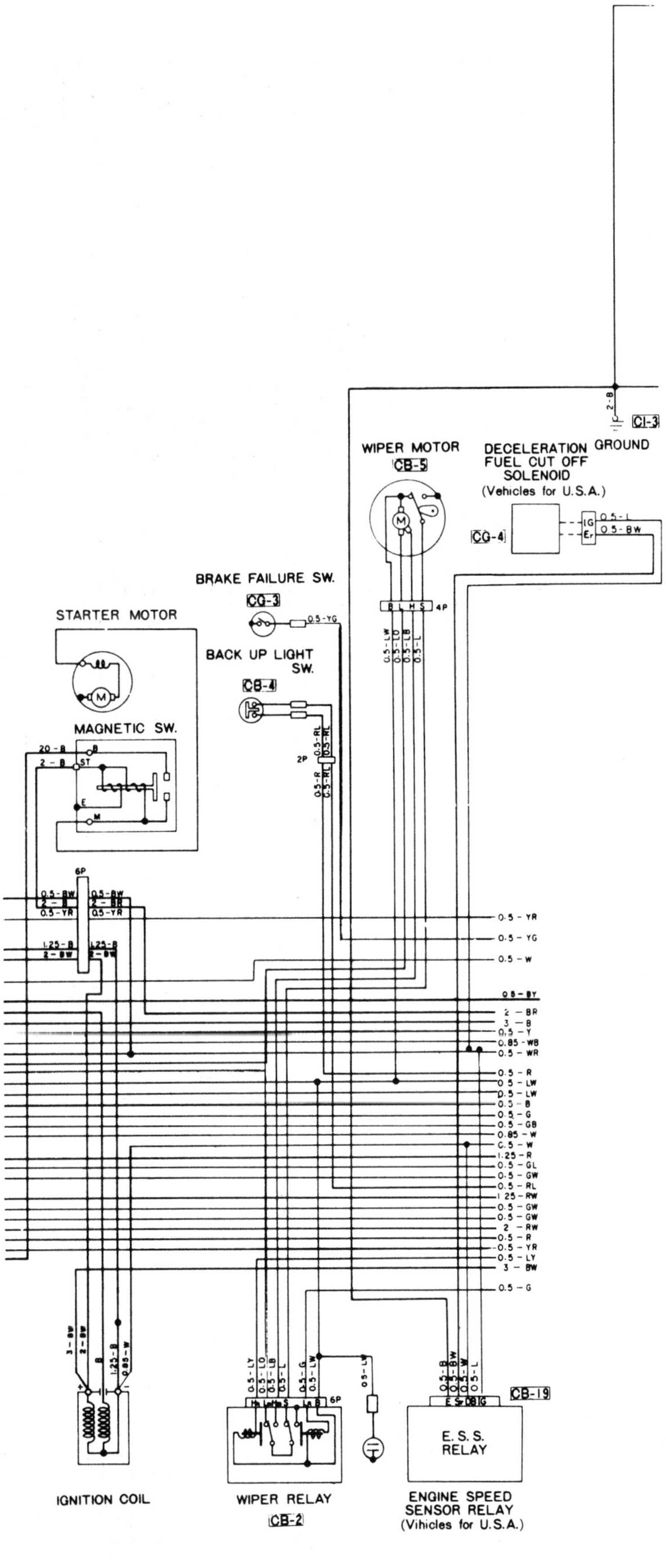

Fig. 10.65 Wiring diagram – 1980 models (continued)

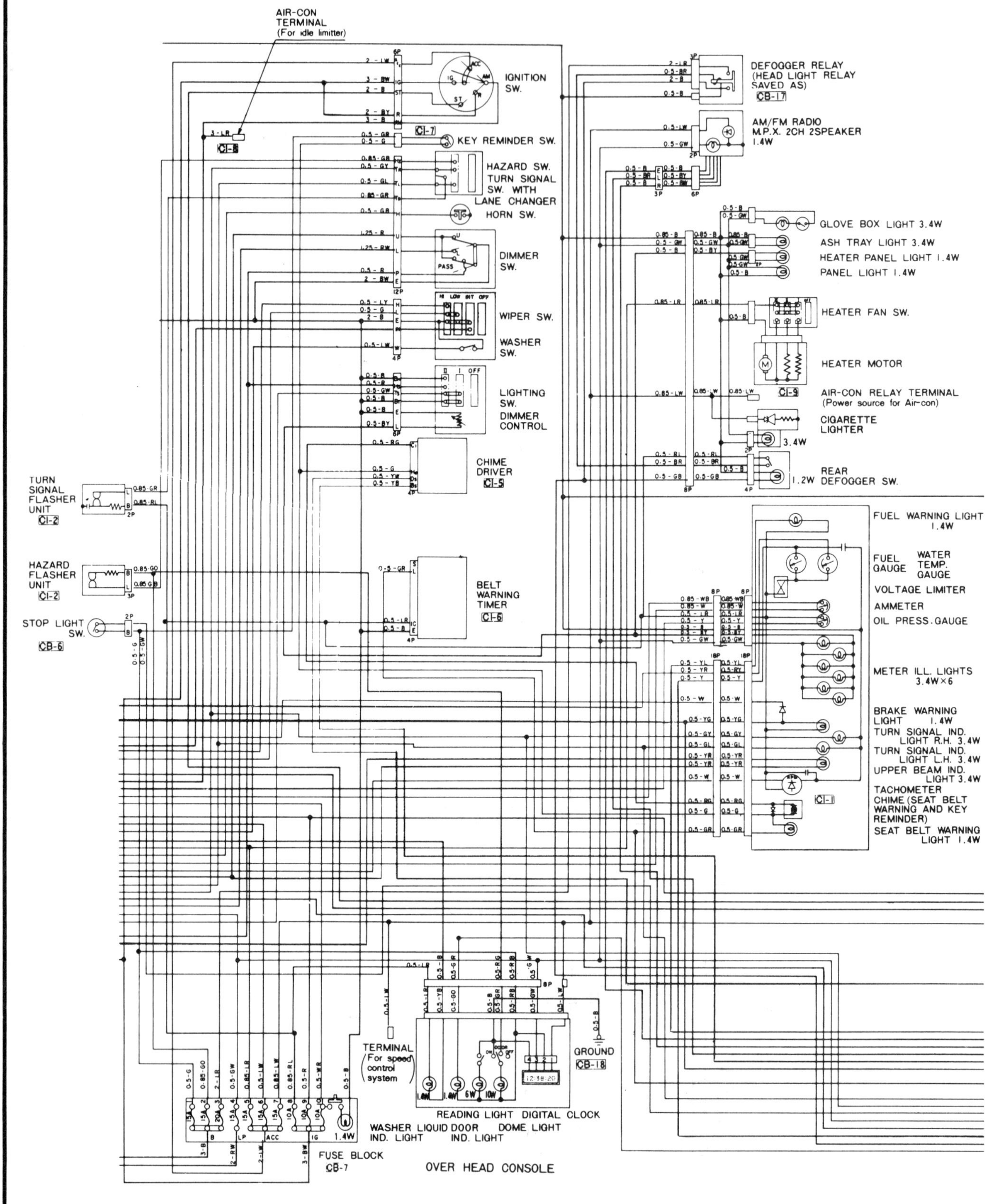

Fig. 10.66 Wiring diagram – 1980 models (continued)

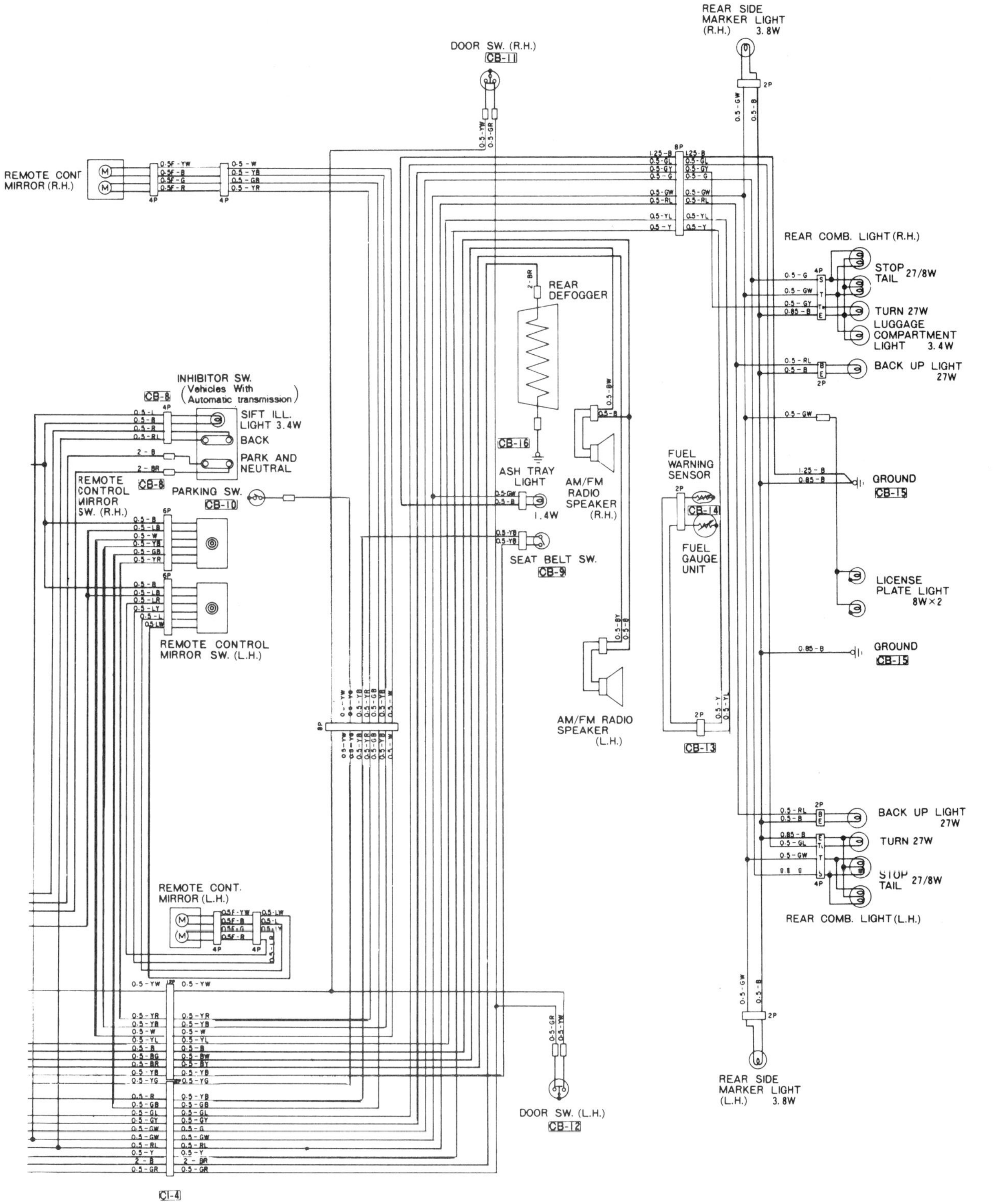

Fig. 10.67 Wiring diagram – 1980 models (continued)

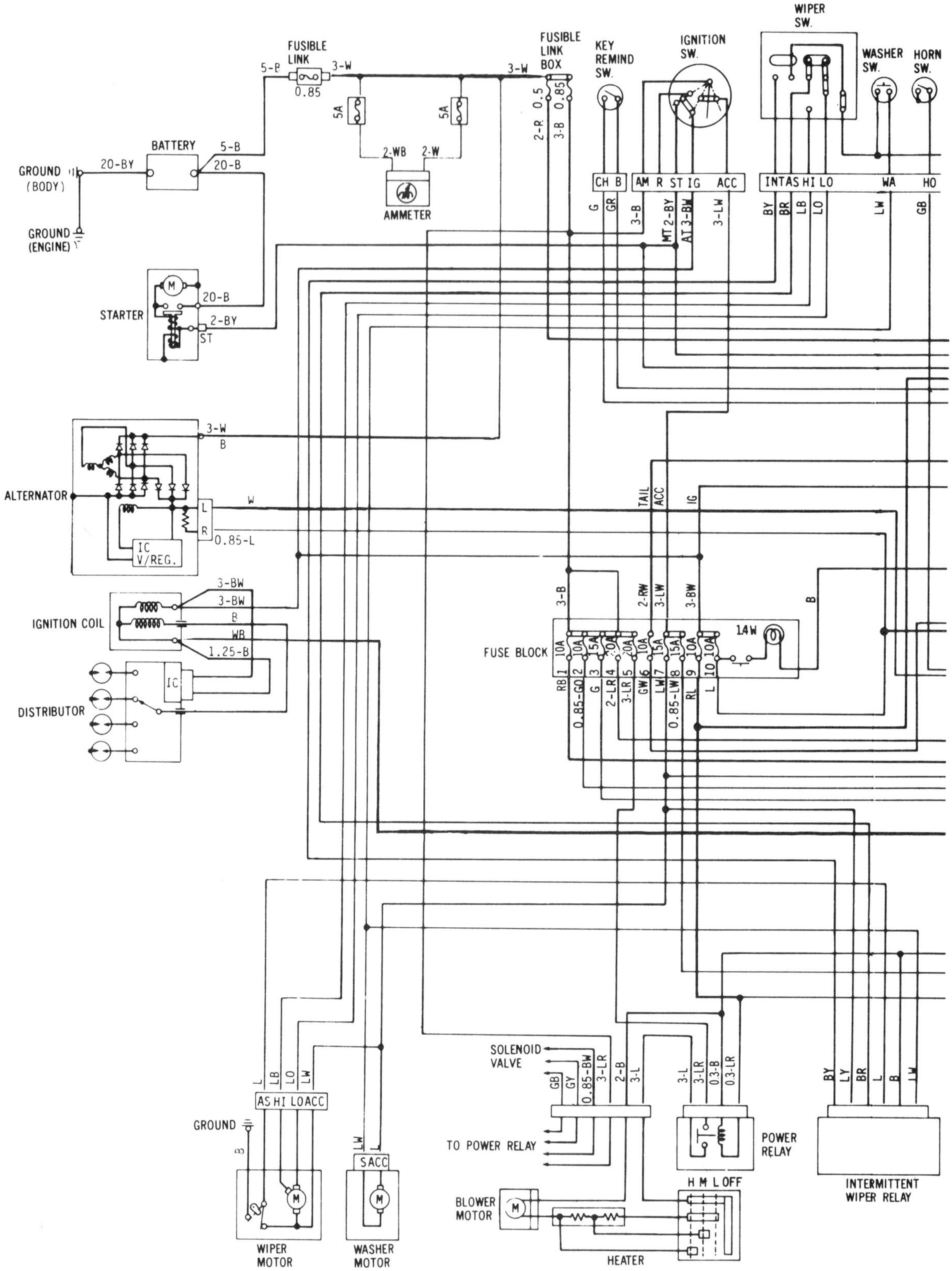

Fig. 10.68 Wiring diagram – 1981 and 1982 models

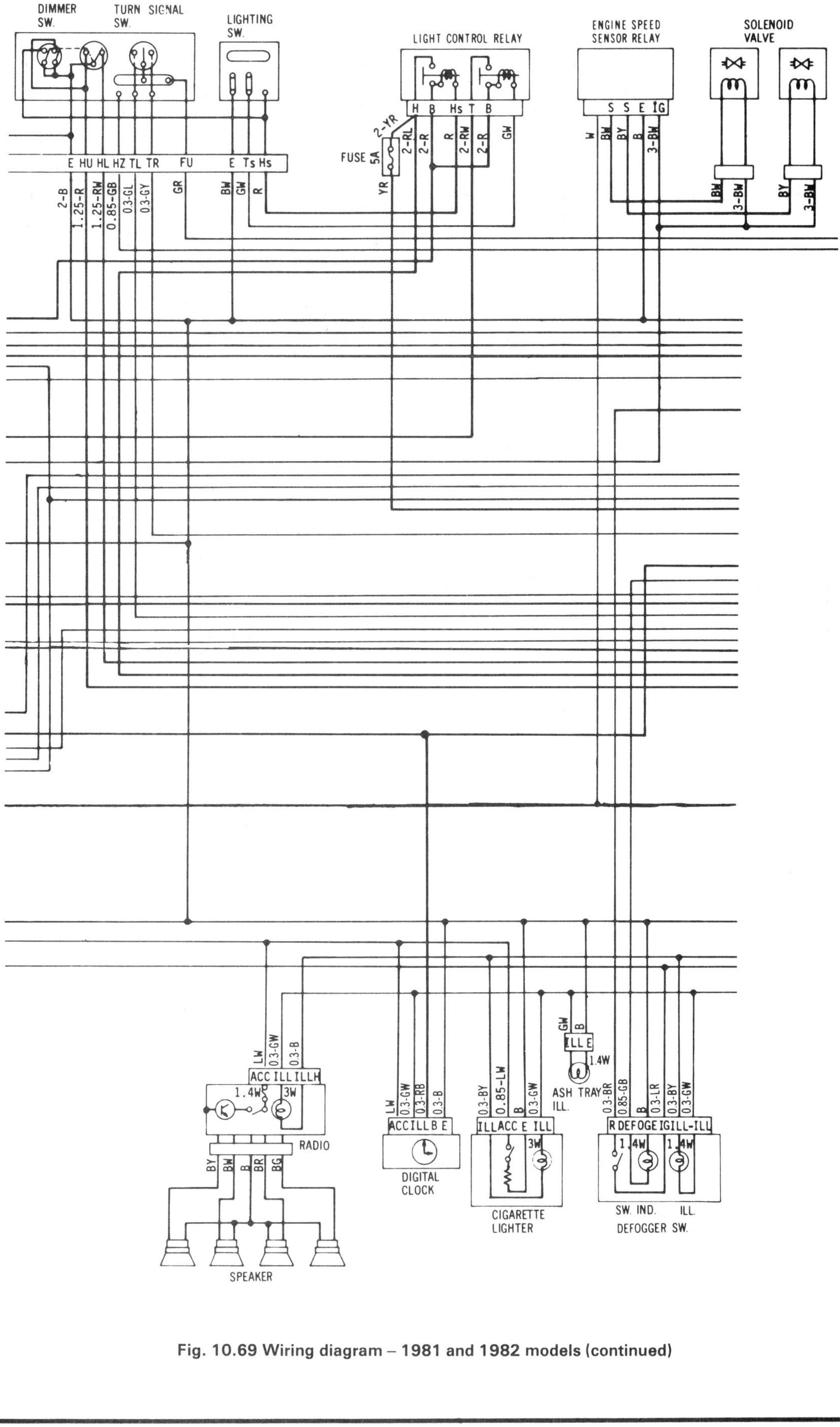

Fig. 10.69 Wiring diagram – 1981 and 1982 models (continued)

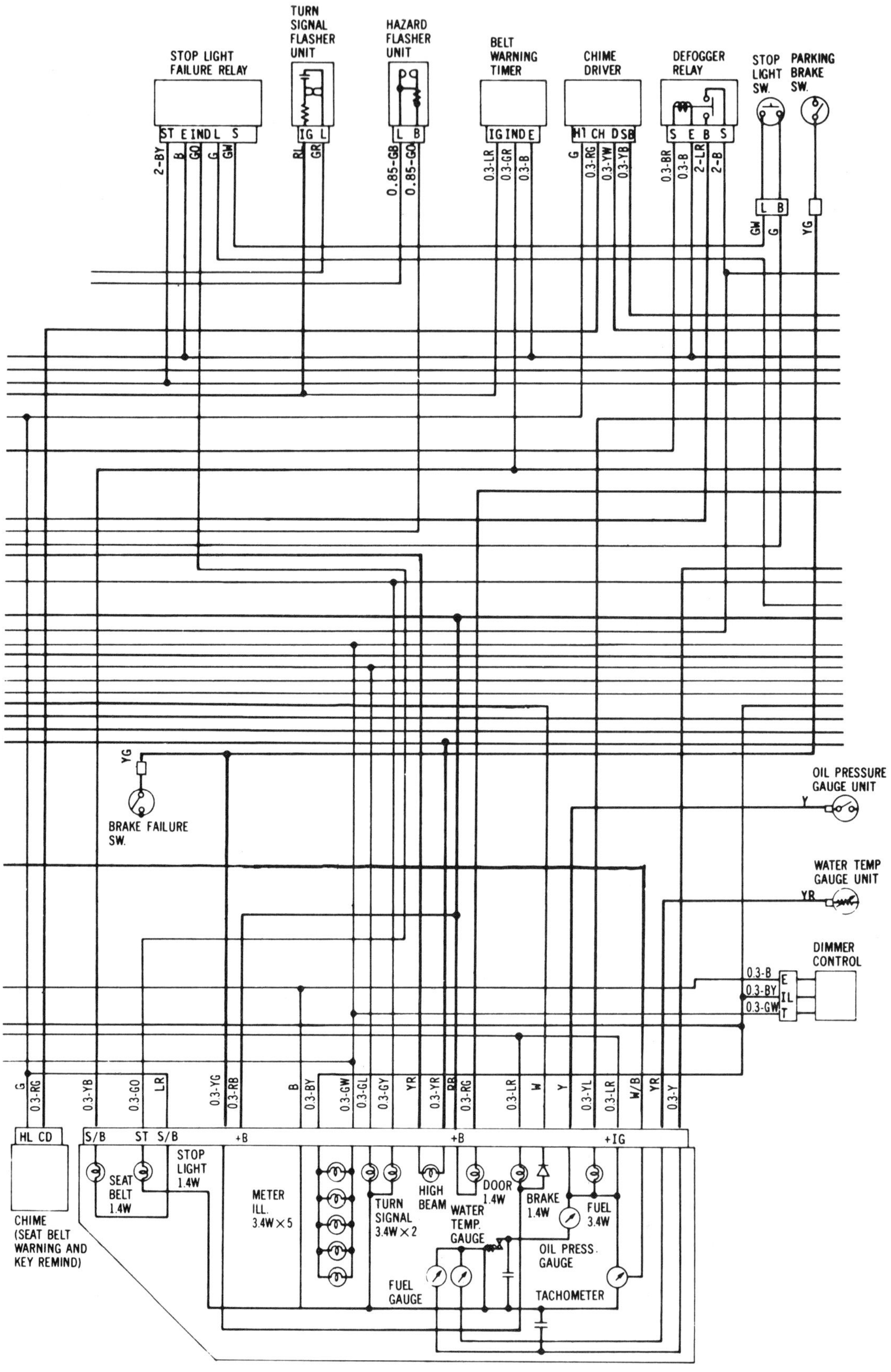

Fig. 10.70 Wiring diagram – 1981 and 1982 models (continued)

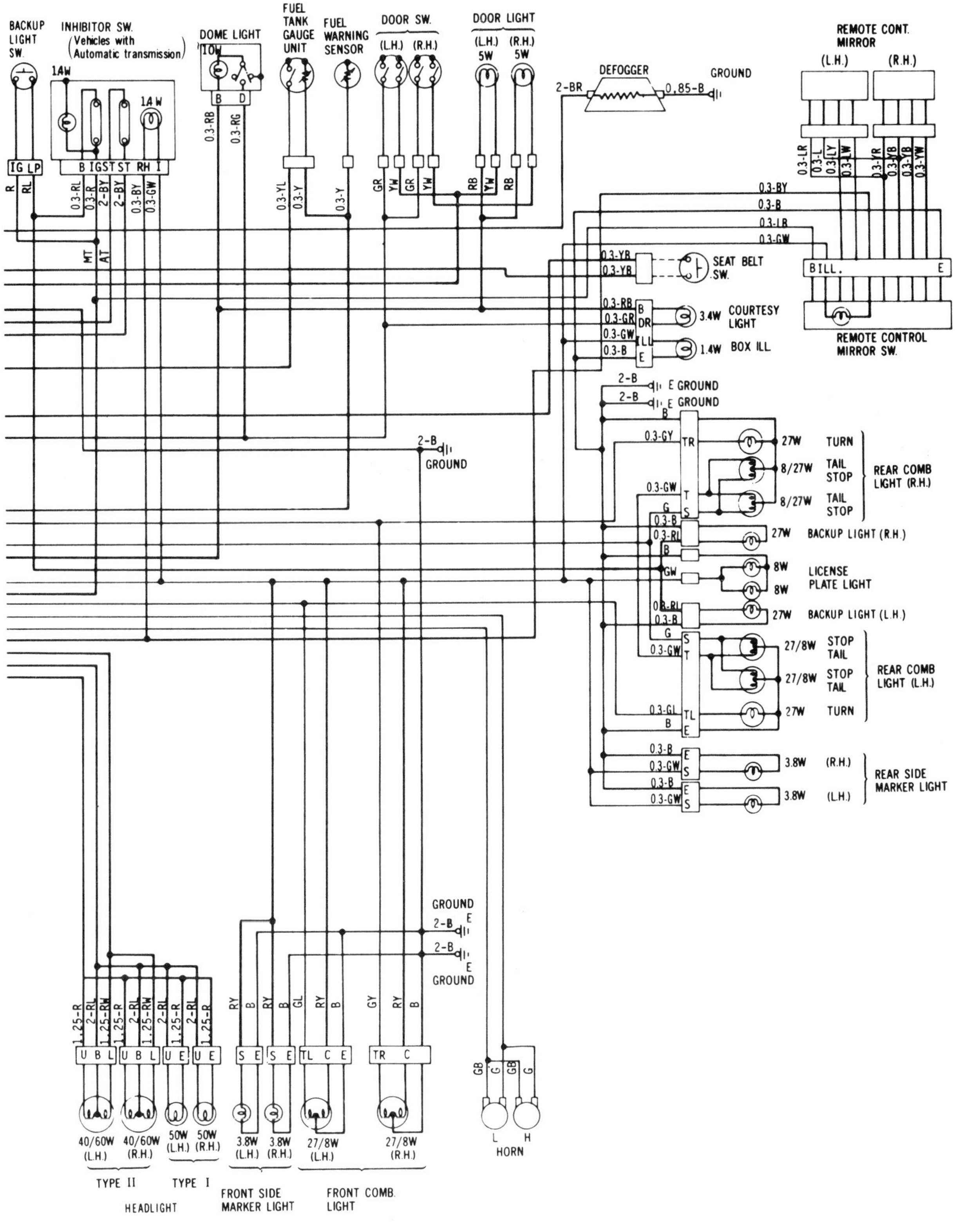

Fig. 10.71 Wiring diagram – 1981 and 1982 models (continued)

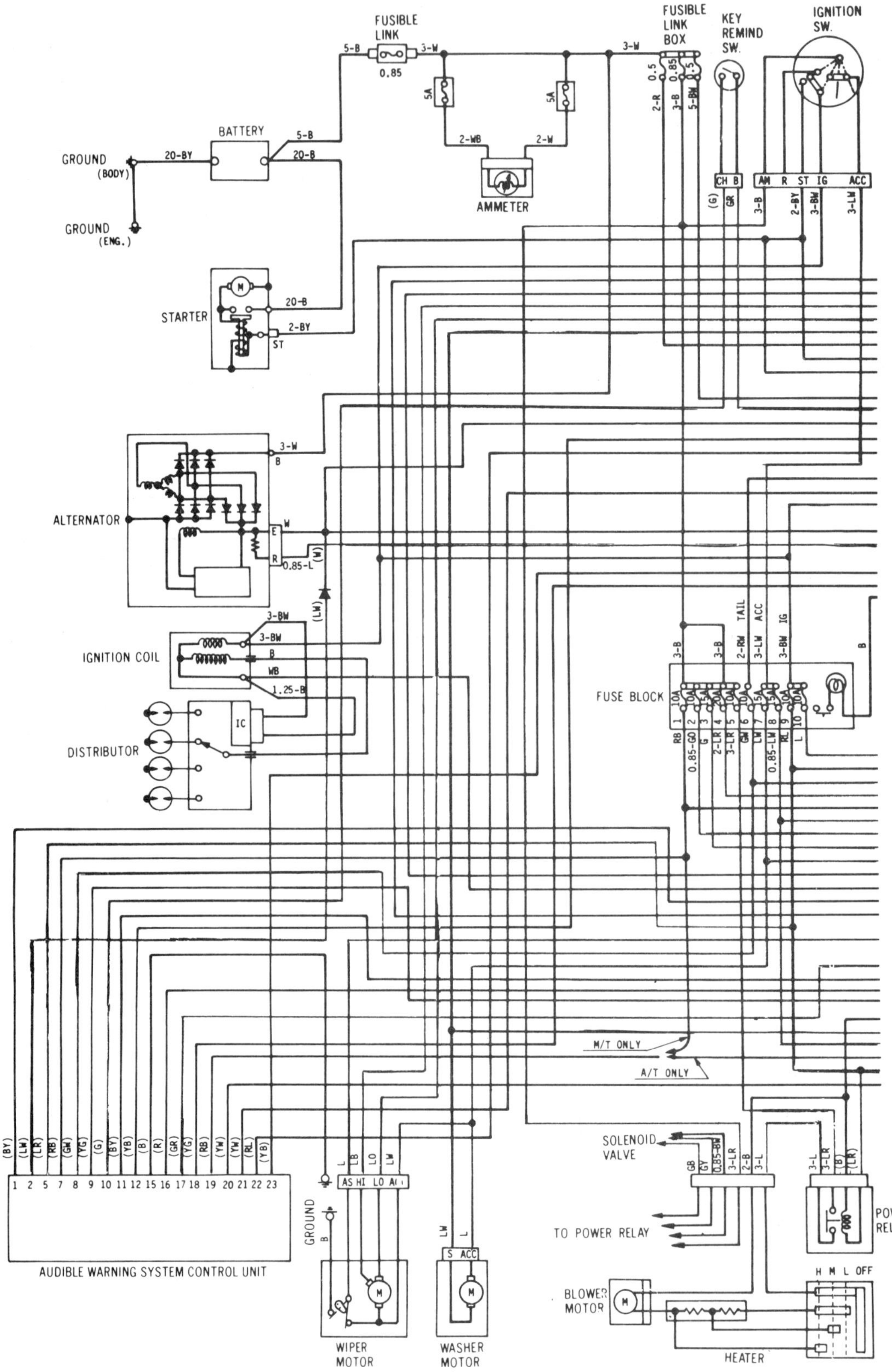

Fig. 10.72 Wiring diagram – 1983 models

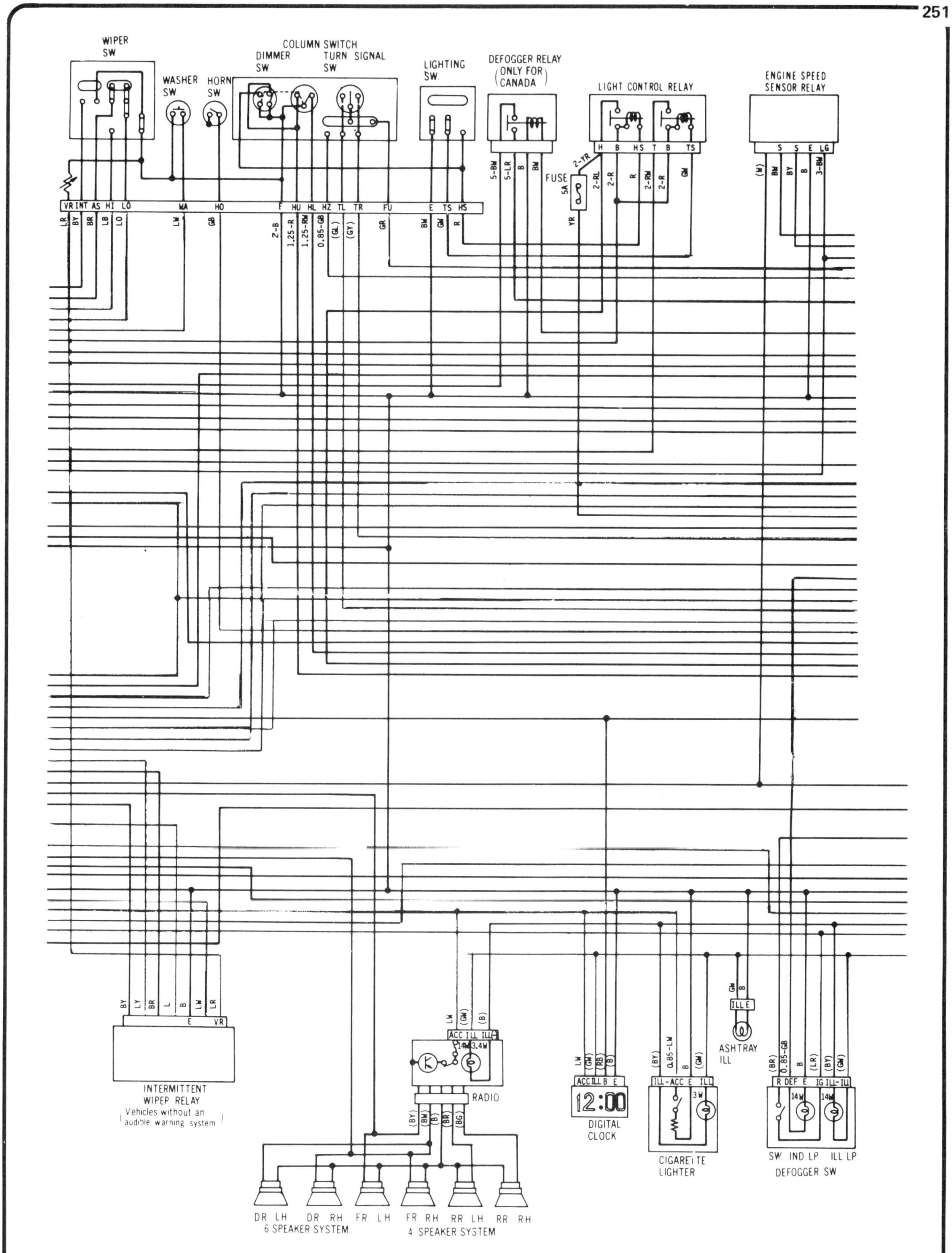

Fig. 10.73 Wiring diagram – 1983 models (continued)

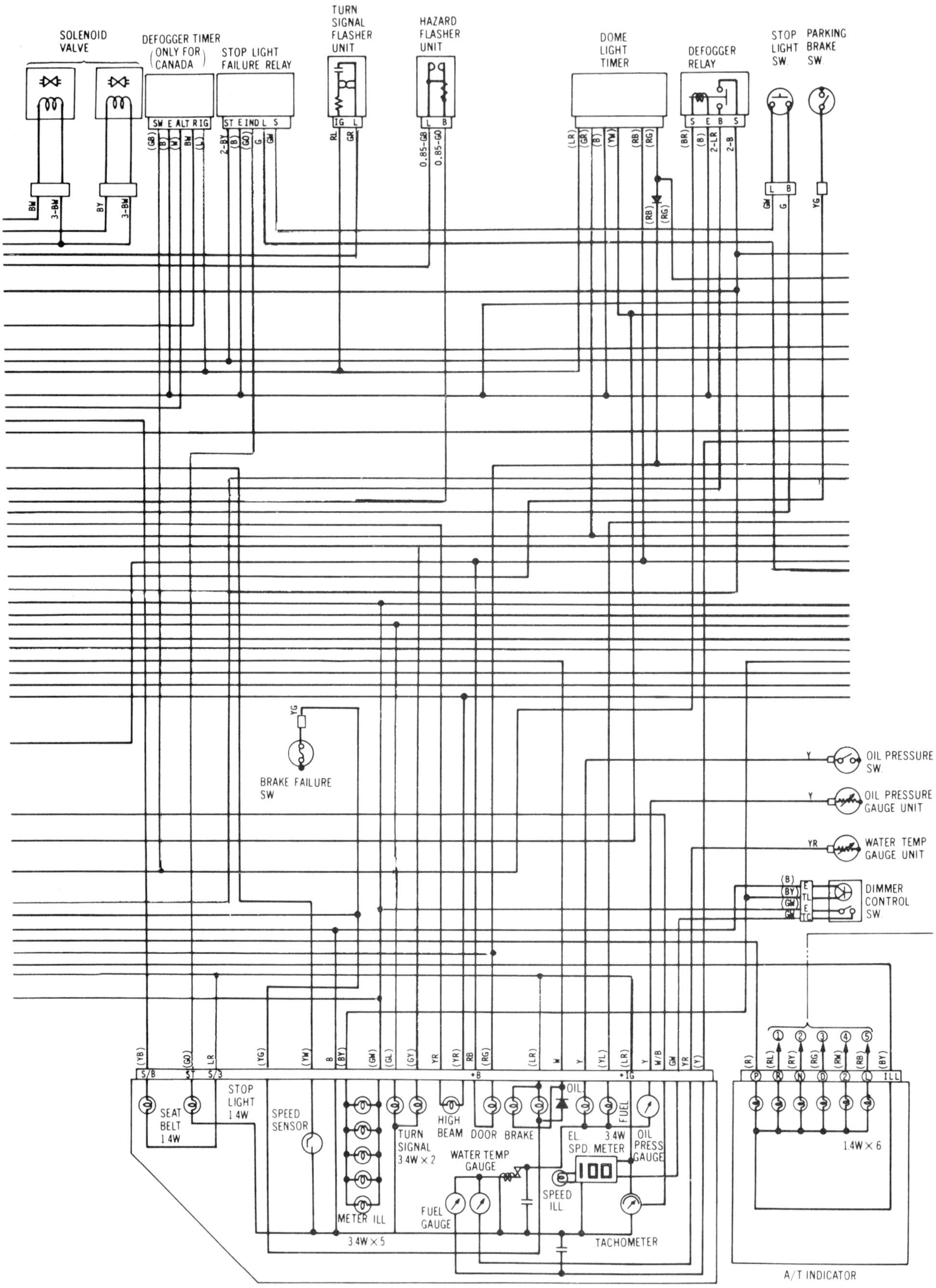

Fig. 10.74 Wiring diagram – 1983 models (continued)

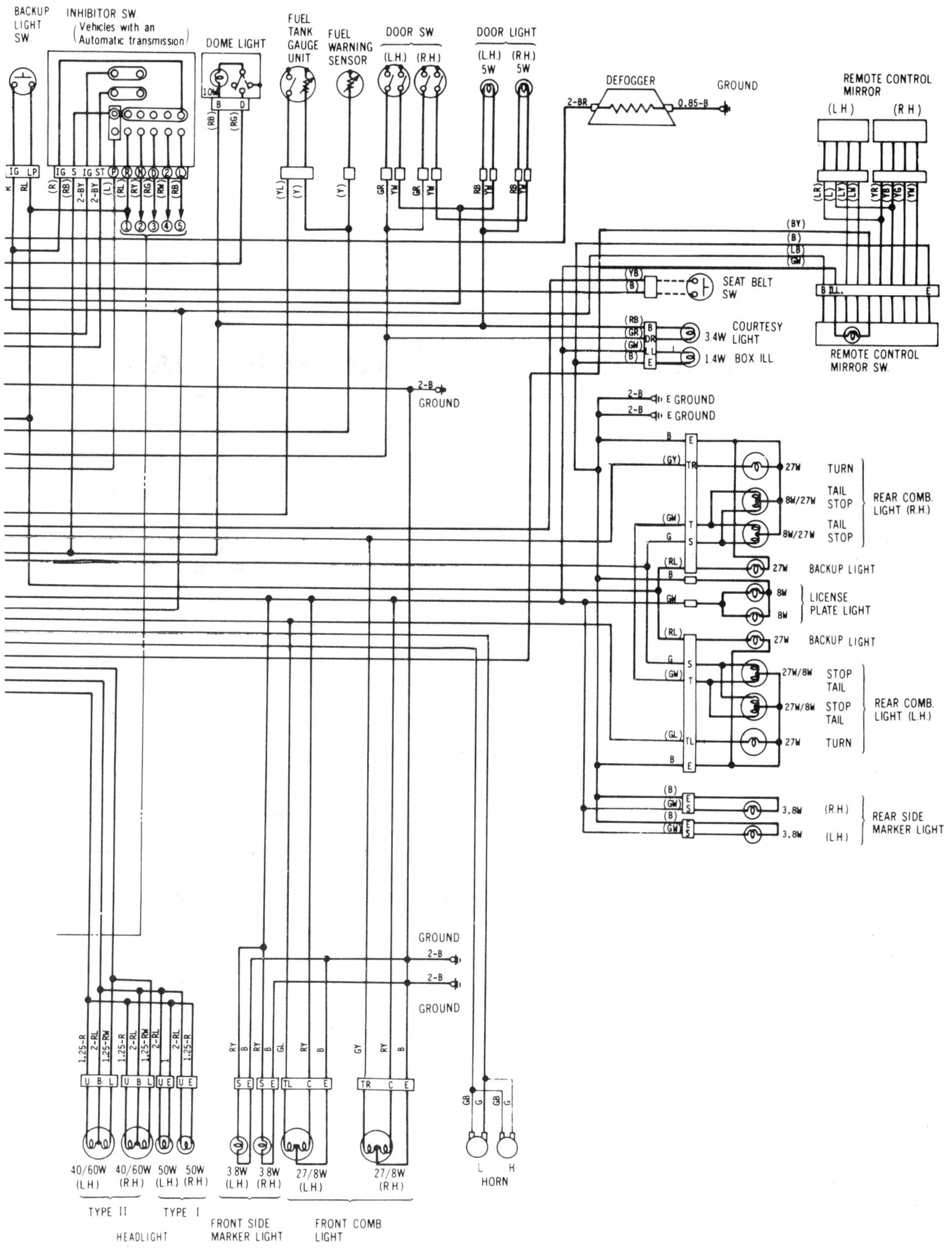

Fig. 10.75 Wiring diagram – 1983 models (continued)

10

Chapter 11 Suspension and steering systems

Contents

Specifications

Front suspension

Coil springs	**1600 cc**	**2000 cc and 2600 cc**
Standard free length		
Right	14.37 in (365 mm)	14.67 in (372.5 mm)
Left	15.26 in (387.5 mm)	15.65 in (397.5 mm)
Color-code		
Right	Yellow-green	Brown
Left	Brown-brown	Gray
Shock absorber strength	**1978 through 1980**	**1981 through 1983**
Expansion	110 lbs (50 Kg)	165 lbs (735 N)
Contraction	66 lbs (30 Kg)	88 lbs (392 N)
Strut bar bend	0.120 in (3 mm) or less	
Allowable distance between stabilizer bar nut end surface and bolt end	0.59 to 0.67 in (15 to 17 mm)	
Maintained distance between strut bar end and end surface of double nut	3.2 in (81 mm)	
Balljoint deflection	0.06 in (1.5 mm)	

Rear suspension

Coil spring free length	11.22 in (285 mm)	
Shock absorber strength	**1978 through 1980**	**1981 through 1983**
Expansion	165 lbs (75 Kg)	143 lbs (637 N)
Contraction	81 lbs (31 Kg)	66 lbs (294 N)
Allowable bushing projections (must maintain on both sides)		
Front lower	0.06 in (1.5 mm) or less	
Rear lower	0.08 in (2.0 mm) or less	
Assist link	0.08 in (2.0 mm) or less	
Silent block	0.04 in (1.0 mm) or less	

Steering	**1978 through 1980**	**1981 through 1983**
Camber	1°28′	
Caster	2°38′	
Toe-in	0.08 to 0.35 in (2 to 9 mm)	0 to 0.28 in (0 to 7 mm)
King-pin inclination	8°25′	9°30′
Steering wheel play		
Standard	1 in (25 mm)	
Service limit	2 in (50 mm)	
Stationary steering effort	6.6 lbs (29 N) or less	
Clearance between center of gear box bolt hole and Pitman arm	0.73 to 0.93 in (18.5 to 23.5 mm)	
Length difference allowed between left and right tie-rod assemblies	0.2 in (5 mm) or less	
Standard distance (L) to be maintained between tie-rod end centers	13.31 in (338 mm)	
Clearance to be maintained between top end of relay rod and lower surface of idler arm	0.15 to 0.17 in (3.7 to 4.3 mm)	

Torque specifications	**ft-lb**	**Nm**
Steering tie-rod nut	36 to 40	49 to 54
Nut at end of strut bar	54 to 61	74 to 83
Front hub-to-brake disc	25 to 29	34 to 39
Front shock-to-top and bottom mount	18 to 25	25 to 34
Strut assembly-to-knuckle arm	58 to 78	78 to 98
Lower arm-to-crossmember	58 to 69	78 to 93
Stabilizer bar-to-lower arm	7 to 14	10 to 20
Lower arm-to-strut bar	43 to 51	59 to 69
Lower arm-to-balljoint	43 to 51	59 to 69
Balljoint-to-knuckle arm	43 to 52	59 to 71
Stablizer bracket	6 to 9	8 to 12
Strut bar bracket	25 to 33	34 to 44
Crossmember	43 to 58	59 to 78
Crossmember-to-engine support	22 to 29	29 to 39
Lower arm-to-arm bracket	94 to 108	127 to 147
Lower arm-to-axle outer bracket	94 to 108	127 to 147
Lower arm-to-axle inner bracket	47 to 58	64 to 78
Upper control arm rod	94 to 108	127 to 147
Rear shock-to-top and bottom mount	47 to 58	64 to 78
Steering pump brace bolt	20 to 30	26 to 40
Steering pump lock bolt	20 to 30	26 to 40
Gear box bleeder screw	2 to 3	3 to 4
Steering wheel nut	25 to 33	34 to 44
Gear box adjustment nut	22 to 32	29 to 44
Pitman arm-to-gear box shaft	94 to 109	127 to 147
Gear box mount	40 to 47	54 to 64
Tie-rod-to-relay rod	25 to 33	24 to 44
Power steering pump bracket	15 to 25	21 to 34
Oil pump pulley nut	20 to 30	26 to 40
Tie-rod adjustment locknut	36 to 40	49 to 54
Relay rod-to-Pitman arm	25 to 33	24 to 44
Relay rod-to-idler arm	25 to 33	24 to 44
Idler arm-to-bracket	29 to 43	39 to 59
Idler arm bracket mount	25 to 29	34 to 39

1 General information

On all models, the front suspension is an independent type, with MacPherson struts, coil springs and a sway bar. Double acting, telescopic shock absorbers are standard.

The rear suspension system is equipped with semi-elliptic springs and double-acting telescopic shock absorbers.

The steering system is conventional in design. Some models have manual steering while others are equipped with power steering.

The power steering pump is driven in the conventional manner by a V-belt from the crankshaft pulley.

2 Tire wear and tire pressure – check

Refer to Chapter 1 to check tires for wear and correct air pressure.

3 Tire rotation

To correctly rotate your tires, refer to Chapter 1.

4 Chassis lubrication – maintenance

To lubricate the chassis correctly, refer to Chapter 1.

5 Suspension – checks

Refer to Chapter 1 to correctly check your suspension and steering components.

6 Front end alignment – general information

Note: *Since wheel alignment and testing equipment is generally out of the reach of the home mechanic, this Section is intended only to familiarize the reader with the basic terms used and procedures followed during a typical wheel alignment job. In the event that your vehicle needs a wheel alignment check or adjustment, we recommend that the work be done by a reputable front-end alignment and repair shop.*

The three basic adjustments made when aligning a vehicle's front end are toe-in, caster and camber.

Toe-in is the amount the front wheels are angled in relationship to the centerline of the vehicle. For example, in a vehicle with zero toe-in, the distance measured between the front edges of the wheels is the same as the distance measured between the rear edges of the wheels. The wheels are running parallel with the centerline of the vehicle. This distance between the front edges of the wheels and the rear edges of the wheels should be within Specifications. Toe-in is adjusted by lengthening or shortening the tie-rods. Incorrect toe-in will cause tires to wear improperly by making them 'scrub' against the road surface.

Camber and caster are the angles at which the wheel and suspension upright are inclined to the vertical. Camber is the angle of the wheel in the lateral (side-to-side) plane, while caster is the angle of the wheel and upright in the longitudinal (fore-and-aft) plane. Camber angle affects the amount of tire tread which contacts the road and compensates for change in the suspension geometry when the vehicle is travelling around curves or over an undulating surface. Caster angle affects the self-centering action of the steering, which governs straight-line stability.

Camber, which is integrated into the strut and knuckle assembly, is pre-set during manufacture and is not adjustable. If the camber is not within specifications, the strut assembly and lower arm must be checked for damage. Caster usually requires no adjustment, although it is slightly adjustable at the threaded end of the strut bar.

7 Shock absorber (front) – replacement

1 Refer to Chapter 1 for a physical check of the shock absorbers. **Note**: *If you find that the shocks are defective, it is not recommended that you overhaul them. Because of the special tools needed to do the job, it is best to let your dealer service department or a service station overhaul them for you.*

2 However, you can remove and install them yourself by referring to Section 8 in this Chapter.

8 Shock absorber (front) – removal and installation

1 The front shock absorber and its related components are shown in the accompanying illustration.

2 Raise and support the front of your vehicle according to the jacking and towing procedures in the front of this book.

3 Remove the front wheels.

4 Disconnect the brake line from the inner retaining bracket of the shock. Plug the hose to prevent contamination and fluid leakage.

5 Remove the caliper support front hub with brake disc, dust cover and disc brake adapter by referring to the appropriate Sections in this book.

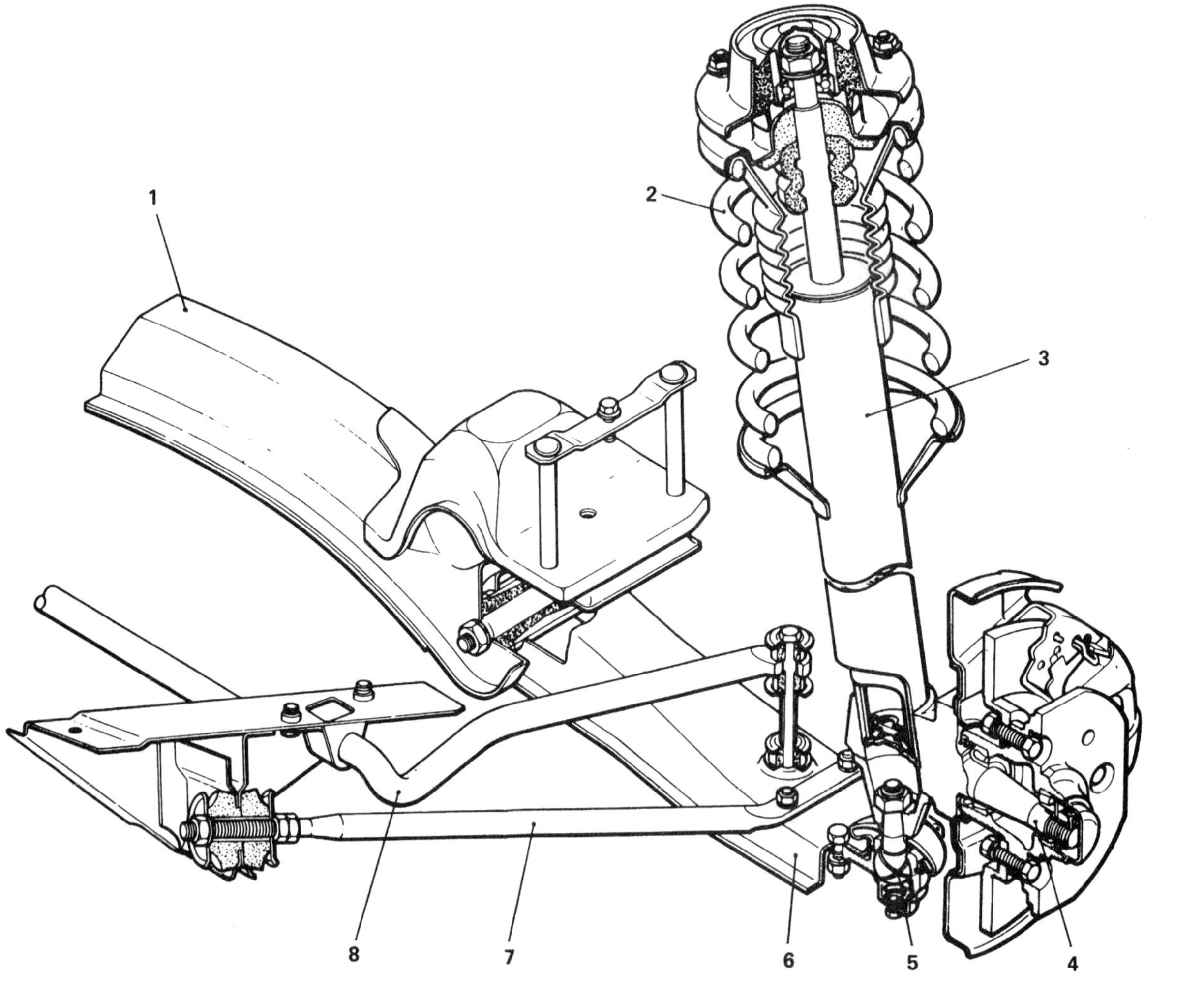

Fig. 11.1 Front suspension components – installed view (Sec 8)

1 Crossmember
2 Front suspension spring
3 Front shock absorber
4 Steering knuckle
5 Balljoint
6 Lower arm
7 Strut bar
8 Stabilizer bar

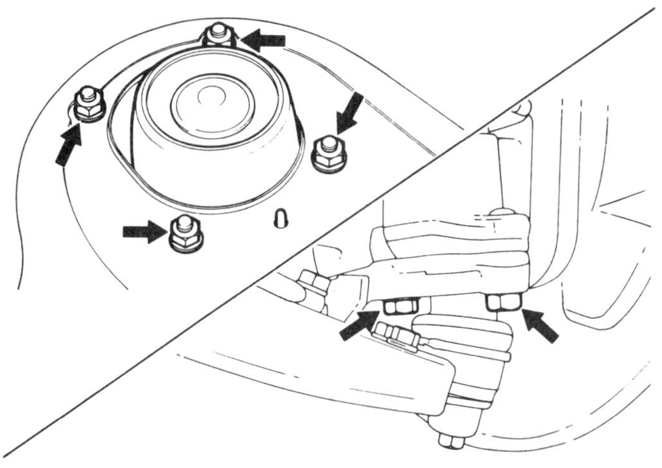

Fig. 11.2 Remove the upper and lower ends of the front shock absorber (Sec 8)

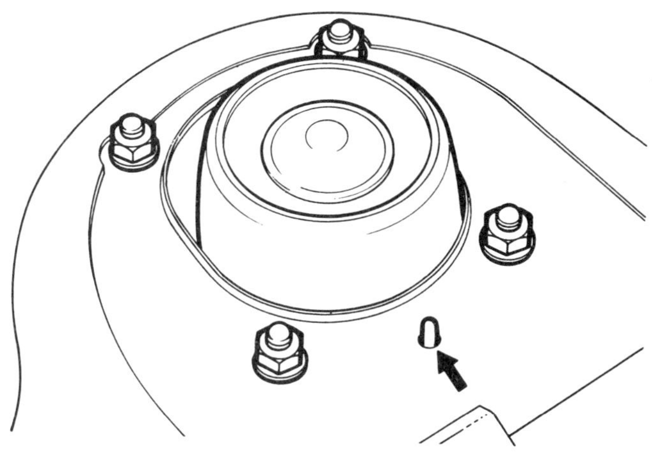

Fig. 11.3 Correct installation of insulator pin in the top of the front shock absorber (Sec 8)

6 Unscrew and remove the top mounting nuts and washers.
7 Unscrew and remove the dust cap.
8 Unscrew and remove the two shock absorber lower mounting bolts and washers. Push down on the suspension lower arm to release the shock absorber at the top and bottom mounts. **Note**: *The bottom mount has two location collars which engage in the bolt holes of the shock absorber lower mount.*
9 Installation is basically the reverse of the removal procedure.
10 Install the top of the shock mounting first and attach and tighten its mounting hardware. **Note**: *Make sure when you attach the top portion of the front shock absorber that you align the insulator pin into the hole of the mounting bracket before you tighten the mounting hardware.*
11 Install the bottom of the shock absorber in its correct mounting and attach its mounting hardware and tighten.
12 Reattach the brake line at the bracket and make sure that no dirt is allowed to enter the lines.
13 Because the brake lines were disconnected, you will have to bleed the brake system by referring to the correct procedure in Chapter 9.
14 If necessary, adjust the caliper and disc assembly.
15 Make sure that all mounting hardware is tightened according to the Specifications.

9 Front hub – removal, inspection and installation

Since the front hub must be removed to service the front wheel bearings, refer to Chapter 1 for the removal and installation procedure.

10 Front wheel bearings – repacking

Refer to Chapter 1 for the procedure to follow when repacking the front wheel bearings.

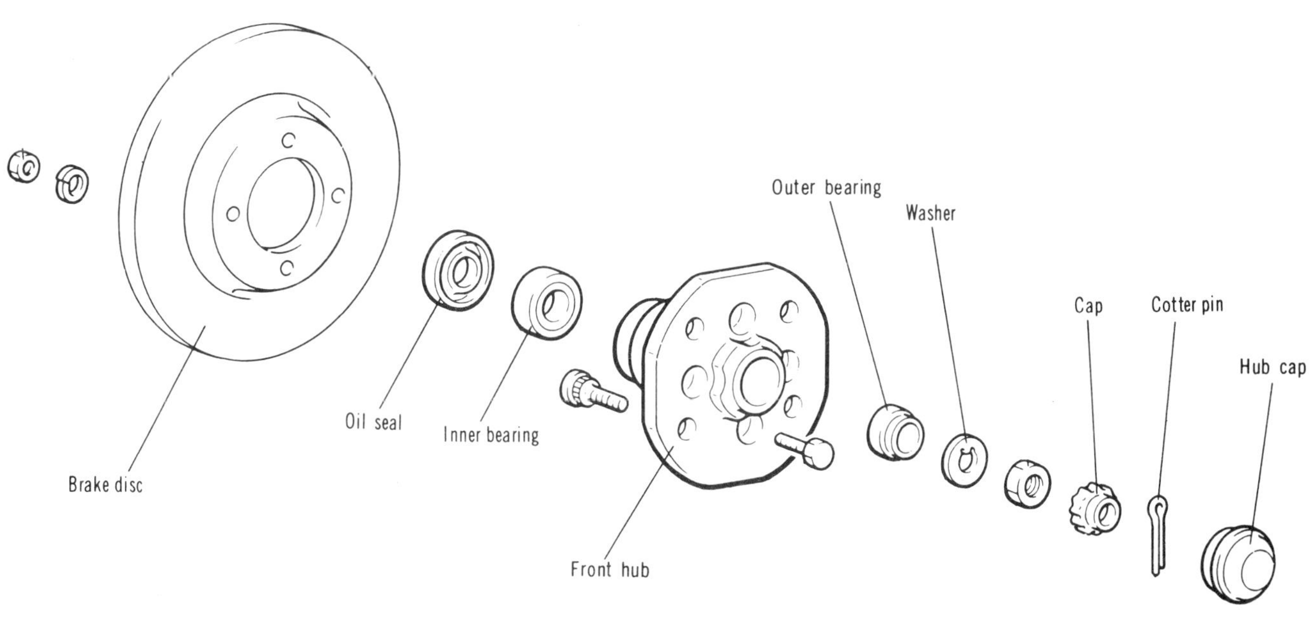

Fig. 11.4 Front hub components – exploded view (Sec 9)

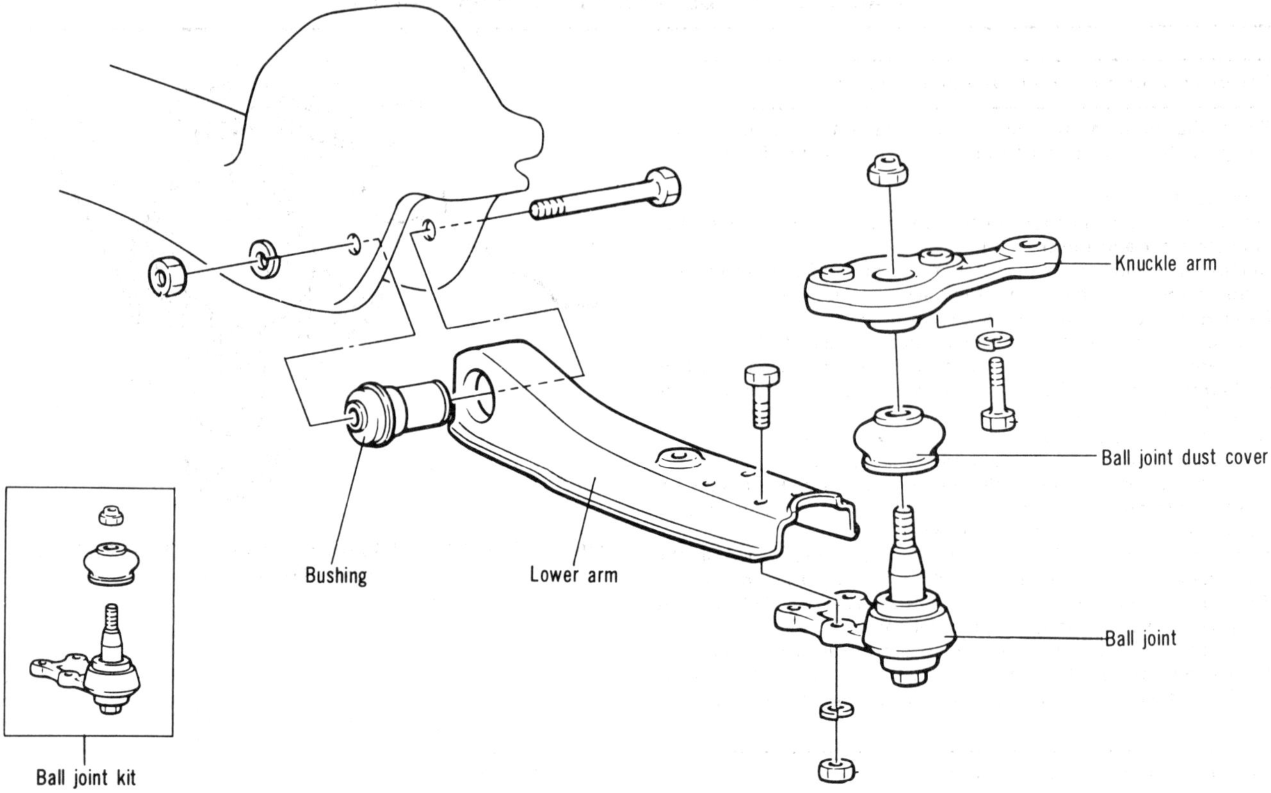

Fig. 11.5 Lower arm components – exploded view (Sec 11)

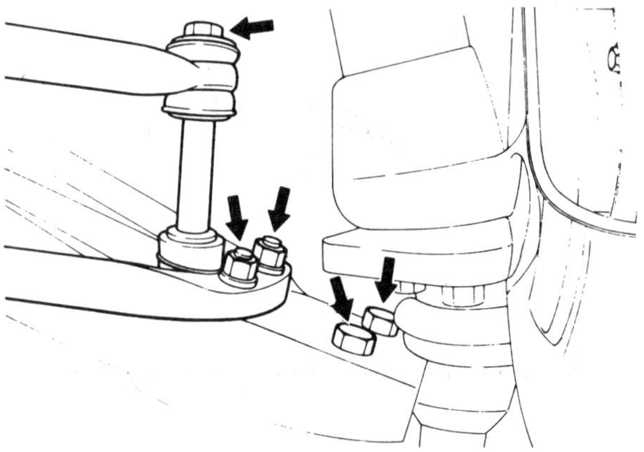

Fig. 11.6 Remove the stabilizer bar, strut bar and balljoint (Sec 11)

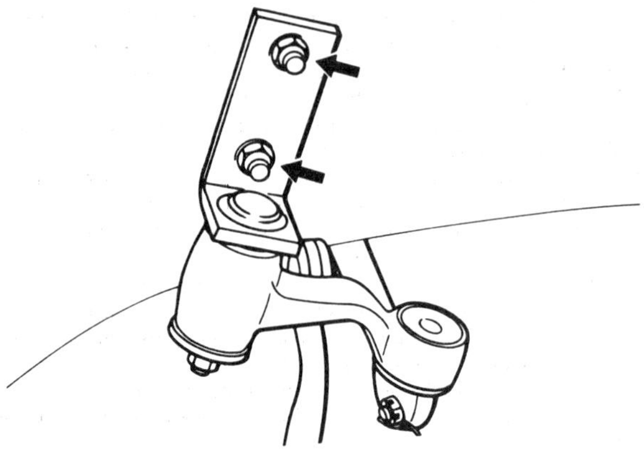

Fig. 11.7 Disconnect the idler arm support (Sec 11)

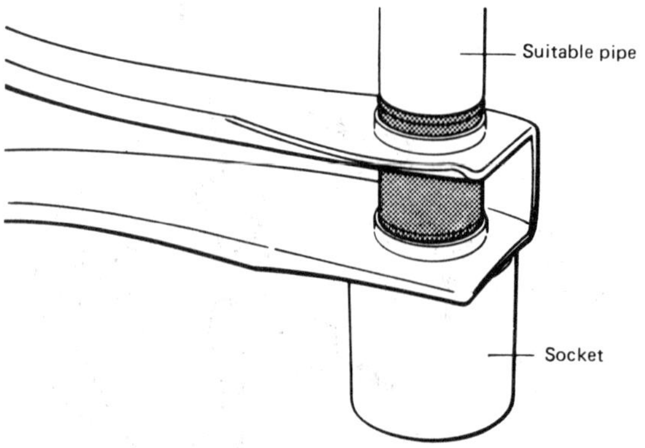

Fig. 11.8 Remove the lower arm bushing only if necessary (Sec 11)

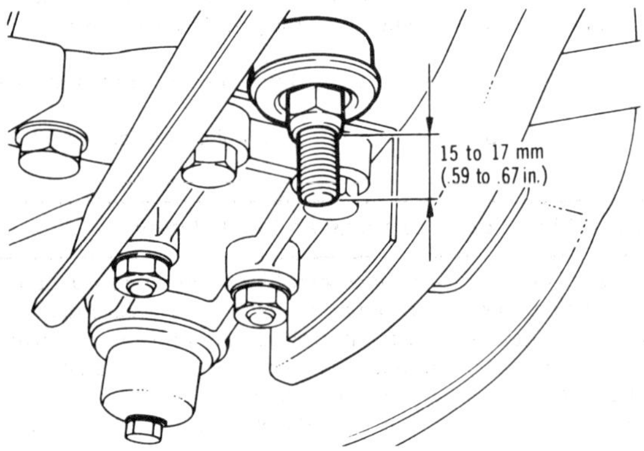

Fig. 11.9 Stabilizer bar to lower arm installation (Sec 11)

11 Lower arm (front) – removal and installation

1 Raise the front of the vehicle and support it on jackstands according to the jacking and towing procedures in the front of this book.
2 Remove the front wheel.
3 Disconnect the connections of the lower arm to the stabilizer bar unit, the strut bar and the balljoint.
4 Remove the idler arm support from the body of the vehicle and move the steering linkage toward the back of your vehicle.
5 Remove the lower arm from the crossmember.
6 Now, push out the bushing using a suitable pipe of 1.25 in outside diameter and a socket with an inside diameter of at least 1.38 in. **Note:** *Do not remove the bushing unless it is necessary. If the bushing is removed, replace it with a new one.*
7 Check the bushing for deterioration, cracks and wear.
8 Check the lower arm for deformation and cracks.
9 Using a pipe of 1.57 in inside diameter and a suitable support, press in the bushing until it contacts the end surface of the lower arm.
10 Installation is the reverse of removal.
11 Remember to tighten the lower arm to the crossmember while the vehicle is raised from the ground but, do not torque tighten yet.
12 Tighten the mounting bolt when the vehicle is solidly on the ground according to the torque Specifications.
13 When attaching the stabilizer bar to the lower arm, tighten the self-locking nut so that the distance from the end of the bolt to the self-locking nut will be the standard value as shown in the illustration.

12 Balljoint – removal and installation

1 Raise and support the vehicle and block the wheels according to the jacking and towing procedures at the front of this book.
2 Remove the front wheels.
3 Remove the caliper support with the caliper assembly and brake hose from the disc brake adapter by referring to Chapter 9.
4 Suspend the caliper assembly from the coil spring with a wire hook, taking care not to damage the brake hose.
5 Disconnect the knuckle arm and steering tie-rod assembly using the special tool shown in the illustration.
6 Remove the bolts installing the knuckle arm to the shock absorber and disconnect them by tapping with a soft-faced hammer.
7 Disconnect the balljoint and the lower arm then remove the balljoint together with the knuckle arm.
8 Loosen the self-locking nut and by tapping on the nut with a soft-faced hammer, disconnect the balljoint and the knuckle arm.
9 Remove the balljoint dust cover by evenly prying the entire outside diameter of the cover with a screwdriver.
10 Check the balljoint dust cover for deterioration or cracks.
11 Check the knuckle arm for deformation or cracks, replace any bad parts with new ones.
12 Installation is the reverse of removal.
13 Before installing a new balljoint, make sure that you install a new balljoint dust cover.
14 Connect the balljoint and knuckle arm by attaching and tightening the self-locking nut to the specified torque. Always use a new self-locking nut.
15 Make sure when installing the caliper support that it is installed correctly.
16 Make sure that all hardware is tightened to the specified torque.

13 Strut/stabilizer bar – removal and installation

1 Raise and support the vehicle and block the wheels according to the jacking and towing procedures at the front of this book.
2 Disconnect the stabilizer bar and the strut bar from the lower arm.
3 Remove the strut bar bracket from the body of the vehicle with the stabilizer bar and the strut bar still attached.
4 Remove the stabilizer bar and the strut bar from the strut bar bracket.
5 Check the strut bar, especially the threaded portion and the connecting portion to the lower arm for cracks and deformation.
6 Check the stabilizer bar for cracks and deformation.
7 Check the rubber bushings, the strut bar bushings and the

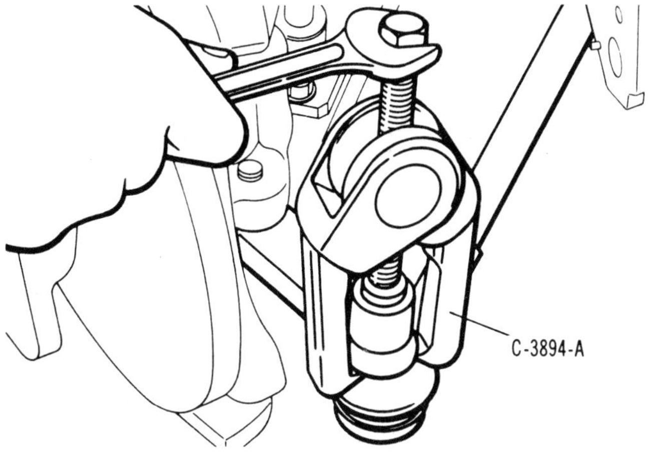

Fig. 11.10 Disconnecting the knuckle arm and the steering tie-rod assembly (Sec 12)

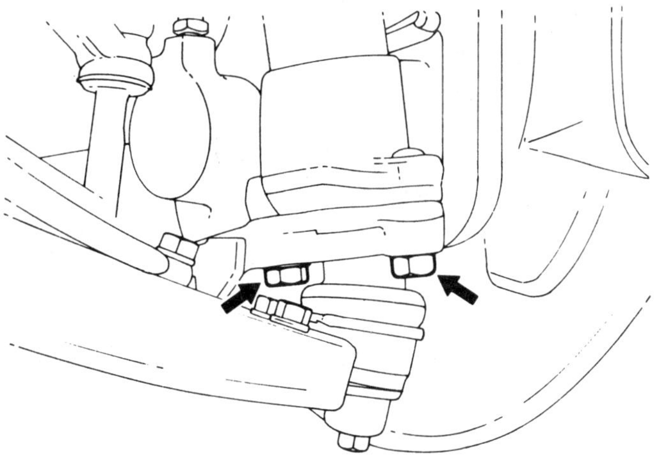

Fig. 11.11 Removing the knuckle arm from the shock absorber (Sec 12)

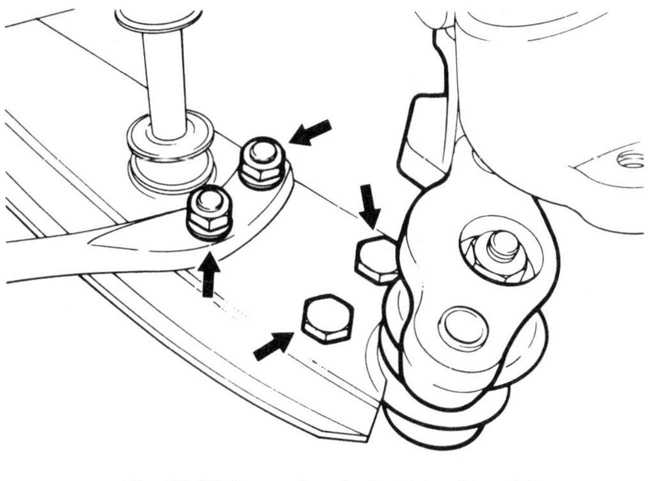

Fig. 11.12 Removing the balljoint (Sec 12)

11

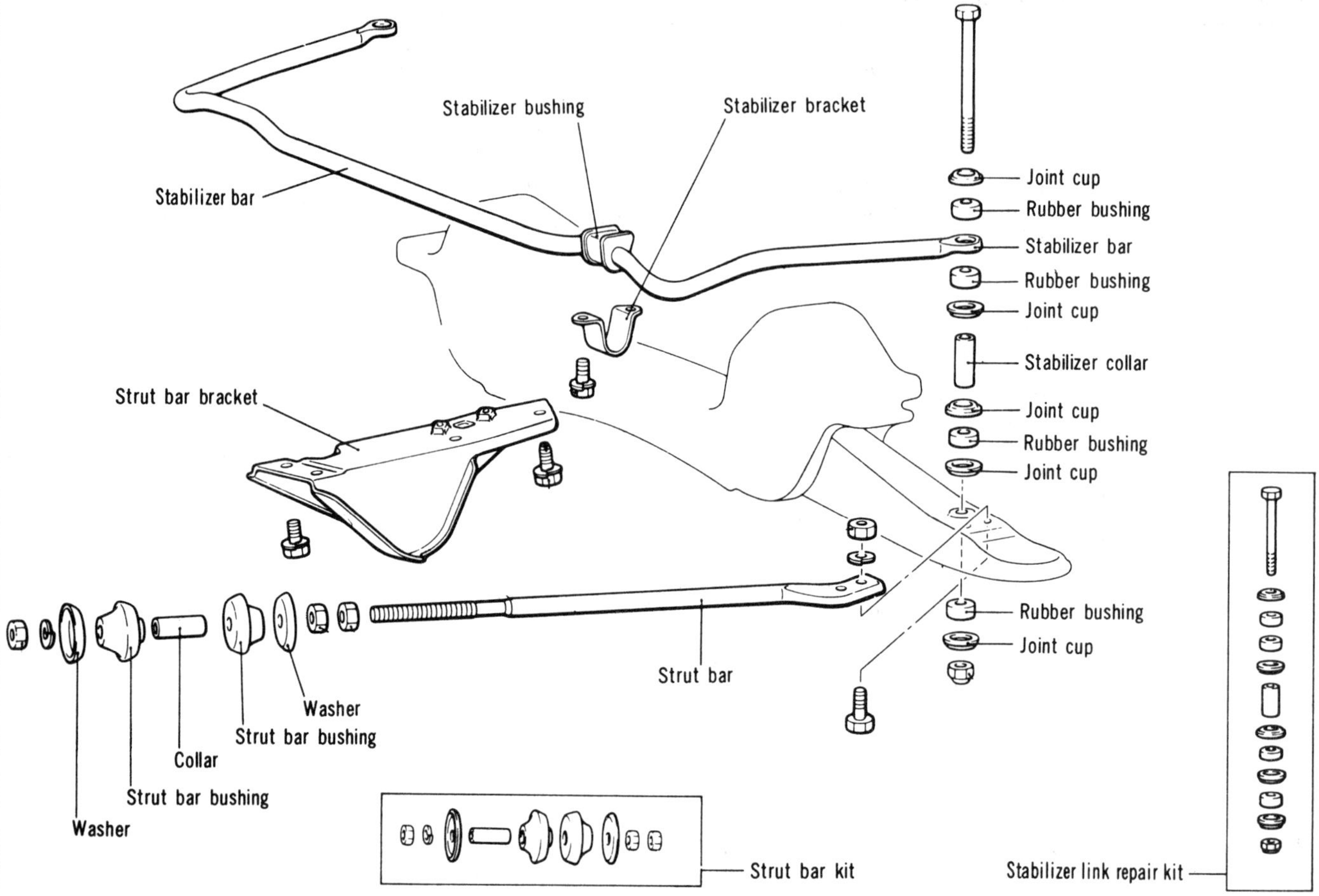

Fig. 11.13 Strut bar/stabilizer bar components – exploded view (Sec 13)

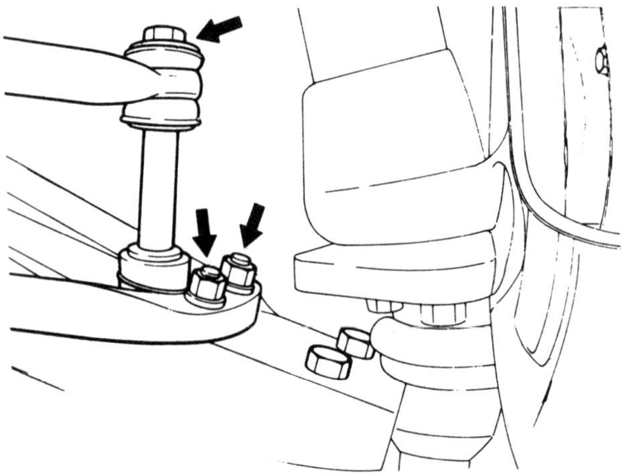

Fig. 11.14 Disconnecting the strut and stabilizer bar (Sec 13)

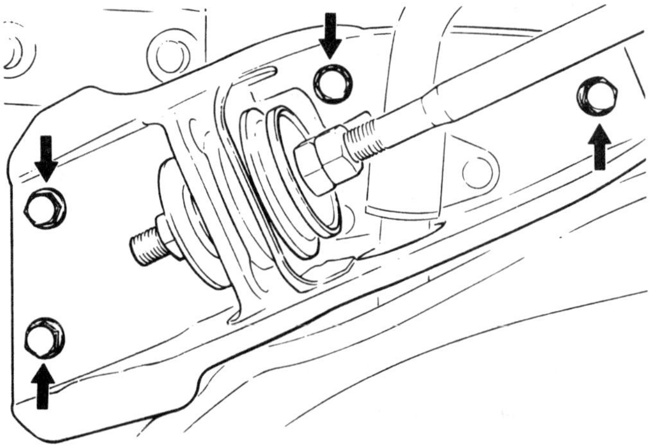

Fig. 11.15 Removing the strut bar bracket (Sec 13)

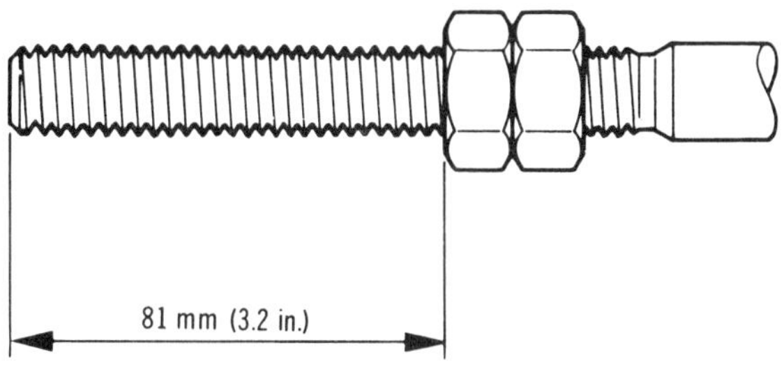

Fig. 11.16 Tightening position of the nut on the strut bar (Sec 13)

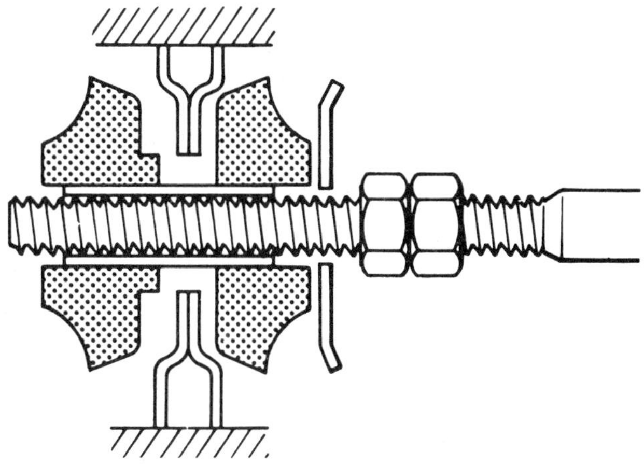

Fig. 11.17 The correct position of the strut bar bushings (Sec 13)

stabilizer bushings for cracks and damage. Replace any bad parts with new ones.

8 Installation is the reverse of removal.

9 Before installing the strut bar, install the nuts to the position shown in the illustration and tighten them to the specified torque.

10 Install the strut bar, paying attention to the identification marks for use on the left or right side of the vehicle.

11 The shapes of the front and rear sides of the strut bar bushings are different. Install as shown in the illustration.

12 Temporarily attach and tighten the nut at the end of the strut bar while the vehicle is off the ground. **Note:** *Do not torque the nut until the vehicle is lowered to the ground.*

13 When attaching the stabilizer bar to the lower arm, tighten the self-locking nut so that the distance from the end of the bolt to the self-locking nut end surface will be as shown in the illustration. **Note:** *Always use new self-locking nuts.*

14 Crossmember – removal and installation

1 Raise and support the vehicle and block the wheels by referring to the jacking and towing procedures at the front of this book.

2 Remove the front wheels.

3 First, remove the lower arms by referring to Section 11.

4 Disconnect the starter cable clamped to the left upper portion of the crossmember.

5 Using a chain block or a block-and-tackle, lift up the upper portion of the engine and place wooden blocks under the oil pan to hold up the lower engine portion with a service jack.

6 Remove the crossmember with the engine support front insulators attached.

7 Now, remove the engine support front insulators from the crossmember.

8 Check the crossmember for cracks, breakage, bends, dents or other damage. Also, check for misalignment by referring to the correct dimensions in the illustration.

9 Installation is the reverse of the removal procedure.

10 Install the crossmember at the specified torque by using new self-locking nuts.

11 Refer to the lower arm installation procedure in Section 11.

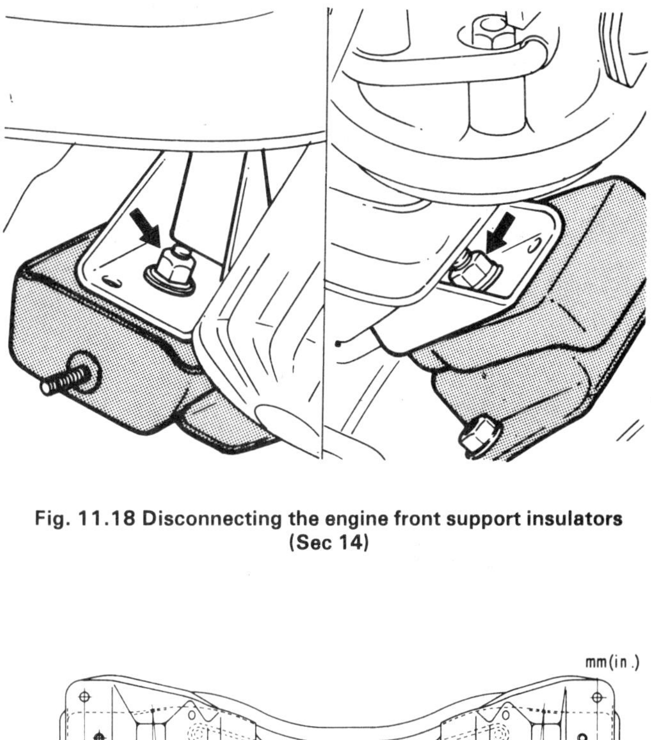

Fig. 11.18 Disconnecting the engine front support insulators (Sec 14)

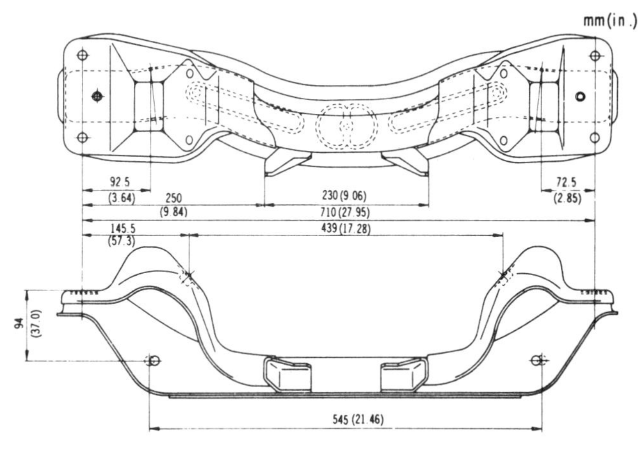

Fig. 11.19 The crossmember alignment checking dimensions (Sec 14)

15 Shock absorber (rear) – removal and installation

1 Using a jack under the rear axle assembly, raise the rear axle slightly. Remove the rear wheels.

2 Remove the shock absorber assembly by first removing the bottom mounting bolts, then remove the top mounting bolts. Pull the shock absorber from underneath the vehicle.

3 Lower the jack which is under the rear axle and remove the coil spring.

4 Check the coil spring for bends, cracks and deterioration.

5 Check the upper and lower rear spring pads for breakage.

6 Check the shock absorber for fluid leaks and noise. Test it manually by moving it throughout its full stroke. The shock absorber must move smoothly with uniform resistance.

7 Installation is the reverse of the removal procedure.

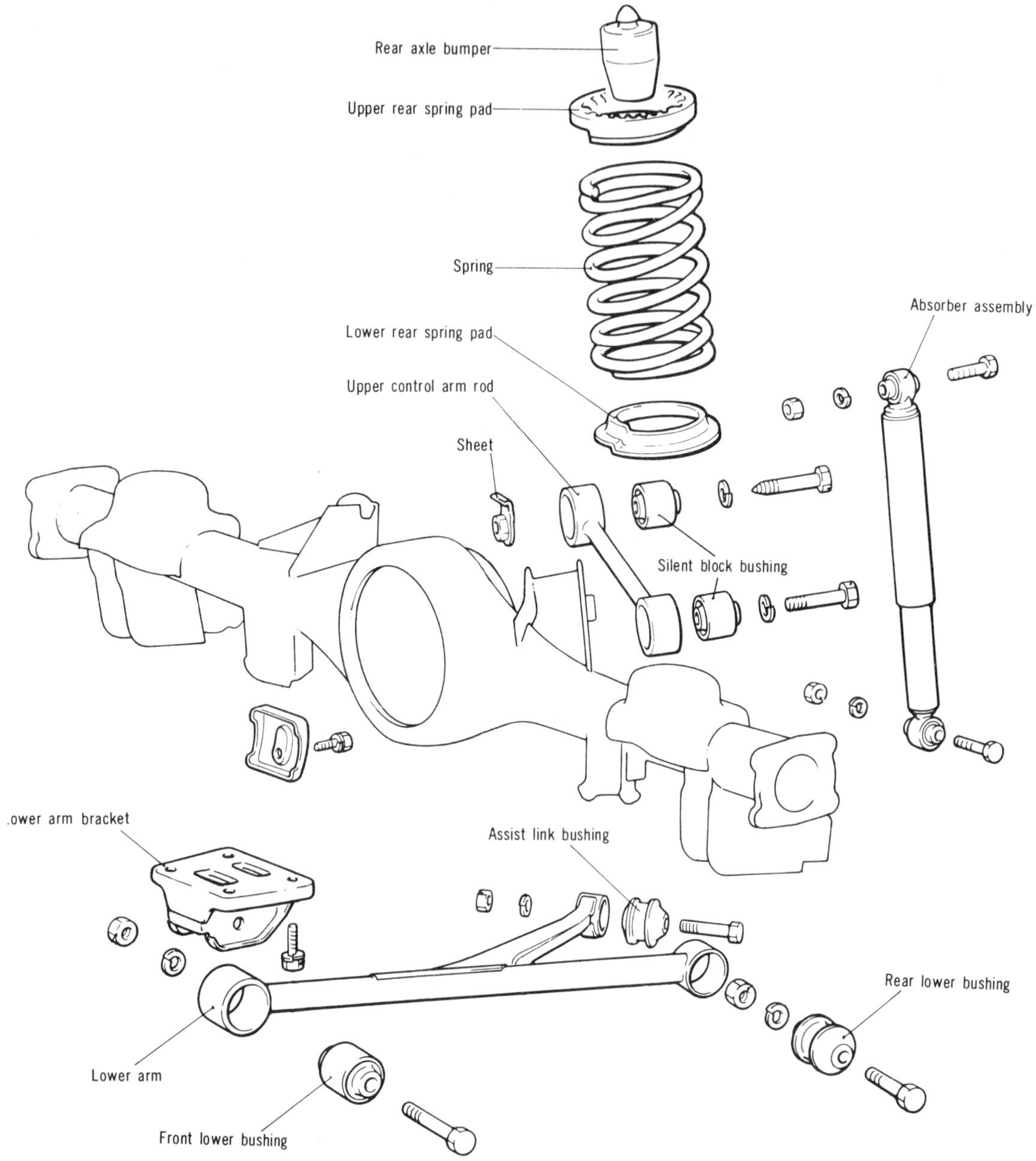

Fig. 11.20 Rear suspension components – exploded view (Sec 15)

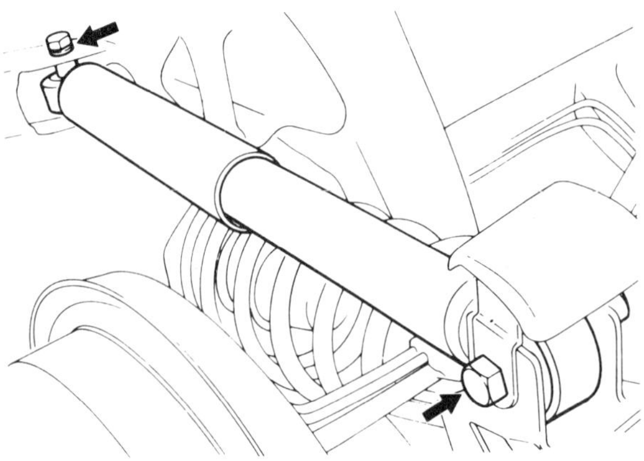

Fig. 11.21 Removal of the rear shock absorber (Sec 15)

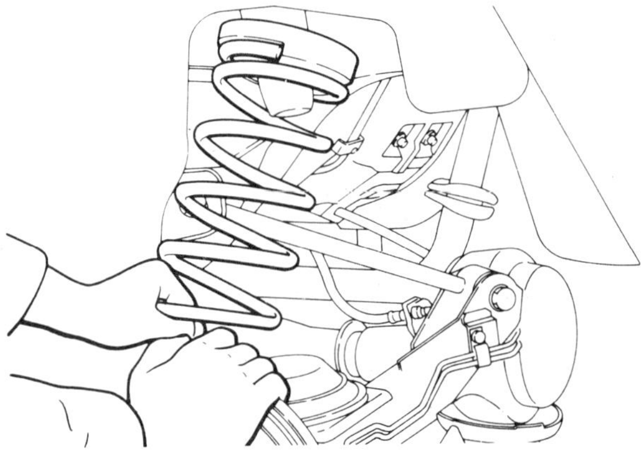

Fig. 11.22 Removal of rear coil spring (Sec 15)

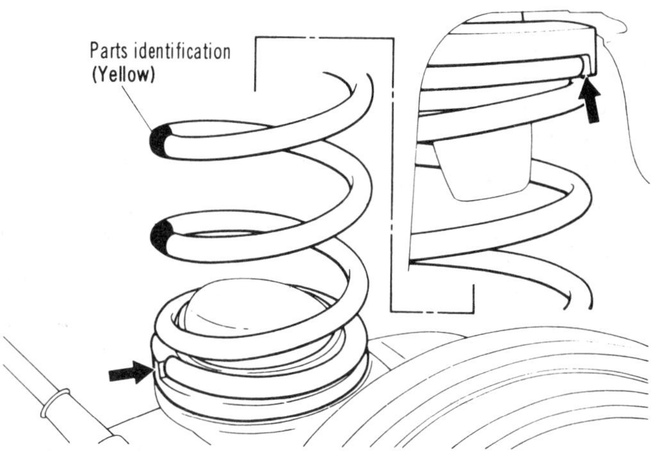

Fig. 11.23 Correct position of the coil spring (Sec 15)

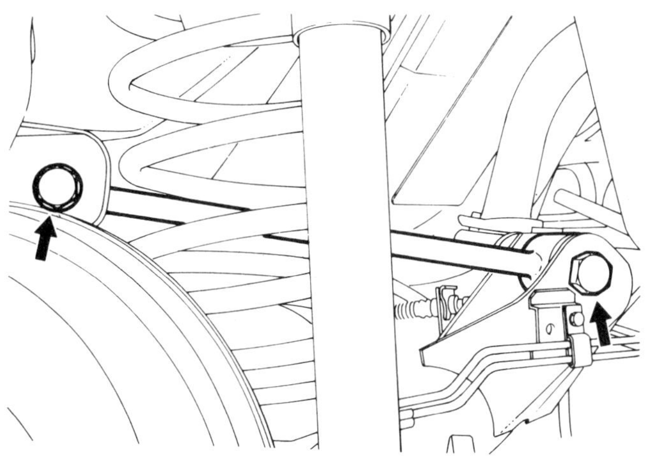

Fig. 11.24 Removal of the upper control arm (rear) (Sec 16)

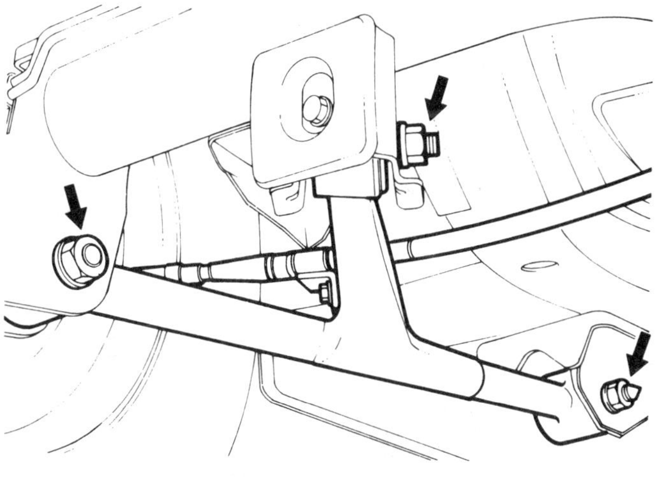

Fig. 11.25 Removal of the lower arm (rear) (Sec 16)

8 Install the lower end of the spring first. Then, correctly position the groove of the upper rear spring pad against the upper mount and install it. **Note**: *The springs are to be selected for their left-right combination by the load classification color marks. Refer to the illustration.*

9 With the springs installed, raise the rear axle with the jack and install the shock absorbers.

10 After temporarily installing the shock absorber, lower the vehicle to the ground and tighten the mounting bolts to the specified torque.

16 Upper/lower control arm (rear) – removal, overhaul and installation

1 Using a jack under the rear axle assembly, raise the rear axle slightly. Remove the rear wheels.

2 Remove the upper control arm rod.

3 On vehicles with rear drum brakes, unhook and put aside the parking brake rear cable from the lower arm.

4 Remove the lower arm from the rear axle housing and from the bracket attached to the body.

5 Check the lower arm and upper control arm for bends and damage.

6 Check the front lower, the rear lower, the assist link and the silent block bushings for deterioration, cracks or missing pieces.

7 If any of these faults are noted in the bushings, replace them with new ones. **Note**: *Do not remove any of these bushings unless they are to be replaced.*

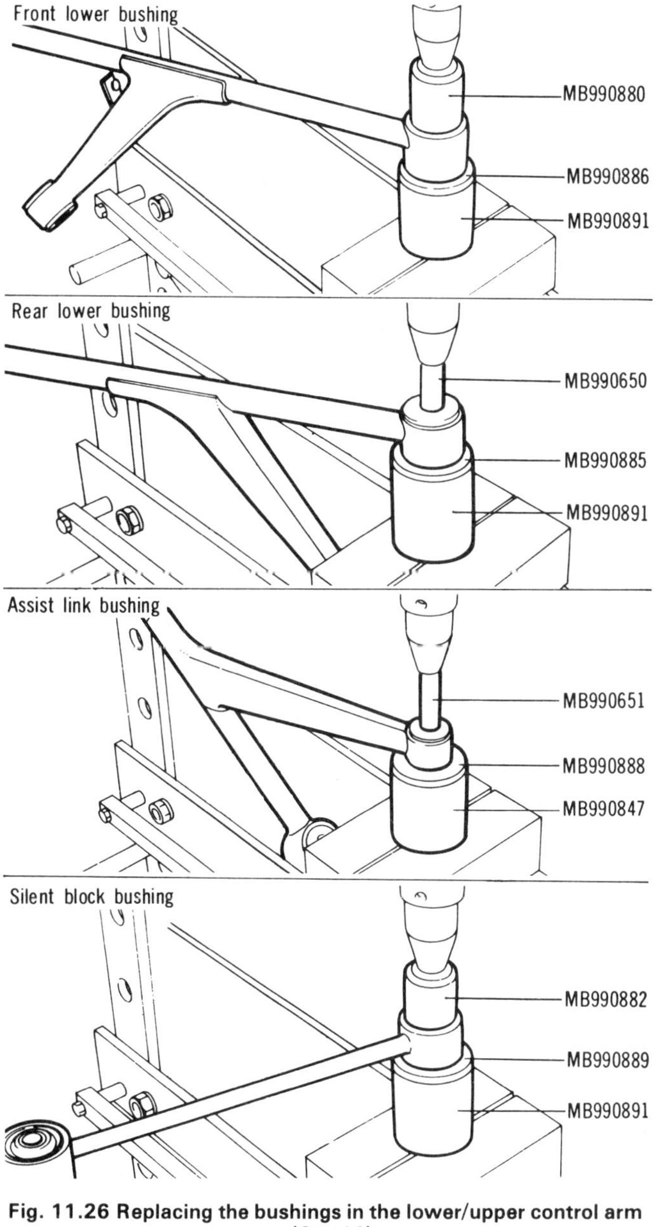

Fig. 11.26 Replacing the bushings in the lower/upper control arm (Sec 16)

11

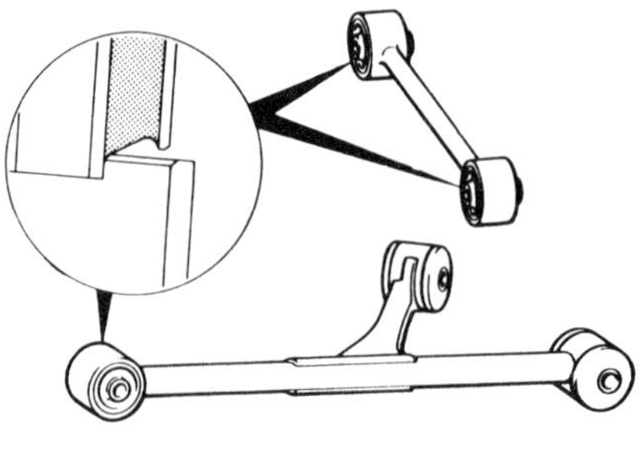

Fig. 11.27 The correct direction for installing new bushings (Sec 16)

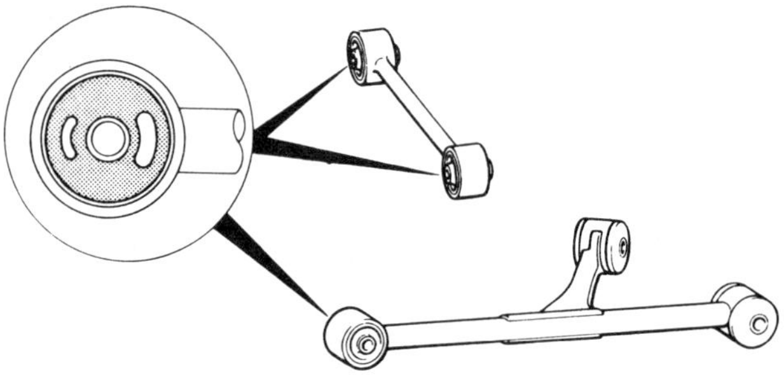

Fig. 11.28 The correct position for installing new bushings (Sec 16)

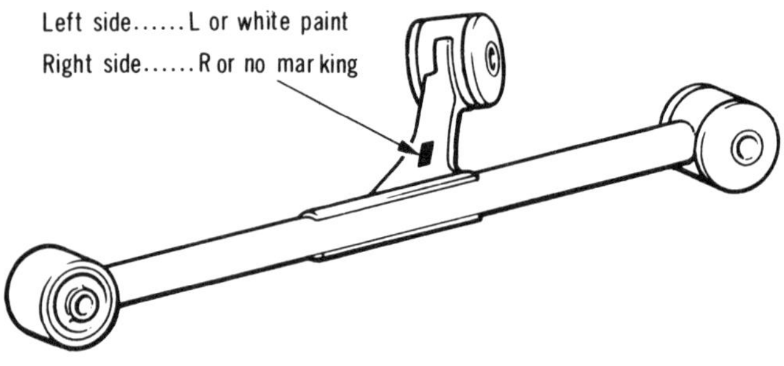

Fig. 11.29 The correct placement of the lower arm onto the vehicle (Sec 16)

8 To remove any of these bushings special tools are required. Refer to the illustration and the following procedure.
9 Press the front lower and the silent block bushings into the chamfered side of the lower arm and upper control rod.
10 Position the holes of the front lower and the silent block bushings as illustrated and press them into place.
11 When finished, make sure that the bushings project equally at both ends (see the Specifications).
12 Installation is the reverse of the removal procedure.
13 With the rear axle jacked up and supported temporarily, install the lower arm. Make sure that the left and right markings are on the left and right sides of your vehicle by referring to the illustration and then tighten the mounting hardware to the specified torque.
14 Reattach the parking brake cable to the lower control arm and install and tighten the upper control arm rod to the specified torque.

17 Coil spring (rear) – removal and installation

To replace or check the rear coil springs, refer to Section 15.

18 Steering wheel – removal and installation

1 Remove the horn pad mounting screws and the horn pad.
2 Remove the steering wheel locknut and the steering wheel by using a steering wheel puller. **Note:** *Do not subject the steering wheel to impact by using a hammer or similar tool.*
3 Installation is the reverse of the removal procedure.
4 To install the steering wheel, place the front wheels in the straight-ahead position.
5 Place the steering wheel onto the shaft and fit the cancel pins of the column switch into the bottom holes in the steering wheel by turning the cancelling ring with a screwdriver.
6 Tighten the steering wheel locknut to the specified torque.
7 Install the horn pad and tighten.

19 Steering wheel lock/column switches – removal and installation

1 In order to remove the steering wheel lock, you first have to remove the steering wheel and both column switches.
2 Remove the steering wheel according to Section 18.
3 Lower the tilt handle to its lowest position and remove the column cover.
4 Remove the column switch mounting screws and the switches themselves by disconnecting and removing the bands around the steering column and also disconnecting all connectors to the switches.
5 To check these switches, refer to Chapter 10.
6 You can now remove the steering wheel lock by using a hack saw and making a slit in the head of each of the mounting bolts.

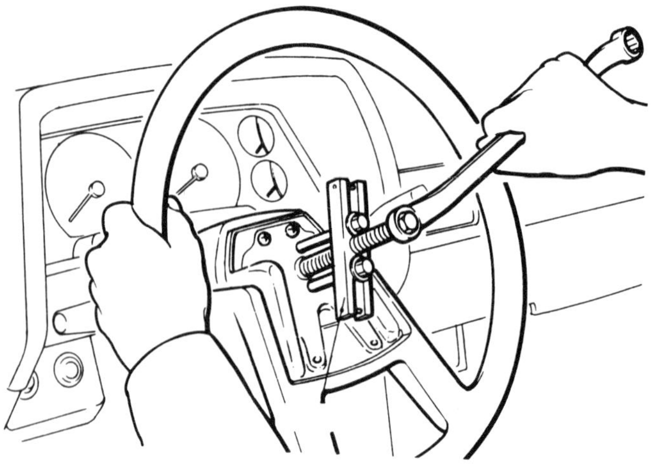

Fig. 11.30 Remove the steering wheel with pullers (Sec 18)

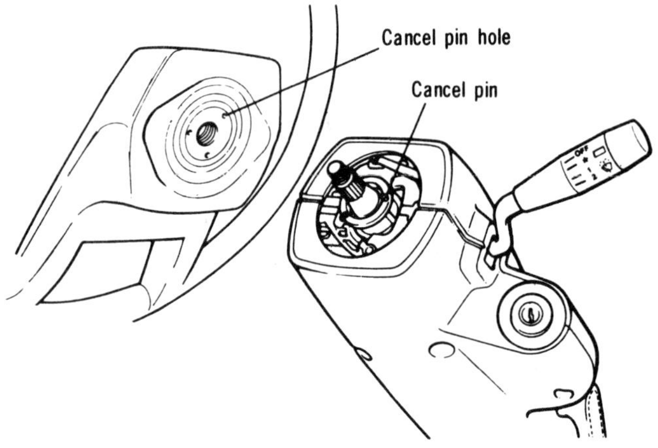

Fig. 11.31 Align the cancel pin hole in the steering wheel with the cancel pin in the steering column (Sec 18)

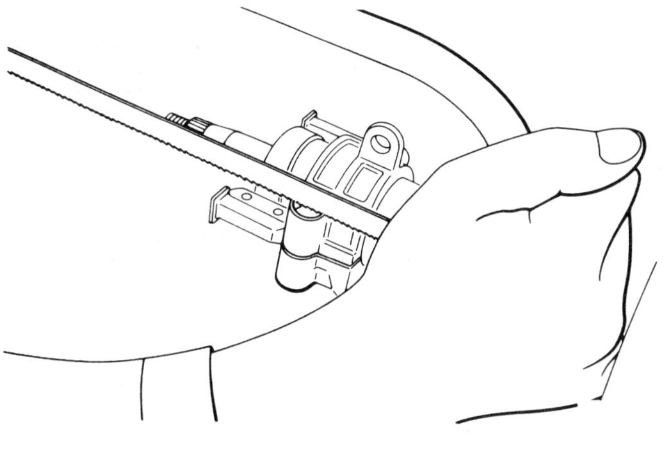

Fig. 11.32 Make a slot in the lock mechanism with a hack saw (Sec 19)

7 Loosen the bolts by using a screwdriver and then remove the steering wheel lock from the column tube.
8 Installation is the reverse of the removal procedure.
9 To install the steering wheel lock, first align the column tube hole with the wheel lock guide dowel for temporary installation.
10 Insert the ignition key to make sure the lock functions correctly.
11 In order to install the steering wheel lock, special bolts will have to be purchased from your dealer.
12 Install the special bolts into the steering wheel lock and tighten them until the heads twist off.
13 Install the steering column switches with their mounting hardware and tighten. Install the mounting clamps for these switches around the steering column and reconnect their individual connectors.
14 Install and tighten the steering wheel.

20 Tie-rods – removal and installation

1 Raise the front of the vehicle according to the jacking and towing procedures at the front of this book and support it with jackstands.
2 Remove the cotter pins from the pin holes of the tie-rod ends and remove the locknuts.
3 Disconnect the tie-rod ends by using special tool C-3894-A.
4 With the tie-rods removed from the vehicle, remove the tie-rod ends. **Note:** *The tie-rod outer end has left-hand screw threads and the tie-rod inner end has right-hand screw threads. The tie-rod end socket is caulked to the plug and cannot be disassembled.*
5 Check the tie-rod ends for damage and deformation. Replace with new ones if necessary.
6 Grip the balljoint with pliers and compress the stud fully, measuring the deflection. If the deflection is out of limit, replace the balljoint with a new one.
7 Check the dust covers for damage and cracks and replace with new ones if necessary.
8 Installation is the reverse of the removal procedure.
9 When installing a new dust cover, coat the cover lip with grease and fill the inside of the dust cover with grease.
10 Temporarily tighten the adjusting nuts so that the standard

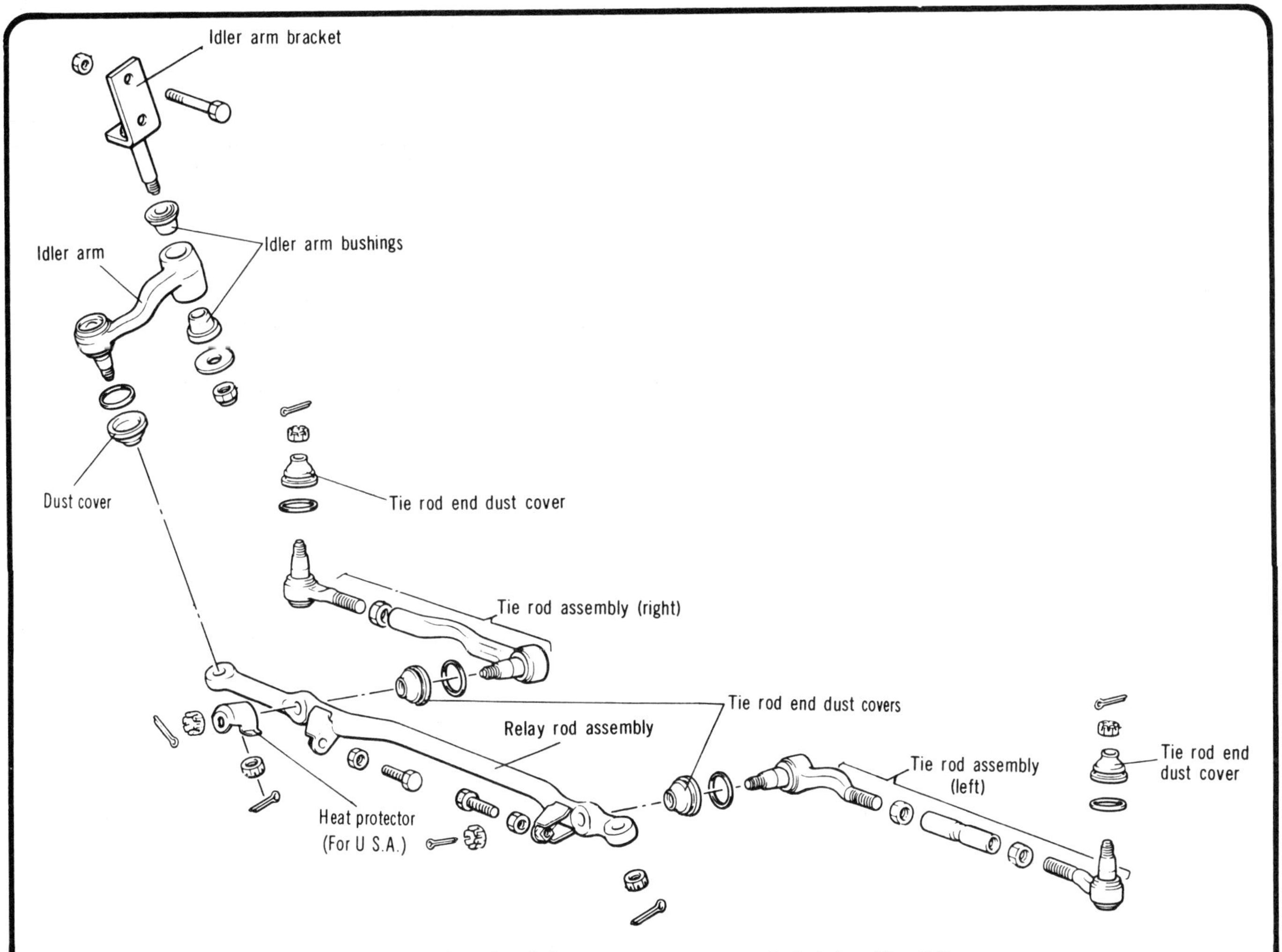

Fig. 11.33 Steering linkage components – exploded view (Sec 20)

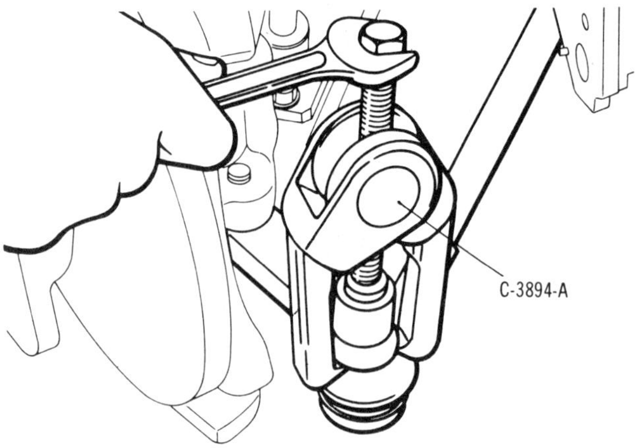

Fig. 11.34 Disconnect the tie-rod assembly with pullers (Sec 20)

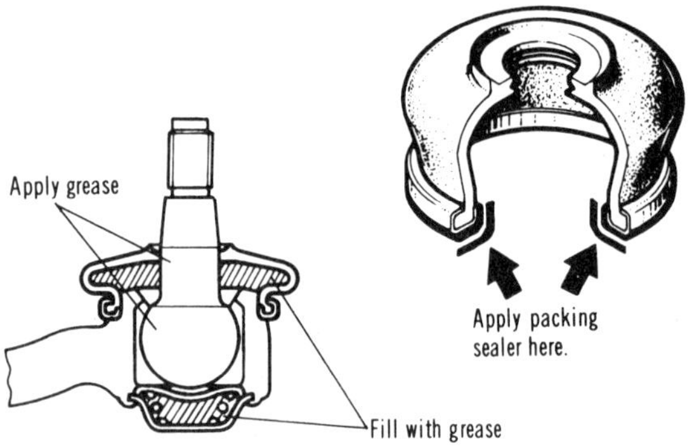

Fig. 11.35 Add grease to a new rod dust cover (Sec 20)

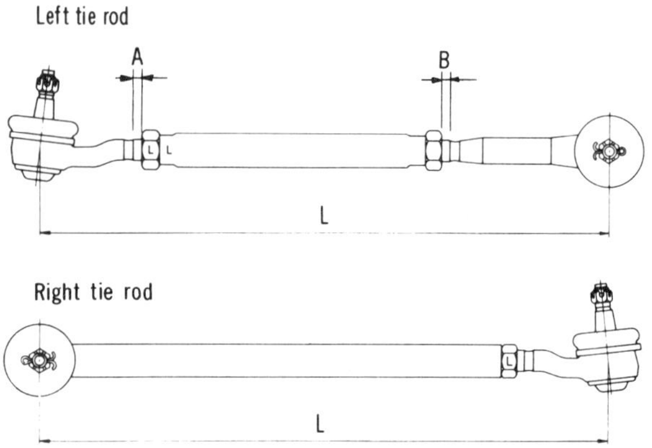

Fig. 11.36 Correct tie-rod adjustment check (Sec 20)

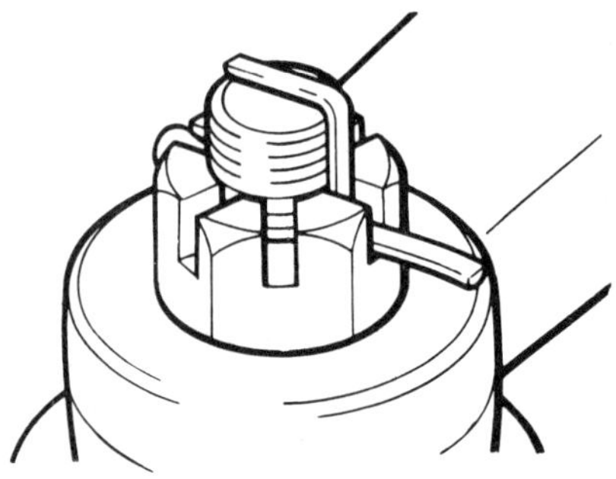
Fig. 11.37 Correct locking installation of cotter pin (Sec 20)

distance is between the stud bolts at both ends of the tie-rods (see illustration).
11 **Note:** *Turn the tie-rod ends inward so that lengths A and B are uniform.*
12 When connecting the tie-rod assembly to the knuckle arm, tighten the nuts to the specified torque, install a cotter pin and open the cotter pin exactly as shown in the illustration.
13 Have the front end aligned by a specialist.

21 Relay rod – removal and installation

1 Raise the front of the vehicle according to the jacking and towing procedures at the front of this book and support it with jackstands.
2 Remove the cotter pins from the pin holes of the tie-rod ends. Remove the pins from the idler arm and the Pitman arm and remove the locknuts.
3 Disconnect the tie-rod ends from the relay rod by using special tool C-3894-A.
4 Disconnect the Pitman arm from the relay rod by using the same special tool.
5 Disconnect the relay rod from the idler arm by using the same special tool and remove the relay rod.
6 Check the relay rod for damage and deformation. Replace the rod with a new one if necessary.
7 Check the dust covers for damage and cracks. Replace the dust covers with new ones if necessary.
8 Installation is the reverse of the removal procedure.
9 When installing a new dust cover, coat the cover lip with grease and fill the inside of the dust cover with grease.
10 Connect the relay rod to the idler arm and the Pitman arm.
11 Connect the relay rod to the tie-rod ends and tighten all the lock nuts to the specified torque.
12 After installation of the relay rod to the Pitman arm and to the idler arm, make sure that there is the right amount of clearance (see illustration).
13 Install the cotter pins and lock them in place by referring to the illustration.
14 Have the front end of your vehicle aligned by an alignment specialist.

22 Idler arm – removal and installation

1 Raise the front of the vehicle according to the jacking and towing procedures at the front of this book and support it with jackstands.
2 Remove the cotter pin from the pin hole of the idler arm and remove the locknut.
3 Disconnect the idler arm from the relay rod by using special tool C-3894-A.
4 Disconnect the idler arm support from the body frame and remove the idler arm assembly.

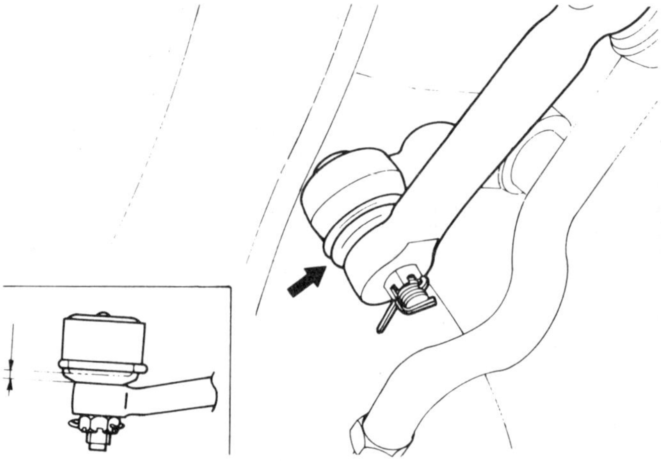
Fig. 11.38 Correct relay rod to idler arm adjustment check (Sec 21)

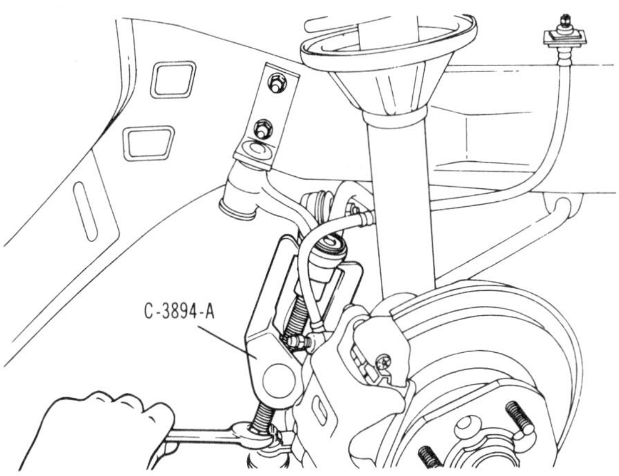

Fig. 11.39 Disconnect the idler arm with pullers (Sec 22)

Fig. 11.40 Remove the idler arm assembly (Sec 22)

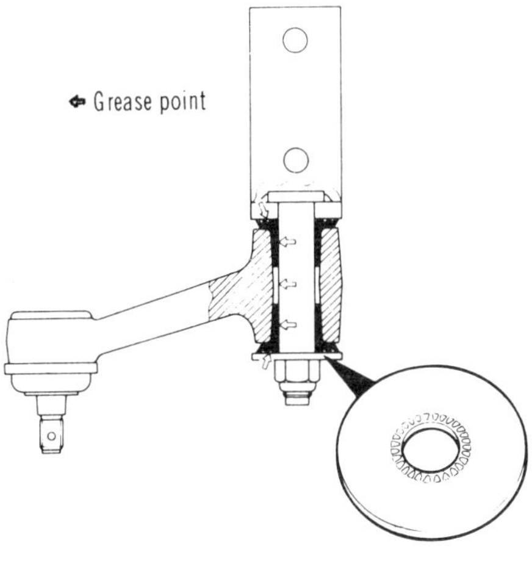

Fig. 11.41 Correct installation position of the idler arm to its support (Sec 22)

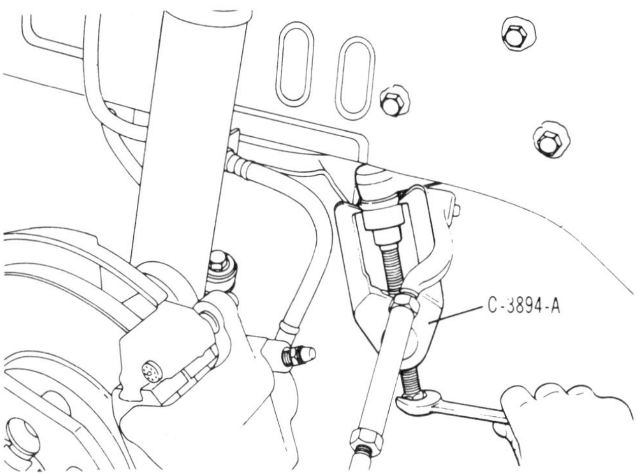

Fig. 11.42 Remove the Pitman arm with pullers (Sec 23)

5 Check the idler arm for deformation and damage. Replace the arm with a new one if necessary.

6 Check the dust cover for cracks and damage. Replace the cover with a new one if necessary.

7 To replace the dust cover with a new one, the idler arm assembly must be disassembled.

8 Reassembly is the reverse of the removal procedure.

9 If new dust covers were installed on the idler assembly, in order to assist in reassembly of the idler arm, apply a thin coat of grease to the inner surface of the idler arm. Also, apply a thin coat of grease to the outer surface of the bushing and insert the bushing up to the flange of the idler arm. If it is hard to insert, use a vice to hold the arm. After the bushing has been inserted, wipe away any excess grease.

10 Also, apply a thin coat of grease to the shaft portion of the arm bracket and the inner surface of the bushing. Set the shaft portion of the bracket so that the arm will be placed in the right position and tighten to the specified torque by referring to the illustration. **Note:** *The washer should be installed with its knurled surface facing the bushing.*

11 The idler arm assembly should be reassembled with a new self-locking nut.

12 Tighten the idler arm support to the body frame at the specified torque.

13 Connect the idler arm to the relay rod. Tighten the locknut to the specified torque.

14 After the idler arm and relay rod have been tightened, check to be sure that the clearance between the bottom surface of the idler arm and relay rod is within the standard range (see illustration).

15 Install a cotter pin and lock it in place by referring to the illustration.

16 Have the front end of your vehicle aligned by an alignment specialist.

23 Pitman arm – removal and installation

1 Raise the front of the vehicle according to the jacking and towing procedures in the front of this book and support it with jackstands.

2 Remove the cotter pin from the pin hole of the Pitman arm.

3 Remove the Pitman arm locknut and disconnect the Pitman arm from the relay rod by using special tool C-3894-A.

4 Remove the Pitman arm retaining nut from the steering gear box assembly.

5 Remove the Pitman arm from the gear box assembly by using special tool CT-1106.

6 Inspect the Pitman arm for any deformation or cracks. Replace it with a new one if necessary.

7 Installation is the reverse of the removal procedure.

8 When connecting the cross shaft to the Pitman arm, align the slit of the cross shaft tip with the marking on the Pitman arm and tighten them to the specified torque.

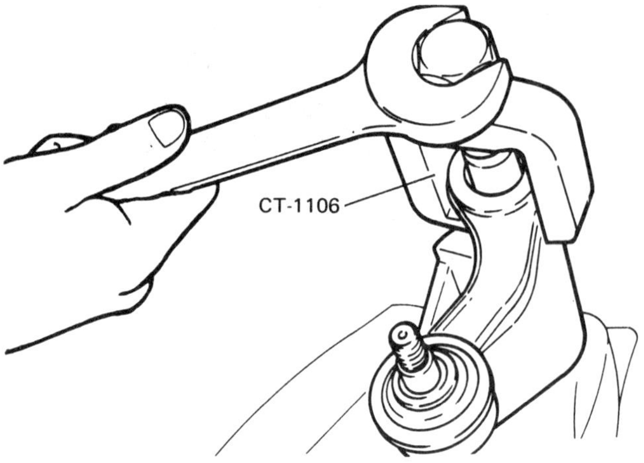

Fig. 11.43 Removing the Pitman arm from the steering gearbox (Sec 23)

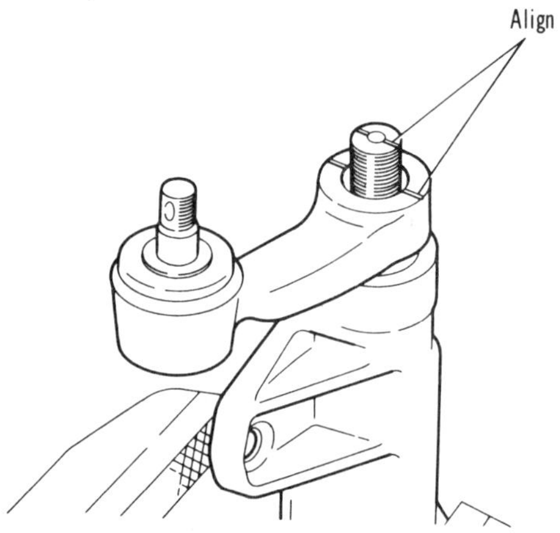

Fig. 11.44 Correct alignment of the Pitman arm to the gearbox cross-shaft (Sec 23)

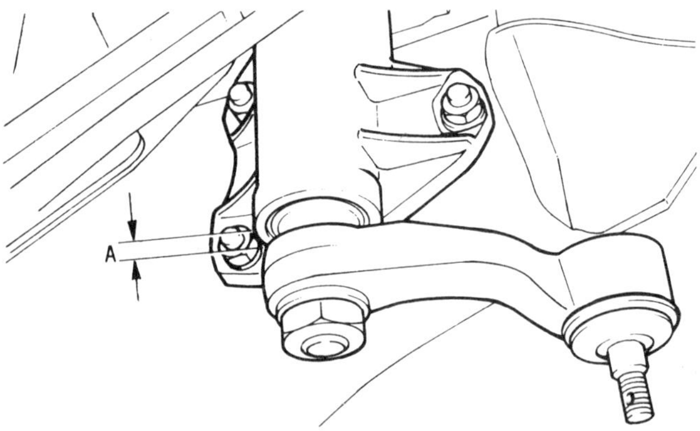

Fig. 11.45 Correct alignment position of the Pitman arm (Sec 23)

9 After tightening the cross shaft to the Pitman arm, make sure that the clearance between the center of the bolt hole in the gear box and in the Pitman arm is within the standard value.

24 Power steering hoses/belt – check, adjustment and replacement

To check, replace or adjust the power steering hoses or belts refer to Chapter 1.

25 Power steering fluid – check and replacement

To check or replace the power steering fluid refer to Chapter 1.

26 Gearbox (manual) – removal and installation

1 Due to the complexity of the component and the special tools and skills required, it is not recommended that the average home mechanic attempt to rebuild a steering gearbox. It would be far more economical, in terms of time and money, to purchase a used, new or rebuilt unit to install in place of the faulty one.
2 Modern steering gearboxes are well-designed and trouble-free, so before concluding that your gearbox is in need or major repairs, check the other steering system components. Worn or damaged shock absorbers, worn or misaligned front-end components, unbalanced wheels, worn or loose wheel bearings and improper tire pressures can produce symptoms similar to those produced by a defective steering gearbox.
3 Raise the front of the vehicle and set it on jackstands. Block the rear tires and set the parking brake to keep the vehicle from rolling.
4 Remove the clamp bolt connecting the steering shaft yoke to the steering gearbox mainshaft.
5 Disconnect the left tie-rod from the relay rod and the Pitman arm from the relay rod by referring to the appropriate Sections in this Chapter.
6 Remove the nuts and bolts that attach the steering gearbox to the frame and remove the gearbox down and out from under the vehicle.
7 To install the gearbox, slip it into place from under the vehicle and insert the bolts that attach it to the frame. Thread on the nuts and tighten them to the specified torque.
8 Connect the Pitman arm and the left tie-rod to the relay rod.
9 Install the clamp bolt in the steering shaft yoke and tighten it to the specified torque.
10 Lower the vehicle to the ground and test drive it.

27 Gearbox (power) – removal and installation

1 As with manual steering gearboxes, it is not recommended that the home mechanic attempt to disassemble or rebuild a power steering gearbox. The gearbox hydraulic components are carefully matched and fitted together at the factory, and unless you know exactly what you are doing, their operation could be adversely affected by taking them apart and putting them back together. If power steering gearbox problems occur, rather than attempting an overhaul, it is advisable to obtain a new or rebuilt unit to install in the vehicle.
2 Power steering pumps are probably the major source of problems encountered with power steering systems, so before deciding to replace or overhaul your power steering gearbox, check the pump and other system components carefully. Improper tire pressure, dragging brakes, faulty balljoints, damaged suspension components and misaligned front-end components can all cause symptoms for which you might at first suspect the steering gear. Again, be sure that the trouble in the system is in the power steering gearbox before rebuilding or replacing it,
3 Place a container under the steering gearbox and remove the fittings that attach the power steering hoses to the steering gearbox. You may find it easier to work from the top of the vehicle when removing the hoses from the gearbox.
4 Raise the front of the vehicle and set it on jackstands. Block the rear tires and set the parking brake to keep the vehicle from rolling.
5 Remove the clamp bolt attaching the steering shaft socket assembly to the power steering gearbox input shaft.
6 Disconnect the left tie-rod from the relay rod and the Pitman arm from the relay rod by referring to the appropriate Sections in this Chapter.
7 Remove the nuts and bolts that attach the steering gearbox to the frame and remove the gearbox down and out from under the vehicle.
8 To install the gearbox, slip it into place from under the vehicle and insert the bolts that attach it to the frame. Thread on the nuts and tighten them to the specified torque.
9 Connect the Pitman arm and the left tie-rod to the relay rod.

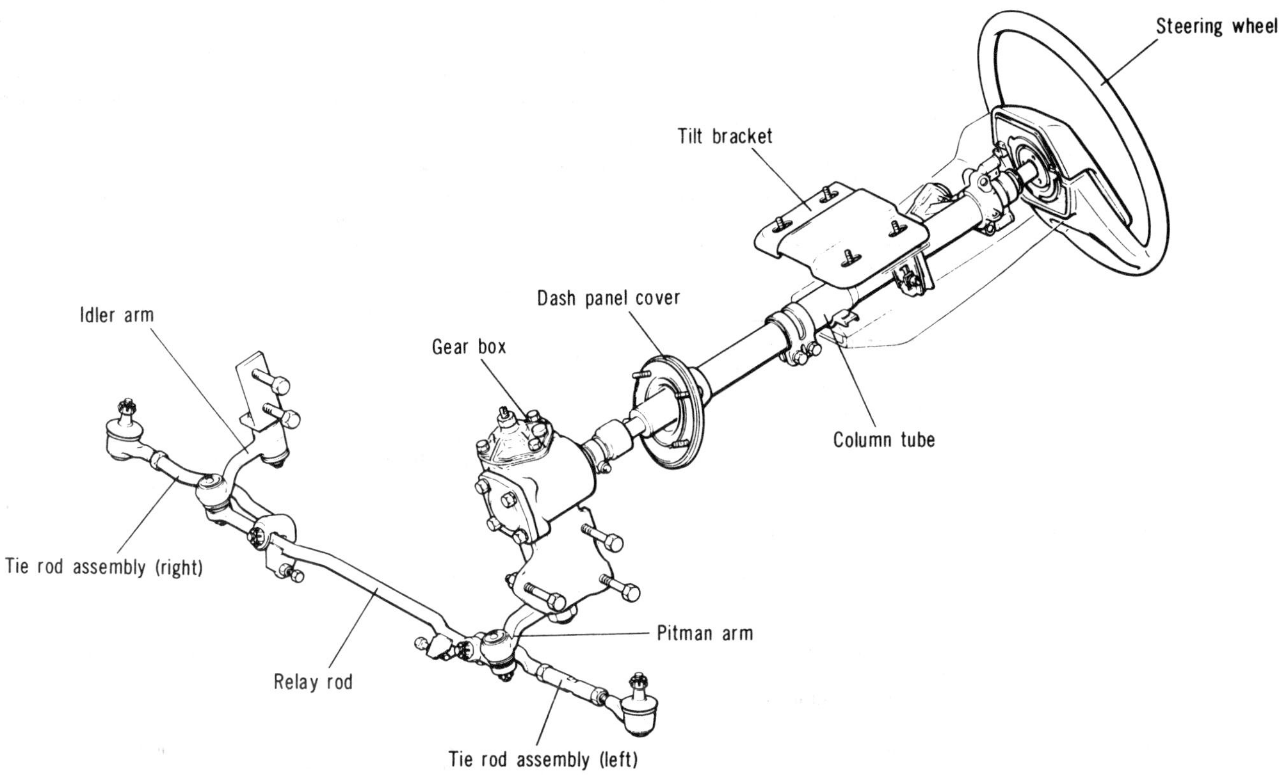

Fig. 11.46 Manual steering system components (Sec 26)

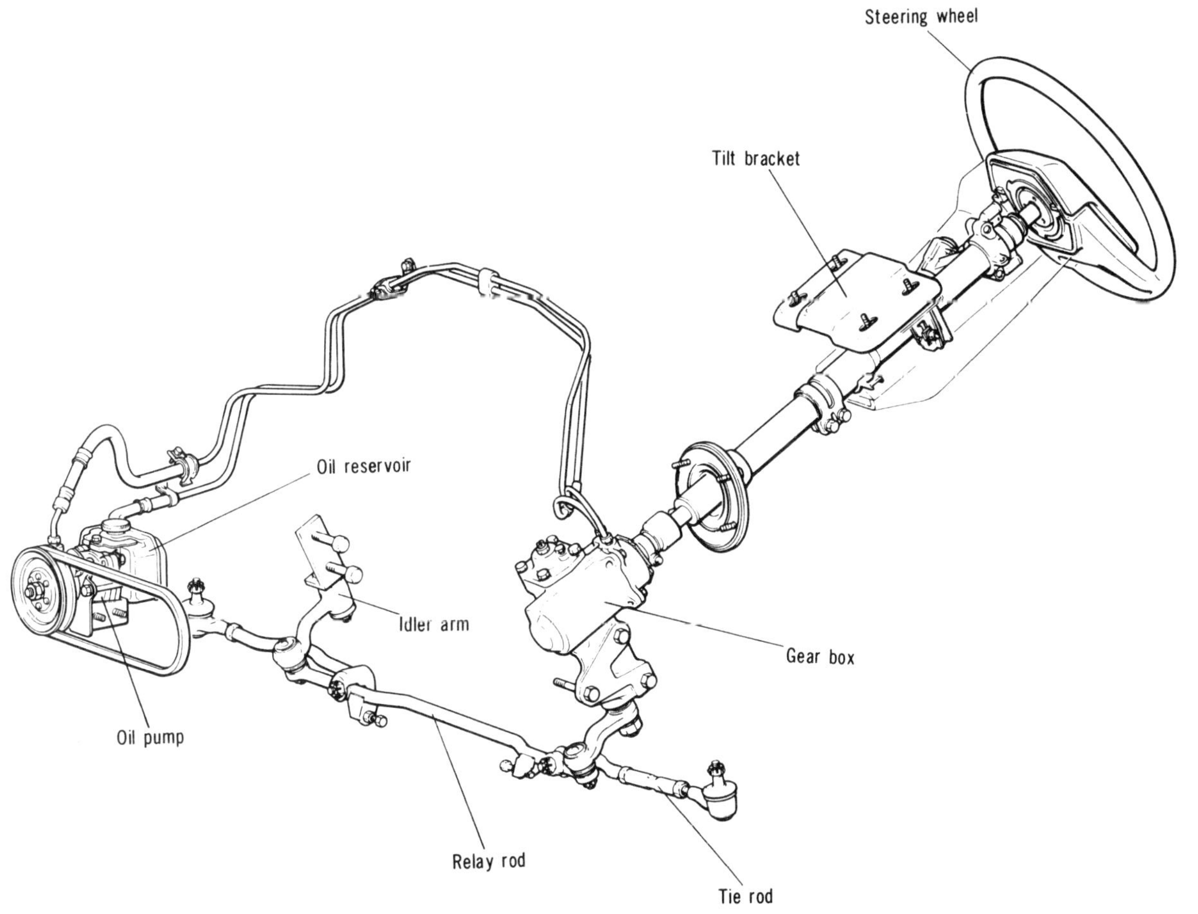

Fig. 11.47 Power steering system components (Sec 27)

10 Install the clamp bolt attaching the power steering shaft socket assembly to the power steering gearbox input shaft. Tighten it to the specified torque.
11 Bleed the system as described in Section 30. Lower the vehicle to the ground and test drive it.

28 Steering – check and adjustment

To check or adjust the steering system, refer to Chapter 1.

29 Pump (power steering) – removal and installation

1 Due to the complexity of the component and the special tools and skills required, it is not recommended that the average home mechanic attempt to rebuild a power steering pump. It would be far more economical, in terms of time and money, to purchase a used, new or rebuilt unit to install in place of the faulty one.
2 Loosen the fittings at the pressure and suction hoses and disconnect the hoses from the pump body. Plug the hoses to prevent the entry of dirt and other contaminants.
3 Loosen and remove the nut and lock washer attaching the pulley to the pump shaft.
4 Loosen the pivot bolts at the bottom of the pump and the adjusting bolt at the top of the pump. Slip the pulley off the pump shaft and separate the pulley from the drivebelt.
5 Remove the adjusting bolt and the pivot bolts and lift the pump out of its mounting bracket.
6 To install the pump, fit it into the mounting bracket and loosely install the pivot bolts and adjusting bolt. Do not tighten them completely.
7 Slip the pulley onto the pump shaft and loosely install the lock washer and nut on the end of the shaft.
8 Slip the drivebelt onto the pulley (make sure it is also on the crankshaft pulley) and tighten the nut on the end of the pump shaft. Squeeze the belt together to keep the pulley from turning while the nut is tightened.
9 Adjust the belt tension by prying the pump body and the engine block with a pry bar or large screwdriver. When the belt has approximately $\frac{1}{4}$ to $\frac{3}{8}$ in of play at the center of its run, tighten the pivot and adjusting bolts securely.
10 Unplug and connect the hoses to the pump body. Do not mix them up. Tighten the fittings securely and make sure the hoses are not twisted or kinked.
11 Fill the reservoir with the specified fluid and bleed the system as described in this Chapter.
12 Test drive the vehicle.

30 Power steering air bleeding procedure

1 Bleeding air out of the power steering system is accomplished in the following manner. Check the fluid level first and add fluid if necessary.
2 Raise and support the front of the vehicle with jackstands.
3 Turn the steering wheel from lock-to-lock two or three times and recheck the fluid level.
4 Start the engine and let it idle. Turn the steering wheel from lock-to-lock again (two or three times) and recheck the fluid level one more time.
5 Lower the front of the vehicle to the ground. Run the engine and again turn the wheels from lock-to-lock two or three times. Recheck the fluid level. Position the wheels in the straight ahead position.
6 Bleeding is complete if the fluid level did not rise, from the Full mark, more than 0.20 in (5 mm) and if no foaming is observed when the engine is stopped.

Chapter 12 Bodywork

Contents

Specifications

Torque specifications	ft-lb	Nm
Door hinge	9 to 19	13 to 25
Front/rear seat belts	17 to 47	23 to 64
Hood latch nut	9.5 to 14	13 to 19

1 General information

The body and frame is of unitized steel, welded, construction. Certain components are particularly vulnerable to accident damage and can be unbolted and replaced with new units. Among these parts are body molding, bumpers, front fenders, doors, hood, trunk lid and glass.

2 Body exterior – maintenance

1 The condition of your vehicle's body is of considerable importance as it is on this that the resale value will mainly depend. It is much more difficult to repair neglected bodywork than to replace mechanical components. The hidden portions of the body, such as the wheel arches, fender skirts, frame and engine compartment, are equally important, although obviously not requiring as frequent attention as the exterior paint.
2 Once a year or every 12 000 miles it is a good idea to have the underside of the body steam cleaned. All traces of dirt and oil will have to be removed and the underside can then be inspected carefully for rust, damaged hydraulic brake lines, frayed electrical wiring and similar problems. The front suspension should be greased after completion of this job.
3 At the same time, clean the engine and the engine compartment with a water-soluble cleaner.
4 The fender wells should be given particular attention, since undercoating can easily come away and stones and dirt thrown up from the wheels can soon cause the paint to chip and flake, and allow rust to set in. If rust is found, clean down to the bare metal and apply an anti-rust paint.
5 The body should be washed once a week or when dirty. Thoroughly wet the vehicle to soften the dirt and then wash it down with a soft sponge and plenty of clean water. If the surplus dirt is not washed off very gently, in time it will wear the paint down.
6 Spots of tar thrown up from the road surfaces are best removed with a cloth soaked in a cleaner made especially for this purpose.
7 Once every six months, or more frequently depending on the weather conditions, give the body and chrome trim a thorough wax job. If a chrome cleaner is used to remove rust on any of the vehicle's plated parts, remember that the cleaner can also remove part of the chrome, so use it sparingly.

3 Upholstery and carpets – maintenance

1 Remove the carpets or mats and thoroughly vacuum the interior of the vehicle every three months (more frequently if necessary).
2 Beat out the carpets and vacuum them if they are very dirty. If the upholstery is soiled, apply an upholstery cleaner with a damp sponge and wipe if off with a clean dry cloth.
3 Consult your local dealer or auto parts stores for cleaners made especially for newer automotive upholstery fabrics. Always test the cleaner in an inconspicuous place.

4 Vinyl trim – maintenance

Vinyl trim should not be cleaned with detergents, caustic soaps or petroleum based cleaners. Plain soap and water or a mild vinyl cleaner is best for stains. Test a small area for color fastness. Bubbles under the vinyl can be corrected by piercing them with a pin and then working the air out.

5 Hinges and locks – maintenance

Every 3000 miles or 3 months, the door, hood and trunk hinges and locks should be lubricated with a few drops of oil. The door and trunk lid striker plates should also be given a thin coat of grease to reduce wear and ensure free movement.

6 Body repair – minor damage

Refer to the accompanying photos which illustrate the following procedures.

Repair of minor scratches

If the scratch is very superficial and does not penetrate to the metal of the body, repair is very simple. Lightly rub the area of the scratch with a fine rubbing compound to remove loose paint from the scratch and to clear the surrounding paint of wax buildup. Rinse the area with clean water.

Apply touch-up paint to the scratch using a small brush. Continue to apply thin layers of paint until the surface of the paint in the scratch is level with the surrounding paint. Allow the new paint at least two weeks to harden, then blend it into the surrounding paint by rubbing with a very fine rubbing compound. Finally, apply a coat of wax to the scratch area.

If the scratch has penetrated the paint and exposed the metal of the body, causing the metal to rust, a different repair technique is required. Remove any loose rust from the bottom of the scratch with a pocket knife, then apply rust inhibiting paint to prevent the formation of rust in the future. Using a rubber or nylon applicator, coat the scratched area with glaze-type filler. If required, this filler can be mixed with thinner to provide a very thin paste which is ideal for filling narrow scratches. Before the glaze filler in the scratch hardens, wrap a piece of smooth cotton cloth around the top of a finger. Dip the cloth in thinner and then quickly wipe it along the surface of the scratch. This will ensure that the surface of the filler is slightly hollowed. The scratch can now be painted over as described earlier in this Section.

Repair of dents

When deep denting of the vehicle's body has taken place, the first task is to pull the dent out until the area nearly attains its original shape. There is little point in trying to restore the original shape completely as the metal in the damaged area will have stretched on impact and cannot be completely restored to its original contours. It is better to bring the level of the dent up to a point which is about $\frac{1}{8}$ inch below the level of the surrounding metal. In cases where the dent is very shallow, it is not worth trying to pull it out at all.

If the underside of the dent is accessible, it can be hammered out gently from behind using a mallet with a wooden or plastic head. While doing this, hold a block of wood firmly against the metal to absorb the hammer blows and prevent large areas of the metal from being stretched out.

If the dent is in a section of the body which has double layers, or some other factor making it inaccessible from behind, a different technique is in order. Drill several small holes through the metal inside the damaged area, particularly in the deeper sections. Screw long self-tapping screws into the holes just enough for them to get a good grip in the metal. Now the dent can be removed by pulling on the protruding heads of the screws with a pair of locking pliers.

The next stage of the repair is the removal of the paint from the damaged area and from an inch or so of the surrounding 'sound' metal. This is easily accomplished by using a wire brush or sanding disc in a drill motor, although it can be done just as effectively by hand with sandpaper. To complete the preparation for filling, score the surface of the bare metal with a screwdriver or the tang of a file (or drill small holes in the affected area). This will provide a really good 'grip' for the filler material. To complete the repair, see the Section on filling and painting.

Repair of rust holes or gashes

Remove all paint from the affected area and from an inch or so of the surrounding 'sound' metal using a sanding disc or wire brush mounted in a drill motor. If these are not available, a few sheets of sandpaper will do the job just as effectively. With the paint removed, you will be able to determine the severity of the corrosion and, therefore, decide whether to replace the whole panel, if possible, or to repair the affected area. New body panels are not as expensive as most people think and it is often quicker and more desirable to install a new panel than to attempt to repair large areas of rust.

Remove all trim pieces from the affected area (except those which will act as a guide to the original shape of the damaged body (ie. headlamp shells, etc.). Then, using metal snips or a hacksaw blade, remove all loose metal and any other metal that is badly affected by rust. Hammer the edges of the hole in to create a slight depression for the filler material.

Wire brush the affected area to remove the powdery rust from the surface of the metal. If the back of the rusted area is accessible, treat it with rust inhibiting paint.

Before filling can be done, it will be necessary to block the hole in some way. This can be accomplished with sheet metal riveted or screwed into place or by stuffing the hole with wire mesh.

Once the hole is blocked off, the affected area can be filled and painted (see the following Section on filling and painting).

Filling and painting

Many types of body fillers are available but generally speaking, body repair kits which contain filler paste and a tube of resin hardener are best for this type of repair work. A wide, flexible plastic or nylon applicator will be necessary for imparting a smooth contoured finish to the surface of the filler material.

Mix up a small amount of filler on a clean piece of wood or cardboard (use the hardener sparingly). Follow the maker's instructions on the package, otherwise the filler will set incorrectly.

Using the applicator, apply the filler paste to the prepared area. Draw the applicator across the surface of the filler to achieve the desired contour and to level the filler surface. As soon as a contour that approximates the correct one is achieved, stop working the paste. If you continue, the paste will begin to stick to the applicator. Continue to add thin layers of filler paste at 20-minute intervals until the level of the filler is just above the surrounding metal.

Once the filler has hardened, excess can be removed using a body file. From then on, progressively finer grades of sandpaper should be used, starting with a 180-grit paper and finishing with 600-grit wet-or-dry paper. Always wrap the sandpaper around a flat rubber or wooden block, otherwise the surface of the filler will not be completely flat. During the sanding of the filler surface, the wet-or-dry paper should be periodically rinsed in water. This will ensure that a very smooth finish is produced in the final stage.

At this point, the repair area should be surrounded by a ring of bare metal, which in turn should be encircled by the finely feathered edge of the good paint. Rinse the repair area with clean water until all of the dust produced by the sanding operation is gone.

Spray the entire area with a light coat of primer. This will reveal any imperfections in the surface of the filler. Repair these imperfections with fresh filler paste or glaze filler and once more smooth the surface with sandpaper. Repeat this spray-and-repair procedure until you are satisfied that the surface of the filler and the feathered edge of the paint are perfect. Rinse the area with clean water and allow it to dry completely.

The repair area is now ready for painting. Paint spraying must be carried out in warm, dry, windless and dustfree atmosphere. These conditions can be created if you have access to a large indoor working area but if you are forced to work in the open, you will have to pick your day very carefully. If you are working indoors, dousing the floor in the work area with water will help to settle the dust which would otherwise be in the air. If the repair area is confined to one body panel, mask off the surrounding panels. This will help to minimize the effects of a slight mismatch in paint color. Trim pieces such as chrome strips, door handles, etc., will also need to be masked off or removed. Use masking tape and several thicknesses of newspaper for the masking operations.

Before spraying, shake the paint can thoroughly, then spray a test area until the technique is mastered. Cover the repair area with a thick coat of primer. The thickness should be built up using several thin layers of primer rather than one thick one. Using 600-grit wet-or-dry sandpaper, rub down the surface of the primer until it is very smooth. While doing this, the work area should be thoroughly rinsed with water, and the wet-or-dry sandpaper periodically rinsed as well. Allow the primer to dry before spraying additional coats.

Spray on the top coat, again building up the thickness by using several thin layers of paint. Begin spraying in the center of the repair area and then, using a circular motion, work out until the whole repair area and about two inches of the surrounding original paint is covered. Remove all masking material 10 to 15 minutes after spraying on the final coat of paint. Allow the new paint at least two weeks to harden, then using a very fine rubbing compound, blend the edges of the paint into the existing paint. Finally, apply a coat of wax.

7 Body and frame repairs – major damage

1 Major damage must be repaired by an auto body/frame repair shop with the necessary welding and hydraulic straightening equipment.

2 If the damage has been serious, it is vital that the frame be checked for correct alignment, as the handling of the vehicle will be affected. Other problems, such as excessive tire wear and wear in the transmission and steering may also occur.

8 Glass replacement – general information

When any windows need to be replaced, it is recommended that it be done by a competent auto glass installer. They will have the right tools and adhesives to get the job done properly.

If you can have the windows installed cheaper with the molding off, refer to the body molding Section in this Chapter and remove the molding yourself before the glass is replaced.

9 Hood – removal, installation and adjustment

1 To remove the hood, first release the springs, then scribe a line (or use paint) around the hinge bolt heads to ensure correct alignment when the hood is installed. Have an assistant hold the hood while the bolts are loosened. Finish removing the bolts while supporting the hood on both sides, then carefully lift it off.

2 Installation is the reverse of removal.

3 To adjust the hood for a good fit, refer to the following procedure.

4 Loosen the hood hinge bolts and move the hood in the desired direction (left or right; forward or backwards).

5 Loosen the adjustment bumper screws at the front corners of the hood to raise or lower the front of the hood until it is even with the tops of the fenders.

6 Loosen the hood lock bolts and move the lock in the desired direction to obtain a snug fit when closed.

10 Trunk lid – removal, installation and adjustment

1 Remove the bolts holding the lid to its hinges and remove the trunk lid.

2 Remove the spring and the lock mechanism from the lid.

3 Installation is the reverse of removal.

4 To adjust the trunk lid for a good fit, refer to the following procedure.

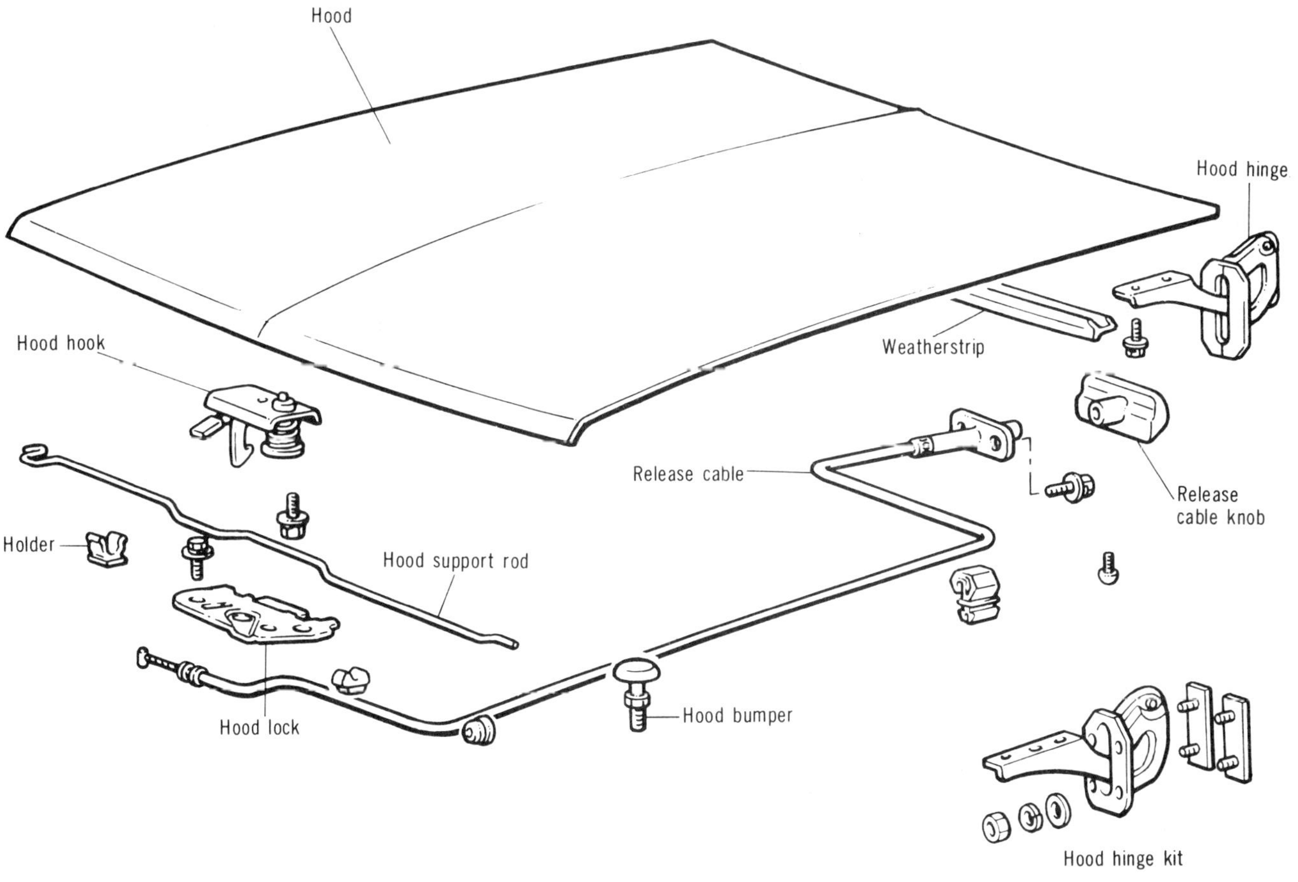

Fig. 12.1 Front hood components – exploded view (Sec 9)

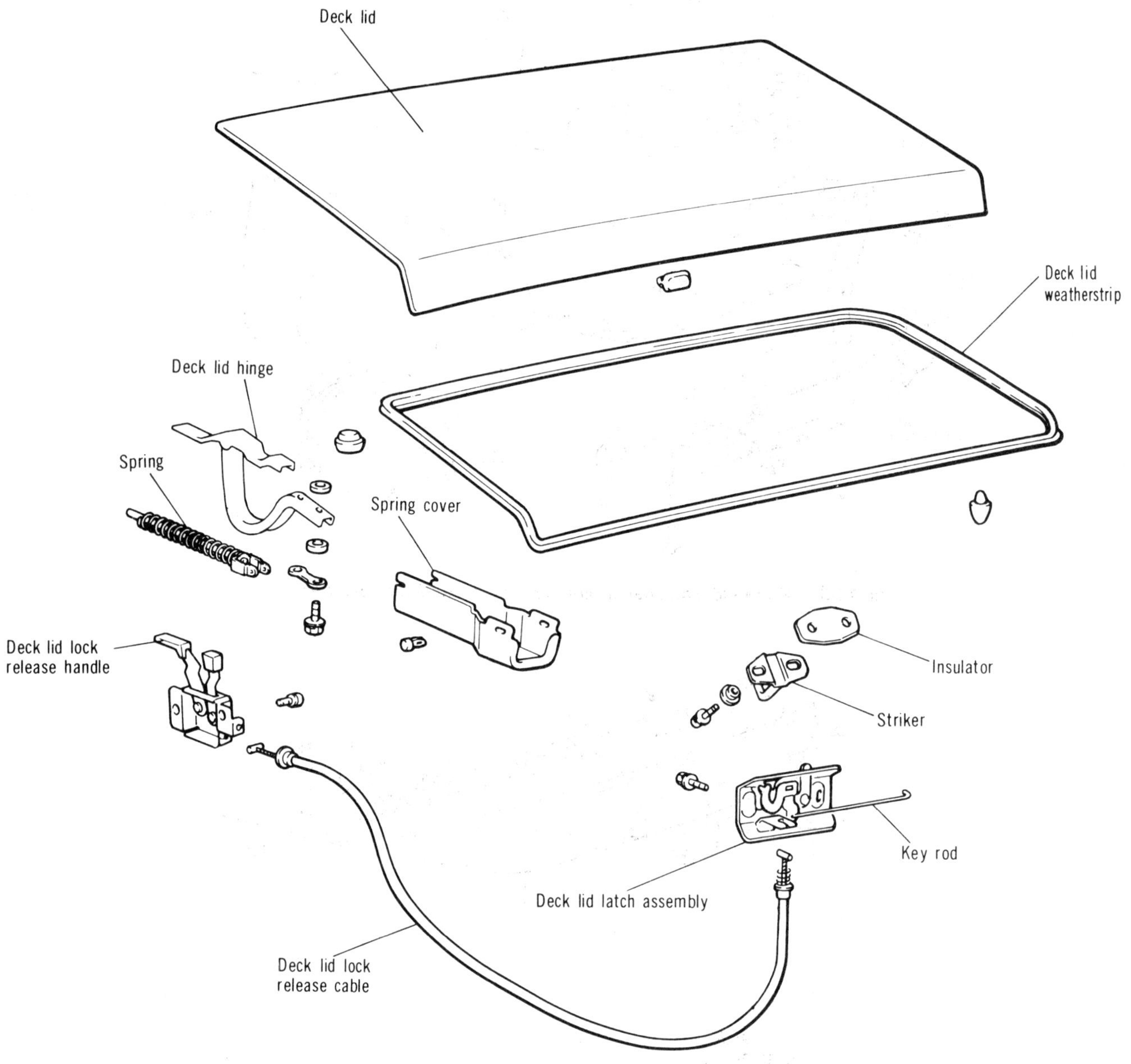

Fig. 12.2 Trunk (deck) lid components – exploded view (Sec 10)

5 Loosen the hinge bolts and move the lid in the direction desired (left or right; forward or backward).
6 Remove the hinge bolts and add spacers (washers) between the hinge and the trunk lid to raise or lower the front.
7 Loosen the adjustment cushions at the rear corners of the lid to raise or lower it.

11 Fenders/front panels – removal and installation

1 In order to remove the front fenders of the vehicle, the front panels must be removed first.
2 Remove the front radiator grill mounting screws. Remove the radiator grill by pulling it forward.
3 Disconnect the front turn signal light connector and then unfasten the harness mounting clip.
4 Remove the bumper by referring to Section 12.
5 Remove the front skirt panel.
6 Remove the front end guide assembly panel.
7 Now remove the fenders by disconnecting the side marker light connectors.
8 Remove the fender mounting bolts and then remove the fender.
9 Remove the fender shield plate and the fender shield rubber.
10 Installation is the reverse of the removal procedure.
11 During installation, touch-up the fender inner surface if the coating is damaged.
12 Since improper sealing of the wheel well portion will cause corrosion, be sure to install the fender shield plate and rubber.
13 When installing the fender to the body, be sure that the clearance between the body and fender is uniform.

12 Front bumper – removal and installation

1 In order to remove the bumper, the radiator grille has to be removed first.
2 Be sure to disconnect the turn signal connectors.
3 Remove the front bumper mounting hardware then remove the front bumper.
4 To disassemble the bumper, remove the turn signal light.
5 Remove the mounting screws which connect the front bumper upper plate and the front bumper lower plate to the reinforcement.

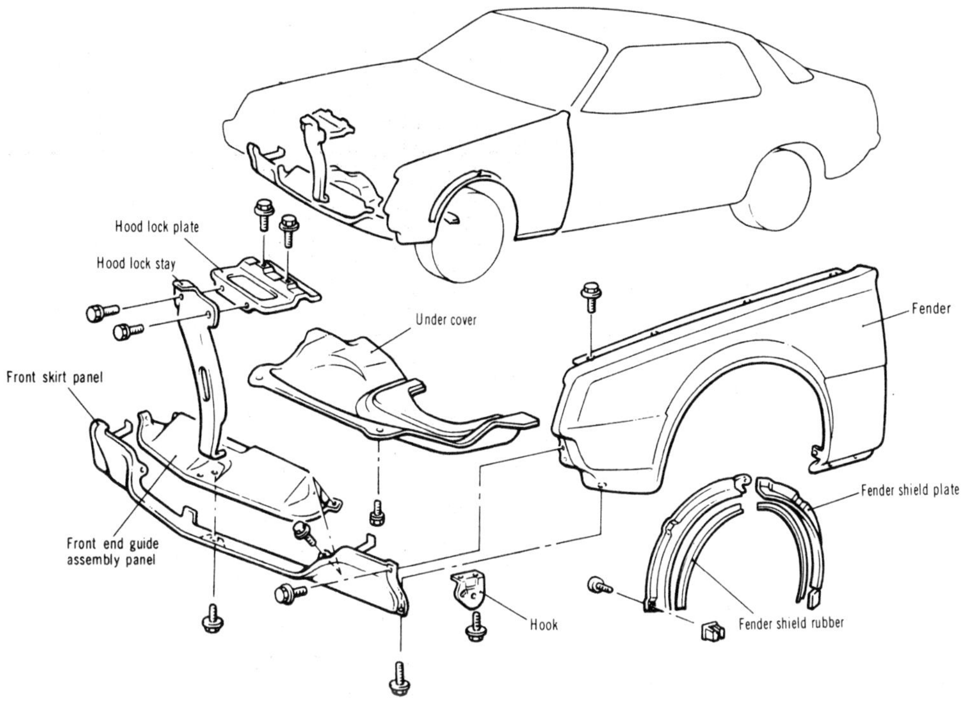

Fig. 12.3 Front fenders and panels components – exploded view (Sec 11)

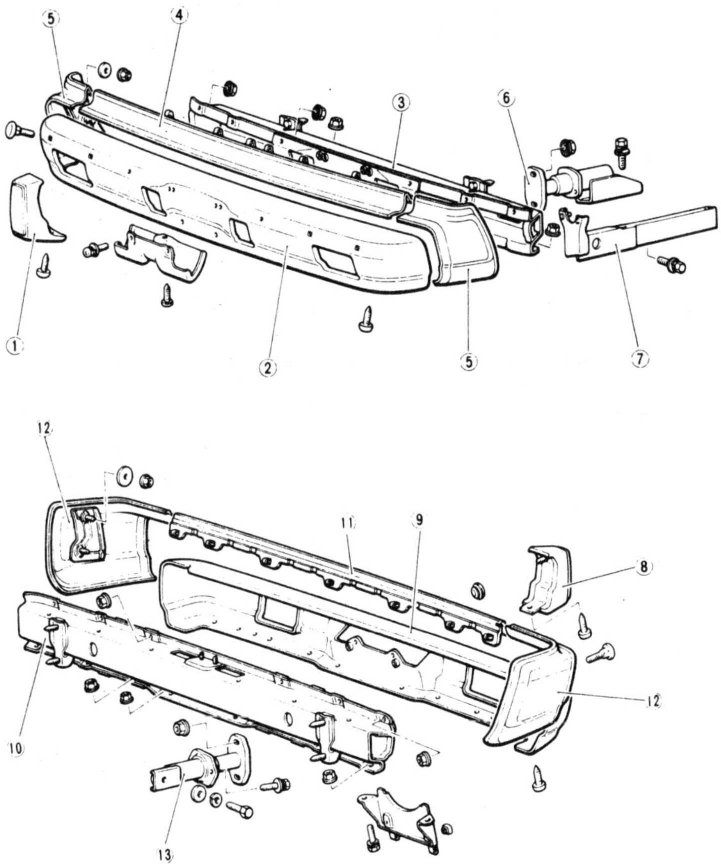

Fig. 12.4 Front/rear bumpers components (1978 through 1980) – exploded view (Secs 12 & 13)

1 Front bumper guard
2 Front bumper face
3 Front bumper reinforcement
4 Front filler, center
5 Front filler, side
6 Front shock isolator
7 Front bumper stay
8 Rear bumper guard
9 Rear bumper face
10 Rear bumper reinforcement
11 Rear filler, center
12 Rear filler, side
13 Rear shock isolator

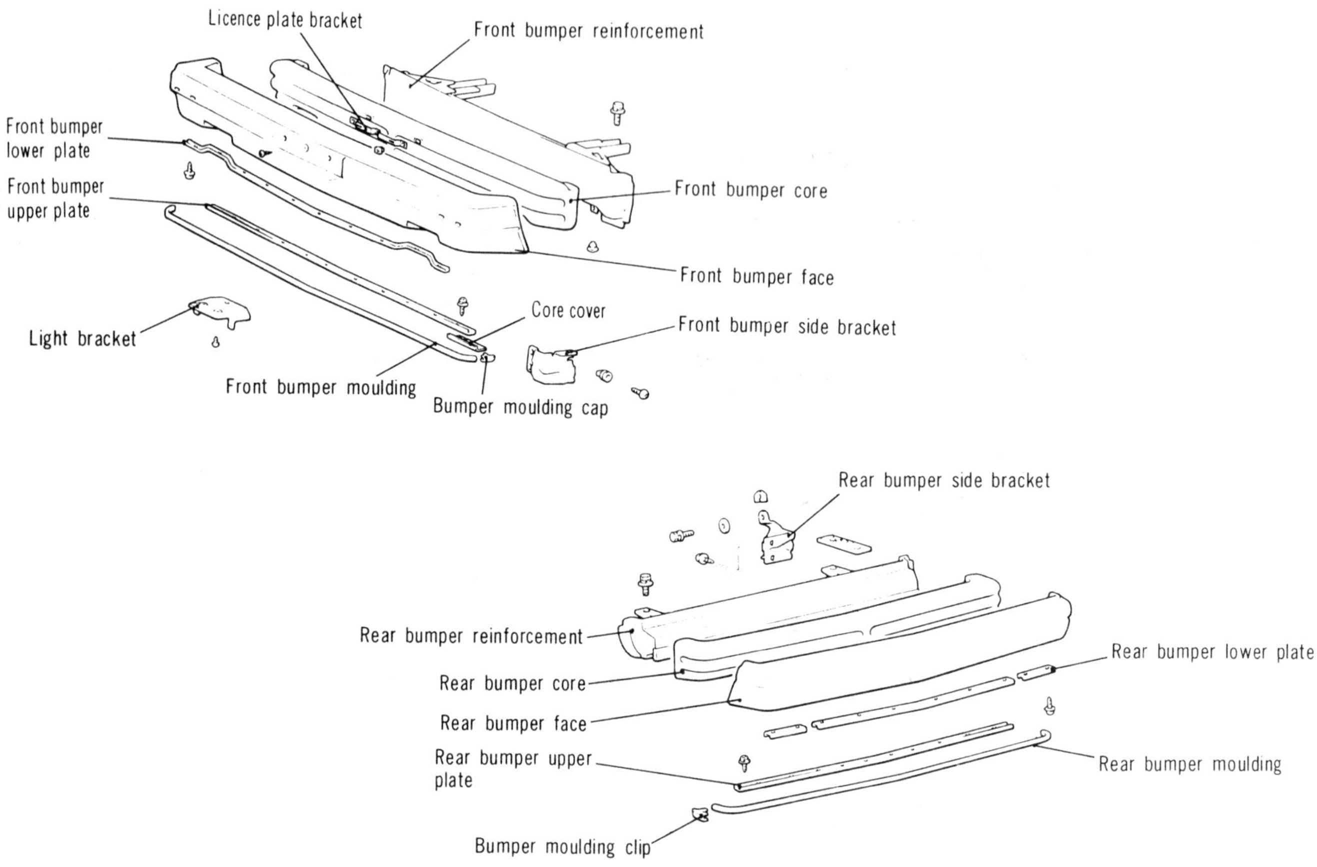

Fig. 12.5 Front/rear bumpers components (1981 through 1983) – exploded view (Secs 12 & 13)

6 Remove the mounting screws which connect the side brackets to the reinforcement and then separate the bumper from the reinforcement. Separate the bumper face from the bumper core.
7 Reassembly and installation of the bumper is the reverse of the removal and disassembly procedure.
8 Be sure to check the bumper alignment prior to final tightening of the retaining bolts.
9 Reconnect the turn signal connector and install the front grille.

13 Rear bumper – removal and installation

1 Remove the bumper stay and the side bracket mounting bolts.
2 Remove the mounting bolts of the tie down brackets from the rear bumper reinforcement and then remove the rear bumper.
3 To dismantle the rear bumper remove the mounting screws which connect the rear bumper upper plate and lower plate to the reinforcement.
4 Remove the mounting screws which connect the side brackets to the reinforcement and then separate the bumper from the reinforcement.
5 Separate the bumper face from the bumper core.
6 Reassembly and installation of the rear bumper is the reverse of the disassembly and removal procedure.
7 Make sure to check the bumper alignment prior to final tightening of the retaining bolts.
8 Reconnect the turn signal indicator connection and the license plate light connection when finished.

14 Body molding – removal and installation

1 The windshield outer molding can be removed by first removing the windshield wiper arm. Then remove the clips from the side, lower and upper molding and detach the molding. Installation is the reverse of removal.
2 The windshield inner molding is removed by first removing the inside rear view mirror. Then remove the front corner pillars and the roof front trim. Installation is the reverse of removal.
3 The rear outer molding can be detached by removing the clips, followed by the molding. Installation is the reverse of removal.
4 The rear inner molding is detached by first removing the rear seat cushion and the backrest. Remove the rear corner pillar, the roof side trim, the package tray board and the package tray pad. After you remove the roof rear trim, the glass can be removed. Installation is the reverse of removal. **Note**: *Be careful not to damage the defogger element.*
5 The quarter window outer molding can be detached by first removing the clips from the molding.
6 The quarter window inner molding is detached by first removing the rear seat cushion and the backrest. Then remove the rear corner pillar and the roof side trim. The glass can now be removed also.
7 The side detached outer moldings can be detached by first removing the clips from the roof drip, the door frame, the door trim, the wheel well, the scuff plate and the rocker panel.
8 The outside door protection molding is removed by inserting a screwdriver behind the molding and then detaching it carefully from the clips.
9 To install the door protection molding, insert the molding clips into the vehicle and then install the molding to the clips.

15 Door trim panels – removal and installation

1 To remove the trim panels, first remove the retaining clip on the window crank then pull off the crank. Remove the arm rest. Detach the inside handle cover, then carefully pry off the door panel.
2 All of the inside door components are easily accessible, but be

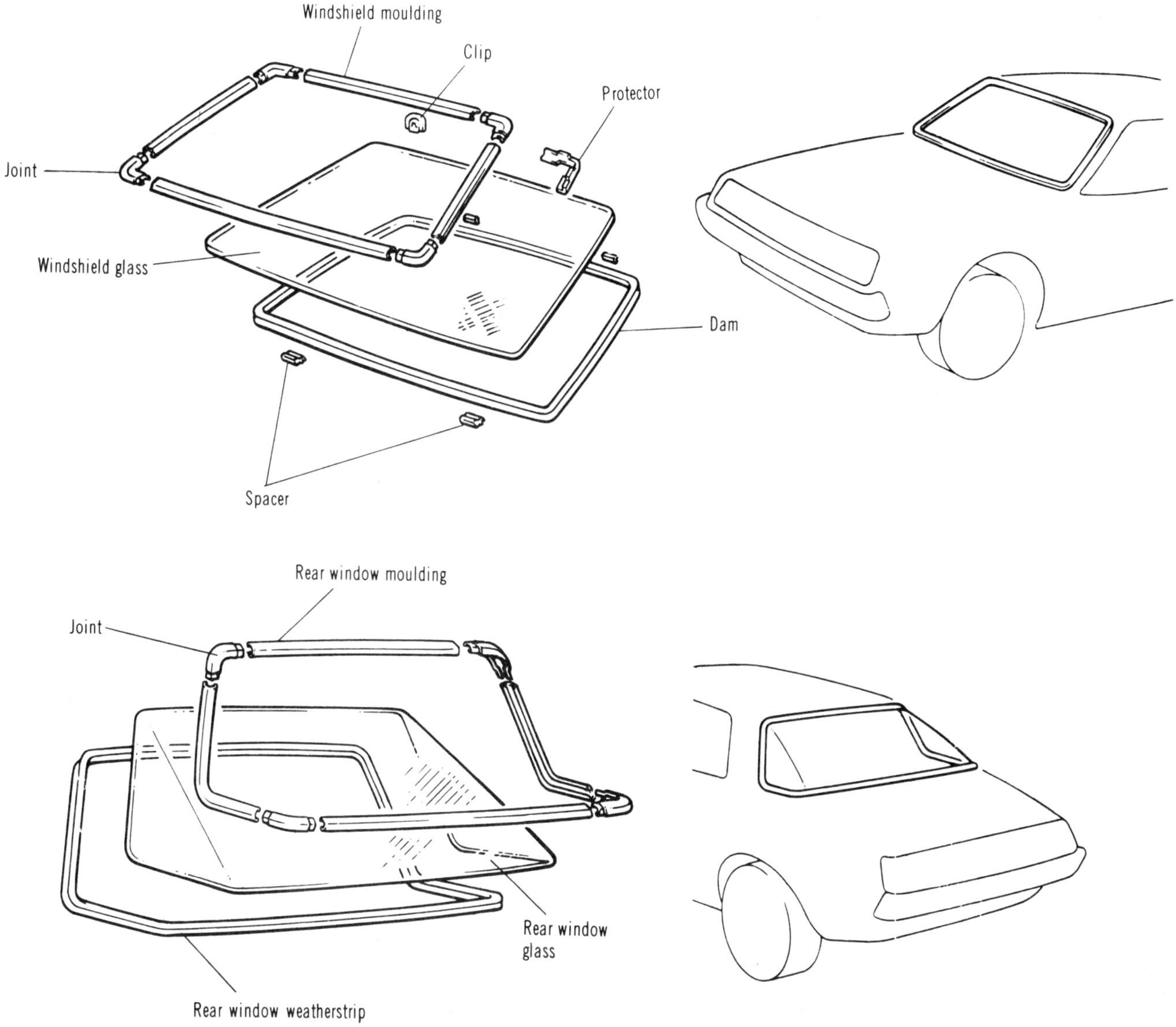

Fig. 12.6 Front/rear window molding components – exploded view (Sec 14)

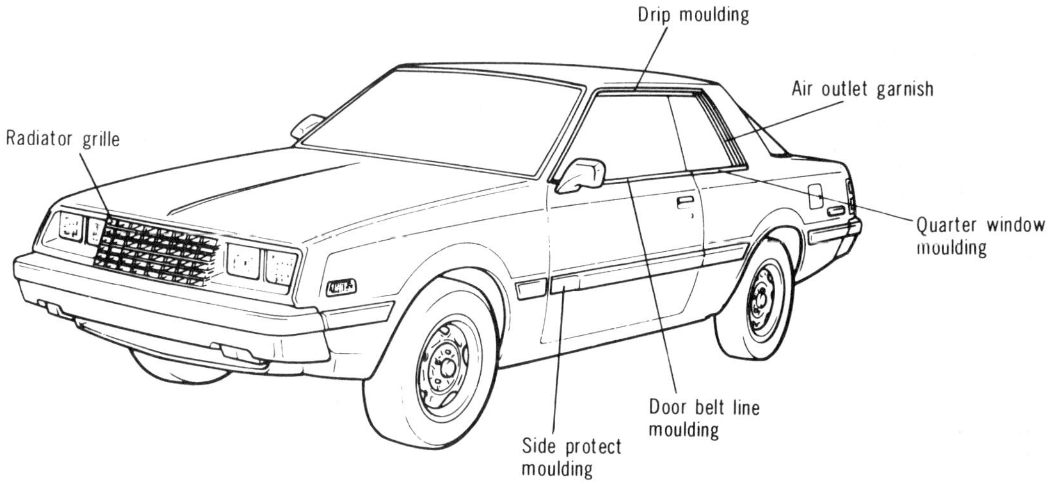

Fig. 12.7 Exterior molding components – exploded view (Sec 14)

These photos illustrate a method of repairing simple dents. They are intended to supplement *Body repair - minor damage* in this Chapter and should not be used as the sole instructions for body repair on these vehicles.

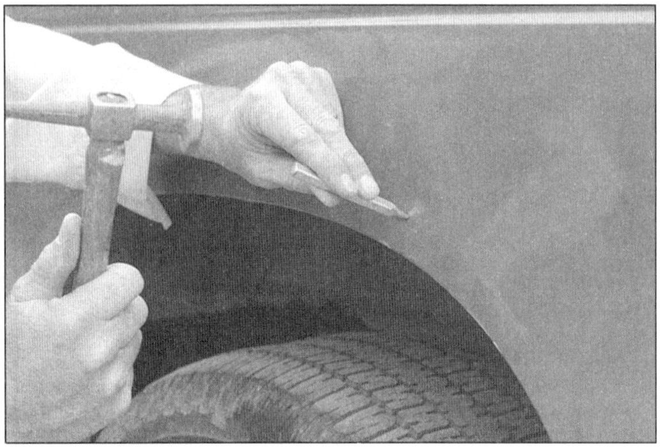

1 If you can't access the backside of the body panel to hammer out the dent, pull it out with a slide-hammer-type dent puller. In the deepest portion of the dent or along the crease line, drill or punch hole(s) at least one inch apart . . .

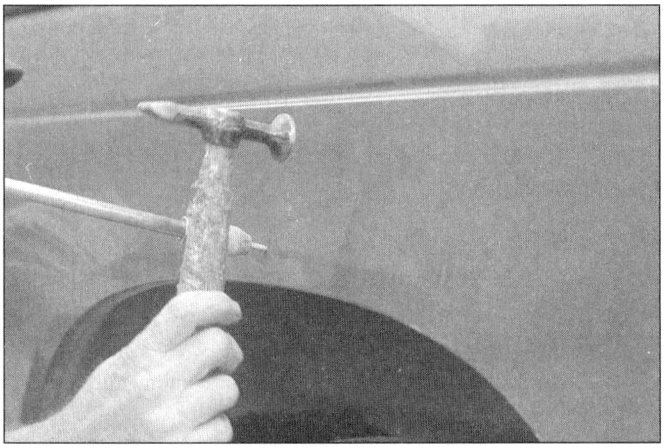

2 . . . then screw the slide-hammer into the hole and operate it. Tap with a hammer near the edge of the dent to help 'pop' the metal back to its original shape. When you're finished, the dent area should be close to its original contour and about 1/8-inch below the surface of the surrounding metal

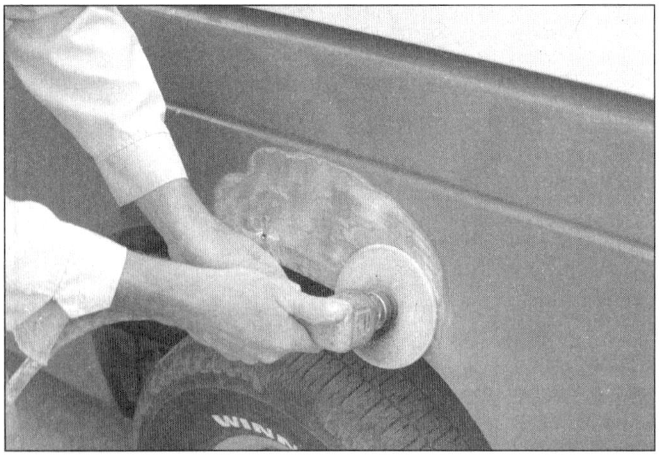

3 Using coarse-grit sandpaper, remove the paint down to the bare metal. Hand sanding works fine, but the disc sander shown here makes the job faster. Use finer (about 320-grit) sandpaper to feather-edge the paint at least one inch around the dent area

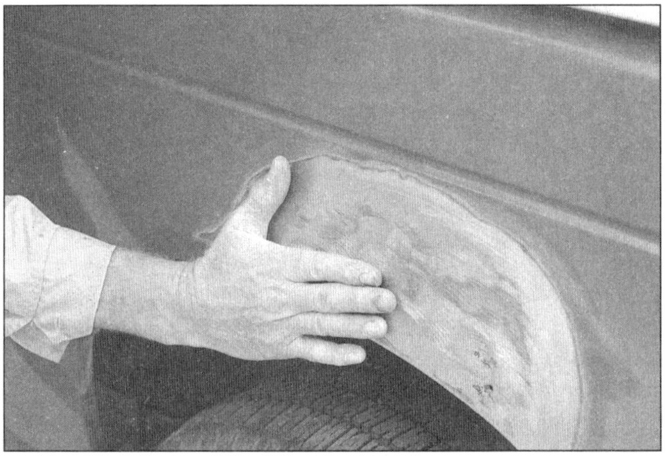

4 When the paint is removed, touch will probably be more helpful than sight for telling if the metal is straight. Hammer down the high spots or raise the low spots as necessary. Clean the repair area with wax/silicone remover

5 Following label instructions, mix up a batch of plastic filler and hardener. The ratio of filler to hardener is critical, and, if you mix it incorrectly, it will either not cure properly or cure too quickly (you won't have time to file and sand it into shape)

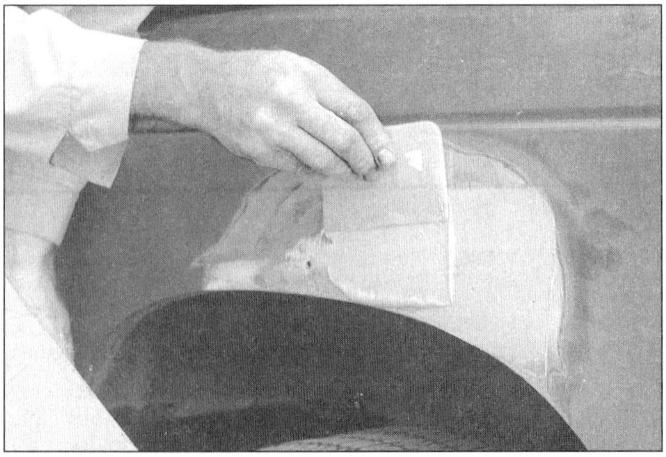

6 Working quickly so the filler doesn't harden, use a plastic applicator to press the body filler firmly into the metal, assuring it bonds completely. Work the filler until it matches the original contour and is slightly above the surrounding metal

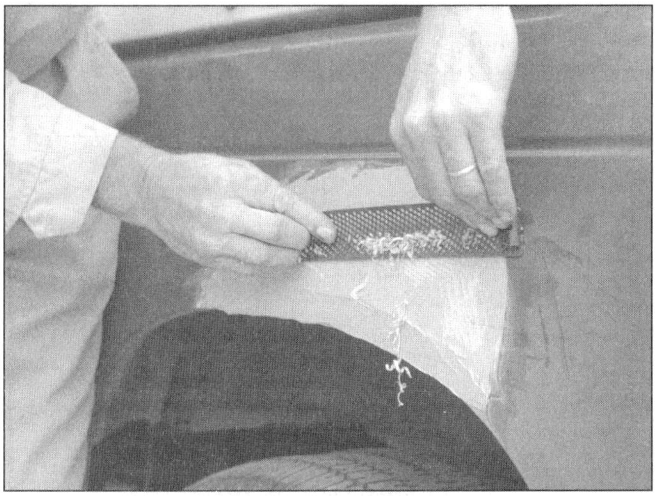

7 Let the filler harden until you can just dent it with your fingernail. Use a body file or Surform tool (shown here) to rough-shape the filler

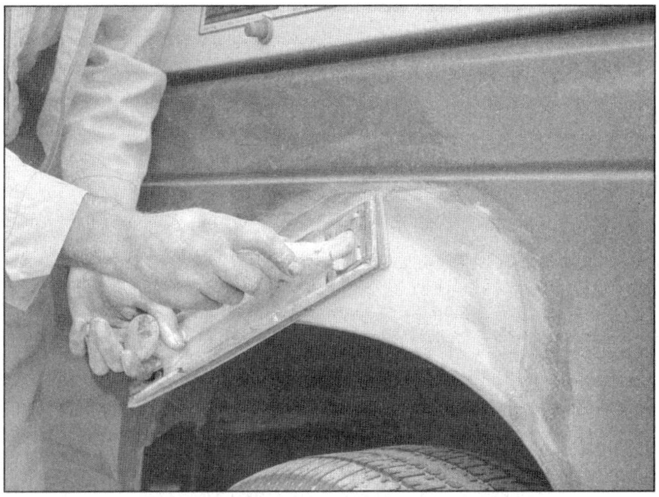

8 Use coarse-grit sandpaper and a sanding board or block to work the filler down until it's smooth and even. Work down to finer grits of sandpaper - always using a board or block - ending up with 360 or 400 grit

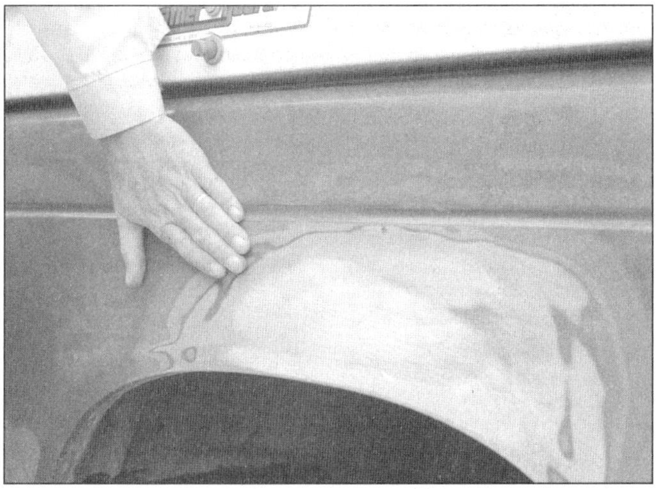

9 You shouldn't be able to feel any ridge at the transition from the filler to the bare metal or from the bare metal to the old paint. As soon as the repair is flat and uniform, remove the dust and mask off the adjacent panels or trim pieces

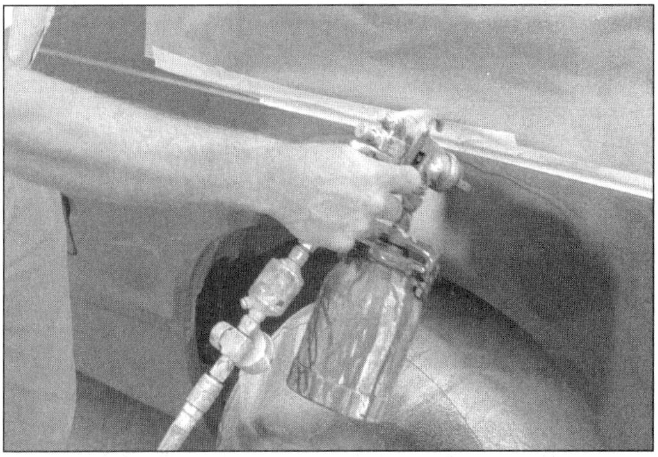

10 Apply several layers of primer to the area. Don't spray the primer on too heavy, so it sags or runs, and make sure each coat is dry before you spray on the next one. A professional-type spray gun is being used here, but aerosol spray primer is available inexpensively from auto parts stores

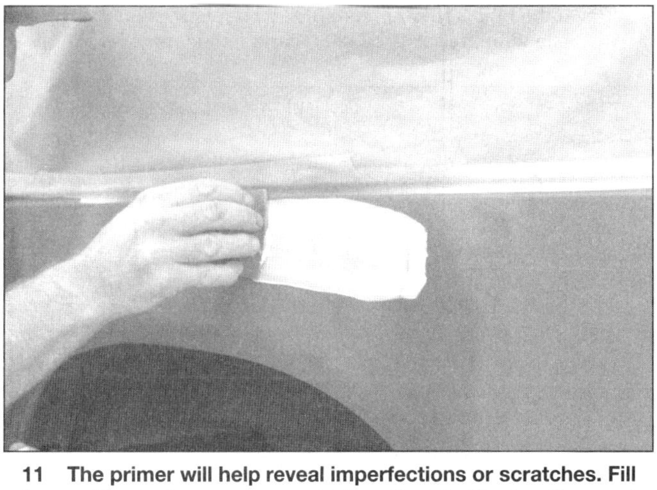

11 The primer will help reveal imperfections or scratches. Fill these with glazing compound. Follow the label instructions and sand it with 360 or 400-grit sandpaper until it's smooth. Repeat the glazing, sanding and respraying until the primer reveals a perfectly smooth surface

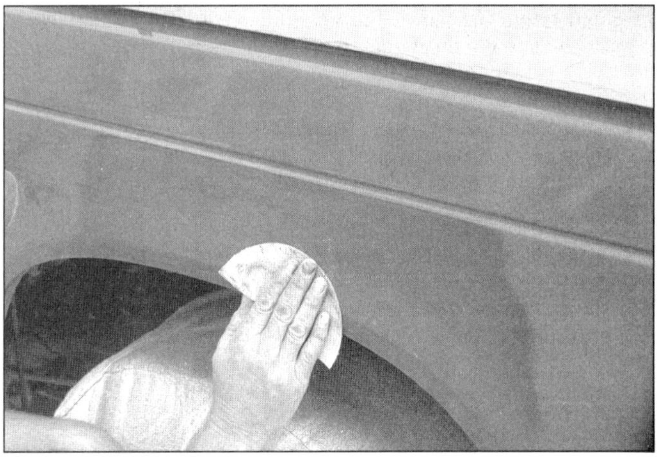

12 Finish sand the primer with very fine sandpaper (400 or 600-grit) to remove the primer overspray. Clean the area with water and allow it to dry. Use a tack rag to remove any dust, then apply the finish coat. Don't attempt to rub out or wax the repair area until the paint has dried completely (at least two weeks)

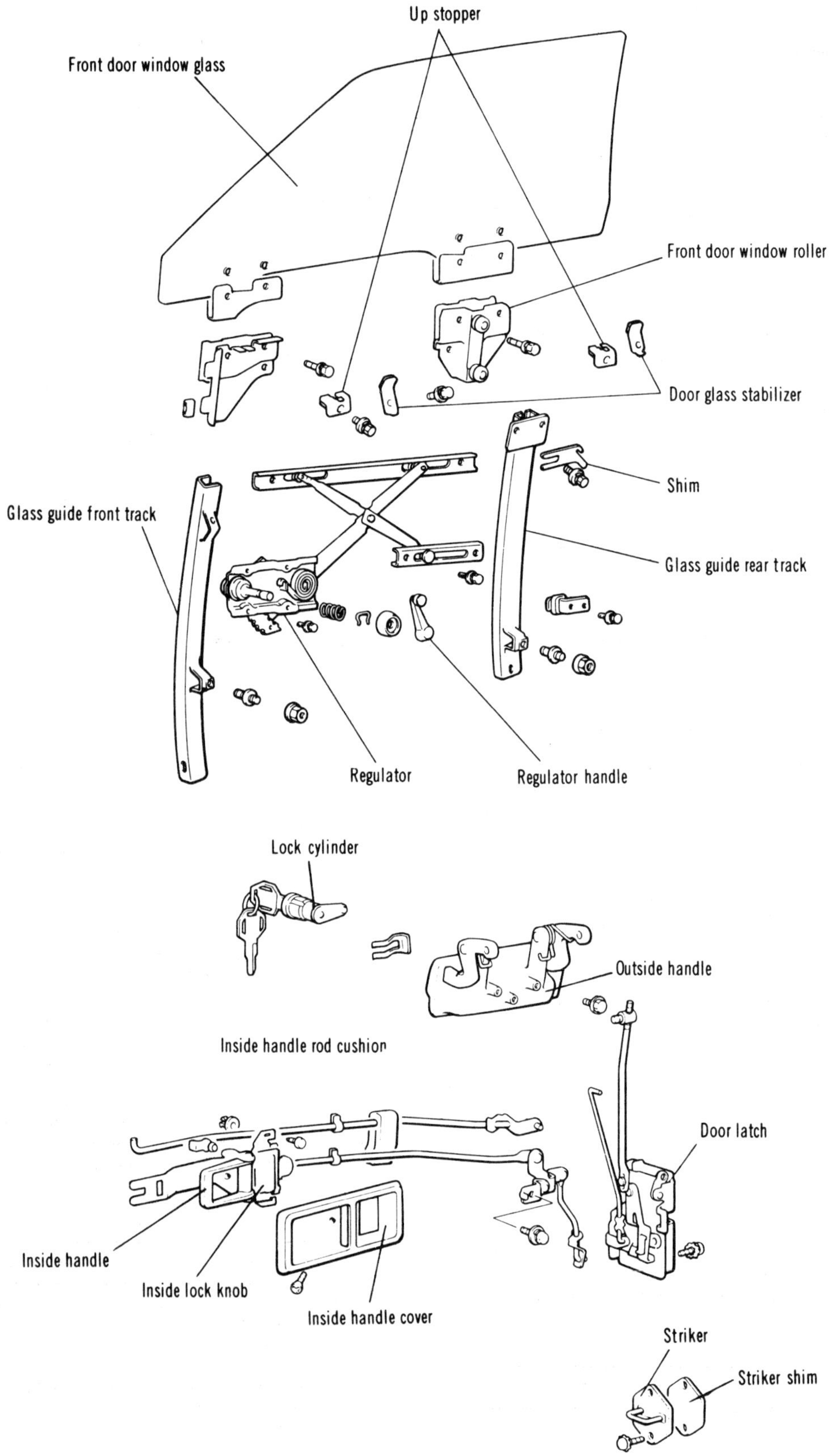

Fig. 12.8 Front door components – exploded view (Secs 15 & 16)

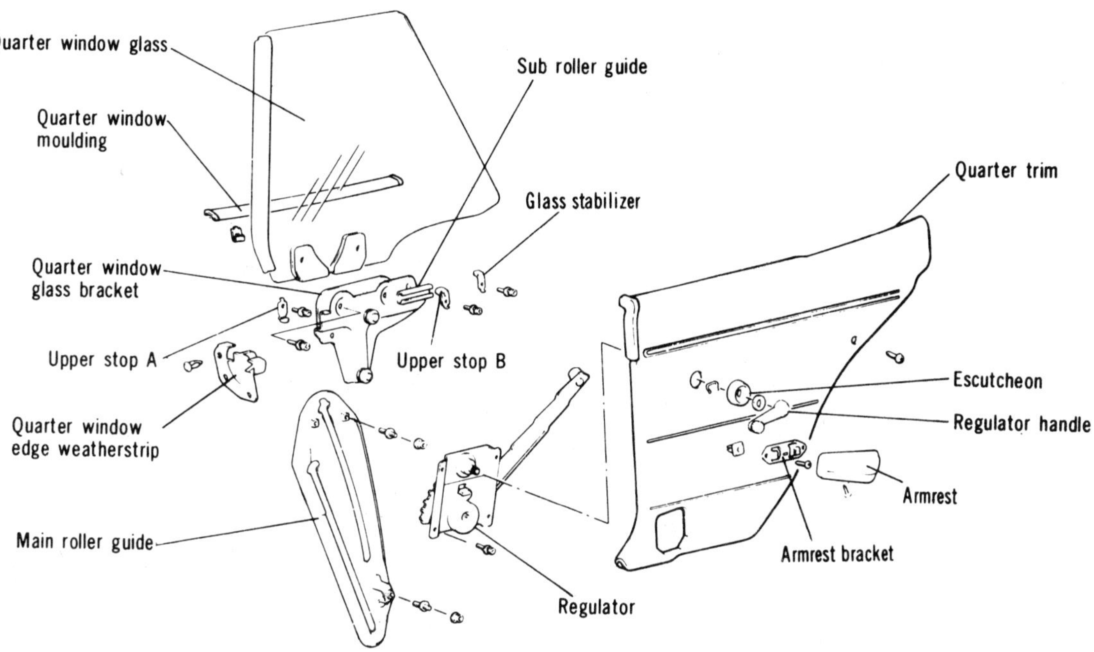

Fig. 12.9 Quarter window components – exploded view (Sec 17)

careful not to tear the weatherproof cover. To install the panels, just reverse the removal procedure.
3 Install the window crank (after the glass is completely raised) at a 30° angle (towards the rear) from the top dead center position. **Note:** *If your vehicle is equipped with door speakers, don't forget to disconnect the speaker connectors in order to completely remove the panel.*

16 Doors – removal, installation and adjustment

1 Refer to the appropriate Section in this Chapter and remove the door trim panel.
2 Remove the window crank mechanism bolts. Remove the crank mechanism and the glass.
3 Remove the door lock mechanism bolts and the door handle bolt. Remove the lock mechanism and the handle.
4 Remove the inside door handle bolts, then remove the inside handle.
5 Remove the door by first placing a jack under the center of the door for support. Remove the door set bolts and carefully lift off the door.
6 Installation is the reverse of removal.
7 Adjust the new door for a good fit by referring to the following procedure.
8 Loosen the body hinge and/or the door hinge bolts and move the door in the direction desired (left or right; up or down).
9 Loosen the door lock striker and move the striker in the direction desired for a tight door fit.

17 Quarter panel/glass – removal and installation

1 Remove the rear seat cushion by removing its mounting bolts and then removing the cushion itself.
2 Remove the quarter panel armrest.
3 Remove the mounting bolts of the rear seat back, and then remove the seat back by lifting it out.
4 Now, remove the window crank, the seat belt retractor and the quarter panel mounting screws.
5 Remove the scuff plate trim rear mounting screw and, lifting the back end of it up, remove the quarter panel by moving it forward.
6 Remove the armrest bracket and the waterproofing plastic sheet.
7 Remove the glass stabilizer and the upper stops A and B.
8 To remove the window, remove the window molding and the edge weatherstrop.
9 Raise the glass to its highest position and remove the glass mounting screws.
10 Lower the window regulator to the mid-way position and pull the glass upward and out.
11 Installation is the reverse of the removal procedure.
12 Position the glass retaining bracket in the mid-way position and then insert the glass from the top. Align the mounting hole of the glass and the bracket and secure it with a bolt.
13 Raise the glass to the top position, insert the front mounting bolt and tighten both the front and the rear bolt.
14 Install the upper stops A and B and also the glass stabilizer. Install the window edge molding and the waterproof plastic sheeting.
15 Install the quarter panel and the scuff rail trim as well as the window handle crank, the seat belt retractor and the quarter panel mounting screws. **Note:** *With the window in the fully up position, install the window crank and the crank knob in a 30° position above the horizontal and forward.*
16 Install the rear seat back and the cushion.

18 Fuel tank filler door cable – removal and installation

1 Remove the lock release cable securing clamp from inside the trunk and slacken the cable.
2 Remove the fuel tank filler door mounting screws and the filler door.
3 Disconnect the lock release cable from the filler door latch and pull it into the inside of the trunk.
4 Remove the left front seat, the left front scuff rail trim, and the left front seat belt. Roll back the carpet.
5 Remove the lock release mounting screws and the lock release handle.
6 Remove the rear seat cushion. Replace the cable with a new one if necessary.
7 Installation is the reverse of the removal procedure.

Conversion factors

Length (distance)

Inches (in)	X 25.4	= Millimetres (mm)	X 0.0394	= Inches (in)
Feet (ft)	X 0.305	= Metres (m)	X 3.281	= Feet (ft)
Miles	X 1.609	= Kilometres (km)	X 0.621	= Miles

Volume (capacity)

Cubic inches (cu in; in^3)	X 16.387	= Cubic centimetres (cc; cm^3)	X 0.061	= Cubic inches (cu in; in^3)
Imperial pints (Imp pt)	X 0.568	= Litres (l)	X 1.76	= Imperial pints (Imp pt)
Imperial quarts (Imp qt)	X 1.137	= Litres (l)	X 0.88	= Imperial quarts (Imp qt)
Imperial quarts (Imp qt)	X 1.201	= US quarts (US qt)	X 0.833	= Imperial quarts (Imp qt)
US quarts (US qt)	X 0.946	= Litres (l)	X 1.057	= US quarts (US qt)
Imperial gallons (Imp gal)	X 4.546	= Litres (l)	X 0.22	= Imperial gallons (Imp gal)
Imperial gallons (Imp gal)	X 1.201	= US gallons (US gal)	X 0.833	= Imperial gallons (Imp gal)
US gallons (US gal)	X 3.785	= Litres (l)	X 0.264	= US gallons (US gal)

Mass (weight)

Ounces (oz)	X 28.35	= Grams (g)	X 0.035	= Ounces (oz)
Pounds (lb)	X 0.454	= Kilograms (kg)	X 2.205	= Pounds (lb)

Force

Ounces-force (ozf; oz)	X 0.278	= Newtons (N)	X 3.6	= Ounces-force (ozf; oz)
Pounds-force (lbf; lb)	X 4.448	= Newtons (N)	X 0.225	= Pounds-force (lbf; lb)
Newtons (N)	X 0.1	= Kilograms-force (kgf; kg)	X 9.81	= Newtons (N)

Pressure

Pounds-force per square inch (psi; lbf/in^2; lb/in^2)	X 0.070	= Kilograms-force per square centimetre (kgf/cm^2; kg/cm^2)	X 14.223	= Pounds-force per square inch (psi; lbf/in^2; lb/in^2)
Pounds-force per square inch (psi; lbf/in^2; lb/in^2)	X 0.068	= Atmospheres (atm)	X 14.696	= Pounds-force per square inch (psi; lbf/in^2; lb/in^2)
Pounds-force per square inch (psi; lbf/in^2; lb/in^2)	X 0.069	= Bars	X 14.5	= Pounds-force per square inch (psi; lbf/in^2; lb/in^2)
Pounds-force per square inch (psi; lbf/in^2; lb/in^2)	X 6.895	= Kilopascals (kPa)	X 0.145	= Pounds-force per square inch (psi; lbf/in^2; lb/in^2)
Kilopascals (kPa)	X 0.01	= Kilograms-force per square centimetre (kgf/cm^2; kg/cm^2)	X 98.1	= Kilopascals (kPa)
Millibar (mbar)	X 100	= Pascals (Pa)	X 0.01	= Millibar (mbar)
Millibar (mbar)	X 0.0145	= Pounds-force per square inch (psi; lbf/in^2; lb/in^2)	X 68.947	= Millibar (mbar)
Millibar (mbar)	X 0.75	= Millimetres of mercury (mmHg)	X 1.333	= Millibar (mbar)
Millibar (mbar)	X 0.401	= Inches of water (inH_2O)	X 2.491	= Millibar (mbar)
Millimetres of mercury (mmHg)	X 0.535	= Inches of water (inH_2O)	X 1.868	= Millimetres of mercury (mmHg)
Inches of water (inH_2O)	X 0.036	= Pounds-force per square inch (psi; lbf/in^2; lb/in^2)	X 27.68	= Inches of water (inH_2O)

Torque (moment of force)

Pounds-force inches (lbf in; lb in)	X 1.152	= Kilograms-force centimetre (kgf cm; kg cm)	X 0.868	= Pounds-force inches (lbf in; lb in)
Pounds-force inches (lbf in; lb in)	X 0.113	= Newton metres (Nm)	X 8.85	= Pounds-force inches (lbf in; lb in)
Pounds-force inches (lbf in; lb in)	X 0.083	= Pounds-force feet (lbf ft; lb ft)	X 12	= Pounds-force inches (lbf in; lb in)
Pounds-force feet (lbf ft; lb ft)	X 0.138	= Kilograms-force metres (kgf m; kg m)	X 7.233	= Pounds-force feet (lbf ft; lb ft)
Pounds-force feet (lbf ft; lb ft)	X 1.356	= Newton metres (Nm)	X 0.738	= Pounds-force feet (lbf ft; lb ft)
Newton metres (Nm)	X 0.102	= Kilograms-force metres (kgf m; kg m)	X 9.804	= Newton metres (Nm)

Power

Horsepower (hp)	X 745.7	= Watts (W)	X 0.0013	= Horsepower (hp)

Velocity (speed)

Miles per hour (miles/hr; mph)	X 1.609	= Kilometres per hour (km/hr; kph)	X 0.621	= Miles per hour (miles/hr; mph)

*Fuel consumption**

Miles per gallon, Imperial (mpg)	X 0.354	= Kilometres per litre (km/l)	X 2.825	= Miles per gallon, Imperial (mpg)
Miles per gallon, US (mpg)	X 0.425	= Kilometres per litre (km/l)	X 2.352	= Miles per gallon, US (mpg)

Temperature

Degrees Fahrenheit = (°C x 1.8) + 32

Degrees Celsius (Degrees Centigrade; °C) = (°F - 32) x 0.56

**It is common practice to convert from miles per gallon (mpg) to litres/100 kilometres (l/100km), where mpg (Imperial) x l/100 km = 282 and mpg (US) x l/100 km = 235*

Index

C

D

E

M

O

P

R

S

HAYNES AUTOMOTIVE MANUALS

NOTE: New manuals are added to this list on a periodic basis. If you do not see a listing for your vehicle, consult your local Haynes dealer for the latest product information.

ACURA

*1776 **Integra & Legend** '86 thru '90

AMC

Jeep CJ - *see JEEP (412)*
694 **Mid-size models,** Concord, Hornet, Gremlin & Spirit '70 thru '83
934 **(Renault) Alliance & Encore** '83 thru '87

AUDI

615 **4000** all models '80 thru '87
428 **5000** all models '77 thru '83
1117 **5000** all models '84 thru '88

AUSTIN

Healey Sprite - *see MG Midget (265)*

BMW

*2020 **3/5 Series** not including diesel or all-wheel drive models '82 thru '92
276 **320i** all 4 cyl models '75 thru '83
632 **528i** & 530i all models '75 thru '80
240 **1500 thru 2002** except Turbo '59 thru '77
348 **2500, 2800, 3.0 & Bavaria** '69 thru '76

BUICK

Century (front wheel drive) - *see GENERAL MOTORS (829)*
*1627 **Buick, Oldsmobile & Pontiac Full-size (Front wheel drive)** '85 thru '93
Buick Electra, LeSabre and Park Avenue; **Oldsmobile** Delta 88 Royale, Ninety Eight and Regency; **Pontiac** Bonneville
1551 **Buick Oldsmobile & Pontiac Full-size (Rear wheel drive)**
Buick Estate '70 thru '90, Electra'70 thru '84, LeSabre '70 thru '85, Limited '74 thru '79
Oldsmobile Custom Cruiser '70 thru '90, Delta 88 '70 thru '85,Ninety-eight '70 thru '84
Pontiac Bonneville '70 thru '81, Catalina '70 thru '81, Grandville '70 thru '75, Parisienne '83 thru '86
627 **Mid-size Regal & Century** all rear-drive models with V6, V8 and Turbo '74 thru '87
Regal - *see GENERAL MOTORS (1671)*
Skyhawk - *see GENERAL MOTORS (766)*
552 **Skylark** all X-car models '80 thru '85
Skylark '86 on - *see GENERAL MOTORS (1420)*
Somerset - *see GENERAL MOTORS (1420)*

CADILLAC

*751 **Cadillac Rear Wheel Drive** all gasoline models '70 thru '92
Cimarron - *see GENERAL MOTORS (766)*

CAPRI

296 **2000 MK I Coupe** all models '71 thru '75
Mercury Capri - *see FORD Mustang (654)*

CHEVROLET

*1477 **Astro & GMC Safari Mini-vans** '85 thru '93
554 **Camaro V8** all models '70 thru '81
866 **Camaro** all models '82 thru '92
Cavalier - *see GENERAL MOTORS (766)*
Celebrity - *see GENERAL MOTORS (829)*
625 **Chevelle, Malibu & El Camino** '69 thru '87
449 **Chevette & Pontiac T1000** '76 thru '87
550 **Citation** all models '80 thru '85
*1628 **Corsica/Beretta** all models '87 thru '92
274 **Corvette** all V8 models '68 thru '82
*1336 **Corvette** all models '84 thru '91
1762 **Chevrolet Engine Overhaul Manual**
704 **Full-size Sedans** Caprice, Impala, Biscayne, Bel Air & Wagons '69 thru '90
Lumina - *see GENERAL MOTORS (1671)*
Lumina APV - *see GENERAL MOTORS (2035)*
319 **Luv Pick-up** all 2WD & 4WD '72 thru '82
626 **Monte Carlo** all models '70 thru '88
241 **Nova** all V8 models '69 thru '79
*1642 **Nova/Geo Prizm** front wheel drive '85 thru '92
420 **Pick-ups '67 thru '87** - Chevrolet & GMC, all V8 & in-line 6 cyl, 2WD & 4WD '67 thru '87; Suburbans, Blazers & Jimmys '67 thru '91
*1664 **Pick-ups '88 thru '93** - Chevrolet & GMC, all full-size (C and K) models, '88 thru '93
*831 **S-10 & GMC S-15 Pick-ups** '82 thru '92
*1727 **Sprint & Geo Metro** '85 thru '91
*345 **Vans - Chevrolet & GMC,** V8 & in-line 6 cylinder models '68 thru '92

CHRYSLER

*2058 **Full-size Front-Wheel Drive** '88 thru '93
K-Cars - *see DODGE Aries (723)*
Laser - *see DODGE Daytona (1140)*
*1337 **Chrysler & Plymouth Mid-size** front wheel drive '82 thru '93

DATSUN

402 **200SX** all models '77 thru '79
647 **200SX** all models '80 thru '83
228 **B - 210** all models '73 thru '78
525 **210** all models '78 thru '82
206 **240Z, 260Z & 280Z** Coupe '70 thru '78
563 **280ZX** Coupe & 2+2 '79 thru '83
300ZX - *see NISSAN (1137)*
679 **310** all models '78 thru '82
123 **510 & PL521 Pick-up** '68 thru '73
430 **510** all models '78 thru '81
372 **610** all models '72 thru '76
277 **620 Series Pick-up** all models '73 thru '79
720 Series Pick-up - *see NISSAN (771)*
376 **810/Maxima** all gas models, '77 thru '84
368 **F10** all models '76 thru '79
Pulsar - *see NISSAN (876)*
Sentra - *see NISSAN (982)*
Stanza - *see NISSAN (981)*

DODGE

400 & 600 - *see CHRYSLER Mid-size (1337)*
*723 **Aries & Plymouth Reliant** '81 thru '89
*1231 **Caravan & Plymouth Voyager Mini-Vans** all models '84 thru '93
699 **Challenger/Plymouth Saporro** '78 thru '83
Challenger '67-'76 - *see DODGE Dart (234)*
236 **Colt** all models '71 thru '77
610 **Colt/Plymouth Champ (front wheel drive)** all models '78 thru '87
*1668 **Dakota Pick-ups** all models '87 thru '93
234 **Dart, Challenger/Plymouth Barracuda & Valiant** 6 cyl models '67 thru '76
*1140 **Daytona & Chrysler Laser** '84 thru '89
*545 **Omni & Plymouth Horizon** '78 thru '90
*912 **Pick-ups** all full-size models '74 thru '91
*556 **Ram 50/D50 Pick-ups & Raider and Plymouth Arrow Pick-ups** '79 thru '93
*1726 **Shadow/Plymouth Sundance** '87 thru '93
*1779 **Spirit & Plymouth Acclaim** '89 thru '92
*349 **Vans - Dodge & Plymouth** '71 thru '91

EAGLE

Talon - *see Mitsubishi Eclipse (2097)*

FIAT

094 **124 Sport Coupe & Spider** '68 thru '78
273 **X1/9** all models '74 thru '80

FORD

*1476 **Aerostar Mini-vans** '86 thru '92
788 **Bronco and Pick-ups** '73 thru '79
*880 **Bronco and Pick-ups** '80 thru '91
268 **Courier Pick-up** all models '72 thru '82
1763 **Ford Engine Overhaul Manual**
789 **Escort/Mercury Lynx** '81 thru '90
*2046 **Escort/Mercury Tracer** '91 thru '93
*2021 **Explorer & Mazda Navajo** '91 thru '92
560 **Fairmont & Mercury Zephyr** '78 thru '83
334 **Fiesta** all models '77 thru '80
754 **Ford & Mercury Full-size,** Ford LTD & Mercury Marquis ('75 thru '82); Ford Custom 500,Country Squire, Crown Victoria & Mercury Colony Park ('75 thru '87); Ford LTD Crown Victoria & Mercury Gran Marquis ('83 thru '87)
359 **Granada & Mercury Monarch** '75 thru '80
773 **Ford & Mercury Mid-size,** Ford Thunderbird & Mercury Cougar ('75 thru '82); Ford LTD & Mercury Marquis ('83 thru '86); Ford Torino,Gran Torino, Elite, Ranchero pick-up, LTD II, Mercury Montego, Comet, XR-7 & Lincoln Versailles ('75 thru '86)
*654 **Mustang & Mercury Capri** incl. Turbo Mustang, '79 thru '92; Capri, '79 thru '86
357 **Mustang V8** all models '64-1/2 thru '73
231 **Mustang II** 4 cyl, V6 & V8 '74 thru '78
649 **Pinto & Mercury Bobcat** '75 thru '80
1670 **Probe** all models '89 thru '92
*1026 **Ranger/Bronco II** gas models '83 thru '93
*1421 **Taurus & Mercury Sable** '86 thru '92
*1418 **Tempo & Mercury Topaz** '84 thru '93
1338 **Thunderbird/Mercury Cougar** '83 thru '88
*1725 **Thunderbird/Mercury Cougar** '89 and '90
*344 **Vans** all V8 Econoline models '69 thru '91

GENERAL MOTORS

*829 **Buick Century, Chevrolet Celebrity, Olds Cutlass Ciera & Pontiac 6000** all models '82 thru '93
*766 **Buick Skyhawk, Cadillac Cimarron, Chevrolet Cavalier, Oldsmobile Firenza Pontiac J-2000 & Sunbird** '82 thru '92
1420 **Buick Skylark & Somerset, Olds Calais & Pontiac Grand Am** '85 thru '91
*1671 **Buick Regal, Chevrolet Lumina, Oldsmobile Cutlass Supreme & Pontiac Grand Prix** front wheel drive '88 thru '90
*2035 **Chevrolet Lumina APV, Oldsmobile Silhouette & Pontiac Trans Sport** '90 thru '92

GEO

Metro - *see CHEVROLET Sprint (1727)*
Prizm - *see CHEVROLET Nova (1642)*
*2039 **Storm** all models '90 thru '93
Tracker - *see SUZUKI Samurai (1626)*

GMC

Safari - *see CHEVROLET ASTRO (1477)*
Vans & Pick-ups - *see CHEVROLET (420, 831, 345, 1664)*

HONDA

351 **Accord CVCC** all models '76 thru '83
1221 **Accord** all models '84 thru '89
2067 **Accord** all models '90 thru '93
160 **Civic 1200** all models '73 thru '79
633 **Civic 1300 & 1500 CVCC** '80 thru '83
297 **Civic 1500 CVCC** all models '75 thru '79
1227 **Civic** all models '84 thru '91
*601 **Prelude CVCC** all models '79 thru '89

HYUNDAI

*1552 Excel all models '86 thru '93

ISUZU

*1641 **Trooper & Pick-up,** all gasoline models Pick-up, '81 thru '93; Trooper, '84 thru '91

JAGUAR

*242 **XJ6** all 6 cyl models '68 thru '86
*478 **XJ12 & XJS** all 12 cyl models '72 thru '85

JEEP

*1553 **Cherokee, Comanche & Wagoneer Limited** all models '84 thru '93
412 **CJ** all models '49 thru '86
*1777 **Wrangler** all models '87 thru '92

LADA

*413 **1200, 1300. 1500 & 1600** '74 thru '91

MAZDA

648 **626** Sedan & Coupe (rear wheel drive) all models '79 thru '82
*1082 **626 & MX-6 (front wheel drive)** '83 thru '91
267 **B Series Pick-ups** '72 thru '93
370 **GLC Hatchback (rear wheel drive)** all models '77 thru '83
757 **GLC (front wheel drive)** '81 thru '85
*2047 **MPV** all models '89 thru '93
460 **RX-7** all models '79 thru '85
*1419 **RX-7** all models '86 thru '91

MERCEDES-BENZ

*1643 **190 Series** 4-cyl gas models, '84 thru '88
346 **230, 250 & 280** 6 cyl sohc '68 thru '72
983 **280 123 Series** gas models '77 thru '81
698 **350 & 450** all models '71 thru '80
697 **Diesel 123 Series** '76 thru '85

MERCURY

See FORD Listing

MG

111 **MGB** Roadster & GT Coupe '62 thru '80
265 **MG Midget & Austin Healey Sprite Roadster** '58 thru '80

MITSUBISHI

*1669 **Cordia, Tredia, Galant, Precis & Mirage** '83 thru '93
*2022 **Pick-up & Montero** '83 thru '93
*2097 **Eclipse, Eagle Talon & Plymouth Laser** '90 thru '94

MORRIS

074 **(Austin) Marina 1.8** all models '71 thru '78
024 **Minor 1000** sedan & wagon '56 thru '71

NISSAN

1137 **300ZX** all models incl. Turbo '84 thru '89
*1341 **Maxima** all models '85 thru '91
*771 **Pick-ups/Pathfinder** gas models '80 thru '93
876 **Pulsar** all models '83 thru '86
*982 **Sentra** all models '82 thru '90
*981 **Stanza** all models '82 thru '90

OLDSMOBILE

Bravada - *see CHEVROLET S-10 (831)*
Calais - *see GENERAL MOTORS (1420)*
Custom Cruiser - *see BUICK Full-size RWD (1551)*
*658 **Cutlass** '74 thru '88
Cutlass Ciera - *see GENERAL MOTORS (829)*
Cutlass Supreme - *see GM (1671)*
Delta 88 - *see BUICK Full-size RWD (1551)*
Delta 88 Brougham - *see BUICK Full-size FWD (1551), RWD (1627)*
Delta 88 Royale - *see BUICK Full-size RWD (1551)*
Firenza - *see GENERAL MOTORS (766)*
Ninety-eight Regency - *see BUICK Full-size RWD (1551), FWD (1627)*
Ninety-eight Regency Brougham - *see BUICK Full-size RWD (1551)*
Omega - *see PONTIAC Phoenix (551)*
Silhouette - *see GENERAL MOTORS (2035)*

PEUGEOT

663 **504** all diesel models '74 thru '83

PLYMOUTH

Laser - *see MITSUBISHI Eclipse (2097)*
Other PLYMOUTH titles, see DODGE

PONTIAC

T1000 - *see CHEVROLET Chevette (449)*
J-2000 - *see GENERAL MOTORS (766)*
6000 - *see GENERAL MOTORS (829)*
Bonneville - *see Buick Full-size FWD (1627), RWD (1551)*
Bonneville Brougham - *see Buick Full-size (1551)*
Catalina - *see Buick Full-size (1551)*
1232 **Fiero** all models '84 thru '88
555 **Firebird** V8 models except Turbo '70 thru '81
867 **Firebird** all models '82 thru '92
Full-size Rear Wheel Drive - *see BUICK Oldsmobile, Pontiac Full-size RWD (1551)*
Full-size Front Wheel Drive - *see BUICK Oldsmobile, Pontiac Full-size FWD (1627)*
Grand Am - *see GENERAL MOTORS (1420)*
Grand Prix - *see GENERAL MOTORS (1671)*
Grandville - *see BUICK Full-size (1551)*
Parisienne - *see BUICK Full-size (1551)*
551 **Phoenix/Oldsmobile Omega** '80 thru '84
Sunbird - *see GENERAL MOTORS (766)*
Trans Sport - *see GENERAL MOTORS (2035)*

PORSCHE

*264 **911** all Coupe & Targa models except Turbo & Carrera 4 '65 thru '89
239 **914** all 4 cyl models '69 thru '76
397 **924** all models incl. Turbo '76 thru '82
*1027 **944** all models incl. Turbo '83 thru '89

RENAULT

141 **5 Le Car** all models '76 thru '83
079 **8 & 10** 58.4 cu in engines '62 thru '72
097 **12** Saloon & Estate '70 thru '80
768 **15 & 17** all models '73 thru '79
081 **16** 89.7 cu in & 95.5 cu in engines '65 thru '72
Alliance & Encore - *see AMC (934)*

SAAB

247 **99** all models including Turbo '69 thru '80
*980 **900** including Turbo '79 thru '88

SUBARU

237 **1100, 1300, 1400 & 1600** '71 thru '79
*681 **1600 & 1800** 2WD & 4WD '80 thru '89

SUZUKI

*1626 **Samurai/Sidekick/Geo Tracker** '86 thru '93

TOYOTA

1023 **Camry** all models '83 thru '91
150 **Carina** Sedan all models '71 thru '74
935 **Celica Rear Wheel Drive** '71 thru '85
*2038 **Celica Front Wheel Drive** '86 thru '92
1139 **Celica Supra** all models '79 thru '92
361 **Corolla** all models '75 thru '79
961 **Corolla** rear wheel drive models '80 thru '87
*1025 **Corolla** front wheel drive models '84 thru '92
636 **Corolla Tercel** all models '80 thru '82
360 **Corona** all models '74 thru '82
532 **Cressida** all models '78 thru '82
313 **Land Cruiser** all models '68 thru '82
200 **MK II** all 6 cyl models '72 thru '76
*1339 **MR2** all models '85 thru '87
304 **Pick-up** all models '69 thru '78
*656 **Pick-up** all models '79 thru '92
*2048 **Previa** all models '91 thru '93

TRIUMPH

112 **GT6 & Vitesse** all models '62 thru '74
113 **Spitfire** all models '62 thru '81
322 **TR7** all models '75 thru '81

VW

159 **Beetle & Karmann Ghia** '54 thru '79
238 **Dasher** all gasoline models '74 thru '81
*884 **Rabbit, Jetta, Scirocco, & Pick-up** gas models '74 thru '91 & Convertible '80 thru '92
451 **Rabbit, Jetta & Pick-up** diesel models '77 thru '84
082 **Transporter 1600** all models '68 thru '79
226 **Transporter 1700, 1800 & 2000** '72 thru '79
084 **Type 3 1500 & 1600** '63 thru '73
1029 **Vanagon** all air-cooled models '80 thru '83

VOLVO

203 **120, 130 Series & 1800 Sports** '61 thru '73
129 **140 Series** all models '66 thru '74
*270 **240 Series** all models '74 thru '90
400 **260 Series** all models '75 thru '82
*1550 **740 & 760 Series** all models '82 thru '88

SPECIAL MANUALS

1479 **Automotive Body Repair & Painting Manual**
1654 **Automotive Electrical Manual**
1667 **Automotive Emissions Control Manual**
1480 **Automotive Heating & Air Conditioning Manual**
1762 **Chevrolet Engine Overhaul Manual**
1736 **GM & Ford Diesel Engine Repair Manual**
1763 **Ford Engine Overhaul Manual**
482 **Fuel Injection Manual**
2069 **Holley Carburetor Manual**
1666 **Small Engine Repair Manual**
299 **SU Carburetors** thru '88
393 **Weber Carburetors** thru '79
300 **Zenith/Stromberg CD Carburetors** thru '76

** Listings shown with an asterisk (*) indicate model coverage as of this printing. These titles will be periodically updated to include later model years - consult your Haynes dealer for more information.*

Over 100 Haynes motorcycle manuals also available

5-94